Human Resources Administration
for Educational Leaders

This text is dedicated to the graduates of College View High School in Lincoln, Nebraska. These special people were instrumental in helping set the personal foundations of motivation, inspiration, and purpose for the author of this text.

Human Resources Administration
for Educational Leaders

M. Scott Norton
Professor Emeritus – Arizona State University

Los Angeles • London • New Delhi • Singapore

For information:

Sage Publications, Inc.
2455 Teller Road
Thousand Oaks,
   California 91320
E-mail: order@sagepub.com

Sage Publications Ltd.
1 Oliver's Yard
55 City Road
London EC1Y 1SP
United Kingdom

Sage Publications India Pvt. Ltd.
B 1/I 1 Mohan Cooperative
   Industrial Area
Mathura Road, New Delhi 110 044
India

Sage Publications Asia-Pacific Pte Ltd
33 Pekin Street #02-01
Far East Square
Singapore 048763

Printed in the United States of America

Library of Congress Cataloging-in-Publication Data

Norton, M. Scott.
Human resources administration for educational leaders / M. Scott Norton.
    p. cm.
Includes bibliographical references and index.
ISBN 978-1-4129-5759-5 (cloth)
    1. School personnel management—United States. I. Title.

LB2831.58.N67 2008
371.2′01—dc22   2007045853

This book is printed on acid-free paper.

08   09   10   11   12   10   9   8   7   6   5   4   3   2   1

Acquisitions Editor:	Steve Wainwright
Editorial Assistant:	Julie McNall
Production Editor:	Catherine M. Chilton
Copy Editor:	Barbara Ray
Typesetter:	C&M Digitals (P) Ltd.
Proofreader:	Annette R. Van Deusen
Indexer:	Jeanne Busemeyer
Cover Designer:	Gail Buschman
Marketing Manager:	Nichole M. Angress

Contents

Preface   **xiii**

Acknowledgments   **xvi**

1. The Human Resources Function:
   Issues, Challenges, and Trends   **2**
   The Human Resources Function in Education: Its Definition   2
   Issues Facing Education and the Human Resources Function   4
      School Governance and Leadership   4
      Relationships and Cooperation   6
      Effective Human Performance   7
      Adequate School Financing   8
      Demands on Professional Personnel   8
      External Mandates and Legal Impacts
         on the Human Resources Function   9
      Developments in Automation and Technology   9
   Challenges Facing Education and
      the Human Resources Function   10
      Influences of the Internal and External Environments
         of the School System   11
      Increasing Diversity in the Workplace   14
      Teacher and Administrator Supply and Demand   16
      Employee Demands for a Balanced Work Life   18
         Flexibility Consideration in Educational Settings   19
         Distance Education and Workplace Flexibility   19
      New Demands for Accountability Within the
         Human Resources Function   21
   Selected New Trends in Human Resources Administration   27
      The Changing Leadership Role of the Human
         Resources Administrator   28
      Administrative Standards and Their Influence
         on the Human Resources Function   29

Competency-Based Performance and the
    Human Resources Function   31
The No Child Left Behind Act   32
Trends Concerning Talent Management
    and the Human Resources Administrator   34
Summary   36
Discussion Questions   37
Case Studies   38
References   40

2. The Human Resources Function: A Historical Perspective   **42**
Personnel Administration Before 1900   43
The Scientific Management Era and Its Impact
    on Personnel Practices   45
The Human Relations Era and Its Impact
    on the Human Resources Function   47
    Contributors to the Human Relations Movement   48
The Behavioral Science Movement and Its
    Contributions to the Human Resources Function   53
    The Contributions of Chester Barnard   53
    Herbert A. Simon   54
    Andrew A. Halpin   54
    Daniel E. Griffiths   55
    Fred Fiedler   56
    Christopher Hodgkinson   57
    Rensis Likert   57
The Postmodern Behavioral Science Era   58
The Human Resources Function and Its Thirteen Processes   60
The Centralization and Decentralization of the HR Function   65
    Organization of the Central Human Resources Unit   65
    Position Description of the Central Unit
        Human Resources Administrator   67
    The Decentralization of the Human Resources Function   69
Standards of Ethical Administration   70
Summary   72
Discussion Questions   72
Case Studies   73
References   75

3. The Human Resources Planning Process   **78**
Definition and Background of the
    Human Resources Planning Process   79
    The Purposes of Human Resources Planning   79
Characteristics of Strategic Human Resources Planning   83
Evolutionary Stage of a School Organization   83
Professional Staff Mix   84

Integrating Human Resources Planning Into the Strategic Plan 84
    Environmental Scanning (1.0) 85
        External Scanning (1.1) 87
        Internal Scanning (1.2) 87
    Strategic and Operational Planning (2.0) 88
        Strategic Plan (2.1) 88
        Operational Plans (2.2) 93
    Implementation (3.0) 95
Correlation With the System Plan 95
Information Needs and Forecasting 96
    Forecasting Personnel Needs 96
    Forecasting Student Enrollments 98
Policy, Regulation, Processes, and Personnel Changes 100
Summary 101
Discussion Questions 101
Case Studies 102
References 105

4. Staffing for Educational Services: the Recruitment Process **108**
An Operations Model for the Recruitment Process 109
    Planning for Recruitment 110
    Organization of the Recruitment Process 111
    Position Descriptions 115
    Recruitment Sources 119
    Recruitment Strategies: Establishing the Recruitment Pool 120
    Controlling the Recruitment Process 122
    The Re-Recruitment of Personnel 125
Summary 128
Discussion Questions 128
Case Studies 129
References 130

5. Staffing for Educational Services: The Selection Process **132**
An Operational Model for the Selection Process 133
    Designing and Organizing the Selection Process 133
    Defining the Behavioral Characteristics to Be Appraised 135
    Compiling Appropriate Selection Data 136
        Letters of Reference 136
        The Interview Guide 137
        Selection Interview Techniques 138
        The Use of Testing in the Selection Process 140
        Legal Considerations and the Interviewing Activity 142
    Preparing Eligibility Lists and Nominations for Submission
        to the Board of Education: Contract Approval 143
        The Background Check 143
    Assessing the Selection Results 144

Summary 146
Discussion Questions 148
Case Studies 148
References 150

6. **The HR Induction, Assignment, Stability, and Protection Processes: Toward the Maximization of Human Potential** **152**
The School as a Social System 153
Human Motivation Theories 154
The Human Resources Induction Process 159
Operational Procedures for Staff Induction 160
Preemployment Activities 160
Postemployment Induction 161
Mentoring Program 162
Policy and Administrative Manual 162
Personnel Information Handbook 163
Orientation for the Beginning Teacher and
Others New to the School System 164
Induction: What the Research Says 165
The Staff Assignment Process 166
Position Assignment 166
Teacher Workload 168
The Douglass Teacher Load Formula 169
The Norton/Bria Formula for Measuring
Elementary School Teacher Load 170
The Human Resources Stability Process 172
Working With Troubled and Marginal Staff Members 172
Employee Assistance Programs 174
Helping the Marginal Teacher 176
Dealing With Conflict and Controversy 177
The Organizational Stability Process:
Teacher Retention 179
Strategies for Reducing Teacher Turnover 180
An Operational Plan for Teacher Retention 181
Retention of Administrative Personnel 182
Why Principals Are Leaving the Position 183
Teacher Absenteeism 184
The HR Protection Process 186
Summary 188
Discussion Questions 189
Case Studies 190
References 191

7. **The Staff Development and Performance Evaluation Processes** **194**
The Purposes of Staff Development 197
Trends in Professional Staff Development 198
Operational Procedures for Staff Development 199

The RPTIM Model for Staff Development 200
Staff Development Methods and Strategies 202
   Consultants 202
   Coaching 203
   Coaching and Mentoring 203
Primary Phases of a Mentoring Relationship 205
Mentor Qualifications 206
The TDP in the Mentoring Process 206
   Quality Circles 209
   Teacher Centers 210
   Assessment Centers 211
   Clinical Supervision 213
   Job Rotation 214
   Peer-Assisted Leadership 215
Adults as Learners 215
The Performance Evaluation Process 217
District Philosophy of Performance Evaluation 218
An Example of an Organizational Plan
   for the Evaluation of Performance 219
The Classroom Observation 223
   Qualified Evaluators 223
   Valid and Reliable Assessment Instruments 225
   Timely Observations 225
   Appropriate Follow-Up Conferencing and Feedback 227
Summary 228
Discussion Questions 229
Case Studies 229
References 231

**8. Organizational Climate and the
Human Resources Function** **234**
Organizational Culture and Organizational Climate 235
The Importance of a Healthy School Climate 236
The Measurement of School Climate 238
Research on School Climate 243
   Characteristics of Schools With Positive Climates 244
   The Impact of School Climate on Student Achievement 245
   The Impact of School Climate
      on the Behavior of Personnel 246
   Dealing With Conflict 247
   School Life and Staff Commitment 248
   The Impact of School Climate on
      Organizational Change and Innovation 249
Improvement of School Climate 251
   Program, Process, and Material
      Determinants of School Climate 251
   School Improvement Models and Strategies 253

Human Resources Responsibilities in the
Improvement of School Climate   253
Summary   255
Discussion Questions   256
Case Studies   257
References   258

9. **The Legal World of Human Resources Administration:**
   Policy and Regulation Development   **262**
   Legal Considerations and the Human Resources Function   263
      Employee Rights   263
      Rights, Responsibilities, and Duties: Academic Freedom   263
      Policies Relating to Staff Protection: Sexual Harassment   264
      Employee Dismissal and Legal Considerations   266
      Drug-Free Workplace Legislation   272
      Legal Considerations Relative to Teacher Transfer   272
      Legal Considerations Regarding the Use of
         Network and Internet   277
   Summary of Selected Legal Statutes, Including Various
      Civil Rights Acts, Relating to the Work of the
      Human Resources Function   279
   The Development of Personnel Policies and
      Regulations   282
      Goals, Policies, and Regulations   283
      Compliance Aspects of Policy   283
      The Benefits of Personnel Policies and Regulations   284
      Criteria That Identify Policies, Regulations, and Bylaws   286
      Topical Headings for Personnel Policies and Regulations   287
      The NEPN/NSBA Policy Codification System   287
      The Davies-Brickell Codification System   290
   How Personnel Policies and Regulations Are Developed   290
   Model for Policy and Regulation Development   291
   The Language of School Policies and Regulations   293
   Summary   294
   Discussion Questions   295
   Case Studies   296
   References   299

10. **Collective Bargaining and the Human Resources**
    Function: Working With Employee Groups   **300**
    Employee Unions Defined   301
    Working Relationships: The Human Resources
       Function and Employee Groups   302
    Collective Bargaining: Definition and Basic Principles   303
    The Two Primary Bargaining Processes   305
    Bargaining By Employee Groups: Historical Perspectives   306

Collective Bargaining in Education and
   the Central Human Resources Unit   309
Collective Bargaining in Education   310
    Distributive Bargaining   312
    Planning and Preparation for Collective Negotiations   313
    Gathering Related Information for Decision
      Making and Cost Analysis   313
    Determining Goals and Objectives
      for Collective Bargaining   314
    Establishing Ground Rules for Conducting
      Collective Bargaining   315
        Authority of Team Representatives   315
        Time and Place of Meetings   315
        Agenda for Meetings   316
        Team Members   316
        Meetings and Meeting Records   316
        Procedural Considerations   316
    Determining the Scope of Collective Bargaining   317
    Clarifying Procedures in Case of Impasse   318
      Mediation   318
      Fact-Finding and Advisory Arbitration   319
      Voluntary Binding and Compulsory Arbitration   319
      Last-Best-Offer Arbitration   320
      Strikes   320
Determination and Recognition of the Bargaining Unit   322
    The Bargaining Agent   324
    Determination of the Composition
      of the Negotiations Team   325
Initial Bargaining Procedures and Appropriate Table Strategies   328
The Contract Agreement   331
    Grievances   332
Impact of Collective Bargaining on Education   333
Summary   336
Discussion Questions   337
Case Studies   338
References   339

11. The Compensation Process: An Operations Model   342
School Finance: The Number One Problem Facing Education   342
Education Is Big Business   343
Competition for the Tax Dollar   344
Operational Model for the Compensation Process   345
    Developing Compensation Policies   345
    Establishing Position Structure   347
    Job Assessment: Determining the
      Value of Employee Positions   348

Compensation Legislation 349
Mandates From State School Boards and the Courts 350
Prevailing Salaries of Related Occupations 350
Collective Bargaining 352
Supply and Demand for Personnel 352
Ability to Pay 353
Standard Cost of Living 354
National Productivity 355
Collateral Considerations That Affect Compensation 355
Establishing Administrative Procedures for
    Implementation of the Compensation Process 356
Controlling the Compensation Process 359
Trends in Salary Scheduling: Alternative
    Compensation Programs 359
History of the Single Salary Schedule 362
Three Basic Models of Salary Schedules 363
Summary 365
Discussion Questions 366
Case Studies 366
References 368

12. **The Classified Staff: An Important Human Resources**
    Administration Responsibility **370**
The Director of Classified Personnel 373
The Classified Job Analysis 375
Job Grading and Salary Ranges 375
Recruitment of Classified Personnel 379
Appraising Candidates in Relation to the Selection Criteria 383
Classified Employee Selection Process 383
    Designing and Organizing the Selection Process 383
        Defining Behavior Characteristics to be Appraised 383
    Employee Eligibility Lists and Nominating Candidates
        for Hiring 387
Assessing the Classified Employee Selection Process 387
The Classified Employee Training Program 388
Employee Evaluation 392
Controlling Classified Employee Development Results 398
Summary 399
Discussion Questions 400
Case Studies 401
References 402

Glossary **404**

Index **417**

About the Author **435**

Preface

Few today argue against the contention that people are an organization's most important asset. It is a fact that organizations will progress as people grow and develop. People are an organization's most important asset, but they are the most costly as well. In most school systems, an average of 80% of the budget is expended on the salary and benefits for its personnel. Because the human resources of the school system are so important to the achievement of school purposes, the human resources processes of planning, recruiting, selecting, inducting, assigning, developing, evaluating, negotiating, protecting, stabilizing, compensating, and climate improvement have become increasingly vital to the strategic planning and programming of the school district's goals and objectives.

This text emphasizes the concept that every leader in a school system is a human resources administrator. Although the human resources process has always been a shared responsibility among and between the central offices and local units of the school system, the increasing demands placed on the human resources function have resulted in new strategic roles for central office administrators and increasing human resources responsibilities for administrators at the local school level. These developments make it essential that all school administrators be knowledgeable and skilled in the required processes of an effective human resources program. In short, an educational leader who is not competent in the area of human resources administration cannot be effective in his or her role as an administrator.

The Organization of the Text

The text is presented in 12 chapters that address each of the 13 primary processes of the human resources function. All of the traditional processes of the human resources function such as recruitment, selection, and compensation are discussed. Also, the human resources processes of staff development, induction, assignment, protection, and stabilizing are discussed in terms of the most recent research and practices in the field. In addition, the text includes a chapter on the classified or support staff of the school system, as well as new trends in such areas as personnel accountability, staff retention, personnel compensation, and collective bargaining.

Each chapter begins with objectives that direct the primary student learning activities. Significant terms are set in bold type throughout each chapter and also are defined in the glossary at the end of the book. Each chapter closes with a summary of the chapter's contents and a section on questions for use in class discussions or as extended learning exercises for students. Simulations in the form of case studies and in-basket exercises provide opportunities for practical applications of chapter concepts. The references included at the close of each chapter provide opportunities for extended reading by the student learner.

A special feature of the text is the inclusion of figures and illustrations that demonstrate and extend learning opportunities for students. Many examples of human resources forms provide students with samples of the tools practicing HR administrators use for planning, recruiting, interviewing, selection, evaluating, compensating, and developing staff personnel.

The text emphasizes five major foundations for the study of the human resources function: (1) the historical development of the function; (2) the current issues, challenges, and trends encountered in the HR function; (3) the nature and strategic significance of the HR function in the organization; (4) the 13 primary processes of the HR function; and (5) supportive research studies and best practices that support the administration of the human resources function.

A note of appreciation is hereby given to Pearson Education, which gave its permission to use material under their copyright in several chapters of the text. Specifically, material in the chapters centering on the planning process, organizational climate, policies and regulations, and collective bargaining added additional quality to the text.

The Special Perspectives of This Text

This text addresses the major responsibilities of school administrators in the area of human resources administration by

- Emphasizing the increasing demands for accountability in the human resources function and ways in which the school administrator can deal with this new challenge.
- Considering the nature of human resources as a strategic rather than a maintenance function and the resulting need for improved knowledge and competency in human resources administration.
- Giving attention to the concept of human resources administration as an increasing responsibility of all school administrators and addressing the need for new HR knowledge and skills on the part of all school leaders.
- Addressing the issues, challenges, and trends related to the human resources function in education and the work of school leaders at all levels.
- Placing emphasis on effective human resources strategic planning and the importance of the internal and external environments in which the school and school system are embedded.
- Examining the historical evolution of the human resources function and the major contributions of many individuals who developed the foundation for contemporary HR practices.

- Describing the significant role of the central human resources unit in the school system and emphasizing its new responsibilities as a strategic unit in school district planning and program implementation.
- Addressing each of the major processes of the human resources function in detail and presenting relevant research and best practices as related to each process.
- Presenting specific examples of practice applications for meeting the personnel needs of enrollment forecasting, compensation scheduling, teacher workload calculations, accountability measurements, and support personnel classification procedures.
- Giving due attention to the nature and importance of the support personnel processes within the school district and underscoring the fact that classified personnel constitute a staff of approximately 50%–100% of the number of certificated personnel.
- Setting guidelines in the form of operational models for use in the planning and implementing of the recruitment and selection processes of the human resources function.
- Underscoring the nature of the human resources function as a people consideration and addressing the importance of human motivation skills in working with employees as individuals with varying personalities and need dispositions.
- Discussing new approaches to staff development in school systems and giving special attention to mentoring, coaching, and the new emphasis on talent management in organizations.
- Supporting the increasing importance of the work of human resources administrators in facilitating a healthy climate for students, employees, and stakeholders of the school.
- Providing a comprehensive discussion on the matter of human resources policy and regulation development and its importance to the support and implementation of effective HR practices.
- Emphasizing the legal world in which the human resources administrator must operate. Employee rights, statutory rights, and contractual rights of employees, including ethical treatment, privacy, freedom of speech, and employee dismissal are discussed in depth.
- Providing examples of compensation approaches and drafting models of salary schedules that delve into the conceptual aspects of employee compensation and provide a foundation for better understanding of the compensation process.

Supplemental Materials

Instructor's resources further support and enhance the learning goals of *Human Resources Administration for Educational Leaders*. The Instructor's Resources CD offers instructors a variety of material that supplements the textbook, including PowerPoint presentations created by educational consultant Larry K. Kelly, sample syllabi for semester and quarter courses, and a test bank consisting of 20 multiple choice and 10 true-false questions for each chapter. All of the materials available for download on the Instructor's Resources CD are also available for you to upload into your course management system.

Acknowledgments

I wish to express appreciation to many people who contributed to the publication of this text. A special note of thanks is extended to educational consultant Larry K. Kelly for conceptualizing and creating the PowerPoint slides to accompany the book. The help and suggestions of the following reviewers are also greatly appreciated: Ronald E. Barnes, Indiana University; Ann Hassenpflug, University of Akron; Joyce P. Logan, University of Kentucky; Angus J. MacNeil, University of Houston; Zach Kelehear, University of South Carolina; James E. Lyons, University of North Carolina at Charlotte; Patrick W. Carlton, University of Nevada, Las Vegas; Stella C. Batagiannis, Indiana University-Purdue University Fort Wayne; John C. Drewes, Nova Southeastern University; Marla Susman Israel, Loyola University Chicago; and Linda R. Vogel, University of Northern Colorado.

Once again, appreciation is expressed to Pearson Education for their permission to use certain copyrighted materials in several chapters of the book. Finally, I wish to acknowledge the editors, Steve Wainwright, Julie McNall, and other personnel of Sage Publications for their support and assistance in the completion of this publication.

M. Scott Norton
Tempe, Arizona

CHAPTER 1

The Human Resources Function

Issues, Challenges, and Trends

Learning Objectives

After reading this chapter, you will be able to

- Describe the major issues and problems facing education and their influence on the important work of the human resources function.
- Understand the major challenges and opportunities facing education and the role of the human resources function in helping to meet these challenges.
- Describe the primary trends within the human resources function and how they have influenced the work of educational leaders.
- Understand the internal environment in which the school is embedded and its influence on factors that tend to inhibit or promote positive outcomes in the human resources program activities.
- Gain a new understanding of accountability as it affects practices of the human resources function and the changing role of human resources administrators.
- Describe the new focus of human resources in education as a strategic function and how it helps the school system achieve its stated goals and objectives.
- Apply the knowledge of national standards such as the ISLLC Standards to the goals and objectives of the human resources function.

The Human Resources Function in Education: Its Definition

Education is a social system that is directly influenced by the environment in which it is embedded. Thus, the issues, problems, challenges, and trends encountered in any social system are also inextricably related to the human resources (HR) function. The human resources function in education is increasingly viewed as vital only to the extent that it supports the guiding goals and objectives of the organization as a whole. In this sense, the issues, problems, challenges, and trends facing a school system become those of its human resources function as well. "The human resources function plays a vital role in helping the system operate within economic structures, meet legal mandates, honor contractual obligations, address pressures of special interest groups, adapt to emerging technologies, and uphold ethical standards while maintaining centrality of purpose" (Young, 2008, p. 1).

The human resources of an organization are its people. The term **human resources** evolved from the term **personnel** mainly because people were being viewed as the primary assets of any system. For the purposes of this text, **human resources administration** is defined as those processes that are planned and implemented in the school system to establish an effective system of human resources and to foster an organizational climate that enhances the accomplishment of the system's educational mission, fosters the personal and professional objectives of the employees, and engages the support of the school community in which the school system is embedded. This perspective emphasizes the vital importance of the human resources function in achieving educational program effectiveness, in viewing the personnel in the school system as an important asset, and in gaining the involvement of the school system's stakeholders in the educational enterprise. The definition includes a major concern for developing a healthy climate within the school system that promotes, first and foremost, the accomplishment of school goals. It is this perspective that this text emphasizes throughout each chapter.

The following section presents the major issues facing education today and discusses their implications for the work of the human resources function. An **issue** is a matter that is in dispute between or among various parties. A **problem** is an unsettled question or obstacle brought forward for inquiry and solution. Specific issues discussed include the following: (1) school governance and leadership, (2) relationships and cooperation, (3) effective human performance, (4) school financing, (5) demands on school personnel, (6) external mandates and legal impacts on the human resources function, and (7) developments in automation and technology. Other sections of this chapter discuss both the major challenges facing human resources administrators and current trends evolving in the field.

Figure 1.1 centers on the relationship between and among the issues, challenges, and trends the human resources function encounters today. Issues and their related problems become challenges for HR administrators. However, challenges can result in new opportunities for improvement and lead to positive change. Figure 1.1 underscores the large possibility of realizing innovations that lead to improved practices. Each of the three phenomena—issues, challenges, and trends—provides opportunities for initiating positive changes in the work responsibilities of human resources leaders.

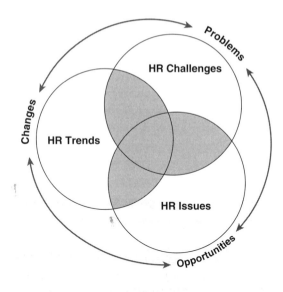

Figure 1.1 Human Resources Issues, Challenges, Trends, and Their Relationships

Issues Facing Education and the Human Resources Function

School Governance and Leadership

School governance and leadership historically have been issues in education in America. Who is to determine education governance policy? Although the Tenth Amendment to the U.S. Constitution states that all powers not reserved for the federal government are to be delegated to the various states, early practices in public education supported the concept of strong local control for determining school policy. Local control was exemplified by the appointment of selectmen to oversee the local schools and to ensure that the schools operated according to the views of the local community. Select committees served as the forerunners of modern-day school boards; personnel responsibilities centered primarily on the hiring of teachers and making certain that daily class lessons taught the values and beliefs of the community. Local school ward boards, which often governed a small number of neighborhood schools, ultimately gave way to the concept of having one school board govern the entire school district. State educational jurisdiction of schools expanded in the early 1800s through the development of county educational systems that gave the state closer supervisory control over local school systems. Historically, the federal government has influenced America's educational programs through mandates related to educational equity, technical and vocational education, special needs programs, and others viewed as important to the welfare of the nation.

Personnel administration as a major function in education is relatively new. Although personnel activities always have existed in education, personnel administration as a coordinated function in school districts has been slow to develop. World War II brought about new approaches to the recruitment, induction, training, compensation, and assignment of both military and nonmilitary personnel. Still, in the early 1960s, it was not unusual for the school district's business manager, school superintendent, or a director of instructional services to perform the personnel responsibilities for the school district. As personnel tasks increased in the early 1970s, a coordinated approach for recruiting, selecting, and inducting personnel into the school system became necessary. Human resources evolved into a major enterprise of school systems as it assumed a more comprehensive function within the school setting. This development demanded new avenues for the preparation of individuals for the work of personnel administrator. Today, the focus on strategic leadership once again is calling for new knowledge, new skills, and new competencies on the part of leaders responsible for human resources processes in education.

The concept that education is a national concern, a state responsibility, and a local function is not as clear today as in previous years. Local school systems presently are under pressure from the state to function according to imposed standards or be placed on probation and possibly be taken over by state authorities. Such pressures add to the fragmentation of the educational system in America. Numerous schooling alternatives are now in evidence nationally. Charter schools, home schooling, magnet schools, schools for homeless children, private schools, special needs schools, gifted schools, traditional schools, and many other special educational alternatives of choice have tended to diffuse educational authority and control. Each of these alternatives has its supporters and detractors.

Some groups are questioning school governance and leadership, as they are presently constituted. Is there a need for the expenses incurred in operating a central unit for personnel operations in a school district? Couldn't the human resources responsibilities be given to the local school administrator? Shouldn't teachers be empowered with the authority to govern a school? Although such ideas appear to have limited support, such suggestions do tend to question the viability of present school operations and support.

School governance has been greatly influenced by the increasing involvement of stakeholders in matters of school policy and practice. Community and parental involvement in school matters is now viewed as a way of life in the making of policy decisions. One such example is the implementation of site-based governance councils in many states. The effectiveness and influence of such involvement, according to reports, vary considerably within the states and within school districts. Nevertheless, site-based councils represent one way in which local communities have attempted to retain their local governance control.

Such matters as teacher empowerment, problems of teacher and administrator shortages and turnover, and calls for human resources accountability have serious implications for education and the work of human resources administrators. Later sections of this chapter, and other chapters of the text, discuss each of these topics.

Relationships and Cooperation

Studies of the work of school administrators over the years have listed concerns with school board actions and board member attitudes on various issues among the most troublesome problems for them. For example, human resources directors in one study named negative working relationships with the school board as one of the three major issues that would likely lead them to leaving the position (Norton, 2004). The same study found school board behaviors and attitudes to be among the five most inhibiting factors for human resources directors. Such terms as micromanagement have been used to describe when school boards spend too much time on matters of administrative procedure rather than school policy. Best practice supports the concept that school boards should contend with the adoption of viable school policy rather than attempting to set forth administrative procedures, a responsibility generally viewed as the responsibility of the school superintendent and professional staff. Chapter 9 focuses on school policy and administrative regulation development.

Teacher strikes continue in education, resulting in the development of negative working relationships whenever they occur. In some instances, unusual actions take place because of poor relationships between school boards and parent groups. Recalls of school board members occur, and in one school district, parents formed a parents' union in an effort to gain a greater voice in school policy. The development of a positive school climate is now considered one of the most important processes of the human resources function in education.

Collective bargaining continues as an adversarial process in the large majority of school districts in the nation, although win-win bargaining approaches are common. Many authorities view collective bargaining as having the greatest influence on the personnel function of any event or educational practice. Many of the problems within collective bargaining have been resolved through experience, legislative statutes, or court actions. Nevertheless, collective bargaining remains problematic for many human resources administrators. A study by Norton (2004) found collective bargaining to be among the leading problems facing human resources directors. For example, should the human resources director serve as the chief spokesperson in collective bargaining? Many authorities contend that such involvement on the part of the HR director is problematic because bargaining remains an adversarial activity and it is not possible to be effective as a staff supporter one day and an adversary the next. Chapter 10 discusses collective bargaining and the pros and cons of various school personnel serving on the school board bargaining team.

Teacher-to-teacher relationships appear to be an increasing problem in many school districts. The problems center on personal conflicts, lack of opportunities to communicate with colleagues, isolation among faculty personnel, and growing competition among personnel brought about by incentive pay practices and teacher load inequities. For example, teacher load studies of high-school teachers have revealed that some teachers carry twice the workload index as other teachers in the same school. High teacher and administrator turnover is closely related to job satisfaction. Job satisfaction studies have underscored the fact that employee and supervisor relations are of more importance to job satisfaction than monetary considerations. Thus, conflict, cooperation, and organizational climate become central to the work of the human resources administrator in education. Chapter 8 emphasizes these topics.

Effective Human Performance

The quality of the teachers and administrative staff and human performance are ongoing concerns in education. Both national and state studies have revealed that "getting quality teachers" is one of the biggest problems in education (Glass, Bjork, & Brunner, 2000; Norton, 2004). This issue often centers on the considerations of teacher certification and performance testing. Who should be permitted to teach? Should there be performance tests for teachers? Critics point to inferior teacher preparation in colleges and universities, and, as a result, some school districts have indicated that they are in the best position and most qualified to determine who should be permitted to teach. The question of who should certify teachers becomes an important debate within the issue of teaching performance as well. Some persons contend that methods classes for prospective teachers are relatively unimportant; they would place the emphasis on the academics or content of the subjects to be taught (e.g., math, science, English, etc.). Others contend that the teacher must be competent in teaching methods and understand how students learn; thus, methods classes are essential.

Performance tests for teachers have become a controversial on-again, off-again issue. In some states, teachers who are given temporary teaching certificates are required to pass a state teachers' test after two years in order to be certified. Proponents of teacher testing argue that such exams help to assure better teachers and lead to higher student performance. They contend that preparation programs in colleges and universities devote little time to teaching methods and classroom management. Others argue that such tests simply discourage teachers from remaining in the profession. Critics of teacher testing also state that teachers are already faced with too many federal and state requirements; additional testing mandates discourage others from entering the teaching field. They point to the fact that certified teachers commonly have to get a college degree, meet certain core and subject requirements, take state government and U.S. Constitution classes, student teach, and update their knowledge and skills periodically through in-service programs or by taking additional college credits.

Teacher shortages give rise to several issues relating to teacher performance. For example, some view alternative routes to teacher certification as a reduction in important preparation standards. In view of the foregoing happenings, school leaders are taking new approaches to retaining quality teachers already on the staff. Although teacher compensation remains among the reasons for teacher loss, research has revealed other nonmonetary reasons for teacher turnover. Thus, school leaders are giving more attention to such matters as organizational climate, teacher morale, induction, assignment, and supervisory relationships. A later section discusses teacher and administrator retention among other challenges facing the HR function.

Public opinion often results in average or below-average ratings of teachers and principals. School personnel directors name teacher quality, administrator quality, troubled workers, and dismissing of incompetent staff personnel among the 20 leading problems facing them in their roles (Norton, 2004).

In view of many of the foregoing problems within the issue of effective performance, new approaches for the screening and selection of applicants for positions in the schools have been implemented. **Re-recruitment**, a relatively new term in education, focuses on efforts to retain key personnel. The screening and selection process now includes more testing approaches and uses of simulations, along with such methods as structured interviews and simulation exercises. Testing requirements for teacher and administrator certification have increased in most states. In an attempt to raise the standards for teaching personnel, testing has resulted in the disqualification of some potential teaching personnel. For example, in one instance in the state of Massachusetts, 59% of the nearly 2,000 teaching candidates failed the state's teacher certification test. Chapters 4 and 5 set forth in detail the human resources processes of recruitment and selection.

Adequate School Financing

Most every study of problems facing education lists school finance as problem number one. Human resources are the most important, but also the most expensive resources in a school system. Directors of human resources in one state named the lack of financial resources as the number one most serious problem facing them (Norton, 2004). The latest national study of the school superintendency listed the financing of schools as the number one factor that inhibited a superintendent's effectiveness; 96.7% of the nation's school superintendents participating in the study were of this view. Compensation is a definite factor in the attraction and retention of qualified administrative leaders (Hertling, 2001; Kimball & Sirotnik, 2000; Norton, 2001; Whitaker, 2000; Yerkes & Guaglianone, 1998). The focus on compensation looms important here because it consumes 80%–95% of the total school district's operational budget, which includes staff salaries.

The public has been reluctant to support additional taxes to pay for underperforming schools. In efforts to find better solutions to the compensation problem, school districts have implemented various approaches to merit pay. Money-saving efforts have included the downsizing of administrative staffs and contracting certain jobs in the school and school district to companies outside the school district. Chapter 11 discusses in detail these topics and others related to the compensation process and staff welfare.

Demands on Professional Personnel

Studies and empirical evidence reveal that human resources personnel are facing increasing demands. The human resources function has grown far beyond the basic process of recruiting, selecting, and dismissing personnel. Chapter 2 presents a comprehensive discussion of the personnel processes that have been added or extended to the responsibilities of human resources administrators. For example, the processes of organizational climate, security and protection, stability, and staff development have been given increased attention in recent years. Background checks, litigation, employee assistance programs, grievance administration, and personal counseling are examples of the additional work responsibilities within the human resources function. Job insecurity can be a primary source for job stress and, if it becomes severe, can result in an employee becoming a troubled worker. In relation to employee relations, job security has become a leading objective of teacher union activity.

Teacher load historically has been a neglected concern of school boards and school administration. As a result, major discrepancies in the workload of the teaching staff are in evidence. Studies of teacher load in many states have revealed the fact that some teachers have teacher load indices twice that of other teachers in the same school. Such inequities lead to the overloading of many of the school's best teachers and result in reducing the performance of quality teachers to a level of actual mediocrity.

Class size has been the dominant concern in teacher load; teachers have been willing to accept larger class sizes so that more money is available for salaries. The debate continues over class size and student learning outcomes, although some studies support the contention that small class size results in important increases in student achievement. In the public schools of America, teacher turnover is above the student dropout rate. Three of 10 teachers do not remain in teaching after the first year. Certainly, workload is likely to have some influence on an individual's decision to leave the profession.

External Mandates and Legal Impacts on the Human Resources Function

Legal impacts on education have permeated virtually every facet of school personnel. The policies of the local school board, as well as state and national legislative mandates, state and national agency rulings, and state and national court rulings serve as both inhibitors and facilitators that influence the work of the human resources function. School superintendents named complying with external mandates as one of the 10 leading problems facing them (Norton, 2001). In a national study conducted by the American Association of School Administrators (Glass et al., 2000), compliance with state and federal mandates was revealed as one of seven factors that tended to inhibit the effectiveness of school superintendents. The factor of external mandates and the question of control relate closely to the issue of school governance as previously discussed. Legal matters, including litigation, were named as third highest among all processes and activities that consume the greatest amount of a human resources director's time (Norton, 2004). Much of the time human resources administrators spend today is concerned with helping to keep the school system in line with external mandates and out of trouble with the law.

The increasing involvement and intervention of external governmental and legal agencies have altered the meaning of the "politics of education." The statement "keep education out of politics" is seldom heard anymore. Education, as one of the social systems operating in society, necessarily must be involved in the competition for tax dollars and other resources needed to accomplish its stated goals and objectives.

Developments in Automation and Technology

The introduction of such technologies as computers, robots, laser scanners, ultrasonic probes, supersonic welding, and others are revolutionizing practices in many fields, and human resources administration is no exception. The use of computer programs for the recruiting and development of personnel is only one example of technological applications in the field. Computer programs for staff development, compensation and benefits programs, substitute teacher programming, computation of teacher load, and numerous other applications have been in place in most school districts for several years. Selection programs utilize scanning techniques for examining resumes of potential candidates for assessing best matches for position openings. Many school districts today will only accept employee applications electronically. Personnel inventories and available applicants can be monitored easily by computer methods. In personnel areas requiring high levels of paperwork, computer programs are being developed to help ease the burden.

Although all of the foregoing outcomes of automation and technology are likely to be viewed positively, human resources administrators are encountering certain problems. For example, new technology makes new demands on employees. Some instances of cyberphobia, or fear of new technology, can occur. Technological advances are likely to make the current skills of the worker outmoded. New skills are required to face changes in the work environment. In many instances, it is not necessary for the worker to come to the office; he or she can complete work just as well or better in another setting. There is less face-to-face conferring, and offices can become less personalized. Distance education, for example, has made some progress in school settings; students complete coursework, do research, communicate with instructors and other students, and complete homework on computers. In some cases, it might be possible for a quality teacher to teach two or three times the number of students via distance education methods. The possibilities for instruction and supervision practices via distance education methodology have barely been tapped to date. Human resources administrators at all levels will continue to face new advances and related challenges in using technology and automation for achieving stated goals and objectives.

Certainly, there are other important issues that carry their own sets of related problems. In many respects, the issues encountered in personnel work often appear to be overwhelming. It seems necessary for educational leaders in the human resources arena to concentrate on a manageable set of issues by devoting their attention to those of most importance. In doing so, the school system and the human resources unit should focus on the organization's major strengths relative to the human and material resources that will most likely allow the achievement of goals at a higher level than before.

Challenges Facing Education and the Human Resources Function

The issues and problems facing human resources administrators are closely related to the challenges encountered in the workplace. For example, the previously discussed issue of relationships and cooperation presents challenges relative to the phenomena of increasing diversity within the work force, managing talent, and fostering a positive organizational climate. In a similar sense, challenges of the human resources function often lead to improved changes in the way things are done. For the purposes of this text, a challenge is a task or summons that is surrounded with difficulties, but is often provocative and stimulating. The following section presents selected challenges facing human resources leaders today: (1) influences of the internal and external environments of the school system, (2) increasing diversity of the workforce, (3) teacher and administrator supply and demand, (4) employee demands for a balanced work life, and (5) new demands for accountability within the human resources function.

Influences of the Internal and External Environments of the School System

The external and internal environments in which the school system is embedded have significant influence on its mission and its different functions. The human resources function of the system is no exception. Figure 1.2 reveals several of the factors that serve to enhance or inhibit a school system's human resources function. As underscored in Figure 1.2, many of the external factors are beyond the direct control of the school system. Although the internal environmental factors are generally open to the input of the school leaders, such influence can be problematic.

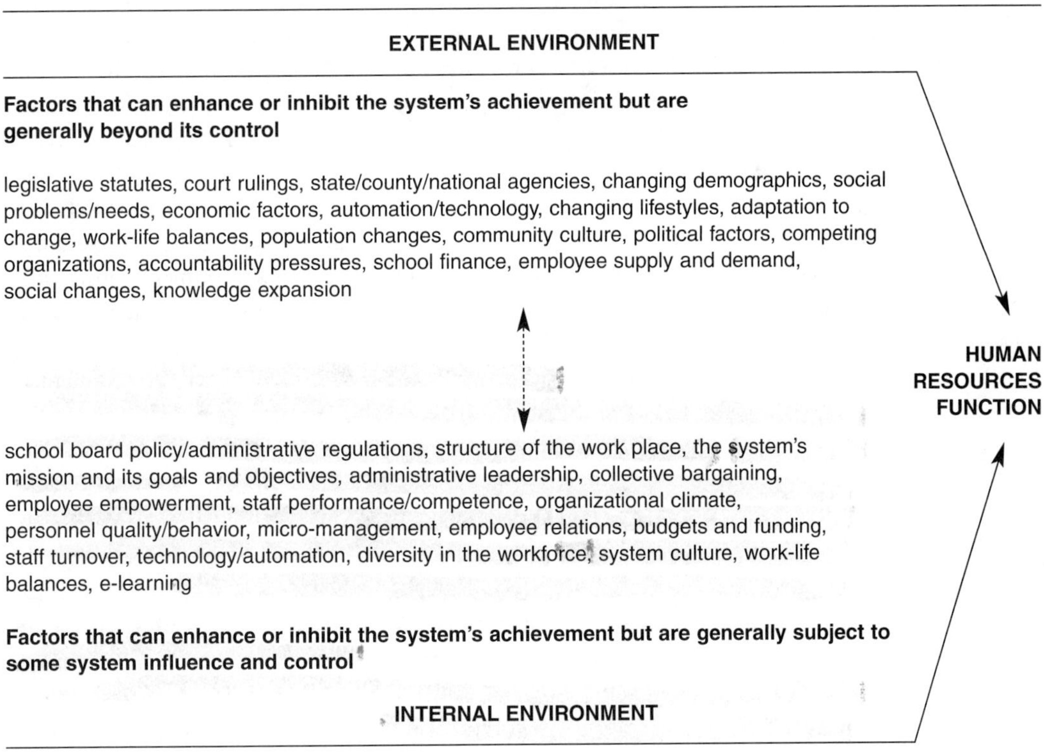

EXTERNAL ENVIRONMENT

Factors that can enhance or inhibit the system's achievement but are generally beyond its control

legislative statutes, court rulings, state/county/national agencies, changing demographics, social problems/needs, economic factors, automation/technology, changing lifestyles, adaptation to change, work-life balances, population changes, community culture, political factors, competing organizations, accountability pressures, school finance, employee supply and demand, social changes, knowledge expansion

HUMAN RESOURCES FUNCTION

school board policy/administrative regulations, structure of the work place, the system's mission and its goals and objectives, administrative leadership, collective bargaining, employee empowerment, staff performance/competence, organizational climate, personnel quality/behavior, micro-management, employee relations, budgets and funding, staff turnover, technology/automation, diversity in the workforce, system culture, work-life balances, e-learning

Factors that can enhance or inhibit the system's achievement but are generally subject to some system influence and control

INTERNAL ENVIRONMENT

Figure 1.2 External and Internal Environment Factors and the HR Function

We noted previously that a school system is a human organization within which a social service is performed. The internal system is composed of a series of interdependent parts including the formal organization, consisting of roles and role expectations, and the informal organization, consisting of people with different personalities and need dispositions. Both the formal and informal dimensions of the organization are embedded within internal and external environments. Changes that take place within these environments influence the behaviors of the persons within the social system. The human resources function is a major subsection of the total school system and is therefore subject to the same influences, conflicts, relationships, and challenges. In the following section, we address several selected challenges facing the human resources function. Before doing so, however, it is necessary to describe briefly the nature of a social system. This discussion serves to describe in more detail the characteristics of a social system and the implications for the challenges facing the human resources function.

Social systems are peopled. People act in roles as teachers, administrators, classified personnel, and students. Each actor has a different personality and possesses a personal set of need dispositions. Social systems are goal oriented; they have a set of goals and objectives that serve to guide their activities and behaviors. Social systems are structured; different components or subsystems are needed to perform specific functions. Social systems are normative; people are expected to behave in a particular manner. Formal rules and regulations prescribe expected behavior. Social systems are sanction bearing; norms for behavior are enforced and controlled through the use of punishment and rewards (e.g., promotion, merit, recognition, termination, demotion, expulsion). Social systems are open systems; the internal and external environments typically supply inputs to the system. Systems of education are affected by the values and beliefs held by the environments in which they are embedded.

Chester Barnard, Jacob Getzels, Egon Guba, and others view a social system as having a structural or institution element and a human or people component that are always interacting. How these two components relate to influence the overall behavior of individuals regarding the achievement of system goals and personal needs is of major interest to behavioral scientists. Figure 1.3 shows the foregoing organizational relationship. Barnard used the term **effectiveness** to describe those things done by an organization to bring about the accomplishment of organizational goals. Effectiveness is the extent to which the observed behavior of the worker is congruent with the expectations of the organization. He used the term **efficiency** to describe those actions implemented to bring about worker satisfaction relative to individual needs. Efficiency, in this context, is the extent to which the worker's behavior is congruent with his or her need dispositions.

The human resources administrator is faced with the challenge of balancing the two dimensions of the system. Barnard (1938) called this phenomenon the **capacity of equilibrium**, the ability to be productive, and at the same time, to satisfy the individual need dispositions of employees. Consider the effectiveness component and those activities or programs that are implemented by the school system to achieve stated goals and objectives. Getzels and Guba (1957) referred to this dimension as the **nomothetic dimension of the organization.** The nomothetic dimension

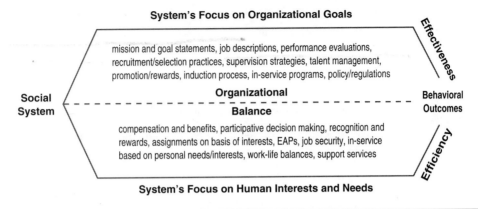

Figure 1.3   Effectiveness and Efficiency and the Human Resources Function

is characterized by well-defined patterns of organization, specific channels of communication, stated methods of operation, and hierarchical decision channels. The following activities or programs serve to foster the effectiveness component of a school system:

1. Development of mission statements with related lists of goals and objectives.

2. Adoption of school policies and administrative regulations.

3. Development of job descriptions that define each position in the organization.

4. Staff in-service programs that center on the development of knowledge and skills related to the goals of the organization.

5. Recruitment and selection policies and procedures that serve to gain the employment of individuals with the necessary skills to meet the goals of the system.

6. Orientation and induction programs that serve to inform employees as to what is important in the organization's mission and ways to achieve it.

7. Advancement policies that reward behaviors that are in tune with the organization's goals.

8. Compensation and merit pay policies that reward behaviors that serve to satisfy organizational goals.

9. The setting of job targets that focus on organization goal achievement.

10. The implementation of supervision strategies that promote desired organizational behaviors.

The efficiency dimension consists of individuals, personalities, and need dispositions. Behaviors that foster group maintenance, mutual trust, respect, positive relationships, and personal friendship exemplify this phenomenon. Other terms used to refer to this dimension are the human dimension, interpersonal domain, consideration, and persons-oriented domain. Efficiency activities and programs implemented to satisfy the needs of individuals in the organization include the following:

1. The implementation of participative management.

2. The implementation of compensation and benefits programs.

3. The provision of job tenure or continuing employment contracts for job security.

4. Employment assistance programs provided to help troubled workers.

5. Provisions and behaviors that serve to foster a healthy organizational climate.

6. Work assignment procedures that place workers in positions on the basis of personal interest and talent.

7. Interest-based in-service programs based on the personal interests and needs of the worker.

8. The provision of fair and equitable workload assignments.

9. Special provisions implemented related to the protection and security of employees.

10. Utilization of clinical supervision techniques and transformational leadership styles that center on building worker initiative and toward higher order need dispositions.

It is not the purpose here to delineate each of the foregoing activities and programs; rather, the purpose is to underscore these entries relative to their influence on the responsibilities of the human resources function. Each of the 20 provisions has important implications for the challenges facing human resources administrators. The list gives additional emphasis to the important challenges of the human resources function, its program provisions, its strategic planning focus, and its important goals and objectives; it underscores the inextricable relationship of the behaviors and activities of the school system and the responsibilities of the human resources function.

Increasing Diversity in the Workplace

Diversity, that characteristic of groups consisting of people who are different from one another, includes variations among people such as race, gender, age, ethnicity, education, and certain physical attributes, as well as the family and society into which individuals are born (Gomez-Mejia, Balkin, & Cardy, 2004). These authors ask the question, "Why manage employee diversity?" They answered the question by stating that, "Unless effectively managed, the presence of diversity among employees may create misunderstandings that have a negative impact on productivity and teamwork. It may also result in overt or subtle discrimination by those who control organizational resources against those who do not fit into the dominant group" (p. 122). Important changes in the nature of the workforce are having profound effects on human resources administration. One such phenomenon is the graying of America—the significant increase of elderly employees actively engaged in the workforce. According to the Bureau of the Census, by the year 2010, 27.8% of the nation's population will be age 45 or older; 14.1% will be 65 years of age or over. The American Association of Retired Persons (AARP) reported that 36% of the U.S. labor force in 2003 were 55 years of age and older (Armour, 2005). The Department of Labor's Bureau of Labor Statistics projects that of all workers in the United States, 46.5% will be 55 years of age or older by the year 2010. Figure 1.4 shows a range of phenomena related to workplace diversity. The following section discusses several of these factors.

Schools are working with a citizenry with a higher level of education; education in America is at an all-time high and "will continue to rise for some time as younger, more educated age groups replace older, less educated ones" (Murray, 2001, p. D7). In 1940, 24.5% of the American population over age 25 had high-school diplomas. That figure jumped to 82.4% in the year 2000. Challenges relating to educational diversity within the U.S. population are demonstrated by the fact that fewer than half of the Hispanic adults who migrated to the United States between 2001 and 2005 had a high-school education (Kaman, 2005). The wide range of differences of opinion regarding the solutions to problems of America's uneducated population will continue to face human resources administrators and other educational leaders in the years ahead.

The distribution of the population by race is another important challenge facing education in America. In regard to the workforce, the Department of Labor's

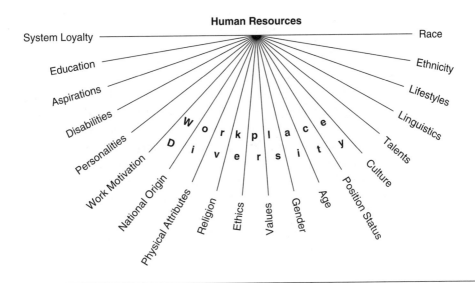

Figure 1.4   Diversity and the Human Resources Function

Bureau of Labor Statistics projects that the number of Asian employees in the United States, including Pacific Islanders, American Indians, and Alaskan Natives, will increase by 44.1% by the year 2010. Hispanic workers will increase by 36.5% and African Americans by 20.7%. These demographic changes have moved the nation to a multicultural, multiethnic society that will necessitate more flexible human resources policies in both public and private institutions in the future.

Why does this chapter give so much attention to the changing demographics of the United States? The primary reason is the fact that the successful school system and human resources function will have to deal with diversity, cultural diversity, ethnic diversity, linguistic diversity, and other such issues, including differences in attitudes about work and its place in one's personal life. The diverse composition of workers will require that new attention be given to the ways human problems are resolved. Human resources administrators will have to address differences in work ethics, organizational loyalty, personal behavior, and perspectives related to professional relationships. The strategies related to human resources planning necessarily must give full attention to the differences that are inevitable in human motivation, work commitment, and family life. Human resources administrators will be challenged to become knowledgeable of diversity management and the strategies that are most effective in achieving desired results.

The changes in demographics present certain problems, but also offer challenges and opportunities as well. Organizational leadership that focuses on the adoption and implementation of policies and procedures that capitalize on diversity is most likely to realize desired results.

Teacher and Administrator Supply and Demand

The U.S. Department of Education continues to report discouraging data regarding shortages of elementary- and secondary-school teaching personnel. Forecasts of teacher supply indicate that only half of the teachers needed in the next five years will be available. Major shortages in specialty areas such as special education, mathematics, science, and foreign languages continue. Efforts by some states, such as California, to reduce class size have been thwarted by the teacher shortage problem. National forecasts indicate that student-teacher ratios will change little if any during the remainder of this decade. The need for teachers will continue to center on student population increases and not on a reduction of pupil-teacher ratios. The challenge for human resources administrators is how to meet the needs for new teachers and at the same time retain the services of quality teachers in the school district.

Teacher shortages consistently rank high in surveys among the serious challenges facing human resources administrators. In a study by Norton (2004), only the problem of the lack of financial resources ranked higher. In one state study, 61% of the participating school principals named teacher shortages as one of the most serious problems facing them (Norton, 2005a).

We contend that the major human resources processes discussed throughout this text play a primary role in teacher and administrator retention. Reports indicate that as many as one-third of the nation's teachers leave the profession after their first year. Several studies have revealed that effective induction programs have a positive impact on teacher morale and retention. More than 30 years ago, Berglas (1973) found that providing personal assistance for new teachers was the single most important factor of all morale factors for those individuals new to teaching. Later, Lemke (1995) reported that well-planned and implemented programs of personnel induction were responsible for raising retention rates from 50% to 85%.

Both research and empirical evidence indicate that the retention of teachers is enhanced when effective human resources processes are implemented. For example, the selection process traditionally has centered on hiring a person who meets the school's needs, with little or no attention given to the candidate's immediate and long-term career goals. If the position does not provide opportunities for the candidate to meet his or her professional career goals over time, there is the possibility of a mismatch. If a mismatch does result, a bonding between the school district and the candidate is unlikely to occur.

School administrator shortages also are personnel concerns of paramount importance. There is some evidence that school principals nationally are seeking early retirement and that a high percentage of assistant principals do not have aspirations of assuming positions of school principal. Administrative quality has become a concern of both public and professional groups. Shortages of quality school administrative leaders have led to questionable practices in administrator preparation. The issue regarding who should prepare administrative personnel is an ongoing topic of debate. Questions concerning the qualifications of college and university personnel for preparing school administrators are common. Some people contend that the college and university personnel in preparation programs do not have personal experience in school administration. Others contend that practitioners in the field are in the best position to prepare school administrators; to them, university preparation is too theoretical. According to some arguments, there are far too many institutions in the work of administrator preparation, and administrator preparation should be done through selective academies or administrator centers similar to military academies, medical centers, or law schools.

Administrator shortages, as is the case with shortages of teachers and other professional personnel, often result in questionable program practices. One example is alternative certification programs that severely reduce the standards for preparation. In some instances, noncertificated persons are placed in administrative positions to do the required work, but are given nonadministrative job titles. If quality preparation and position certification are not important, the question arises whether certain central administrative or supervisory positions are really needed. Such actions often lead to cuts in middle management positions in the school and school district.

Some people contend that low salary is the crucial factor that militates against attracting personnel to the teaching profession. However, national studies have indicated that workplace conditions are the primary ingredients of job satisfaction for teachers. The more favorable the conditions of supervisory leadership and support, school climate, autonomy of teachers in the classroom, student relationships and parental support, the higher the teachers' satisfaction scores (Perie & Baker, 1997). Later chapters discuss topics related to employee supply and demand, such as teacher recruitment, teacher and administrator retention, compensation, and classified personnel turnover.

Employee Demands for a Balanced Work Life

Today's employees are seeking a balance between work and family life. The old adage of "living to work" has changed to "working to live." Some organizations have found solutions to the balance problem through various approaches to flexible scheduling, by varying work hours, job sharing, part-time teaching schedules, and telecommuting. Flexible scheduling helps employers meet the demands of employees for more control over their personal time. Some school systems are vowing to decrease their teacher shortages by supporting the tuition for educational expenses incurred for members who are working on advanced degrees in their area of expertise or are teacher aides working toward a Bachelor's degree and teacher certification. Some school systems are finding that providing incentives for teacher referrals can be effective in finding and hiring new personnel.

The nature of the American worker is changing, and these changes have become evident in the people who are employed in education. Accompanying these changes are changes in the workplace itself. For example, the average life expectancy in 1900 was 47.3 years, and in 2000 life expectancy was 76.5 years. The percentage of women working outside the home increased from 18.3% in 1900 to 63.0% in 2000. Keith Green, a spokesperson for the Society of Human Resources Management, believes that demographic changes are the biggest employee relations issues today, and that generational changes are very high on the list of issues facing organizations (Robertson & Moos, 2005).

Among the needs and often the demands of today's employees is the opportunity to have a balance between work and aspects of their personal lives. The concept of **workplace flexibility** has become a new challenge for human resources administrators in education. Flexible arrangements are being witnessed in many school districts. Employee contracts with such alternative work arrangements as more time off, variations in the number of hours worked, additional use of virtual means of communication techniques such as telecommunications and the outsourcing of some work activities, Internet communication techniques, freelance teams that serve as alternatives to permanent workers, concierge services made available to employees, child and dependent care benefits, job and task assignments rather than a specific number of assigned hours per week, and others such as full-time and part-time alternating work schedules are in evidence in organizations today.

Data concerning popular work life benefits being provided by companies were reported in a study of human resources executives in 45 states covering more than one million employees (Gannett News Service, 2004). Fifty-eight percent of the companies had established alternative work arrangements for employees, 58% provided work leave for attending school functions, 57% had established wellness programs, and 55% had telecommuting services. Such work life benefits are indicative of the provisions that are increasingly evident in educational organizations and are likely to be expanded in school settings during the next decade. Other challenges facing human resources administrators in the area of employee life-career policies are increased services relative to personal counseling, including mentoring and coaching, and other ongoing professional development support services. Each of these provisions necessitates new skills on the part of administrative personnel and increased funding for their accomplishment.

Although flex-time programs were operative in 29 million companies in 2001, this figure dropped to 27.4 million in 2004 primarily because of threats of employee layoffs in some companies and the fact that the use of outsourcing tended to obviate the need for flexible hours to cover off hours. It is clear that the economics of the time greatly influence the work arrangements implemented in all organizations (Armour, 2005). We contend that education is no exception and that the more traditional work arrangements in most school settings can be altered to become more conducive to positive work life balances.

Flexibility Consideration in Educational Settings

Research evidence regarding pressure and stress on the part of administrative and teaching personnel in teaching is invariably high. In one state study (Norton, 2004), 87.8% of the human resources directors described their job pressure/stress as being "very high" or "high." Studies of school superintendents, principals, and teachers have revealed similar statistics in this regard. The need for many people, according to Collier (2005), is a short sabbatical to renew their zest for life. In the same work, Collier refers to Jon Van Cleve's beliefs that organizations that provide sabbaticals get "newly recharged employees where their mind is clear and they're ready to embrace new ideas and concepts" (Collier, 2005, p. D3). In addition, companies are finding that time off can be an important benefit for attracting and retaining employees, especially in high-stress fields. The underlying concept of time off is that a rested employee is more effective; they are more ready to address new ideas and program changes. Some people argue that school personnel already have enough time off; after all, they contend, teachers are contracted for only nine months of the year and school administrators generally work only 11 months. We submit that times have changed; educational personnel have extended work assignments during the summer months or are completing advanced degree requirements or other credits tied to such programs as the No Child Left Behind Act, special language programs, or other professional development requirements relative to the demands of their current position. Dedicated school employees, teachers, administrators, and other support personnel see the necessity for ongoing professional growth and skill development. Although the concept of time off is a difficult sell in education, finding ways for employees in education to receive time off is an action long overdue.

Distance Education and Workplace Flexibility

Certain questions arise concerning innovations of part-time and flexible work time arrangements. How do such schedules affect the productivity of the school system and student achievement? Does flexibility in work schedules really result in improved employee retention? How would such flexibility actually work in school settings? Won't such work schedules tend to inhibit needed organizational communication? How do part-time work and distance education arrangements affect employee and school system bonding and commitment? More study is needed in order to provide better answers to such questions. An early study of part-time women employees did give some positive information in this regard (Steen, 2000). Many of the women in the study remained with their employers for many years, and approximately half were promoted during the time that they were employed part-time. Most reported that they were satisfied with the arrangement and that they believed they could return to full-time work if they so desired. Indeed, half of the women employees in the study did return to full-time employment after their part-time work experiences. **Boomerang hiring** is being witnessed throughout the educational professions. Estimates indicate that as many as 5% of former teachers in many school districts are rehires. Boomerang hiring provides one positive response to the teacher shortage problem. Former teachers who are rehired save both time and money in induction and professional development costs. In most cases, the teacher who returns to teaching has a different perspective and a more positive attitude. They often are among the school's most ardent supporters and are instrumental in recruiting new teaching personnel to the school and school district.

Innovations in distance education programming, whereby both the teacher and students work outside the traditional classroom using various means of telecommunications, permit quality teachers to reach more students. Computer technology is a way of life for most students today, and this fact permits an increased use of technology for instructional purposes. Schools will be challenged increasingly to become virtual systems, incorporating telecommunications, computer technology, and other distance-learning strategies in the delivery of instruction to larger audiences at all levels. Instructional time for students, for example, can be increased through the elimination of many of the administrative tasks and classroom interruptions evidenced in many traditional settings. Several years ago, the Mesa School District became the first district in Arizona to offer full-time distance learning for secondary schools. Some students take all of their course work through the Internet. The use of video streaming, a technique that allows students to view the teacher and communicate as well, is one way to compensate for the lack of one-to-one teacher-student contacts (Gayle, 2000).

Virtual teams, employee teams that use various technologies to work cooperatively when separated from one another, are another example of distance learning. Consider a human resources virtual team given the task of recommending criteria for performance evaluation of school principals. Time and travel expenses might be saved through the use of a number of technologies that expedite communication during the early stages of task organization and planning.

The outsourcing of learning programs, whereby students take advantage of local community learning settings or move to some alternative school program for a specified period of time, represents opportunities to utilize more effectively the learning resources in the local school community. Part of the resolution to the teacher shortage rests in the creative use of teaching talent within the school community. Who might be in the best position to instruct students in computer programming, for example? How might community resources become part of science education for some students? Many local sources might be tapped. Empirical evidence indicates that community organizations generally welcome the opportunity to become partners with the school. Through such extensions, students gain additional knowledge and skills, qualified talent within the community helps bring relevance to the school program, and local enterprises benefit through fostering the potential of new interest and competency of potential employees for their business enterprise. Such outsourcing requires the professional supervision of the local school and is subject to the rules and regulations of the school board and state agencies relative to instructional programming.

New Demands for Accountability Within the Human Resources Function

Pressures for human resources accountability will escalate in the years ahead. Increasingly, school system leaders, school boards, and other stakeholders are asking questions about the productive outcomes of human resources activities. Accountability, as it relates to the work of the human resources function, is revealed in the extent to which it establishes procedures and initiatives to deal with changes in the workplace, to contend appropriately with diversity, and to implement programs that provide specific evidence of their contributions to the goals of the school system. Although accountability measures are not new to the human resources function, the movement is now apparent in both public and private organizations. As early as 1966, a University of Michigan research program was instituted to develop and implement human resources accounting in industry. The first known seminar on human resources accounting, conducted by the Foundation for Research on Human Behavior, occurred in 1966 in Ann Arbor, Michigan (Brummet, Flamholtz, & Pyle, 1969). Among the participants at this HR accountability seminar were Rensis Likert, Director of the Institute for Social Research, University of Michigan; R. Lee Brummet, Professor of Accounting and Research Associate in the Institute for Social Research, University of Michigan; William C. Pyle, Human Resources Accounting Director, University of Michigan; and Eric G. Flamholtz, Assistant Project Director, Institute for Social Research, University of Michigan. As Pyle stated in his presentation to seminar participants:

> The first task of the research is to develop an operational model which will facilitate human resources management by guiding both the collection and reporting of relevant data . . . information which reflects how well human resources are being required and developed in the organization . . . and which indicates how adequately these resources are being utilized to achieve the objectives of the enterprise. (Brummet et al., 1969, p. 23)

These objectives still underlie the rationale for HR accounting measures today: the use of accounting to facilitate the effective management of human resources. However, contemporary perspectives are placing increased emphasis on HR's ability to provide specific evidence of its contributions to the "bottom line" of the organization's goals and objectives. As Pyle further stated, "If human resources are so important . . . why have conventional accounting systems failed to provide meaningful information about the firm's human resources?" (Brummet et al., 1969, p. 26).

We believe that HR administrators in education will be further challenged to produce evidence of HR's accountability to the goals of the school system and its stakeholders using methods similar to those used in other fields. Accountability related to the measurement of program results will be an ongoing challenge. Human resources administrators must be able to answer such questions as, "what procedural changes and program results are to be achieved through the implementation of this program proposal?" For example, the HR function will be asked to demonstrate its **return on investment (ROI)**. Terms such as ROI, bottom-line contribution, program impact, benefits versus costs, performance standards, and worth will inevitably be placed on the table of accountability of human resources personnel in education. The question will not be, "Did the HR unit provide performance management programs for its school principals?" but "Did the performance management programs result in improved practices, and to what extent?" Not, "Did the school principal and other HR administrators provide an effective induction program for new and continuing teaching personnel?" but "Did the planned induction program result in improvements in the first-year retention rate and overall teacher morale?"

Although soft measures such as job satisfaction levels, perceived values of training sessions, and opinions regarding the usefulness of certain program provisions will continue to be applied to assess HR processes and activities, hard data measurements that center on the difference between the monetary value of services provided or goods produced and the total dollar cost of all the materials and resources necessary to produce the services or goods will be addressed. Although this consideration is often difficult or seemingly impossible to determine in education, it is clear that more meaningful hard measures for assessing the effectiveness of HR processes will evolve as more attention and effort are given to this endeavor.

Behavior costing is a term Cascio (2003) used for attaching the economic estimates to the consequences of employee behaviors. He emphasizes the point that the benefit from determining costs related to the employee rests in being able to demonstrate positive results (e.g., financial gains, improved behavior) from the wise applications of human resources management methods. It is a mistake to assume that such processes as personnel recruitment are of no real cost to the school district because HR administrators are already salaried. Recruitment is a definite district cost. The expenses incurred in the writing and submission of advertisements for teaching positions, the process of developing and processing employee applications, the expenses involved in travel and per diem related to recruitment activities, telephone costs, software costs, reference checks, time and materials for interviewing candidates, and other related recruitment activities require time and money. For example, the activity of interviewing 25 candidates for one hour each at an estimated cost of $45 per hour results in an expense of $1,125. Assessments of this nature have an objective of ascertaining answers to such questions as, "Can we improve our recruitment and selection procedures so that we are able to reduce the time and personnel necessary for these activities and yet retain or improve the quality of hires generated? Can we adjust recruitment and selection procedures in order to realize a more specific focus on hiring needed minority candidates or special needs in certain subject-matter areas or reduce the number of candidates withdrawing at certain points in the recruitment and selection processes?"

It is not within the scope of this chapter to detail all of the various approaches to accountability that the HR function might take in school systems; later chapters of the text discuss many approaches. Because of its increasing importance of accountability, however, two examples of the possible uses of accountability measures are presented here: one focusing on the identification of future employee success and the other on calculating the costs of teacher absenteeism.

Over the past 85 years, researchers have tried to identify valid predictions for future job-related performance (Lohaus & Kleinmann, 2002). These writers use the term **potential analysis** in relation to the capability of a person to perform in a job at a certain level of competence. That is, potential analysis attempts to determine the extent to which an individual's skills that already exist or do not exist will develop or could be developed in the future. Schmidt and Hunter (1998) used intelligence tests, integrity tests, work sample tests, conscientiousness tests, structured employment interviews, biographical data measures, and assessment center results to assess the validity of such predictions. A combination of a general intelligence test and an integrity test had the highest validity relative to predictions of employee future job performance, a validity statistic of 0.65. A test of general mental ability had the highest prediction validity of 0.51 for jobs of average demands. General intelligence tests had a validity statistic of 0.58 for predicting the future job performance of managers in organizations. Using standard multiple regression, Schmidt and Hunter (1998) combined the general intelligence test validity results with each of the other testing methods. The combination of the general intelligence test and integrity test, for example, resulted in the highest validity statistic of 0.65. The general intelligence test combined with the work sample test or the structured employment interview validity score resulted in a 0.63 validity statistic. Although the assessment center validity statistic was the lowest, 0.37, when combined with the general intelligence test, it resulted in a validity statistic of 0.53.

Another example of the use of accountability is related to assessments of teacher absenteeism. As later chapters of the text will discuss, HR directors, school principals, and school superintendents view teacher absenteeism as a major problem and challenge of primary importance. In one study (Norton, 2004), HR directors named absenteeism of staff among the leading 10 major problems facing them.

Absenteeism is the failure on the part of any employee to be at work as scheduled, regardless of the reason for such absence. Absence for any reason results in a loss of productivity and an added expense for the organization. Although absences from work are most often viewed as being inevitable in education, empirical evidence suggests that personal illness is the reason used for many absences that are actually taken for other reasons. HR accountability necessitates being knowledgeable of the approximate cost of absenteeism as well as the determination of causes and possible improvement strategies.

Using certain approximations and assumptions, consider the cost of absences for a school district of 1,800 teachers who work 40 hours per week and average 8 hours per day. Assume that employee absenteeism accounts for 1.75% of the scheduled work hours (Cascio, 2003) and that the average hourly pay of teachers for the district is $31.50.

40 hr × 40 weeks = 1,600 hr

2 weeks' vacation or 40 hr × 2 = 80 hr

5 paid holidays or 5 × 8 hr = 40 hr

1,600 hr − (80 hr + 40 hr) = 1,480 hr

1,480 hr × 1,800 teachers = 2,664,000 total scheduled hours

2,664,000 × 0.0175 = 46,620 work hours lost per year

Using the hourly salary figure of $31.50, the loss per year, not counting expenses for substitute teachers and other related expenses, would cost the district $1,468,530.

The purpose of presenting the foregoing examples of accountability measures, of course, is not to argue whether teachers do or do not work more or less than 40 hours per week; rather, the purpose here is to demonstrate ways in which certain important information can be gathered relating to potential human competency projections or the costs of teacher absenteeism, teacher turnover, teacher in-service programs, and other HR processes and activities. The discussion serves to emphasize the matter of human resources accountability and the challenges therein. In cases in which accountability measures are inappropriate for educational applications, they should be rejected with reason. On the other hand, it seems clear that many appropriate accountability applications can add immeasurably to the assessment of HR practices and lead to positive improvement of the function. Accountability assessments do not just happen; just like other programs and functions in education, accountability assessments require administrative planning, implementation, and evaluation.

Later chapters of the text demonstrate in detail the challenges related to human resources accountability measures in several ways. We contend that terms such as added value, quality management, recruitment and selection yield ratios, and performance management will become part of the daily vocabulary of practicing HR administrators. More attention will be placed on outcomes of human resources program results. Questions such as the following need to be asked: "What do the hard data reveal regarding the expenses incurred for implementing the recruitment program and the number of applicants selected for the recruitment pool? How many applicants were selected from the pool as potential candidates for positions in the school district? What percent of the candidates was actually offered positions in the school district? What percent of the candidates who were offered positions accepted contracts? What were their performance ratings of contracted employees for the first year in the district? What percent of the employees remained in the school district after year one?"

Answers to the foregoing questions would provide important data for needed change and improvement in the recruitment and selection processes. If the present recruitment and selection processes do not add to the value of the school district's specified objectives, their effectiveness becomes questionable. The reality of this concern in business, industry, and now in education is illustrated by increasing recommendations in some quarters for eliminating the central office human resources function and placing its responsibilities in the local schools or outsourcing many of the current HR processes.

The implications for human resources administrators are clear. Accountability measures must be given much more attention than they receive at present. Hard data about program results must be gathered, examined, and reported objectively. Accountability measures are presented in several chapters of the text.

An Operational Model for Assessing Accountability Effectiveness. Human resources administrators have the responsibility for evaluating the effectiveness of the accountability measures implemented in the program. Similar to any effective program in educational settings, effective accountability programs require administrative planning, implementation, and evaluation. The following operational model begins with the determination of the selection of processes, activities, and target area to be measured and ends with controls that serve to assess the effectiveness of the end results. Like other operational models, this accountability model serves as a guideline for the implementation of important activities and presents opportunities for alterations that meet the unique needs of different situations in different school settings.

Step 1—(a) Selection of the human resources processes, problems, or target areas to be measured. Delimit the target areas to be included in the assessment. Is the focus to be related to a specific HR process such as recruitment or to an identified problem such as teacher turnover, a service such as an employee assistance program (EAP), a program such as incentive pay, or the contribution of the HR function to a specifically stated school district goal? (b) Consider the nature of the data and information that need to be gathered relative to the target area(s) selected. Are the data and information available and can they be measured? (c) Determine to whom the final report will first be submitted (i.e., central human resources unit administrators, school superintendent, central administration cabinet, school board, etc.).

Step 2—(a) Selection of the assessment team members. Some persons would consider this as the first step in the assessment process. Commonly, one or more individuals first identify the target areas to be addressed in the assessment, and the selection of appropriate team members follows. (b) Team member characteristics: temperament, experience, ability, and motivation. Team relationships loom important in assessment activities; poor temperament has been identified as the number one reason for unsuccessful teamwork. It is essential that members have experience in human resources administration and the specific target area(s) to be addressed. People selected for team membership should have a prior record of interest in the target area(s), and their record of accomplishment should reveal a specific motivation in HR and the specific target areas to be measured. (c) Does the present work schedule allow for a commitment of the individual to the time commitments required in the assessment work schedule, or can the work schedule of the individual be altered satisfactorily to permit the member to participate? (d) Does the potential team member possess unique talents necessary for the completion of the assessment that other members might not possess?

Step 3—(a) Data collection and related sources of support. In view of the target area(s) to be assessed, what methods of data collection will be most productive? What information is already available in organizational documents, business reports, HR data files, and other research methods? What data collection instruments will be required? (b) Collect needed data and information through the use of well-designed questionnaires, structured interviews, pre- and post-test strategies, and other research methods.

Step 4—(a) Compile and analyze data using appropriate statistical methods (percentages, correlations, variations relative to collected descriptive data). Use appropriate instrumentation such as t-tests to determine significant differences. Be certain that data analysis is consistent and accurate. Attempt to keep statistical presentations as direct and simple as possible. The use of central tendencies such as means, medians, modes, and correlations is preferable for presenting descriptive data. (b) Use appropriate graphs, figures, and illustration to help explain the data including before and after graph illustrations. Use all data collected including those that are not necessarily positive. (c) Double-check the accuracy of data and information collected and statistical results. One error in the assessment report can result in a negative reaction to the entire report.

Step 5—(a) Complete a preliminary written draft of the assessment results. Carefully review the draft within the assessment team; make needed revisions. (b) Share the preliminary report with appropriate others (e.g., HR personnel directly involved in the work of the target area(s) assessed, HR director if not a team member, school superintendent, etc.). (c) Have the assessment team debrief input from others and make appropriate changes in the draft as necessary.

Step 6—(a) Completion of the final assessment report with recommendations as fits the case. Recommendations might include suggestions for follow-up assessment activities or priority suggestions for improvement of the target area(s) assessed. Feedback should be timely in relation to school board agenda schedules, community concerns, and budgetary timelines. (b) Keep the media in mind. Reports of this nature are viewed as public documents. Special feedback sessions with the media are advisable. Reports must be objectively and honestly presented.

Step 7—(a) Decisions regarding target area(s) improvement plans. The accountability assessment team may or may not be directly involved in the decisions regarding needed program improvements set forth in the assessment report. In most cases, the team's recommendations will give consideration to this issue. That is, what is the most appropriate unit within the school district to make decisions concerning the improvement needs, and how will specific decisions be made in this regard? (b) Written reports most often include the following major sections: introduction with purposes and background information, assessment methods that were implemented, data collected and the statistical analysis of the data, study resources required included related expenditures, assessment findings, assessment conclusions, and related study recommendations.

Step 8—(a) Evaluation of the assessment procedures and the effectiveness of the assessment results. A follow-up evaluation of the effectiveness of the assessment activities is an important final step in the operations model. Both an objective team evaluation of its work and feedback from appropriate others relative to the work of the team and the study results are needed. An assessment of the assessment is recommended. (b) Criticism of accountability activities in education will likely occur. That is, some groups and individuals will point to the fact that education is not a for-profit business. Rather, education's purpose is people oriented and directed toward the goal of student achievement, not the sale of products or services for financial gain. Questions will be asked, such as how can the monetary value of teachers and other school employees be determined in relation to the business concept of added value? How can the long-range value of an in-service activity really be assessed? Aren't there far too many variables involved in the determination of the efficacy of an employee induction program or a performance evaluation program to determine outcomes objectively? Although such questions are legitimate and difficult to answer, the fact is that current challenges regarding pressures for human resources accountability are inevitable and certain to increase during the decade ahead. Proactive leadership on the matter of accountability by human resources administrators will become an increasing requirement. Different chapters throughout the text discuss applications of accountability measures in the area of human resources administration.

Selected New Trends
in Human Resources Administration

We previously noted that issues, challenges, and trends in education are inextricably related. Various problems are related to each issue. Problems can lead to many challenges, and their solutions can lead to improved practices. A **trend** is a general movement or detectable change in thinking or practice. It is a tendency that has emerged in the field of practice and later may become a prevailing practice. The challenges discussed in the preceding section could be viewed as trends in human resources as well. For example, dealing with workplace diversity, efforts to increase the retention rates of teachers and administrators, the increasing use of automation and other technologies in HR practices, work-life balance provisions, and increases in the implementation of distance education practices all represent trending developments in HR administration.

At the outset of the first decade of the 21st century, Losey (2000) set forth the future leadership role of all human resources administrators. He stated that, "While maintaining the special body of HR knowledge, professionals in human resources management must also be generalists who understand economics, politics, social and cultural trends, government mandates in labor laws, diversity management, health care management, privacy concerns, international trends, and a myriad other issues. For HR professionals of today's business environment [it is essential] to understand and manage the important interaction of technology, work flow, organizational strategies and, most important, people" (p. 17). Losey's contention remains relevant today: human resources administration in education will continue to deal with an ever-expanding HR agenda, but also will have to address the concerns of a changing workforce.

The following section emphasizes three specific trends in education generally that have significantly influenced practices within the human resources function as well. The first trend centers on the changing role of the human resources administrator in education, including the responsibilities of those leaders at the local school level. This consideration includes the corresponding need for increased competence on the part of all HR administrators. Thus, a second major trend discussed in the following section is competency-based performance related to state and national administrative standards such as the ISLLC standards for school administrators. In addition, the impact of the No Child Left Behind Act (NCLB) is discussed. A third trend is that of talent management.

The Changing Leadership Role of the Human Resources Administrator

The foregoing discussions related to issues and challenges revealed several changes in the leadership role of the human resources director. A major trend in the leadership role of the HR function during the next 10 years will be the ongoing change from a support and maintenance function to a strategic leadership role. Through the implementation of such developments as automation and outsourcing, central office HR directors will spend less time on such basic maintenance activities as record keeping, dealing with employee benefits, and the recruiting, screening, and selecting of employees. Technology will permit entire HR processes to be automated, enabling many present tasks to be completed more efficiently and at less cost. HR administrators will become more directly concerned with policy matters related to talent development, compensation practices, staff retention strategies, and other HR policy matters that focus on the school system's primary goals and objectives. This movement brings about a leadership function that has commensurate system responsibilities in strategic planning and decision making. As a result, new leadership will require new knowledge and new skills on the part of all HR administrators. If the HR function is to become an effective partner in the policy decision process of the school system, continuous growth and development on the part of its administrators not only will be an expectation, but will become a requirement. As Schramm (2005) noted, "if planning and strategy are two elements in the process affecting how organizations respond to changes . . . day after day, HR's role in strategic planning may become even more important to the organization—the intellectual and productive capacity of its work force. HR will be central to understanding the future of an asset that is increasingly important to the organization—the intellectual and productive capacity of its work force" (p. 152).

Dana and James Robinson (2005) have underscored the increased attention given to learning and performance. As these writers note, "Just as 'personnel administration' transformed into 'human resource strategy' to reflect the profession's changing role in the organization, so too will 'training and development' change over the next decade" (p. 65). As we previously noted, function accountability for fostering organizational growth and development will increase the need to focus on outcomes rather than just the activity. The learning and performance focus will be integrated into the administration procedures of the organization at a strategic level. That is, learning will be embedded directly into the program tasks that employees must perform; learning and doing will become seamless (Robinson & Robinson, 2005).

A variety of learning methods, including coaching, mentoring, on-the-job experiences, job rotation, programmed class sessions, university courses, distance learning programs, and other technology, will greatly increase. Computer technology will permit immediate access to best practices in relation to an immediate problem or need. Users will enter their query into a computer and receive information in seconds. Authorities are now speaking of knowledge management, learning programs, and classroom delivery. **Knowledge management** involves the processing of information readily from one unit to another. Learning programming will be closely tied to the goals, objectives, and business requirements of the school system. Classroom delivery, programmed for the professional development of the employee, will be centered more strategically in that it will reflect the present needs and challenges facing the system. Its purpose will be to gain knowledge and skills that will be immediately applicable to workplace needs.

Administrative Standards and Their Influence on the Human Resources Function

Along with the many legislative mandates and legal requirements that affect policies and administrative procedures of human resources administration, almost every state has adopted standards to guide the planning, restructuring, and evaluation for the preparation and licensing of school leaders. Trends such as the establishment of the national ISLLC standards have had a major influence on the preparation and practices of human resources administrators. As Norton (2005b) stated, "Although criticized by some authorities for their limitations relative to a comprehensive perspective of the work of school leaders, by 2004 more than 40 states had either adopted or recommended the use of the ISLLC standards for the improvement of leadership preparation programs in both university-based and non-university based settings" (p. 64). Because the standards have many implications for the work in human resources administration and for the preparation of leaders in this area, these standards are set forth in the following section along with their knowledge requirements and the specific chapters in this text in which specific HR implications apply.

ISLLC Standards and Their Knowledge Requirements for School Leaders

Standard 1: A school administrator is an educational leader who promotes the success of all students by facilitating the development, articulation, implementation, and stewardship of a vision of learning that is shared and supported by the school community.

Standard 1 Knowledge

- learning goals in a pluralistic society (Chapters 1, 2, 6, and 9)
- the principles of developing and implementing strategic plans (Chapters 1 and 3)
- systems theory (Chapters 1 and 2)
- information sources, data collection, and data analysis strategies (Chapters 1, 3, 5, and 9)
- effective communication (Chapters 1, 6, 7, and 8)
- effective consensus building and negotiations skills (Chapters 7 and 8)

(Continued)

(Continued)

Standard 2: A school administrator is an educational leader who promotes the success of all students by advocating, nurturing, and sustaining a school culture and instructional program conducive to student learning and staff professional growth.

Standard 2 Knowledge

- student growth and development
- applied learning theories (Chapter 2)
- applied motivational theories (Chapter 2)
- curriculum design, implementation, evaluation, and refinement
- principles of effective instruction
- measurement, evaluation, and assessment strategies (Chapters 1, 3, and 8)
- diversity and its meaning for educational programs (Chapters 1 and 8)
- adult learning and professional development models (Chapter 7)
- the change process for systems, organizations, and individuals (Chapters 1 and 3)
- the role of technology in promoting learning and professional growth (Chapters 1 and 3)
- school cultures (Chapters 1 and 8)

Standard 3: A school administrator is an educational leader who promotes the success of all students by ensuring management of the organization, operations, and resources for a safe, efficient, and effective learning environment.

Standard 3 Knowledge

- theories and models of organization and the principles of organizational development (Chapters 1, 2, and 3)
- operational procedures at the school district level (all chapters)
- principles and issues relating to school safety and security (Chapters 1 and 6)
- human resources management and development (all chapters)
- principles and issues relating to fiscal operations of the school (Chapters 1, 10, and 11)
- legal issues affecting school operations (Chapter 9)
- current technologies that support management functions (Chapter 2)

Standard 4: A school administrator is an educational leader who promotes the success of all students by collaborating with families and community members, responding to diverse community interests and needs, and mobilizing community processes.

Standard 4 Knowledge

- emerging issues and trends that may affect the school community (Chapter 1)
- the conditions and dynamics of the diverse school community (Chapters 1, 8, and 9)
- community resources (Chapters 7 and 8)
- community relations and marketing strategies and processes (Chapters 1 and 8)
- successful models of school, family, business, community, government, and higher education (Chapters 1, 2, and 8)

Standard 5: A school administrator is an educational leader who promotes the success of all students by acting with integrity and fairness and in an ethical manner (Chapter 9).

Standard 5 Knowledge

- the purpose of education and the role of the leadership in modern society (Chapter 1)
- various ethical frameworks and perspectives on ethics (Chapters 2 and 6)
- the values of the diverse school community (Chapters 1 and 6)
- professional codes of ethics (Chapter 6)
- the philosophy and history of education (Chapter 2)

Standard 6: A school administrator is an educational leader who promotes the success of all students by understanding, responding to, and influencing the larger political, social, economic, legal, and cultural context.

Standard 6 Knowledge

- principles of representative governance that undergird the system of American schools (Chapters 1 and 6)
- the role of public education in developing and renewing a democratic society and economically productive nation (Chapters 6 and 9)
- the law relating to education and schooling (Chapters 6 and 9)
- the political, social, cultural, and economic systems and processes that affect schools (Chapters 1, 2, 9, and 10)
- models and strategies of change and conflict resolution as applied to the larger political, social, cultural, and economic contexts of schooling (Chapters 1, 2, 8, 9, and 10)
- global issues facing teaching and learning (Chapter 1)
- the dynamics of policy development and advocacy under our democratic political system (Chapter 9)

NOTE: The Interstate School Leaders Licensure Consortium (ISLLC) Standards were developed by the Council of Chief State School Officers (CCSSO) and member states. Copies may be downloaded from the Council's website at www.ccsso.org.

SOURCE: Council of Chief State School Officers. (1996). *Interstate School Leaders Licensure Consortium (ISLLC) standards for school leaders*. Washington, DC: Author. Reprinted by permission.

Each ISLLC standard is accompanied by a knowledge statement that serves to define the specific skills required of the leader as well as those dispositions related to the fundamental beliefs, values, commitments, and skills that reflect the concomitant behaviors related to the standard. Although parts of each chapter of this text add to the accomplishment of the six ISLLC standards, several chapters deal directly with specific ISLLC standards. For example, Standard 3 centers on ensuring a safe, efficient, and effective learning environment in the school. Chapter 6 discusses the stability and protection processes of the HR function, and Chapter 8 centers on human resources development set forth in ISLLC Standard 3.

Competency-Based Performance and the Human Resources Function

Trends related to the implementation of state and national standards also are noted in the increasing focus on competency-based performance in education.

Competency-based performance is revealed in HR programs and activities in several ways. For example, the concept has influenced the assessment of administrative effectiveness. The tasks, skills, and indicators of skills of the human resources function are identified and used as the criteria for performance evaluations. First, a relevant statement of human resources tasks, skills, and indicators of competency required in the role of all HR administrators is determined. The specific responsibilities, obligations, or requirements of the position, termed **tasks**, are delineated. Each task is accompanied by relevant **competencies** or abilities needed to accomplish the task at a satisfactory level of performance. The products or behaviors that illustrate one's capacity to perform competently, termed **indicators of competency**, are identified. The indicators of competency, along with a determined evaluation procedure, are used to evaluate the human resources administrator's performance. Competency-based statements are used for other purposes as well. Because the tasks in each competency statement contain the primary responsibilities of the human resources position, the statement is an excellent source for the development of job descriptions. Competency-based statements help define the role of the human resources administrator and underscore the areas of personal development required for effective performance.

Figure 1.5 shows a statement of selected skills related to the role of human resources administration. Although the skills focus on the work of the central office human resources unit, many of them apply equally well to school principals and other human resources personnel.

In Figure 1.5, the major task required of the HR director is the process of filling vacancies. Related competencies include the ability to research and develop a staffing needs inventory and the ability to identify viable sources for recruiting qualified applicants for school system needs. Competency indicators, relating to the ability to research and develop a staffing needs inventory, would include such indicators as "reviewing research regarding staffing patterns and allocations, conducting and calculating forecasting strategies related to enrollment projection and employee transition statistics" (Norton, 2005b, p. 100).

Although competency-based performance has been used for several years, such growing trends as talent management, performance assessment, and accountability have brought it to the forefront. It is apparent that state and national administrative standard statements are always competency based.

The No Child Left Behind Act

The No Child Left Behind Act (NCLB), signed by President George W. Bush in January 2002, has had a major impact on education and the human resources function in education. Although the NCLB's primary purpose is to commit schools to bringing all students up to grade level or better in reading and math by 2014, it reaches far into many aspects of the human resources function. Part A of Title II of the Elementary and Secondary Education Act (ESEA) provides funds to ensure that all teachers are qualified and effective. Other parts of the NCLB emphasize such human resources activities as professional development for teachers and multiple

1.1   Ability to research and develop a staffing needs inventory.

1.2   Ability to identify viable sources for recruiting qualified applicants for school system needs.

1.3   Ability to develop with others an appropriate process for the screening of the best candidates for a given position.

1.4   Ability to develop with others an effective induction program for new and continuing personnel.

1.5   Ability to plan and implement with others a continuing process for staff development and growth.

1.6   Ability to plan and develop with others an effective program of assessment and evaluation for staff personnel.

1.7   Ability to provide effective counseling, EAPs, and mentoring programs that focus on the needs and interests of staff personnel.

1.8   Ability to assist in the development of a strategic planning program for the human resources function of the school district in relation to the strategic plan of the school district.

1.9   Ability to plan, develop, and administer with others an effective program of compensation and benefits program for system personnel.

1.10   Ability to participate in the collective bargaining process as fits the case of the particular school system.

1.11   Ability to disseminate and educate others regarding the provisions of the negotiated agreement between the school board and the employees' association and to support others in its administration.

1.12   Ability to take the lead in the development of effective policies for the human resources function for consideration and adoption by the school board.

1.13   Ability to develop an effective and efficient records management system for the school or school district.

1.14   Ability to administer effectively the personnel resource processes of the human resources function.

1.15   Ability to plan, prepare, and present an appropriate budget to support the work of the human resources function.

1.16   Ability to develop appropriate metrics for the measuring of accountability within the many programs and activities of the human resources function.

Figure 1.5   Selected Competencies of the Human Resources Administrator

career paths toward becoming a career teacher, mentor teacher, or exemplary teacher. Although it is beyond the scope of this chapter to detail all of the HR provisions that are encompassed within the NCLB, several of the purposes and provisions within the various titles are noted as follows:

Staff Development—Provision of high-quality professional development. The focus is on strategies that will help with the adoption and implementation of more effective teacher development activities.

Teacher Advancement Activities—Use of program funds for teacher advancement initiatives that foster professional development and emphasize continuous career path growth.

Merit-Based Performance—State funds are authorized to assist local educational agencies to develop merit pay or differential pay systems in "high poverty" schools and districts.

State Testing of Subject-Matter Competence or Assistance in Meeting State Certification Requirements—Such activities may be done under the stated regulations of ESEA Title II.

Special Teacher Preparation—Use of funds to increase opportunities for minorities, individuals with disabilities, and other underrepresented individuals in teaching.

Scientifically Based Research—Use of funds to do research that involves the application of rigorous, systematic, and objective procedures to obtain reliable and valid knowledge relevant to education activities and programs.

The regulations and definitions used in the NCLB and related titles are both specific and comprehensive. For example, the term "high quality professional development" means professional development that meets the criteria contained in the definition of professional development in Title IX. Professional development includes, but is not limited to, activities that

- Improve and increase teachers' knowledge of academic subjects and enable teachers to become highly qualified.
- Are an integral part of broad schoolwide and district-wide educational improvement plans.
- Give teachers and principals the knowledge and skills to help students meet challenging state academic standards.
- Improve classroom management skills.
- Are sustained, intensive, and classroom-focused and are not one-day or short-term workshops.
- Advance teacher understanding of effective instruction strategies that are based on scientifically based research.
- Are developed with extensive participation of teachers, principals, parents, and administrators. (U.S. Department of Education, Improving Teacher Quality State Grants, ESEA Title II, Part A, Revised, October 5, 2006)

As we noted at the outset of this chapter, the issues, problems, challenges, and trends that the HR function encounters are closely related. Other considerations ahead in human resources administration include changes in such matters as health care, employee benefits, personnel offices in local school locations, technology-enabled learning for employees, implementation of HR metrics, and increased attention to compliance with local, state, and national laws. Various chapters discuss these and other concerns.

Trends Concerning Talent Management and the Human Resources Administrator

Talent management is an effort to measure an employee's individual work performance against the specific objectives determined by the organization and the individual. The underlying objective is to discern the personal strengths of the employee, to capitalize on these strengths in work assignments, and to improve individual weaknesses that could serve to derail or inhibit the ultimate success of the employee. Talent management also includes staff retention and development and succession planning ("Critical Issues in HR," 2006). Thus, talent management becomes an important challenge for practicing administrators of personnel. Identifying and capitalizing on unique skills of personnel within the school system can facilitate team building and self-managed work teams that serve to raise important questions and suggest new solutions for the issues and problems being encountered.

Organizational reform most often necessitates a change in organizational structure. Such restructuring requires expertise in talent management; effective deployment of human resources is of paramount importance. We submit that a major challenge facing the human resources function in education is that of performance management.

Many writers have proposed guidelines for performance management. However, the six components Stephen and Roithmayr (1998) set forth several years ago remain viable. These authorities emphasized that human resources administrators must be competent in implementing the following:

1. Planning, the setting of performance objectives. Cooperative decision regarding the performance expectations of the employee accomplishes several positive ends. First, it provides a two-way discussion between the supervisor and the employee concerning the important aspects of the work itself. Second, it serves as a basis for fostering personal initiative on the part of the worker in the accomplishment of objectives that tie closely to the overall goals and objectives of the organization. Third, the setting of objectives serves toward the end of work accountability. Performance is reviewed and evaluated on the basis of objectives that were cooperatively determined at the outset.

2. Measuring, the determination of methods of assessing results. Although this factor focuses on best practices as revealed by research and empirical evidence, the emphasis is on the end results. Research has shown that effective employees are most willing to accept responsibility for the performance results for which they have had input and appropriate personal control.

3. Developing, establishing individual development plans. This factor centers on the continuing growth and development of the employee. It permits the worker to take responsibility for his or her own personal development. It sets the stage for objectively evaluating personal performance.

4. Reviewing, evaluating achievements against objectives. When the foregoing steps are implemented, they provide valuable data and information for reviewing and evaluating performance results. Professional employees want to become better performers in their fields. When given the opportunity, they will take charge of their own personal destiny.

5. Coaching, giving appropriate feedback to the individual employee. Coaches use their techniques to help other individuals by using a combination of education, cheerleading, and listening to help individuals ask and then answer important

questions about their work and their behaviors. Although coaches give feedback to the individual, the goal is to help the individual think through a situation toward the goal of self-resolution. The activity provides an opportunity for the employee to view improvement as personal; self-esteem is fostered.

6. Rewarding and recognizing, compensating for individual contributions realized. Employees want to know how well they are doing. Research studies reveal that the worker needs to know that personal productivity contributes to the overall goals and objectives of the organization; the work is important. When high levels of performance are realized, appropriate rewards and recognition serve to reinforce such behavior. (Adapted from Stephen & Roithmayr, 1998, p. 231.)

HR Focus ("Critical issues in HR," 2006) underscored other significant HR challenges and priorities. The number one priority for HR directors was talent drive, including staff retention, staff development, and succession planning. Other challenges for the HR function included employee engagement and enhanced productivity (how to get more from current employees); leadership training and development at all levels; using technology for efficiencies and cost saving; how to develop and implement the "right" metrics to provide information required by system leaders regarding human capital contributions to the system; compliance with federal, state, and local laws; and automated hiring functions including applications and testing.

Summary

The important work of human resources administrators is revealed in large part in the issues, problems, challenges, and trends encountered in the function. Education, as one of the most significant institutions nationally, is a social system that must deal with the political, economic, and social issues of the time. Human resources, as a major function of education, must deal responsibly with the same issues, problems, challenges, and trends that affect education.

The primary issues that influence policies and practices in human resources administration include changes in the governance and leadership of education; existing relationships and cooperation among and between individuals and agencies; financial support; the increasing demands made on personnel in the field; legal mandates and requirements made by various local, state, and national bodies; and the extraordinary expansions of automation and technology worldwide. Each issue carries with it different problems that must be analyzed and resolved.

Issues and problems result in challenges from internal and external forces that most often seriously affect the work responsibilities of the HR function. Diversity within the community and workforce demands changes in the way the human dimension of the organization is administered. The emergence of such positions as Vice President of Talent Acquisition and Diversity, as the Dennis Corporation created in 2006, might well become a growing practice. Other developments, such as teacher and administrator supply and demand, the increasing calls for accountability of the HR function, demands by employees for a more balanced work life, and the expanding implementation of distance education methods for increasing employee learning opportunities, are among the challenges facing HR administrators in organizations.

Trends in education emerge, grow, and develop, and often become daily practice. It is clear, however, that the role and responsibilities of the contemporary human resources leader are changing. Strategic processes within the school and school district place the HR administrator in an important role in the planning and implementation of school community goals. Although the traditional responsibilities of the maintenance role of the HR function will continue, innovations in technology will permit such processes as recruitment, selection, and compensation and benefits to be accomplished more quickly and efficiently and at less cost to the school district.

State and national requirements such as state, regional, and national standards and movements for increasing teacher and administrator competency are influencing HR practices in many ways. Such trends will necessitate an ongoing program of professional development for all school employees. Accountability within the HR function will be a way of life in the future.

Discussion Questions

1. Identify the primary social trends in a school and community with which you are most familiar. What is the nature of such trends? Which of these trends do you view as being most important and why? How are these trends influencing educational practices in the school and school system? What specific school district policies or regulations have been adopted and implemented as a result of the trends that you have identified?

2. The chapter discusses diversity and speaks of "the management of diversity." Review the section in the chapter that centers on this challenge. Then, analyze the extent to which you believe schools and school districts in America are meeting this challenge. Be specific in your answer by citing examples and current practices.

3. The chapter content addresses the topic of the school as a social system. First, review the theoretical concept of a social system and its dimensions. Next, specifically consider the idiographic or human dimension of a social system. What specific provisions and programs might be provided within the system for employees that promote the improvement and effectiveness of the human dimension?

4. Consider ISLLC Standard 5 and its knowledge standard related to "the values of the diverse school community." First, list several values of a diverse school community. Then, be specific in describing several ways in which the strategic goals and objectives of the HR function in the school district might promote the list of such diversity values.

5. Assume the role of HR director in the Fairbanks School District. You have been asked to report on the outcomes of an administrators' academy program that included all school principals two years ago. The two major experiences provided by the academy centered on recruiting quality teachers and retaining their services in the school district. What metrics and accountability measures might you prepare and include in the forthcoming report?

Case Studies

CASE 1.1

MISSING PERSONS REPORT

The Fairbanks School District's student enrollment has 9,500 students in grades K–12, 55% of whom are minorities. The school district is located just south of a large metropolitan school district with similar student diversity statistics and adjacent to two other suburban school districts with minority student populations of 25% and 20%, respectively. Each district has grades K–12. Although the student enrollments in the metropolitan school district and the two adjacent school districts have increased substantially during the last several years, the Fairbanks School District declined in population from 11,275 to 9,500 within the same time period.

Several recent personnel problems have resulted within the Fairbanks School District. Some school parents and other stakeholders have equated the enrollment loss with an underperforming school district, although state test scores show the achievement of students in the Fairbanks district to be at the same level as the surrounding school districts. The salary schedule provisions at the competing schools are quite comparable to the salary provided by the Fairbanks district.

Superintendent Rodriguez has asked you to report at a forthcoming school board study meeting and lead a discussion on the matter of declining enrollment and the issues, challenges, and problems that it is presenting in the district. The superintendent has asked you, as the district's personnel director, for an assessment of the issues and related problems surrounding the present status of enrollment decline, rather than having specific solutions at this point.

Questions

1. In view of the key factor of school decline, what are some special issues and related problems that you might have encountered to date, or ones that you would forecast for the future unless viable solutions are implemented? What specific challenges might you note?

2. What additional information and data might be important in the preparation of your report to the school board? For example, what accountability measures might be used in this case at this time?

3. Some might argue that it is simply a matter of demographics; the Fairbanks School District has a much higher percentage of minority students than surrounding districts. What is your response to such an argument?

CASE 1.2

ENOUGH IS ENOUGH!

Dylan Joseph, principal of Whittier Middle School, was in attendance at the monthly school board meeting. One topic focused on the updating of job descriptions for all administrators in the school district. A task force of representative administrators within the district had gathered information relative to the major job responsibilities of the school principal and the central human resources director. Taking a clue from recent trends to have the personnel function become more strategically related to the district's decision-making process, the task force recommended that the school district's central personnel office turn over the HR processes of recruitment, induction, selection, assignment, and others to the local school principals. The central office HR director would serve in the superintendent's cabinet for strategic purposes.

The discussion that followed the recommendation was somewhat heated. Board member Krieser commented, "Yes, and this could save money in several ways. Perhaps the central office personnel staff could be reduced in size." The director of personnel, Ted Sutton, immediately stated, "Well, of course, we could not reduce the central staff anymore than it is already, but the idea of placing personnel in the middle of important administrative decisions is a trend nationally." Principal Bassett asked the question, "Hasn't anyone examined the list of recommended responsibilities for school principals? Taking on the work of the central office personnel director doesn't make sense. Enough is enough."

Questions

1. In view of the limited information revealed in Case 1.2, discuss the issues and problems involved in gaining a workable perspective among and between the respective individuals and offices within the school system. Consider the nature of the human resources function. How can the function of human resources be administered effectively under the concept that "every administrator is a human resources administrator"?

2. Human resources is often viewed as a shared responsibility. In your opinion, is such a statement merely a cliché or can it be implemented realistically?

CASE 1.3

WHAT'S HAPPENING?

Fairbanks Middle School

MEMO

To: Virginia Bassett, Principal

From: Raul Cruz and Gwen Storer (Grade 8 Social Studies and Fine Arts, respectively)

RE: Issue of Merit Pay

Several of us on the staff have been discussing what we view as a detrimental move for the Fairbanks Middle School teaching staff. We have heard that talks on merit pay for teachers have been taking place at various levels in the school district.

(Continued)

(Continued)

Although our information is based on hearsay, we understand that the school's Site-Based Advisory Committee is considering the recommendation of merit pay for teachers at our school. The Fairbanks Middle School teaching staff has two specific questions at this time. First, if and when a merit pay proposal becomes a reality, how do you plan to include representation from the faculty? A highly important question in our opinion is, "Would you support such a movement for schools and why?"

Too many decisions that involve the professional teachers seem to be implemented without our knowledge. Both state and national agencies have proposed merit-pay plans under the guise of career development, quality performance, and other plans. As you know, merit pay in education is an issue that has not been well received and likely would not really work here either.

Since your leadership opinion would weigh heavily on any decision about merit pay in our school, we ask that you inform us of your stand on this issue.

Questions

1. Assume the role of Principal Bassett and draft your response to the appropriate persons. Avoid merely stating that you know nothing of the matter and cannot respond at this time. The intent here is to have you think through the issues and problems related to merit pay and related pay-for-performance plans.

2. Develop a list of what you perceive as the pros and cons of merit pay and pay-for-performance programs.

3. Are you aware of a merit pay or pay-for-performance program that has been implemented successfully in a school system? Briefly describe the plan. Has it been universally accepted by the personnel involved in the plan? Why or why not?

References

Armour, S. (2005, July 31). Flex-time hours wane, report says. *Arizona Republic, USA Today*, p. D1.

Barnard, C. I. (1938). *The functions of the executive.* Cambridge, MA: Harvard University Press.

Berglas, W. W. (1973). A study of relationships between induction practices and the morale of the beginning teacher. *Dissertation Abstracts International, 34*(5), 2189-A.

Brummet, R. L., Flamholtz, E. G., & Pyle, W. C. (1969). *Human resources accounting.* Ann Arbor, MI: Foundation for Research on Human Behavior.

Cascio, W. F. (2003). *Managing human resources: Productivity, quality of work life, profits* (6th ed.). New York: McGraw-Hill/Irwin.

Collier, J. G. (2005, February 5). Small steps can lead to contentment. *Arizona Republic*, p. D3.

Critical issues in HR drive 2006 priorities: #1 is talent drive. (2006, January). *HR Focus, 83*(1), 1, 13.

Gannett News Service. (2004). Popular work life benefits of workers. *Arizona Republic*, Section D.

Gayle, J. S. (2000, September 12). More students choosing school from a distance. *Arizona Republic*, Section Tempe, p. 1.

Getzels, J., & Guba, E. (1957). Social behavior and the administrative process. *School Review, 65*(4), 423–441.

Glass, T. E., Bjork, L., & Brunner, C. (Eds.). (2000). *The study of the American school superintendency.* Arlington, VA: American Association of School Administrators.

Gomez-Mejia, L. R., Balkin, D. B., & Cardy, R. L. (2004). *Managing human resources* (4th ed.). Englewood Cliffs, NJ: Prentice Hall.

Hertling, E. (2001). Retaining principals. ERIC Digest, 147. Retrieved June 17, 2001, from http://eric.uoregon.edu/publications/digests/digest147.html

Interstate School Leaders Licensure Consortium. (1996). *Standards for school leaders.* Washington, DC: Council of Chief State School Officers.

Kaman, J. (2005, March 28). Migrants lack diplomas. *Arizona Republic,* p. A1, A6.

Kimball, K., & Sirotnik, K. A. (2000). The urban school principal: Take this job and. . . ! *Education and Urban Society, 32*(4), 535–543.

Lemke, J. C. (1995). Attracting and retaining special educators in rural and small schools: Issues and solutions. *Rural Special Education Quarterly, 14*(2), 25–30.

Losey, M. (2000). HR comes of age. In F. Maidment (Ed.), *Human resources: 00/01* (10th ed.). Guilford, CT: Sluice Dock.

Lohaus, D., & Kleinmann, M. (2002). Analysis of performance potential. In S. Sonnetag (Ed.), *Psychological management of individual performance.* West Sussex, UK: Wiley.

Murray, M. (2001, April 29). An added benefit for workers: Flexibility. *Arizona Republic,* p. D7.

Norton, M. S. (2001). *The school superintendency in Arizona: A research study.* Tempe: Arizona State University, Division of Educational Leadership & Policy Studies.

Norton, M. S. (2004). *The human resources director in Arizona: A research study.* Tempe: Arizona State University, Division of Educational Leadership & Policy Studies.

Norton, M. S. (Ed.). (2005a). *Competency based preparation of educational administrators: Tasks, competencies, and indicators of competency.* Tempe: Arizona State University, Division of Educational Leadership & Policy Studies.

Norton, M. S. (2005b). *Executive leadership for effective administration.* Boston: Allyn & Bacon.

Perie, M., & Baker, D. P. (1997). Job satisfaction among America's teachers: Effects of workplace conditions, background, characteristics, and teacher compensation (NCES 97471). Washington, DC: U.S. Department of Education, National Center for Educational Statistics.

Robertson, J., & Moos, B. (2005, July 18). New day: Execs are younger than help. *Arizona Republic,* p. D1, D5.

Robinson, D., & Robinson, J. (2005). A heightened focus on learning and performance. *HR Magazine, 50*(73), 65–67.

Schmidt, F. L., & Hunter, J. F. (1998). The validity and utility of selection methods in personnel psychology: Practical and theoretical implications of 85 years of research findings. *Psychological Bulletin, 124,* 262–274.

Schramm, J. (2005, October). Planning ahead. *HR Magazine, 50*(10), 152.

Steen, M. (2000, September 10). Part-time needn't damage career. *Arizona Republic,* p. D5.

Stephen, A., & Roithmayr, T. (1998). Escaping the performance management trap. In M. Butteriss (Ed.), *Re-inventing HR: Changing roles to create the high-performance organization* (pp. 229–249). Etobiocke, Ontario: John Wiley & Sons, Canada, Ltd.

U.S. Department of Education. (2006, October 5). *Improving teacher quality state grants, ESEA Title II, Part A, Revised.*

Whitaker, K. (2000). Where are the principal candidates? Perceptions of superintendents. *NASSP Bulletin, 85*(625), 82–92.

Yerkes, D. M., & Guaglianone, C. L. (1998, November/December). Where have all the high school administrators gone? *Thrusts for Educational Leadership, 28*(2), 10–14.

Young, I. P. (2008). *The human resource function in educational administration* (9th ed.). Upper Saddle River, NJ: Pearson Merrill Prentice Hall.

CHAPTER 2

The Human Resources Function

A Historical Perspective

Learning Objectives

After reading this chapter, you will be able to

- Gain an appreciation for the contributions many individuals and groups have made to the development of personnel administration historically.
- Understand how contemporary industrial and business practices in the United States and other countries set the stage for early personnel practices that later were greatly influenced by the sciences of psychology and sociology.
- Identify specific practices in today's human resources processes that were researched and put into practice as early as the 19th century.
- Define and describe the major processes of the human resources function.
- Gain knowledge of the specific standards that guide practices of the human resources function as set forth by the American Association of School Personnel Administrators.
- Gain knowledge of the ethical standards that guide the relationships and program provisions of the human resources function.

Policies and practices in education are inextricably related to the social, economic, and political influences of their time, and the human resources function is no exception. The evolution of human resources administration is revealed in four major eras of administrative history. This chapter discusses these eras and the significant contributions to personnel administration that individuals made during these time periods. Such terms as job descriptions, division of labor, span of control, incentive pay, bureaucracy, hierarchy of authority, and accountability, which are common terms in personnel literature today, were among the personnel concepts introduced into personnel practices as early as the 19th century. This chapter details contemporary organizational processes of the human resources function. It places emphasis on the responsibilities of the central office human resources unit and on the increasing responsibilities of the local school district. In addition, it examines the standards that guide the practices of the human resources function along with the ethics required of human resources administrators.

Personnel Administration Before 1900

Before 1900, religious groups, community influentials, and parents assumed the primary responsibility for overseeing the proper education of children and youth and only reluctantly permitted outsiders to give instruction outside the home. The title **selectmen** was given the influential persons asked to supervise what was to be taught and how instruction was to be presented. Although the selectmen knew little about education, they closely monitored the instructional process and the work of the teachers who served in the schoolroom. Personnel work consisted mainly of hiring the teacher, assigning the working conditions and value lessons to be taught, determining the salary to be paid, and firing an incompetent teacher when they considered it necessary.

Professional administration in the early 1800s was slow to develop. The nation was in the early stages of moving from a rural to an urban population. In the early decades of the 1800s, the cities of Baltimore and Cleveland tried to hire a school superintendent, but the city councils were reluctant to do so. A common procedure at the time was to use a member of the select committee to manage special aspects of the business of the school, including certain personnel tasks.

By 1870, only 29 school superintendents served schools across the nation. Local schools relied heavily on the county superintendent to help with such personnel matters as the training of teachers. Teachers in the 19th century were marginally prepared, many with only a high school education. Although teachers generally were required to be licensed, few held college degrees. Even as late as 1900, no state required a degree for teaching elementary school, and only two states required a degree for secondary school teaching. By 1920, no states required an elementary school degree and only 10 states required a secondary school degree for teaching. By 1965, all states required a degree for secondary school teaching, and 45 did so for teaching at the elementary school level.

As the various states attempted to control their schools, they found the state school board and state superintendent of schools overwhelmed with education's growing demands. The logical answer was the creation of the county superintendent's office. Delaware had the first recorded county superintendent in 1829. By 1879, 34 of the 38 states had created the office. For the next 75 years, the county superintendent of schools provided useful services to local schools, including specific contributions to teacher preparation. Although the two-year normal school reached prominence by 1870, much in-service training was done through teacher institutes sponsored by the county superintendent's office. In the early 1840s, Henry Barnard, Connecticut's state superintendent of schools, made a suggestion to the Connecticut legislature to begin a Teachers' Institute. When refused, Barnard reportedly used his own funds to call a three-day meeting at which he and others taught lessons on the basics, globes, and "school keeping." Later, county township institutes provided similar experiences for teachers. "Among the means provided for enhancing the efficiency of the public school of Indiana none are capable of affording the teachers and schools more benefit than the Township Institute" (Bloss, 1882). Laws in many states required the county sponsorship of such teacher institutes.

During the early decades of the 19th century, administrative management was in disarray and without professional direction. Many local schools had principals who also taught full time; most had little formal administrative preparation. Yet, it was a common practice to have the school principal assume personnel duties. As schools began to increase in number and size because of the nation's population increases, education became too complex for laymen to handle; more administrative personnel were needed to administer the school programs.

With the advent of the public high school in the late 1800s and the development of larger, more comprehensive school systems, the influence of the county school superintendent waned and local "specialists" began to assume local roles in school administration. Yet, before 1900, there was little evidence of organized central office personnel services in school systems. Personnel services were assumed largely by the local school principal or by other central office personnel of the school district. For example, the coordination of personnel services often became part of the responsibilities of the school business official, the director of instruction, or the school superintendent. World War I prompted new concerns for the handling of large numbers of workers for the war effort. This development led to the implementation and ultimate growth of the centralization of personnel units in school districts. However, separate personnel units were not found in many school districts of size even in the 1950s. During the early 1960s, personnel came to be recognized as an important function for quality school districts. Some universities began to provide coursework in the personnel area and recommended that personnel positions be instituted in local school districts. By 1966, an estimated 250 such central personnel offices existed nationally. Today, an estimated 3,000 central office personnel director positions exist in the nation's school districts. Although the personnel function has always been viewed as a shared responsibility, today local school administrators have assumed many of the personnel responsibilities for school districts. This topic is discussed later in the chapter. As mentioned previously in Chapter 1, the term "personnel function" evolved into the term "human resources," which gave more emphasis to the people assets of the organization.

The Scientific Management Era and Its Impact on Personnel Practices

The **scientific management era,** which dominated organizational thought primarily from 1890 to 1920, greatly influenced practices in personnel administration. Although many individuals contributed to the scientific management concepts of the time, Frederick Taylor is historically viewed as the father of scientific management. At the turn of the 20th century, the nation was facing a critical, cost-conscious public; there was alleged mismanagement of all government institutions; the cost of living was on the rise; and the American people were calling for reform. These conditions set the stage for Taylor and his concepts of task management and efficiency.

Taylor's system of **task management** centered on the concept of efficiency, the best way to do a task at the lowest possible cost. Taylor published his work, *The Principles of Scientific Management,* in 1911. He set forth 13 steps in his management plan, one of which included the distributing of minute, specialized tasks, which, when taken together, would get the job done more efficiently. Another important step was the coordinating or ordering of these numerous, small tasks to the entire job. Such task considerations led to the piece-rate principle, time and motion studies, and the division of labor between management and the worker. Included within the task concept was performance evaluation that resulted in the implementation of incentive pay or merit pay programs. Businesses and industrial organizations readily adopted these concepts, and by 1912, national leaders in education were endorsing them as best practices for school systems. For example, topics for the 1912 NEA/Superintendents' annual meeting included, "The Principles of Scientific Management Applied to Teaching Music," "Securing and Maintaining Efficiency in the Teaching Force of Normal Schools," and "A Study of Adolescent Efficiency" (Callahan, 1962).

Other people made important contributions to personnel administration of the scientific management era, including Lyndall Urwick, Henri Fayol, Max Weber, Frank and Lillian Gilbreth, Henry Gantt, and others. Lyndall Urwick wrote on the seven principles of management. Two of the primary principles were the **principle of definition**, every individual performs a single function, and the **principle of organization,** duties and responsibilities should be clearly and completely defined in writing—the initial concept of personnel job descriptions (Urwick, 1937).

Henri Fayol was the managing director of a French mining and metallurgic company from 1888 to 1918. The English version of his work, *General and Industrial Management,* was first issued in 1949. Fayol divided all activities within the undertakings of industrial management under six major groups: technical, commercial, financial, security, accountability, and managerial. Fayol listed five major elements of managerial activities, ultimately termed POCCC: to plan and forecast, to organize, to command, to coordinate, and to control. Later, in 1938, Luther Gulick elaborated on Fayol's concept and set forth the acronym POSDCoRB: planning, organization, staffing, directing, coordinating, reporting, and budgeting. Staffing centered on the personnel responsibilities of the school administrator. These primary elements have been instrumental in guiding administrative practices since their inception. Fayol also coined or extended the importance of such terms as the division of work, unity of command, unity of direction, subordination, scalar chain, equity, stability of tenure, initiative, and esprit de corps. Many authorities believe that Fayol's contributions, along with Max Weber's concept of bureaucracy, were the essence of mechanistic organizations of the scientific management era.

Weber's concepts of authority in organizations and the ideal organization remain relevant in organizational theory today. He was concerned with human frailty and the unreliability of human judgment due to biases, favoritism, and incompetence. His answer was to bring **rationality** into the organization through such developments as depersonalization. He viewed the bureaucratic structure as being more predictable and able to bring about a climate with less friction and confusion. Weber described the ideal organization as having the following five elements: (1) a hierarchical structure with well-defined lines of authority; (2) functional specialization exemplified by a division of labor based on competency; (3) prescribed competence exhibited by certification of competency; (4) impersonal relations whereby personal, emotional, and irrational elements are eliminated; and (5) rules of behavior evidenced by a system that prevents the unpredictability of the individual worker and reduces human error (Weber, 1910/1947). Most people would agree that school districts today exhibit many of the foregoing bureaucratic characteristics.

Frank and Lillian Gilbreth, both industrial engineers, were friends of Frederick Taylor and endorsed his task concepts for effective organizational practices. Frank Gilbreth (1911), through his time and motion studies, demonstrated worker efficiency, job simplification, and cost reduction procedures in organizations. In his memorable study of bricklayers on the job (Gilbreth, 1909), he observed every facet of the work requirements of bricklaying, including the worker's physical movements, the tools used in the trade, and the relative production of each worker. As a result, job standards and techniques were recommended that reportedly increased the work efficiency of bricklayers and their production fourfold. Lillian Gilbreth was a highly competent engineer and industrial psychologist in her own right. She worked with companies in the designing of more efficient kitchens in the home and helped disabled women accomplish common household tasks. She was the recipient of many awards and honorary degrees during her career. Frank and Lillian Gilbreth often are remembered because their lives and concern for efficiency were portrayed in the popular movies *Cheaper by the Dozen* and *Belles on Their Toes*, which were based on books written by their children.

Henry L. Gantt was an industrial engineer who also became acquainted with Frederick Taylor and his work at the Midvale Steel Works in Pennsylvania. Gantt set forth many of his organizational concepts in his work, *Gantt on Management*, published in 1961. The work set forth concepts of planning and control, task setting, cost accounting, task bonuses, and charting. His contributions in the area of charting are perhaps most memorable. His chart concepts remain in use in all facets of business, industry, and education today. He recommended and devised charts for recording worker production, worker behavior, worker progress, company inventories, ordering, machine efficiency, machine costs, and many others. Management concepts of structure and efficiency were the underlying features of Gantt's work.

There were many other contributors to the scientific management era. Among the contributions of these persons were concepts related to controlled conditions of work, line and staff positions, departmentalization, prescribed competence, CEO (chief executive officer of the organization), specialization, accounting, forecasting, worker discipline, centralization and decentralization, the exception principle (executive management deals with a matter only if it cannot be handled at a lower level), principle of subordination, and many other personnel considerations. Although Frederick Taylor and the concepts associated with the scientific management era are sometimes criticized in the literature for their apparent lack of human consideration, the era was responsible for setting the foundation for many of the contemporary practices in educational administration and the administration of the human resources function.

The Human Relations Era and Its Impact on the Human Resources Function

Several factors underscored the gradual move from the scientific emphasis in management to the human relations movement that focused on people. As we previously mentioned, scientific management came under severe criticism for what many perceived to be the inhumane treatment of the worker. At one time, Frederick Taylor was called before a congressional committee to explain and defend scientific management procedures that some people viewed as asking workers to behave like machines. Most authorities today agree that Taylor's focus on management overlooked the human factors important to worker motivation and productivity. However, his contributions to the matter of worker efficiency and the use of scientific approaches to the study of management were far-reaching.

Thinkers and writers such as Mary Parker Follett began to expound on the concept that "organizations are people." Follett, along with other authorities such as Elton Mayo, Fritz Roethlisberger, William Dickson, Kurt Lewin, Ralph White, Douglas McGregor, Ronald Lippitt, and Frederick Herzberg, was instrumental in changing approaches to administration in all organizations and added new dimensions of thought to the relationships between administrative supervisors and the employees in the organization.

Terms such as coordination, informal and formal groups, the Hawthorne effect, motivators and hygienes, job satisfaction, Theory Y, basic needs, commitment, and others were among those initiated or emphasized in the theories and concepts that various individuals set forth in the human relations era.

The spirit and urgency of the human relations movement were expressed pointedly by Tead and Metcalf in the early 1920s.

The new focus in administration is to be the human element. The new center of attention and solicitude is the individual person, the worker. And this change comes about fundamentally for no sentimental reasons, but because the enlistment of human cooperation, of the interest and goodwill of the worker, has become the crux of the production problem. . . . Present development is in the direction of a new science and a newly appreciated art—the science and art of personnel administration. (p. 1)

Contributors to the Human Relations Movement

Mary Parker Follett was among "the women who made an impact on the management discipline in spite of the cultural constraints of the era" (Parks, 2001, p.1). She was a strong advocate of employee empowerment and the use of integrative conflict resolution strategies. She espoused the use of coordination within organizations as opposed to the hierarchical authority that existed in the early 1920s.

In regard to leadership, Follett spoke of "power with" rather than "power over" other members of the organization. In her work, *Creative Experience*, she related "power over" to **coercive control**, which she termed the curse of the universe (Follett, 1924). Power with or **coactive power** was considered as genuine power that she viewed as the enrichment and advancement of every human soul. A problem or conflict is best resolved through integrative methods. Integration requires the interaction of group members with one another to achieve common goals. Both management and the workers together must study the situation and search for the real values on both sides of an existing situation in order to bring about a mutual resolution to the matter. According to Follett, only through such a self-governing principle can the growth of individuals be facilitated and the members of a group fulfilled.

The primary concern of management, according to Follett, should be the building and maintenance of dynamic yet harmonious relationships. Her views on coordination were revolutionary at the time she proposed them in 1924. She believed that specific concepts of coordination were instrumental in focusing methods of personnel practices on the positive goals of organizational harmony. The four views of coordination that Follett (1940) stipulated are as follows:

Follett

1. *Coordination by direct contact.* Persons responsible for the work must be in direct contact regardless of their level of authority within the organization. Both horizontal and vertical communication within the organization are necessary if positive coordination is to be achieved.

2. *Coordination at the time of the formulation of policy decisions.* The persons responsible must be directly involved at the time of the formulation of policy decisions, not merely informed after a decision has been determined. Involvement will serve to enhance motivation, commitment, and morale.

3. *Coordination as the reciprocal relationship of all factors in a situation.* Existing relationships in a situation must be carefully weighed and examined. All factors

surrounding a situation must be related to one another and the inputs and probable outcomes carefully considered as to their effects on these factors.

4. *Coordination as a continuing process.* Factors of coordination such as individual and group participation, individual and group relationships, and internal and external communications must be viewed as ongoing, continuous responsibilities of the administrator.

Because many of Follett's ideas were revolutionary at the time of their introduction, they were not always readily accepted. By 1933, her ideas had become less acceptable in the thinking of management and organization. Some authorities believe that she was "too far ahead of the times." Follett's concepts of organizations as cooperative systems with existing human relationships and organizational coordination are generally accepted in management theory today.

Elton Mayo was an industrial researcher who came to the United States from England. He is often called the father of the human relations movement. As a member of the faculty at Harvard University, he and his associates studied personnel problems related to worker turnover, work incentives, employee boredom, employee motivation, employee production, group behavior, and other aspects of human behavior on the job. Mayo was especially interested in the ideas of Mary Parker Follett and, as early as 1923, he and others investigated working conditions in a textile plant in Philadelphia. The plant reportedly was experiencing high levels of employee turnover due to monotonous work that led to boredom and low production. Mayo introduced rest pauses and made a full-time nurse available to aid employees and to act as a listener to personal needs. As a result, both production and morale improved. When the employees were allowed to participate in deciding the frequency and duration of the work pauses, more improvement was realized. According to reports, in a few months the turnover rate was reduced to that of other units in the mill. The initial explanation of the turnaround was that the work pauses and other changes served to remedy the monotony and improve the mental outlook of the workers. However, a follow-up study at the Hawthorne plant of Western Electric Company in Chicago was to alter the foregoing explanation.

Between 1923 and 1926, Mayo and an associate, Fritz Roethlisberger, carried out various experiments in an attempt to answer the question, "What effects did illumination have on the worker and worker production?" Variation of more or less lighting for one group and constant lighting for another group was implemented; they found no significant differences in the work production of the two groups. Regardless of the extent of the lighting, production increased in both cases.

The foregoing study was followed by a series of studies by Mayo and his associates (Mayo, 1933; Roethlisberger & Dickson, 1939). In one investigation, Mayo's team inserted a variety of variables into a setting that included six females working on assembling telephone relays. During this five-year experiment, the team maintained a detailed record of the variables and resulting conditions. One variable was a special group incentive plan; others were rest pauses, shorter hours, and the provision of refreshments. The experimenters reportedly went out of their way to discuss the changes with the women before their implementation. Production invariably increased.

In another part of the experiment, Mayo inserted the same conditions that were in effect at the very outset of the research. The employees were put back on an eight-hour day, six days a week with no rest pauses and no refreshments. As a result, worker output went to its highest level recorded to that time. The researchers concluded that the physical conditions of room lighting, rest periods, and other such factors were not significant for worker efficiency and production. What went on inside the worker was more important than the outside conditions of the work itself.

Overall, the work of Mayo and his associates focused attention on the importance of human relations, morale, and informal networking in all organizations. The importance of human motivation in a social system brought attention to the importance of worker aspirations and communication among and between management and employees. The experiments revealed that under certain conditions, increased group responsibility and improved work production come from within the group itself. The topic of informal organizations became an important aspect of organizational research.

Other major contributors to the human relations movement were Kurt Lewin and his colleagues Frederick Herzberg and Douglas McGregor. The following section discusses the contributions of each of these individuals.

Kurt Lewin, Ronald Lippitt, and Ralph White (1939) conducted early research on leadership styles and their effects on work outcomes and personal behavior of personnel. Their 1939 study examined the behaviors of 10-year-old boys in relation to leadership styles termed **authoritarian**, **democratic**, and **laissez-faire**. Authoritarian leadership was defined as the use of directed behavior whereby the leader set the goals and the procedures for accomplishing them. Democratic leadership was characterized by organized but cooperative approaches to decision making. Laissez-faire leadership was defined as a free-rein approach that encouraged personal initiative with few restrictions on individual or group choices. The researchers avoided labeling the leadership styles "best" or "wrong." By having teachers use the specific characteristics associated with each of the leadership styles, procedures relating to the development of lesson goals, lesson procedures, partnerships, and work production were implemented. The major finding of the experiment was that different leadership styles do indeed lead to different behavioral outcomes (White & Lippitt, 1960). Although authoritarian leadership did result in higher levels of production, personal outcomes resulted in lower levels of cooperation and morale, higher levels of frustration, and less self-direction. Democratic leadership brought about positive behaviors such as superior morale, cooperation, group unity, and self-direction. In addition, outcomes of higher levels of work quality and self-direction resulted. Inferior work quality, less productivity, and a higher degree of dissatisfaction were evident when the laissez-fair style of leadership was implemented. The results of these studies were far-reaching; democratic leadership and democracy in organizations became the focus of best practice in all organizations, including school settings. The terms democratic schools, democratic administration, democratic supervision, democratic teaching, and democratic personnel administration led practices within the human relations era and continue in contemporary personnel practices.

The Two-Factor Theory of Job Satisfaction was reported in Herzberg, Mausner, and Snyderman's book, *The Motivation to Work* (1959). Its impact on employee

Herzberg stated that the factors leading to job satisfaction and those leading to job dissatisfaction are different. Those factors related to job satisfaction (motivators) and job dissatisfaction (hygienes) by accountants and engineers are identified in Part "A". Part "B" reveals the same factors as revealed in a study of teachers by Thomas Sergiovanni. Part "C" shows these factors for school administrators as found in a study by Gene Schmidt.

MOTIVATORS	HYGIENES
A. Accountants and Engineers	A. Accountants and Engineers
1. Achievement 2. Recognition 3. Work Itself 4. Responsibility 5. Advancement 6. Salary	1. Company Policy and Administration 2. Technical Supervision 3. Salary 4. Interpersonal Relations With Subordinates 5. Working Conditions
B. Teachers	B. Teachers
1. Achievement 2. Recognition 3. Work Itself 4. Responsibility	1. Interpersonal Relations With Students 2. Interpersonal Relations With Peers 3. Company Policy and Administration 4. Technical Supervision
C. Administrators	C. Administrators

1. Achievement
2. Recognition
3. Advancement
4. Interpersonal Relations With
   Subordinates
	1. Company Policy and Administration
	2. Interpersonal Relations With
	   Supervisiors
	3. Interpersonal Relations With Peers
	4. Interpersonal Relations With
	   Subordinates

Figure 2.1   Herzberg's Two-Factor Theory of Job Satisfaction

SOURCE: Herzberg, Mausner, and Snyderman (1959), Sergiovanni (1967), and Schmidt (1976).

motivation and job satisfaction is reflected both in today's administrative practices and by the great number of follow-up research studies that tested the theory in most every professional field. The Two-Factor Theory's major hypothesis was as follows: The factors leading to positive attitudes (toward work) and those leading to negative attitudes are different. The study pursued the question of whether different kinds of factors were responsible for bringing about job satisfaction and job dissatisfaction. Herzberg and colleagues' study population included engineers and accountants who were interviewed for the purpose of determining the factors that they associated with job satisfaction and job dissatisfaction. Figure 2.1 reveals job satisfaction and dissatisfaction factors for accountants and engineers as found in the early studies by Herzberg and associates and for teachers and administrators in studies by Sergiovanni (1967) and Schmidt (1976). As revealed in Figure 2.1, achievement, recognition, work itself, responsibility, advancement, and salary appeared to be important in fostering job satisfaction. The central focus of these factors is on the job itself: accomplishments and outcomes of the work, recognition for doing the work, having meaningful work, having personal responsibility for the work, moving upward on the job, and being appropriately compensated for the work. Because these factors served to bring about job satisfaction, they were termed

motivators. Those factors associated with job dissatisfaction included bad company policy and administration, poor methods of employee supervision, inadequate salary, poor interpersonal relations with supervisors, and poor working conditions. These factors, termed **hygienes**, will bring about job dissatisfaction.

The factors in Herzberg's study that fostered satisfaction of people in their jobs were different than those factors that made people dissatisfied. For example, an employee who had neither negative nor positive attitudes toward his job would become a satisfied worker if the factors of achievement, recognition, meaningful work, job responsibility, and advancement were present. However, the absence of these motivators would simply bring the worker back to a neutral position, but not to job dissatisfaction. Similarly, the existence of negative hygiene factors on the job would result in a dissatisfied employee. According to the theory, however, the positive existence of the hygiene factors would not create a satisfied employee but would simply bring the employee back to a neutral position. It is interesting to note that similar studies of school administrators, school teachers, nurses, and other professional employees have found results quite similar to those of the Herzberg study. A contemporary study of the job satisfaction of teachers in America's schools revealed that administrator support (relationships with supervisors) and leadership, student behavior, the school climate, teacher autonomy (teacher control over classroom conditions), and parental support related to job satisfaction for teachers (Perie & Baker, 1997). Workplace conditions were key factors in the determination of job satisfaction. The more favorable the working conditions, the higher the satisfaction scores. Compensation and benefits were only modestly related to job satisfaction.

Douglas McGregor (1960) opened new thinking about leadership styles and human potential in his theory of motivation published in his work, *The Human Side of Enterprise.* McGregor's **Theory Y** was most significant in the fact that it went beyond merely satisfying individual needs. Rather, it revealed a new confidence for the intelligence and initiative of the individual worker to contribute in extraordinary ways to the organization in a pursuit toward self-direction and personal fulfillment. McGregor's Theory Y concepts are as follows:

- The expenditure of physical and mental effort in work is as natural as play or rest.
- External control and the threat of punishment are not the only means for bringing about effort toward organizational objectives. People will exercise self-direction and self-control in the service of objectives to which they are committed.
- Commitment to objectives is a function of the rewards associated with their achievement.
- The average human being learns, under proper conditions, not only to accept but to seek responsibility.
- The capacity to exercise a relatively high degree of imagination, ingenuity, and creativity in the solution of organizational problems is widely, not narrowly, distributed in the population.
- Under the conditions of modern industrial life, the intellectual potentials of the average human being are only partially utilized. (pp. 47–48)

Several key human resources implications are revealed in McGregor's Theory Y contentions. First, they underscore the vital significance of the human resources function and the confidence that can be placed in the human element of the organization. Second, it suggests both the potential of employee talent and its availability throughout the organization. Third, it emphasizes the fact that the human resources function is a shared responsibility, and fourth, it encourages the human resources concept that higher achievement is likely to follow higher expectations.

The Behavioral Science Movement and Its Contributions to the Human Resources Function

We noted previously in this chapter that social systems have an organizational or institutional element and a human or people element that are continuously interacting. Behavioral scientists are interested in studying just how these two elements interrelate to influence human behavioral outcomes and organizational goal achievement. The work of two important contributors to the behavioral science era, Jacob Getzels and Egon Guba, was discussed earlier in the chapter. Most authorities consider the work of Chester Barnard (1938) to be one of the most important contributions to behavioral science and to the educational administration profession in general. The following section discusses Barnard's work and the works of several other organization and motivation theorists.

The Contributions of Chester Barnard

Chester Barnard is recognized as being among the first to view an organization as having a structural or formal dimension and a human or informal dimension that are always interacting. His seminal work, *The Functions of the Executive* (1938), motivated others to study how these two dimensions interrelate to influence the overall behavior of individuals and groups regarding the achievement of system needs and goals.

Barnard's concepts of organizational cooperation are of special interest to human resources administration. He contended that the individual possesses a limited power of choice; environmental factors and man's physiological makeup make cooperation imperative. For example, protection, security, and the maintenance of other human needs depend on cooperative behavior.

According to Barnard (1938), cooperation depends on the system's leadership to obtain a balance of equilibrium between these two phenomena. If the system fails to provide effectiveness and efficiency, system cooperation is not possible. Therefore, Barnard submits, every executive must perform three key functions:

1. *Formulation of organizational purposes.* The essential basis of cooperative action is cooperative purpose. Acceptance of purpose by members of the organization is essential.

2. *Maintenance of communication in the organization.* Communication is vital for translating purpose into action. Decision making depends on communication. As Simon (1957) stated, without communication there can be no organization.

3. *Obtaining the necessary performance from members.* Commitment involves securing the essential services from members through bringing them into cooperative relationships and motivating them to surrender control of personal conduct in order to achieve **superordinate goals.**

Each of the foregoing executive functions relates directly to the work and responsibilities of human resources administrators. Barnard's work served to underscore the importance of individual behavior in effective organizations. His concepts emphasized the fact that organizations are composed of people who have individual needs and motivations. His work supported the contention that authority exists only to the extent that the workers are willing to accept it. Barnard motivated others to study these relationships. The following section presents a summary of the contributions of several others to the behavioral science movement.

Herbert A. Simon

Simon, a winner of the Nobel Prize, published *Administrative Behavior* in 1947. Simon used economics, psychology, and sociology to analyze administrative theory. Like Barnard, he focused on the organization's capacity of equilibrium and the belief that motivation was a matter of exchanging incentives for work commitments. Simon, like Weber and others, was concerned with rationality in organizational decision making. He held the view that most decisions must be made without complete information; only a few of the many available alternatives can be considered. In addition, people cannot attach accurate values to results. People are willing to accept what is "good enough" rather than reaching for rationality in their decision making. It was Simon's opinion that the sciences could serve a positive purpose by bringing rationality into the decision-making process.

Andrew W. Halpin

The topic of organizational climate in school settings developed rapidly following Halpin's early studies in the 1950s. This work led to the ultimate design of the Organizational Climate Description Questionnaire (OCDQ) that has been used in numerous climate studies in school settings and other organizations (Halpin & Croft, 1962). The original OCDQ consisted of 64 items presented in relation to a Likert-type scale from "rarely occurs" to "very frequently occurs." Eight subscales were determined (e.g., hindrance, disengagement, esprit, production emphasis, consideration, etc.), as well as six prototypes of various climates(e.g., open, autonomous, controlled, familiar, paternal, and closed). For example, an open climate featured the subscales of low hindrance, average intimacy, low disengagement, high esprit, low production emphasis, low aloofness, high consideration, and high thrust. The characteristics of a closed climate were virtually opposite those of an open climate, with the exception of intimacy, which was also "average."

The Leadership Behavior Description Questionnaire (LBDQ), initially created by Hemphill and Coons (1950) and later revised by Halpin and others (1952), has also been widely used for determining leadership styles. The LBDQ centered on the two

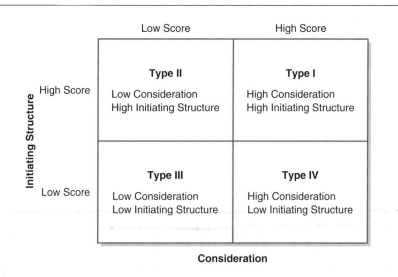

Figure 2.2   Andrew W. Halpin's Four Leadership Styles (LBDQ)

SOURCE: Halpin, Andrew. (1956). *Leadership Behavior of School Superintendents*. Chicago: University of Chicago Press.

organizational dimensions of initiating structure and consideration for measuring leadership behavior. Initiating structure, as we previously noted, centers on the leader's attention to organizational goals, procedures, patterns of communication, and other formal matters. Consideration centers on the human aspects of behaviors of the leader. The leader's attention is given primarily to individual and group relationships, work conditions, team building, friendships, and other people needs.

Halpin identified four types of leaders. For example, if an individual scored above the means for initiating structure and consideration on the LBDQ, the individual was categorized under type-1 leadership. A score above the mean for consideration and below the mean for initiating structure categorized the individual as a type-4 leader (see Figure 2.2). Halpin's studies were important because of their emphasis on the human dimension of organizations and the related importance of the human resources function.

Daniel E. Griffiths

Daniel E. Griffiths contributed extensively to the literature on the theory of administration, especially in relation to decision making in organizations and scientific research methods. He believed that the use of theory in administration had many benefits and stated that "theory can serve the administrator as a guide to action, as a means for clarifying and analyzing a problem or situation being encountered in practice" (1959). Griffiths (1988) focused on the importance of the application of theories and emphasized the point that the real value of theory is to be judged by the way it is useful in practice. He made it clear that theory was not something that tells the administrator what ought to be done. Rather, the focus is on the "if this, then this" consideration. That is, theory can guide the individual through the process of clarification, "If this is done and/or applied, I can expect this to happen." Both decision-making and research methods have gained increasing importance in the area of human resources. If, indeed, the HR administrator is to serve a major role in the strategic planning of the school system, effective decision making is paramount. In addition, the new calls for accountability in human resources activities necessitate attention to objective, hard data. Research results will serve an important purpose in achieving this end.

Fred Fiedler

Fred Fiedler (1974) used the concept of a task-motivated leader and a relations-oriented leader to develop a contingency leadership model. He held the belief that three factors—leader-member relations, task structure, and the leader's power position—combined to determine the favorableness of a particular situation. Through research and empirical testing, he found that certain leadership styles were more effective in some situations than others. For example, task-motivated leaders performed best when conditions were viewed as being unfavorable. When moderately favorable conditions existed, relations-oriented leaders performed best (see Table 2.1). A highly favorable situation exists when leader-member relations are good, the task is structured, and the power position of the leader is strong. Fiedler's contingency model sets forth eight possible octants of favorableness. The primary implications for human resources leaders are that they must know and understand their own leadership style. It is important that they study the existing situation relative to their power relationship and its structure. In view of this information, the leader might decide to delegate the matter to another individual whose leadership style fits the situation. Or, there might be ways to alter the existing situation to make it more compatible with the leader's style.

Table 2.1   Contingency Leadership Octants

The Favorableness of the Situation	Octant	Leader-Member Relations	Task Structure	Power Position
	1	Good	Structured	Strong
	2	Good	Structured	Weak
Favorable	3	Good	Unstructured	Strong
	4	Good	Unstructured	Weak
Moderate	5	Poor	Structured	Strong
	6	Poor	Structured	Weak
Unfavorable	7	Poor	Unstructured	Strong
	8	Poor	Unstructured	Weak

SOURCE: Fiedler and Chemers (1974). Reprinted by permission.

Fiedler did not accept the idea that leaders could simply change their style to meet the situation at hand. On the contrary, he argued that one's leadership style was a natural phenomenon and changing it to meet a situation was not realistic. He did suggest, however, that leadership styles could indeed be determined and that a situation could be altered to fit the leader's style. Other studies have supported Fiedler's views in this regard (Short & Greer, 2002). Contingency or situational leadership has received considerable attention in educational theory. Its implications for the human resources function center on its relevance to team building, participative management, and human relationships.

Christopher Hodgkinson

Is HR administration a science or an art? Hodgkinson viewed the management aspects of administration as a science and its administration as an art. In his work, *Towards a Philosophy of Administration* (1978), Hodgkinson devoted much attention to values, ethics, beliefs, and judgments and discussed their influence on leadership decision making and its outcomes. He was of the opinion that administration cannot be completely rational, that administrators' values, ethics, and experiences directly influence their behaviors and ultimately affect the administration of the system as a whole. As Hodgkinson (1978) stated:

> An organization can have neither "consciousness" nor a "will." These can only be properties of its individual members. The implications of this distinction for administrative philosophy are crucial, for it bears on problems of organizational morality and responsibility. (p. 17)

Hodgkinson made it clear for all human resources administrators that their personal ethics and values assume a vital role in how they administer a program; that the HR function is indeed a human consideration.

Rensis Likert

Likert's broad range of contributions to the behavioral sciences era and to personnel administration are best represented in his publications, *New Patterns of Management* (1967b) and *The Human Organization* (1967a). For example, in *The Human Organization*, Likert set forth an eight-item assessment scale that was based on four organizational types from Exploitive-Authoritative to Participative. The eight major characteristics used to assess an organization's profile included such personnel behaviors as leadership, motivation forces, communication, cooperative teamwork, decision making, goal setting, control practices, and performance goals. Likert was among the first to speak of human resources as assets rather than costs of an organization. He viewed people as an organizational investment and developed Likert scales to measure these assets objectively.

In relation to the characteristic of communication, Likert recommended a linking-pin concept to ensure horizontal and vertical communication within the system. As revealed in Figure 2.3, each unit within the organization was organized so that one

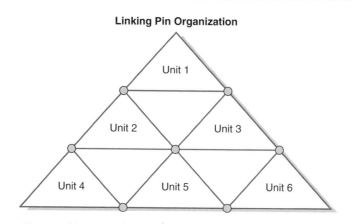

Linking Pin Organization

Figure 2.3   Overlapping Group Structure

SOURCE: Adapted from Likert (1967b).

member of the unit also belonged to another unit. In this manner, this member could serve as a link between his or her primary unit and another unit for purposes of communication and collaboration.

Likert-type assessment scales are commonly used in human resources administration and other functions within the school system. Many of the surveys used by school districts to assess parent, teacher, and community opinion use a Likert-type response design.

Many other authorities contributed directly to the behavioral science era. Chris Argyris, James March, Henry Minsberg, Gareth Morgan, Roald Campbell, Edwin Bridges, Amitai Etzioni, and others were influenced by the formal and informal organizational challenges that led to the postmodern era in the history of human resources administration.

The Postmodern Behavioral Science Era

Postmodernism views administration as complex, unpredictable, unstable, and uncertain. Thus, it presents a direct challenge to traditional assumptions about the administration of organizations and leadership behaviors, and questions the values on which many of the prevailing assumptions are founded. An era of thought termed **critical theory** has challenged the validity of many contemporary leadership concepts. The purpose of such criticism purportedly is to learn the real truth about human behavior of organizations and to expose biases that have permeated previous studies (e.g., biases related to gender, power relationships, and structural, social, and political relationships that influence leader and follower behaviors; Norton, 2005, pp. 41–42).

Among the perspectives that are part of postmodernism are systems theory, concepts of pluralistic leadership, and other concepts of leadership including

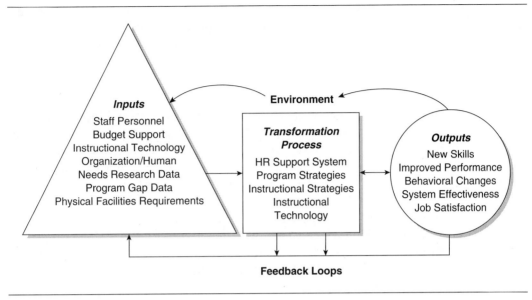

Figure 2.4   Systems Model for Staff Development

transformational leadership, critical constructivism, and learning organizations. The following section summarizes each of these perspectives.

Although systems theory has expanded in many directions since the early 1950s, it builds on the basic concept that organizations are influenced by the environment in which they are embedded (Morgan, 1987; von Bertalanffy, 1950). Systems that are open to their environment are termed **open systems**. Systems that do not have appropriate relations with their environment are termed **closed systems.** Organizations that focus exclusively on their internal environment, such as many of those in the scientific management era, are viewed as closed systems. An open system theory focuses on three primary considerations (Morgan, 1987). First, an open system emphasizes the environment; it organizes with the environment clearly in mind. Second, an open system views the system in terms of its interrelated parts: their relationships to all parts of the system and to the system as a whole. Third, an open system uses the systems approach and attempts to establish relationships between different systems in order to identify and avoid possible organizational dysfunctions.

Systems theory permits the expansion of new and creative ways to think about organizations. Rather than viewing the system only from an internal, closed perspective, it permits different approaches to the concepts of structure, communication, relationships, and change. Figure 2.4 illustrates a systems model relative to a human resources point of view for the process of staff development.

Environmental inputs are represented by such sets as human and physical resources, financial needs, technology, and program contents and methods. The procedures and technologies that are applied to the environmental inputs are changed through the *transformation process* that consists of the strategies, tools, and programs designed to achieve desired *outputs*. Each part of the system is interrelated and dependent on all of the other parts of the system and the system as a whole. The **inputs** related to the staff development process, for example, would include such environmental resources as staff leadership personnel, budgetary support allocations, organizational and human needs information, research data, program gap data, and physical facility requirements. **Transformational processes** center on the organization's human support systems, instructional technologies, program strategies, instructional strategies, and other related processes. **Outputs** of the staff development system process are exemplified by identifiable new skills and improved performance on the part of the human support system as well as changes in human behavior related to positive changes in self-confidence and job satisfaction. Measures taken resulting from performance and attitudinal changes are viewed as **feedback**. Measures encompass the use of various analyses, diagnoses, data reports, and other accountability assessments that serve as indicators of the viability of the outcomes achieved. As we mentioned previously, feedback in this sense is exemplified in the outcome factors related to improved human performance and increased levels of system achievement.

Webb and Norton (2004) note four specific benefits of systems theory for the human resources function:

1. Establishing interpersonal and interdepartmental work patterns that enhance organizational communication and understanding.

2. Gaining insight into system functions that can lead to the identification of organizational strengths and weaknesses.

3. Helping the entire organization to focus on its primary goals and objectives.

4. Helping human resources personnel to utilize human resources in ways that enhance possibility of more productive outputs in relation to the related costs of inputs and transformation process expenditures. (p. 18)

The Human Resources Function and Its Thirteen Processes

Human resources administration was defined previously as those processes that are planned and implemented in the organization to establish an effective system of human resources and to foster an organizational climate that enhances the accomplishment of educational goals. This definition establishes the HR function as existing of specific processes that together result in a healthy organizational climate and strategically center on goal achievement.

The primary human resources processes can be categorized under three classifications: human resources utilization, human resources environment, and human resources development. These classifications and their corresponding processes are inextricably related. Figure 2.5 shows the 13 processes and the major classifications with which they are closely related.

Although later chapters discuss each of the HR processes in detail, the following section presents a brief description of each process.

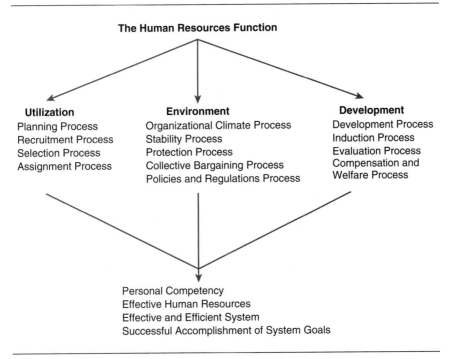

The Human Resources Function

Utilization
Planning Process
Recruitment Process
Selection Process
Assignment Process

Environment
Organizational Climate Process
Stability Process
Protection Process
Collective Bargaining Process
Policies and Regulations Process

Development
Development Process
Induction Process
Evaluation Process
Compensation and
Welfare Process

Personal Competency
Effective Human Resources
Effective and Efficient System
Successful Accomplishment of System Goals

Figure 2.5   The Human Resources Function and Its 13 Processes

Human Resources Planning. This is the formation of a strategy or program for the accomplishment of prescribed outcomes. It consists of two essentials: (1) setting goals and objectives and (2) developing strategies for the implementation of the prescribed outcomes determined. Planning is a foundational process that serves to focus the energies and resources of the school system on achieving the desired results. HR planning is an ongoing process that occurs at various levels, namely, strategic planning, short and long-range planning, and operational planning. Chapter 3 comprehensively discusses HR planning.

The Recruitment Process. The recruitment process is designed to develop a pool of qualified applicants to fill the various position needs within the system. Recruitment is the process by which qualified personnel are informed of positions available and their interest and qualifications are assessed. Recruitment procedures generally center on an effort to gain a balance in staffing relative to such factors as preparation, experience, cultural background, and gender. From the viewpoint of many authorities, a thorough job of recruiting and ultimate selection can significantly reduce the problems that school administrators and others must face. Chapter 4 discusses the recruitment process.

The Selection Process. The selection process involves the finding and hiring of personnel who best fit the school and school system. The concept of fit, of course, includes competency for the position, but organizational fit is of paramount importance as well. "Person-organization fit is a state of congruence between the overall personality, goals, values and interpersonal skills of the individual and the climate/culture of the organization" (Villanova & Muchinsky, 1997, pp. 257–258). Selection must consider the interests and career aspirations of the candidate; if these factors are not considered or are left undone, it is unlikely that a bonding between the candidate and the system will materialize. Chapter 5 centers specifically on the selection process.

The Induction Process. This process encompasses the complex of activities designed to gain congruence between institutional objectives and employee needs. Induction often is referred to as orientation or preservice programming. Induction activities begin at the outset of the prospective employee's contact with the school system and continue until the employee and the system no longer view it as necessary. Induction ties closely with the ongoing staff development process. Pre-employment induction includes information about the nature of the school and school system's mission, the demographics of the community, the makeup of the school's population, availability of instructional resources, and other faculty and student information. Post-employment induction activities include the provision of information relative to the specific working environment, staff relationships, school and district policies and procedures, personal assistance information, and other services that facilitate the transition of employees into their respective roles within the school and school system. Chapter 6 discusses the induction process.

The Assignment Process. The assignment of personnel centers on the placement of individuals in positions that best suit their personal talents and interests and enhance the achievement of the school's goals and objectives. Assignment of personnel includes the deployment of talent in the best interests of the employee, the school system, and the student. Conditions of work such as workload, staff supervision, organizational climate, and performance evaluation methods all relate to the effective utilization of personnel. Chapter 6 further develops the assignment process.

The Performance Evaluation Process. Both formative and summative evaluations of employee performance are necessary responsibilities of human resources administrators. Formative evaluation systems focus on outcomes that improve the personal performance of the employee and school or school district practices. Summative evaluation systems are implemented at specified times to provide data and information relative to the continuation of employment, tenure, or employee dismissal. Because evaluation practices have been criticized as being ineffective, a variety of more objective methods has been implemented in performance evaluation programs. Effective performance evaluation programs serve an important purpose in the overall operation of a school and school system. Chapter 7 further develops the topic of performance evaluation.

The Collective Bargaining Process. **Collective bargaining** is the process whereby matters of employee relations are determined mutually by representatives of employee groups and their employers within the limits of the law. Two primary approaches to collective bargaining are practiced in education, distributive bargaining and integrative bargaining. **Distributive bargaining** is modeled after the process used mainly in the private sector that is designed to realize maximum gain through use of authority, power, sanctions, or withdrawal of services. Power-based bargaining and fractional bargaining are associated with distributive bargaining, and each has its own purposes and related bargaining strategies. In education, quasi-distributive bargaining has been the most common practice; it does involve a *quid pro quo* strategy, but attempts to avoid a test of power between the two bargaining parties. **Integrative bargaining** is win-win bargaining that encompasses strategies with varying terms such as interest-based bargaining, collaborative bargaining, consensus-based bargaining, and problem-solving bargaining. Quasi-integrative bargaining is similar to quasi-distributive bargaining in that both commonly use *quid pro quo* strategies, but the former places more emphasis on problem solving. Early studies in collective bargaining in education focused on whether or not bargaining was instrumental in gaining improvements in salary and conditions of work for employees. Chapter 10 presents the answer to this question and an in-depth discussion of collective bargaining in education.

The Protection Process. The protection process focuses on the physical security of employees as well as the liberty and property rights of personnel under the law. Protection from physical harm and employee wellness programs are examples of provisions within this process. Academic freedom and protection from sexual harassment are related to the protection process as well. The Fourteenth Amendment of the U.S. Constitution sets forth the entitlement of due process to protect individuals; no state shall deprive anyone of life, liberty, or property without fair procedures and rightful protection. Chapter 6 discusses the protection process in more detail.

The Stability Process. The stability process has the purpose of ensuring the retention of system quality and program continuity within the organization. The human resources stability process centers on the retention of quality staff, the reduction of teacher absenteeism, managing conflict, services for troubled workers, and dealing with marginal employees. Health, safety, and welfare provisions represent one facet of the stability process. Another dimension is that of employee retention. The human resources function has a major responsibility for providing a high quality of program services to ensure needed continuity within the school system. Chapter 6 develops the concepts of stability in depth.

The Organizational Climate Process. The organizational climate process strives to create an environment within the system that supports the achievement of school goals and objectives. **Organizational climate** is defined as the collective personality of a school or school system, the atmosphere that prevails in the system as characterized by the social and professional interactions of the administration, faculty, and students. Empirical evidence has confirmed that school climate can be assessed. Researchers have identified variations of school climate and the external and internal conditions that influence school climate positively or negatively. The implications of school climate for the work of human resources directors are far-reaching. For example, studies of student achievement have found a relationship between organizational climate and student achievement. Other studies have underscored the importance of working conditions and worker job satisfaction. Chapter 8 comprehensively presents the topic of organizational climate.

The Compensation Process. The compensation process of the school system is designed to accomplish several purposes. The hiring and retaining of quality personnel are among those purposes. In order to achieve these ends, a competitive compensation program is essential. The increasing cost of benefits (COB) is a growing concern for most every school district. Benefits provisions have increased substantially during the last several decades. Costs of benefits have resulted in the reduction of payments for certain employee benefits; employees are being asked to assume a larger proportion of benefit costs. The salaries, wages, and benefits provided in most school systems represent 80%–90% of the school system's budget for operations. Some people contend that the compensation process is the most challenging of all the HR processes. Although the responsibilities of the compensation process are shared with others in the school system, the impact of the process on the HR function is significant. Chapter 11 examines the employee and compensation process.

The Policies and Regulations Process. Goals, policies, administrative regulations, and by-laws are integral governance provisions for all organizations. The human resources function is no exception. Some people contend that a school district's personnel policies are a direct reflection of how it values its human resources. The trend relating to the positioning of human resources as a strategic function includes the fact that participation in policy development is an increasing responsibility of HR administrators. For this and other reasons that are discussed in Chapter 9 of the text, policy and administrative regulation development is an important concern of all HR administrators in education.

Governing board policies directly affect the work and life of school employees. Viable personnel policies and regulations give the professional staff the guidelines and freedom to implement program initiatives. Chapter 9 discusses the criteria of good policies, the coding of school policies and regulations, and the development of HR policies for the school system.

The Staff Development Process. Staff development is sometimes called professional growth, in-service education, advanced preparation, or other terms that imply continuing educational experiences for employees. Effective school programs depend on the continuous professional growth of all employees. Although staff development takes place in a variety of programs and is directed by different units of the school system, the human resources unit often shares responsibility for in-service training, mentoring programs, curriculum development sessions, skill assessment centers, administrator academies, clinical supervision clinics, and other programs that center on the personal and professional improvement of employees. Chapter 7 discusses staff development in detail.

The Centralization and Decentralization of the HR Function

Each major human resources process relates directly or indirectly to virtually every other function in the educational enterprise, making the human resources function a shared responsibility. The responsibility for certain personnel tasks or activities commonly is assumed in part by units other than HR. For example, the central office personnel unit generally assumes the primary responsibility for the recruitment process. The central human resources unit commonly develops position analyses and job descriptions, but the responsibility for hiring generally is shared with the instructional unit, local school administrators and staff, and other system personnel. The sharing of activities in the staff development process is another example of shared responsibility.

In Chapter 1, we noted that new governance movements portend considerations for even greater changes in roles and operations of the central human resources unit. Although the central human resources unit is viewed as the keystone to an effective personnel program, this text fully supports the contention that every school administrator or supervisor is a "director" of human resources. Neglect of the human resources processes at any level in the system ultimately militates against the successful operation of the school system's mission. The following section discusses the organization, responsibilities, and guiding ethics and standards of the human resources function.

Organization of the Central Human Resources Unit

There is no specific model for the organization of the central human resources unit in school districts; the central unit organization varies widely in relation to the size of the school district, organizational level, and the placement of the unit within the organizational structure. For example, some school districts delegate personnel responsibilities among various administrative personnel throughout the system. Other arrangements include dividing the human resources responsibilities between the superintendent and assistant superintendent of schools, placing the personnel unit within the school business office, or placing the human resources unit within the office of a line administrator such as an assistant superintendent or director of instruction. More common, perhaps, is the practice of organizing human resources as a separate unit under the direction of an assistant superintendent or director who is a specialist in personnel administration.

Figure 2.6 illustrates one organization model in which the director of human resources serves as a staff administrator as opposed to a line administrator. A **line administrator** is one who is in the hierarchical line of authority; this person has specific decision-making authority and has other personnel, both line and staff, reporting to that office. A **staff administrator** is not in the hierarchical line of authority; rather, this person serves in an advisory and support role for other line personnel. Although the staff administrator does have specific responsibilities, this person commonly does not have other line personnel under his or her supervision. Nationally, human resources directors tend to view themselves as staff administrators, although

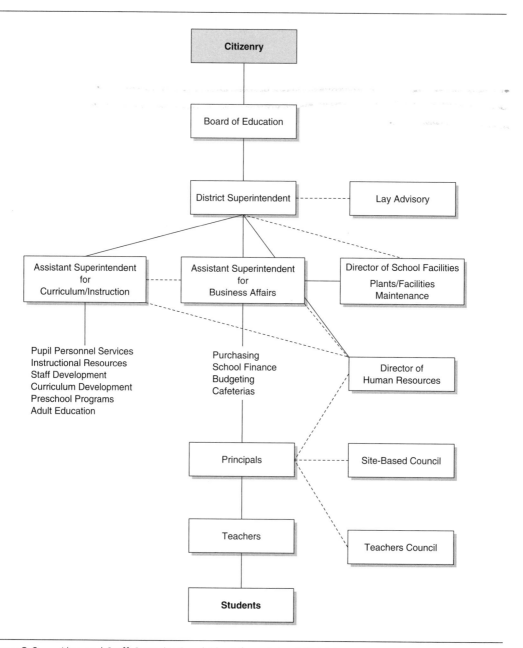

Figure 2.6   Line and Staff Organizational Chart for a School District

the exceptions are numerous. In a statewide study in Arizona, nearly two-thirds of the participating human resources directors viewed themselves as line administrators (Norton, 2004). Titles for central office human directors vary widely. Personnel Director is the most common title, but titles such as HR Specialist, assistant superintendent for human resources, supervisor of personnel, and assistant superintendent of human resources are also typical.

A study of personnel directors in one state (Norton, 2004) found the following:

1. Their average age was 48 years.

2. They entered their first position as a human resources director at the average age of 43.

3. 22% held a doctoral degree.

4. 63% had served as a personnel director for five years or less.

5. 43% were in their first three years of service in the directorship.

6. The highest percentage, 22%, had been school principals just prior to entering the directorship; only 11% entered from an assistant director's role.

7. The typical HR director was a married white female who had been in the position for an average of 4.68 years.

8. Only one-fourth were of the opinion that they were well prepared to assume the role of HR director.

9. Job stress was "very high" or "high" in the position.

10. HR directors reported most often to the superintendent of schools.

11. Two-thirds of the directors served on the school board's negotiating team.

12. Directors averaged 52 hours per week on work responsibilities.

13. The five primary position responsibilities included recruitment of personnel, human resources planning, record keeping, policy development, and the substitute teacher program. However, the separation of personnel, employee benefits program, and personnel counseling were primary responsibilities of at least 50% of the directors.

14. The five most serious problems facing the HR directors were the lack of financial resources, teacher shortage, personal workload, external mandates and requirements, job pressure or stress, and teacher retention.

Position Description of the Central Unit Human Resources Administrator

A position analysis is the process of examining the contents of a position or job and breaking it down into primary tasks. It is a scientific, in-depth analysis of a position, its constituent parts, and surrounding conditions. A position analysis includes such considerations as the duties required in the job itself, job qualifications including levels of experience and education, the knowledge and skills required in accomplishing the work, effects of the job on the worker, the position schedule, kinds of internal and external contacts required, conditions of work, staff and line relationships, and the terms of employment.

A **position description** evolves from the position analysis. As emphasized throughout this chapter, the central unit's human resources position is not characterized by a single description. Figure 2.7 is an example of a position description for a central unit HR director that includes many common elements relative to the HR director's position title, major duties, evaluation responsibilities, coordination activities, record-keeping requirements, special assignments, and position qualifications. Supervision received and supervision given are also included in the job description.

Wymore School District

Position Description for the Human Resources Director

POSITION TITLE: Director of Human Resources

CONTRACT: 12 months

GENERAL STATEMENT OF RESPONSIBILITIES:

To plan, coordinate, and supervise the operation of the central human resources unit in such a way as to enhance the morale of school district personnel, promote the overall efficiency of the school system, maximize the educational opportunities and benefits available to the individual student, and foster the working climate for all employees and students.

QUALIFICATIONS:

1. An advanced degree in administration with an emphasis in personnel administration.

2. Prior experience in administration, and personnel work in education or related experience in other fields. Teaching experience is preferred.

3. Demonstrated knowledge and skill in the processes of human resources administration, including strategic planning, salary and benefits allocations, collective bargaining, working conditions, staff development, employee records, legal aspects of the employee relations, and other aspects of personnel administration.

SUPERVISION:

The director is directly responsible to the school superintendent and supervises those employees assigned to the human resources office. Serves as a member of the Superintendent's administrative cabinet.

PRIMARY DUTIES AND RESPONSIBILITIES:

1. Supervises and directs:
   a. the planning process related to all aspects of the human resources function.
   b. the recruitment, screening, and processing of all personnel recommended for candidacy for positions within the school district.
   c. works with local school administrators and other district personnel in the selection of personnel for various positions within the school system.
   d. coordinates personnel activities in the areas of personnel reports, budgeting, contracts, and salary placement for both certificated and classified personnel.
   e. works cooperatively with the school district business unit relative to the matters of employee benefits, certification, unemployment compensation, substitute teaching, employee dismissal, and other matters relating to school law.

2. Evaluates:
   a. all applications for prospective placement in employee recruitment pools.
   b. substitute teacher applications.
   c. current policies and proposed policies relating to the human resources function in the school district.
   d. personnel working within the human resources unit of the school district.

3. Coordinates and assists:
   a. in the selection of certificated and classified personnel.
   b. in the review of requests for transfer or promotions of personnel.
   c. as a representative of the school board in the collective bargaining process.
   d. in the personal of personnel and the school district's Employee Assistance Program.
   e. in the budgeting process for the employee benefits program.
   f. in the design and implementation of research activities related to personnel matters such as salary and benefits, professional standards, personnel trends.
   g. in the planning and implementation of the school district's induction process.
   h. in the writing and recommendation of personnel policy and administrative regulations relating to the human resources function.

4. Develops and maintains:
   a. an appropriate system for personnel records for current and former school district employees.
   b. an applicant file for prospective candidates for school district positions.
   c. salary schedules for certificated teachers, supervisory-administrative personnel, and classified staff personnel.
   d. position descriptions for all personnel positions.
   e. personnel policies and administrative regulations.
   f. personnel handbooks for employees.
   g. records of personnel performance evaluations and other legal and counseling records related to employees' performances.

5. Coordinates and collaborates:
   a. with other units and administrators in the assessment of the working environment and implementation of a positive working climate within the school district.
   b. in the review of all staff evaluations and makes recommendations relative to continued employment status or other appropriate status.
   c. in the determination of recommendations for termination or employees, assembling and substantiating information for dismissal of employees, and arranging for the implementation of due process proceedings as fits the case.
   d. as a hearing officer as appropriate on employee appeals of disciplinary action and coordinates district grievance and complaint processes.

Figure 2.7   Position Description for a Human Resources Director

The Decentralization of the Human Resources Function

The human resources function historically has been a shared responsibility. The most common practice is that of a balance between a centralized and decentralized HR function (Norton, 2000). In recent years, local school principals have assumed increasing responsibilities for many of the HR processes. For example, in one study (Norton, 1999), 100 school principals were asked to identify the human resources processes that were considered part of their job description. Table 2.2 shows the specific HR process and the percent of the school principals who reported that the process was required in their role.

Table 2.2   School Principals' Primary Responsibilities in Human Resources Administration

Human Resources Processes	Percent Reporting
Staff Selection	96%
Assignment of Staff Personnel	92%
Organizational Climate	92%
Performance Evaluation	88%
Staff Development	84%
Staff Protection (safety, liberty/property rights)	62%
Stability of Staff (retention, transfer, continuing employment)	59%
Recruitment of Staff Personnel	54%
Staff Compensation (re: merit pay, extra pay)	16%
Collective Bargaining	1%
Others	9%

SOURCE: Norton, M. S. (1999). The Work of the School Principal in the Area of Human Resources Administration in Arizona. *The NASSP Bulletin*, 83(603), pp. 108–113. Copyright © National Association of Secondary School Principals. All rights reserved. Reprinted by permission of Sage Publications.

As indicated in Table 2.2, 96% of the participating principals listed staff selection as a primary responsibility. The assignment of staff, organizational climate, staff evaluation, staff development, and staff induction received responses of 92%, 92%, 88%, 84%, and 84%, respectively. It is clear that school principals are highly involved in the human resources function. On average, school principals were spending 31%–40% of their time on personnel matters. Staff evaluation, organizational climate, selection of staff, staff development, and personal counseling were viewed as those HR processes and activities demanding the most of the principals' time.

Standards of Ethical Administration

The American Association of School Personnel Administrators (AASPA) was first established in 1959, although it evolved from the Conference of Teacher Examiners that was organized in 1940 for the purpose of improving the qualifications and selection of teachers for America's schools (AASPA, 1988). Human resources administration is a growing field. It can be safely estimated that there are 2,500 directors of personnel presently serving in school districts nationally. The number of personnel employees working in central personnel units far exceeds that figure.

The AASPA is the primary national professional organization for human resources administrators, although such organizations as the National Staff Development and

STATEMENT OF ETHICS FOR SCHOOL ADMINISTRATORS/PERSONNEL

A human resource administrator's organizational behavior must conform to an ethical code. The code must be idealistic and at the same time practical, so that it applies to all educational administrators. The administrator acknowledges that the schools belong to the public for the purpose of providing educational opportunities to all. However, the administrator must assume responsibility for providing leadership in the schools and community. The responsibility requires the administrator to maintain standards of exemplary conduct. It must be recognized that the administrator's actions will be viewed and appraised by the community, associates, and students. To these ends, the administrator subscribes to the following statements of standards.

1. Makes the well-being of students the fundamental value of all decision-making and actions.
2. Fulfills responsibilities with honesty and integrity.
3. Supports the principle of due process and protects the civil and human rights of all individuals.
4. Obeys local, state, and national laws and does not join or support organizations that advocate, directly or indirectly, the overthrow of the government.
5. Implements the board of education's policies and administrative rules and regulations.
6. Pursues appropriate measures to correct those laws, policies, and regulations that are not consistent with accepted educational goals.
7. Avoids using his/her position for personal gain through political, social, religious, economic, or other influences.
8. Accepts academic degrees or certification only from duly accredited institutions.
9. Maintains the standards and seeks to improve the effectiveness of administration through research and continuing professional development.
10. Honors all contracts until fulfilled or released.

Approved by the AASPA Executive Committee, June 2003

Figure 2.8   Standards for the Ethical Administration of the Human Resources Function

SOURCE: "Statement of Ethics for School Administrators/Personnel" reprinted with permission of the American Association of School Personnel Administrators, from *Standards for School Personnel Administration* (AASPA, 2004).

Training Association (NSDTA) provide human services training and extensive staff development programs for human resources professionals as well.

AASPA membership includes human resources administrators, school superintendents, principals, personnel support staff, attorneys, business personnel, and others interested in human resources administration. The AASPA has been interested in advancing research and practice in personnel administration since its establishment. One of the association's contributions to the field was a statement of ethics and practice to guide administrators generally (AASPA, 1988). The ethics statement includes practices related to honesty, human rights, loyalty, endorsement of school policy, use of position influence, and maintenance of standards.

Another AASPA contribution to human resources administration was its statement of ethical standards for human resources administration. These standards have been updated and revised three times since 1960; they define and further clarify the purposes, processes, responsibilities, and significance of the HR function. The standards (Figure 2.8) serve as a benchmark for establishing and accomplishing the goals and objectives of the total organization. Such standards are instrumental for the development of guiding school district policies and administrative regulations.

Summary

This chapter emphasized the evolution of the human resources function and the significant contributions made to personnel administration by many people during the scientific management, human relations, behavioral science, and postmodern eras historically. Contemporary human resources practices find their roots in the research and concepts established by such individuals as Frederick Taylor, Henri Fayol, Max Weber, Frank and Lillian Gilbreth, Henry Gantt, and others who contributed to the scientific management era and its emphasis on task management and organizational efficiency. The human relations era served to place the human factor in human resources administration. The contributions of Mary Parker Follett, Elton Mayo and associates, Frederick Herzberg, Douglas McGregor, Kurt Lewin, and others emphasized the human dimensions of all organizations and the concept that organizations are people. Chester Barnard was one of the leaders of behavioral science, a concept that all organizations have structural and human dimensions. Effective organizations maintain a balance between these two dimensions. Postmodernism focuses on concepts of social reconstruction; it is characterized by challenges regarding unequal relationships as applied to race, gender, nationalism, class, and other socioeconomic factors.

The human resources function was defined in terms of its responsibility for effectively administering 13 processes and establishing an organizational climate that enhances the accomplishment of organizational goals and objectives. This chapter presented an overview of these processes—planning, recruitment, selection, induction, assignment, development, protection, security, compensation, organizational climate, collective bargaining, policies and regulations, and performance evaluation.

The specific responsibilities of directors of central human resources units were discussed. The centralized work of the human resources function was presented, as well as the increasing trend toward the decentralization of the function. The human resources function was described as a shared responsibility. Local school principals are assuming a large proportion of the responsibility for such HR processes as personnel selection, assignment, development, evaluation, and organizational climate.

Statements of ethics and professional standards for the human resources administrators, as set forth by the AASPA, were presented. Such statements provide both a foundation and a direction for setting policy and guiding the work of human resources administration.

Discussion Questions

1. The HR processes are viewed as being closely related to one another. Consider the HR processes of recruitment, induction, and assignment. Describe how these processes are interrelated.

2. Christopher Hodgkinson viewed management as a science and administration as an art. Explain the conceptual differences between management and administration as conceived by Hodgkinson. Use illustrations relating to human resources administration in your response.

3. Mary Parker Follett used the term "integration" as the best process for resolving conflict in organizations. Review Follett's concepts in this regard and then explain their application to organizational conflict.

4. Consider the responsibilities of a central unit HR director in a school district with which you are most familiar. In your opinion, is a line or a staff HR director most effective in the position? Does the position description for a human resources director provided in the chapter reflect the position as you know it? State several reasons in support of your response.

5. In view of this chapter's information regarding the work and responsibilities of human resources administrators, give thought to the matter of preparation for this administrative role. What subject matter and professional experiences appear to be most essential for effective administration as a human resources administrator?

Case Studies

CASE 2.1

THIS IS A REAL DILEMMA; WHAT DO YOU THINK WE SHOULD DO?

Whittier Middle School is experiencing problems of morale, increased absenteeism, and other aspects of job dissatisfaction on the part of the school staff. Assistant Principal Gwen Bassett went to the school principal's office after school to discuss the situation. "The attitudes of our faculty members are at a low ebb," said Gwen Bassett. "I was unable to get a single volunteer for the parent-teacher advisory committee and only one teacher said she would be willing to work on the faculty social this semester. Even Donna Erickson, one of our most cooperative teachers, indicated that faculty satisfaction overall was not the best."

"Yes, I have been worried about this situation for some time," responded Principal Manuel Ruiz. "I just don't know how to begin. Gwen, what suggestions do you have in mind?"

Questions

1. As Assistant Principal Gwen Bassett, what would be your response? What concepts of the chapter would be helpful in suggesting what might be done in this situation? For example, how might the Herzberg theory of job satisfaction serve in this case?

2. Consider the HR process of organizational climate as it might relate to this case. Although certain school conditions are implied in the case scenario, how might an organizational climate assessment be useful in helping to improve the situation at Whittier?

CASE 2.2

A Case for Organization

Clyde Benson was in his first year as superintendent of the Grand Island School District. He was selected superintendent over three other finalist candidates partly because of his reputation as a great manager. During the first six months of his service in the Grand Island School District, Benson had revised several sections of the school district's policies that were ultimately adopted by the school board. Among other administrative actions, Benson guided the development of a new mission statement and the revision of job descriptions for school principals and other school administrators; he also worked with the human resources director in drafting a staff development plan that he believed would serve to improve many aspects of the school system.

During the next few months, however, Superintendent Benson and the school board became concerned about several developments within the school system. Although student achievement was beginning to improve, faculty attitudes toward work and interpersonal relationships became problematic. In a study session with the school board, the problems in the area of personnel were placed on the agenda. Board members expressed concerns about personnel conflicts and complaints that they had heard about.

Superintendent Benson was asked to comment on the situation. "Well," responded Benson, "I was asked to come to Grand Island and bring needed organization into place. I was asked to improve student achievement and this is beginning to take place. I have reorganized certain offices and updated the district's mission statement. I think that I have accomplished what I was called on to do."

Questions

1. First, give thought to the case at hand regarding the administrative style and accomplishments of Superintendent Benson. In view of the limited information set forth in the case, analyze Benson's style in relation to what Chester Barnard terms the "capacity of equilibrium."

2. Review the theoretical concepts of Andrew Halpin, Fred Fiedler, and others. What do these concepts reveal about the Superintendent's leadership style?

3. Consider the human resources organization and operations in a school district with which you are most familiar. Describe the organization of the HR function from the viewpoints of centralization and decentralization. Examine the research reports in the chapter relative to the HR responsibilities of the central unit HR director and other administrators in the district, such as the school principal. Do the research studies compare favorably with the practices identified with the school district that you selected?

CASE 2.3

Induction for Whom?

MEMO

TO: Emory Ziegler, Principal

FROM: Ad Hoc Committee on Faculty Affairs, Joan Hershey, Chair

RE: Committee's Discussion on Faculty Affairs

As you likely are aware, the Wymore Middle School Ad Hoc Committee on Faculty Affairs has been meeting periodically during the year to examine its charge and to discuss several items relating to the affairs of the faculty. Among the topics discussed informally this year were student discipline, teacher load, and teacher evaluation, although no definite recommendations were determined in these areas.

The matter of teacher induction was brought to the table by two new members of the committee, Wilma Andrus and Wilson Black. As you know, both Wilma and Wilson are new to Wymore this year. Both of these teachers were of the opinion that the orientation activities provided them by the school and school district did not deal with matters of importance to them. Rather, the focus seemed to be on "district and school needs" as opposed to the questions and problems of importance to them. For example, one day of the induction program was spent on the topics of teacher membership in the state teachers' association, school and district goals, and the school-community survey taken last spring. Topics such as student discipline procedures, instructional resources, teacher-parent expectations, mentoring services, and student grading were not discussed, although they were mentioned in the teachers' handbook distributed at the first faculty meeting.

Our committee believes that this matter indeed is one of concern. How do you view this matter and what suggestions do you have regarding the improvement of this important aspect of faculty affairs? We hope to meet next week to review your response. Thanks for your immediate attention to this matter.

cc: Members of the Committee on Faculty Affairs

Questions

1. Assume the role of Emory Ziegler, the school principal, and set forth the specific procedures that you would implement in responding to Joan Hershey and the Ad Hoc Committee. Specifically, what actions appear to be in order in this situation and what steps would you take administratively?

2. What steps might school leaders take to ensure the involvement of staff members in the process of employee induction? How might they gather ideas for the activities for induction programs? What ongoing program assessments might be useful in this regard?

References

American Association of School Personnel Administrators (AASPA). (1988). *Standards for school personnel administration.* Virginia Beach, VA: Author.

American Association of School Personnel Administrators (AASPA). (2004). *AASPA standards for ethical administration of the HR function.* Olathe, KS: Author.

Barnard, C. I. (1938). *The functions of the executive.* Cambridge, MA: Harvard University Press.

Bertalanffy, L. V. (1950). An outline of general systems theory. *British Journal of the Philosophy of Science, 1*(2), 34–164.

Bloss, J. M. (1882). *Thirteenth report of the superintendent of public instruction of the state of Indiana to the Governor.* Indianapolis: State of Indiana.

Callahan, R. E. (1962). *Education and the cult of efficiency.* Chicago: University of Chicago Press.

Fayol, H. (1949). *General and industrial management.* London: Sir Isaac Pitman and Sons. (Original work published 1916)

Fiedler, F. E., & Chemers, M. M. (1974). *Leadership and effective management.* Glenview, IL: Scott, Foresman.

Follett, M. P. (1924). *Creative experience.* New York: Longmans, Green.

Follett, M. P. (1940). The meaning of responsibility in business management. In H.C. Metcalf & L. Urwick (Eds.), *Dynamic administration: The collected papers of Mary Parker Follett* (pp. 146–166). New York: Harper and Brothers.

Gantt, H. L. (1961). *Gantt on management.* New York: American Management Association and the American Society of Mechanical Engineers.

Getzels, J. W., & Guba, E. G. (1957). Social behavior and the administrative process. *School Review, 65,* 423–441.

Gilbreth, F. B. (1909). *Bricklaying system.* Easton, PA: Hive.

Gilbreth, F. B. (1911). *Motion study: A method for increasing the efficiency of the workman.* New York: D. Van Nostrand Co.

Griffiths, D. E. (1959). *Administrative theory.* New York: Apple-Century Crofts.

Gulick, L., & Urwick, L. (Eds.). (1937). *Papers on the science of administration.* New York: Columbia University Press.

Halpin, A. (1956). *Leadership behavior of school superintendents.* Chicago: University of Chicago Press.

Halpin, A., & Croft, D. B. (1962). *The organization climate of schools.* U.S. Office of Education Research Project (Contract # SAE 543-8639). Chicago: University of Chicago, Midwest Administration Center.

Halpin, A., & Winer, B. J. (1952). *The leadership behavior of the airplane commander.* Washington, DC: Human Resources Research Laboratories, Department of the Air Force.

Hemphill, J. K., & Coons, A. E. (1950). *Leader behavior description.* Columbus: Ohio State University Personnel Research Board.

Herzberg, F., Mausner, B., & Snyderman, B. (1959). *The motivation to work.* New York: Wiley.

Hodgkinson, C. (1978). *Towards a philosophy of administration.* Guilford, England: Billing & Son.

Lewin, K., Lippitt, R., & White, R. (1939). Patterns of aggressive behavior in experimentally created "social climates." *Journal of Social Psychology, 10,* 271–299.

Likert, R. (1967a). *The human organization.* New York: McGraw-Hill.

Likert, R. (1967b). *New patterns of management.* New York: Garland.

Mayo, E. (1933). *The human problems of an industrial civilization.* New York: Macmillan.

McGregor, D. (1960). *The human side of enterprise.* New York: McGraw-Hill.

Morgan, G. (1987). *Images of organization.* Newbury Park, CA: Sage.

Norton, M. S. (1999, January). The work of the school principal in the area of human resources administration in Arizona. *NASSP Bulletin, 83*(603), 108–113.

Norton, M. S. (2004). *The human resources director in Arizona: A research study.* Tempe: Arizona State University, Division of Educational Leadership & Policy Studies.

Parks, C. A. (2001). *Management pioneers: Women as early contributors to the management discipline.* Retrieved November 18, 2007, from http://westga.edu/bequest/2001/women.htm

Perie, M., & Baker, D. P. (1997). *Job satisfaction among America's teachers: Effects of workplace conditions, background characteristics, and teacher compensation.* Washington, DC: National Center for Education Statistics. (ERIC Document Reproduction Service No. 412181)

Roethlisberger, F. J., & Dickson, W. J. (1929). *Management and the worker.* Cambridge, MA: Harvard University Press.

Short, P. M., & Greer, J. T. (2002). *Leadership in empowered schools: Themes from innovative efforts.* Upper Saddle River, NJ: Merrill/Prentice Hall.

Simon, H. A. (1957). *Administrative behavior* (2nd ed.). New York: Macmillan.

Urwick, L. F. (1937). *Organization as a technical problem.* In L. Gulick & L. F. Urwick (Eds.), *Papers on the science of administration* (pp. 47–88). New York: Institute of Public Administration, Columbia University.

Villanova, P., & Muchinsky, P. M. (1997). Person-job fit. In L. H. Peters, C. R. Greer, & S. A. Youngblood (Eds.), *The Blackwell Encyclopedic Dictionary of Human Resource Management* (pp. 257–258). Oxford, England: Blackwell.

Webb, L. D., & Norton, M. S. (2004). *Human resources administration: Personnel issues and needs in education* (4th ed.). Upper Saddle River, NJ: Merrill Prentice-Hall.

Weber, M. (1947). *The theory of social and economic organization* (T. Parsons, Ed., A. M. Henderson & T. Parsons, Trans.). New York: Free Press. (Original work published 1910)

White, R., & Lippitt, R. (1960). *Autocracy and democracy: An experimental inquiry.* New York: Harper & Row.

CHAPTER 3

The Human Resources Planning Process

Learning Objectives

The information in this chapter will enable you to

- Understand the changing role of the HR director from a support and maintenance function to a leadership role in the total operations of the school system.
- View strategic HR planning as a process inextricably tied to the general goals and purposes of the school district.
- Define strategic and operational planning and relate their use in the planning and implementation of the various human resources processes of the HR function.
- Gain an understanding of external and internal scanning as it relates to strategic planning and the human resources function.
- Gain skill in the strategies for forecasting personnel needs.
- Plan and implement HR strategies that enable the school to gain a competitive edge in gaining available resources and achieving stated goals.
- Visualize how strategic human resources planning fosters personnel principles related to staff involvement, staff development, organizational climate, visioning, and other organizational positive outcomes.

This chapter discusses the human resources planning process and its vital importance to the effectiveness of the HR function. The chapter begins with a discussion of the primary purposes of HR planning and its relationship to other processes of the HR function. The definition of human resources planning, the six characteristics of human resources planning, and a discussion of professional staff mix provide the background for a general strategic planning model that highlights the integration of human resources planning into the strategic plan of a school system. A graphic illustration depicts the strategic planning model, and the accompanying discussion reviews the model's three main elements: environmental scanning, strategic and operational planning, and implementation. A general operations model for the planning process is also presented.

The next section presents methods of forecasting personnel needs and technological approaches to projecting enrollments. This discussion incorporates a Markovian analysis of personnel attrition. Additionally, models for forecasting student enrollments are discussed.

How does the school system determine its direction and practices? What kinds of data and information are essential for the successful completion of the human resources tasks and responsibilities? The human resources planning process serves to answer such questions.

Definition and Background of the Human Resources Planning Process

Planning is a comprehensive, continuous process that is characterized by flexibility and responsiveness to change. It centers on the formation of a strategy or program for the accomplishment of desired outcomes. Planning consists of two essential activities: (1) setting essential goals and program objectives, and (2) developing blueprints and strategies for the accomplishment and implementation of the goals and objectives.

Planning is a methodological mechanism for projecting intentions and actions rather than reacting to causes and events affecting education and the schooling process (Young, 2008, p. 62). **Strategy**, on the other hand, "is the process that serves to determine what decisions, programs, activities, and resources are necessary to achieve the desired results (Norton, 2005, p. 102).

The planning process differs from the plan. A **plan** is a product of the planning process; it is a fixed entity that is time and place specific. The aim of planning is to focus the energies and resources of the school system on the right results. When the school system uses proper planning procedures, it encourages accountability on the part of personnel. The primary intent of human resources planning is the same as any other type of organizational planning: to help decide in advance what is to be done and to clarify the school system's expectations of what it envisions the total system and its parts to be and to do. In this sense, planning is the school system's way of projecting its purposes.

The Purposes of Human Resources Planning

Effective human resources planning places the HR function in a position of being proactive. Planning has the potential of anticipating a problem or condition before it occurs. Effective HR planning is an important forerunner for positive change. Human resources planning provides (1) a basis for agreement as to the ultimate goals and purposes of the school system, (2) a clear definition of options and alternatives available for decision making, (3) an identification of system strengths on which an improved program can be built, and (4) a systematized procedure for setting objectives. Planning is the central focus of the human resources function because all of its related processes depend on it.

Previous chapters discussed the concept of human resources as a strategic function. What, then, is strategic planning? Pfeiffer, Goodstein, and Nolan (1986a) provided a foundational perspective of strategic planning when they defined the term in the following way:

> *Strategic planning is the process by which an organization envisions its future and develops the necessary procedures and operations to achieve that future.* This vision of the future state of the organization provides both the direction in which the organization should move and the energy to begin that move. (p. 2)

Strategic planning is a dynamic process for helping a school system shape its future. Through techniques of strategic management, school systems can effectively adjust to the unpredictable demands brought on by environmental changes. Strategic HR planning serves to tie the specific objectives of the HR function to the overall purposes and objectives of the school system. It focuses on how the HR objectives are to be achieved. Thus, strategic planning is a process that serves to guide an organization in an environment of rapid and continuous change. Strategic planning focuses on established objectives and the system's strengths in terms of human and material resources.

> Organizations need strategic planning because the world changes constantly. It is foolhardy and unrealistic to assume that economic conditions, consumer needs and expectations, competition, . . . or a host of other factors will be the same two, three, or five years from now as they are today. A strategic planning process is a systematic effort by an organization to deal with the inevitability of change and an attempt to envision its own future. The importance of this process is that it enables an organization to help *shape* its own future rather than simply *prepare* for the future. (Pfeiffer et al., 1986b, p. 24)

Sibson (1992), who worked with more than 500 companies over a period of 32 years, underscored the importance of strategic planning in his statement that, "Every one of these companies that engaged in *real* strategic thinking . . . has been successful by every measure of enterprise performance. . . . Every company that has shunned strategic activities in their management processes has *failed* and is no longer in business" (pp. 1–2).

Any effort by a school system to respond effectively to change must include a careful analysis of information about its environment. The results of this analysis will have an important impact on the system's strategic plan and will be critical to effective human resources planning. "Organizations tend to commit resources to counter productive or conflicting activities when organizational changes are not consistent with its strategic plan" (Kreitner & Kinicki, 1998, p. 621). Norton and colleagues (1996) noted that although

> some consider long-range planning to be the same as strategic planning . . . there are some key distinguishing characteristics. Long-range planning is a form of operational planning typically involving a time span of more than one

year. . . . Strategic planning is used to set the compass heading for the institution. Long-range planning is typically of lesser import and subservient to the direction set in strategic planning. (p. 133)

As with strategic planning, strategic human resources planning is concerned with the effective utilization of human resources and their contributions toward the accomplishment of educational goals. Planning involves forecasting, designing, strategizing, organizing, participating, and collaborating. **Designing** is the creation of plans of action directed toward specific goals. **Forecasting** is an activity that centers on looking to the future and assessing probabilities. **Strategizing** is the defining of activities to meet stated system goals. **Organizing** involves the use of a systematic approach to decision making. **Participating** involves **cooperating** with those affected for the best implementation, and **collaborating** is using all possible resources in order to achieve the best results. Each of these factors necessitates a knowledge and understanding of the system's internal and external environments. As Norton (2005) noted, for a school executive to attempt a significant change in the school's program or operations without having an intelligent fix on the environments in which the school is embedded would be a serious mistake.

Strategic human resources planning is not necessarily the making of future decisions; it is focused on current decisions and their future implications. Strategic human resources planning produces current decisions about what should be done now to realize desired outcomes in the future. Accordingly, the purpose of human resources planning is to ensure the most effective use of personnel resources to move an organization toward its mission and achieve its strategic objectives. As early as 1968, Hanlon's classic work, *Administration and Education*, underscored the most difficult part of planning: conceptualization. Hanlon used an idea advanced by Leonardo da Vinci "that the execution of a work of art is the easiest part of the artist's job, while the most difficult part is the conception and composition of that work" (p. 29). Hanlon pointed to the conception as the original vision that the artist wishes to communicate and the composition as the plan of the work. The artist's conception and plan permit the artist to judge the correctness of various aspects of the work that gives the artist the ability to resolve problems that occur during its execution. Without the conception and plan, it makes little difference which strokes of the artist's brush are used, because none results in a better painting than any other. Hanlon makes the point that the conception of a plan and the plan itself provide a standard for judging and evaluating behaviors and actions taken by people in the organization in relation to what the organization wishes to become. Strategic planning is based on a similar rationale.

A **strategic plan** is "a long-term plan outlining actions needed to achieve planned results" (Kreitner & Kinicki, 1998, p. 621). Strategic human resources planning is based on information that justifies conclusions about existing trends, which in turn form a rationale for predicting future events. "Strategic planning, properly done . . . can be the means of moving to the future and determining what that future will provide for children and youth" (Norton et al., 1996, p. 133). And, as Young (2008) stated, a strategic school system plan is designed to accomplish several specific ends. Among these ends are (1) utilizing a school system's mission statement to guide a strategic planning process for the human resource function, (2) placing in perspective different goals of the human resource function as linked to a school district's mission, (3) identifying general objectives of the human resource function pertaining to most human resource goals, and (4) specifying operational functions necessary for accomplishing both specific goals and general objectives (pp. 19–20). Strategic human resources planning is a system's function and is inextricably tied to the system's guiding strategic plan.

Strategic human resources planning evolved from strategic business planning in the early 1970s. Strategic planning was an important tool for relating management decisions to organizational objectives. The process was developed to bring about an improved allocation of financial and other material resources for maximizing planned organizational outcomes. It provided ultimate accountability for the effectiveness of management decisions. The changes in net product-line profits measured in dollars gained or lost have been regarded as evidence of management's performance.

The concept served the private sector well until recent years. A number of changes and national trends have emphasized the importance of the human element in strategic planning. Concurrently, the federal government and other agencies increasingly are involved in regulating many aspects of human resources management. Each of the several human resources processes—selection and recruitment, compensation systems, promotion policies, collective bargaining, evaluation, and others—has been affected by such external mandates. Laws, court decisions, and executive orders of the last several national administrations have made the elimination of job discrimination a national priority. Also, societal changes prompted by emerging trends in the family structure and the shifting age distribution of the population are a few among many considerations that have focused attention on improving human resources planning. Such considerations have had a profound effect on the operations of many organizations. Moreover, the social conscience of a growing number of organizational decision makers has been raised to include such factors in the framing of strategic objectives that are characterized by a sense of social responsibility (e.g., protecting the environment).

Data about factors of human resources have become an important part of the overall strategic human resources planning process. The educational institution is a personnel-intense industry. In most instances, school systems establish mission statements to guide their commitments of time, energy, and human and material resources. Within this context, strategic objectives are defined for the numerous subunits of the organization as a focus for operational plans. The factors that affect sound human resources planning are as important to strategic planning in education as they are in business. Strategic human resources planning must be integral to the strategic educational planning process and must possess certain characteristics to ensure its effectiveness.

Service agencies such as the public school system have a vital interest in the development of workable models of strategic human resources planning. Such models will provide school systems with the benefits of a focused program, targets for improvement, and knowledge of the makeup and expectations of its constituencies. School systems will also have the advantage of becoming proactive rather than reactive.

Characteristics of Strategic Human Resources Planning

Several characteristics specific to strategic planning have direct application to the processes of planning human resources strategically. The human resources planning process should be *comprehensive*. It must include the many subunits of the organization, for example, schools, departments, and divisions. All planning is done so that changes in one unit can be anticipated from planned or observed changes elsewhere in the system.

Human resources planning is a process that is *integrative*. All parts should interrelate to form a whole. It is not simply a collection of plans from the several subunits of the organization, but rather a single plan reflecting personnel recruitment, selection, allocation, compensation, and development for all units.

The process is *continuous* and usually conforms to the organization's planning cycle. Data are continuously updated so that decisions can be made with the highest degree of currency and accuracy.

A *multiyear planning format* is essential to the continuous process of planning and should reflect activities and developments over a period of one to five years. This plan usually becomes less specific as it projects into the latter part of the five-year cycle. The plan is updated annually for each successive year of the planning cycle, and a new year is added annually to maintain the five-year planning perspective.

The many constituencies affected by the plan should have input in the formulation process. Thus, the plan must be *participatory* to gain individual commitment to implementation. Involvement in the planning process is a good investment that yields important dividends in commitment.

Finally, *flexibility* must be integral to the planning process. The plan should provide for modification and change as required by changes in the school system's internal and external environments and the specific needs of its constituencies. This flexibility should also be evidenced in the plan's sensitivity to the evolutionary stage of the school system and changes required in the professional staff mix, the topic of the next section.

Evolutionary Stage of a School Organization

The process of strategic human resources planning, as we previously noted, is founded on premises and basic assumptions that reflect on the history of the organization and the anticipation of its future. Such a foundation helps to clarify the predictions for future human resources needs so that processes can be developed and implemented to fulfill these needs.

How will future needs be derived from the consideration of a school district's life cycle? A school system on the fringe of a major metropolitan area that is struggling with continuous enrollment increases will be at a different evolutionary stage than a well-established central city district that is trying to retain a quality program in an environment of declining enrollment. The expanding system may need leadership personnel who are flexible, innovative, and committed to program development. On the other hand, the city system may desire educational leaders who can work with communities in the closing of schools and yet maintain high-quality programs through such transitions. Thus, a strategic consideration is to match personnel with the requirements dictated by the evolutionary stage of the organization.

Professional Staff Mix

Baird, Meshoulam, and DeGive (1983) were among the first to portray a portfolio mix of human resources as one in which personnel with specific skills, abilities, and expertise can be moved among units of the organization to achieve the organization's strategic objectives. Specifically, procedures are established so that personnel can be transferred among units of the organization to optimize the use of their talents.

Developing the mix involves balancing the best human resources talents with program needs to achieve the strategic objectives of the school system. Similar to the example discussed earlier, several attendance areas of a school system may be growing rapidly while several others are struggling with enrollment declines. An analysis of the professional staff mix would take into consideration the strategic objectives of both the school system and the individual schools involved to determine the optimum mix of professional staff. This analysis may suggest changes in staffing to help achieve strategic objectives.

The professional staff mix frequently receives special considerations. One such consideration relates to those school districts that are under a court order to provide a particular racial blend of professional staff members in all schools. Another district may be required to balance the professional experiences of faculty members among the schools of the district. Apart from court orders, it is often worthwhile educationally to balance staff on the basis of age, ethnicity, gender, and teaching load.

Despite the need for improving the professional staff mix in a school system, the reality that many school organizations face may militate against such efforts. School board policies, contract agreements, past practices, and traditions can make it difficult to optimize the professional staff composition. Although transfer and assignment policies can be difficult to modify, traditions and past practices will certainly be more difficult if not nearly impossible to change. The human resources administrator must exhibit careful planning, expert leadership, and sensitivity to realize such changes.

Integrating Human Resources Planning Into the Strategic Plan

The professional literature is replete with models for applying techniques of strategic planning to education. Figure 3.1 presents a model that was formulated to represent a synthesis of key elements of the strategic planning process rather than an elaboration on the many models found in practice. Figure 3.1 graphically represents the relationship among the various elements of a general strategic planning model for a school system with emphasis on integrated strategic human resources planning (operational planning). The major elements of the model include *1.0* **Environmental Scanning** with its sub-elements *1.1 External Scanning* and *1.2 Internal Scanning*, and *2.0* **Strategic and Operational Planning** with sub-elements *2.1 Strategic Plan* and *2.2 Operational Plans.* The last major element of the model is *3.0* **Implementation**. The following discussion will elaborate on the model presented in Figure 3.1.

Strategic human resources planning must be done within a context, and it is this context that forms a basis for establishing a school system's mission and developing its strategic and operational plans. The context is gained from an **environmental scan**. The interpretation of the environmental scan will influence a school system's mission and all aspects of the planning process. It is clear that environmental scanning provides important information for use in the ultimate development of a strategic plan for administering the human resources function. Specifically, the planning process entails the development of human resources operational plans that are consistent with the overall strategic plan. These operational plans are dynamic because they interact with those of other organizational units. In addition, operational plans are monitored continuously and can be modified to reflect changing conditions in the school system's environment.

Environmental Scanning (1.0)

A school district's environment is viewed from two perspectives that are best illustrated by the acronym **SWOT**. *S*trengths and *W*eaknesses are regarded as internal environmental factors, whereas *O*pportunities and *T*hreats are the key factors of the external environmental scan. Based on an interpretation of the environmental scan, assumptions can be developed to guide all planning efforts. A careful analysis of scanning information provides a school system with information that supports the development of a rationale for operating assumptions. These assumptions are used to assess the viability of the strategic plan. The assumptions relate to the external sociocultural, economic, technological, and political-legal areas, and to the selected factors of the internal scan, such as human and financial resources.

From a strategic perspective, a school organization must be attuned to its environment. A description of a school system's educational environment includes many considerations that can be viewed simultaneously as constraints and opportunities. In each instance, strategic plans must be developed to minimize the negative effect of constraints and maximize the positive impact of opportunities.

Some of the obvious environmental factors include state board policies and regulations, the state aid funding model for education and other state legislation, relationships with teacher training institutions, services of intermediate service agencies, competition from surrounding school systems that draw from the same teacher pool, the school tax digest, and federal program regulations.

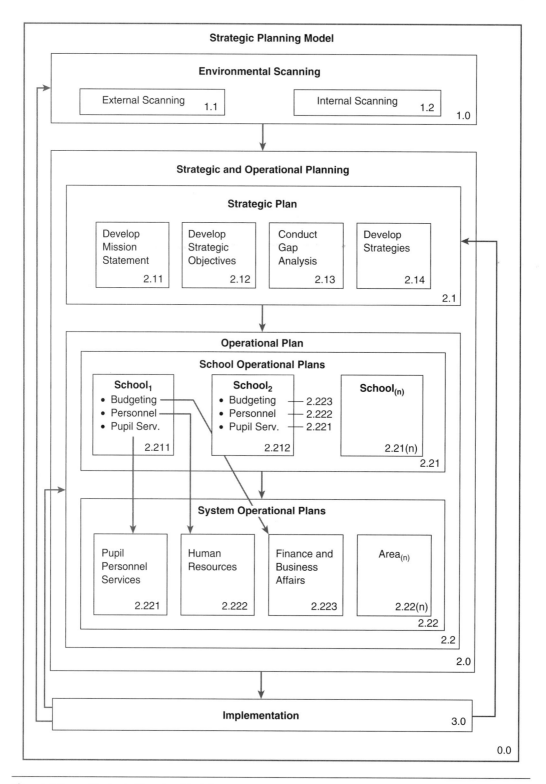

Figure 3.1　　Strategic Planning Model

Other environmental factors relate to the demographic features of the constituencies that the school system serves, including, among others, racial and ethnic composition of the community, age distribution of residents, and socioeconomic status.

The processes of external and internal environmental scanning are continuous and fixed to the school district's planning cycle. Typically, the planning cycle is five years. Like the multiyear planning format, this plan is updated for each successive year of the planning cycle. A new year is added annually to maintain the five-year strategic planning perspective. In each repetition of the planning cycle, all elements of the strategic plan are updated to reflect changing conditions, new directions, and emerging basic beliefs about the educational processes. Environmental scanning is included as an integral part of the strategic planning model, and it affects all elements of the planning process (see Figure 3.1).

External Scanning (1.1)

External scanning is the monitoring, evaluating, and disseminating of information from the external environment to key people within the organization. It is a tool used to avoid strategic surprises and to ensure the long-term health of the school district. Typically, the external scan focuses on emerging trends that present *opportunities* for the school district and potential *threats* to its continued effectiveness. Central to the process of the external scan are four focal points of investigation: sociocultural, economic, technological, and political-legal. Changing demographics such as age, gender, ethnicity, education, culture, and supply and demand of workers are other important scanning areas.

Internal Scanning (1.2)

Internal scanning is usually done by the staff of the district, but it can be done by outside groups or organizations. It addresses the questions of *strengths* that support strategies and *weaknesses* in the organization that constrain strategies. Specifically, this scan investigates the structure of the organization to determine the extent to which it facilitates the implementation of the organization's developed strategies. Every school organization has a unique culture, and the several schools of a school system often develop subcultures within the system's organization. Moreover, the system's culture is represented by the values, ideology, and goals shared by the members of the organization, including the patterns of behaviors for getting work done.

Early studies have suggested an examination of certain organizational artifacts to gain insight into an organization's culture. This evidence can be uncovered not only in an organization's policies, but also by employee greetings, dress, language, ceremonies, gossip, and jokes. It has been suggested that an understanding of culture can be found in the practices of administrators. For example, *how* decisions are made is an indication of culture. Some school organizations value collegiality, working together in groups, and opportunities for participatory decision making.

However, others might be characterized by a number of individuals working independently within some formalized decision-making process. Rituals of the organization can be a part of the culture and vary greatly from system to system. Some may provide public commendations for exemplary accomplishments or promotions.

Another aspect of the culture is the control of information in the school system. Some control information very tightly; others are more open. Additionally, patterns of communication among members of the system characterize a cultural value. Some exhibit a top-down pattern of communication; a bottom-up pattern prevails in others. In a similar vein, some school systems tend to operate democratically, whereas others are more autocratic.

Although influenced by the system's overall culture, an individual school often develops its own subculture. Different elements of the system's culture can exist in a similar form at the individual school level. For example, if a school system places great value on the accomplishments of staff members, an individual school may give great recognition to the achievements of students. This system value is transmitted to its organizational members and is evidenced through the emphasis placed on recognizing student accomplishments.

Strategic and Operational Planning (2.0)

Strategic and operational planning are key components of the strategic planning process. The strategic plan is consistent with the assumptions derived from an analysis of the environment, and it forms the bases for relating all operational plans.

Strategic Plan (2.1)

The four elements of the strategic plan, as illustrated in Figure 3.1, are *2.11* **Develop Mission**, *2.12* **Develop Strategic Objectives**, *2.13* **Conduct Gap Analysis**, and *2.14* **Develop Strategies**. The actual strategic plan is published in a relatively brief document (usually 25 pages or fewer) that gives direction to all operational planning activities. Each operational plan relates to the strategic objectives and strategies in the strategic plan.

Mission Statement (2.11). A critically important factor in the development of a school system's strategic plan is its educational mission. The mission statement provides direction based on a perception of the environment. Specifically, it is a reflection of the top leaders' interpretation of the educational environment. By virtue of their position, leaders influence the system's culture and can respond to their perception of the environment in ways that manifest their beliefs and values about the nature of educating young people, the task of education, and its processes. Consequently, the identified mission directly influences the major direction of a school system. For example, one system may state its primary mission as vocational education, whereas others may concentrate on basic skills, college preparation, special education, or community education.

Over a period of time, all school systems experience changing environmental factors. These environmental shifts can create a need to redefine the general mission of the school system. For example, a school system that has moved beyond the period of expansion in its life cycle may begin to see population shifts away from the central city to suburban areas with expanding pockets of non-English-speaking populations. This important environmental change should bring about an examination of the system's mission. If a new mission statement results, the system needs to make changes in its strategic plan. On the other hand, if the leaders of the school system misinterpret or ignore the changing environment and do not refocus the system's mission, obvious conflicts will invariably arise between the system and its constituencies. "Regardless of the status of the mission statement, the statement needs to be reviewed by the strategic planning council to determine if it contains vision focus, and clarity deemed appropriate in light of the strategic analysis" (Norton et al., 1996, p. 139).

As Burns (1998) pointed out,

Human resources needs to play a key role in any major change initiative. . . . Human resources is the in-house centre of expertise on human issues and . . . it is the human dimension of change which so often confounds organizations. HR must be present throughout the change management process, but particularly in the crucial planning phases. (p. 153)

In full consideration of the realities of the external environment, a mission statement for a particular school system is developed. A written mission statement helps the system define its vision for the future, provides a clear focus for the system's personnel, and identifies a rallying point for committing the human and material resources of the district. Establishing a mission and implementing it through planned strategies permits a school system to shape the organization that it wants to become. It provides a perspective for the future of the system and a vision for the continued existence of the system. Norton and Kelly (1997) noted that every administrator must have a vision. "That vision will often include expectations concerning: (1) student success, (2) the overall climate or environment of the school, (3) the processes by which decisions are made, and (4) the ways in which the administrator envisions individuals and groups interacting together" (p. 4).

Deciding what function the school system serves within its environment is the first step in deriving a mission. This function focuses on the current and emerging educational needs of the community. With a vision in mind, the question of whom it serves becomes germane. Environmental changes require a school system to reevaluate its mission statement periodically. The mission statement should be reviewed every five years to ensure that it meets the needs of the communities it serves. One essential ingredient of the mission statement is an identification of the segment of the population served. No school system can be everything to everyone. Market segmentation requires a review of the actual population the school system serves as well as whom it might potentially serve. In addition to geographical boundaries, the school system must know the ages of the people it serves; it must know the ethnic makeup of the community; it should have a good sense of the community's financial resources; and it should fully understand the values of the people. The school system completes its mission statement by determining how it will perform its function. The "how" response in the mission statement is expressed in general terms and gives guidance to material and personnel resource allocations; for example, the district will use the latest technologies whose effectiveness is supported by research findings and will employ the most qualified teachers who demonstrate a readiness to use the technologies.

The mission statement is carefully studied by the school system in relation to the realities of the external environment. A careful examination of the mission statement should be conducted to determine if it satisfies the following criteria set forth by Smith (2005):

1. A mission statement must be stated in specific and definitive terms.

2. It must be the motivational focus that encourages all points of view and still maintains a coherent organization moving toward common aims.

3. Any mission statement should include the following three primary elements: schools are for kids, schools belong to the people, schools are people developers.

4. To receive commitment to a mission, people in the organization need to go through four steps: (1) awareness that the mission exists, (2) written communication to all in the organization of what the mission is, (3) planned and intermittent reinforcement of the intended mission, and (4) power to perpetuate the mission.

5. The mission statement must be developed by a team effort if there is going to be commitment to that statement.

6. Out of the mission statement should come strategic objectives that are clear and measurable. (pp. 27–29)

The following partial example is excerpted from the mission statement of the Chandler Unified School District, Chandler, Arizona. The guiding statement of the school district's mission statement is, "To provide students with the knowledge, skills and attitudes necessary to be lifelong learners and responsible citizens." The mission statement includes six sections including student achievement, school climate, program enhancement, staff development, communication, and resource utilization. The sections on staff development and school climate are as follows.

Staff Development

Student achievement and school climate will be improved by professional growth activities designed to enhance, maintain, and refine staff competencies.

Key Results

A. All schools will identify a staff development focus based on Teach for Success data and develop a plan to include:
   1. Site staff development
   2. Follow-up Teach for Success data collection

B. By 2009, 75% of secondary math and science classroom teachers will have participated in high quality content literacy staff development.

C. By 2009, 75% of 4–12 classroom teachers will have participated in high quality content literacy staff development.

D. By 2007, 75% of K–3 classroom teachers will have participated in high quality staff development focused on the National Reading Panel's five core elements of a reading program.
   1. Vocabulary
   2. Phonics
   3. Fluency
   4. Phonetic awareness
   5. Comprehension

E. By 2009, 75% of K–6 classroom teachers will have participated in high quality mathematics staff development focused on algebraic reasoning and conceptual understanding.

F. By August 2009, 100% of staff will have completed the full SEI endorsement (60 hours) required by the state.

School Climate

District will provide a safe working and learning environment and students will apply the principles of responsible citizenship and self-discipline.

A. All schools will develop a plan to improve trends identified in the student discipline data.

B. Student dropout rate will not exceed 3.0%.

C. Student daily attendance rate will be at or above 95% measured through the 100th day report.

D. The District will reduce or maintain its Recordable Case Incident Rate (RCIR) to be at or below the national average RCIR for the K–12 education industry as reported by the Alliance.

Develop Strategic Objectives (2.12). A school system's strategic objectives should focus on critical success indicators. These indicators are translated into specific objectives that provide directions for the use of the school system's resources (time, energy, and money). Achievement of these strategic objectives demonstrates the system's success in achieving its mission.

Objectives are usually focused on outcomes and are client centered and positively stated. Moreover, the strategic objectives should be related to those indicators against which the school system's constituencies evaluate its success (e.g., improved test scores, low dropout rate, scholarships and awards, employment after graduation, college entrance, etc.).

Leithwood, Aitken, and Jantzi (2001), in their book, *Making Schools Smarter: A System for Monitoring School District Progress,* provide an excellent, practical tool for helping schools and school districts determine an image that serves decision making relative to goal prioritization, and needed changes to accomplish the image and improve school accountability. As the authors state, "'*Making Schools Smarter*' is a monitoring system designed to help schools and districts acquire the information they need to better realize their intentions for improvement, accountability, and school restructuring" (p. 3). In brief, a monitoring system serves to provide a description of what the school "really should be" along with a process to help determine what the school "really is." Such tools can help schools and school districts acquire, analyze, and interpret information needed to achieve strategic planning and related accountability. For example, concepts and tools available in the above-mentioned resource can be especially useful to school leaders in the determination of mission, objectives, and continuous program monitoring, which are essential components for effective planning.

Conduct Gap Analysis (2.13). The gap analysis applies reality to the strategic planning process. It involves a review of each strategic objective by comparing the desired outcomes to current outcomes in light of internal scanning information. In other words, the analysis reveals the gap between the outcomes desired and current outcomes in relation to available human and material resources, technologies, and instructional processes. One question frequently raised is whether the objectives provide sufficient challenge to stretch the creative thinking of the organization's members during the development of strategies. A response to this question may suggest that the outcomes sought by the strategic objectives be increased to press for greater challenges or, perhaps, lowered to reflect certain realities.

Develop Strategies (2.14). Strategies are statements about how the proposed strategic objectives will be achieved. If the objective of increasing the reading scores of middle-grade students by a specified amount in a given period of time is established, one strategy might be to evaluate the middle grade's reading curriculum; another may stipulate the creation of an intensive staff development program in reading for middle-grades teachers; and a third might create a new screening and selection program for processing applicants to teach in the middle grades. Certainly, there could be others. Strategy selection is dependent on the expertise of the system's strategic planners, the creativity and competencies of its staff, and their interpretations of both external and internal data from environmental scans. Strategies are the most important tools for coping with change, and they provide important bases for mitigating extraneous demands on the school system. Therefore, school administrators must learn to manage strategically; that is, their day-to-day decisions must relate consistently to the strategies adopted for the system's strategic objectives, and their decisions should move the organization in the direction of its mission.

The function of human resources must be integral to the school system's strategic plan by providing direction for future developments of human resources in conjunction with the system's identified mission, strategic objectives, and strategies. There is a consensus among planners today that human resources is an important consideration in the development of strategic objectives and strategies.

Human resources planning must be part of the organization's strategic plan. The human resources operational plan is just as important as a curriculum or a financial plan and should be developed in ways that are consistent with objectives of the system's strategic plan. Additionally, system strategic objectives and strategies provide specific direction for the development of individual school operational plans, which also reflect the need for human resource considerations.

Operational Plans (2.2)

Operational plans are developed for all functional areas of the school system. These include central office departments or units as well as individual schools. To develop operational plans for the several subunits of the school system (e.g., departments, program divisions, and schools), each subunit engages in crafting plans to achieve the integrating function of the overall strategic plan.

Operational plans are specific to one or more of the established strategic objectives and strategies. The aggregate impact of all operational plans particular to the same strategic objective will contribute to achieving that objective. This concentration of effort is the appeal of strategic planning. It brings important system-wide priorities into focus through operational plans that affect in different ways the achievement of mutually agreed on objectives. For example, if some area of student achievement is a priority, then the human resources department can develop an operational plan to direct its staffing practices for improving the personnel mix serving this area of the curriculum; the staff development unit could frame operational plans to improve instructional strategies or the knowledge base of teachers in the area; the curriculum unit might map this area of the curriculum to find possible incongruencies; the administration may establish an operational plan to increase public awareness; and the finance unit may work with another unit of the school system to seek external project funding. Each of these approaches can take the form of operational plans for individual functional units of the system or represent plans of cross-functional areas. We present this example to show how many parts of the organization develop operational plans that target a single strategic objective, but use several strategies.

The operational plans include goals to give direction to the overall effort, objectives to establish targets or outcomes sought by the plan, procedures for implementation, policy considerations, time schedules, implementation constraints, and monitoring procedures for control and evaluation. All plans are reviewed so that a coordinated effort can be used to minimize program overlap.

School Operational Plans (2.21). The school is the primary unit for delivering services in a school system. Each school will have its own operational plan, which reflects strategic objectives that are consistent with the system's strategic objectives. An individual school's plan will focus on the unique needs of its students and will be in harmony with its immediate environment.

As operational plans vary from school to school, people with different skills and abilities will be required to achieve the school's strategic objectives. The requirements for a professional staff mix for two elementary schools might be quite different. For example, suppose a primary component of a system's mission is basic skills, and the system has the strategic objective of raising reading scores on a standardized achievement test to the national mean in five years. One school might identify reading as a strategic priority. Another school that has maintained a mean achievement score in reading that is well above the national norm may focus its energy and resources on another strategic priority. Accordingly, each school may require a different professional staff mix. Such considerations have important implications for staff development, recruitment, and selection. Thus, the strategic human resources plan should reflect these considerations. In practice, the balancing of the professional staff mix has not been widely implemented, despite its importance to strategic planning. Strong school board policies that reflect the importance of professional staff mix to strategic planning may help to promote a more balanced mix in the future.

This situation can serve as another example for understanding a school's operational plan. Certainly, the strategic objective of increasing scores on basic skills tests has implications for site-based budgeting, possible curricular or organizational changes, and of course personnel. Figure 3.1 shows how these considerations become inputs into the operational plans of the system's functional areas.

System Operational Plans (2.22). Each functional area at the system level must have an operational plan for integrating all of the school unit strategies. The need for a different professional staff mix, as we mentioned in the previous example, is again used for purposes of illustration. If shifts in staff are required to optimize the mix, the personnel function would incorporate in its operational plan changes that accommodate all school units at an optimal level. Similar changes in the areas of curriculum or budgeting could affect any number of functional areas. Consequently, the specific strategies of each of these functional areas may have implications for an integrated human resources strategy. "Operational planning may be an outgrowth of a strategic planning effort. Typically once a strategic plan has been developed in which strategic goals have been specified and prioritized, operational planning teams are selected to devise a plan for reaching the identified objectives or goals" (Norton et al., 1996, p. 133).

The **human resources (2.222) operational plan** reflects an integration of the various school unit plans and the system functional plans. The model does not represent a linear flow of information; on the contrary, there is neither a beginning nor an end. It is a continuous process of integration that supports the school system's strategic plan. Each unit and functional area of the system provides input to the human resources operational plan and has a role to play in its formulation and subsequent implementation.

Norton and colleagues (1996) identified three basic components to the strategic human resources planning process: (a) the strategic analysis, (b) clarifying the mission, and (c) strategic management. "Strategic analysis is a process in which the strategic planning council reviews all the environmental considerations they feel have a significant influence on the school system" (p. 138). The mission statement is then reviewed for the purpose of assessing its reflection of the vision, focus, and clarity as determined by the results of the strategic analysis. Strategic management, the third phase of the process, focuses on the implementation of the strategic plan and making the plan operational.

The human resources operational plan should accomplish three objectives. First, it should correlate with the strategic plan of the system. Second, it should enumerate required changes in personnel, school board personnel policies, and administrative regulations and processes so that the system's strategic objectives can be achieved. Third, it should provide a master plan for recruiting, selecting, compensating, and developing human resources.

Implementation (3.0)

The results of implementing operational plans provide both product and process data that become feedback to other elements of the model. This feedback gives evidence to support a need for the refinement, modification, or reformulation of other aspects of the plan. In some instances, objectives will be changed. On occasion, the mission statement will be rewritten, or new strategies will be developed.

Correlation With the System Plan

School systems generally have not extensively involved their human resources units in the development of strategic plans. Despite the obvious and important advantages of integrating strategic planning and human resources planning, the educational literature suggests that such involvement has evolved rather slowly, yet, today, substantial progress is being realized.

In a study of HR directors in one state, one-fourth of the respondents reported that the HR function had moved toward much greater involvement in the school district's policy arena within the last few years (Norton, 2004). In the same study, approximately two-thirds of the HR directors viewed themselves as being a line instead of a staff member in the school system, and a large majority were of the opinion that they had "much influence" on the school district's actions that affected human resources policy decisions. Historically, human resources administrators have not been involved in strategic decisions. Most decisions of a strategic nature usually involved the superintendent and a small group of others, such as those responsible for finance or curriculum. Dyer (1984) underscored the importance of human resources involvement in school districts' policy decisions more than 20 years ago, but emphasized that, if the human resources plan is to be integrated with the system's strategic plan, human resources administrators must give attention to four basic tasks.

The first task is to discover how the school system's educational strategies are determined. Many decisions are based on formal planning procedures that are presented to the superintendent and board of education for approval. By contrast, many strategic decisions result from a response to a crisis or an ad hoc effort of a temporary taskforce. Thus, the human resources administrator must be aware of both the formal and informal decision-making processes.

The second task is to determine how much consideration is given to human resources in the strategic planning process. Do the plans include factors of professional staffing, development, recruitment, and selection? Are appropriate data collected and correctly analyzed? Are these data used to forecast future human resources needs and supply of personnel? Are the results of such analyses used in decision making?

A third task is to decide the amount of consideration that human resources should receive. Although education is a personnel-intense industry, different strategies will dictate different levels of involvement. A strategic plan to close several low-enrollment schools may dictate different human resources requirements than a plan for a bond election to renovate school facilities. Both would require human resources consideration, but the former may be more critical when considering human resources than the latter.

The fourth task is to work toward closing the gap between the amount of consideration that should be given and what is actually given to human resources in strategic educational planning. This gap can be closed by continuously giving attention to the credibility of the human resources organization. The professional staff must be regarded as competent. They must be knowledgeable about education and educational issues as well as most other aspects of the educational processes in the school system, including curriculum design and development. In order to integrate the human resources plan with the system's strategic plan, the human resources plan must be viewed as a shared plan rather than one relating only to the human resources unit.

Information Needs and Forecasting

Collecting and analyzing valid and current human resources information relative to the school system's strategic objectives can provide a basis for ensuring that the human resources development efforts correlate with strategic educational plans. Human resources information must be collected from the different units of the organization, compared, and reported in a form that supports strategic decisions. Compensation, professional staff mix, and performance appraisals are important factors around which specific data are collected.

Forecasting Personnel Needs

Forecasting serves to project future events for the purposes of program planning (Krazewski & Ritzman, 1996). Personnel forecasts are needed to provide a basis of maintaining productivity levels, identifying future professional staff mix, preventing staff shortages, minimizing the costs of overstaffing, and complying with equal employment opportunity goals (Rothwell & Kazanas, 1988). Another factor includes forecasting the attrition of personnel. Attrition results from personnel who move to new positions within the organization, leave the organization for positions elsewhere, or retire. An investigation of such changes requires the human resources unit to develop expertise in forecasting.

Two methods of forecasting supply include quantitative and judgmental techniques. **Quantitative techniques** for forecasting future demand for human resources include such statistical procedures as regression analysis and ratio analysis. For example, when two variables are correlated, regression analysis can be used to forecast future personnel needs if the number of a previous variable is known. **Judgmental techniques** for determining employee demands center on the evaluation of relevant employee hiring, dismissal, and turnover data. Examples of judgmental supply forecasting are executive techniques, succession techniques, and vacancy analysis. **Vacancy analysis** is the technique of making judgments about the likely movements of employees in the short- and long-range future. Best judgments about employee shortages or surpluses are estimated by comparing them to estimates of employee demand.

Markovian analysis represents another quantitative technique for forecasting employee supply. A forecast of changes in personnel provides human resources administrators with information that can be used to guide action to achieve the strategic objectives of the system. Such changes are often studied through the use of cohort analyses, census analyses, or more complex procedures related to Markov chains. The foundational work of Feuer, Niehaus, and Sheridan (1984) provides a comprehensive review of forecasting practices. The following discussion is a simple example of a Markovian analysis for forecasting personnel changes.

Table 3.1 illustrates the movement of six classifications of personnel in a school system. In this example, the hypothetical system has 1,460 professional employees including 300 primary teachers, 250 intermediate-level teachers, 230 upper-level teachers, 500 secondary teachers, 80 supervisors, and 100 administrators. These employee classifications and current employment levels are listed in columns *a* and *b*. Data in columns *c–h* are probability factors for each of the classifications. The factors are based on the mean percentage of personnel changes for the past five years, and it is assumed that these transition probabilities remain stable over time. Column *c* shows a probability of 0.60 (60%) for primary teachers to remain on the job during the year, 0.15 (15%) for primary teachers to move to an intermediate-level teaching position, 0.05 (5%) to move to an upper-level teaching responsibility, 0.01 (1%) to become supervisors, and 0.19 (19%) to leave the system. In a similar manner, the intermediate-level teachers (column *d*) have a probability of 0.10 for moving to primary teaching, 0.70 to stay on the job, 0.10 to move to upper-level teaching, and 0.10 to leave the organization.

Projections by classifications for the following year are presented in column *i*. The projection for each classification is based on the sum of the products of the probability factors and their corresponding employment level for the current year.

Table 3.1   Markovian Analysis of Personnel Attrition

Role	Current	Primary	Intermediate	Upper	Secondary	Super.	Admin.	Projection
a	b	c	d	e	f	g	h	i
Primary	300	0.60	0.10					205
Intermed.	250	0.15	0.70	0.10				243
Upper	230	0.05	0.10	0.70	0.05	0.01		227
Secondary	500			0.06	0.75			389
Supervisors	80	0.01			0.01	0.90		80
Admin.	100			0.01	0.01	0.05	0.85	96
Exit		0.19	0.10	0.13	0.18	0.04	0.15	220

For example, a projection of the number of primary teachers available the next year is $(0.60 \times 300) + (0.10 \times 250) = 180 + 25 = 205$. Similarly, a projection of upper-level teachers is $(0.05 \times 300) + (0.10 \times 250) + (0.70 \times 230) + (0.05 \times 500) + (0.01 \times 80) = 15 + 25 + 161 + 25 + 1 = 227$. Using this procedure for the other classifications, the projection for intermediate-level teachers is 243; secondary teachers, 389; supervisors, 80; and administrators, 96.

In the case of a Markovian analysis involving more classifications of personnel, an electronic spreadsheet such as Lotus 1-2-3 would render the analysis an easy task. The use of a spreadsheet would also allow the human resources planner to ask "what if" questions where different assumptions about attrition could be investigated.

Forecasting Student Enrollments

One cannot dispute the importance of making reliable enrollment projections because they are related to strategic decisions about staffing, curriculum, facilities, and financing. Most projections are made from extensive data sets incorporating 10 years or more of data that may include past school enrollments, current enrollments, parochial and private school enrollments, nonresident enrollments, children per dwelling unit, resident live births, socioeconomic indicators, shifts of population, mobility of families, in/out migration, housing starts, transfer rates, home resales, and student retention rates. Additionally, selected factors such as building patterns, types of dwellings, community patterns, transportation changes, integration, and national trends are frequently used to temper the statistical treatment of the historical data for localizing projections.

Strevell (1952) discussed some of the earliest forecasting methods, including the use of data related to class projections, retention ratio projections, housing projections, and total population forecasts. About the same time, Linn's (1956) approach for making enrollment projections included school enrollment trends over a 20-year period, current enrollments, parochial and private school enrollments, nonresident enrollments, birth rate trends, residential construction, children per dwelling unit, and the number of preschool children. Approximately two decades later, Leggett (1973) and Engelhardt (1973) asserted that accurate forecasts could be made by using birth rate trends and cohort survival ratios. Later, Strong and Schultz (1975) demonstrated the effectiveness of a regression model that used previous years' enrollments, increases in population of children by age, students not promoted, and students entering the labor force.

The **cohort survival** method, sometimes termed the percent-of-survival method, has been a popular forecasting technique for much of the past 30 years. The cohort survival method is based on certain assumptions, namely, that certain statistics will continue to be similar to what they have been in former years (e.g., birth rates, death rates, student migration, grade retention policy, student retention, and other population influx or outflux). Thus, any major fluctuations in population growth pose problems in the ability to predict accurately the enrollment data. As Seyfarth (1996) noted, "The accuracy of any prediction diminishes as the distance from the predicted event increases. Predicting enrollments one year in advance is more accurate than predicting enrollments 5 or 10 years ahead" (p. 28). The use of any forecasting method necessitates the application of both experience and judgment of professionals who can adjust retention ratios on the basis of their specific knowledge of the school community. Consider the following situation: during a period of 15 years, on average, 97% of the students enrolled in kindergarten continued in the first grade the following year, and 94% of the students enrolled in first grade continued on to second grade during the same 15-year time period. Assuming that there are 500 students in kindergarten, we can predict that 485 students will enroll in grade one next year, and of 485 first-grade students, 459 will appear in grade two the next year. Table 3.2 illustrates a cohort technique for forecasting kindergarten enrollments based on annual birth rates over a period of six years.

In Table 3.2, the cohort retention ratio is calculated by dividing the kindergarten enrollment by the number of births for any specific year (e.g., 2001, 3,380 divided by 3,400 = 0.9941). The figures for the years 2001 through 2005 represent the actual statistics for those years. To calculate the projected enrollment for 2006, find the average cohort retention ratio by adding the five previous ratios and dividing by 5.

Table 3.2 Kindergarten Enrollment Projections

Year of Birth	No. of Births	Kindergarten Year	Enrollment	Cohort Retention Ratio
1996	3400	2001	3380	0.9941
1997	3450	2002	3401	0.9857
1998	3600	2003	3503	0.9730
1999	3701	2004	3650	0.9862
2000	3800	2005	3701	0.9739
2001	4000	2006		

The average cohort ratio is 0.9786. Then multiply the number of births five years previously, 4,000, by the mean enrollment ratio, 0.9786. The 2006 kindergarten projected enrollment is 3,914.

Because of such factors as student mobility, rapid population increases within the school community, declining student enrollment, major changes in business or industry growth or decline, school district reorganization and other environmental events, major school district policy change, and objective historical data, cohort survival methods that rely on normal enrollment succession are not always appropriate. In such cases, such strategies such as the **Bayesian estimation process (BEP)** are implemented. Bayesian processes are used in a wide variety of instances to forecast such things as the economy and the time for which a specified process is likely to go out of control. The BEP is a nonlinear technique that relies on information and data from both historical and environmental factors for forecasting student enrollments, such as those we previously mentioned (e.g., school reorganization, major policy changes, major businesses leaving the school district, etc.). The BEP uses the following four major strategies: (1) development of the basic data matrices (objective historical information, cumulative data aggregated for each grade level over a specified time period, usually five years, and statistics utilized by BEP in forecasting nonlinear enrollment results); (2) determination of the environmental factors that will likely influence the enrollment of the school district or a specific school building; (3) calculation of net enrollment statistics; and (4) combining normalized objective information based on historical statistics with normalized subjective information based on related perceptions and judgments of school leaders (Young, 2008).

Because of the improved reliability and ease of using such forecasting systems, the work of the educational planner can be greatly facilitated through their application in making strategic decisions. Certainly, there are other similar systems available, and there will be more and improved systems in the future. It is most important for all school administrators to be aware of such developments and their potential for facilitating administrative decision making.

Forecasting of staffing needs is not always complex. For example, assume that a school district has 15,000 students and a staff of 750 teachers. Best projections indicate that student enrollment will increase by 5,000 in the next ten years. Using a 20:1 pupil to teacher ratio, 250 teachers will be needed plus the expected teacher replacements due to teacher turnover.

Policy, Regulation, Processes, and Personnel Changes

School policies and regulations are inextricably related to the human component of organizations. Therefore, the strategic plan of a school system will invariably require that certain school board policies and administrative regulations be changed or new ones developed so that strategic objectives can be accomplished. As a part of the strategic plan, the section of the document related to human resources should enumerate the need for these changes with specific recommendations.

For instance, the human resources plan may include the objective to raise the minimum level of formal preparation for instructional personnel. This objective is to be fully implemented within a specified period of time. Also, an analysis of school board policies may suggest that there are inadequate policies and corresponding regulations for guiding the implementation of the objective. The human resources operational plan would include recommended additions or changes to policies and administrative regulations. Chapter 9 presents the human resources process of policy and administrative development.

Summary

The planning process is foundational to the success of all other human resources processes and to the ultimate success of the school district's primary educational goals. Strategic human resources planning is a process of preparing a school system for activities in the future, and its decisions related to the use of personnel must show evidence of contributing to the system's objectives. Generally, its purpose is to ensure that the human resources of the school system are employed efficiently and effectively in pursuit of identified outcomes.

The effective planning of human resources requires a system for maintaining relevant system-wide data and information. This information is used to forecast trends on which to base decision making, to provide for an optimal professional staff mix, and to support other functions, such as recruitment, selection, induction, assignment, and compensation.

The implementation of strategic human resources planning must be based on an analysis of the environment. It should be sensitive to the culture of the school system. In addition, the human resources objectives must be consistent with the system's mission and its strategic objectives.

The planning process should be comprehensive and include all subunits of the school system. The plans for each subunit should be integrated to form an overall plan for the total organization. The process is continuous and should conform to the planning cycle of the system, with a multiyear emphasis of five years. Finally, the process should be flexible and participatory to accommodate change and expert staff involvement.

Discussion Questions

1. Either individually or in small discussion groups, identify two different school systems in your immediate area and describe the evolutionary stages that each school system has experienced. Share these descriptions with the class. Discuss how they are alike and how they are different. Can you predict the emerging evolutionary stage of each school system?

2. Based on the descriptions in question 1, what are some of the most important human resources needs for each system during the next two to five years? What priorities should be given to optimizing the professional staff mix? What will be the most important human resources needs in 10–15 years?

3. In discussion groups, make a list of cultural elements that exist in your school or school system. Discuss the differences in each list and how the several elements affect the behaviors of personnel.

4. This chapter presented methods of forecasting staff and student numbers. Without question, such activities necessitate both time and resources. Consider, however, the results of not gaining such information. What are the likely impacts on both human and monetary resources?

Case Studies

MIXED EXPECTATIONS

Dylan Thomas was filled with excitement as he hung up the telephone. Dr. Tyler Woods, the superintendent, had just asked him to chair the newly created planning committee for strategic planning. As the director of human resources for the College View School District, he felt that he would now be able to play an important part in shaping the future of the district.

As Dylan reflected on the challenges facing the committee, he felt that strategic planning would help the district to become proactive by carefully considering its primary thrust. In the past, Dylan had argued to narrow the focus of the district. He felt there were so many demands being made on the limited resources of College View that every program ended up with only limited financial or personnel support. Now, he hoped that strategic planning would help the school district to narrow its focus by deciding what was important and making a serious commitment to the goals of highest priority. The community has high expectations for the school district and has been willing to support requests for funds to improve nearly all academic programs. Parents have been very pleased with the apparent rigorous demands made of students. The district has always had a very strong college preparatory program, with 78% of its graduates entering college on graduation, and a sizable number of the district's seniors have been successful in getting admitted to some of the more prestigious colleges.

Despite the fact that the curriculum has always been geared to the college-bound students, a number of pressure groups have been successful in getting the board of education to install a vocational program that has been a drain on the district's financial resources and, according to some citizens, is "taking money away from the more important challenge of preparing students for college." On the other hand, an emerging group of young parents has been working with the coaches to get more emphasis placed on athletics. Some board policies make it difficult for students to fully participate in interscholastic competition. Recently, two star football players were not allowed to participate because of poor grades in academic courses.

The first meeting of the committee was held in a retreat setting at a country lodge, where Superintendent Woods welcomed the committee. He also talked about the importance of the committee's work and requested their total commitment to the strategic planning process. Dylan knew that the superintendent's strong statement showing a commitment to and belief in strategic planning nearly ensured a good kickoff meeting.

After the superintendent spoke, Dylan led the group in a discussion of strategic planning by presenting an applied model for school district planning. This model was the one recommended by the State Department of Education in a workshop that Dylan attended last year. This was followed by several group exercises that involved the members in a discussion of values related to educational issues. All the exercises were focused on consensus decision making that precipitated much more discussion and heated debate than Dylan anticipated.

Later, Dylan administered a strategic planning readiness instrument and wrote the group's results on the chalkboard. At this point, Dylan led a discussion of the results. He was surprised that the scores showed such a high degree of readiness for the team to plan strategically. This was the last activity of the day and the meeting was adjourned.

During the morning session on the next day, Dylan explained environmental scanning by using the acronym SWOT. He talked about the importance of knowing both the external and internal environments of the school district. This led to a lengthy discussion of many aspects of the district's environment.

Following lunch, Dylan introduced the concept of a mission statement and its relationship to strategic planning. He emphasized the importance of addressing the questions of What? Who? and How? He asked the planning team members to each develop a written response to the What? question. Dylan told the committee to write their statements on the chalkboard, and they would discuss their responses after the coffee break.

As Dylan scanned the statements posted, he was surprised to find statements that were very diverse. This concerned him because he feared that a discussion of these statements would deteriorate into serious arguments. Thus, he decided to ask the committee members to read only their responses, and he told them that he would make copies of these statements for the next meeting. Dylan wanted to give some careful thought to how he might handle the obvious conflicts that would emerge.

Andrew Scott read his statement first. He said, "College View is committed to providing programs that meet the needs of students by developing excellence in both physical and academic abilities through challenge and competition."

Melanie Rose followed with, "It is the purpose of College View to provide quality education with an emphasis on the basics."

Board member Greg Stephen followed by very forcefully stating, "College View School District is committed to providing quality educational programs that will support gainful employment of its graduates."

The teacher of the year, Sara Olivia, followed with, "It is our purpose to provide a comprehensive educational program that will satisfy the social, psychological, physical, and educational needs of our children."

Pamela Nor read, "The College View School System is committed to helping students to develop a strong self-concept and a sense of self-esteem."

Principal Elaine Herr offered, "We are committed to providing programs of quality basic education in an environment that supports trust and mutual respect."

Randall Craig showed his strong interest in vocational education when he read his statement. "College View School District will provide a program to support the development of job-related skills that are augmented by skills in basic education."

Angeline Wilson then read her statement, "Our school system commits itself to providing quality programs that support the educational development and personal interests of all citizens of the community."

Finally, Dr. Woods stated, "We at College View commit ourselves to providing the highest quality of education for our students that is focused on student interests and academics."

Dylan then thanked the group and told them that he would have the statements reproduced for the next meeting in six weeks. At this point he was glad that no discussion followed because he didn't want to end the meeting in controversy. As he drove home, he wondered if any of the statements really reflected what the College View community wanted. For the next several days, he was preoccupied with thoughts of what to do next.

(Continued)

(Continued)

Questions

1. What problem(s) will Dylan have to deal with at the next meeting?

2. What are some symptoms of the problem(s)?

3. What are all of the possible actions that Dylan might take to solve the problem(s)?

4. What consequences should Dylan anticipate from implementing each of the actions?

5. What action should Dylan attempt?

CASE 3.2

THE STATE MANDATE

Elaine Ora, a seasoned human resources administrator, attended several workshops on strategic human resources planning that the State Department of Education offered. She tried for several years to convince the superintendent to consider strategic planning in the district because she strongly valued the process and felt that it would greatly help her district. Also, she had reliable information from a friend at the State Department of Education suggesting that it was only a matter of time before the State Board of Education would mandate that all school districts develop annual strategic plans.

Elaine knew that the superintendent did not value any type of serious planning. She frequently recalled one of the superintendent's rebuttals to her planning suggestions, "We tried that comprehensive planning once, and it was a waste of time. The governor even had a conference on it. Then we had to submit that huge report that was probably never read."

As expected, the State Board adopted a regulation that required all school districts in the state to plan strategically and submit their plans to the Department of Education for approval.

When the superintendent received notification of the requirement from the State Superintendent of Public Instruction, he asked the assistant superintendent for administrative services, the assistant superintendent for business affairs, and the director of finance to write the plan. Elaine was not asked to be involved.

Questions

1. Did the superintendent make a good decision? Why or why not?

2. What problems can be anticipated from the superintendent's decision?

3. What are the possible actions that Elaine might take?

4. What consequences can be anticipated from each action?

5. What is your recommendation regarding what Elaine should do?

CASE 3.3

SARA'S NEW ASSIGNMENT

At the last meeting of the board of education, Sara Olivia was appointed as the new assistant superintendent for human resources. The board's approval was another vote of confidence for Dr. Tyler Woods, who was appointed superintendent only a year ago.

Superintendent Woods's decision to recommend Sara was based on her strong background in strategic planning and previous experiences as the director of personnel in a neighboring school system. Previously, she had directed the strategic planning effort of a large school system in another state.

During her first day on the job, Sara was arranging her personal belongings in a beautifully redecorated office when Dr. Woods stopped by to give her the old "Welcome aboard" greeting. After a few minutes of casual conversation, he said, "Oh, by the way, I need your help. The board is eager to support my suggestions on strategic planning for the district. They asked me to give them a set of recommended board policies that they can consider for getting this effort underway. This is going to be one of the most important things that this school system has ever done, and the community will be watching it closely. You'll have to be a key player in this effort. So, what I'd like you to do is set up whatever committees you need for developing the policies and get back to me as soon as possible."

Questions

1. What considerations should Sara give to forming the committee? Who should be involved?

2. What should be the committee agenda at the beginning of the committee's work?

3. What policy areas should be reviewed in preparation for making policy recommendations to the board?

References

Baird, L., Meshoulam, I., & DeGive, G. (1983). Meshing human resources planning with strategic business planning: A model approach. *Personnel, 60*(5), 14–25.

Burns, S. (1998). Effective change management. In M. Butteriss (Ed.), *Reinventing HR: Changing roles to create the high-performance organization* (Chapter 7). Etobicoke, Ontario: John Wiley and Sons.

Dyer, L. (1984). Linking human resource and business strategies. *Human Resource Planning, 7*(2), 79–84.

Engelhardt, N. L. (1973, June/July). How to estimate your future enrollment. *School Management*, pp. 38–41.

Feuer, M. J., Niehaus, R. J., & Sheridan, J. A. (1984). Human resource forecasting: A survey of practice and potential. *Human Resource Planning, 7*(2), 85–97.

Hanlon, J. M. (1968). *Administration and education.* Belmont, CA: Wadsworth.

Krazewski, L. J., & Ritzman, L. P. (1996). *Operations management: Strategy and analysis* (4th ed.). Reading, MA: Addison-Wesley.

Kreitner, R., & Kinicki, A. (1998). *Organizational behavior* (4th ed.). Boston: McGraw-Hill.

Leggett, S. (1973, January). How to forecast school enrollments accurately—and years ahead. *American School Board Journal*, pp. 25–31.

Leithwood, K., Aitken, R., & Jantzi, D. (2001). *Making schools smarter: A system for monitoring school and district progress* (2nd ed.). Thousand Oaks, CA: Corwin.

Linn, H. E. (1956). *School business administration.* New York: Ronald.

Norton, M.S. (2004). *The human resources director in Arizona: A research study.* Tempe: Arizona State University, Division of Educational Leadership & Policy Studies.

Norton, M. S. (2005). *Executive leadership for effective administration.* Boston: Allyn & Bacon.

Norton, M. S., & Kelly, L. K. (1997). *Resource allocation: Managing money and people.* Larchmont, NY: Eye on Education.

Norton, M. S., Webb, L. D., Dlugosh, D. G., & Sybouts, W. (1996). *The school superintendency.* Needham Heights, MA: Allyn & Bacon.

Pfeiffer, J. W., Goodstein, L. D., & Nolan, T. M. (1986a). *Applied strategic planning: A how to do it guide.* San Diego: University Associates.

Pfeiffer, J. W., Goodstein, L. D., & Nolan, T. M. (1986b). *Applied strategic planning: A new model for organizational growth and vitality.* In J. W. Pfeiffer (Ed.), *Strategic planning: Selected readings* (pp. 1–25). San Diego: University Associates.

Rothwell, W. J., & Kazanas, H. C. (1988). *Strategic human resources planning and management.* Englewood Cliffs, NJ: Prentice Hall.

Seyfarth, J. T. (1996). *Personnel management for effective schools* (2nd ed.). Boston: Allyn & Bacon.

Sibson, R. E. (1992). *Strategic planning for human resources management.* New York: American Management Association.

Smith, R. E. (2005). *Human resources administration: A school-based perspective.* Larchmont, NY: Eye on Education.

Strevell, W. H. (1952, March). Techniques of estimating future enrollment. *School Board Journal*, pp. 35–38.

Strong, W. B., & Schultz, R. R. (1975). Models for projecting school enrollments. *Educational Evaluation and Policy Analysis, 3,* 75–81.

Young, I. P. (2008). *The human resource function in educational administration* (9th ed.). Upper Saddle River, NJ: Pearson Merrill Prentice Hall.

CHAPTER 4

Staffing for Educational Services

The Recruitment Process

Learning Objectives

After reading this chapter, you will be able to

- Describe the challenges facing human resources administrators relative to problems of employee supply and demand.
- Describe the purposes of human resources recruitment and the importance of training personnel for recruiting.
- Identify and implement an operational model for the recruitment process and describe its importance as a reflection of the school district's strategic plan.
- Identify various strategies for personnel retention, including the re-recruitment of personnel.
- Use various interviewing techniques in the recruitment process.
- Differentiate between a job analysis and a job description, including the benefits of each.
- Identify several measures for use in evaluating the accountability of the recruitment process.

Personnel recruitment is the human resources process that informs personnel of positions available and assesses their interest and qualifications. It is a systematic method of identifying and attracting personnel in order to create an applicant pool for vacant positions in the school system. It is the first step in the hiring process. The development of an applicant pool is not merely a matter of luck. Rather, there is a close association between recruitment planning and the educational returns related to the process.

Recruitment screening serves the purpose of narrowing the recruitment pool to only those applicants who are minimally qualified for the position openings.

This procedure encompasses two specific tasks. One task is that of person-job fit. **Person-job fit** centers on narrowing the applicant pool to those who are best qualified for the position opening in question. "**Job-Person-Job Fit** is a state of congruence between job demands and resources on the one hand, and individual abilities and proclivities on the other" (Villanova & Muchinsky, 1997, p. 257). The second task centers on **person-organization fit** or the further narrowing of the applicant pool to those applicants who both fit the requirements of the position and also fit the organization. "Person-organization fit is a state of congruence between the overall personality, goals, values, and interpersonal skills of the individual and the climate/culture of the organization" (Villanova & Muchinsky, 1997, pp. 257–258). Organization analysis looms important because of its potential for enhancing the creation of a bond between the position applicant and the organization. If there is a mismatch between the school system and the individual, personnel problems are likely to occur and employee retention is jeopardized. Several kinds of questions that can serve organizations in their attempt to analyze short- and long-term personnel needs have been suggested (Kossek & Block, 2000, pp. 257–258):

1. What are the short- and long-term goals of the school system?

2. What types of capabilities does the school system need in order to implement its chosen strategy?

3. What are the school system's specific human resources needs?

4. What tasks does the school system need to accomplish?

5. What knowledge, skills, and other characteristics does the school system need for job performance?

6. What aspects of the school system's environment affect the administration of its human resources function?

7. What characterizes the climate and culture that exist in the school system?

The answers to such questions provide important information that enhances the achievement of organization-fit and person-fit objectives.

An Operations Model for the Recruitment Process

An effective recruitment process necessitates the important steps of planning, organizing, identifying productive recruitment sources, determination of recruiting activities, processing of applications, evaluating applications for the recruitment pool, and evaluating recruitment results through accountability measures. The following operations model sets forth these important steps, each of which is discussed in-depth later in this section.

Step 1—Planning for Recruitment. Policies are developed and adopted that state the purposes that the recruitment process is to accomplish, the list of factors required to ensure a balance in staffing, the need to give attention to recruitment on a broad basis, and the desired specifications for persons who are to be involved in the recruitment process.

Step 2—Organization of the Recruitment Process. Clear directions for the responsibilities of the central human resources director, local system personnel, and others are determined. Financial support requirements are determined and approved. An inventory of position needs is completed; job analyses and job descriptions are developed as required. Recruitment interview instruments and report forms are developed. Interviewers are trained. Re-recruitment activities are planned.

Step 3—Determination of Recruitment Sources. The most viable sources for applicants are identified. Special attention is given to strategies for recruiting quality personnel for special needs areas and job positions that have been problematic for recruitment in the past. Strategies for announcing position openings are established and supply sources are contacted.

Step 4—Establishing the Applicant Pool. Processing of the recruitment applications is implemented. Recruitment interviewing methods are determined. Preliminary interview rating forms are designed. Criteria are identified for the purpose of refining the applicant pool to only those who are qualified for the respective positions. The progress of the pool development is monitored.

Step 5—Control of the Recruitment Process. Results of the recruitment process are assessed in terms of stated purposes and expected outcomes. Procedures are evaluated in terms of their effectiveness in producing desired outcomes. Accountability measures are applied and analyzed. Cost-effective data are calculated.

Planning for Recruitment

A recruitment policy states what the recruitment process is to accomplish; it centers on expectations of the end results. Figure 4.1 is an example of a school board recruitment policy that includes many of the common characteristics of such policies: responsible persons or units, what the process is to accomplish, special purposes, required legal and qualification checks, and the authority for final approval of appointment.

The foregoing policy avoids setting forth the specific procedures for accomplishing the desired ends of recruitment. In most cases, the administrative regulations for implementing board policies are left to the discretion of the school superintendent and the professional staff. However, it has become more common for personnel policies for such personnel processes as recruitment, selection, evaluation, and dismissal to include specific procedural statements. In some instances, school board policies cite verbatim the specific state statutes regarding these employee matters in order to avoid violations specified by legal processes.

Personnel Recruitment Policy

Code 4112

In order to develop a pool of the best qualified personnel for positions in the Wymore School District, efforts will be taken to gain a balance in staffing relative to such factors as experience, preparation, gender, diversity, and personal interests. Recruitment should be on a broad basis geographically and include a variety of recruitment sources such as career placement offices, media advertisement, student teaching, job fairs, staff referrals, career day activities, and other sources that serve to identify qualified applicants and help to achieve staff balance. Although a variety of personnel should participate in the recruitment process, only qualified personnel who have been trained in the recruitment process should be involved in the ultimate selection of applicants for the various applicant pools. Special recruitment activities should result in meeting the personnel shortages in the school district due to the school district's increasing enrollments and special needs areas. The ultimate goal of the recruiting process is to develop a pool of the best qualified applicants for the ultimate selection for position openings in the school district. Legal activities relating to position licensing requirements and background check are necessary in the selection of personnel for the various applicant pools. The school superintendent and those qualified personnel delegated by that office will be responsible for administering the recruitment process and achieving its stated goals and objectives.

Ref: Statute 15–000

Date Adopted: April 20, 20____

Figure 4.1   Personnel Recruitment Policy

Given the potential for legal challenges, it behooves those responsible for the recruitment and selection of employees to be knowledgeable about federal and state legislation pertaining to the recruitment and selection process both from a practical perspective relative to fulfilling system needs and obligations for staffing the organization. (Young, 2008, pp. 95–96)

Goals and purposes of the recruitment process evolve directly from the school board policy and the purposes and objectives set forth in the human resources strategic plan. For example, the personnel goals set forth in the board policy and strategic plan (e.g., staff balance, talent retention, qualified recruiters, school-community culture, etc.) are discussed. Information collected from previous recruitment assessments is reviewed for purposes of possible improvement of the ongoing recruitment process.

Organization of the Recruitment Process

The school system commonly is one of the largest employers of the community. It is essential to define specific responsibilities and determine the wide variety of task assignments for the recruitment of personnel. Both centralized and local units of the school district often share the responsibility for recruiting personnel, although the central human resources unit commonly coordinates the recruitment process and the prescreening of applications. As Chapter 2 noted, nearly 83% of the central office human resources directors in one state named recruitment of personnel as a primary responsibility (Norton, 2004).

The recruitment process requires funding for position advertising, travel costs, development and printing of recruitment instruments and records, clerical services, personnel services, and other expenses related to the process. Various studies have estimated the loss of first-year teachers at approximately 30%. "Such turnover is expensive: replacing workers costs 25% of each person's salary. Lose 6% of your 1,000 teachers making $25,000 per year, and you face a replacement bill of $375,000, money that would be welcomed in other budget lines" (Norton, 1999). Budgeting for such expenses is essential.

The use of employee attrition analysis, such as set forth in Chapter 3 in the section on Markovian analysis, is useful in determining staff recruitment and selection needs (see Table 3.1). Employee attrition and retention statistics are compared to projected program needs in order to determine the number and necessary qualifications of employees to be recruited. The equation is quite simple: PCE + NPN = TNE (the number of personnel currently employed in school district positions plus the number of personnel needed as replacements or for new programs equals the total number of district employees projected for the coming year).

Included in organizational activities is the development of appropriate position analyses and position descriptions. A **position analysis** is the process of examining the contents of a position and breaking it down into significant tasks. It is a scientific, in-depth analysis of the position and includes its constituent parts and surrounding conditions. The information to be examined depends largely on the specific purpose of the analysis. Typically, the contents of a position analysis include

1. Information about the position itself—primary duties, tools and technology, environment, terms of employment.

2. Qualifications—knowledge, special skills, physical requirements, experience, education requirements.

3. Schedule of activities and time requirements—related tasks that influence the position, day or night commitments, months per year.

4. Effects of the position or work on the employee—stress, illness records, turnover, relationships, safety, peer relationships.

5. Conditions of work—workload, environment, hazards, inside or outside, turnover, illness records.

6. Relation to the organization—coordination, supervision required, supervision given, line and staff relationships, reporting, support services, responsibilities.

7. Relation to the community—communication, contacts, support agencies, services rendered, public demands.

The information and data garnered from a position analysis serve multiple purposes. Its value to the employer includes the following:

1. It provides a position focus relative to goals of the system, ties the position strategically to these goals, and serves as the basis for role examination and its effects on the employee. It provides specific evidence relative to the workload demands of the person in the position.

2. It provides a basis for evaluating the position and improving its conditions and employee performance. It can point to position situations that require restructuring. It can clarify specific qualification required in the position.

3. It serves as a basis for recruitment and selection of professional and support personnel by identifying specific position responsibilities and qualifications.

4. It serves as the basis for relevant employee development activities that are more relevant for the given position.

5. It can serve to identify problems related to system security, personal protection, and safety hazards.

6. It becomes a legal statement for the school system on questions of hiring, performance appraisals, counseling, and dismissal. It can assist in the development of performance instruments that are closely job related.

The value of a position analysis for the employee includes the following:

1. It provides position applicants with important information about the work requirements and performance expectations. It reveals the position's effects on the employee and the conditions under which the position takes place.

2. It sets forth direction as to how the position links to other units in the school system and to the system's overall strategic objectives.

3. It provides more freedom for the employee regarding the use of personal creativity and innovation in the position by setting forth expected results as opposed to procedural requirements.

4. It serves as a sounding board for determining personal and professional growth and development needs and opportunities.

5. It serves as a communication tool relative to position changes, possible position improvements, available resources, career opportunities, and agreements relative to work outcomes.

A position analysis is not complete until verified by an appropriate supervisor. Figure 4.2 indicates several kinds of questions that the supervisor must answer. All appropriate parties must fully discuss any differences between the supervisor's views of the position and those resulting from the position analysis. The parties make changes in the position analysis depending on the clarifications and agreements determined. Both the employer and the employee benefit from this discussion because a better understanding of the nature of the position generally results.

The extent to which position analyses are common practices in human resources administration in education is not completely clear. From a conceptual point of view, job analysis should be an ongoing activity performed by qualified human resources personnel. In reality, the activity in education is sporadic and most often associated with positions of support personnel.

Position analyses precede the activities of position grading and position assessment or valuing. **Position grading** centers on the analysis of a position or family of positions and determining the range level for each specific position (e.g., clerk 1, clerk 2, administrative assistant, lunch worker 1, lunch worker 2, food service clerk,

To the supervisor: Please examine the attached questionnaire of the employee under your supervision. Comment on each section as indicated by the specific question. Add additional comments on additional sheets if necessary.

1. Is the position description of _____ in the position of

    (name of employee)

    _____ essentially accurate? _____ Yes _____ No

    (official position title)

    If you answered "no," correct the statement as necessary with explanations as appropriate. What modifications of the employee's statements should be made?

    _____

    _____

2. What specific aspects of the position were omitted in the position analysis or should not be included in the statement?

    _____

    _____

    _____

3. Should more emphasis be placed on aspects within the position analysis than on those shown by the employee?

    _____

    _____

    _____

4. Are the skill and educational requirements listed by the employee in the position analysis adequate for this position? What additional knowledge and/or skills are necessary, if any?

    _____

    _____

    _____

5. How readily available are replacement personnel for this type of position (Supply and Demand)?

    _____ supply is plentiful   _____ demand (need) is high

    _____ supply is adequate   _____ demand is moderate

    _____ supply is limited   _____ demand is low

6. What special circumstances, conditions, or qualifications should be considered in connection with this position (other than those that might have been mentioned previously)?

    _____

    _____

    _____

7. Is the present classification of this position a correct one in your opinion? Please explain.

    _____

    _____

    _____

8. Given the basic qualifications and responsibilities for the position, what particular induction information and/or training sessions might be necessary for any new employee who was new in the position?

    _____

    _____

    _____

9. Please make other comments and/or observations relative to the analysis of this position that you might find necessary.

    _____

    _____

    _____

    _____

Supervisor's signature: _____   Date: _____

Figure 4.2   Supervisor's Verification of Completed Position Analysis Questionnaire school lunch cashier, food service operation assistant, etc.). **Position assessment** or valuing ascribes monetary values to each position. Chapter 12 includes a comprehensive discussion of position grading and assessment.

Position Descriptions

A position description is a written statement containing facts pertaining to the position's responsibilities, context, and requirements. It evolves from the position analysis and commonly includes the job title, general and specific position responsibilities, position qualifications, and supervisory relationships. Among many uses, position descriptions

1. Provide the basis for recruiting and interviewing position applicants or candidates.

2. Clarify employee responsibilities and specific duties.

3. Provide a point of comparison between the expected duties of the position and the actual duties performed by the position incumbent.

4. Help a staff member view the position in terms of its relation to the school's and school system's overall goals and objectives.

5. Help set fair and objective standards for supervising and evaluating job performance.

6. Clarify lines of authority and important channels of communication.

7. Help identify program and employee needs relative to professional development.

8. Inform the school board and others about the actual work responsibilities performed by school system employees.

9. Provide reliable information on the content and requirements of a position that is useful in managing ongoing change within the system.

10. Provide legal safeguards for dealing in a just manner with employee retention and dismissal.

11. Enhance opportunities for employee creativity by focusing on the expected outcomes of the position as opposed to specifying procedural guidelines.

Figure 4.3 shows the contents typically found in a position description for a classroom teacher: position title, position qualifications/knowledge/skills, supervisor, position goals, performance responsibilities/duties, terms of employment, and performance evaluation.

Figure 4.4 shows an example of a position description for a high school principal. The contents are typical of most position descriptions for school principals, although the job description in Figure 4.4 classifies work responsibilities under four major classifications: curriculum and instruction, school administration and management, student personnel, and staff personnel. Specific duties of the school principal in the classification of staff personnel include recommendations for hiring and dismissal, staff development, supervision of all personnel, recommendations

<u>Position Title</u>:	Teacher
<u>Qualifications</u>:	Teaching certificate as required by state law
	College degree with major in subject area of teaching
	Experience as determined by the local school board
	Other qualifications as might be determined as necessary by the school board
<u>Immediate Supervisor</u>:	School principal or person designated by the school principal
<u>Persons Supervised</u>:	Students assigned and teacher aide if assigned
<u>Position Goal</u>:	To guide and assist students in learning subject matter and skills that will contribute to their personal development as active, responsible citizens.
<u>Position Responsibilities</u>:	Responsibilities include:

*Meeting and instructing students in assigned classes in the locations and at the times designated.

*Planning a program of study in accord to state and local school guidelines that meets the individual needs, interests and abilities of the students.

*Creating a classroom environment that is conducive to learning and is appropriate to the maturity and interests of the students.

*Guiding the learning process toward the achievement of stated goals through the establishment of clear objectives for all lessons and curricular experiences.

*Directing students to set and maintain appropriate standards of behavior in and outside the classroom.

*Employing a variety of instructional models and strategies that provide for the needs of students in relation to their capabilities, personal interests, and needs.

*Understanding and applying knowledge relative to student growth and development.

*Assessing the accomplishment of students on a regular basis and providing reports and feedback to students and parents as appropriate to the requirements and the situation.

*Enforcing the guidelines of safety and protection of students including physical safety, health and general welfare.

*Maintaining accurate, complete, and appropriate records as required by state law and local school board policy and administrative regulations.

*Assisting the school board and the local administration in the implementation of all policies, administrative regulations, and school rules relating to student conduct, responsibility, and academic progress.

*Maintaining a personal and professional self-improvement plan that results in the development of new knowledge and needed skills for the teaching position assigned.

<u>Special Knowledge/Skills</u>:	Specific skills related to human relations, judgment, problem analysis, ability, written communication, oral communication, decision making, planning and organization, and leadership are important for effectiveness in the position.
<u>Terms of Employment</u>:	Salary is determined by the school district's approved salary schedule for teachers on an annual basis. Teachers are eligible to receive additional compensation for assuming special assignments in such areas as coaching, extra-curricular programs, and achievements related to the school district's Master Teacher Program.
	The work year is established by the school board annually in accordance with state law.
<u>Evaluation</u>:	Performance evaluations are implemented according to the provisions set forth in the Board of Education's policy on Evaluation of Professional Personnel.

Figure 4.3   Position Description for a Classroom Teacher

TITLE: School Principal

GENERAL STATEMENT OF THE RESPONSIBILITIES: The school principal serves as the instructional leader of the school in providing leadership in the planning, implementation, monitoring, and evaluation of the curriculum and instructional services. The principal is responsible for the supervision of the staff members employed in the school and for maintaining a safe and caring learning environment. The principal carries out the administrative procedures approved by the school superintendent and the professional staff and supports the policies adopted by the board of education. The goals and objectives developed by the school principal and staff are tied directly to the overall strategic goals and objectives of the school district.

POSITION QUALIFICATIONS:

   *Appropriate degree and administrative certification;

   *Has a minimum of three years of classroom teaching experience;

   *Three years of prior administrative experience is preferred;

   *Demonstrated ability to establish and maintain an effective school learning environment;

   *Demonstrated ability to work cooperatively with staff personnel and members of the school community;

   *Demonstrated skills of administrative leadership including judgment, planning and organizational ability, human relations, decision making, written and oral communication, and problem analysis;

   *Demonstrated the knowledge and ability to establish a viable set of school goals and objectives that tie strategically to the overall goals and objectives of the school system.

THE POSITION DUTIES:

Curriculum and Instruction

   *Implements and coordinates the instructional program of the school;

   *Coordinates professional staff development activities in collaboration with the central office instructional unit and the human resources unit;

   *Supervises the instructional assignment of instructional personnel;

   *Oversees the evaluation of the instructional program including specific internal and external assessments, the testing program, and goal achievement;

   *Establishes an effective teacher performance evaluation system designed as a formative, staff improvement procedure;

   *Gathers and analyzes student achievement data and uses such information for improving instructional programs and teacher performance;

   *Develops the master schedule for the school including instruction, extra-curricular, and related school meetings and programs.

Management

   *Ensures that all programs and activities provided by the school are in compliance with the laws of the state, regulations of the State Board of Education, and the policies of the school district's Board of Education;

   *Assists in the development of the budget for the school in collaboration with the central office human resources unit, the business office, and the office of the superintendent of schools;

   *Represents the school in its dealings with other public entities and institutions, as well as community organizations and the school's stake holders;

   *Ensures the proper maintenance of school records, including property, personnel, student, budget, supplies, and other required school records;

   *Directs the completion of various reports required by the school, school district, state and other official agencies;

   *Supervises the proper care and maintenance of the school facilities;

   *Develops and interprets the purposes and needs of the school to the superintendent and other appropriate bodies within the school system;

(Continued)

(Continued)

*Serves as a member or ex-officio member of various committees within the school;

*Serves as the general supervisor of all support personnel.

Student Personnel

*Establishes rules and guidelines for proper student conduct and maintaining discipline;

*Establishes an effective program of student personnel in the school including guidance services and career services information;

*Establishes programs and activities that foster a positive school climate and positive relations among students, staff, and the school administration;

*Ensures an effective program of articulation with feeder schools that promotes student understanding, growth, and development;

*Develops schedules for students that maximize learning and personal development;

*Promotes a positive relationship between the school and parents and works collaboratively with parents in fostering healthy parent-child relationships.

Personnel Administration

*Recommends to the school superintendent all appointments, transfers, and dismissals of professional and support members of the school staff;

*Assigns all members to their instructional assignments and develops effective methods of determining equitable workload assignments;

*Recommends all promotions, demotions, changes of personnel status, and salary changes to the school superintendent and central human resources unit;

*Establishes and maintains an effective communication system with school staff personnel, students, and parents;

*Establishes an effective induction program for all staff members new to the school in collaboration with the central human resources unit and other appropriate school administrative personnel;

*Serves as the communication link between the school superintendent's office, the school staff personnel, and students in the school;

*Establishes a system of re-recruitment of personnel designed to retain quality personnel in the school program;

*Maintains such personnel records that are required by the school, school district, or state agencies as required by law;

*Activity supports the Employee Assistant Program of the school district in order to serve the special needs and problems of staff personnel.

EVALUATION OF PERFORMANCE:

The performance evaluation of the school principal will consist of a "system assessment" that includes input from the school staff, students, and parents of the students (Board Policy GBCD).

SUPERVISION RECEIVED:

The school principal is directly responsible to the Superintendent of Schools.

SUPERVISION GIVEN:

The school principal supervises all professional and support personnel of the school staff.

CONTRACT PROVISIONS:

The school principal's position is a 12 month contract position. Two weeks of vacation time are given each year subject to the approval of the school superintendent.

The school principal's compensation is determined by the official school principal's compensation schedule, approved by the school board annually.

Figure 4.4   Position Description for a School Principal for changes of status, record keeping, staff assignments, communication, teacher-parent conference scheduling, and performance evaluation.

Recruitment Sources

Past success often dictates the specific recruitment sources for a particular school district. However, changes in supply and demand, special program needs, personnel turnover, competition for scarce staff personnel, and other factors often necessitate changes in recruitment sources.

Empirical evidence suggests that "walk-ins" constitute one of the best sources for new personnel, but heavy reliance on this source may not meet the school board's policy requiring an attempt to provide staff balance or to recruit on a broad basis.

Common recruitment sources include placement bureaus, job fairs or round-ups, advertising in newspapers or other media, student teachers, college recruiting, position posting in various locations including in-district postings, employment agencies, professional journals, internal faculty referrals, teacher aides, local talent, ex-teachers, and word of mouth. A growing recruitment source is the Internet. Several pros and cons of online recruiting are summarized as follows.

Pros	Cons
1. Definitely in place as a contemporary practice. Immediate access to a ready supply of applicants.	1. Same applicants are available to many other districts. National competition.
2. Cost savings in terms of travel, paper, postage, and so forth.	2. The electronic forms established by the school district may not be used by the applicant.
3. Use of clerical personnel during early stages of recruiting.	3. Availability for personal interviews questionable. Travel costs problematic.
4. Broadened geographic search increases chances of diversity and kinds of experience.	4. Distance tends to complicate interview methods for some applicants. Is too impersonal.
5. Some guarantee of quality.	5. No guarantee of quality.
6. Online applicants are likely to have good computer skills.	6. Some good applicants may not have good computer skills.
7. Empirical evidence suggests that online recruitment is more successful for higher level or specialized personnel.	7. Use of e-mail does not ensure that the applicant is the one responding to the application and interview questions.

It is a common practice for human resources directors and school principals to network with other principals and directors about recruitment. For example, a school district that does not have a particular position opening for an applicant may refer the applicant to another district in the network. Some high schools have Future Teachers of America (FTA) chapters that foster students' interest in teaching.

Students engage in learning activities and experiences related to the nature of teaching and opportunities in the teaching profession. A growing human resources effort is that of re-recruitment, which is the subject of a later section.

Recruitment Strategies: Establishing the Recruitment Pool

Initial recruitment screening strategies include the gathering of applicant information through such activities as the recruitment application, resumes, college transcripts, references, confirmation of certification, and the recruitment interview. Among the most common types of information gathered are

- Application information including name, address, e-mail address, teaching degree and major, related specialties and certifications, college activities, personal references, and special interests.
- Last position and reason for leaving.
- Student teaching information and teaching record.
- Specific position for application and teaching areas of interest.
- Related work experience.
- Professional activities, memberships, and conferences.
- Co-curricular interests and experiences.
- Special recognition, honors, and awards.
- Date of availability.
- Career aspirations.

Recruiting interviews are frequently conducted via personal or conference calls. Figure 4.5 is an example of a recruitment interview that serves several screening purposes. Such instruments can be administered in short time periods and yield initial information about the applicant's oral communication skills, philosophy about instructional methods and classroom management, and views of personal strengths.

Recruitment in some instances is more challenging because of the location of the school or school district, the district's ratings on student performance, its reputation, or other factors that include districts located in poor economic areas or with low salary scales. In such instances, special recruitment measures are necessary.

Although there are no guarantees that special recruitment strategies will succeed, a few strategies are presented as follows:

- Make recruiting everyone's business. Provide training in recruitment.
- Have a guaranteed interview if one applies for a position in the school district.
- Reduce the workload of first-year teachers (e.g., provide a teacher aide, provide one less hour or class to teach, establish an effective mentor program).
- Make special efforts to get retired teachers to return for short-term or part-time assignments.
- Promote the concept that multicultural and multilingual teaching is a rewarding career. Emphasize how such teachers can make a positive difference.

Name _____ Recruiter _____ Location _____

Date _____ Applying for Position _____ Certification(s) _____

Degree(s) _____ Major _____ Minor _____

1. What is your assignment preference (e.g., subjects, grade level, extracurricular)?
2. How do you determine the student's instructional levels?
3. What two or three instructional methods do you prefer? Why?
4. What techniques would you use for classroom management?
5. What materials do you use in teaching?
6. If you could change these materials, what would you change?
7. What do you believe to be your teaching strengths?
8. How would you meet the needs of all students in the classroom? (Academic, social, emotional, physical)
9. Briefly describe your professional/career aspirations at this time in your life.

Comments on applicant's presentation of answers, speech patterns, oral communication, etc.

General comments and observations

Overall recommendation: Outstanding _____ Good _____ Average _____ Below Average _____

Figure 4.5   Recruitment Interview

- Develop programs with local universities and colleges that bring graduate school preparation programs to the school district. Encourage university–school district collaboration.
- Work with local schools to sponsor scholarship programs to work with FTA chapters and other potential teachers. Assign a mentor teacher to work with prospective teachers during their college years. Have social studies units on education in the regular school program.
- Request the civic and community organizations in the district to help recruit by providing both human and monetary resources.
- Invite candidates for teaching to tour the school district and visit with faculty personnel and community members.
- Issue a challenge to those who think they can measure up to the needs of the school district and contribute to the school district's goals. Work at getting prospective teachers to buy in to the school district through identification with the district's goals and the recruit's personal aspirations.
- Send successful teachers of the school district to job fairs with pictures and portfolios. Let them sell the school district.

- Develop a video that tells about the quality of the schools within the school district and the school district's programs. Have the video placed in appropriate teacher placement offices. Develop a school district binder that highlights school programs, successes, programs, traditions, opportunities, and benefits and make it available in placement centers (Norton & Kelly, 1997).
- Develop movie screen recruitment ads that can be shown at local and regional theaters.

Information and data gathered from the foregoing recruitment activities must be summarized in a form that is easily accessible and useful for making decisions about the inclusion of the applicant in the district's recruitment pool. Figure 4.6 shows the common contents of summary recruitment reports. The recruitment interview summary report should include an evaluation of the information relating to college data, teaching experience, personal traits of the applicants, special data relative to the applicant's creativity and career focus, and ratings for candidacy. All information and data are synthesized and used for gaining consensus as to whether or not to place the applicant in the recruitment pool. As indicated in Figure 4.6, applicant priority ratings range on a continuum of Priority One, Two, or Three or Not Recommended. Depending on the case at hand, those recommended for the pool are so informed. From an ethical standpoint, those applicants who are not recommended should be notified that they are not being given further consideration for the respective position. Legal authorities recommend that individuals not recommended for retention in the recruitment pool for a particular position not be given specific reasons for this decision.

Controlling the Recruitment Process

The importance of the recruitment process and its related cost factors make it important that some methods of assessing and controlling its effectiveness be implemented. To what extent were the purposes of the recruitment process realized? To what extent did the recruitment process result in achieving the human resources strategic goals? How many of the total number of position applicants were selected for the applicant pool? How many of the people in the applicant pool became employee candidates? How many of the employee candidates were offered contracts with the school district, and how many accepted? One straightforward accountability measure is the calculation of the number of pool applicants who actually become position candidates. For example, if 45 pool applicants actually were selected as candidates for 35 position openings, the recruitment rating would be approximately 128%. On the other hand, if only 20 pool applicants became position candidates for the 35 openings, the rating would drop to approximately 57%.

Breaugh (1997) suggests the use of yield ratios to assess the success of recruitment and selection activities. For example, Figure 4.7 shows the applicant flow data beginning with the number of original applicants who continue in the process at each stage of the recruitment process. If 200 of 300 applicants ultimately qualify for the applicant pool, the yield ratio is 200 to 300 or 67%. Similarly, if 100 of the 200 pool applicants become position candidates, the yield ratio is 100 to 200 or 50%; if

RECRUITMENT APPLICATION/INTERVIEW SUMMARY REPORT

Date: _____

Desired Position: _____

E1 _____ MS _____ Sr _____ Other: _____

Interviewed at: _____

Interviewer (s): _____

_____

_____

Credentials Complete: Yes _____ No _____

I. Personal Data

Name: Mrs.

Miss

Mr.

Dr. _____ Phone: (   ) _____

Last   First   Md.

II. College Data

Bachelors _____ Masters _____ Doctoral _____ Other: _____

College of Highest Degree: _____ Date: _____

Certifications Held: _____

Student Teaching: Where _____ Subject/Grade _____

III. Teaching and Related Experience (Give type and length): _____

_____

_____

_____

IV. Traits:

Key: 1-Excellent,   2-Very Good,   3-Good,   4-Fair,   5-Poor

1	2	3	4	5

a. Appearance, Grooming, Neatness, Dress _____

b. Personality, Poise, Enthusiasm _____

c. Oral Communication, Grammar, Speech _____

d. Quality of Responses to Questions _____

e. Emotional Stability, Maturity _____

f. Professional Attitude _____

g. Professional Awareness _____

h. Quality of Experience, Extra-Curricular _____

i. Other Languages, speak, read, write _____

(Continued)

(Continued)

V. Comments: (Identifiable skills, including knowledge, creativity, goal orientation, human relations, problem analysis, judgment, and so forth) _____

_____

_____

_____

_____

VI. Overall Evaluation (Use foregoing key, 1-excellent etc.)

Interview: 1   2   3   4   5   Credential/References 1   2   3   4   5

VII. Selection Pool Recommendations: Priority One _____ Priority Two _____

Priority Three _____ Priority Four _____ Priority Five _____

Report Form Completed by: _____

Figure 4.6   Recruitment Application/Interview Summary Report for Certified Personnel

Number of Original Position Applicants
300

Number of Applicants Placed in Applicant Pool
200..Yield Ratio 67%

Number of Pool Applicants Who Became Position Candidates
100..Yield Ratio 50%

Position Candidates Who Became Position Finalists
50..Yield Ratio 50%

Number of Position Finalists Who Were Offered Contracts
20..Yield Ratio 40%

Number Who Accepted Contracts After the Offer
18..Yield Ratio 90%

Number Who Accepted Contracts and Remained After First Year
12..Yield Ratio 70%

Number of Employees Who Remained After Year Three
9..Yield Ratio 75%

Figure 4.7   Application Flow by Stages With Accountability Measures

50 of the 100 position candidates become finalists, the yield ratio is 50 to 100 or 50%; if 20 of the finalists are offered contracts, the yield ratio is 20 to 50 or 40%; if 18 of the 20 finalists who are offered contracts accept the offer, the yield ratio is 18 to 20 or 90%; if 12 of the persons who accepted positions remain after one year, the retention yield ratio is approximately 70%; and finally, if 9 of the 12 persons are still on the job after three years, the retention ratio is 9 to 12 or 75%.

Recruitment is a definite district cost. Recruiting costs, such as those discussed previously, must be considered in terms of their relationship with the effectiveness of the recruitment plan and procedures. Can the recruitment process be improved so that it is possible to reduce the time and number of personnel necessary for these activities and yet retain or improve the number and quality of the recruitment pool? Can an adjustment be made in the recruitment plans and procedures in order to realize a more specific focus on hiring personnel in special needs areas or reduce the number of applicants withdrawing at certain points in the recruitment process? Is the recruitment problem related to the low number of available applicants being prepared? Is there a greater need for the training of interviewers or other personnel involved in recruitment activities?

Many other cost comparisons can be implemented in the evaluation and control of the recruitment process. For example, the costs of traveling to various sites for recruitment or interviewing of applicants can be compared to the actual returns from such visitations. The number of applications received compared to the actual costs of advertising for classified personnel in movie theaters and regional newspapers is another indicator of value received. Did the additional expenditures and personnel time related to the recruitment of mathematics and special education teachers for the school district result in more applicants than in previous years? The answers to these and other questions provide important information that can lead to changes and improvements in the recruitment process. In the long run, the success of the recruitment process resides in the extent to which quality personnel are hired and retained in the school system. This kind of control requires the tracking of the success of the employees hired as well as the recruitment procedures and the successful recruitment decisions made by the personnel involved in the recruiting and selection processes.

The Re-Recruitment of Personnel

Although recruiting new personnel is a major challenge in school districts today, equally important is the ability to retain those teachers and staff personnel who are already in the system. The serious personnel problem of teacher and staff retention has brought more attention to the matter of re-recruitment, also termed strategic staffing. **Re-recruitment** activities center on retaining quality personnel; every effort is made to reduce employee turnover. Re-recruitment is becoming a primary competency for human resources administrators (Ettore, 1997).

Reasons for voluntary teacher turnover vary, but they typically are based on the facts that (1) teaching was not a satisfying experience for them; (2) teaching for them was devoid of opportunities for success, career advancement, and recognition for their contributions; and (3) they found work outside education that was more highly compensated and rewarded. Each of these reasons holds implications for reducing teacher turnover and increasing teacher retention.

The human resources function has a primary responsibility for resolving the problem of teacher turnover. For example, early studies underscored the fact that an employee induction program that specifically provides personal assistance is the single best factor of all morale factors for personnel new to the teaching profession (Berglas, 1973). Approximately 20 years later, Lemke (1995) reported that, "carefully planned programs of orientation have been known to raise the retention rates from 50% to 85%" (p. 25). Some authorities refer to orientation as a socialization process. "Socialization is the process wherein individuals become aware of the prevailing norms and do their best to assimilate" (Mahoney, 2006, p. 30). **Induction** serves the purpose of helping the new employees bond with the school system, bringing them toward the belief that they are important members of the school system's team.

> Employees who are appropriately matched to their jobs exhibit higher levels of job satisfaction and performance. . . . An appropriate and productive job match means that the required tasks of the position relate directly to the personal strengths and interests of the employee. (Webb & Norton, 2004, p. 330)

Organizational climate plays a major role in the determination of job satisfaction and ultimately in the decision of personnel to leave the system. The consensus of most climate studies is that the more favorable the conditions of work, the higher the level of employee job satisfaction. Even though individuals may have been attracted to teaching because they wanted to work with children and youth, when they encounter intolerable working conditions, find themselves embedded in a school system with a poor image, are placed in ill-advised personnel assignments, do not receive the support needed to become successful as a teacher, or are assigned to teach subjects or grades outside their areas of strength and interest, many leave education for work in other fields.

Spitzer (1996) noted that traditional reward practices, although costly, have not resulted in long-term employee motivation. He speaks of power rewards that release employee energy and are empowering rather than manipulative. Power rewards avoid excessive dependence on money rewards, giving more attention to motivators that (1) create a climate of appreciation, (2) help employees understand the importance of their work, (3) add variety and interest to their work, (4) increase employee responsibility and authority, (5) encourage continuous learning and personal improvement, and (6) allow them to use personal initiative and to set their own goals. Research studies support the contention that organizational climate is inextricably related to job satisfaction. By providing personnel with meaningful opportunities to grow intellectually and through the employee's commitment to learn from daily interactions, motivational benefits above those of monetary compensation are possible. Organizational climate is the major topic of Chapter 8.

Robinson and Galpin (1996) set forth five specific considerations for re-recruitment leadership:

1. Security—Employees in the system must be made aware early that they are an integral part of accomplishing the mission of the system.

2. Inclusion—People want to be in on things. Participation in important decisions and ongoing participation are paramount to the dynamics of the system.

3. Control—Talented people want to maintain some autonomy over how things are done. Creativity is an important motivator.

4. Ego—The understanding of the statement, "I play an important role in the success of the system," must be effectively communicated.

5. Doing the Right Things—Providing rationale for decisions helps individuals to see that staying with and committing to making changes successfully are the "right things to do." (p. 90)

One suggestion for assessing the interest in the teacher's current position assignment is to use a brief survey questionnaire that is administered at least annually. Figure 4.8 is an example of an assignment interest questionnaire. This questionnaire is designed as a teacher request. Although the local school administrator and the central human resources director cannot always meet the specific requests and interests of the teacher at the time, they are alerted to the employee's interests. Feedback to the employee about possible assignment changes within the school or school system is of paramount importance. Serious attention to the teacher's program and career interests is vital in the re-recruitment activity.

Instructions: The school and school district are interested in learning about your present personal and professional interests in relation to your position assignment(s), Please complete the following questionnaire related to teaching and extra-curricular assignments. Although it may not be possible to meet specific requests for assignment changes at this time, each request will be considered and reported, to the central human resources unit in the district for their consideration.

Name of Employee: _____

Present Position: _____ Location: _____

Time in Present Position: _____ Grade(s)/Subjects Taught: _____

Teaching Assignment Interests and/or Requested Changes

    Grade Level Change (please explain) _____

    _____

    Subject-Area Interest and/or Change (please explain)_____

    _____

    Supervisory and/or Administration Interests (please explain)_____

    _____

    Certifications Held _____

    Special Interests/Changes in Extra-Curricular Assignments (please explain) _____

    _____

    _____

Comments/Clarifications: _____

_____

Principal/Supervisor Comments or Recommendations _____

_____

    _____   _____

    Supervisor/Principal Signature   Date

Figure 4.8   Inventory of Personnel Status Regarding Position Assignment and Professional Interests

The recruitment operational plan calls for an assessment of potential employees' career aspirations at the outset of their employment. These interests must be tracked and kept in mind. Empirical evidence strongly suggests that individuals actually do pursue personal goals relative to their career aspirations. Personnel retention and re-recruitment success relate closely to the extent to which the school system itself helps meet these personal aspirations. The considerations of person-organization fit and organization-person fit, which we discussed earlier in this chapter, are two-way considerations. Both the organization's needs and the personal and professional needs and interests of the employee are important concerns of the recruitment process.

Summary

Recruitment is the human resources process that informs personnel of positions available and assesses their position interests and qualifications. It represents the first step in the hiring process. Two important tasks of the recruitment process are person-organization fit and organization-person fit. That is, both the applicant's qualifications for a position and the personal interests and aspirations of the candidate are important. Both considerations are necessary in order to establish a bonding between the organization and the candidate.

The recruitment process operations model includes several key steps: (1) planning for recruitment, (2) organizing the recruitment process, (3) identifying recruitment sources, (4) establishing the recruitment pool, and (5) controlling the recruitment process. Each of these steps must be effectively implemented if the recruitment process is to be successful. The adoption of a viable recruitment policy by the school board is an important activity of recruitment planning. Position analyses and position descriptions are essential developments within the many required organizing activities. The identification of reliable recruitment sources and effective recruitment procedures is vital to the development of the school district's recruitment pool of applicants. Controlling the recruitment process includes a comprehensive assessment of how well it is accomplishing its stated purposes. Both descriptive and quantitative measures can provide important information and data useful in making decisions about needed improvements in the recruitment process.

Recruitment is a foundational process of the selection process. Many practitioners view recruitment and selection activities as among the most important tasks that they perform. Not only does recruitment serve as the first step in the hiring of school system personnel, but an effective job of recruitment and selection can reduce substantially the administrative problems encountered within the school district.

Discussion Questions

1. (Class Project Discussion) Each class member is to draft a position description for a school principal. Focus primarily on the specific responsibilities

and duties of the school principal. Discuss the various results obtained. Then, check the common responses of the class members with the principal's position description set forth in Figure 4.4. Discuss differences and similarities.

2. Give thought to the responsibilities of the recruitment process as presented in the chapter. Set forth several specific suggestions for the training of individuals who participate in the recruitment process.

3. The chapter suggests that a step of paramount importance in the recruitment process is the adoption of a recruitment policy for the school district. Defend this recommendation. What specific purposes does a policy adopted by the school board serve in regard to the recruitment of personnel?

4. Consider the several strategies set forth in the chapter related to recruiting in school districts experiencing difficulties due to geographical, financial, and other such problems. Select two or three of the strategies that you believe might be most effective and support your selection.

Case Studies

CASE 4.1

NO NEED TO FREEZE THE JOB IN PLACE

Principal Perez received a call from the district human resources director, Irene Romero. Lincoln Elementary School had just been approved for an assistant principal's position, the first in the school's history. Irene Romero queried Principal Perez about the possibility of his sending a draft position description for the new position. She suggested that Perez give some thought to the project and then send it to her for examination. Principal Perez asked Romero about the content areas of the position description that she had in mind. She indicated that the contract months, major goals of the position, specific duties to be performed, supervision responsibilities, and performance evaluation considerations should be part of the description.

"Well," said Principal Perez, "Don't get me wrong, but I never did see the importance of these job descriptions. Don't they just serve to freeze the possibility of creativity and initiative in the position?"

Questions

1. Assume the position of the human resources director, Irene Romero. What is your response to the statement of Principal Perez?

2. Name several ways in which creativity and personal initiative can be encouraged in a position description.

A NEW APPLICANT

MEMO

TO: Carl Sutter, Director of Human Resources, Wilson District

From: Joan Royce, Math Teacher, Wilson High School

RE: Interest in Administrative Assignment

I wanted to let you know that I have completed the work and internship for administrative certification for the role of supervisor or school principal and would like to be considered for work in these areas. As you know, I have taught math at Wilson High School for six years and assisted in the administration of the Adult High School math program for two years now.

The College View University Career Services unit informed me of two supervisory positions in the Union and King Creek school districts, but I would prefer to remain with the Wilson District in some administrative role.

I was hoping that you might be able to help or inform me about opportunities in our school district. I would appreciate the opportunity to visit with you on this matter.

Thank you.

cc: Principal Lyon, Wilson High School

Questions

1. Assume the role of Carl Sutter, Director of Human Resources. What steps might you take in response to the teacher's memo?

2. List several ideas that a school district might take to retain personnel talent within the district.

References

Berglas, W. W. (1973). A study of the relationship between induction practices and the morale of the beginning teacher. *Dissertation Abstracts International, 34*(5), 2189-A.

Breaugh, J. A. (1997). Yield ratios. In L. H. Peters, C. R. Green, & S. A. Youngblood (Eds.), *The Blackwell encyclopedia of human resources management* (pp. 257–258). Oxford, England: Blackwell.

Ettore, B. (1997, May). How are companies keeping the employees they want? *Managing Review, 86*(5), 49–53.

Kossek, E. E., & Block, R. N. (2000). EEO in the workplace: Employment law changes. In E. E. Kossek (Ed.), *Managing human resources in the 21st century: From core concepts to strategic choice* (pp. 257–258). Cincinnati, OH: Southwestern College Publishing, Thompson Learning.

Lemke, L. C. (1995). Attracting and retaining special educators in rural and small schools: Issues and solutions. *Rural Special Education Quarterly, 14*(2), 25–30.

Mahoney, D. (2006). *Ethics and the school administrator*. Lanham, MD: Rowman & Littlefield Education.

Norton, M. S. (1999). The work of the school principal in the area of human resources administration. *NASSP Bulletin, 83*(603), 108–113.

Norton, M. S. (2004). *The human resources director in Arizona: A research study*. Tempe: Arizona State University, Division of Educational Leadership & Policy Studies.

Norton, M. S., & Kelly, L. K. (1997). *Resource allocation: Managing money and people*. Larchmont, NY: Eye on Education.

Robinson, D. C., & Galpin, T. (1996, July). In for a change: Re-recruiting your "human capital" during turbulent times. *HR Magazine, 41*(7), 90–93.

Spitzer, D. R. (1996, May). Power rewards: Rewards that really motivate. *Management Review, 85*(5), 45–50

Villanova, P., & Muchinsky, P. M. (1997). Person-job fit. In L. H. Peters, C. R. Green, & S. A. Youngblood (Eds.), *The Blackwell encyclopedic dictionary of human resource management* (p. 257). Oxford, England: Blackwell.

Webb, L. D., & Norton, M. S. (2004). *Human resources administration: Personnel issues and needs in education* (4th ed.). Upper Saddle River, NJ: Merrill Prentice Hall.

Young, I. P. (2008). *The human resource function in educational administration* (9th ed.). Upper Saddle River, NJ: Merrill Prentice Hall.

CHAPTER 5

Staffing for Educational Services

The Selection Process

Learning Objectives

After reading this chapter, you will be able to

- Utilize an operational model as a guide for administering the selection process of the human resources function.
- Describe the importance of a school district policy that guides the administration of the selection process.
- Identify the common criteria used in the assessment of a candidate's qualifications for a teaching position.
- Describe the difference between a recruitment interview and a behavioral selection interview used for the selection process.
- Describe the purposes and uses of different interviewing methods in the selection process.
- Understand the importance of having trained interviewers with specific personnel skills participate in the selection process.
- Identify the several "checks" required as part of the selection of qualified personnel.
- Understand the vital importance of planning in the implementation of the selection process.
- Understand the interrelationship between and among the planning, recruitment, selection, induction, and assignment processes of the human resources function.

A common comment by practicing school administrators is that the selection of personnel is their most important responsibility. Quality staffing of classroom, administrative, and support positions in the school system is a vital step in ensuring a quality education for students. Without capable personnel, the educational goals of the school system cannot be fully realized. **Selection** is the process of making decisions about the hiring of personnel. It includes a series of steps, activities, and assessments related to the position itself, the school system's goals and objectives, and the further evaluation of the applicants selected from the recruitment pool.

As Norton (2005) stated:

> The selection process becomes much more than filling vacancies; it necessitates the hiring of individuals with those qualities needed for achieving the organizational purposes, not just meeting the requirements of one particular job. In addition, the system must give full consideration to the aspirations of the applicant. Commitment to the organization's purposes and the retention of services require such consideration. (p. 103)

An effective process of personnel selection can achieve several important purposes:

1. It is a way to encourage change and improvement in the school system's educational programs.

2. It can reduce substantially the personnel problems faced by school administrators and others in the school system.

3. It can foster a bonding between the school system and employees that results in a reduction of employee turnover.

4. It can improve the organizational climate of all schools within the school system.

5. It can serve to change the climate of the school and school system by fostering improved interpersonal relationships between and among staff and administrative and student personnel.

An Operational Model for the Selection Process

An effective selection process is a planned, organized, and controlled process. The following section discusses six specific steps of the selection process: (1) designing and organizing the selection process, (2) defining the behavioral characteristics to be appraised, (3) compiling appropriate selection data and appraising candidates in relation to the selection data, (4) preparing the eligibility list, (5) nominating the selected candidates for hiring and receiving contract approval by the school board, and (6) assessing the selection results.

Designing and Organizing the Selection Process

An effective selection process is guided by a viable selection policy, specific goals and objectives, and strategic plans for the implementation of the process under the direction of qualified administrative leaders. A viable selection policy states what the selection process is to accomplish. Figure 5.1 is an example of a typical selection policy that includes the assignment of responsibility for the process, the desired results concerning personnel quality and diversity, expectations concerning personnel licensing, legal requirements, and the finalization of contracting for personnel services.

The individual states have been given the primary responsibility for determining a teacher's qualifications and eligibility for employment in public schools. State boards of education and departments of education have been delegated the responsibility to assure local school boards that individuals who hold teaching certificates are qualified to do so.

Personnel policy, like any other policies adopted by the school board, should be legislative in nature. A policy states what is to be done as opposed to the specific administrative procedures required for its implementation. The selection policy in Figure 5.1 stipulates that, "Efforts will be made to maintain staff balances relative to preparation, experience, gender, race, and personal background." The school superintendent, director of human resources, and other professional staff members commonly draft the administrative regulations necessary for implementing the policy. For example, selection procedures concerning staff preparation balances would necessitate the consideration of the candidates' earned degrees, the institutions providing the preparation, degree majors and minors, academic records, and other criteria relating to preparatory backgrounds.

Code 4001

The school superintendent is authorized to determine the human resources needs of the school district and, in cooperation with the central human resources unit, establish a recruitment pool from which qualified personnel will be recommended to the school board for employment. The school board will employ persons best qualified for the position to be filled. The school district administration shall make special efforts to maintain staff balances relative to preparation, experience, gender, race, and personal background.

The school superintendent or central human resources unit will assure that each person nominated for employment holds appropriate certification for respective positions and that required background checks have been ordered and evaluated before board contracts are offered.

Finalization of employment of any person becomes official when an employment contract has been offered and signed by the potential employee, the background check has been cleared, and the governing board has taken action to approve the appointment.

Administrative regulations, established by the school superintendent and professional staff, should include specific procedures for implementing this policy, including administrative procedures for assessing the accountability of the selection process.

Figure 5.1   Policy for Personnel Selection

A school board policy guides the development of the goals and objectives of the selection process. Selection goals and purposes differ from school district to school district depending on policy, purposes, and strategic plans. For example, a general goal might state that, "It is the goal of the human resources selection process to hire and retain quality personnel who match the qualifications for available positions and whose career aspirations are compatible with the opportunities available within the school district." Although general in nature, the goal underscores a commitment to hiring personnel who meet the person-fit and organization-fit concepts of personnel selection. Other selection objectives might be more specific. For example, a statement that, "an objective of the selection process is to hire personnel who are committed to the teaching of reading skills as they pertain to the specific content of their subject-matter area," sets forth a specific knowledge and skill of reading criteria and serves as one criterion for candidate selection.

The plans for the implementation of the selection process include (1) a thorough review of the applicant information gathered during the recruitment process, (2) the selection responsibility assignments, (3) the organization of search teams, and (4) the naming of search team leaders. Plans are made either to conduct selection interviews of all pool applicants or to determine applicants to be interviewed on the basis of highest ratings received during the recruitment process.

Defining the Behavioral Characteristics to Be Appraised

Position descriptions serve as ready resources for defining the behavioral characteristics to be used for the rating of position candidates. The information to be compiled and the questions to be answered are identified and included in the appraisal instruments utilized in the selection process. Common sources for gathering selection information for inexperienced teachers include (1) the personnel application, (2) the personal interview, (3) the student teaching experience record, (4) the academic records of the candidate, (5) work history and past performance, and (6) letters of recommendation. The testing of knowledge and skills related to teaching methodology has increased as a data collection method. Common data information sources for experienced teachers are similar to those of inexperienced teachers, although teaching references are of paramount importance in selecting experienced personnel.

Studies of the characteristics viewed as important for teacher selection somewhat surprisingly are limited. An early study by Kowalski, McDaniel, and Reitzug (1992) listed preferred teacher characteristics as viewed by school principals. Table 5.1 shows 21 characteristics rated on a Likert-type scale from 1 = low to 5 = high. School principals in the study listed respect for students, honesty, emotional stability, professional commitment, and professional pride among the top 10 characteristics. The challenging question for selection personnel is just how the characteristics of respect for students, honesty, emotional stability, and others are to be assessed. The selection planning team must decide which position criteria can be assessed in the interviews and which should be assessed by the use of other techniques. Data gathering activities include a variety of information sources. Application information, interview results, letters of reference, and professional vitas are common data sources. Other sources such as testing, simulation activities, and structured interviews are among the strategies also discussed later in the chapter.

Compiling Appropriate Selection Data

Letters of Reference

Letters of reference continue to be among the leading information sources used in the selection process for both inexperienced and experienced personnel. In many

Table 5.1   Important Characteristics for Teacher Selection as Viewed by Principals

Characteristic	Mean Score (1 = low, 5 = high)
1. Respect for students	4.94
2. Honesty	4.88
3. Ability to work with peers	4.80
4. Verbal communication	4.79
5. Quality of previous experience	4.79
6. Emotional stability	4.69
7. Commitment to the teaching profession	4.69
8. Professional commitment	4.69
9. Ability to assess pupil progress	4.68
10. Professional pride	4.60
11. Willingness to be a team leader	4.58
12. Effective discipline	4.54
13. Written communication	4.54
14. Ability to retain confidentiality	4.53
15. Knowledge of child growth and development	4.47
16. Understanding of subject matter	4.46
17. Ability to use questioning techniques	4.44
18. Pleasant personality	4.41
19. "Model" of several models of teaching	4.37
20. Ability to be a decision maker	4.35
21. Potential for professional growth	4.32

SOURCE: Kowalski, McDaniel, & Reitzug (1992).

instances, school administrators and other school personnel are reluctant to write letters of reference, especially when a nonsupportive response is required. Court rulings have made it clear that it is a responsibility of school officials to give honest responses in letters of recommendation. In a Wisconsin case, a superintendent was listed as a reference for a former employee whose contract had not been renewed. The superintendent sent a negative response to the prospective employer's letter of inquiry. As a result, the former employee filed a libel suit. The court ruled that, "Public policy . . . requires that malice not be imputed in such a case situation, for otherwise one who enjoys a qualified privilege might be reluctant to give a sincere, yet critical response" (Peterson, Rossmiller, & Volz, 1978, p. 279).

Three guidelines serve those school leaders and others who are asked frequently to send letters of reference to other schools and organizations for former employees: (1) contents of letters of reference must be based on factual information that can be documented in the personnel records of the school system, (2) any intent to damage the reputation of a former employee by asserting untrue information is unlawful, and (3) the courts have made it clear that not only should school officials participate in the writing of recommendations for former employees, positive or negative, but they have a professional responsibility to do so.

The reliability of personal references as a viable source for employment purposes has been an ongoing concern. Few studies have been conducted on the value of references in the process of teacher evaluation and selection. An early study by Vukovich (1970) is worthy of mention. This study concluded that

1. Teacher references or evaluations have certain identifiable characteristics that can be used as a guide in selection.

2. Teacher references or evaluations are sufficiently predictive to enable employing officials to use them successfully as predictive devices.

3. Teacher references or evaluations for the more successful teachers are equally as predictive as are those for less successful teachers.

4. Teacher references or evaluations that are innocuous and short in length and contain reserved statements are predictive of less successful teachers.

5. Teacher references or evaluations that contain many superlative modifiers are predictive of more successful teachers. (p. 1)

Empirical evidence suggests that personal references are useful in the determination of teaching performance. Performance evaluations and records of teaching experience also tend to be valuable in determining future success in teaching. However, not all sources of data and employee information are equally predictive of teacher performance. For example, the number of years of experience in teaching reportedly influences the assessment results of teacher perceiver assessments.

The Interview Guide

An interview guide that includes procedures for assessing the criteria identified relative to each position opening, and provides guidelines for specific questions to be used in each interview, serves several purposes. For example, an interview guide enhances continuity in the interviewing activities by helping each interviewer focus on the selection criteria for the specific position opening. The use of multiple interviewers increases the potential of more detailed and accurate information resulting from the interview. The interview guide is also a valuable learning resource for inexperienced interviewers.

The training of interviewers is an important activity of the selection process. Empirical evidence has revealed major differences in interviewers' judgments relative to the rating of a single candidate. The lack of interview training and dependency on the use of a "sixth sense" for determining the best candidate are among the reasons for poor selection results. All interviewers must be knowledgeable of the position criteria being assessed, the importance of the physical setting for the interview, and how to enhance the interactions between the interviewee and themselves. Both one-on-one interviews and group interviews require qualified interviewers. Training in the administration of interviewing instruments is necessary in order to accomplish a high level of inter-rater reliability among interviewers who use the same instrument.

Selection Interview Techniques

The Talent Attraction and Selection System (TASS) suggests three different approaches to position selection and related interviewing of candidates. One approach centers on a **short interview technique** initially conducted as a telephone interview. A brief review of the candidate's professional qualifications serves as an opener for the interview. The criteria and characteristics necessary related to the position opening are identified by asking questions about performance. For example, the interviewer might ask, "How do you determine the interests and special needs of students?" or "How do you establish student discipline in the classroom?" A record of the interviewee's responses is completed and placed in the candidate's file. Empirical evidence suggests that a telephone interview can be completed within a 30-minute time period. Thus, several interviews can be administered in a relatively short time.

Those candidates who score appropriately in the telephone interview typically are invited to participate in a brief, on-site **performance interview**. For example, a mathematics candidate might be asked to "teach us why we invert and multiply in the division of fractions." An elementary school candidate might be asked, "Show us how you would proceed with a lesson on phonics in grade two or three." Again, ratings are recorded for performances relative to oral communication, poise, knowledge of subject matter, and instructional methodology.

Another interview strategy in the TASS approach is the **long interview technique,** which takes from two to as many as six hours. Various strategies are implemented to determine the candidate's strengths and weaknesses. The applicants chosen from the recruitment pool generally are interviewed by an interdisciplinary committee consisting of school administrators, teachers, parents, and, in some instances, students. The candidates interact during the interview time period with committee members and appropriate others. Consensus assessments are determined for each candidate and submitted to the school principal or other appropriate person. The long interview allows broad involvement of representative personnel in the selection process and an in-depth observation of candidates. This interview strategy provides an opportunity to observe the candidate in a variety of situations and circumstances.

A third strategy recommended by TASS is the **group interview**. Specific qualification "tests" are used depending on the purpose at hand. For example, a middle school mathematics candidate might be asked to "teach the binary system right now." An elementary school candidate might be asked to "teach a reading lesson." In some interviews, the characteristics of stress tolerance or poise are observed by purposefully "attacking" certain beliefs about student retention in grade or by asking the candidates their views concerning the instructional benefits of the self-contained classroom. Other characteristics are assessed through the use of simulation activities. For example, an English teacher candidate and a music candidate are brought together and asked to resolve an interdepartmental problem: "You, the music teacher, need more time to work with the Glee Club. If you get more time, you, the English teacher, will lose half your students on Friday afternoons. How does each of you feel about that?" Such strategies are used for specific purposes. Conflict management, judgment, sensitivity, poise, and decision making are among the characteristics tested through such methods.

An example of a **subject-specialty interview** report form shown in Figure 5.2 is designed for a teacher of English. Sections one and two of the form are related to the candidate's knowledge of the subject matter and the experience and preparation for the teaching of English. The entries listed on the report form represent a synthesis of information gathered from a variety of sources, including performance activities that serve to assess the behavior characteristics of the applicant. For example, part three of the form might be assessed in part by asking the candidate to demonstrate a lesson in grammar, literature, or English composition.

A **structured interview** uses pre-prepared questions and specific "look-fors" to assess teacher candidates on such characteristics as mission, empathy, individualized perception, listening, focus, innovation, and others that are difficult to assess through other interview strategies. The process includes a structured, stress-free interview used to identify the success patterns or basic life themes within a person. Similar questions are asked over and over and a final profile of results is charted. Structured interviews, such as the Teacher and Administrator SRI Perceivers, provide a keen understanding of each candidate's strengths, motivations, and values. The original teacher perceiver instrument was designed by Donald Clifton and William Hall, then members of the faculty at the University of Nebraska. The instrument was based on many years of research on high-performing teachers. Its administration requires comprehensive training in both the procedures and the recording of the interviewee's responses. School systems throughout the nation have employed the instrument. The teacher perceiver and the administrator perceiver instruments are administered under the supervision of the Gallup Organization, now located in Omaha, Nebraska.

Candidate's Name: _____

Interviewed for Position of: _____

Interviewer(s): _____

Date: _____

1. Screening Dimension Number 1: Knowledge and Skills Related to the Subject Matter
   a. Degrees and Majors/Minors
   b. GPAs in English Courses
   c. Knowledge of English Curriculum
   d. Knowledge of Teaching/Learning Methodology in English
   e. Knowledge of Specific Subject(s) to be Taught (e.g., English Composition, English Literature, Speech, Communication Skills, Grammar, Reading)

2. Screening Dimension Number 2: Experience and Preparation
   a. Specific Experience as a Member of a Curriculum Team in English
   b. Clarifications Concerning Previous Teaching Experiences
   c. Memberships and Participation in Professional Organizations (e.g., state and national English teachers' associations)
   d. Clarifications of Previous Teaching Experiences (Areas of English Taught, Grade Levels, and Methods)

3. Screening Dimension Number 3: Personal Characteristics and Qualifications
   a. Personal Appearance, Poise, and Stability
   b. Communication Skills—Voice, Clarity of Ideas, Use of English Language, Aspects of Voice
   c. Personality-Sensitivity
   d. Leadership Traits—Judgment, Goal Orientation, Team Member, Initiative

4. Synthesis for Each Dimension (5 = high, 1 = low)
   Dimension 1____
   Dimension 2____
   Dimension 3____

Figure 5.2   Contents for a Behavior Interview Report Form: English Teacher

The Use of Testing in the Selection Process

Several states use testing to determine candidates' knowledge and competency in various subject areas for purposes of licensing and certification. In most cases, such tests are closely tied to state or regional standards such as the Interstate School Leaders Licensure Consortium (ISLLC), the National Council for Accreditation of Teacher Education (NCATE) standards, or teaching and administrative standards set forth by a particular state.

Research over the past 85 years has tried to identify valid predictions for future job-related performance (Lohaus & Kleinmann, 2002). Although such testing is not a common practice in education today, trends in all fields indicate that testing is becoming increasingly important for personnel selection. Lohaus and Kleinmann (2002) use the term "potential analysis" in relation to the capability of a person to perform in a job at a certain level of competence. **Potential analysis** attempts to determine the extent to which an individual's competencies that already exist or do not presently exist will develop or could be developed in the future.

Schmidt and Hunter (1998) did one of the most comprehensive studies for determining employee potential. They used intelligence tests, integrity tests, work sample tests, conscientiousness tests, structured employment interviews, biographical data measures, and assessment center results to assess the validity of future job performance. Table 5.2 shows the validity results for various combinations of the tests that were administered.

A combination of a general intelligence test and an integrity test had the highest validity, 0.65, for predictions of employee future job performance. A test of general mental ability had the highest validity of 0.51 for jobs of average demands. A general intelligence test had a validity statistic of 0.58 for predicting the future job performance of managers in organizations. Using standard multiple regression statistics, the general intelligence test validity results were combined with each of the other testing methods. The combination of the general intelligence test and integrity test, for example, resulted in a 0.65 validity statistic. The general intelligence test combined with the work sample test or the structured employment interview validity score resulted in a 0.63 validity statistic. Although the assessment center validity statistic was the lowest, 0.37, it resulted in a validity statistic of 0.53 when combined with the general intelligence test.

It is unclear to what extent such testing will be implemented in educational settings in the future. The answer depends in part on the extent to which accountability measures are mandated for the human resources function, the extent to which talent management practices influence the human resources function of education, and the extent to which appropriate testing instruments are developed for such special use in education.

Table 5.2   Predictability of Future Job Success Through Testing

Type of Test Administered	Performance/Success Statistic
General Intelligence Test	0.58 (Prediction for managers)
General Intelligence Test	0.51 (Prediction for jobs with average demands)
Assessment Center Methods	0.37
General Intelligence Test + Integrity Test	0.65
General Intelligence Test + Work Sample	0.63
General Intelligence Test + Assessment Center Methods	0.53

SOURCE: Schmidt, F. L. & Hunter, J. F. The Validity and Utility of Selection Methods in Personnel Psychology: Practical and Theoretical Implications of 85 Years of Research Findings. *Psychological Bulletin, 124*, 262–274. American Psychological Association.

Legal Considerations and the Interviewing Activity

The matter of legality regarding interview questions is problematic. Laws relating to employment interviews vary from state to state. It is of paramount importance that interviewers be knowledgeable of the employment laws in their local jurisdiction. Hanson (2007) warns that asking the wrong question can result in litigation problems for the organization. Hanson recommends that, "To avoid potentially problematic hiring practices, make sure that your hiring managers are versed in what interviewing practices are legal and proper" (p. 1). Hanson suggests a number of topics to avoid in interviews because they could trigger close scrutiny by the Equal Employment Opportunity Commission (EEOC):

1. "Do you have children under 18? What are you plans for child care?" Questions such as these could be viewed as discriminatory if the employer asks them only of women. Federal law prohibits employers from making pre-employment inquiries into child care.

2. "Are you pregnant? Do you plan to have children?" Discrimination based on pregnancy is unlawful under Title VII.

3. "Have you ever been arrested or convicted of a crime?" Unless the employer has a valid job-related reason for asking such a question, it could be viewed as discriminatory.

4. "What is your date of birth?" Questions that give away an applicant's age could indicate unlawful discrimination on the basis of age.

5. "When did you graduate from high school or college?" These kinds of questions tend to give away the applicant's age and could be considered discriminatory.

6. "Are you available to work on weekends?" This question appears to be innocent, but according to the EEOC, may demonstrate intent to discriminate by discouraging applicants of certain religions from applying.

7. "What is the lowest salary you would accept?" Because women have traditionally been paid less than men for the same work, they might be willing to accept lower pay. This is viewed as discriminatory by the EEOC.

8. "Have you ever filed a workers' compensation claim?" This question is unlawful because it is likely to reveal information about the applicant's disabilities.

9. "Do you have a disability? What is the nature of the disability?" The Americans with Disabilities Act forbids employers from making any pre-offer inquiries into an applicant's disability. (Hanson, 2007, pp. 1–2)

Hanson recommends that providing standardized interview questions is one way of avoiding costly lawsuits.

Preparing Eligibility Lists and Nominations for Submission to the Board of Education: Contract Approval

The candidates who have been selected to fill specific position openings are placed on an eligibility list. In some instances, more than one person is placed on the list for a specific position opening. Thus, there is a need to prioritize candidates on the basis of rating results and search team consensus. The search team makes a tentative offer of a position to a candidate subject to the approval of the school superintendent and ultimately the district's school board.

The school superintendent or delegated school representative nominates selected candidates to the school board for employment. The school board acts officially on the hiring of the nominees. Formal action by the school board is recorded in the school board minutes, the candidates are notified of the hiring, and a contract is rendered to the people hired with appropriate provisos including background check clearances, immunizations, and others such as the completion of the required teaching degree and position certificate as fits the case.

As Fischer, Schimmel, and Stellman (2003) have noted, "a contract is not valid until the school board approves it. . . . Because school boards act as public bodies, they cannot accept (or ratify) a contract without taking official action" (p. 17). However, unless state law requires a teacher's contract be in writing, an oral contract is legally binding if it includes all the legal requirements that define a contract. In contract law, a teacher's contract must have (1) a meeting of the minds of both parties, (2) valid consideration, (3) legal subject matter, (4) competent parties, and (5) definite terms (Fischer et al., 2003, p. 16). In addition, it must be remembered that, "A contract is binding on both parties, and either party who fails to meet the contractual obligations has *breached* (broken) the contract" (Fischer et al., 2003, p. 18).

The Background Check

Estimates indicate that up to 40% of applicant resumes contain false or tweaked information. Cases of the hiring of personnel who did not have the required credentials for the position in question, who had not reported past records of child molestation or other criminal activities, who submitted false information concerning their previous work history, or who reported other erroneous information on their job applications have made comprehensive background checks a requirement for hiring in almost every school district nationally. Unfortunately, state laws concerning background checks vary. Minimally, a background check serves to verify the candidate's social security number. On the other hand, a background check might verify the accuracy of the applicant's work history, provide a complete criminal record, check the candidate's credit report, and verify the validity of the references submitted in the candidate's application (Doyle, 2007).

The Privacy Act prohibits the solicitation of the candidate's school records without permission to do so. State laws vary on the checking of criminal history. In some instances, there is a date restriction for checking on the past criminal offenses. In other instances, criminal checks depend on the specific job. For example, it is reasonable to find out whether a school system candidate has a history of child sexual abuse, but there is some question about the legality of soliciting a candidate's credit report. State laws and the rationale for knowing such information would determine the reasonableness of such an inquiry. The military can disclose information about a candidate's name, rank, salary, assignments, and awards without the candidate's consent. The same is true with driving records (Doyle, 2007). The Fair Credit Reporting Act (FCRA) views a background check as a consumer report. A candidate must be notified in writing and give his or her authorization before a background check is conducted. If there is information that the candidate does not want disclosed, he or she can withdraw the application.

Figure 5.3 is an example of a criminal background check designed to be completed by the position applicant. A formal background check would serve to verify the accuracy of the candidate's entries. Because of the increasing number of serious problems being experienced in the nation's schools, an Arizona school board discussed the toughening of their fingerprint policy after the arrest of a former employee on charges of raping a 15-year-old student (Clark, 2007). It is common to find that fingerprint cards of some certified and classified personnel have expired. Thus, it is imperative that school district human resources units check the validity of fingerprint cards on an annual basis.

Assessing the Selection Results

The final step in the selection process is to assess its success in terms of accomplished purposes and benefits received. Chapter 4 briefly discussed specific accountability measures. For example, what percent of the recruitment pool became active candidates, and what percent of the active candidates were offered positions in the school district? It also was suggested that retention statistics are another measure of person-position match and person-organization match. What percent of the candidates hired remained after year one and after year three?

Other control measures include the assessment of job performance after the employee's first year in the position. What are the performance ratings of the persons that were selected? Has the quality of the personnel improved as a result of the selection procedures used? For example, if all of the newly hired teachers received high performance ratings for the first year, the result provides evidence that the interviewers and data analyzers were effective in their selection role. Did the selection training sessions result in better selection decisions?

A debriefing of the recruitment and selection procedures should be an ongoing activity. What activities and programs were especially effective and why? What activities did not result in the desired ends and why? What changes or additions to these human resources processes are in order? What changes in the training of selection personnel are necessary? What were the most successful recruitment sources? To what extent were the original goals and objectives of the selection process realized?

An assessment instrument, often overlooked as a valuable tool for improving current selection practices, is the exit interview. An **exit interview** is administered

---

Certification in Accordance With State Statutes

Name: _____   Telephone: (   ) _____

Mailing Address: _____

City: _____

State: _____   Zip: _____

1. _____ Check here if the following statement is true:

I am not awaiting trial on and I have never been convicted of or admitted committing any of the criminal offenses in this state or similar offenses in another jurisdiction in Question 2 below.

2. _____ Check here if the following statement is true:

I am awaiting trial on or I have been convicted of or admitted committing any of the criminal offenses in this state or similar offenses in another jurisdiction which are checked below:

___a. Sexual abuse of a minor
___b. Arson
___c. Sexual assault
___d. Contributing to the delinquency of a minor
___e. Felony offenses involving the distribution of marijuana or other narcotic drugs
___f. Burglary
___g. Robbery
___h. Molestation of a child
___i. Child abuse
___j. Sexual conduct with a minor
___k. First or second-degree murder
___l. Kidnapping
___m. Commercial exploitation of a minor
___n. Rape
___o. Any other dangerous crime against children, including crimes against a minor, aggravated assault resulting in a serious physical injury or committed by the use of a deadly weapon or dangerous instrument, taking a child for the purpose of prostitution, or involving or using minors in drug offenses.

I certify that the above statements are true. I understand that information inconsistent with that received from the official background and fingerprint checks may result in termination.

_____   _____
Signature   Date

To be completed by a Notary Public:

The above-named person, who is known to me or who has provided proper identification, signed his/her name on this document in my presence on this day of _____, 20___.

Notary Public: _____
My commission expires: _____

Figure 5.3   Criminal Background Check to Be Completed by Applicant With Notary Public Signature Verification to employees who have decided to leave the school system voluntarily. Why are you leaving the school system? What aspects of the induction program were most beneficial to you? To what extent did the school system meet or serve your career aspirations? Did you find the information given to you about the school and school system during the recruitment and selection processes to portray accurately the actual conditions and practices within the school system? What information or changes in the selection process that you experienced might you recommend? Feedback from those persons leaving the system in response to the foregoing questions and others could lead to important changes in the recruitment and selection activities. Figure 5.4 is an example of an exit interview that is specifically designed for those teachers who decide to leave the system during the first three to five years.

Finally, it is highly recommended that the results of the selection appraisal be reported to the school board. This action accomplishes several purposes. First, such a summary report shows the school board and the citizenry that the school district has the school board's selection policy in place and has assumed responsibility for meeting its stated goals and objectives. Second, it demonstrates that the accountability of the human resources function has been given priority attention. Third, it alerts the school board and others to the specific staffing-related challenges and problems facing the school district; it provides evidence for the necessary monetary support required to administer a successful selection process.

Summary

The selection of personnel for positions in the school system is one of the most important responsibilities of human resources administrators in the school system. Selection is a planned, organized, and controlled process that includes a series of steps, activities, and assessments related to the school district's stated goals and objectives.

An effective selection process has the potential of supporting positive change within the school system, reducing the problems school system administrators face, increasing program effectiveness, creating a more positive organizational climate, and enhancing a bonding between the employee and the organization.

This chapter included a comprehensive discussion of a selection operational model that included activities and assessments related to the design and organization of the selection process, defining behavioral characteristics for system positions, compiling information and data for candidate appraisals, preparing candidate eligibility lists, nominating candidates for employments, contracting for positions, and assessing selection results.

It also emphasized the importance of developing an interview guide and training persons to serve as interviewers. Several interview strategies, including the TASS interviewing methods, were discussed. Legal considerations related to the administration of candidate interviews were presented; the importance of background checks for each potential employee was emphasized.

Activities for assessing the results of the selection include the use of certain metrics for judging the effectiveness of various steps in the selection process. The

---

Exit Interview

Conducted with (Name, Title): _____

Date: _____ Conducted by (Name): _____

1. *(Ask of voluntary resignations)* For what reasons are you leaving the school/school system?

2. *(If employee was subject to disciplinary procedure)* What is your understanding of events which have led to separation?

3. How would describe the kind of supervision that you received?

4. To what extent was the supervision received beneficial to you in the performance of the duties of your position?

5. What is your opinion of the organizational climate in the school and/or position in which you were serving?

6. What did you like or dislike most about the school and/or the position in which you were serving?

7. What is your opinion about the training or mentoring you received?

8. Do you believe that appropriate opportunities for advancement were available?

9. Did the position assignment match with your personal and professional strengths and interests? Why or why not?

10. How might the school and/or school leadership have been more helpful to you in meeting your position responsibilities?

11. What other comments or suggestions might you have regarding the school system, school, or particular position in which you served?

12. Would you share your immediate and/or long-range plans with us?

13. *(If the individual is moving to a new position)* What factors in the new position attracted you the most?

Figure 5.4   Personnel Exit Interview Form

reporting of selection process results to the school board can enhance the board's confidence in the selection process by revealing that the board's selection policy is in place and the human resources administration is cognizant of its need to be accountable for outcomes.

Discussion Questions

1. How does the information that can be obtained from a position application differ from that which can be obtained from a selection interview?

2. What steps or procedures can be implemented in the selection process to make it more objective and less subjective?

3. Identify several ways in which the selection process can enhance the bonding between the employee and the school and school system.

4. Consider the design of a behavioral interview to be administered in the selection of a second-grade elementary school teacher. List four primary knowledge or behavioral characteristics that you might suggest for this position. Prioritize your listing. How might you rate your priority listing for selection purposes?

5. What are the advantages and disadvantages of having a site-based team of 5–10 members serve on the interview team for a given position?

Case Studies

CASE 5.1

A RECOMMENDATION FOR A BALANCE IN PERSONNEL SELECTION

HELP

Hispanic Educational Leadership Program

Ward Henson, Principal

Wymore Middle School

Wymore, Lafayette

Dear Principal Henson:

As you are aware, nearly 40% of the students at Wymore Middle School are Hispanic and, reportedly, only 15% of the teachers are Hispanic. The Hispanic Educational Leadership Program (HELP) has two goals for the ensuing year as follows:

1. Increase the percentage of Hispanic faculty in the school proportionally to that of the Hispanic student enrollment, and

2. Increase the program of bilingual education to accommodate all students in the school.

At this time, HELP requests your support in achieving these important goals. May we hear from you at this time regarding your thoughts and your action plans for the Wymore Middle School relative to the above-stated goals?

Sincerely,

Raul Rodriguez, Chairman

HELP

cc: Emanuel Evans, Supt. of Schools

Duard Smith, Pres. of the School Board

Questions

1. Assume the position of Ward Henson in this case. How would you respond to Raul Rodriguez? What other action would you see as important in this situation?

2. What information presented in this chapter would be helpful to you in deciding on your response?

CASE 5.2

WHY WASN'T I SELECTED?

Virginia Lee, Director

Human Resources Office

College View School District

Lincoln, Lafayette

Dear Dr. Lee:

Recently I was interviewed for the position of math teacher in the College View School District. I was under the impression that my interviews went well. However, just today, I received a letter indicating that I had not been hired for the position. I would appreciate knowing why I wasn't selected.

I understand that my references were good, and my grade point average for my junior and senior years was 3.0. As I mentioned, my interviews seemed to be good.

Your answer to my questions is appreciated.

Sincerely,

Charles Recheck

(Continued)

(Continued)

Questions

1. Assume the role of HR director, Virginia Lee. What action would you take in this situation? Be specific in answering the question. For example, if you decide to write a letter to Charles Recheck, actually write the letter.

2. What legal considerations seem important in this case?

3. Most authorities recommend that a non-hired candidate not be told why they were not hired. What is the rationale of this recommendation?

References

Clark, R. (2007, February 13). Higley school board may toughen fingerprint policy after man's arrest. *Arizona Republic*, p. B6.

Doyle, A. (2007). Your guide to job searching. Retrieved November 19, 2007, from http://jobsearch.about.com/cs/backgroundcheck/a/background.htm

Fischer, L., Schimmel, D., & Stellman, L. R. (2003). *Teachers and the law* (6th ed.). Boston: Allyn & Bacon.

Hanson, E. M. (2007). *Educational administration and organizational behavior* (6th ed.). Boston: Allyn & Bacon.

Kowalski, T. J., McDaniel, P., & Reitzug, U. C. (1992). Factors that principals consider most important in selecting new teachers. *ERS Spectrum, 10*(2), 34–38.

Lohaus, D., & Kleinmann, M. (2002). Analysis of performance potential. In S. Sonnentag (Ed.), *Psychological management of individual performance*. West Sussex, UK: Wiley.

Norton, M. S. (2005). *Executive leadership for effective administration*. Boston: Pearson, Allyn & Bacon.

Peterson, L. J., Rossmiller, R. A., & Volz, M. M. (1978). *The law and public school operation* (2nd ed.). New York: Harper & Row.

Schmidt, F. L., & Hunter, J. F. (1998). The validity and utility of selection methods in personnel psychology: Practical and theoretical implications of 85 years of research findings. *Psychological Bulletin, 124*, 262–274.

Vukovich, E. (1970). *Teacher selection process: How to use references*. Paper prepared by Eli Vukovich and sponsored by the American Association of School Personnel Administrators, Richard A. Schromm, Director.

CHAPTER 6

The HR Induction, Assignment, Stability, and Protection Processes

Toward the Maximization of Human Potential

Learning Objectives

After reading this chapter, you will be able to

1. Explain the various concepts of human motivation.

2. Explain the importance of planned induction for persons new to the school system and identify specific program provisions in this area of human resources.

3. Identify the primary considerations for effective assignment of school personnel.

4. Identify factors that constitute teacher load and methods for calculating the workload of teachers.

5. Understand the importance of gaining stability within the organization and ways of decreasing personnel turnover.

6. Describe the place of the HR protection process from the standpoints of liberty and property rights of the organization's personnel.

7. Understand strategies for dealing with controversy and conflict within the school environment and their importance for promoting organizational effectiveness.

A major responsibility of the human resources function is maximizing the human resources of the school system. Human resources administration was defined in Chapter 2 as those processes that are planned and implemented in the school system to establish an effective system of human resources and to foster an organizational climate that enhances the accomplishment of the system's educational mission, fosters the personal and professional objectives of the employees, and engages the support of the school community in which the school system is embedded. This definition emphasizes the purposeful utilization of people, through positive motivation, appropriate assignments, establishment of organizational stability, and provisions for the safety and protection of employees in order to achieve the organization's goals and employees' self-fulfillment.

Effective administration relative to staff induction, assignment, stability, and protection is of paramount importance in accomplishing this objective. The growing emphasis on maximizing human resources emanates from the realization that organizations progress to the extent that they are able to motivate and develop people. It is for this reason that the HR processes of induction, assignment, stability, and protection are important. Each of these processes is inextricably tied to human motivation. It is essential, therefore, that human resources administrators understand these basic processes as they relate to both the organization and the personal needs of school employees. For this reason, several motivation and human behavior concepts are discussed at the outset of this chapter. Following the discussion of human motivation is a discussion of the essential human resources processes of staff induction, staff assignment, organizational stability, and personnel protection, with special attention to teacher workload, the troubled staff member, the marginal employee, and other considerations that serve to promote or inhibit the realization of human potential. Chapter 7 presents the staff development process, which is of paramount importance to the maximization of personnel.

The School as a Social System

We note throughout this text that human resources administration focuses on humans and human behavior. Researchers note that human behavior in organizations is influenced by both institutional and human factors. Getzels and Guba (1957) described this concept in their social systems model presented in Figure 6.1.

According to the Getzels-Guba social systems model, the actual behavior outcomes (B) within a social system are determined by the institutional role (R) and the individual's personality (P); $B = f (R \times P)$. The role represents position, office, or status within the institution (e.g., superintendent, principal, supervisor, teacher, etc.) and is defined by both role expectations and the nature of the institution. The institutional role and the unique individual need disposition constitute the two dimensions of the Getzels-Guba model. The role and role expectations of the institution are termed the nomothetic dimension. The individual personality and need disposition are termed the idiographic dimension (Getzels & Guba, 1957).

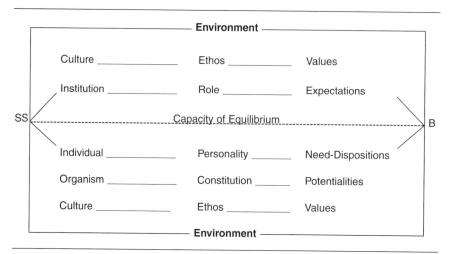

Figure 6.1   Social Systems Model

SOURCE: Getzels, J. W., & Guba, E. G. (1957). Social behavior and the administrative process. *School Review*, 65(4), 423–441. University of Chicago Press. Reprinted with permission.

The Getzels-Guba social systems model is a useful framework for explaining what leadership is needed in human resources administration to maximize the human potential of a school system. According to these theorists, "The unique task of administration at least with respect to staff relations, is just this: to integrate the demands of the institution and the demands of the members in a way that is at once organizationally productive and individually fulfilling" (Getzels & Guba, 1957, p. 430). The implications of the social systems model for the human resources administrator are far-reaching. The administrator who considers only the institutional dimension without giving equal consideration to the individual aspects within the school system is likely to be insensitive to the environment, its elements, and its conditions. Such an individual not only will be indifferent to the various signals that indicate problems and needs within the school system, but also will be unable to effect possible resolutions and improvements. Both the nomothetic and idiographic dimensions must be fully considered if equilibrium within the system is to be realized. As defined by Barnard (1938), equilibrium is the organization's capacity to be productive and at the same time satisfy individual employee motives.

Human Motivation Theories

School administrators who understand human behavior will be much more effective in making positive differences in the school climate and maximizing human potential. Chapter 1 included a brief discussion of human motivation as conceptualized by Herzberg, Mausner, and Snyderman (1959) and by McGregor (1960).

Numerous other human motivation theories were set forth in the literature in the 1950s and 1960s when the human relations movement was prominent.

Some theories centered on outcome behaviors that are influenced by individuals' perceptions of past events or how they perceive future outcomes relative to their personal needs and beliefs. Other theories view behavior as an action that can be changed through interventions that modify an individual's responses. The terms behavior modification, drive-reinforcement theory, operant conditioning, and behaviorism all relate to the concept that the behavior of an individual can be altered through reinforcement of desired actions. The following discussion considers several leading motivation theories.

Probably more than any other single concept in personnel literature, Maslow's hierarchy has established a direct focus on the basic needs of human beings and their importance in human behavior. According to Maslow's hierarchy, a need is a potential motivator until it is realized or satisfied. As the need is satisfied, it becomes less effective as a motivator, and the next higher order need becomes the motivator for the individual (Maslow, 1954/1987). Figure 6.2 illustrates Maslow's hierarchy and the five basic needs from lower to higher order. Thus, if the individual has specific needs relative to personal safety and security, Maslow argues that attempts to motivate a person at the esteem needs level would be ineffective.

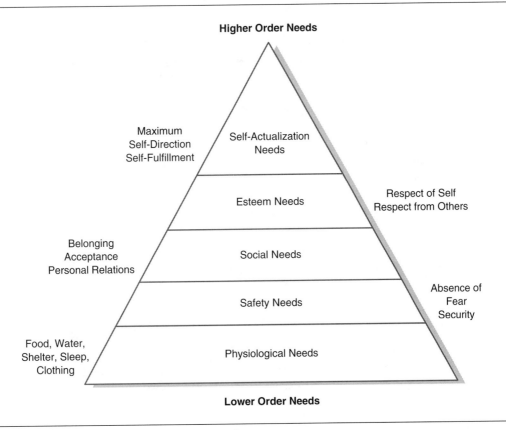

Figure 6.2   Maslow's Hierarchy of Basic Needs

SOURCE: Maslow (1954/1987). Reprinted by permission.

Alderfer's (1972) ERG theory (existence, relatedness, and growth) relates closely to the concepts Maslow proposed. Existence needs include, in general, Maslow's physiological and physical safety needs (Figure 6.2); relatedness needs encompass the social needs, safety needs, and esteem needs, as they relate to relations with others; and growth needs are concerned with self-actualization needs and esteem needs, as they are reflected in positive self-concepts. ERG views motivation as being present within all of the three levels depending on the extent to which various needs have been satisfied or remain unsatisfied. This view differs from Maslow's concepts, however, in that individuals may seek needs at higher levels even though some needs at a lower level have not been met.

Vroom proposed his expectancy theory of motivation in *Work and Motivation* (1964). Vroom stated, "we view the central problem of motivation as the explanation of choices made by organisms among different voluntary responses" (p. 9). Vroom's expectancy theory incorporated three component concepts: (1) valence, a person's affective orientations toward a goal or a desired outcome; (2) instrumentality, the extent to which a person believes the effort put forth will lead to desired consequences or prevent undesirable results; and (3) expectancy, a belief concerning the likelihood that a particular act will be followed by a particular outcome. The expectancy theory of motivation is based on the proposition that effort, performance, and rewards are inextricably related. This concept of motivation argues that effort and performance depend on individuals' perceptions of their potential for meeting personal reward outcomes. Expectancy theory suggests that effort and performance in a particular activity (e.g., obtaining a degree or credential) depend on the individual's perception of whether that activity will increase the realization of personal goals. For example, an individual who has a certain career goal is likely to be highly motivated toward obtaining the credentials needed for the desired position and will exert the required effort and performance. In brief, expectancy theory supports the belief that employees put forth more effort and are more productive when they perceive a relationship among effort, performance, and reward. Figure 6.3 illustrates Vroom's motivational theory.

Brayfield and Crockett (1955), among others, believed that motivation depends on the individual's pursuit of important goals. They stated that, "we might expect high satisfaction and high productivity to occur together when productivity is perceived as a path to certain important goals and when these goals are achieved" (p. 416). This rather straightforward view supports the concepts of goal commitments that are important aspects of expectancy theory, Theory Y, and needs theory. McGregor's Theory Y places emphasis on fostering individual self-direction and full potential exceeding the mere satisfaction of personal needs. McGregor explained his theory in *The Human Side of Enterprise* (1960).

Administrative concepts such as management by objectives (MBO) are based on path-goal theory. In *Managing by Objectives*, Raia (1974) contended that, "whether or not the behavior is actually satisfying to the individual depends upon his latent motives and needs" (p. 97). Raia viewed MBO as being consistent with the path-goal theory of motivation, because MBO is based on the establishment of clearly defined work objectives, progress assessments, a relationship between appraisal and development and compensation, and the element of participation in cooperative goal setting.

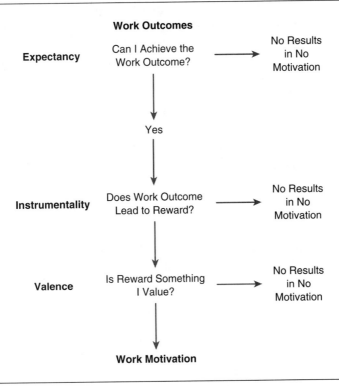

Figure 6.3   Vroom's Expectancy Theory of Motivation

SOURCE: Vroom (1964). Used by permission.

Ouchi's (1981) Theory Z has received much acclaim in business and industry and has provided an impetus for rethinking traditional approaches to management and employee relations. Theory Z organizations develop within the employee the important factor of commitment to organizational goals and high productivity through the use of such incentives as lifetime job tenure, personal participation in decision making and problem solving by all employees, the use of team efforts to complete tasks, and a focus on the personal concerns of employees. According to Ouchi (1981), trust, subtlety, and intimacy exist in every Theory Z organization. These components are exemplified by certain characteristics that had provided for the remarkable success of business and industry in Japan. He emphasized that positive human relations, not technology, make for increased production. The activities of participative management, consensus decision making, and reduced organizational "bureaucracy" promote job satisfaction and motivate the worker to make personal sacrifices that lead to extraordinary success for the organization.

B. F. Skinner's initial work, *The Behavior of Organisms* (1938), as well as his later works, advanced the proposition that an individual's behavior is modified through immediate rewards of favored responses and by no response to unfavorable behavior. Positive reinforcement, through personal reward, praise, recognition, or extended authority, is used to solidify the continuation of desired behavior. Undesirable behavior is dealt with by use of extinction, whereby the behavior is merely ignored. Skinner's concepts also suggest that desired responses can be learned through shaping. When favored responses are seldom or never demonstrated, initial rewards are given for behavior responses similar to the desired behavior. Finally, only the desired response is reinforced through appropriate rewards (Skinner, 1953, 1969).

Behavior modification suggests that providing careful feedback of positive job results to an employee would reinforce that behavior, that pay incentives or other rewards for exemplary attendance would reduce employee absence, and that rewards given an employee for reaching a desired skill level would lead to a continuation of positive personal development.

Behavior modification research provides several suggestions for administrative practice:

1. The kind of behavior desired should be determined as specifically as possible.

2. If the desired behavior is not currently present or is seldom demonstrated, shaping techniques should be used to bring about changes in behavior similar to the desired behavior. Similar behavior should be positively reinforced.

3. Desired behavior should be reinforced immediately. Material rewards and "psychic" or "social" rewards, such as benefits, commendations, authority, carefully designed personal feedback, responsibility, and recognition should be scheduled as reinforcers.

4. Results should be measured and assessed and decisions reached concerning the appropriate schedule of reinforcements needed to ensure the continuation of the desired behavior.

The discussion of motivation reemphasizes the concept previously stated that "schools are people." Effective human resources administration requires an understanding and concern for the individual needs of personnel. Such understanding must be present when implementing programs of staff induction or placing personnel in specific work assignments. In this respect, the often-heard maxim "know your staff" assumes a more comprehensive, purposeful meaning. The maximization of human resources within the school system requires a meaningful integration of the system's goals and the employees' need dispositions. When these considerations are brought into relatively close congruence, achievement of goals and personal fulfillment are more likely to be realized. The variables of individual behavior and the realities of human organizations often defy simple analysis. Yet the realization of the full potential of human resources requires that the concepts and theories relating to human motivation and behavior be understood, applied, and evaluated in all human resources processes.

McClelland (2005) speaks of achievement-motivated people and affiliation-motivated people. Achievement-motivated people are more concerned with personal achievement than with the rewards of success. Affiliation-motivated people favor social or attitudinal feedback. According to McClelland (2005), achievement-motivated people have the following characteristics: (1) the capacity to set high ("stretching") but obtainable goals, (2) the concern for personal achievement rather than the rewards of success, and (3) the desire for job-relevant feedback (how well am I doing?) rather than for attitudinal feedback (how well do they like me?).

McClelland's concepts relate closely to Herzberg's motivation-hygiene theory in that high-motivated persons tend to be most interested in those motivation factors of the job itself.

The Human Resources Induction Process

The HR induction process serves a major purpose in getting staff members new to the school off to the best possible start. Induction has been shown to be instrumental in fostering staff morale and reducing staff turnover. This section discusses the process.

Staff induction begins with the job application, and then continues through job candidacy and, on an ongoing basis, for as long as the employee or the organization views it as necessary. "The purposes of induction are to create a good first impression, relieve anxiety, set expectations, encourage socialization and team building, build identification with the employee, and prevent problems" (Starcke, 1996, p. 111). Although the entry of new employees into the school system requires special orientation considerations, the process is not limited only to new employees; nor should it be viewed only as a first-year induction activity. Rather, the induction needs of individual employees are ongoing and the induction process is continuous. Induction activities serve as important links to recruitment and selection as well as a complement to staff assignment and development.

If effectively planned and implemented, the staff induction process serves several basic purposes:

1. It encourages individuals with qualifications congruent with district expectations to consider employment in the system.

2. It integrates effectively and efficiently new and experienced staff personnel into their respective roles in the school system.

3. It develops understanding and commitment to the stated goals and objectives of the school system.

4. It reduces or removes problems and conditions that tend to inhibit personal effectiveness and job satisfaction.

5. It identifies the specific talents of each employee and builds these abilities into the overall educational team.

6. It acquaints personnel with the important considerations of personal, professional, and community relationships within the school community.

7. It ascertains specific needs of school personnel and analyzes these needs in relation to the school system's expectations.

8. It identifies for each employee those human and physical resources that can enhance personal effectiveness.

9. It provides opportunities to identify specific strengths and personal professional interests of employees.

10. It provides information and services that promote instruction and learning.

Induction is a planned process that is based on the school system's stated goals and the roles of its human resources. The maximization of the system's human resources serves as the foundation and rationale for induction activities and services.

Operational Procedures for Staff Induction

The staff induction process begins with the prospective employee's first contact with the school district and continues throughout employment, as needed. Properly planned and implemented, the process involves all members of the staff, appropriate community members, and employee associations. The general administrative procedures for planning, implementing, and evaluating the induction process can be classified into four steps as follows:

1. *Step 1.* The governing board adopts policies that commit the school system to effective induction practices and indicate what the school system desires from the process. The board of education, school employee personnel, and community representatives develop specific goals for the induction process cooperatively.

2. *Step 2.* All information that would assist in identifying the induction program needs is determined. The clarification of specific position assignments and responsibilities for program implementation is completed. Individual problems and needs are identified through informal interviews or other means such as mentoring programs.

3. *Step 3.* Previously determined plans and procedures are implemented. Individualized programs for providing special services are determined and administered.

4. *Step 4.* Information that can be used to evaluate the program's results is collected. Objective assessments of feedback relative to the accomplishment of program objectives and meeting individual needs are completed. These findings are used in debriefing sessions and other evaluation activities for improving future programs.

Preemployment Activities

Preemployment induction activities generally are provided during the period between initial contact with the school district and the time the individual assumes a specific role in the school system. On initial contact with the school district, information is provided to a potential employee to build an understanding of the school district's nature, community makeup, and educational expectations; the general working environment; faculty-student information; and professional opportunities within the district, including compensation levels and benefits.

Preemployment induction necessitates a variety of program provisions. Face-to-face communication, use of printed materials, group sessions, audio-visual technology, and other practices are common for both gaining and disseminating information. Various strategies are employed for carrying out preemployment induction programs. The following five procedures are examples of contemporary practices.

1. Over a specified time period, school district employees are surveyed as to what information and personal assistance proved most beneficial to them as well as what communication and assistance should be added prior to employment. Results are analyzed and program activities designed to provide the most beneficial information and assistance for the employee.

2. During the initial contact with the school district, a potential employee completes a brief questionnaire to ascertain the kinds of information and personal assistance that might prove most helpful (e.g., employment benefits, community information, school district policy and procedures, student evaluation procedures, etc.). Those individuals or offices assigned the responsibility for the requested information provide the information to groups and individual applicants.

3. Various offices and personnel gather information concerning the most frequently asked questions during preemployment, major problem areas regarding entry transition, and specific school district information of high priority. This feedback is synthesized, and appropriate induction activities are planned to provide the necessary feedback to prospective employees.

4. Every effort is made to personalize preemployment induction. Initial inquiries are expedited. To the fullest extent possible, internal personnel are assigned specific duties regarding preemployment orientation and communication. Briefing sessions are planned, one-on-one conferences are scheduled when feasible, and other special efforts are made to put the prospective employee at ease with the school system.

5. Induction teams, representative of both internal and external members of the school district, are established. Each team serves as the primary information resource for a specific area of the preemployment induction. In some instances, one particular resource member serves as the liaison person for one or more prospective employees.

Postemployment Induction

Following the district's decision to hire an individual, postemployment induction must be implemented. Specific information relative to the employee's assignment, the environment in which the person will be working, professional resources available, formal staff relationships, policy and regulation resources, personal responsibilities, and provisions for personal assistance are among the induction information and activities of importance at this time. Postemployment induction focuses on facilitating an effective, efficient transition of personnel into their respective roles within the school system and community. Its primary purpose is to assist new employees in the achievement of optimal success as members of the school community. Provisions and practices that add to the induction program following employment include mentor programs, policy and regulation manuals, and personnel information handbooks.

Mentoring Program

Many school districts have a long history of providing a "helping-teacher" for new personnel, but the mentor program concept presents a more comprehensive approach to induction and staff development. A **mentor** is an experienced professional who guides the personal development of a less experienced individual through coaching and advising. In a mentor program, each new employee is "teamed" with an experienced peer on the staff who serves as a sponsor, a teacher, and an adviser. Mentoring provides help in building communication channels of importance to continued growth, allows for new knowledge relative to teaching approaches, develops a system of personal support and increased self-confidence, extends insight into district purposes, and provides a relationship with a master teacher who can serve as a role model for teaching. The mentor benefits through increased personal self-esteem and recognition as a successful teacher and contributor to the school's program. Mentoring requires keeping up to date on best practices in teaching and necessitates refinement and improvement of personal knowledge and skills.

Overall, the school system benefits through increases in staff knowledge about the school district, increased confidence and morale of staff members, and improved staff member effectiveness. Successful mentor programs most often are based on the special needs and interests of the new or inexperienced staff member. Mentoring, as a facilitator of professional growth in staff development, is discussed in more detail in Chapter 10.

Policy and Administrative Manual

A properly codified, comprehensive policy and regulation manual can serve as one of the primary induction resources for school personnel. Policy and regulations are of special significance to the human resources function generally, but they contribute to the induction process by

1. informing school personnel as to what the school district wants to accomplish;

2. providing a common basis for understanding and a basic reference for effective communication;

3. clarifying the division of labor between the school board and professional administrative staff;

4. establishing a basis for action, effective school operations, and meaningful evaluation;

5. providing information concerning professional responsibilities and opportunities;

6. setting forth guidelines and procedures for completing specific practices and meeting personal responsibilities that meet the standards of the school system; and

7. providing specific procedures for personnel in such areas as student evaluation, securing instructional resources, community participation, transfer, and professional development.

Chapter 9 contains a comprehensive treatment of policy and regulation development relative to the human resources function.

Personnel Information Handbook

The importance of the personnel information handbook in the induction process demands that its development and dissemination be given high priority by human resources administrators. The value of the personnel handbook extends beyond its contributions to the induction process; its potential for orienting both new and continuing staff is far-reaching.

A personnel information handbook serves a variety of important purposes including the fostering of employee initiative in decision making, identification of special service resources, and the improvement of continuity relative to employee responsibilities in the many and various activities of the school's program.

Although the personnel handbook often includes some information related to school district policy and administrative regulations, the handbook and the policies manual are different documents. The policies manual is the governance document for the district and sets forth the legislative (policy) and executive (regulations) guidelines under which the district is to operate. The personnel handbook is designed to provide information that answers questions about (1) the school district's goals, services, and facilities; (2) the community and its makeup; and (3) procedures relating to securing substitute teachers, obtaining curriculum materials, completing grade reports, the school calendar, professional growth activities, insurance plans, and other information that the school district has determined to be of value to employees. Figure 6.4 shows a sample of one section of a personnel handbook. The sample focuses on the employee assistance program in a school district.

The human resources director, school principals, teaching staff, support personnel, and other supervisory staff members need to participate in the determination of content for the handbook, the dissemination of the information, and the evaluation of the handbook's effectiveness. The central human resources unit that serves as the clearinghouse for needed additions, clarifications, and changes most often coordinates the development of the handbook. Such practices as using brief questionnaires to gain feedback from new personnel, various school district units, and experienced personnel are most useful in assessing the handbook's effectiveness.

Employee Assistance Program

The Lincoln School District understands that school personnel may encounter personal problems that need professional attention. The school district's employee assistance program is designed to help resolve personal problems that tend to adversely impact on job performance. Services are available to all personnel who might need professional counsel in such areas as problem drinking, marital-family problems, personal crisis situations, financial problems, drug dependency, work-supervisor relations, peer relations, and medical health. Such services are provided for employees at all levels. Dependents of employees also may take advantage of these private and confidential services. In some cases, services are provided by professional agencies other than school district personnel. In any case, confidentiality is strictly maintained. Employees are encouraged to take advantage of the EAP services before any problem becomes too difficult. EAP services are provided as part of your employee benefits. Employees may take advantage of these special services by contacting the Lincoln School District Human Resources Office or by calling (480) 838-AIDE.

Figure 6.4   *Sample Section of an Employee Personnel Handbook*

Orientation for the Beginning Teacher and Others New to the School System

Induction often is given such labels as orientation, preservice program, staff development, or introduction of employees. Induction is defined as the complex of activities designed to gain congruence between institutional objectives and employee needs. It begins with the job application and continues on an ongoing basis for as long as the employee or the organization views it as necessary. Thus, the induction process assumes a comprehensive perspective as opposed to the traditional practice in some schools of scheduling one or two days of informational sessions for employees at the outset of a school year. We view these one or two day sessions for employees as orientation activities. Such orientation activities must be provided for beginning teachers and other personnel new to the school district. Some activities, which later become routine, often pose considerable frustration for new personnel and detract attention from important position responsibilities. Empirical evidence reveals several common problems that face teachers new to a school district, such as the following:

1. Procedures and expectations concerning student homework regulations, required records, and reports.

2. Available instructional resources and services.

3. Parental communication.

4. Ways of securing instructional materials.

5. Reporting student absences and tardies.

6. Policies and procedures for student grading, student promotion, and student retention.

7. Student discipline regulations.

8. Extracurricular duty expectations.

9. Sources for personal assistance relative to financial aid, childcare, and health programs.

Induction activities must be designed to provide personnel with the necessary guidelines for action, but also must ensure that personal assistance and support are available to staff members. The teaching environment, teacher workload, work schedule, position assignment, and other conditions of work also influence the effective transition of personnel into the school system. The workload of staff members new to teaching, for example, is often found to be the heaviest among all the teaching staff. These considerations are discussed later in this chapter.

Relationships with other staff members and administrators often pose problems for beginning teachers. Induction activities that establish attitudes of cooperation and team spirit are essential. The mentoring provision, previously discussed, can be instrumental in serving this need. Position descriptions, communication channels and resources, and an explanation of personnel and office relationships are invaluable in this respect.

New personnel also need community information such as educational support services, recreational and cultural opportunities, civic activities, demographic data, medical facilities, governance structure, and community/school support information. Faculty handbooks and planned community tours can be sources for such information.

Induction: What the Research Says

Induction has gained added attention in view of research results that underline the importance of planned induction activities during the early years of service because beginning teachers and other employees need help with special problems. Personal problems, such as financial needs, can inhibit effectiveness on the job. During induction, information should be provided about educational credit associations within the school system or community agencies. In addition, services provided through employee assistance programs (EAPs) should be explained. As Norton (2001) emphasized, "sensitivity to learning and addressing the needs of novice teachers may improve teacher retention, as teachers with high levels of job satisfaction are the most likely to remain in teaching" (p. 20). Such positive programs can result in a reduction of turnover rates, improved job satisfaction, higher levels of job performances, and less time and money spent on remedial approaches to staff development.

Breuer (2000) reported on a study conducted by the Coca-Cola Retailing Council that found that employee turnover costs the typical supermarket $198,977 a year. That figure reflects a national cost of $5.9 billion annually. Furthermore, the study concluded that, "the first week of a new employee's experience is the most vital factor in retention" (Breuer, 2000, p. 32). More than 30 years ago, Berglas (1973) found that the personal assistance given to teachers new to the school system was the single most important factor in fostering teacher morale. The induction process serves as an important link between recruitment, selection, and staff assignment.

The Staff Assignment Process

Staff assignment is the human resources process that maximizes human resources through the (1) deployment of talent and competency in the best interests of the total staff and student population; (2) identification of staff talent and assignment of individual employees to facilitate an effective instructional program; (3) assessment of roles, including the identification of inhibitors and facilitators, to permit optimal utilization of resources; (4) recognition of individual staff differences and implementation of leadership styles that best fulfill the potential of all personnel; (5) utilization of available research, tools, and skills to provide the best possible working conditions; and (6) examination of staff workloads that facilitate rather than inhibit effective work performance. This activity includes the consideration of environmental conditions that increase personal motivation, effort, and productivity: specific assignment, workload, and personal problem resolution.

Staff assignment is closely linked to other personnel processes. Selection, induction, evaluation, development, and organizational climate especially complement the activities and purposes of staff assignment. Although staff assignment clearly reaches beyond the singular consideration of matching the individual and a specific position, because of its paramount importance, position assignment is discussed in detail in the following section.

Position Assignment

Human resources authorities agree that one of the most effective means by which human resources administrators can assist the organization to achieve its stated goals and maximize employee potential is through the determination of appropriate position assignments. Employees who are appropriately matched to their jobs and to the organization exhibit higher levels of job satisfaction and performance. An appropriate and productive job match means that the required tasks of the position relate directly to the personal strengths and interests of the employee. One of the keys for helping individuals reach their fullest potential and contribute most toward personal and organizational goals is to assign them to positions in which their knowledge and skills can best be utilized. Gannett News Service (Lowe, 2001) reported on tips provided by businessman Peter Lowe, who underscored the importance of matching the person to the position as follows:

Match the person to the position: don't tailor the position to suit the person. One of the most common hiring mistakes takes place when you interview a bright, talented individual you like and, even though they aren't quite right for the position, you hire them anyway. It's an understandable mistake. A good candidate in the wrong position is a bad employee. (p. D2)

Position assignment requires several essential considerations: (1) the specific nature of the position, including role expectations, necessary knowledge and skills, and conditions under which the role is performed; (2) the professional preparation, competencies, and interests of the employee; (3) the relationship of the position and the employee's characteristics and competencies; (4) the extent to which the assignment provides for the personal motivation needed by the employee and the extent to which success can be realized in the position; and (5) consideration of the forces of organizational culture and informal group structure.

While securing personnel who possess the knowledge and skills needed in the assignment, recruitment and selection must also be aimed at providing an opportunity for the employee to use the knowledge and skills that are most personally rewarding. Individuals generally have developed personal competence in a large number of task areas. Most persons also have competencies that they most enjoy using and that tend to bring both the highest levels of productivity and personal satisfaction. Position assignment necessitates the careful examination of both the general qualifications of the individual and the specific competencies most rewarding to that person. When a match is found between the competencies required by the job and those most satisfying to the individual, both the school system and the employee are likely to benefit. The meeting of the foregoing conditions commonly is viewed as providing meaningful work for the employee.

The implementation of an effective process of teacher assignment is enhanced by the adoption of an official school board policy. Such a policy sets forth the specific objectives concerning what is to be accomplished in the assignment process. As noted in Figure 6.5, an assignment policy gives attention to the importance of the position description and employee qualifications, workload, program needs, staff balance, and student relationships. In addition, the personal talents and interests of the employee are underscored.

Information about the individual's specific qualifications for the position and his or her specific competencies is gathered through a variety of sources: placement credentials, job application forms, personal resumes, appropriately designed job questionnaires, structured interviews, examination of job references, and assessment methodology. Accurate information about job and employee competencies is necessary for proper position assignment. Position placement is a planned process that uses objective measurements and evaluations of position needs and individual competencies to match positions and individuals.

The goals, beliefs, traditions, and values of a particular school are important factors in the assignment of employees to that school. If an individual employee's personal characteristics and beliefs are significantly incongruent with the culture of the school, personnel problems most likely will develop. The local building administrator's leadership style and the employee's followership style are also important assessments in position assignment. The time taken to gather information concerning the matter of organizational culture, employee characteristics, and leadership/followership styles will produce positive dividends for the school district and the employee by enhancing job satisfaction and productivity.

The matter of teacher workload is a consideration of paramount importance for the maximization of personnel. Workload is discussed in the following section.

Effective employee assignment is instrumental in ensuring a positive match between personnel, the school district, and the school in which the employee is assigned. Deployment of talent in the best interests of the school district, the employee, and the students is an essential human resources responsibility. The placement of individuals in positions that best suit their personal strengths and interests is a primary objective of the school district. Position qualifications, as described in position descriptions, educational program needs, staff balance, and staff/student relationships are important factors in appointing employees to school district positions.

In assigning employees to positions within the school district, consideration also should be given to such factors as working conditions that include both instructional workload and extracurricular duty assignments. Fair and equitable workload assignments that facilitate effective work performance, increase personal motivation, and foster the retention of quality personnel are of primary importance. Other factors such as the goals, traditions, and environments of a particular school are important factors in the assignment of employees to a particular school/community.

Both initial assignments and reassignments of personnel are of importance to effective educational programming. Thus, the school board encourages programs relative to the re-recruitment of current employees that foster the retention of quality personnel.

Figure 6.5   Sample Policy for the Assignment of Personnel

Teacher Workload

Staff assignment requires that careful attention be given to teacher load. Without such consideration, inequities in the workload are certain to persist, and personnel who are most qualified to carry out an effective educational program in the school often are so overburdened that their efforts are forced to a level of mediocrity. Equity of assignment is not the only personnel consideration that underscores the importance of teacher load. Load reductions are advisable in certain situations, including the case of individuals new to teaching.

Maximization of human resources is inhibited seriously if inequitable distribution of load exists, or if load is unwisely allocated. A comprehensive examination of the teacher's workload also serves to assess what teachers actually do in meeting the responsibilities of their assignment. Such data loom important in accounting for the work contributions of the teaching staff relative to both in-class and extracurricular responsibilities. Human resources administrators need this information to make intelligent and defensible decisions concerning the ways in which the talents of each staff member are used. In addition, teacher load information is useful concerning the assignment of extra duties, reveals imbalances between the teaching load and extra duty load of a teacher, and serves as evidence for the need for additional staff.

The actual load of the teacher includes more factors than just class size and number of classes. Other load factors are the number of subject matter preparations required, the length of class periods, the nature of the subjects taught, the nature of the students taught, extracurricular or additional duty assignments, and, at the elementary school level, such factors as the number of grades taught, including the combination of grades within one classroom. With the general exception of class size and number of classes taught, little attention has been given to these other important factors in considerations of teacher load and staff assignments. However, if staff assignment is to be considered in a more "scientific" and equitable manner, objective measures must be used to assess these factors and must become a part of rational and justifiable decisions concerning workload assignments. The makeup of teacher load has certain commonalities that can be measured with reasonable objectivity. Two such measures are the Douglass teacher load formula and the Norton/Bria formula for elementary teacher load, discussed briefly in the following sections.

The Douglass Teacher Load Formula

As early as 1928, Harl Douglass developed a formula to measure teaching load in high schools. Since that time, the formula has been refined, validated, and tested through numerous empirical studies; it is the most carefully developed means available for measuring teacher load in grades 7–12. The result of the formula computation of load for each teacher is an index of load that may be directly compared among teachers, departments, and schools, or with national norms. Several states have developed teacher load norms based on the Douglass formula for all major subject matter areas that individual schools can use to compare their school load with those of other state schools. The Douglass formula (1951; see also Jung, 1949) is

$$TL = SGC \, [CP - DUP/10 + (NP - 25 \, CP)/100]$$
$$[(PL + 50)/100] + 0.6PC \, [(PL + 50)/100]$$

Application of the Douglass Load Formula. Determine the index of teacher load for a teacher who has the following duties:

- Teaches two classes of 12th-grade English with 25 and 27 students. Each class meets five times per week. The teacher has only one preparation, because one class is a duplicate. Each class period is 60 minutes.
- Teaches three classes of 11th-grade social studies with 30, 27, and 23 students. Each class meets five times a week. Two classes are duplicates. Each class period is 60 minutes.
- Spends an average of 360 minutes per week in nonteaching duties during the semester.

Determine the values for the variables:

SGC = 1.1 for 12th-grade English and for 11th-grade social studies

CP = 25 (the teacher instructs five periods each day and each period meets five times per week: CP = 5 × 5 = 25)

DUP = 15 (there are three duplicate classes per day, one English and two social studies. Thus, there are 15 duplicates for the five-day week: 3 × 5 = 15)

NP = 660 (the teacher instructs 25 + 27 + 30 + 27 + 23 = 132 students each day for the five-day week. Thus, the weekly total is 660 students: 132 × 5 = 660. PL = 60 minutes)

PC = 6 (The teacher's 360 minutes of cooperative duties is the equivalent of six class periods, where one class period is 60 minutes: $360 \div 60 = 6$)

Substituting into the formula,

$$TL = 1.1 [25 - 15/10 + (660 - 625)/100]$$
$$[(60 + 50)/100] + (0.6 \times 6)[(60 + 50)/100] = 32.82 \text{ units}$$

As one gains experience using the Douglass formula, it takes only a few minutes to calculate the load of each teacher. With computerization, the time consideration is inconsequential. The computer can readily provide the administrator with subject area central tendency comparisons, school-to-school load comparisons, and, when available, school load comparisons with other states. Because the Douglass formula does not apply to the elementary school grades, other tools such as the Norton/Bria formula are available.

The Norton/Bria Formula for Measuring Elementary School Teacher Load

The Norton/Bria Formula (Norton & Bria, 1992) considers the load factors of assigned hours of teaching, time spent in preparation for teaching, cooperative or extracurricular duties of a noninstructional nature, the number of students taught, and the load related to extra grades taught in a single classroom by one teacher. Unlike the Douglass formula, the Norton/Bria formula measures teacher load in hours of time spent per work in teaching rather than index load units. The Norton/Bria formula is written as

$$TLH = 3/2 \text{ ATH} + (SL \times PH)/CM + F \text{ or } F'(OG \times PHs) + 0.6 \text{ (CH)}$$

where TLH = total load hours of time per week,

ATH = assigned teaching hours in the classroom per week,

PH = preparation hours (one-half the actual time for assigned hours in the classroom per week: 1/2 ATH),

SL = actual number of students taught above or below the average class size for any given grade (class sizes can be altered according to local or state class size norms),

CM = standard class mean size,

OG = other grades taught in a single classroom under the direction of one teacher (e.g., for a teacher who teaches grades 2 and 3 simultaneously in one room, OG = 1),

F = 1/16 (use for small and medium-sized school districts),

F' = 1/13 (use for larger school districts),

CH = cooperative hours spent in non-instructional duties such as meetings, playground supervision, parental conferences, and other nonteaching assignments.

Application of the Norton/Bria Formula. A third-grade teacher with an enrollment of 32 in a small school district begins teaching at 8:30 a.m. and ends at 2:45 p.m. The teacher has a 30-minute lunch break and has supervision duties for a 20-minute recess in the morning and again in the afternoon. Additional duties including faculty meetings, PTA, chairing a curriculum group, advising the science club, and district-level meetings require 675 minutes weekly.

Load calculation:

ATH = 25 hr 25 min [Assigned teaching hours per week are 5 days × 6 hours 15 minutes/day (8:30 a.m.–2:45 p.m.) less 5 days × 40 minutes/day for recess and 5 days × 30 minutes/day for lunch.] PH = 1/2 ATH = 1/2 (25 hr 25 min) = 12 hr 43 min.

SL = 7 [Student load is based on the actual number of students above or below the average class size for grade 3. It is calculated as a fractional measure of the time needed for preparation. The average class size for grade 3 is 25 (see below). Average class size data can be altered to reflect local norms.]

$$7 \times (12 \text{ hr } 43 \text{ min})/25 = 3 \text{ hr } 34 \text{ min}$$

Table for Average Class Size

Grade	Students
1	24
2	25
3	25
4	27
5	28
6	28

CM = 25; OG = 0 (no extra grades taught); F′ = 1/16; CH = 6 hr 45 min (0.6 × 675 min/week) = 405 min/week = 6 hr 45 min.

Substituting into the formula and rounding any fractional minutes to the nearest whole minute,

$$\text{TLH} = 3/2 \ (25 \text{ hr } 25 \text{ min}) + (7 \times 12 \text{ hr } 43 \text{ min})/25$$
$$+ \ 1/16 \ (0 \times 12 \text{ hr } 43 \text{ min}) + 6 \text{ hr } 45 \text{ min}$$
$$= 38 \text{ hr } 8 \text{ min} + 3 \text{ hr } 34 \text{ min} + 0 + 6 \text{ hr } 45 \text{ min}$$
$$= 48 \text{ hr } 27 \text{ min per week}$$

Tools such as the Douglass and Norton/Bria formulas have been neglected in human resources practices. Subjective load assignment practices in education have resulted in load inequities. In view of the time given to other utilization activities, the neglect of teacher load is indefensible. Teaching is demanding work; equity of assignments is imperative. The workload of teachers and other personnel must be a priority of any human resources program concerned with maximizing human potential. Equity in employee deployment requires an evaluation of teacher load from the standpoint of several perspectives. Equitable workload assignments, balance, alterations, and support evidence for needed employee staffing depend on information and data that can be determined from valid measures and analyses of teacher load.

Inequitable and burdensome workload militates against quality teacher performance and the stability of teachers in the profession. The following section discusses the HR stability process.

The Human Resources Stability Process

How does the school system maintain a viable workforce over a long period of time? What conditions and programs serve the stability of the school system, and what conditions militate against the continuation of high-level educational services? Once the human resources function secures the needed personnel for the operation of the school system, the responsibility for maintaining an effective work force becomes vitally important. The HR stability process centers on the retention of a quality staff, the reduction of teacher absenteeism, services for troubled workers, dealing with marginal employees, EAPs, and other personnel activities that serve to provide a high quality of program services and assure needed continuity within the organization. The following sections discuss each of these personnel activities.

Although stability encompasses a wide variety of program provisions, Young (2008) points out that such personnel considerations include two clusters of activities: "entitlement (employment, protection, retirement incentives, leave entitlements) and privileges (medical coverage, employee assistance, and leave privileges)" (p. 296). These clusters include all provisions that serve to keep the system viably staffed. Inhibitors such as marginal employees, conflict within the school system, and excessive employee turnover militate against the establishment of a stable organization. The significance of employee stability was underscored by one company executive in the statement that, "sales and profit are our number one objective, but retention is our number one priority" (Breuer, 2000, p. 29). The education parallel to the foregoing statement might be, "teaching and student learning are our number one objective, but employee retention is our number one priority." The following section discusses the stability process as related to troubled and marginal staff members.

Working With Troubled and Marginal Staff Members

A growing problem for human resources administrators at all levels is that of the troubled staff member. Figure 6.6 illustrates the interrelation between the work life and the personal life of the employee, and the effect of problems in each.

As Figure 6.6 illustrates, work-related problems have negative effects on the personal life. Personal life problems, in turn, contribute further to both job stress and the quality of job performance. Although the pattern between personal and work life is not exact, problems related to the employee's personal and work life are nonetheless interdependent and interrelated.

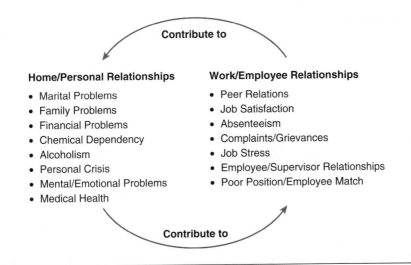

Figure 6.6   Home/Personal and Work/Employee Life Interrelationships

Medical health and stress related to mental and emotional problems commonly are leading problems for teachers and administrators considered as troubled employees. "Another set of symptoms associated with teacher stress is turnover, early retirement, sickness absenteeism, and intention to leave—all forms of withdrawal" (Travers, 2001, p. 136). Although a 7%–8% turnover rate is viewed as common for most organizations, a 25%–33% turnover of first-year teachers frequently is reported. The leading problem areas for troubled workers, including teachers, administrators, and support staff, are shown in Table 6.1.

Table 6.1   Leading Problem Areas for Troubled Workers in Education

Problem Area	Number of School Districts Reporting
Medical health and/or personal injuries	52
Problem drinking, alcoholism	50
Mental-emotional problems	47
Marital-family problems	46
Employee-supervisor relationships	29
Personal crisis	21
Financial problems	17
Drug-chemical dependency	17
Work-peer relationships	11
Others	10

SOURCE: Norton, M. S. "Employee Assistance Programs—A Need in Education." *Contemporary Education* (1998), *60*, p. 24. Reprinted by permission.

Employee Assistance Programs

Fortunately, the number of employee assistance programs (EAPs) offered by school district programs is increasing. Often these programs are administered jointly with employee organizations. EAP service arrangements include the provision of referral services to outside professionals, in-house counseling programs staffed by local district professionals, consortia that include cooperative funding for services within or outside the school districts, and the use of approved consultants who provide the necessary EAP services.

As Chapter 11 will discuss, many school districts provide EAP services as part of the fringe benefit program. Such personal assistance is integral to the maximization of human resources within the school district. Although the central human resources unit most often coordinates the EAP, local human resources administrators, such as the school principal, are instrumental in the program's success. Because the building principal works most closely with many troubled personnel, identification, referral, counseling, and mentoring all become part of the principal's human resources responsibilities. EAPs are supported by viable school board policies that underscore the importance of providing confidential services for troubled workers and delegate responsibilities for implementing such services. Figure 6.7 is an example of an EAP school board policy. Although the policy states the aim of the EAP program, it leaves the discretion necessary for the professional staff to set forth appropriate administrative regulations for its implementation.

Not only did the number of employee assistance programs increase during the 1990s, but also the services provided by these programs increased significantly since their earlier singular focus on the treatment of employee alcohol problems. Doolittle (1996) noted that EAPs provide services for employees in all areas in which behavioral or personal problems exist. He suggested that the "next logical step is to use EAPs to integrate all organizational functions related to employee health and productivity" (p. 22). In this approach, the EAP is involved throughout the employee's referral and treatment process. That is, the EAP serves as liaison between the employee, treatment provider, and employer in the coordination of services from the identification of the problem to the treatment and the return to health in the most effective way possible.

Code: GCBC

The Employee Assistance Program in the College View School District No. 105 recognizes that unresolved problems may adversely impact the job performance of employees at all levels of responsibility. These problems may include, but are not limited to chemical dependency, and marital, family, legal and/or financial concerns. To facilitate a timely resolution to these problems, the district provides employees and their dependents with the benefit of confidential counseling and assistance provided by the Employee Assistance Program. Employees are encouraged to take advantage of the services before any problem becomes overwhelming. Every person using the program is assured total confidentiality. For additional information call the Personnel Office or call CONTACT, Inc. 840-0000.

Ref: Board Policy GCBC and Regulation GCBC-R.

Figure 6.7   Employee Assistance Program School Board Policy

In a study of HR professionals, the respondents were asked to name the specific values of EAPs for the organization. The HR professionals named referral services, short-term personal counseling, and financial counseling as most valuable organizationally. When asked which services of their EAP were most valuable to them, they named the 24/7 emergency services, referral services, short-term counseling, and critical incident interventions.

When asked what services the HR professional wished their EAPs would provide, they named added educational training programs and health promotion programs that could be used throughout the company workplace (Citrin, Crook, & Winn, 2004). Rumsey (1992) noted that the HR professional is in a delicate position relative to gaining the employee's trust and then creating enough distance so that the employee will accept the EAP referral without feeling unsupported. When the professional has enough information to understand the employee's problem, Rumsey recommends the following steps:

- Identify the concerns.
- Identify possible solutions.
- Develop strategy for the employee to look for and resolve in treatment.
- Match the employee with the provider(s) (case matching).
- Discuss providers.
- Explore resistance.
- Decide the next step.
- Refer to the provider(s). (p. 42)

The following principles and personnel procedures aid the HR staff stability process in serving the troubled staff members and providing positive leadership in this developing area:

1. Maintain a positive viewpoint regarding troubled staff personnel. The responsibility of the human resources function is to assist and develop human potential at all levels. The personal worth and dignity of troubled employees must be protected.

2. Establish procedures for ascertaining signs of personal problems demonstrated in the employee's behavior and effectiveness. Behavioral signals such as irritability, lack of motivation and interest, decreased physical energy, lack of commitment, loss of concentration, and self-deprecation serve as clues for needed action. Decreased effectiveness is revealed in such tendencies as setting low goals, inferior or deteriorating work, avoidance of difficult tasks, and increased human error.

3. Be fully aware of the assistance resources available for troubled personnel within the school system and through external agencies. Provide the necessary leadership for gaining personal counseling services. Work to promote a positive attitude toward the use of personal assistance counseling and services. Promote the view that the use of expert help, when needed, is good judgment.

4. Use appropriate principles of effective human resources administration in working with troubled staff members. Proper position assignment, workload, and use of appropriate mentors are among the important considerations. Make certain that the employee knows about the support services available for counseling and guidance. Take special measures to establish open communication with the troubled worker. Use a sensitive approach that best fits the situation.

Helping the Marginal Teacher

Marginal teachers are those individuals who are performing unsatisfactorily in one or more areas so that learning for students is inhibited. Among the first to identify characteristics of the marginal teacher was Smith (2005). The marginal teacher commonly

- Does not teach to the curriculum in general and to the specific objectives in particular.
- Lacks enthusiasm for students and teaching.
- Has poor personal relations with students.
- Exhibits poor teaching skills.
- Has unorganized classroom and lessons.
- Does not establish expectations for student behavior; discipline is usually a major problem.
- Lacks knowledge of the subject matter. (p. 213)

Empirical evidence suggests that, in many cases, the marginal teacher is not always fully aware that he or she is performing incompetently. One reason given for this condition is the nature of the performance evaluation itself. That is, the procedures used in the performance evaluation often are flawed because they may not clearly identify specific problems. If this occurs, the teacher becomes confused about both improvement needs and possible remedies. There is considerable evidence, both clinical and experimental, relating to the individual's ability to shut out or completely dismiss certain messages that are threatening; some of these studies indicate that, as vague awareness of a situation becomes more clear, the individual can arrest the process, so a well-defined awareness does not occur and perhaps at this point the threatening message is rejected or even demolished as though it never took place.

A competent professional must administer clinical procedures. If not, the marginal teacher is likely to continue to perform unsatisfactorily. Five considerations are necessary in helping the marginal teacher toward improvement: (1) implement effective performance evaluation methods that result in a clear identification of the teacher's strengths and specific needs and problems; (2) develop an improvement plan that specifies, among other things, what the teacher must do personally to improve in the problem areas and also what the school will do to help the teacher reach the improvement objectives as determined; (3) give specific attention to those strengths that the teacher might possess in order to enhance the chances for improvement; (4) help the teacher establish functional and supportive relations with other teachers; and (5) make certain that the school principal provides administrative support exemplified by a demonstrative attitude of caring, personal commitment to and interest in effective classroom teaching.

We would emphasize the need to make certain that the teacher clearly understands the specific problems related to teaching performance and what must be done to improve. As previously noted, the teacher who is not aware of problems regarding their teaching performance may be completely surprised to be the target of such charges; thus, gaining an understanding of the problems is a first prerequisite for remediation.

Chapter 7 discusses the purposes of performance evaluation, the evaluation plan, and standards for the development and operation of a sound evaluation system, along with the identification of personal strengths and needs for professional improvement in relation to assessment center techniques. Assessment center methods are also discussed briefly later in this chapter.

As Chapter 7 will discuss, clinical supervision emphasizes system-wide instructional improvement through improved staff performance. Clinical supervision necessitates a cooperative relationship between the teacher and the supervisor.

There are times when it is necessary to develop a comprehensive remedial plan for the marginal teacher. Although a remedial plan differs from case to case, it includes those items that are unsatisfactory according to the overall performance evaluation. Among those areas commonly included in such plans are (1) professional preparation and scholarship, (2) instructional skill, (3) classroom management, (4) handling of student discipline and attendant problems, and (5) effort toward improvement when needed. Figure 6.8 is an example of a remedial plan for Area 4, handling of student discipline and attendant problems.

Dealing With Conflict and Controversy

A closed climate is defined as one that is characterized by low staff morale, limited and inadequate communication, and limited socialization. In such a climate, one might expect that conflict and controversy among staff personnel would occur. Yet, because of the dynamics and individual differences that exist in any organization, differences of opinion and personal conflict also occur in schools with open climates. Attempts to meet the needs of the school system often conflict with the need dispositions of individuals in the system. For example, the need to increase class size because of budgetary conditions might be contrary to the need to reduce faculty workload, or school budget priorities might differ in the minds of the administration, teachers, and various school stakeholders. Thus, role, personality, priority, authority, procedural, and other types of conflict are inevitable in most every organization.

Although conflict resolution is dependent on many variables, including leadership style, several considerations or strategies can be used to capitalize on controversy and conflict. An open climate, for example, expects and respects individuals' rights to disagree, and human resources administrators must recognize the

A. Your performance reflects an inability to consistently establish order and discipline in the classroom.

B. I recommend that your handling of student discipline be improved during the probationary period to reflect an ability to consistently establish order and discipline in the classroom.

C. Suggestions that would assist you in correcting the above deficiencies include:

1. Communicate to students appropriate expectations for conduct and behavior. These would include the following:

   (a) Students will arrive at class punctually

   (b) Students will take their seats in a timely and orderly fashion

   (c) Students will sit in their seats properly and remain in their seat unless otherwise instructed

   (d) Students will be quiet and attentive when you are instructing

   (e) Students will not be loud, disrespectful, or engage in rough housing

2. Misbehavior should result in appropriate and consistent consequences. This is best accomplished through a process of progressive discipline depending on the nature of the offense. Follow the adopted school sequence for dealing with discipline:

   (a) student reprimand

   (b) conference with student

   (c) detention-give notice; maximum 30 minutes

   (d) parent contact

   (e) referral to principal

3. Maintain a current log on each student that you have disciplined. Each entry should state the date of the misconduct, the nature of the misconduct, and action taken.

Figure 6.8   Remedial Plan for Handling Student Discipline and Attendant Problems

SOURCE: Smith, R.E. (2001). *Human Resources Administration* (3rd ed.). Larchmont, NY: Eye on Education, p. 226.

right of employees to do so. Any effort to limit the right of disagreement likely will lead to other negative relationships rather than to build organizational trust and confidence. Open systems seek ways to gain input from workers through the use of system surveys, think tanks, shadow groups, and other viable suggestion systems.

Controversy in an open climate can be useful. Progress in terms of goal achievement and new understandings is often generated by full reflection on existing problems, issues, and alternative solutions. Supervisors need special training to help prepare them to deal with the sensitive issues that often are the center of organizational conflict. In this way, school leaders can make controversy more constructive. School leaders must work to broaden the base of staff and community understanding through purposeful assessment of criticism. Understanding the "facts" surrounding a situation can serve to ward off unfair criticism because it helps to distinguish between constructive and destructive proposals.

Such an assessment necessitates keeping personally informed of the existence and concerns of criticisms that are expressed. Open channels of communication can serve as the school system's nervous system; problems can be identified in their early stages. Such awareness allows for further assessments and appropriate responses as well as an opportunity to keep minor criticisms to manageable proportions. Action must be taken to counteract unfair or irresponsible criticism. A planned strategy for such action includes the gathering of accurate information, soliciting help on the matter from appropriate groups and individuals, and then setting forth an action plan as appropriate to the case.

The school leader's overall task in dealing with conflict and controversy is to maintain the integrity of the system and the confidence of the school system's stakeholders in an atmosphere in which critics have a right to disagree as well as to have access to the system's open channels of communication. Conflict and controversy can help lead to better solutions to existing problems. A positive approach to such matters serves to maximize the efforts of personnel and the productivity of the school system's efforts. In short, the leader's best defense in dealing with conflict and controversy is to maintain a communications initiative with both employees and the school's publics.

The Organizational Stability Process: Teacher Retention

Increasing problems related to teacher shortages have resulted in critical attention to the retention of quality personnel in education. The loss of intellectual capital in organizations has become known as brain drain. In a recent study of HR directors in Arizona, teacher retention ranked eighth among 18 of the most serious problems facing them (Norton, 2004). Most U.S. corporations expect 6% of their employees to quit each year. Studies of teacher loss in education, however, indicate that approximately 25% to 33 1/3% of those persons entering teaching leave after their first year, and that 33 1/3% to 50% leave the profession by the end of the fifth year. No organization can lose that proportion of its professional employees and expect to remain stable and effective.

It is estimated that it costs 25% or more of the teacher's salary to replace him or her; the cost of replacing a school principal or other mid-management supervisor is estimated to be much higher. By using the 25% figure, lose only 10% of a staff of 130 teachers making an average salary of $36,000 and the bill is $117,000, money that would be welcomed in other budget lines. Although the loss of monetary capital is problematic, the corresponding loss of intellectual capital perhaps is even more crucial. The loss of the knowledge base, system experience, and personal talent inhibits the accomplishment of the stability goals of the school system. The paramount importance of staff stability and its significance as a powerful competitive strategy is understood more clearly today than ever before. An article in *HR Focus* (Stum, 1998) noted the concept of customer loyalty and that competent people are needed to serve the organization's stakeholders in order to gain their loyalty. Customers who believe that they are not being well served add to our stress and may take their business elsewhere. When staff personnel remain in the system long enough to know the school's customers and the community being served, outcomes become more attainable.

Strategies for Reducing Teacher Turnover

The literature is replete with recommendations for reducing teacher turnover. Chapters within this text are devoted to gaining school system commitment on the part of staff personnel through the improvement of school climate, by implementing such activities as staff induction programs, fair and equitable compensation practices, and positive climate programs, all of which are directly related to the retention of quality personnel. Employee retention starts the first day a potential applicant makes contact with the school system. Effective teacher retention ties closely with all of the primary HR processes and their related activities. Thus, the need to gain commitment on the part of both new and experienced personnel is everyone's business.

A unique study by Stum (1998) identified what were termed the top five commitment drivers that affect workforce performance. Stum's research findings suggest several important components for building a bonding between the employee and the school system. Stum contended that the true drivers of commitment include

1. The extent to which the organization encourages personnel to challenge the way things are done; being able to speak up about the status quo without fear of retribution. A healthy school climate encourages such input.

2. The extent to which the organization works to improve employee job satisfaction; providing opportunities for employees to soar with their strengths, giving less attention to overcoming weaknesses. Such considerations are likely to reap many rewards. People who are doing what they really like to do, are doing it well, and enjoy the work, are more likely to stay with the organization.

3. The extent to which the organization provides the employee with opportunities for personal growth and development. When the drivers to motivate reside solely in the employee's supervisor, both productivity and morale are likely to decline. For new personnel, especially, professional development that centers on structuring of systematic assistance in professional growth is of paramount importance. Studies of teacher turnover often identify teachers' feelings of isolation and abandonment as primary reasons for so many teachers leaving education after one or two years.

4. The extent to which organizational direction is evident. Without an understanding of goals, it is comparable to running a race without any of the contestants knowing the length of the course. On your mark, get set, go! But where? A sure way of obstructing motivation is to fail to gain an understanding of system goals.

5. The extent to which the organization recognizes work-life balance needs. This is an occurring change from the perspective of "living to work" to "working to live." The retention of personnel in education requires special attention to work-life balance. Unless realistic solutions to restrictive teacher work schedules and job requirements are found, many will continue to choose work elsewhere.

An Operational Plan for Teacher Retention

Although there are no panaceas for resolving the teacher turnover problems facing education today, there are important steps that will assist in moving ahead constructively in attempts to reduce teacher turnover. The following practices are recommended:

Step 1. Adopting and implementing a guiding school board policy for retaining quality teacher personnel. The retention of teaching talent in the school system must be viewed as a district priority. The adoption of a specific personnel policy on teacher retention by the school board serves to place this matter on the agenda as a district priority. The district policy sets forth the aim of the retention program—what the program is to accomplish. A viable district policy serves as the forerunner for the administrative actions needed to implement effective retention policies. Figure 6.9 is an example of a policy on teacher retention.

Step 2. Designing and Implementing a Retention Plan. A retention plan must give full consideration to the administrative regulations for implementing the board policy, budget requirements, and the delegation of leadership responsibilities.

Although the development of administrative procedures is the primary responsibility of the administrative staff, completed regulations should be brought to the school board for review to assure continuity between policy aims and regulative procedures. Program strategies that include attention to the work environment, employee career opportunities, nonmonetary rewards and personal recognition, work-life balance, induction/selection/assignment practices, and supervisory relationships must be implemented.

The Lincoln School District recognizes that the district's personnel are vital to the successful accomplishment of its educational mission. The retention of quality personnel is among the school district's highest priorities. Thus, the board of education supports those programs and activities that serve to keep employee turnover at the lowest possible rate. In order to accomplish this goal, school leaders are responsible for designing and implementing effective programs that serve to attract and retain quality personnel at all levels.

Under the direction of the superintendent of schools, effective programs of personnel recruitment, selection, induction, assignment, development, and organizational climate should be implemented. Periodic assessments of personnel work interests should be implemented. School principals and other supervisory personnel should give necessary attention to the climate of the schools and/or units of the district's employees. Such plans are to be reviewed annually by the school superintendent or by persons delegated this important task.

Job satisfaction surveys that gain the input of the school district's employees relative to organizational climate, peer and supervisor relationships, staff participation, and other factors should be administered periodically. Programs of employee recognition and reward for superior work are encouraged as part of this policy statement.

The Lincoln School Board understands the importance of compensation and work benefits, including a balanced work life for employees, as related to employee retention.

Figure 6.9   Example of a Teacher Retention Policy

Step 3. Monitoring Staff Turnover. Close monitoring of staff turnover serves to establish program accountability through assessments that support positive retention activity results. Records of teacher turnover must be maintained and used in diagnosing turnover patterns and problem areas at the local school level. Accountability is demonstrated through the use of hard data; those practices that have resulted in a reduction of teacher turnover must be identified and put into practice as appropriate throughout the school system.

Step 4. Individualizing the Retention Activities. Staff members leave the school system for different reasons, so the retention program, including the re-recruitment of personnel, must be personalized. Ongoing assessments of the intentions of employees concerning job satisfaction, assignment interests, career development aspirations, and other related factors must be administered both formally and informally. An example of a survey of current employee interests and intentions was presented previously in Figure 6.5. The administration of such questionnaires provides clues as to the employee's current attitudes about work assignments and career aspirations. Appropriate follow-up by the school principal or other supervisor holds re-recruitment potential; administrative behaviors that demonstrate an active interest in the welfare of the employee can yield positive results as well.

Step 5. Establishing Guidelines for Personnel Services. The working definition of human resources administration must not only include the terms "recruit," "select," "assign," "induct," and "develop," but must also underscore the important term, "retain personnel." Each of the several processes of the HR function must give necessary consideration to the reduction of teacher turnover. For example, as mentioned previously, the induction process is of paramount importance in assuring high morale for teachers during their first years of teaching.

Step 6. Implementing Specific Strategies for Teacher Retention. Although employee compensation is an important consideration in the attraction and retention of teachers, nonmonetary factors can influence positive teacher job satisfaction as well. Important considerations, according to Robinson and Galpin (1986), are inclusion, control, and ego. Teachers are concerned about job security; they want to participate in the decision-making process, they view working conditions as of utmost importance, they need autonomy that fosters the opportunity for personal creativity, they seek an understanding of their role and its contributions to the scheme of things that take place in the school, and they are motivated by being part of doing the right things to accomplish worthy end results.

What keeps teachers in the school system? (1) Knowing what is expected at work, (2) having materials needed to do the work, (3) having an assignment that provides opportunities to do what one does best, (4) knowing that their opinion counts, and (5) having received recognition for work well done.

Retention of Administrative Personnel

The seriousness of turnover in the administrative area of education is revealed by statistics showing high percentages of turnover on the part of school superintendents, principals, HR directors, and other supervisors. For example, a study of HR directors in one state reported that the average tenure in the same position was only 4.68 years (Norton, 2004). Nearly 42% of the HR directors had been in their present role for three years or less. The average tenure for superintendents in the states of Illinois, Texas, and Arizona was 5.9, 6.33, and 5.89 years, respectively (Norton, 2001). The latest national study of the school superintendency in the United States (Glass, Bjork, & Brunner, 2000) reported the tenure of school superintendents to be five to six years per district. The researchers divided the total years in the superintendency by the number of superintendencies held in calculating the tenure statistics.

Why Principals Are Leaving the Position

As Hertling (2000) stated, "Today's principal is faced with the complex task of creating a school wide vision, being an instructional leader, planning for effective professional development, guiding teachers, handling discipline, attending events, coordinating buses, tending to external priorities such as legislative mandates, and all the other minute details that come with supervising a school" (p. 1). Kennedy (2000) pointed out five major reasons for the lack of principal retention and why school principals often say, "it just isn't worth it": (1) the changing demands of the job, (2) salary, (3) time, (4) lack of parent and community support and the negativity of the media and pupils toward schools, and (5) lack of respect.

In a study of 170 high school assistant principals, only 30% of the participants indicated that they had a career goal to seek a high school principalship (Pounder & Merrill, 2001). This fact supports Whitaker's (2000) study that reported a "somewhat extreme" or "extreme" shortage of principal candidates. Overall, 90% of the superintendents in the study rated the principal shortage problem from "moderate" to "extreme."

In another study of 110 elementary, middle, and secondary school principals (Norton, 2004), the participants were asked to identify the position provisions that would serve to retain their services in the role. Being able to make a difference, the conditions of challenges and opportunities in the role of leadership, relationships with students, personal satisfaction in the role, and compensation for the position led the principals' responses (see Table 6.2). When asked for recommendations for keeping quality principals in the role, the respondents listed the following: providing needed resources, reexamining the principal's role, providing public support, adding benefits and incentives, gathering principal feedback regarding job status and conditions, improving retirement benefits, educating the public as to the demands of the job, providing mentoring services, and outsourcing certain work within the role.

Various studies have underscored the serious problems facing school principals. Problems facing school principals that often lead to their leaving the position include the lack of supervisor or board support, the lack of work-life balance, increasing or changing job demands, time requirements of the position, lack of respect shown for the position, external mandates or interference in the role, lack of staff support, and overall stress in the role. Unless each of these inhibiting factors is addressed, turnover in the principalship most likely will continue at its present level.

Table 6.2 Recommendations for Keeping Quality School Principals in the Role: By Organizational Level

Recommendations	K–6	7–8	9–12	Rank
Increase Salaries	2	1	2–3	1
Provide Resources	1	2	2–3	1–2
Reexamine the Role	3	5	1	3
Provide Public Support	4	3	5–9	4
Add Benefits/Incentives	8–10	4	4	5
Gather Principal Feedback	6	6–7	5–9	6
Attractive Retirement	5	9	5–9	7
Educate Public of Demands	7	8	5–9	8
Mentoring Services	8–10	6–7	5–9	9
Outsource Certain Work	8–10	10	10	10

SOURCE: Norton, M. S. (2004). How Can We Attract and Retain Quality School Principals: What Do Principals Say? *Educational Considerations*, Spring 2004, 31(2), 25–30.

Teacher Absenteeism

Research studies have found that teacher absenteeism is a growing concern among the nation's educators (Norton, 2005). One statewide study named teacher absenteeism among the 10 problems facing human resources directors in school systems today (Norton, 2005). Podgursky (2005) reported that teachers' paid sick leave and personal leave time averaged approximately 5% of their salaries, compared to about 2% for personnel in other professions. Podgursky, an economist associated with the University of Missouri-Columbia, based his findings on data from the Bureau of Labor Statistics and other school and staffing surveys to reach this conclusion. Current higher salary levels for teachers, higher substitute salaries, and trends toward higher numbers of teacher absences result in significant increases in monetary expenditures for school districts.

Various studies of teacher absenteeism historically have revealed the following results:

1. Overall, male teachers had significantly fewer absences than female teachers. There was a significant difference in the occurrence of absence for men between the ages of 21 and 39. The number of absences claimed by female teachers increased with age (Scott & McClellan, 1990; Unicomb, Alley, Avery, & Barak, 1992).

2. Elementary teachers averaged 6.63 days of absence per year compared to 3.32 days for secondary personnel. Teachers were absent on Wednesdays more frequently than any other day. Mondays were the least claimed days for absence. November, January, and April were peak months for teacher absences (Unicomb et al., 1992). Research has not been consistent concerning years of experience and absenteeism (Porwoll, 1980).

3. Some research has shown that teacher absenteeism ties closely to school leave provisions. For example, teachers who had accumulated the maximum days of absence tended to use additional sick leave days indiscriminately (Jacobson, 1990).

4. Individuals who received low performance evaluations were associated with higher levels of absenteeism (Pitkoff, 1993).The rate of teacher absenteeism was found to be highest in elementary schools, schools with lowest student achievement, schools composed of economically disadvantaged and minority students, schools that do not require teachers to speak to their immediate supervisor about pending absence, urban school districts, and districts consisting of more than 257,000 people (Pitkoff, 1993).

Research studies on the specific effects of teacher absences on student achievement are limited, and the few that have occurred tend to differ in their findings. It is difficult to design studies that control the many variables related to teacher absenteeism and associate them with student achievement. A study of 323 human resources executives found that personal illness topped the reasons for unscheduled employee absences at work (Personal illness tops absentee list, 2006); 35% were due to personal illness, 21% to family issues, 18% to personal needs, 14% to entitlement mentality, and 12% to stress. Other studies have found that organizational climate and teacher absenteeism are related (Imants & Van Zoelen, 1995). Collegial relations and leadership style of the school principal were found to be associated with teacher absenteeism. Although the topic of teacher absenteeism needs closer examination and in-depth research, the studies that have been completed, along with empirical evidence, suggest certain provisions that school leaders should consider in attempts to improve teacher absenteeism (Norton, 2004):

- School districts should develop clear guidelines concerning employee attendance, including measures to deal with excessive absenteeism. In cases of excessive employee absence, factors such as leave policy and school leadership practices should be examined carefully.
- Most authorities recommend close monitoring of leave. Empirical evidence suggests that absenteeism is reduced when school employees are required to report their absence to their supervisor. Records of absenteeism should be maintained and used for diagnosing attendance patterns and problem areas at the school level.

- Employee assistant programs should be established in the school district that provide for personal counseling for employees who have excessive absences. Counseling could result in the identification of the major cause of absence and possible solution to the existing problem.
- Evidence suggests that incentives hold some potential for improving teacher absenteeism. School districts should pilot various incentive programs and assess their impact on absence reduction. For example, child-care services in cooperation with parent groups and other community agencies might be extended to employees of the district.
- Buy-back of unused sick leave should be considered as a means of discouraging indiscriminate use of sick leave by employees. Although an expensive provision monetarily, such a step could help keep teachers on the job to serve the instructional program of the schools.

The HR Protection Process

How are school employees protected from unfair treatment and physical harm? The human resources protection process has received increased attention because of personnel issues related to employee rights and personal security. Such matters as tenure, employee grievances, due process, academic freedom, job safety, and capricious treatment have been the center of litigation cases and new policy actions by school districts. Most school boards nationally have now adopted official policies on the protection of employees who are threatened with harm by an individual or group while carrying out assigned duties. An example of an administrative regulation related to threats is as follows:

Any employee who is threatened with harm by an individual or group while carrying out assigned duties shall immediately notify the building principal or supervisor. The principal or supervisor shall then notify the Superintendent's office of the threat and together they will take immediate steps in cooperation with the employee to provide every reasonable provision for the employee's safety. Precautionary steps, including any advisable legal action, shall be reported to the Superintendent's office at the earliest possible time.

Concern for workplace violence has resulted in school efforts to set forth precautionary measures in cases of violence and threats, including efforts to identify the characteristics of individuals who might be threats to the safety of students and employees. Empirical evidence has revealed that the type of firearm used in most all threats is a handgun; such weapons are easily concealed. Nearly 60% of workplace violence involves a male suspect 40 years of age or older; approximately 15% of the suspects have a mental health history, and approximately 10% display well-known warnings before acting. Such information supports precautionary measures that school personnel might implement.

Lessening personal employee anxiety and forecasting a more positive climate have always been objectives of effective human resources administration. These concerns associated with personal protection, however, have broadened in scope and are now reflected in virtually every process of the human resources function. Protection concerns include grievance procedures, transfers, dismissals, separation, liability protection, reduction in force, promotions, employee discipline, personal safety, background checks, and tenure decisions.

As previously noted, a growing area of the protection process is that of security from bodily harm. Incidences of attacks on teachers, administrators, students, and other school personnel are growing problems for school districts nationally. Aon Consulting Worldwide's Loyalty Institute has underscored the importance of employee safety and security by listing this need as one of the five steps of the "performance pyramid" of workplace practices for evaluating an organization's efforts on the commitment and employee loyalty front. As Aon Consulting stipulates, "the foundation of any good workplace is recognizing employees' need for a safe, non-threatening work environment" (Cole, 2000, p. 48). The responsibility for maintaining a safe, healthy, and secure school environment is basic to the human resource protection process.

As Chapter 5 noted, efforts of organizations to ensure the safety of all persons in the school community have resulted in the widening use of background checks. The primary purpose of background checks is to make certain that those persons hired in the school district do not present liability or security risks. The number of organizations using background checks is increasing dramatically, especially for those employees who work with children. Percentages of employers who investigate backgrounds of potential employees increased from 66% in 1996 to 96% in 2004, an increase of 30% ("Background checks widening," 2005).

Safety culture awareness is aimed at minimizing workplace injuries, but it also serves to reduce medical expenses, limit school liability for negligence, and reduce employee absenteeism. As most every HR administrator would agree, safety consciousness is simply the right thing to do. Chapter 9 discusses legal considerations in regard to legal protection.

Protection issues also include procedures for protecting both students and employees from injury due to unsafe conditions within the school district facilities and while participating in activities such as vocational, technical, and industrial education, and in science laboratory activities. Administrative policies usually set forth stipulations concerning the wearing of protective eyewear and the storing of potentially dangerous chemicals.

Every school board policy manual stresses compliance with the requirements of the Occupational Safety and Health Administration (OSHA). Employees, who as a result of their employment are exposed to bloodborne pathogens (such as Hepatitis B or Human Immunodeficiency Virus), commonly are required to report the details of the exposure in writing to the school district and required to follow postexposure evaluation and follow-up activities in accordance with state and federal laws. An employee who chooses not to complete the required reporting requirements is at risk of losing any claim to rights. Workers injured in the workplace are usually required to follow similar reporting procedures or be at risk of losing worker's compensation benefits.

Most school districts have specific local policies to ensure compliance with state and federal laws related to the transmission of communicable diseases. For example, requirements, such as proof of immunization against rubella, are set forth in adopted policies in most school districts today. State and federal laws in most states require a report within 24 hours of outbreaks for such diseases as giardiasis; haemophilus influenzae, type b, invasive disease; hepatitis A; measles (rubeola); meningococcal invasive disease; mumps; pertussis (whooping cough); rubella (German measles); scabies; and shigellosis. Policies and procedures concerning HIV/AIDS in school settings were set forth in detail previously. The foregoing information serves several purposes relating to the safety and protection of school personnel, one purpose of which is to illustrate the growing comprehensive efforts of school districts nationally to safeguard both students and employees.

In addition to policies and procedures pertaining to employee and student safety in schools, many school districts provide other guides relating to procedures for dealing with crisis situations. For example, the Tempe Elementary School District in Tempe, Arizona publishes a Quick Response Guide that includes specific directions for meeting crisis situations relating to weapons in school; fire, smoke, or gas odor; sheltering; chemical, biological, or radiological incidents; CPR/first aid; hostage taker; evacuation and relocation center; lockdown procedures; and threatening calls including bomb threats. For each instance, specific behavioral procedures are set forth and are accompanied by the district's crisis-line telephone number along with a complete list of related emergency phone numbers.

Chapter 9 discusses the liberty and property rights of personnel, including the topic of academic freedom.

Summary

The provision of policies, conditions, and programs that serve to maximize the human assets of the school system pays dividends for both the employer and the employee. The primary purposes of the assignment, induction, stability, and protection processes center on fostering human potential and promoting the achievement of school system goals. When the worker is assigned to a role where his or her primary strengths and interests are utilized, both job satisfaction and self-fulfillment are likely to result. Important results of proper staff assignment include retention of staff, high morale, employee commitment, goal achievement, and higher productivity. According to research results, teachers new to a school who are given personal assistance through effective orientation activities and induction programs have higher morale than those who do not receive such help. High morale is instrumental in reducing the major problem of employee turnover.

Teacher turnover militates against a stable organization; no organization can lose quality personnel and expect to remain effective. This chapter presented the reasons that many personnel leave the teaching and administrative professions, but also underscored various steps that schools must take to ameliorate the problem of employee turnover.

Instability, as revealed in an inability to retain quality personnel, excessive employee absences, and ineffective personnel policies, is a growing concern for the human resources administrator. If the school system is to develop an effective system of human resources, it must take measures to maintain personnel stability at all levels. The rights, safety, and protection of employees are inextricably tied to the establishment of stability within the school system. Personal safety and the protection of liberty and property rights are of paramount importance for achieving school system purposes.

As has been emphasized in this chapter and throughout this textbook, schools are people and school systems will develop as people progress. As revealed in the definition of human resources administration set forth in this text, it is the responsibility of all human resources administrators to work toward the development of an effective system of human resources within the school system and to build a climate that fosters the accomplishment of educational goals. The personnel processes discussed in this chapter—assignment, induction, stability, and protection—play a major role in realizing these intentions.

Discussion Questions

1. Examine the definitions of personnel assignment, induction, stability, and protection as discussed in the chapter. Give several illustrations in which one process is related to another. For example, how does the induction process relate to and support the stability process?

2. Research studies in the area of teacher load reveal that teachers new to the profession often have the heaviest teacher loads. Identify several reasons that such inequities too frequently exist. What are the likely problems of such a practice in both short- and long-term results?

3. Consider the stability process as discussed in the chapter. First, describe several possible program actions on the part of school leadership that might serve to reduce teacher turnover. Then, set forth a specific procedure for demonstrating the accountability of one of the program actions that were described.

4. The chapter described several protection program activities that have been implemented in school districts nationwide. Consider the school or school district with which you are most familiar. What protection activities, discussed in the chapter, are present in the school or school district in question?

5. Class Exercise: As noted in the chapter, school districts might lose as many as one-third of their first-year teachers. Divide the class members into two groups; ask one group to develop a list of factors that would tend to personally keep them on the job as teachers, and ask the second group to develop a list of factors that would tend to motivate them to start thinking about leaving a teaching position. Ask each group to personalize their responses to the

greatest extent possible. Use the lists of the two groups to examine the matter of teacher turnover. Which items on the listing of the first group appear to be realistically "reachable"? Which items on the listing of the second group appear realistically "avoidable"?

6. A high school teacher of social studies has two classes of grade 10 history with 26 and 32 students and three classes of government with 26, 31, and 33 students. The subject-grade coefficient for social studies is 1.1. Class periods are 55 minutes in length. On average during the semester, the teacher spends 11 periods per week in cooperative duties. Use the Douglass load formula to calculate this teacher's units of teacher load. (Note: The answer is 35.40 units.)

Case Studies

CASE 6.1

A MATTER OF LOAD

Greg Stephen, teacher of band at College View High School, was asked by Principal Virginia Lee to see her in the office at his first convenience. When Greg arrived at the principal's office, Principal Lee greeted him warmly and asked him how the band and orchestra program was going this year.

"Just fine," responded Greg, "although this year seems to be busier than last year. The band marched in the Fiesta Day Parade and performed for the downtown Rotary Club just last week."

"Let's see," said Principal Lee. "You have one class of beginning band, a class of advanced band, and the orchestra class, I believe. They each meet for two hours twice each week. Is that correct?"

"Yes, that's right," answered Greg. "But the advanced band is required to perform at halftime at each football game in the fall and the orchestra presents a school assembly program each spring. And then I get all these other requests to perform by various local groups. Just yesterday I agreed to have the beginning band perform at the next Parent-Teacher Organization meeting."

"I have been receiving requests for more student opportunities in beginning band," said Principal Lee. "I'd like you to consider this growing request."

"I just don't know how I could consider such a load increase," responded Greg. "My plate is running over as it is."

"Well," said Principal Lee, bringing the meeting to a close, "let's give this some additional thought and talk again next week."

Questions

1. What information should Principal Lee have on hand when she meets with Greg Stephen again next week?

2. In view of what you learned about the calculation of teacher load in the chapter, speculate about the results that such a calculation of Greg's load might reveal.

CASE 6.2

NOT AGAIN!

Lee Bassett, first-year principal of the Wittier Elementary School, has been receiving an increasing number of calls from parents of children in Edith West's third-grade class regarding her strict discipline measures and unfriendly relationships with both parents and children. General complaints have centered on Miss West's inability to work with slow learners in the class and her record of giving abrupt responses to questions posed to her by the children's parents. As one parent complained, "Miss West is unapproachable. She takes it as an affront when I place a call to her and immediately goes on the defense."

Miss West had served as a teacher in the Lafayette School district for 11 years; three years at Longfellow Elementary School, three years at Park Elementary School, two years at Grace Elementary School, three years at Meadowlark Elementary School, and is now in her first year at Whittier Elementary School. She was transferred from each of the foregoing schools at the request of the school principals because of what was viewed as a "situation where the teacher needed a new atmosphere in which to work." Her performance evaluations over the years, based on a scale of 1 = excellent to 5 = poor, have averaged 3.3. Of Miss West's four prior principals, two viewed her as a marginal teacher in their recommendation of transfer sent to the school superintendent.

Principal Bassett sat back in his chair and thought about what he should do at this time. He called his secretary and asked her to bring a transfer recommendation form to him. On receiving the form, Principal Lee sat back once again as if to give more thought to the matter of Miss West.

Questions

1. Assume the role of Principal Bassett and take steps that you believe are most appropriate in this case. Be specific in describing what action you will take at this time.

2. Review the section on the marginal teacher set forth in the chapter. How might the recommendations in the chapter be of help to you as principal at this time?

References

Alderfer, C. P. (1972). *Existence, relatedness, and growth: Human needs in organizational settings*. New York: Free Press.

Background checks widening. (2005, November 21). *Arizona Republic*, pp. D1–D2.

Barnard, C. I. (1938). *The functions of the executive*. Cambridge, MA: Harvard University Press.

Berglas, W. W. (1973, November). A study of the relationship between induction practices and the morale of the beginning teacher. *Dissertation Abstracts International, 34*(5), 2189-A.

Brayfield, A. H., & Crockett, W. H. (1955). Employee attitudes and employee performance. *Psychological Bulletin, 55*, 416.

Breuer, N. L. (2000). Shelf life. *Workforce, 79*(8), 29–32.

Castetter, W. B., & Young, I. P. (2000). *The human resource function in educational administration* (7th ed.). Upper Saddle River, NJ: Merrill/Prentice Hall.

Citrin, R. S., Crook, J., & Winn, S. (2004). Grading EAPs. *EAP Digest, 24*(3), 21.

Cole, C. L. (2000). Building loyalty. *Workforce, 79*(8), 48.

Doolittle, T. M. (1996). Critical connections: Linking EAP with workplace health. *EAP Digest, 16*(5), 22–24.

Douglass, H. R. (1928). Measuring teacher load in the high school. *The Nation's Schools, 2*(4), 22–24.

Douglass, H. R. (1951). The 1950 revision of the Douglass high school teaching load formula. *NASSP Bulletin, 35*, 13–24.

Getzels, J. W., & Guba, E. G. (1957). Social behavior and the administrative process. *School Review, 65*(4), 423–441.

Glass, T. E., Bjork, L., & Brunner, C. C. (2000). *The study of the American school superintendency.* Arlington, VA: American Association of School Administrators.

Hertling, E. (2000). Retaining principals. *ERIC Digest 147.* Retrieved June 17, 2001, from http://eric.uoregon.edu/publications/digests/digest147.html

Herzberg, F., Mausner, B., & Snyderman, B. (1959). *The motivation to work* (2nd ed.). New York: Wiley.

Imants, J., & Van Zoelen, A. (1995). Teachers' sickness absence in primary schools, school climate and teachers' sense of efficacy. *School Organization* (UK), *15*(1), 77–86.

Jacobson, S. (1990). Attendance incentives and teacher absenteeism. *Planning and Changing, 21*(2), 78–93.

Jung, C. W. (1949). *The development of a proposed revision of the Douglass formula for measuring teacher load in the secondary school.* Unpublished doctoral dissertation, University of Colorado, Boulder.

Kennedy, C. (2000). *Summary of responses to NAESP/NASSP/NMSA survey questions.* Washington, DC: Principals' Leadership Summit.

Lowe, P. (2001, February 25). Workplace browser, *Arizona Republic,* p. D2.

Maslow, A. H. (1987). *Motivation and personality* (3rd ed.). New York: HarperCollins. (Original work published 1954)

McClelland, D.C. (2005). *Employee motivation, the organizational environment and productivity* (abstract). Retrieved December 13, 2007, from http://accelteam.com/human relations/hrel-06-mcclelland.html

McGregor, D. (1960). *The human side of enterprise.* New York: McGraw-Hill.

Merriam Webster's Collegiate Dictionary (10th ed.) (1994). Springfield, MA: Merriam Webster.

Norton, M. S. (2001). *The school superintendency in Arizona: A research study.* Tempe: Arizona State University, Division of Educational Leadership & Policy Studies.

Norton, M. S. (2004). *The HR director in Arizona: A research study.* Tempe: Arizona State University, Division of Educational Leadership & Policy Studies.

Norton, M. S. (2005). *Executive leadership for effective administration.* Boston: Pearson Allyn & Bacon.

Norton, M. S., & Bria, R. (1992). Toward an equitable measure of elementary school teacher load. *Record in Educational Administration and Supervision, 13*(1), 62–66.

Ouchi, W. (1981). *Theory Z: How American business can meet the Japanese challenge.* Reading, MA: Addison-Wesley.

Personal illness tops absentee list. (2006, May 5). *Arizona Republic,* p. D1.

Pitkoff, E. (1993). Teacher absenteeism: What administrators can do. *NASSP Bulletin, 77*(551), 39–45.

Podgursky, M. (2005, March). *Are school teachers underpaid? Some evidence and conjectures.* Paper presented to the American Education Finance Association's Annual Meeting, Louisville, Kentucky.

Porwoll, P. J. (1980). *Employee absenteeism: A summary of research.* Arlington, VA: Educational Research Service.

Pounder, D. G., & Merrill, R. J. (2001). Job desirability of the high school principal: A job choice theory perspective. *Educational Administration Quarterly, 37*(l), 27–57.

Raia, A. P. (1974). *Managing by objectives.* Glenview, IL: Scott, Foresman.

Robinson, D. C., & Galpin, T. (1986, July). In for a change. *HR Magazine, 47*(7), 90–93.

Rumsey, M. J. (1992). Making EAP referrals work. *EAP Digest, 12*(5), 42–43.

Scott, K. D., & McClellan, R. I. (1990). Gender differences in absenteeism. *Public Personnel Management, 19*(2), 229–253.

Skinner, B. F. (1938). *The behavior of organisms.* New York: Appleton-Century-Crofts.

Skinner, B. F. (1953). *Science and human behavior.* New York: Free Press.

Skinner, B. F. (1969). *Contingencies of reinforcement: A theoretical analysis.* Englewood Cliffs, NJ: Prentice Hall.

Smith, R. E. (2005). *Human resources administration: A school-based perspective.* Larchmont, NY: Eye on Education.

Starcke, A. M. (1996). Building a better orientation program. *HR Magazine, 41*(1), 107–114.

Stum, D. L. (1998). Five ingredients for an employee retention formula. *HR Focus, 75*(9), S9–S12.

Travers, C. J. (2001). Stress in teaching: Past, present, and future. In J. Dunham (Ed.), *Stress in the workplace* (chapter 8). London: Whurr.

Unicomb, R., Alley, J., Avery, P., & Barak, L. (1992). Teacher absenteeism: A study of short-term teacher absenteeism in nine Nova Scotia schools which shows that teachers are absent significantly less than workers in other professions. *Education Canada, 32*(2), 33–37.

Vroom, V. H. (1964). *Work and motivation.* New York: Wiley.

Whitaker, K. (2000, May). Where are the principal candidates? Perceptions of superintendents. *NASSP Bulletin, 85*(625), 82–92.

Young, I. P. (2008). *The human resource function in educational administration* (9th ed.). Upper Saddle River, NJ: Pearson, Merrill Prentice Hall.

CHAPTER 7

The Staff Development and Performance Evaluation Processes

Learning Objectives

After reading this chapter, you will be able to

- Describe the importance of the staff development process in relation to its link to the achievement of school district goals and its relation to serving the needs and interest of employees.
- Utilize an operational model for the implementation of an effective staff development program in a school or school district setting.
- Identify and describe several strategies for providing professional development opportunities for school staff personnel.
- Understand the important considerations in developing and implementing staff development programs for adult learners.
- Implement a mentoring relationship with a teacher or administrator.
- Describe the importance of the performance evaluation process for improving the internal operations and overall effectiveness of the school system.

Staff development in education has come to be viewed as indispensable if the goals of the organization are to be realized and the need dispositions of the employees are to be met. According to studies from management consultants the largest single factor driving job satisfaction is the opportunity for growth and career development (Bathurst, 2007). The staff development process in education has many facets as evidenced by the numerous terms in the literature that name the process. Such terms include professional growth, in-service education, continuing education, recurrent education, on-the-job staff training, human resources development, staff improvement, renewal, talent management, and other combinations of these terms.

Harris (1989) attempted to differentiate between and among the terms *staff development, staffing, in-service training,* and *advanced preparation.* He viewed the term *staff development* as embracing much more than *in-service education.* One component of staff development, according to Harris, is staffing, which includes several of the human resources processes (i.e., selecting, inducting, assigning, developing, evaluating, etc.). The other side of staff development includes two kinds of training, in-service education and advanced preparation. In-service training is considered to be any planned program provided for the purposes of improving the skills and knowledge of employees on the job. For Harris, however, advanced preparation differs from in-service in terms of its goals and objectives, which are intended to anticipate future needs of the school system or needs brought about by changes in workplace assignments.

For the purposes of this text, **staff development** is defined as the process of providing opportunities for employees to improve their knowledge, skills, and performance in line with the goals and values of the organization and in relation to the interests and needs of the employee. This definition submits that the growth of employee development must be linked to the school district's strategic plan and to the short- and long-range workforce assets. Such a concept requires an ability to anticipate gaps in the knowledge and skills of the workforce and how the changing school system's demographics, economic status, and present employee inventory will impact the accomplishment of stated goals and objectives. In this sense, staff development places an emphasis on organizational learning and is provided at the identified time of need either by the organization, by an employee group, or by the individual worker. It emphasizes the premise that organizations will progress to the extent that people grow and develop.

The term *staff development* generally is preferred to the term *training* in professional fields, although definitions of the two terms often are quite similar in the literature. For example, as previously noted, Harris speaks of staff development as having two kinds of training, one of which is in-service training. Among the trends in human resources administration today is tying staff development to the motivation, deployment, and alignment of people within the system to increase the system's productivity. A relatively new term for this relationship is ***talent management.*** The fact that organizations will realize greater personnel performance by developing and using the strengths of its human assets rather than focusing on their weaknesses is a concept developed by Clifton and Nelson in their work, *Soar With Your Strengths* (1996).

Historically, staff development has been a reactive program. The inadequacies in the preparation of teachers before 1900 and many years thereafter required major remediation programs. As early as 1882, Bloss noted in his annual report to the Governor of Indiana, that "The fact that so large a portion of the teachers are inexperienced is not the only difficulty, since the statistics for the past three years show . . . the majority of teachers licensed to teach are by no means the most competent" (p. 156). In fact, the need to provide the "missing education" for the ill-prepared teachers dominated in-service programs in most school districts during much of the first half of the twentieth century. Such motivation unfortunately continues in many schools today. As a result, participants in such programs often approach in-service with little motivation and considerable passivity.

Staff development must be proactive rather than reactive; its effectiveness depends on the extent to which it is personalized and based on positive constructs. It is not that concern for deficiencies in staff preparation and the need to update skills are not appropriate concerns of staff development; rather, remediation should not assume the dominant role. The human resources planning process must project and predict as accurately as possible the human skills and talents necessary to meet system needs in the immediate and long-range future. Armed with this information, along with important ongoing recommendations from building-level personnel, staff development joins other personnel processes to build the human resources necessary to keep the school system alive and vital. These program activities become cooperative endeavors that account for personal interest as well as for local building and organizational program needs.

The position taken in this text is that staff development is self-development. Each individual must assume the primary responsibility for his or her continuous personal growth. When this occurs, a school system truly begins to demonstrate the characteristics of a learning organization whereby the needs in the system are readily identified by the system personnel and the personnel initiate steps to correct or improve the identified concerns.

This discussion of staff development, then, is based primarily on the following concepts:

1. The staff development process is developmental in that its emphasis is on a continuously growing individual. In this sense, staff development is an ongoing process as opposed to a one-time project. It focuses on projected needs and objectives that will help the school system remain creative and productive. Individual growth that meets these projected needs provides employees with a personalized opportunity to reach higher levels of self-fulfillment and gratification. Staff development is viewed as an important investment in the school system's future.

2. Effective staff development places greater emphasis on the extension of personal strengths and creative talents than on the remediation of personal weaknesses. The major focus of growth is on what the individual can do and how these strengths can be further developed and used.

As mentioned above, effective staff development is self-development. Growth is personal in the sense that what motivates each individual is a personal matter and each person's self-image is instrumental in determining what incentives will encourage personal growth. Staff development is self-development in that growth begins with a personal need, and individuals develop by being willing to take responsibility for their own personal growth. This concept does not mean that personal development is not to be enhanced through the support of others, but that personal growth is mainly an intrinsic rather than an extrinsic phenomenon.

Staff development, from the foregoing perspectives, can be illustrated through the concepts of the Getzels-Guba (1957) social systems model. Each individual employee has unique need dispositions based on personality factors. The institution has certain expectations for the purposes of the organization and what it desires from each employee. The areas of agreement between personal needs and institutional expectations for the employee constitute areas of high potential for progress. As illustrated in Figure 7.1, as each person realizes new knowledge and skills, new and broadened aspirations of development become possible. Through the use of effective motivation and a system of rewards related to improved performance, personal development becomes an ongoing, continuous process.

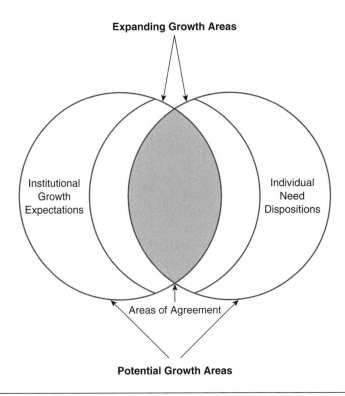

Figure 7.1   Professional Growth: Areas of Agreement and Areas for Potential Growth

The Purposes of Staff Development

The important purposes of the staff development process can be summarized as follows:

1. To provide planned staff development opportunities that provide the learning necessary to enable the employee to perform at the level of competency required in current and future position assignments.

2. To foster a climate that facilitates personal self-fulfillment, institutional effectiveness, human creativity, and system renewal.

3. To serve the school system's primary goals: enhancing and achieving quality teaching and learning for students.

4. To save money. It is costly to hire and then dismiss employees who do not work out. It also is costly to lose good employees because they are frustrated by the lack of opportunity for professional growth. It is wasteful to accept barely satisfactory work as the norm (NSBA, 1996). It also is wasteful not to provide opportunities that lead toward the objective of optimal development on the part of each individual.

5. To establish viable and meaningful programs that enable system personnel to work cooperatively toward achieving the system's goals and their own personal goals in the areas of achievement, satisfaction, and self-fulfillment.

Trends in Professional Staff Development

Several changes in the approaches to staff development have become evident, both conceptually and in practice. Several of these practices or trends are noted in the following comparative statements. Staff development has moved:

- Away from in-service training toward staff development as talent management.
- Away from staff development as a single event toward staff development as a continuous process.
- Away from a focus on remediation toward a process of building on personal strengths.
- Away from sporadic and uncoordinated activities toward the planning and utilization of systematic strategies that center on defined objectives.
- Away from a singular focus toward a multiple approach with varied programs and leadership strategies.
- Away from a passive approach toward a proactive approach based on personal initiative and professional interests.
- Away from staff development as an isolated activity toward staff development activities linked with other human resources processes.
- Away from limited control and evaluation toward both self- and system-evaluation and control.

Several trends are revealed in the foregoing staff development changes. For example, there is a clear indication that staff development has become an expected, ongoing process. Individual initiative and motivation serve important roles in the determination of successful staff development activities.

Operational Procedures for Staff Development

The operational procedures for the staff development process progress through a series of five steps: (1) adopt a guiding policy for staff development; (2) develop a statement of program goals and objectives; (3) plan the program activities, encourage collaborative participation, provide delivery systems, and determine program responsibilities; (4) implement program activities, schedule and deliver plans and programs that encourage personal initiative for individual growth activities; and (5) evaluate the staff development process and implement appropriate changes. Each of these steps is discussed in the following section.

Step 1. The guiding policy for staff development is adopted as an official school board action that establishes the goals of the program. Policy is used by the school district staff to determine specific procedures through which to implement the program throughout the school system.

An example of a board of education staff development policy is as follows:

> The board of education supports the principle of continuous personal growth and development for all personnel employed in the school district. Such development programs and activities that serve to enhance the goals and objectives of the school district and to meet the immediate and future needs of district personnel should be made available through cooperative planning and implementation by members of the school district staff. A variety of programs and delivery methods is encouraged, which provide opportunities for employees to meet professional interests and needs and foster personal initiative toward the goal of self-development.

The general responsibility for the administration of the staff development program belongs to the school superintendent who delegates program responsibilities among the staff as appropriate and who recommends, with proper input from employees, minimal requirements for development to meet changing certification requirements, to adjust to program changes, and to gain the future knowledge and skills necessary to ensure the viability of human resources in the district.

This policy sets the guidelines for the administrative discretion necessary for its implementation. It emphasizes the need for development programs that relate directly to the strategic plans of the school system and its goals and objectives. Such major administrative considerations as minimal requirements, needs assessments, program activities, implementation procedures, incentives, and resources are concerns primarily of the school district personnel. Staff development is a shared responsibility, with local school personnel assuming much of the responsibility for program design and implementation. The extent to which the central human resources unit assumes major responsibility for staff development is a function of the individual school district. Nevertheless, effective staff development is not viewed as something that the school or school district does to the individual, rather the district sets the stage for a variety of opportunities for employee growth.

Step 2. Step 2 of the operational procedure includes creating goals and objectives for staff development relative to identified system and employee needs and interests. In-service programs that focus on the immediate, realistic, personal needs and local school problems are likely to be more effective than others. Further, programs that consider both the interests and needs of the organization's personnel and the needs of the organization provide an important organizational balance in staff development.

Step 3. Step 3 links closely with Step 2. Programs, activities, and delivery systems must be planned and programmed with the individual employee in mind. Both school and individual responsibilities must be determined. Ideally, school systems should have a unit/department whose primary responsibility is staff development. School district size, governance structure, and other factors, however, determine the extent to which this recommendation is possible. Sometimes the human resources unit or instructional unit serves the purpose of program coordination. In other instances, participants of a team teaching program might assume the responsibility for their own professional development. In any case, the need for close cooperation and mutual sharing of program activities and responsibilities is important for program success.

Step 4. Step 4 puts the plans and program options into place. The activities, experiences, learning programs, and personal initiatives are made available and implemented. Staff development activities are both formal and informal. They include workshops, conferences, peer teaching, mentoring, independent study activities, assessment methodology, internships, job rotation, college courses, think tanks, e-learning technology, and other program pursuits. Selected program options are presented briefly in the next section of this chapter.

Step 5. Step 5, evaluation of the staff development process, focuses on the assessments necessary to judge the extent to which the stated goals for the program are being met. As emphasized throughout this text, programs such as staff development increasingly will be called upon to show the "return on investment." That is, what hard data were gathered that demonstrate the contribution of the staff development program to the bottom line of school and/or school district goals and objectives? For example, to what extent did a specific staff development program result in the implementation of improved instructional methodology in the classroom? Did the program result in improved student achievement outcomes?

The RPTIM Model for Staff Development

The RPTIM model for staff development, created by Woods, Thompson, and Russell (1981) more than 20 years ago, remains as one of the most comprehensive models for effective staff development. This model conceptualizes staff development into five stages and 38 practices. The 38 practices within each stage of the RPTIM model are research based, and the National Development Council and the

Council of Professors of Instructional Supervision endorse these as practices that should serve as the basis for effective staff development in schools (see Figure 7.2).

The five stages of the RPTIM model are (1) readiness, (2) planning, (3) training, (4) implementation, and (5) maintenance. Each stage focuses on several practices. For example, the readiness stage centers on the development of a positive climate before the staff development activities are attempted. Activities associated with this stage include the establishment of goals for future program improvement, current school practices and those practices not yet found in the school are examined to determine which ones are congruent with the school's goals for improvement before staff development activities are planned, the collaborative writing of goals for school improvement, assessments of group or individual motivation regarding the proposed program, and the determination of the leadership and support needed.

When readiness is considered to be at a high level, specific planning activities are implemented. Although planning is inextricably tied to the goals and objectives of the HR function and the school district as a whole, different plans for various development activities are designed. The planning stage includes such activities as the examination of differences between desired and actual practices in the school to identify staff development needs, the learning styles of participants are considered, specific objectives of various staff development activities are determined, and the leadership is shared among teaching and administrative personnel.

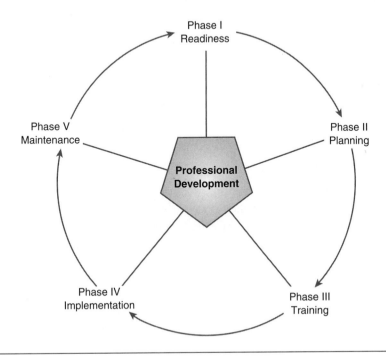

Figure 7.2   The RPTIM Model of Professional Development

SOURCE: Wood, F. H., Thompson, S. R., & Russell, F. (1981). Designing effective staff development programs. In B. Dillon-Peterson (Ed.), *Staff development/organization development*. Alexandria, VA: Association for Supervision and Curriculum Development.

The training of personnel relative to the required delivery methods required in the program as well as the actual staff development activities is then completed. Individual staff personnel choose objectives for their own professional learning. Leaders of staff development activities are determined according to their expertise and, as the individual or group becomes increasingly confident in their abilities, they assume more responsibility for their own development. The application or implementation of the new training is put into practice. Resources are allocated to support the implementation of new practices and work behaviors. School staff personnel use peer collaboration to assist one another in implementing new work behaviors.

As a final step in the RPTIM process, evaluations of procedures and program outcomes are assessed and changes are recorded for the purpose of improving future staff development efforts. In the maintenance stage, a systematic program of instructional supervision is used to monitor and support new work behavior. The results relative to new practices and behaviors are assessed through a variety of methods, which include changes in student behavior and achievement. Other methods and strategies for staff development are discussed in the following section.

Staff Development Methods and Strategies

The comprehensiveness of the staff development process and the variety of approaches utilized to achieve its purposes have been described in numerous publications. This section presents a description of several approaches to staff development, including the use of consultants, mentoring, coaching, quality circles, teacher centers, assessment centers, career development planning, clinical supervision, personnel appraisal methods, taskforce and shadow groups, job rotation, and peer-assisted leadership. Other development activities not discussed here, but that are somewhat self-explanatory, include college and university course work, sabbaticals, exchange teaching, conferences and conventions, and the reading of professional journals and materials (NSBA, 1996).

Consultants

There are various ways to help individuals and groups improve professionally. Consultants, mentors, and coaches are available to help as particular personnel needs are identified. Consultants focus on answering the question, "What do you need to know?" A consultant could be an internal or external specialist called upon to impart needed skills or knowledge that will move the school's program toward a particular goal. Generally the consultant is trained in a relatively narrow field of expertise and sees his/her role as a teacher who has a specific method or special knowledge, which can be taught, applied, and tested. Consultants frequently offer diagnostic tests following the consultancy that serve to measure one's level of professional proficiency in a particular field. For example, a consultant might be used to develop qualified teacher performance evaluators. Following the training experience, the knowledge and skills gained by each participant might be tested by having them evaluate the performance of a practicing teacher and then having their completed performance evaluation report compared with those of other experienced, qualified evaluators.

Coaching

Coaches serve to help answer the question, "Where do you want to go?" Through the use of key listening techniques, coaches help guide the individual as he/she focuses on a desired career direction. By listening and asking key questions and encouraging action toward the individual's goal, the coach acts as a cheerleader by focusing on the present and future rather than on the past. Although coaches most often work with individuals on a one-to-one basis, there are team coaches who work with school teams such as assistant principals or teams of support personnel. An individual might work with a coach for a few months and find success or might choose to work with the coach over a longer period of time to gain ongoing insight into the individual's career.

Coaching and Mentoring

Coaching and mentoring are terms often used synonymously, although there are differences between these two strategies. **Mentoring** generally refers to the art of helping to steer a subordinate or a colleague in the same field. **Coaching**, on the other hand, uses techniques for professionals or clients in a full range of backgrounds (A. Allegra, personal communication, 2005). For instance, a qualified coach might not only counsel professionals within their own occupational specialty, but also may be prepared to work with individuals in a variety of fields. Through the use of a combination of education, cheerleading, and listening, the coach may help an individual to think about certain important questions and then help him or her in answering them. Such queries could include the following:

- What challenges and problems am I facing now?
- What opportunities are available to me right now?
- What I am grateful for this week?
- What didn't I get done, but intended to do?
- What do I want this coaching call to accomplish?

Such broad queries inevitably lead to specifics, which the coach then discusses in relation to the person's career and special interests. A coach might help a person develop and implement worthy goals, provide feedback or listen to feedback, help a person think through alternative solutions, give personal counsel, provide support and encouragement, help develop priorities, give career information, help the person identify and implement personal strengths, or suggest improvements in the area of personal relations. Quite often, an individual brings a specific problem facing him/her to a coach with hope of finding a solution. A coach can be someone internal or external to the organization in which the individual is employed. The following operational model provides guidelines for dealing with the problem at hand.

Step 1. Discussion of the problem. Although the individual in this case initiated the contact with the coach and indicated that a problem did indeed exist, the coach and the individual use problem analysis techniques to help clarify the problem and ascertain if the problem, as defined by the individual, is indeed the problem that really exists.

Step 2. Once there is some agreement concerning the nature of the problem, both the coach and the individual consider the wisdom of various options available for resolving the problem. Each option is viewed in terms of its perceived pluses and minuses.

Step 3. The coach and the individual consider the preferred option for solution and reach a mutual understanding of follow-up procedures for its implementation. They then determine the best timing for implementing the first steps of the preferred option.

Step 4. Depending on the case at hand, a follow-up session to assess the results is determined. The coach gives positive feedback regarding the successful behaviors demonstrated by the individual. Coaching can reinforce the good work of an employee and build self-confidence toward a goal of self-development.

Mentoring. Mentoring assumes a variety of forms in staff development. As Smith (2005) points out, "Developmental relationships such as between a mentor teacher and a protégé can be powerful stimuli for change and learning. Research indicates that mentors as well as beginning teachers find that the program enhances their classroom abilities, increases their enthusiasm for teaching, and that they experience positive results involving their teaching, professional growth, and impact on the profession" (p. 141).

Antonio Allegra (personal communication, 2006) states that a mentor helps one to answer the question, "How can you best network?" That is, mentors work with individuals in a given field of expertise. They offer their experience, expertise, and friendship to help others who seek inner knowledge of the art of a particular niche of professional education. Several functions of a mentor include: (1) developing an improved self-esteem on the part of the protégé, (2) teaching specific management skills related to effective teaching or administration, (3) serving as a role model for the protégé, (4) encouraging the protégé's personal and professional growth through effective feedback and personal support, (5) helping the protégé to develop a plan for continuous professional growth and development, (6) helping the protégé to gain an understanding of the social and political environments in which the profession of teaching takes place, and (7) providing appropriate program activities for the protégé that result in opportunities to assume new and challenging responsibilities.

The mentor-protégé relationship is a rewarding endeavor that enhances each person's career. Both the mentor and the protégé learn more about themselves, improve their personal skills, and gain professional recognition. Bush (2005) commented that Carla Snyder, a Vice President for Career Services in Scottsdale, Arizona, recommends that personnel should volunteer as a mentor within an organization.

Offering a few hours of your time each week or month to a junior employee pays dividends. Besides helping to meet people outside your department, mentoring signals to company executives that you are a motivated, enthusiastic team player. . . . By mentoring a worker in a different area of the company, you can also broaden your awareness of the company's scope. (p. ED1)

Mentoring has several specific purposes: (1) to improve the quality of teaching and leadership in the school system, (2) to develop a pool of well-qualified professional teacher and administrative personnel, (3) to provide an on-the-job professional development opportunity for certificated and classified system personnel, (4) to create linkages between theory and practice in school leadership at all levels, and (5) to recognize the expertise of experienced teacher and administrator personnel in the school system.

Primary Phases of a Mentoring Relationship

During phase 1 of the mentoring relationship, several activities are implemented for the purpose of fostering a bonding relationship between the mentor and the protégé. Phase 1 begins by the mentor and protégé sharing background information and discussing the expectations of both parties. The strengths and areas of need on the part of the protégé are identified, and related goals and the protégé's objectives are established. An emphasis is given to the development of a talent development plan (TDP) for the protégé that sets forth potential development opportunities. It is important to have a focus in the mentoring process; one cannot merely "wing it" and accomplish important ends. The TDP serves to help the protégé determine where he or she wants to go and what he or she hopes to accomplish. The TDP is carefully reviewed and clarified, and the mentor and protégé reach an agreement regarding its implementation.

Phase 2 of the mentoring relationship centers on the actual implementation of the TDP. During this phase, the mentor observes the protégé's behavior in a variety of situations, listens to the protégé's analysis of his or her own behavior and concerns, and gives behaviorally specific feedback as fits the case at hand. For example, the mentor might reinforce the protégé's effective behavior and achievements, offer suggestions for referencing ineffective behavior, or merely listen to the protégé talk and reflect on his or her own personal behavior. As extensions of phase 2, the mentor might share understandings of the organizational structure of the school system, including its culture and subcultures. It often is appropriate to introduce the protégé to other experienced teachers or administrators as necessary.

The final phase, phase 3, centers on the cultivating of a collegial relationship on the part of the protégé and other teachers and educational leaders. The protégé is encouraged to continue to participate in challenging professional development activities through mutual professional support and sharing with others in the school system and educational profession.

Mentor Qualifications

Arguably, a major reason that all too many mentoring activities are ineffective is that the person assigned to serve as the mentor is ill-prepared to do so. Teaching and/or administrator experience alone does not guarantee mentoring success. There are six knowledge and competency areas that practicing mentors of new teachers should possess, the six Ts: training in mentoring, teaching experience, technical know-how, tact in mentoring, teaching of adults, and time commitment.

Training in the methodology of mentoring is of paramount importance. Successful mentors understand that mentoring is a planned, developmental process that takes place over a period of time. They have a good understanding of the procedures related to the protégé's TDP as described in the following section of this chapter.

We submit that teaching experience provides the mentor with a better understanding of the needs of teachers new to the profession and the problems that most new personnel encounter at the outset of their career.

Technical know-how in educational methodology for effective teaching and student learning can serve the mentor in many ways.

Mentors must use tact when working with a diverse population of teaching personnel. Caring, patience, and confidentiality are among those interpersonal skills most important for developing positive mentor-protégé relationships.

As this chapter discusses in some detail, adult learners view learning experiences in unique ways. For example, they seek new knowledge and skills that can be applied to practice. Adult learners are motivated by those experiences that use their personal strengths and provide opportunities for self-direction and personal initiative. Mentors should have a good knowledge of these and other adult learning purposes as they work with protégés who are motivated by gaining new knowledge and skills for success in the classroom.

Perhaps one of the most difficult problems facing the implementation of effective mentoring programs is that of time commitments. Successful mentoring requires the use of valuable time on the part of those persons who most often are already among the busiest people in the organization. However, just as the school system must provide time for staff development opportunities on an ongoing basis, so must the school arrange for time for talented mentors to work effectively. In the long run, the protégé, the mentor, and the school system benefit in terms of personal and organizational achievement.

The TDP in the Mentoring Process

Because the TDP plays such an important part in guiding an individual's professional and personal growth, the steps in its development and implementation are discussed further in the following section. There are four primary steps in the TDP as follows: Step 1, establishing the mentor-protégé relationship; Step 2, preparing the protégé to work on the TDP; Step 3, identifying talent development areas; and Step 4, establishing goals and objectives and determining an action plan.

Step 1: Establishing the Mentor-Protégé Relationship. As previously stated, establishing a positive mentor/protégé relationship is of paramount importance. At the first meeting, the mentor and protégé discuss the purpose and value of mentoring. The mentor shares the highlights of his or her professional experience and why he or she has chosen to be a mentor. The mentor specifies ways in which he or she will be able to assist the protégé in his or her talent development program. The several phases of the mentoring relationship are outlined, and any special features of the school system's mentoring policies and features are explained. The protégé is asked to describe what he or she would like to accomplish in the mentoring relationship. The protégé is encouraged to ask any questions about the mentoring program or about the mentor-protégé relationships.

Step 2: Preparing the Protégé to Work on the TDP. The mentor discusses the purposes and structure of a TDP with the protégé, emphasizing that, although the mentor will be readily available to provide suggestions and to answer questions, the protégé is responsible for developing the individual talent development program in relation to personal strengths and interests. Recommendations for assessing personal strengths are set forth, and the mentor suggests an approach for working on the TDP (e.g., collecting related information such as a personal resume, assessments, reports, work samples, performance evaluations, etc.). It is important to emphasize the need to schedule uninterrupted blocks of time to give thought to the development of the TDP.

The first meeting should be closed on a positive note that includes the determination of the protégé's understanding of the purpose of the TDP and questions related to the process of completing a strengths and needs analysis. A discussion of the time and place for the next meeting, the agenda for the second meeting, and the responsibilities of the mentor and protégé for the next meeting are clarified. Communication information is exchanged and the meeting is closed on a positive note that includes the mentor's mention of his or her enthusiasm about being a mentor and the growth opportunities the talent program provides for the protégé.

Step 3: Identifying Talent Development Areas. Through the use of appropriate questions and probes, the protégé is helped to use what he or she learned from preparing the TDP background information to identify personal strengths and areas for development. Questions may include the following: "What was your overall reaction as you considered your background of experiences, performance evaluations, and assessment instruments? How do your strengths and needs for improvement impact on your job performance? How do they relate to your professional development?" The mentor uses active listening to determine how the protégé ties strengths and needs to his or her development on the job. Can the protégé give examples of effective and ineffective behavior as related to teacher or administrator skill dimensions and professional knowledge?

In order to help the protégé identify on-the-job issues that are key to his or her effectiveness as a teacher or administrator, the mentor might ask directly, "What are some primary issues related to your job?" The mentor listens in order to determine the protégé's ability to identify and articulate important issues and how well he or she is able to make a connection between the level of effectiveness and their level of development. Can he or she identify behaviors that are important for dealing successfully with particular issues? Can he or she relate his or her identified strengths to potential behaviors that might serve to deal with the identified issues?

After listening to the protégé's remarks, the mentor gives feedback on his or her responses to specific questions. Feedback commonly takes the form of a developmental question: "What specific personal skills do you think were most often revealed in the answers that you provided?" The mentor's purpose is to allow the protégé to give thought to the relationship between his or her personal skills and behavioral responses rather than having the mentor provide this insight.

Step 4: Establishing the TDP Goals and Objectives and Determining an Action Plan. During the activities related in Step 3, the TDP goals are established and an action plan to implement the goals is determined. The protégé identifies a limited number of skill dimensions and key behaviors that he or she chooses to highlight in the TDP. The mentor and protégé review the value of the development of personal strengths and note special needs that require attention. The mentor asks the protégé to discuss the rationale for the goals and objectives that they have selected and listens for whether the protégé incorporates identified strengths, interests, and needs in the goal statement. If not, why not? In addition, the priorities of the protégé are examined in relation to the goals and objectives set forth.

At this point, the development of an action plan for implementing the stated goals is necessary. How the protégé plans to pursue his or her TDP goals and objectives while working on job-related concerns and interests is determined. The protégé is asked to identify resources he or she has identified to help accomplish the intended objectives. What will be done? How will it be done? Who will be involved? Where will it be done? When will it be done? How will it be monitored and evaluated?

The mentor helps determine if the action plan has been carefully thought out. Is the plan ready for implementation? Is there a plan for monitoring and evaluating progress? How will the mentor and protégé continue to work together?

Ebmeier (2000) found that school principals influence the personal efficacy of teachers by providing improvement assistance through mentoring and praise. Such factors as confidence, commitment, and satisfaction are obtained primarily by the extent to which teachers believe the principal is interested in and is actually supportive of teaching. The interaction between the mentor and the classroom teacher, exemplified by effective mentoring techniques, is perceived as administrative support by the teacher and can lead to improved teaching and innovative practices.

A mentor in education uses similar strategies, and although advice and guidance are offered as appropriate to the case, helping the individual teacher think through a situation toward the goal of self-resolution of the problem or question is foremost. Thus, active listening techniques serve significant purposes. It should be noted that both mentoring and coaching sessions frequently take place through distance methods such as the use of the telephone or e-mail.

Assume that a teacher is having serious problems with organizing and presenting effective teaching lessons. The mentor, in this case, might initiate a session by asking the teacher to describe the planning process being used to develop each lesson. The mentor might ask, "How do you determine the objectives for each lesson, and how are these objectives supported in follow-up learning activities?" During this time, the mentor serves as a listener, and the teacher is the speaker. Clues about short-term unit objectives and their relationship to the school's instructional goals can be assessed from the teacher's responses. If it is determined that the development of classroom objectives and learning experiences for students are in need of attention, the mentor can assist the teacher in the process of planning a well-designed daily lesson.

In some cases, depending upon the situation at hand, mentors might go through any number of exercises with the teacher: working on lesson planning, role playing the actual introduction to a planned lesson, suggesting follow-up activities such as observing other teachers at work, recommending appropriate readings, or critiquing a proposed lesson plan with a follow-up classroom observation.

The emphasis in mentoring should be that of providing a positive experience for both the mentor and the teacher or administrator. Ultimately, the goal is to have the protégé seek such collaboration and become enthusiastic about the potential of self-improvement.

Empirical evidence has shown that individuals can shift from an area of weakness to one of strength, from a lack of confidence to personal self-confidence. Thus, mentoring can result in changes of behavior: hesitant innovators can become more creative in their instructional approaches, and poor disciplinarians can develop into the classroom authorities that they were but didn't know it.

In summary, a mentor is selected to work with an individual staff member or small group of members for the purpose of personal growth and continuous networking. The mentor becomes the primary counselor and (1) ascertains the special areas of interest and need regarding the protégé's personal development; (2) works with the protégé to design the most viable plan for individual growth; (3) assesses the most appropriate resources for meeting growth objectives, including other mentors in the network; and (4) serves as a sounding board and constructive critic in evaluating progress and commitment. The need for a nonthreatening relationship and personal confidence is foremost.

Quality Circles

Quality circles originated in Japan, where small groups participate actively in planning, designing, and implementing work procedures in business and industry. The use of quality circles for staff development in education is a technique that places the primary responsibility for personal growth on individuals linked together for the improvement of teaching and student learning. Members of a circle might include the teaching and support staff of one unit of a multiunit elementary school, the teachers within a department of mathematics in a local school, a group of primary grade level teachers in a local school, foreign language teachers from several schools within a district, or others whose common work interests or personal growth objectives can be enhanced through cooperative activities.

Quality circles generally are established and operated within the following guidelines:

1. The circle members focus on an area or program of instruction that is determined to be important to the school's objectives and to their personal interests. The members identify areas of special need, sources of knowledge, and skill development. Individual members, or the group as a whole, determine responsibilities for personal learning. At times, individuals serve as resource persons for all group members. Members determine responsibilities for teaching subject area content.

2. A variety of methods and procedures can provide practice of the skills and knowledge required to implement the desired program or teaching methodology. Modeling, simulation, observation, and video techniques provide opportunities to practice in classroom and nonclassroom settings.

3. Constructive feedback is provided through a systematic procedure of self-evaluation and group review.

4. Specific provision is made for implementing the behaviors or methods desired. Mentoring, peer counseling, or coaching is structured through a system that places primary responsibility for improvement on the individual, with full support of the circle members.

Quality circles can serve several important purposes and provide numerous benefits to the system and its human resources, including the following:

1. The development of new knowledge and skills to enhance present and future job performance, as viewed by staff members themselves.

2. The establishment of the individual's responsibility for personal development through a process of "team mentoring" and individual leadership. That is, the group itself determines its development interests and needs and delegates various individuals to take the leadership in these areas of development.

3. The promotion of personal motivation and work satisfaction through opportunities for achievement, relevant growth, and appropriate rewards for improved performance.

4. The improvement of personal performance and work quality to meet school goals and objectives that have been established by consensus.

5. The general improvement of staff communication, human relationships, and trust through opportunities to be a member of the local school and school district teams and to be a significant member of the decision-making process.

Teacher Centers

Another way to place the primary responsibility for personal development on the individual teacher is through the teacher center, an enriched environment of resources, personal involvement, and peer communication. The teacher center concept makes the teacher an active participant in decisions and activities relating to personal growth. A teacher center need not be a permanent site or facility, but conceptually constitutes a teaching resource bank where teachers informally participate in activities that enhance their performance in the classroom. Teachers, alone or in groups with similar interests, examine instructional materials, design teaching aids, read materials on teaching methods and strategies, develop new lesson plans, and communicate with other teachers and support personnel concerning creative ideas in an area of instructional interest. Based on the proposition that professional staff personnel are best qualified to determine the necessary training needed by their colleagues, the teacher center concept is governed primarily by teachers.

A teacher center might be a temporary site, such as a school district's reading center, used for a specified period of time for a specific instructional development purpose. It might be a self-contained room with a professional library, film and visual materials, a work design area for making instructional aids, and other resource banks available for examination and classroom use. In those school districts that have established extensive educational facilities for teaching and learning centers, facilities for examining instructional technology of various kinds, computer facilities, curriculum resource banks, research libraries, conference and workshop rooms, instructional design facilities, media resources, and support staff personnel are available for teacher and staff use. Not all activities in a teacher center are informal. Teachers generally give high ratings to specific workshops, designed to develop new teaching concepts and skills.

The positive aspects of teacher centers are numerous. The concept of teachers helping teachers is supported by research. Intrinsic motivation that leads to personal development activities is one important criterion for proactive growth. One concern, however, is the possible absence of research-based development programs. Conceptual frameworks founded on tested theory, research, and empirical applications are essential. If the delivery system for staff development depends exclusively on individual opinions of "effective practice," the potential exists for misdirected effort and practice.

Assessment Centers

Assessment center techniques were first adopted by the military as well as business and industry to select and promote administrative personnel. In education, the first use of assessment centers was also in personnel selection—the selection of school administrators. As we previously noted, beginning in the 1970s, the National Association of Secondary School Principals (NASSP) assumed a major leadership role in the development of assessment techniques to select school principals. Since then, assessment center methodology has proven beneficial to assess performance in teacher and administrator preparation programs and in staff development.

In a typical assessment center, participants work through tasks designed to elicit behavior considered important for the job involved. Assessors observe the process and take notes, using specially designed observation forms . . .

assessors compare observations and make a final evaluation of each candidate for that exercise. At the end of the process, the assessors develop a summary report on each candidate. (Brown, 1992, p. 35)

Such a center is not a fixed physical location; rather, assessment activities are conducted in various settings, whenever and wherever a qualified group of assessors meets to assess the performance of an individual or group of individuals for a stated reason.

An assessment center is characterized by several activities:

1. Behaviors and skills, determined to be relevant to a specific job, are assessed through standard methods and activities.

2. Multiple assessment techniques are utilized to gain performance data, such as interviews, leaderless group activities, individual task exercises, in-basket simulation, pencil-and-paper tests, personality tests, and other simulation exercises.

3. A group of assessors participates in the evaluation procedures. Such individuals are specifically trained and certified in the methods used and the procedures followed.

4. Information and individual assessor results are pooled through a process of "jurying" that leads to a final consensus of performance results.

5. If the assessment is for staff development purposes, the person assessed receives a system of thorough feedback.

Mentoring, in particular, appears to have considerable potential as a growth model in conjunction with assessment methodology. One major advantage of such a relational approach is its potential for personalizing the growth process by the professional involvement of a specially selected mentor who works with a protégé on the strengths and needs as revealed in assessment results.

Assessment centers can also play a major role in the preparation of school administrators. The assessment center method can be used to both diagnose students' entrance and exit competencies and assess the effectiveness of the preparation program (Sirotnik & Durden, 1996; Wendel & Uerling, 1989).

Some authorities consider behavioral assessment methods, such as seeing how a potential employee acts in a given situation, to be a better measure of abilities than an interview or even a pencil-and-paper test. Some HR administrators view simulations, although expensive and time-consuming, as a more reliable predictor of effective performance than other traditional screening methods. Although some researchers would not support this contention, the fact is that assessment center methodology, such as the use of in-basket and role-playing exercises, does provide effective ways to assess administration and teaching skills through simulations of on-the-job situations. Among the primary benefits of assessment center methodology are (1) the use of multiple assessors serves to reduce the possibility of rater bias; (2) candidates demonstrate their knowledge and competency through involvement in several different activities and exercises (e.g., in-basket exercises, leaderless group exercises, assigned role exercises, etc.); (3) all candidates perform the same exercises or activities, and all have a fair opportunity to excel; (4) a wide variety of administrative skills can be assessed (e.g., problem analysis, leadership, organizational ability, oral and written skills, human relations skills, and others); and (5) research has demonstrated that assessments center methodology is among the highest rated methods for job fit.

Clinical Supervision

Effective technical supervision significantly facilitates staff development and maximization of human resources. Clinical supervision emphasizes system-wide instructional improvement through improved staff performance. Assessments provide information relative to the achievement of mutually determined teaching objectives. Clinical supervision is a cyclical procedure.

Step 1. The cooperative relationship between the teacher and supervisor, which is essential to the procedure, is fostered. During this phase, they discuss the nature of clinical supervision, clarify follow-up procedures and responsibilities, specify purposes and focus on development objectives, and discuss uses of classroom observation information.

Step 2. The teacher plans an instructional unit with constructive input by the supervisor. Instructional objectives, teaching methods, instructional materials, monitoring strategies, and other teaching and learning considerations are determined. On the basis of this information, the supervisor and teacher determine the procedures for the actual classroom observation.

Step 3. The focus in this step is on planning the observation procedures. Information on student learning needs or problems as well as the physical setting is collected.

Step 4. The supervisor makes the actual classroom observation. In this step, the agreed on methods for collecting information are implemented. Following the observation, both the supervisor and the teacher examine the recorded information individually to interpret the data relative to the teaching activities that took place and the objectives of the intended lesson.

Step 5. The supervisor incorporates the data collected into the most meaningful and reportable format, which the teacher can readily understand.

Step 6. The supervisor plans the postobservation conference with the teacher. The specifics to be discussed in the conference, the approach to be used, and the conference objectives are established under the terms of the original planning agreement. Strengths and areas for improvement are analyzed for discussion purposes.

Step 7. The postobservation conference provides an opportunity for the teacher and supervisor to review the information collected and evaluate the results in relation to predetermined objectives. The supervisor serves as an instructor, helping the teacher interpret the results of the classroom observation. Through a mutual discussion of actual classroom events, the teacher and supervisor focus on the kinds of changes needed in the follow-up classroom performance to achieve desired learning objectives.

Step 8. The teacher and supervisor plan the next teaching lesson and the behaviors and methods to be implemented in an effort to realize continually improved results. This final step leads to new directions in planning, the reestablishment of the relationship for the future, and the reimplementation of the steps in the **clinical supervision cycle.**

Career Development Planning

Career development planning includes such activities as personal counseling, self-concept and assessment workshops, career opportunity seminars, and close coordination of the organization's human resources processes with employee career aspirations. The work experience and the employee's personal development program are planned to facilitate the individual's career goals in relation to the organization's future human resources needs.

Personnel Appraisal Methods

The organization's appraisal process focuses primarily on gathering formative information that can direct the employee's growth and development. Rather than using summative ratings to determine job continuation, the appraisal process becomes a cooperative procedure that encompasses self-evaluation and mentoring feedback to motivate continuous employee development. A later section of this chapter presents a comprehensive discussion of the performance evaluation process.

Taskforces and Shadow Groups

Service on taskforce groups that focus on the creation of better, more effective methods has viable personal development potential. Representatives from community, administrator, teacher, and student groups concentrate on an educational objective through cooperative problem-solving activity.

Industry especially has benefited from the use of "shadow groups," which generally involve the simulation of an activity by members of the organization. For instance, employees might assume the roles of the governing board members and conduct a board meeting using a proposed future agenda. The process helps management anticipate problems prior to the actual board meeting and gain insight on important employee perspectives on the issues and agenda items. Employee participants and other representatives are able to gain appreciation for the agenda issues, develop a better understanding of the organization's problems, and gain new perspectives about their growth needs in relation to the goals of the organization.

Job Rotation

Industry has experienced success in the practice of moving employees and managers to various positions to enhance organizational effectiveness and employee development. Education has not generally endorsed the practice; however, the idea has received some favorable acceptance as a positive growth practice for school administrators. After a certain time period, both the individual and the organization benefit when the employee can exercise personal talents and meet new challenges in a different assignment. Additionally, experience and knowledge of the different educational units and school programs are spread to more people in the district. Arguments against the practice of job rotation center on the possible disruptive effects it might have on the local school community. Authorities suggest that the practice of job rotation in the future will tie closely to personal competency. That is, the task at hand will determine required skill needs, and personnel will be assigned to such tasks accordingly.

Peer-Assisted Leadership

Peer-assisted leadership (PAL) describes the basic concept of this development process—participants helping other participants in the improvement of their personal skills. In 1983, the instructional management program at the Far West Laboratory in San Francisco established PAL in order to (1) help administrators develop skills that they can use to analyze their own and others' management behaviors, (2) give participants opportunities to learn how other administrators lead in their positions, (3) enable administrators to gain support from colleagues, and (4) provide a means for assisting administrators in the understanding of effective behavior in their specific setting. Since that time, PAL activities have been proven effective with other professional staff personnel. Instruction relative to data collection through interviews, shadowing, reflective interviewing, and advanced reflective interviewing is provided. In early meetings, participants are introduced to the model of the general framework for program leadership. PAL differs from mentoring in that PAL is not a mentor-protégé arrangement. Rather, peers are placed in partnerships or triads, and each participant helps others examine and reflect on personal behaviors, skills, and activities in relation to the school environment, specific skills being implemented, and expected program results. PAL goals include helping participants to develop skills for analyzing personal behavior; enabling participants to gain support and insight from colleagues; and providing participants an opportunity to learn how others lead, teach, and create. Participants of PAL programs report that it serves to increase awareness of their own behavior, style, and intentions. It serves as an important self-evaluation tool and leads to the learning of new strategies and personal skills.

The field of education has numerous methods and strategies for implementing staff development. Although most of the discussion in this chapter has focused on teacher development, such programs as assessment centers, peer-assisted leadership, job rotation, internships, taskforce groups, career development planning, and mentoring apply equally well to administrative personnel. Perhaps the underlying importance of staff development in education is reflected in the basic concept that schools will improve as people progress.

Adults as Learners

Because school system personnel are adult learners, staff development activities must use the basic principles that facilitate optimal learning and growth for them.

An understanding of adults and how they learn is as vital to successful adult professional development as the knowledge of children and adolescents at the K–12 level is to their successful learning. "Knowing who is likely to participate in our programs, why adults choose to participate, and what barriers must be overcome before they can participate is knowledge that educators can put to good use in planning and delivering programs" (Merriam & Brockett, 1997, p. 129).

Research on adult learning has shown that adult learners need

1. To be involved in the determination of their learning activities; they must have a voice in the determination of learning goals, program content, learning experiences, and appropriate evaluations.

2. To be considered as individual learners; each adult brings a varied background of experiences and knowledge to any learning situation. They are activity oriented and need to be actively involved in the learning process.

3. To see the value of the learning experiences; they need to know that the activities and experiences will be applicable to their work and the resolution of problems in their work environment.

4. To see tangible outcomes from the learning activities and experiences; they need to receive some indication of their personal achievement toward learning goals. They are goal oriented and are focused on the accomplishment of specific goals.

Authorities in the area of adult education point to several important differences between **pedagogy**, the art and science of teaching children, and **andragogy**, the art and science of helping adults learn. Knowles and Associates (1984) emphasized four underlying assumptions of andragogy that differ from those of pedagogy and their implications for adult learning.

1. *Regarding the Concept of the Learner.* As the individual grows and matures, his or her self-concept moves from one of dependency to one of increasing self-directedness. The psychological need to be perceived and treated as a person capable of taking responsibility for himself or herself holds important implications for adult learning programs. For example, situations that do not allow the individual to be self-directing tend to produce tension between that situation and the individual's self-concept.

2. *Regarding the Role of the Learner's Experience.* As the adult engages in an ever-expanding variety of experiences, he or she is more able to relate to new learning experiences. Adults enter into an educational activity with both a greater volume and a different quality of experience from youth. New transmittal techniques for adult learners must include an emphasis on experiential strategies that capitalize on the rich resources of experiences of the learner. Thus, the use of active, participative activities such as simulation, discussion, problem solving, and team projects is favored over lectures and other more passive instructional methods.

3. *Regarding Readiness to Learn.* As the individual matures, readiness to learn becomes more dependent on the tasks required for the performance of his or her evolving social role. That is, adult learners are ready to learn because the roles they are approaching or serving set forth the "need." They become ready to learn when they experience a need to know or to do something in order to perform more efficiently. As Knowles and Associates (1984) pointed out, the critical implication of this assumption is the importance of timing learning experiences to coincide with the learner's developmental tasks in social roles as teachers, leaders, organizational members, and so forth.

4. *Regarding Orientation to Learning.* For the most part, adults do not learn for the sake of learning. They learn in order to perform a task, solve a problem, or live in a more satisfying way. Thus, the immediacy of application is a critical learning motivator, and a problem-centered orientation is of primary importance. (Knowles and Associates, 1984, pp. 11–12)

These guidelines for working with adult learners underline specific questions that staff development program personnel must answer: (1) To what extent is the staff development program relevant to learner needs? (2) To what extent has the program been personalized as well as individualized; is there an opportunity for self-direction based on personal needs, problems, and interests? (3) To what extent does the program relate to the background of experience possessed by the learners? (4) To what extent does the program provide for active learning on the part of the learners? (5) To what extent does the program provide for assessment and feedback relative to learning and behavioral changes?

In brief, the facilitation of learning experiences for adults requires knowledge of the social role development, problems, and needs of the individual. Thus, to be able to plan, organize, and implement effective staff development programs for adult personnel, human resources administrators must be prepared to respond in creative ways to the unique needs and interests of the individual learner. In this sense, knowledge must be personalized, not just individualized. Personalization requires that learning strategies focus on the background and experience unique to the adult learner.

The Performance Evaluation Process

Teacher performance evaluation has two primary purposes that are revealed in the goals for formative evaluations and summative evaluations. **Formative evaluation** goals center on professional development purposes and are exemplified by such activities as improving teaching skills, emphasizing student outcomes, focusing on teaching excellence, and identifying teacher in-service activities. Because formative evaluation is viewed as a self-improvement process, the individual being evaluated commonly is directly involved in the evaluation process.

Summative evaluation goals, on the other hand, are associated with making decisions relative to job continuation, tenure, placement on the specific tracks of the school system's evaluation plan, and defining teacher compensation levels.

Summative evaluations are more formal in nature and administered by a qualified evaluator of the school or school system. Most authorities contend that, since the goals of formative and summative evaluations are different, different evaluators should be used for their administration. Empirical evidence, however, reveals that this practice is uncommon.

District Philosophy of Performance Evaluation

Guidelines for a school district's evaluation program commonly are stated in the state's legislative statutes, a school board policy, or a statement of philosophy included in the school district's evaluation plan. Figure 7.3 contains an example of a philosophy of evaluation. The philosophy centers on four key intentions: (1) that performance evaluation and staff development are essential for the improvement of instruction and professional growth, (2) that performance evaluation and staff development are cooperative efforts, (3) that performance evaluation should recognize the fact that individuals are different, and (4) that district-wide commitment is required for the performance evaluation program to be effective.

EMPLOYEE PERFORMANCE EVALUATIONS

INTENDED OUTCOMES — To improve the level of job production and skill performance of the individual through a planned program based on the premise that all employees have a commitment and responsibility to continuing improvement in work performance.

PRIMARY PURPOSES — Performance evaluations are designed to provide an opportunity for supervisors and employees to develop performance goals that center on the further development of the employee's work performance.

Performance evaluations are designed to determine both the strengths of the employee's performance and those aspects that need improvement.

RELATED PURPOSES — To use the performance evaluation data as an aid in the development of a plan of assistance designed to serve the employee in correcting identified deficiencies.

To identify the employee's special skills and personal strengths that might be employed in other work positions that require specialized skills and knowledge.

ADMINISTRATIVE PROCEDURES
a. All employees are to be evaluated at least once each year, but may be evaluated twice per year (1 formative and 1 summative).
b. The evaluation is to be administered by an administrator or other approved evaluator.
c. The employee shall receive a copy of the evaluation and shall have the right to request a conference with the administrator responsible for the area in which the employee works.
d. Evaluation plans are to be reviewed annually for updates and changes.

Figure 7.3   Performance Evaluation: Philosophy and Purposes

SOURCE: Adapted from the statement, *Purpose of Classified Evaluation Plan,* Anderson County Public School District, July, 2006, Lawrenceburg, KY.

An Example of an Operational Plan
for Evaluation of Performance

The fact that state legislation commonly requires the development of performance evaluation programs was previously stated. Figure 7.4 is an example of a state's procedural requirements for the evaluation of performance of certificated personnel (Arizona Statute 15-537, 2006).

The following operational performance evaluation plan is adapted from the evaluation process utilized in the Mesa Public School District in Arizona. The plan sets forth six primary activities: (1) the teacher evaluation system orientation, (2) the classroom

---

ARS 15-537, 2007 Arizona State Legislature

A. The governing board of a school district shall establish a system for the evaluation of the performance of certificated teachers in the school district. The objectives of the teacher performance evaluation are to improve instruction and maintain instructional strengths. The governing board shall involve its certificated teachers in the development and periodic evaluation of the teacher performance evaluation system.

B. The governing board shall prescribe specific procedures for the teacher performance evaluation system which shall include at least the following elements:

   1. A reliable evaluation instrument including specific criteria for measuring effective teaching performance in each area of the teacher's classroom responsibility.

   2. An assessment of the competencies of teachers as they relate to the specific criteria for measuring teacher performance prescribed in paragraph 1 of this subsection.

   3. A specified minimum number and minimum duration of actual classroom observations of the certificated teacher demonstrating teaching skills by the persons evaluating the teacher.

   4. Specific and reasonable plans for the improvement of teacher performance.

   5. Appeal procedures for teachers who disagree with the evaluation of their performance, if the evaluation is for use as criteria for establishing compensation.

C. A regular evaluation of the performance of each certificated teacher as provided in this section shall be performed at least twice each year for a teacher who has not been employed by the school district for more than the major portion of three consecutive school years. The governing board may provide for additional teacher performance evaluations as it deems necessary.

D. The governing board shall designate persons who are qualified to evaluate teachers to serve as evaluators for the district's teacher performance evaluation system. The governing board shall ensure that persons evaluating teachers are qualified to evaluate teachers.

E. An evaluation made as provided in this section shall be in writing, and a copy shall be transmitted to the certificated teacher within five days after completion of the evaluation. The certificated teacher may initiate a written reaction or response to the evaluation.

F. Each evaluation shall include recommendations as to the areas of improvement in the performance of the certificated teacher if the performance of the teacher warrants improvement. After transmittal of an assessment a board designee shall confer with the teacher to make specific recommendations as to the areas of improvement in the teacher's performance. The board designee shall provide assistance and opportunities for the certificated teacher to improve his performance and follow up with the teacher after a reasonable period of time for the purpose of ascertaining that the teacher is demonstrating adequate classroom performance.

(Continued)

(Continued)

G. Copies of the assessment and evaluation report of a certificated teacher retained by the governing board are confidential, do not constitute a public record and shall not be released or shown to any persons except:

1. To the certificated teacher who may make any use of it.

2. To authorized district officers and employees for all matters regarding employment and contracts and for any hearing which relates to personnel matters.

3. For introduction in evidence or discovery in any court action between the governing board and the certificated teacher in which either:
   a. The competency of the teacher is at issue.
   b. The assessment and evaluation were an exhibit at a hearing, the result of which is challenged.

Figure 7.4   Performance of Certificated Teachers: Evaluation System

SOURCE: Arizona State Revised Statutes, 15-537, 2007.

observations, (3) collection of data, (4) the completion of the evaluation summary form, (5) the final evaluation activities, and (6) the inadequate classroom performance process. The following plan is comprehensive in its provisions and generally meets the requirements set forth in the state statute described in Figure 7.4.

I. TEACHER EVALUATION SYSTEM ORIENTATION

Teachers must be oriented to the evaluation instruments and to the specific procedures to be used in their performance evaluation. In particular, they must be made aware of the evaluation components, competencies, and indicators for measuring effective teaching performance. The intent is to make teachers aware of those competencies that are to be assessed and those components of classroom performance and professional conduct that must meet district standards and are viewed as essential to successful teaching.

II. CLASSROOM OBSERVATIONS

For probationary teachers, evaluator(s) must annually complete a minimum of two classroom observations with postobservation conferences. At least one observation is scheduled with the teacher, and it should be approximately one class period or teaching segment in length.

For continuing-status teachers in the goal setting and goal review years, the evaluator annually completes a minimum of two "walk-through" observations no more than a standard class period or teaching segment. A walk-through evaluation is used to check several aspects of instruction. Figure 7.5 is an example of a classroom walk-through evaluation. Although not every "look for" on the checklist is observed during any one walk-through visit, those look-fors that are observed are noted and feedback is provided to the teacher in a follow-up conference. In some cases two or more walk-through visits are completed before a follow-up conference is scheduled. In this way, a more complete picture of the teacher's instructional methodology and learner behaviors is possible. During the observation/conference year, the evaluator completes at least one scheduled observation lasting approximately one class period or teaching segment in length and at least one walk-through evaluation annually.

III. COLLECTION OF EVALUATION DATA

The collection of evaluation data is to be completed through multiple sources. The major sources of evaluative data include: (a) classroom observations, (b) teacher artifacts, (c) documentation of student growth, (d) goal achievement, (e) professional standards, (f) completion of required knowledge modules, and (g) growth plan results, if required. Much data collection is accomplished through the use of Evaluator Worksheets for each of the foregoing sources.

Classroom Observations. See II above.

Teacher Artifacts. Documentation of teacher artifacts includes lesson plan models/samples; instructional materials such as handouts and worksheets; visual displays in the form of bulletin boards, charts, models and murals; and instructional technology aids.

Student Growth. Student growth and achievement data are collected through student work samples, grade records, grade distribution analysis, and student performance on district, state, and nationally normed tests. Formal documents analyzing student achievement must be presented as evidence of student growth and achievement.

Goal Achievement. Goal achievement is a three-year process, a continuous cycle repeated throughout the continuing status teacher's career in the school system. Goal achievement is the culmination of the evaluation process, including professional growth and instructional improvement as well as improvement of the level of student achievement.

Professional Standards. The professional standards component is separate from classroom performance and addresses professional attitudes and behaviors, skills, and ethics that are outside the classroom performance element of the Teacher Evaluation System. The evaluator completes the Professional Standards Worksheet, which lists the competencies and indicators under the two major areas of professional ethics and professional attitude and behavior.

Acquired Knowledge Module. The Acquired Standards component is designed to provide professional growth in instructional planning and instructional techniques, with a focus on the school system's curriculum standards. Probationary teachers entering the school system have a contractual obligation to successfully complete the Acquired Knowledge Module during the first two years in the school system (see p. 11 of the evaluation handbook).

Growth Plan Results. Growth plans reflect areas where improved job performance is desirable, based on the most recent Evaluation Summary Form. The purpose is to provide clear direction and expectation for improved job performance.

IV. COMPLETION OF EVALUATION SUMMARY FORM

The evaluator reviews the multiple data sources and completes the teacher Evaluation Summary Form. The document must assist the teacher in the areas where improved performance is desirable. The document must assist the teacher in (1) understanding what has to been done well and why that behavior is important, (2) understanding what area(s) need attention, (3) understanding why improved performance is important, and (4) giving clear directions as to how the performance can be improved.

V. FINAL FORMAL EVALUATION ACTIVITIES

The evaluator and the teacher must schedule a final evaluation conference to review and discuss the Evaluation Summary Form. The teacher must sign the form to indicate that he or she has read the evaluation documents. Copies of the Evaluation Summary Form shall be provided for the teacher, and the original copy must be sent to the Human Resources Office for inclusion in the teacher's personnel file. If the teacher feels the evaluation is inaccurate or unfair based on procedural and/or substantive issues, he or she may submit a written rebuttal to accompany the evaluation form.

VI. INADEQUATE CLASSROOM PERFORMANCE PROCESS

At any time that the evaluator believes a teacher's classroom performance is inadequate, the evaluator initiates the Procedures for Dealing with Inadequate Classroom Performance for Probationary or Continuing Teachers.

(Continued)

(Continued)

Classroom Walk Through Evaluation Form

Name of Teacher: _____ Subject/Grade Level _____

I. Teaching Objective
    A. Teaching Lesson Objective Stated   Yes _____ No _____
    B. Lesson Plan Present   Yes _____ No _____

II. Anticipatory Set
    A. Tie to Previous Lesson   Yes _____ No _____
    B. Authentic/Real World Experiences   Yes _____ No _____

III. Text/Materials
    A. Materials Aligned to Grade/Level   Yes _____ No _____
    B. Multiple Opportunities   Yes _____ No _____
    C. Clear Product Standards   Yes _____ No _____
    D. Choice   Yes _____ No _____
    E. Novelty and Variety   Yes _____ No _____

IV. Instructional Strategies
    A. Setting Objectives   Yes _____ No _____
    B. Generating and Testing Hypotheses   Yes _____ No _____
    C. Identifying Similarities/Differences   Yes _____ No _____
    D. Summarizing and Note Taking   Yes _____ No _____
    E. Cooperative Learning   Yes _____ No _____
    F. Questions, Cues, Advanced Organizers   Yes _____ No _____
    G. Homework and Practice   Yes _____ No _____
    H. Provisions for Individual Differences   Yes _____ No _____

V. Learner Engagement
    A. Active Learning   Yes _____ No _____
    B. Student Self-Assessment   Yes _____ No _____
    C. Small Group Activities   Yes _____ No _____
    D. Independent Study   Yes _____ No _____
    E. Meaningful Practice   Yes _____ No _____
    F. Time on Task   Yes _____ No _____
    G. Personal Interest   Yes _____ No _____

VI. Learning Environment
    A. Organized for Learning   Yes _____ No _____
    B. Current/Relevant Displays   Yes _____ No _____
    C. Student Work Displayed   Yes _____ No _____
    D. Classroom Behavior Standards Displayed   Yes _____ No _____
    E. Safe and Orderly   Yes _____ No _____
    F. Courtesy in Evidence   Yes _____ No _____
    G. Humor, Praise, Positive Reinforcement   Yes _____ No _____
    H. Positive Behavior of Learner   Yes _____ No _____

VII. Comments

_____
_____
_____
_____
_____

Evaluation: _____ Date of Walk Through: _____

Figure 7.5   Example of a Classroom Walk-Through Evaluation Form

The Classroom Observation

Many authorities view teacher evaluation as one of the most important respon-sibilities of the school principal. Most persons would agree that both **formal** and **informal classroom observation** are the leading activities for collecting teaching performance information and determining the quality of performance. Performance evaluations require four basic components: (1) a qualified eval-uator, (2) valid and reliable assessment instruments, (3) timely observations, and (4) appropriate follow-up conferencing and feedback. The following section dis-cusses each of these components.

Qualified Evaluators

State legislation on performance evaluation commonly mandates that people evaluating teachers be qualified to do so (see Figure 7.6). As a result, university administrator preparation programs, state departments of education, state admin-istrator associations, and other agencies have instituted programs and workshops for the certification of qualified evaluators. Such state mandates have directed school systems to present evidence that viable personnel evaluation programs are in place and that provisions for certifying evaluators for these programs have been implemented.

Qualified evaluators should be able to demonstrate their knowledge and skill of performance evaluation in the following ways: (1) know and understand the basic requirements of the state concerning the teacher evaluation process and the phi-losophy of the school district relative to the purposes of the evaluation process; (2) have a thorough understanding of the design, criteria and standards, and imple-mentation of the school or school district's performance instruments; (3) know the similarities and differences between and among the different evaluation instru-ments in practice, including norm-referenced, criterion-referenced, and self-referenced systems; (4) understand the use of various ranking systems, including forced distribution, simple distribution, alternate ranking, and paired ranking tech-niques; (5) know and understand rating systems, including graphic rating, check-lists, narrative systems such as work portfolios, goal and objective techniques, and work journals; (6) have knowledge and understanding of the principles of student learning and effective instructional methodology; and (7) maintain appraisal objectivity, including the concepts of content validity and construct validity of eval-uation instruments.

Along with the foregoing criteria, other considerations for determining the selection of qualified persons for personnel evaluation include the following:

1. *Time.* Do the individual's job responsibilities provide adequate time to per-form the many requirements of the performance evaluation process? Pre-evaluation conference planning, classroom observation time requirements, time for observation analysis, and postevaluation conference feedback are among the time demands for performance evaluators. For example, a pre-evaluation conference commonly requires time to review the teacher's job description, discuss lesson goal expectations, review classroom management

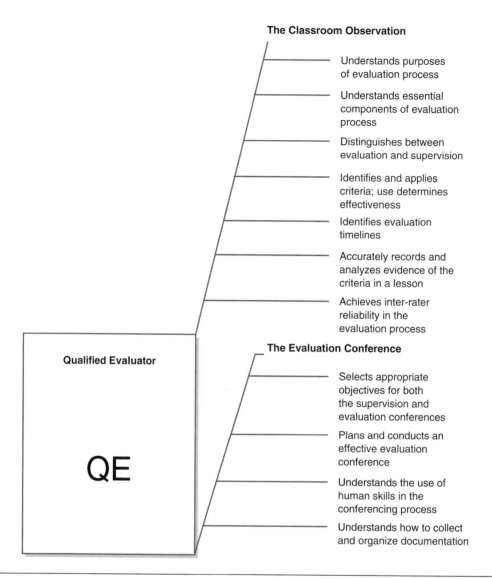

The Classroom Observation

Understands purposes of evaluation process

Understands essential components of evaluation process

Distinguishes between evaluation and supervision

Identifies and applies criteria; use determines effectiveness

Identifies evaluation timelines

Accurately records and analyzes evidence of the criteria in a lesson

Achieves inter-rater reliability in the evaluation process

The Evaluation Conference

Selects appropriate objectives for both the supervision and evaluation conferences

Plans and conducts an effective evaluation conference

Understands the use of human skills in the conferencing process

Understands how to collect and organize documentation

Qualified Evaluator

QE

Figure 7.6   Knowledge/Skill Criteria for a Qualified Evaluator

SOURCE: Adapted from the Knowledge/Skill Criteria for a Qualified Evaluator Program provided by the Arizona School Administrators, Inc., 2008, Phoenix, Arizona.

procedures, identify special student needs, determine instructional resources, review instructional methods, and discuss other related instructional procedures.

2. *Qualifications.* Does the individual possess the knowledge and skills for participating as an evaluator in the performance evaluation process? Is he or she a certified evaluator? Position in the school system does not necessarily qualify a person as a performance evaluator.

3. *Sensitivity.* Does the individual possess the human relations skills, poise, and temperament necessary for serving in the performance evaluation process? Is the individual capable of being sensitive to the feelings of persons being evaluated and yet retain objectivity in the process?

4. *Performance Record.* What is the individual's personal record concerning evaluation results? That is, over time, how do the performance evaluation results of the evaluator correlate with those of other qualified evaluators? Do the evaluator's classroom evaluation results compare favorably with other aspects of the teacher's overall performance and effectiveness?

Valid and Reliable Assessment Instruments

According to Young (2008), the basic categories of performance appraisal systems are (a) ranking systems, (b) rating systems, and (c) narrative systems. Ranking systems center on comparing the work performance of one employee with that of other employees in the same job classification.

Rating systems are criterion-referenced and use standards, traits, competencies, or other criteria to rate the employee on rating scales that use some legend for differentiating knowledge or skills levels, such as 10 = high to 1 = low or a Likert-type scale such as 5 = behavior always demonstrated to 1 = behavior not demonstrated. Empirical evidence suggests that rating systems are by far the most common performance evaluation systems used in education.

Narrative systems are self-referenced in that they center on the work of the individual employee in relation to the expectations of the job. An example of one narrative evaluation technique is the job portfolio, which includes a statement of specific job purposes, samples of work production, and assessments of the accomplishment of job requirements. "Portfolio assessment involves a content analysis of the integration of means, methods, and outcomes used by and produced by the employee when fulfilling assigned work duties" (Young, 2008, p. 218).

Figure 7.7 is an example of a rating system type performance evaluation instrument used by the Laramie County School District #1 in Wyoming. The instrument features four primary performance categories and a Likert-type rating scale from U = Unsatisfactory to D = Distinguished performance. Each Performance Benchmark (1a, 1b, 1c, etc.) is related to one or more of the 10 Performance Standards of the school district. For example, teacher performance Standard I states that "All teachers will demonstrate knowledge, skills and attitudes which enhance pupil self-esteem and confidence and promote constructive interaction among people of differing social, racial, ethnic and religious backgrounds." The school district's Standard V states that "All teachers will demonstrate knowledge of the standards and content areas they teach and methods of teaching."

Timely Observations

As previously noted, school district policy and regulations most often set forth the number and frequency requirements for conducting performance evaluations.

Track I Summative Evaluation

Name _____ School _____ Date _____

Whenever a "U" or "D" is given, comments describing the performance are required.

Key: U– Unsatisfactory B– Basic P– Proficient D– Distinguished

				Designing Knowledge Work
U	B	P	D	
				1a Demonstrating Knowledge of Content and Pedagogy (ST: V, VI, VII)
				1b Demonstrating Knowledge of Students (ST: I, II, VI, VII)
				1c Selecting Instructional Goals (ST: II, V, VI, X)
				1d Demonstrating Knowledge of Resources (ST:IX)
				1e Designing Content Instruction (ST: I, II, III, IV, V, VIII, IX, X)
				1f Assessing Learning Using Student-Generated Products (ST: V, VI, X)
				Creating a Safe and Orderly Environment for Learning
U	B	P	D	
				2a Creating an Environment of Respect/Rapport (ST: I, III, IV, VI, VII)
				2b Establishing a Culture for Learning @ District Mission (ST: V, VI)
				2c Managing Classroom Procedures (ST: III, IV, V, VI, VII, IX, X)
				2d Managing Student Behavior (ST: I, II, III, IX, X)
				2e Managing Physical Space (ST: III)
				Facilitating Knowledge Work
U	B	P	D	
				3a Communicating Clearly and Accurately (ST: II, VI)
				3b Using Questioning and Discussion Techniques (ST: I, II, VI, VIII, IX)
				3c Engaging Students in the Work (ST: V, VI, VII, IX)
				3d Affirming the Performance of Students (ST: I, IV)
				3e Demonstrating Flexibility/Responsiveness Through Monitoring and Modifying the Work (ST: I, II, IV, V, VI, IX)
				Professional and Leadership Responsibilities
U	B	P	D	
				4a Reflecting on Teaching (ST: III)
				4b Maintaining Accurate Records (ST: III, IV, VIII)
				4c Communicating with Families (ST: IV)
				4d Growing and Developing Professionally (ST: I, II, III, IV, V, VI, VIII, IX, X)
				4e Showing Professionalism (ST: I, II, III)

Figure 7.7   Rating System for Teacher Performance Evaluation

SOURCE: Adapted from the Laramie County School District #1 Track I Summative Evaluation, Cheyenne, Wyoming.

Note: The Laramie County School District uses 10 standards for benchmark alignment purposes. For example, Standard I states "All teachers will demonstrate knowledge, skills, and attitudes which enhance pupil self-esteem and confidence and promote constructive interaction among people of differing economic, social, racial, ethnic, and religious backgrounds."

These requirements commonly differ for nontenured and tenured teaching personnel and for teachers who are participating in special performance programs such as Master Teacher programs and other performance-based or incentive-pay programs. Typically, initial contract teachers are evaluated twice a year and continuing contract teachers are evaluated once each year, although such practices differ within states and school districts nationally. As previously noted, walk-through evaluations provide opportunities for the evaluators to observe classroom instruction more frequently.

Ideally, performance evaluations for nontenured personnel should include three classroom evaluations annually. The first evaluation should occur at the time the teacher is initiating a new instructional unit or lesson. It is at this time that instructional objectives are established and intended instructional activities and student expectations are identified. The evaluator should plan a second classroom visit near the middle of the unit or lesson after the teacher has had the opportunity to introduce the major content of the new unit and implement his or her teaching methodology. A final timely classroom visit should occur at the close of the instructional unit or lesson when the teacher is synthesizing and assessing goals and objectives. In this way, the evaluator is able to gain a broader perspective of the teacher's knowledge and skills in planning, organizing, teaching, and assessing classroom instruction.

Appropriate Follow-Up Conferencing and Feedback

Every informal or formal classroom observation should result in appropriate feedback to the teacher. Although a primary objective of performance evaluation is that of professional development and personal improvement, the reinforcement of teaching excellence should not be overlooked. Follow-up conferencing provides opportunities to praise outstanding teaching performance, to identify the specific strengths of the teacher, and to discuss why excellent teaching is so important to the overall success of the school and school district.

The follow-up conference centers on an analysis of the observation results and setting goals for improvement. Smith (2005) suggests that the following five factors serve to determine the appropriate approach for the evaluator to use during the conference:

1. What is the purpose of this postobservation conference?

2. What are the needs and communication style of the person being evaluated?

3. What are the situational elements to be considered (e.g., past observation, incidences or events of the work environment)?

4. What is my communication or behavior style, and what strengths do I bring to the post conference (e.g., the communication strengths that I bring to the post conference, knowledge of instructional methodology)?

5. What behaviors do I bring to the post conference that promote success? (pp. 181–183)

Summary

The maximization of human resources in the school system is a primary responsibility of the human resources function. This concern emphasizes the purposeful development and utilization of people within the organization. It also underlines the perspective set forth throughout this text that the human resources function is a primary responsibility of all personnel in the school system. An organization's progress depends on the extent to which people are positively motivated and developed.

Because the school is a social system, the behavior of individuals is influenced by the institution's expectations and the individuals' personal need dispositions. Staff development serves to establish congruence between organizational roles and personal needs toward the goal of developing behaviors that harmonize with stated organizational purposes and personal self-fulfillment.

Each of the human resources processes contributes uniquely to the maximization of human resources. Staff development is the comprehensive complex of activities designed to maximize the strengths of the human assets within the school system for the purpose of increasing the system's potential for meeting its objectives and fulfilling employee needs.

Approaches to staff development that emphasize remedial programs generally have proven to be ineffective. A focus on employee strengths and self-fulfillment fosters self-development from a positive perspective. Potential growth best occurs when the individual's dispositions agree with the organization's growth expectations.

The implementation of the staff development process consists of a planned sequence of procedures that begins with commitment by the board of education; continues through cooperative goal setting, program design, and delivery; and culminates in opportunities to practice the knowledge and skills gained in a wide variety of learning activities. Evaluation leads to necessary program changes and ensures continuous program improvement. All activities require basic principles of adult learning.

Staff development methods and strategies are virtually limitless and are provided through the local school district, institutions of higher learning, employee associations, and other agencies. However, effective staff development is a personal activity that focuses on the individual's strengths and interests. Such strategies as coaching, mentoring, quality circles, teacher centers, assessment centers, peer-assisted leadership, and clinical supervision are among the viable approaches for meeting the purposes of the staff development process. As previously stated, school systems will progress as people in the system develop.

Performance evaluation is one of the most important responsibilities of human resources administrators. An effective personnel evaluation process can serve as motivation toward employee professional development, program improvement, and school system effectiveness. Similar to any other effective human resources process, the evaluation process is a planned program that includes employee orientation to the evaluation plan, pre–classroom observation conferencing, the classroom observation, the data collection, post–classroom observation conferencing, and dealing with inadequate performance.

Discussion Questions

1. Staff development was discussed as a proactive experience rather than a reactive one. Discuss your personal staff development experiences. Have these experiences met the proactive criteria? Why or why not?

2. Assume that you have been asked to serve as a mentor for a teacher new to the teaching profession. What factors will influence your decision to serve in this capacity? For instance, what personal or professional benefits might you expect to receive in such an assignment?

3. Think about the question of staff development and accountability. Assume that you have been asked to defend staff development in terms of its return on investment. What "hard data" might you cite as possible proof for specific staff development activities?

Case Studies

CASE 7.1

I'LL JUST SIT THERE AND LET THEM GROW ME

The district schedule of in-service programs for Wymore School District had just been announced. It called for four full days of in-service for all teachers in the district for one day each in September, November, January, and March. The in-service days for all elementary school teachers would focus on the use of technology in the classroom. Secondary teachers would have "experts" speak to them according to their subject area specialties. All teachers are required to attend each of the four days of in-service. They are not paid for in-service training days; the four days were part of a negotiated agreement whereby teachers were given four days of personal leave in exchange for the four days of in-service.

Although the in-service programs of previous years had received evaluations by participants in the average to below average range, no changes in the program planning or delivery were made for the current year. As one teacher commented to a colleague, "I'll show up at each of the in-service days as required, sit down, and let them grow me." It could be said that "apathy" was the best description of the teachers' attitudes.

Questions

1. First, in view of the somewhat limited information regarding the staff development program at Wymore, give your assessment of the situation in terms of apparent problems facing the school district's program.

2. In view of the descriptions of successful staff development programs set forth in the chapter, design a plan that you believe is needed to renew the staff development program in the school district. How might you initiate such a renewal program plan? Who would you involve? What assessments do you see as necessary at this time?

   a. What specific practices and relationships would you examine at the outset to ameliorate the problems indicated in the case description?

   b. What recommendations would you offer for obviating the problems described in the case?

CASE 7.2

TIME TO TEACH

As assistant director of human resources, you receive the following memorandum. Examine the memo and then present your ideas of follow-up in this case. Keep in mind the specific principles set forth in the chapter concerning effective in-service programs as well as the principles of adult learning.

MEMO

To: E. O. Herr, Assistant Director

From: Verna Petrov, Grade 3 Teacher, Union Elementary

Re: Program suggestion

I'd like to make a suggestion for you to consider in planning some of our in-service days. I know that you have run a survey of perceived needs in the district that has given you some general or overall ideas, but for some of us, surveys don't always fit our needs as individuals.

Here are a couple of things I see as needs:

1. When we test with the battery of the Columbus Test of Basic Skills, and place so much empha-sis on it, teachers tend to start teaching to the test, and I'm not sure that is good.

2. I don't want to sound negative, but when I have 27 children from residents in our district in my class and then get two or more who can hardly speak English, it is becoming impossible for me to take care of the class; the few non–English-speaking students require all my time. Then, many of them will be gone again in a few weeks or months.

Please don't misunderstand me. I'm not saying we need in-service on working with these few children. I want help working with the whole class. Why not set up a training program for children with limited ability in English, and when they get up to grade level, place them in appropriate classes? It seems to me that the least restricted environment is one that would help these deserving students learn best.

Thanks!

Verna Petrov

Questions

1. What specific problems do you determine from this scenario?

2. From the somewhat limited evidence provided, what necessary staff development practices appear to have been overlooked in this case in the past? Discuss the alternatives for action at this time. As the school principal, outline a brief action plan that you would recommend in Ms. Petrov's case.

CASE 7.3

JUST LEAVE US ALONE, WE'RE PROFESSIONALS

MEMO

TO: Mildred Ross, HR Development Office

FROM: Kim Geston & Clara Sutter, Co-Chairs

Teachers' Ad Hoc Development Committee

RE: Your request for feedback on in-service programming

Date: September 23

Please know that our Development Committee has met twice in follow-up of your memo of September 2 asking for the committee's recommendations for in-service programs during the ensuing year. As you are well aware, teachers in the Wymore School District spent a great deal of time in-servicing last year and the year before. The effectiveness of these programs, in our opinion, was minimal. As professionals, we respectfully request that we be allowed to participate in our own way in development activities this year; that is, let each teacher use his or her own initiative in this regard this year and the years ahead.

At the end of the school year, each teacher would be asked to submit a brief report on his or her individual growth activities. We believe that such a professional approach encourages personal initiative and allows each individual to focus on his or her own personal interests.

Question

1. Assume the role of Mildred Ross and set forth the specific actions that you will take in view of the memorandum received from Geston and Sutter. If you decide to respond in writing to them, actually draft the letter that you will send. If, for example, you want to meet with the "committee," set forth the specific statements that you plan to make at the meeting and the questions that you will ask. Are there others that you want to involve in this matter at this time? In brief, set forth your follow-up action plan.

References

Bathurst, P. (2007, March 11). Training is the key at top firms. *Arizona Republic*, p. ED1.

Bloss, J. M. (1882). Thirtieth report of the superintendent of public instruction of the state of Indiana to the governor: State of Indiana.

Brown, M. (1992). Only the best. *American School Board Journal, 179*(3), 35–36.

Bush, C. (2005, November 6). Stay put: New jobs, old workplaces. *Arizona Republic*, p. EC1.

Clifton, D. O., & Nelson, P. (1992). *Soar with your strengths.* New York: Dell.

Ebmeier, H. (2000, November). *How supervision works in schools: An investigation of a path model through structured equation modeling.* Paper presented at the Annual Conference of the University Council for Educational Administration. Albuquerque, NM.

Getzels, J. W., & Guba, E. G. (1957). Social behavior and the administrative process. *School Review, 65*(4), 423–441.

Harris, B. M. (1989). *In-service education for staff development.* Boston: Allyn & Bacon.

Knowles, M., & Associates. (1984). *Andragogy in action: Applying modern principles of adult learning.* San Francisco: Jossey-Bass.

Merriam, S. B., & Brockett, R. G. (1997). *The profession and practice of adult education: An introduction* (1st ed.). San Francisco: Jossey-Bass.

National School Boards Association. (1996). *The school personnel management system.* Alexandria, VA: Author.

Sirotnik, K. A., & Durden, P. C. (1996). The validity of administrator performance assessment systems: The ADI as a case-in-point. *Educational Administration Quarterly, 32,* 539–564.

Smith, R. E. (2005). *Human resources administration: A school-based approach* (3rd ed.). Larchmont, NY: Eye on Education.

Wendel, F. C., & Uerling, D. F. (1989). Assessment centers—Contributing to preparation programs for principals. *NASSP Bulletin, 73,* 74–79.

Wood, F. H., Thompson, S. R., & Russell, F. (1981). Designing effective staff development programs. In B. Dillon-Peterson (Ed.), *Staff development/organization development.* Alexandria, VA: Association for Supervision and Curriculum Development.

Young, I. P. (2008). *The human resource function in education* (9th ed.). Upper Saddle River, NJ: Pearson Prentice Hall.

CHAPTER 8

Organizational Climate and the Human Resources Function

Learning Objectives

After reading this chapter, you will be able to

- Differentiate between organizational climate and organizational culture.
- Delineate the importance of organizational climate in the improvement of the HR function and the achievement of school goals.
- Discuss how the climate of a school or school system can be determined.
- Understand more clearly the inevitable event of "conflict" in school settings and how some conflict can serve to initiate positive change.
- Describe how fostering a positive school climate is related to positive student achievement and employee behavior.
- Describe how the climate of a school system can be improved.

Human resources administration is those processes that are planned and implemented in the organization to establish an effective system of human resources and to foster an organizational climate that enhances the accomplishment of district goals. This definition emphasizes the responsibility of the human resources function to foster an environment in which relationships among personnel, students, and others lend support to the work of the human resources function and the achievement of stated objectives. The complex of personal and organizational relationships within the school is necessarily a concern of the human resources function. Human resources administrators throughout the school system must assume a major role in the development of a healthy school environment in which everyone works cooperatively to achieve desired ends.

This chapter discusses organizational climate as it relates to the work of human resources administrators in education. First, a distinction is made between organizational culture and organizational climate, and the importance of a positive climate is discussed. Next, the research on school characteristics associated with a healthy school climate and the assessment of climate is reviewed. This is followed by a discussion of the impact of climate on student achievement, the behavior of school staff, organizational conflict, and organizational change and innovation. The final section discusses the improvement of school climate, with special attention given to the role of human resources administrators in this process.

What do school systems do to foster a healthy working environment for employees? How can the school become a better place to work? What effect does organizational climate have on employee performance? This chapter addresses the answers to these questions.

Organizational Culture and Organizational Climate

Organizational climate, organizational culture, syntality, school atmosphere, school health, and others are among the terms found in the literature to describe human behavior in organizations. In some instances, these terms are used interchangeably. Yet, definitions of the term "culture" vary. For example, to Cunningham and Cordeiro (2000), culture is "a continuous process of creating meaning in social and material contexts" (p. 94). Kleiman (2000) defined culture as "a society's set of assumptions, values, and rules about social interactions" (p. 412). Pai and Adler (2001) defined culture "as that pattern of knowledge, skills, behaviors, attitudes and beliefs, as well as material artifacts produced by human society and transmitted from one generation to another" (p. 21). Robbins (2001) stated that "organizational culture refers to a system of shared meaning held by members that distinguishes the organization from other organizations" (p. 510). "Culture is not interchangeable with ethnicity. It is dynamic and changing, dependent on place, time, and the influence of other groups" (Decker, Decker, & Brown, 2007, p. 31). "Ethnicity refers not to race, but to selected cultural and sometimes physical characteristics used to classify people into ethnic groups or categories" (Decker et al., 2007, p. 30). In this text, culture is the set of important assumptions, beliefs, values, and attitudes that members of the school or school system share.

The human resources function benefits in several ways from knowing and understanding the culture. Deal and Peterson (1999) point out that the group's culture can serve to

1. Foster school effectiveness and productivity.

2. Improve collegial and collaborative activities that improve communication and problem-solving practices.

3. Foster successful change and program improvement efforts.

4. Build employee commitment and closer identification among staff, students, and administrators.

5. Amplify the energy, motivation, and vitality of a school staff.

6. Add the focus of daily behavior and attention on what is important and valued. (pp. 7–9)

As Norton (2005) noted, the organization's primary goals, beliefs, and values are reflected in the cultural assumptions that support the important programs and daily work of staff personnel. The culture of the organization allows its members to commit themselves to meaningful purposes and superordinate goals above and beyond personal, vested interests.

Organizational climate is the collective personality of a school or school system. It is the school atmosphere as characterized by the social and professional interactions within it. The collective behavior of a school is the school's personality or its **syntality**. The healthy organization gives due attention to meeting its required tasks and fulfilling its organizational and human needs by emphasizing continued growth and development. The school that is meeting its task needs has a clear goal focus—communication adequacy—and fosters a climate that enhances positive human relationships. Climate is a phenomenon that is influenced by both the internal and external environments of the school system. Although climate is relatively enduring, these internal and external influences can lead to changes in the climate of the school over time.

Table 8.1 illustrates differences between school culture and school climate, as well as the characteristics that serve to link the two. As depicted in Table 8.1, school climate is characterized by the social and professional interactions of people in the school community, whereas school culture extends beyond the interpersonal life that takes place in the school setting. Culture is more normative than climate in that it goes beyond interpersonal relationships.

The Importance of a Healthy School Climate

Why is school climate such an important consideration for the human resources function? Why does the environmental setting within a school system require the special attention of human resources administrators? How can school climate be instrumental in the improvement of the HR function in the school system? Several reasons can be identified:

1. Because schools, departments, and offices are staffed by people, school climate in a real sense is a human condition. The kind of climate in the school sets the tone for the human considerations of importance to human resources administration. An important part of the work of human resources administrators is to determine the facilitators and inhibitors of school effectiveness, those strengths and weaknesses that affect the climate of the school system. The determination of school climate is the forerunner of the determination of the strategies for school improvement generally and improvement of conditions in the workplace specifically.

Table 8.1   Links Between School Culture and School Climate

School Culture	Links	School Climate
Culture is the set of important beliefs and values that members of the school system share. **Culture** is more normative than climate in the sense that it is a reflection of the shared values, beliefs, and underlying assumptions of school members across an array of organizational dimensions that include but go beyond interpersonal relationships.	• People • Socialization • Shared goals • Interpersonal relations • Environmental factors • Influenced behaviors • Attitudes • Individual needs • Artifacts • Traditions • Sanctions	**Climate** is the collective personality of a school or school system. It is the atmosphere that prevails as characterized by the social and professional interactions of people. **Climate** is more interpersonal in tone and substance than culture. It is manifested in the attitudes and behaviors of teachers, students, administrators, and community members. **Climate** is concerned with the process and style of a school's organizational life, rather than its content and substance.

2. The school climate sets the opportunity for growth and renewal. Human resources administrators must work to promote a school environment that fosters positive personnel development in order to remain vital and alive. The healthy school serves to stimulate people's best efforts by providing meaningful work, motivating challenges, and continuous opportunities for learning. Through an ongoing program of people development, the school system has the ability to innovate and change as needed within a changing society.

3. Effective communication requires a climate of trust, mutual respect, and clarity of function. Such communication is inhibited in schools where distrust and poor human relations exist. Effective communications is an important component of an open, positive climate; it serves to tie the school community together.

4. Climate conditions the school environment for creative efforts, innovation, and change. These behaviors serve as foundations for organizational goal achievement. A positive school environment encourages innovative practices that serve toward the achievement of new goals. Rather than attempting to initiate change and then realizing subsequent failure, school leaders should examine the school climate first and, if it is less than favorable, take steps to improve it before attempting program innovation.

5. Positive school climate implies positive team building in that goal development and achievement are cooperative tasks that require mutual trust and respect among faculty personnel. Human resources administrators can foster a climate of trust by demonstrating trustworthy behavior in their leadership roles.

Thus, school climate is important to school systems and to the human resources function because it affects all of the important reasons that schools exist. As a study of school climate by Wynn and Carboni (2006) reported, teachers are more likely to remain in the profession when they are satisfied with the school principal's leadership and with the school climate.

Human resources leaders have an important role in determining what the school system is and what it might become. In order to have a positive influence, however, they must understand why organizational climate is important to school effectiveness as well as to the effectiveness of the HR function, how it can be determined, and how to foster a positive environment within the system.

The Measurement of School Climate

In order to gain knowledge about the nature of school environments, the characteristics associated with different kinds of climate, and the impact various leadership styles have on personnel behaviors, school systems have administered numerous empirical climate assessment instruments.

Among the leaders in the study of organizational climate were Andrew W. Halpin and Don B. Croft, who developed the most widely used instrument for measuring climate in schools, the Organizational Climate Description Questionnaire (OCDQ), in 1962. Halpin and Croft focused primarily on school climate as the relationships held among group members and relationships between the school principal and the teaching staff.

The OCDQ comprises 64 Likert-type items to which teachers respond, describing the climate of the school from their perspectives. It yields school mean scores that are averages of the scores for all teachers' responses on eight subtests related to principal and teacher behavior. For example, two of the subtests are **disengagement** and **intimacy**. Disengagement refers to the teacher's tendency to "not be with it." This dimension describes a group that is going through the motions but is not in gear with respect to the tasks at hand. Intimacy refers to the teachers' enjoyment of friendly relationships with each other.

Halpin and Croft (1962) developed six prototypic profiles to describe climates on a continuum from open to closed using the profiles of 71 schools. An **open climate** is one in which the staff enjoys extremely high morale, works well together, enjoys friendly relations but does not engage in a high degree of socialization, and possesses the incentive to work things out and to keep the school moving. Kreitner (2001) noted that open climates have four characteristics:

1. *Interaction With the Environment.* Open systems have permeable boundaries, whereas closed systems do not. Organizations depend on the environment for survival.

2. *Synergy.* An open system adds up to more than the sum of its parts. Only when all parts are in place and working in concert can the winning edge be achieved.

3. *Dynamic Equilibrium.* In open systems, dynamic equilibrium is the process of maintaining the internal balance necessary for survival by importing needed resources from the environment.

4. *Equifinality.* Open systems can achieve the same results by different means. (pp. 282–284)

In contrast to the open climate, a **closed climate** is characterized by low staff morale, limited and inadequate communication, and limited socialization. In addition, closed systems are typified by impermeable boundaries and static equilibrium. A climate in which workers have excessive workloads, tight deadlines, unreasonable supervisors, unrealistic targets for productivity, and unattainable goals is often termed a **toxic climate.**

The work of Halpin and Croft (1962), and the wide use of their OCDQ in hundreds of empirical studies, contributed significantly to the foundational concepts of school climate and served to motivate other researchers to study the topic from a variety of perspectives, including the characteristics associated with positive climates, the impact of climate on personnel, and the climate characteristics associated with effective schools: innovation and change. Later sections of this chapter review selected research related to these considerations.

Other early assessment instruments addressed a variety of perspectives of organizational climate. Among these instruments were the following:

The High School Characteristics Index (HSCI) (Stern, 1964). The HSCI was one of the first climate instruments developed at the Syracuse University Psychological Research Center as a standardized instrument to measure climate in schools. The HSCI's 30 scales relate to seven factors of school climate, including group life, personal dignity, achievement standards, and so on. Such data can be invaluable in providing a school profile of existing conditions from the perspectives of the school's most important clients, the students.

The Purdue Teacher Opinionaire (PTO) (Bentley & Rempel, 1980). The PTO is designed to provide a measure of teacher morale. The instrument includes 10 factors related to the school environment. Data collected from teachers in one school result in norms that can be compared with those of the entire school system or with selected faculties in the system. The 10 climate factors include teacher rapport with the principal, satisfaction with teaching, teacher load, rapport among teachers, teacher status, community support of education, community pressures, and others. The instrument can be useful to school administrators, school staffs, and researchers who desire an objective and practical index of teacher morale. Comparisons can be made among teachers when grouped by schools, grade levels, subject areas, and tenure status. The reliability and validity of the PTO have been empirically tested and retested in hundreds of school settings since its first form was developed in 1961. The Purdue Research Foundation also developed the Purdue Evaluation Scale (PES), which is completed by students. The instrument provides evaluative information in six climate areas including ability to motivate students. The PTO and the PES are available through the Office of Technology Commercialization at Purdue University in West Lafayette, Indiana.

The CFK Ltd. School Climate Profile. The Charles F. Kettering School Climate Profile (Phi Delta Kappa, 1973) can be completed by teachers, students, and parents. Although designed more than 30 years ago, the School Climate Profile remains among the most comprehensive climate survey instruments available today. It focuses on general, program, process, and material determinants of school climate. For example, the respondent uses a Likert-type scale in the general climate section to assess such factors as respect, trust, morale, school renewal, and caring.

The Harrison Instrument for Diagnosing Organizational Ideology. The Harrison Instrument for Diagnosing Organizational Ideology (Harrison, 1985) differs from the aforementioned instruments in that it helps staff personnel compare their organization's values and their own personal values with four different "cultures" or ideologies. The aim is to enable participants to clarify where their organization stands on a number of important value issues and to identify differences between the organization's ideology and their own. Organizational ideologies include (1) power orientation, (2) role orientation, (3) task orientation, and (4) self-orientation. Results enable the organization to identify potential problem areas and to take steps to resolve areas of conflict.

Organizational Health Inventory (OHI-S). The OHI-S (Hoy, Tarter, & Kottkamp, 1991) is administered to teachers and uses a Likert-type scale to assess seven climate areas: (1) institutional integrity, (2) principal influence, (3) consideration, (4) initiating structure, (5) resource support, (6) morale, and (7) academic emphasis. Profiles of results for each of the seven climate areas can be determined and compared with other schools in the district. The OHI is a useful tool for measuring school climate because it measures key dimensions of organizational health and was specifically designed, developed, and tested in the schools.

Revised Versions of the OCDQ. Revised versions of Halpin and Croft's OCDQ were completed by Hoy and Clover (1986), Kottkamp, Mulhern, and Hoy (1987), and Hoy and Tarter (1997). The updated OCDQ-RE was designed specifically for use in elementary school, the OCDQ-RS for secondary schools, and the OCDQ-RM for middle schools. OCDQ-RE uses four climate prototypes: (1) open, (2) engaged, (3) disengaged, and (4) closed. For example, a disengaged climate, which exemplifies ineffective attempts by the principal to control faculty behavior, contrasts directly with behaviors of personnel in engaged climates. Each of the newer OCDQ climate instruments has been tested thoroughly for validity and reliability for use at their respective school levels.

The OCDQ-RS is a 34-item instrument designed to assess climate in secondary schools. It focuses on five dimensions of behavior including the supportive and directive behaviors of teacher personnel. Two of the dimensions describe the behaviors exhibited by the principal and three center on teacher behaviors, specifically teacher relationships with students, colleagues, and supervisors. Resulting data provide descriptions of the openness and intimacy of the school climate. As we previously defined it, intimacy refers to the level of satisfaction that teachers obtain from their friendly relationships with other teachers in the school.

The OCDQ-RM (Hoy & Tarter, 1997) represented an effort to create a climate instrument especially designed for use in middle schools. More information about the OCDQ-RM and the OCDQ-RE is available in the publication, *Healthy Schools* (Hoy & Tarter, 1997).

In addition to those described, a number of other climate assessment instruments has been developed and tested for use in schools. Among those still widely used are the *School Discipline Climate Survey: Toward a Safe Orderly Learning Environment* (Grossnickle, 1993); the *School Climate and Context Inventory* (Bobbett & French, 1992); the *Tennessee School Climate Inventory* (Butler & Albery, 1991), the *Group Openness and Trust Scale* (Bulach & Malone, 1993); and the *Comprehensive Assessment of School Environments* (National Association of Secondary School Principals, 1987).

In many cases, school districts have found it convenient to design their own climate survey tools. Such instruments can be useful for gaining feedback from a variety of school stakeholders, but they have the disadvantage of lacking state or national norms for comparative purposes. Figure 8.1 illustrates a district-designed climate assessment instrument. Surveys designed by school personnel can be administered to teachers, students, and parents. They compare results in a variety of ways, including the perceptions of school climate by students in relation to the perceptions of the faculty.

Peoria School Improvement Climate Study

School _____

Grade _____

Directions:

Circle the number that best describes how you feel about your school. Do not circle more than one number for each statement.
Value of the number:
(1) Strongly disagree, (2) Disagree, (3) Don't know, (4) Agree, (5) Strongly agree

I. School Atmosphere	
1. Our school has a friendly atmosphere.	1 2 3 4 5
2. Our school is a place where students want to be and a place where they can learn in a pleasant environment.	1 2 3 4 5

(Continued)

(Continued)

3. The students and staff take pride in our school.	1 2 3 4 5
4. School spirit and morale are high in our school.	1 2 3 4 5
5. Students and staff members in our school are usually happy.	1 2 3 4 5
II. Student Staff Relationships	
1 Staff members and students trust and respect one another.	1 2 3 4 5
2. Teachers in our school care about students and go out of their way to help them.	1 2 3 4 5
3. Teachers and other personnel in our school treat students fairly and as persons.	1 2 3 4 5
4. Students and staff in our school frequently participate in activities that solve problems and improve our school.	1 2 3 4 5
5. The principal of our school is respected by students and staff members and is looked upon as an effective leader.	1 2 3 4 5
III. Student Behavior/School Rules	
1. There are relatively few disciplinary problems in our school.	1 2 3 4 5
2. The rules in our school are clearly defined and fair.	1 2 3 4 5
3. Most students in our school obey the school rules.	1 2 3 4 5
4. Student attendance is good in our school.	1 2 3 4 5
5. Visitors in our school consider our students well-behaved and courteous.	1 2 3 4 5
IV. Peer Relationships	
1. The students in our school get along well with each other.	1 2 3 4 5
2. The students in our school are treated with respect regardless of race, religion, or physical or mental handicaps.	1 2 3 4 5
3. Students in our school are willing to give a helping hand to other students.	1 2 3 4 5
4. There is little friction or hostility between groups of students in our school.	1 2 3 4 5
5. New students are made to feel welcome and a part of our school.	1 2 3 4 5
V. Student Achievement/Learning Environment	
1. Student achievement is high in our school.	1 2 3 4 5
2. Students feel that our school program is meaningful.	1 2 3 4 5
3. The teachers in our school make learning enjoyable.	1 2 3 4 5
4. I like who I am and feel good about myself.	1 2 3 4 5
5. Students in our school seem to like and feel good about themselves.	1 2 3 4 5

Figure 8.1   Student School Climate Survey Instrument

There are other assessment strategies for gaining input from staff personnel that tie closely to one or more of the human resources processes and can result in findings that serve to improve current practices and ultimately lead to climate improvement. For example, valuable information can be gathered from employees who have decided to leave the system through the use of well-designed exit interviews. Information gained from an exit interview can help to determine why employees are leaving and what the school system might have done to retain them. Questions such as the following tend to serve such purposes:

1. What did you like best about working here? What did you like least?

2. What steps would you suggest to improve the workplace in this system? What changes might you suggest?

3. To what extent were you able to realize your career goals while working here?

4. What opportunities did you have for discussing your career goals and teaching interests with others in the school system?

Because much more of human resources administrators' time is being spent on people management and efforts to make the school system a place where professional personnel and other workers want to be, more attention necessarily will be directed to assessments of the workplace environment and its competitive ability to attract and retain quality personnel.

Research on School Climate

Mary Parker Follett and others questioned the emphasis placed on the technical aspects of work for fostering productivity, as exemplified by Taylor's task system in the scientific management era. Follett contended that the central problem of any enterprise is the building and maintaining of dynamic yet harmonious human relationships. Her concepts of coordination for refocusing methods of supervisory and personnel practices to achieve organizational harmony were revolutionary. She introduced the concept of integration for dealing with conflict and initiated foundations for contemporary practices such as participatory management, commitment to superordinate system goals versus personal vested interests, and integrative approaches to problem solving, including collective negotiations. Follett's work spurred many subsequent investigations that sought a better understanding of the relationship between the human element and organizational health and productivity.

Throughout the 1920s and during the next three decades, much attention was given to organizational concepts in the areas of democratic leadership. Informal group influences, the school as a social system, and other organizational characteristics were among the topics studied in relation to school climate. Much of the contemporary thought relating to organizational climate had its beginning in the 1960s.

Since that time, numerous climate studies have centered on (1) the characteristics of schools with positive climates, (2) the impact of climate on student achievement, (3) the impact of climate on the behavior of personnel, and (4) the impact of school climate on school program innovation and change. The following sections discuss research studies related to each of these areas.

Characteristics of Schools With Positive Climates

Many of the studies of climate, completed during the late 1970s and 1980s, centered on the effective school movement. Walberg and Genova (1982) found that the use of professional knowledge by teachers was significantly associated with such climate characteristics as equality of staff treatment, integration of staff cooperation, goal direction, and learning orientation.

School climate is a key factor in the difference between effective and ineffective schools. These results were supported by Farrar and Flakus-Mosqueda (1986), who found that the one element all successful school improvement programs had in common was the development of a positive climate in which problems and issues could be identified and resolved. Short and Greer (1997) contended that, "In the healthy organization, challenges are addressed, solutions to problems are found, and new methods and innovations are initiated. . . . Thus, a healthy organization not only has effective processes but also is likely to have a high trust culture" (p. 63).

Rutherford (1985) studied perceptions of effective and less effective principals relative to five characteristics. One characteristic was the establishment and maintenance of a supportive school climate. He found that effective principals differed from less effective principals in their views of school climate. For example, less effective principals were much more concerned with maintaining a nonthreatening, "keep clear of problems" environment. Taylor and Tashakkori (1994) collected data on the factors affecting climate from 9,987 teachers and 27,994 students. They found that the leadership of the school, the collegiality of the faculty, and student discipline were the major factors influencing school climate (Winter & Sweeney, 1994). Such support is exemplified in principals who recognize achievement, back up teachers, encourage teachers, care for teachers, and administer school rules fairly. Sweeney (1992) reported research results from a study of more than 600 schools nationally. The principal's effectiveness in learning environment administration, instructional leadership, and human resources management correlated highly with a positive climate. In fact, human resources management was the principal behavior most highly correlated with a positive school climate.

These research findings describe many characteristics that promote positive climates in schools and school systems, including such factors as the establishment of clear school goals; high expectations for human performance; a high level of interpersonal relations and cooperative work efforts founded on trust; contacts with the culture in which the school is embedded; a supportive, caring school leader; a problem-solving capacity within the school; and the existence of high esprit within the school community. The following sections discuss the research and practices relating to organizational climate and student achievement.

The Impact of School Climate on Student Achievement

The definition of human resources used in this text emphasizes the fostering of organizational climate for the purpose of enhancing the accomplishment of school goals. Most everyone agrees that student achievement ranks high among the goals for schools. Over the past 30–40 years, numerous research studies have centered on the relationship between school climate and student achievement. Hopkins and Crain (1985) described efforts in a suburban high school to improve test scores through improvements in the school's climate, including such strategies as student participation in decision making. A 10-year high of ACT scores, improved student attendance, significant decrease in the dropout rate, and other positive student outcomes were attributed to the positive climate changes made by the school administrators.

Studies by Hoy and Appleberry (1970), Lunenburg (1983), and Deibert and Hoy (1977) support the general findings of Hopkins and Crain (1985). For example, Lunenburg's research demonstrated that students' perceptions of humanistic school climate related in a positive manner to their personal motivation, task orientation, problem solving, and attitude toward learning.

Paredes and Frazer (1992) examined school climate over a four-year period. They found that (1) high schools with positive climates had higher student achievement and lower dropout rates, (2) student achievement was affected most directly by teacher expectations of student success and the instructional goals of teachers, and (3) school climate scores were better predictors of student dropout rates. Newman and Associates (1996) extended the foregoing findings in their report of a five-year study related to school success and school culture. Researchers found that commitment to high student expectations, support for staff innovation and creativity, an ongoing search for new ideas, and a climate of caring and collaboration among staff were among those conditions directly related to school success.

Such factors as due process procedures for students and efforts to develop clearly written school rules and procedures, along with specific efforts to disseminate them, led to improved climates in nine schools in Kentucky and Tennessee (Bobbett & French, 1992). Bulach and Malone (1994) used three survey instruments to study the impact of the principal's leadership style on school climate and student achievement; they found a significant difference between leadership style and the subscale of school climate.

Many local school districts have reported increases in student achievement following concerted efforts to improve the climate of the school. Winter and Sweeney (1994) summarized the results of the research on the relationship between climate and student achievement:

> For more than a decade, studies have proven that climate makes a difference in secondary school. Climate affects student achievement and behavior independent of student's intelligence or home environment. It is also reflected in the shared attitudes, beliefs, and values of the people of the school. (p. 66)

We submit that the foregoing research findings are of paramount importance for the work of school leaders. Practitioners who seek practical research results should carefully examine the findings of organizational studies such as those reviewed in the foregoing sections. The research on climate is clear; what is needed is a serious implementation of the research findings.

The Impact of School Climate on the Behavior of Personnel

Herzberg, Mausner, and Snyderman (1959) pointed out more than 40 years ago that interpersonal relationships with one's superior and the technical aspects of supervision were organizational **hygienes** associated with job dissatisfaction. In 2000, the Gallup Organization gave this contention major support. Gallup interviewed 200,000 employees and concluded that the length of an employee's stay with an organization is determined by the quality of the relationship with his or her immediate supervisor (Buckingham, 2000).

The impact of the workplace environment on employee satisfaction, commitment, and loyalty is no longer a matter of debate. Virtually every study of employee attitudes and behavior reaches the same conclusion: work conditions, in the long run, loom more important to job satisfaction and worker retention than do salary and other monetary incentives. "And, the organizational climate of the school often is disrupted when high turnover occurs because the efforts to develop positive interpersonal relationships and collaborative support networks in the school system and community for the purpose of delivering effective learning environments are thwarted" (Norton, 2001, p. 16).

It is clear that success in organizations today depends on a working environment that encourages input of the best ideas regardless of the sources of these ideas, and the collaboration of workers and team efforts to implement these ideas in the most optimal ways. Such working relationships are not possible in school systems with unhealthy school climates.

Organizational climate has been found to affect staff in a variety of ways. As we noted in the foregoing discussion, job satisfaction is directly related to conditions of work. Conditions of work include the nature of the supervision received, administrative support, parental support, interpersonal relationships, participation in the system's decision making, and consideration of one's work and life needs. Patrick (1995) found that the principal's administrative style had much influence on the job satisfaction of teaching personnel. In related studies, researchers have found that school climate factors, such as the principal's leadership, the collegiality of the faculty, student discipline, and staff placements in school settings that provide the opportunity for them to use their personal and professional strengths and to do what they do best, were major determinants of staff job enjoyment and satisfaction.

Previously, we discussed the OCDQ-RE climate assessment instrument. Hoy and Clover (1986) developed four prototypes of climate that result in various teacher behaviors. For example, the open climate features cooperation and respect within the faculty and between the faculty and the school principal. Teacher behavior fosters open and professional interactions among faculty members. The open climate promotes cooperative behavior among faculty members and meaningful engagement in their work. In the engaged climate, teachers tend to ignore the principal's attempts to control faculty behavior. Teachers respect each other's professionalism and competence. Attention to tasks is high, and the faculty members are professionally responsive despite the principal's restrictive behaviors. In disengaged climates, relationship behaviors in the school are negative. Teachers are not engaged in the tasks, and teacher behaviors are exemplified by divisiveness, intolerance, and noncommitment. Teacher behaviors in closed climates are quite similar to those in disengaged situations: task commitment is low, intimacy is low, and collegiality also is low.

Hoy and Miskel (2001) summarized the research on school climate and its impact on staff personnel as follows: "Recent research . . . shows that open school climates are characterized by higher levels of loyalty and trust, both faculty trust in the principal and in colleagues, than closed climates" (p. 150). They stated further that research clearly indicates that open schools generate higher levels of school commitment, and the openness of the climate is related to teacher participation in decision making as well as higher ratings of school effectiveness.

Dealing With Conflict

Conflict is an antagonistic state or action that is exemplified by divergent ideas and interests of individuals or groups. Hoy and Miskel (2001) point out that, "Administrators are faced with the classic confrontations between individual needs and organizational expectations; consequently, they spend a substantial amount of time attempting to mediate conflict" (p. 245). These authors also note additionally that power and politics are facts of organizational life, and, thus, conflict in organizations is inevitable. We discussed open and closed systems earlier in this chapter; both types of systems are subject to conflict, but open systems are much more prepared to deal with it.

Schools with unhealthy climates find it difficult to deal with conflict because personnel do not work well together. In these climates, rules and regulations set the manner in which things are done, and the systems lacks a needed problem-solving capacity. Thus, problems are "resolved" through mandate as opposed to an integration of ideas and alternatives, and conflict is often resolved in these environments by employee turnover. In an open school climate, disagreement and the expression of other points of view are not only expected, but are solicited. That is, the system purposely seeks input from all staff personnel through such means as suggestions systems, the use of "think tanks" for problem solving, and the use of shadow group techniques that place general staff personnel in role-play exercises to examine problems that the system and its administrative personnel face. Healthy school systems realize that any attempt to discourage disagreement will most likely result in negative outcomes such as poor relationships and lack of confidence in the system's leadership.

In a healthy school climate, the consideration of controversial matters can be useful. Progress in terms of goal achievement and new understandings is often generated through opportunities to reflect on problems and alternative solutions. Thus, the HR administrator can help make disagreements constructive in a number of ways. One need is for the HR administrator to broaden the base of stakeholder understanding through purposeful assessment of criticism the school or school system receives. In this way, the HR administrator is in a much better position to limit unfair criticism, because assessment strategies serve to distinguish between constructive and destructive proposals.

Human resource administrators must implement viable methods for learning about the existence and specific concerns of criticism. The advantage of an open climate in this regard is that open channels of communication are most likely already in place; these channels serve as the system's nervous system whereby school leaders are more able to discern conflict at an early stage and make an immediate, appropriate response to any attack, as well as keep such conflict more manageable. In those instances when criticism is unfair or based on irresponsible behavior, a planned strategy is necessary. The gathering of accurate information concerning the situation at hand, obtaining the participation of knowledgeable groups and individuals on the matter, and strategizing for appropriate counteraction are among the steps needed in such cases.

Public relations personnel have learned that attempts to cover up school problems, or to use the tired phrase of "no comment" when working with the media and others, only tend to exacerbate the problem. Thus, the overall task of HR administrators is to work to maintain integrity and stakeholder confidence in a climate where critics have the right to disagree and to access the school system's open channels of communication. Conflict and controversy can be helpful in leading to preferred solutions. Schools that maintain a communications initiative such as suggested here are much more likely to deal effectively with the inevitable conflict they will encounter as a social institution.

School Life and Staff Commitment

The importance of gaining the commitment of staff personnel to the school system and its purposes is emphasized throughout this text. Although staff commitment is the result of various influences, research findings point out that worker loyalty is tied closely to how employees perceive that their supervisors are supporting inside and outside work life (Laabs, 1996). In fact, a workforce commitment study by Aon Consulting Worldwide (1998) found that the biggest driver of employee loyalty was having managers who recognize employees' need to balance work with home life. This climate conditioner differs drastically with earlier views that the worker was never to let family or home life interfere with the job. Work-life matters have become ones of paramount importance to employees generally. It is certain that structured work schedules for teachers and other school staff members must be reevaluated in view of the changing attitudes of today's employees toward work and life balances. New innovations in work schedules and instructional delivery in schools must be implemented. If not improved, job satisfaction will lessen and school climate will suffer. The implications for work-life management by HR administrators include the following:

1. Studies reveal that both workplace and home life support by the organization increases employee loyalty. Thus, failure to recognize this fact will harm school climate and staff commitment to the school system.

2. Schools must give full attention to work-life benefits in school settings in order to attract and retain quality personnel. Recruiting, selection, and retention processes must give high priority to "advertising" how the school system is giving attention to benefits in the area of work life. Policy decisions and HR strategies must recognize the inextricable relationship between the work and personal life of staff personnel. The HR processes of recruiting, selection, and retention necessarily must emphasize the needs of staff members, not only the needs of the school system.

3. HR administrators must realize that giving attention to school climate and to staff commitment by recognizing work-life balances is not just something they *should* do, but rather something they *must* do in order to keep the school system alive and vital.

The Impact of School Climate on Organizational Change and Innovation

Several investigators have examined the relationship between types of school climate and the rate of innovations in schools. As early as 1966, Marcum studied innovative and noninnovative schools in a five-state area and found a significant difference between school climates of the most innovative and least innovative schools. School faculties judged innovative schools as having open climates. Bennett (1969) and Christian (1972) also studied innovation in relation to school climate. Bennett found a higher positive relationship in both number and types of innovations in the more open types of climate. Christian used Halpin and Croft's OCDQ to study climate in elementary schools relative to the introduction and use of innovative educational practices. He found a significant positive relationship at the 0.01 level between openness and the rate of introduction and utilization of innovations in the school studied. The climate factors of disengagement and esprit were most closely related to the *rate* of use of innovations; the characteristics of aloofness and thrust, as related to positive principal behaviors, were most directly related to the *degree* of school innovativeness (see Table 8.2).

During the 1980s and 1990s, considerable climate research focused on school change as related to school reform. Bulach and Malone (1994) studied the relationship between several school climate characteristics (e.g., group openness and group trust) and the implementation of reform efforts in Kentucky. Thirteen schools and 292 teachers participated in the study. The researchers stated that, "the results of this study lead to the conclusion that school climate is a significant factor in successfully implementing school reform" (p. 7). The researchers cautioned that higher climate scores could have been the result of successfully implementing school reform. They were not certain which was cause and which was effect.

Those involved in school reform have also noted the importance of climate. For example, Akin (1993) expressed the opinion that administrators who expect to be successful in school site-based management projects must first understand their school's climate and know how to change a negative climate to one that exemplifies the positive characteristics of healthy organizations. Similarly, Stevens (1990)

Table 8.2 The Behavior of School Principals and Resulting Teacher Behavior

Principal Behaviors	Teacher Behaviors
Supportive Behavior	*Collegial Behavior*
Avoids the assignment of meaningless routines and burdensome duties to teachers.	Teachers help and support each other.
Allows flexibility and freedom to act independently.	Teachers respect the professional competence of their colleagues.
Gives teachers respect and support in both personal and professional tasks.	Teachers accomplish their work with vim, vigor, and pleasure.
Listens and is open to teacher suggestions.	Teachers have a high level of esprit de corps.
Gives genuine and frequent praise.	Teachers are highly committed to the work of the school.
Allows teachers freedom to perform without close scrutiny.	Teachers are engaged in creative efforts, innovation, and change.
Provides facilitating leadership behavior devoid of bureaucratic red tape.	Teachers assume a responsibility for their own personal and professional development.

SOURCE: Adapted from *Instructional Leadership* by Hoy, A. W., and Hoy, W. K. (2003), Boston, MA: Allyn & Bacon, pp. 286–287.

argued that giving attention to important climate considerations is a significant forerunner of school reform.

Hoy and Miskel (2001) stated that, "The principal of a healthy school provides dynamic leadership—leadership that is both task oriented and relations oriented. Such behavior is supportive of teachers and yet provides directions and maintains high standards of performance" (p. 200). Yet they were cautious in suggesting that the idea of changing organizational culture, or even bringing about real change, is simplistic. And, as other researchers have noted, "something that emerges as an abstract, unconscious, and complex expression of needs and beliefs, it is not a maneuverable or manageable entity" (Norton, Webb, Dlugosh, & Sybouts, 1996, p. 75). Nevertheless, certain empirical truths have been discovered in relation to climate and organizational change: (1) change in organizations is much more readily realized and effective if personnel understand what the change is all about and why it is necessary, (2) successful implementation of change and innovation requires that attention be given to special training needs that serve to provide the necessary knowledge and skills to implement new goals and programs, and (3) strategies for recruiting, selecting, assigning, retaining, compensating, and developing personnel must focus on the changes and innovations in question.

This chapter has focused on organizational climate, and research is clear that it can be assessed and improved. The following section discusses successful programs and practices for improving school climate and the responsibilities of HR administrators in achieving this end.

Improvement of School Climate

The improvement of school climate is a responsibility of all school personnel. However, the school principal, as a human resources administrator, must assume a leadership role in assessing the climate and taking action for improvement based on the implications of assessment results. This contention is problematic in many ways: because the condition of school climate ties closely to the quality of the principal's leadership and ability to work with the human element, principals in some instances might be reluctant to survey staff personnel on this matter.

As we saw in the previous discussion on measuring school climate, most climate instruments focus on the leadership and human skills of the principal in large part. The following section provides a review of the CFK Ltd. School Climate Profile, followed by a discussion of operational models that can be used to improve the climate in school settings.

Program, Process, and Material Determinants of School Climate

As we previously noted, one of the landmark publications in the area of school climate improvement is Phi Delta Kappa's publication, *School Climate Improvement: A Challenge to the School Administrator* (1973). Although the publication was first marketed nearly 30 years ago, its conceptual foundations remain applicable for practice in contemporary school settings. The publication, based on many of the climate concepts set forth in an earlier Charles F. Kettering Ltd. publication, sets forth school climate factors under three categories: **program, process, and material determinants.** Figure 8.2 presents each of the three climate dimensions and the provisions that accompany them. The CFK Ltd. instrument includes each of the climate determinants set forth in Figure 8.2.

Climate improvement begins with assessing the school's climate for the purposes of ascertaining areas targeted for improvement, determining a foundation for the purposes of ascertaining areas targeted for improvement, and determining a foundation for evaluating climate improvement changes resulting from specific program actions. Improvement procedures include the following action steps:

1. Human resources administrators must gain an understanding of school climate and its determinants. They must also be knowledgeable of climate assessment procedures.

2. Human resources administrators must examine their leadership role in a program of climate improvement. Such an examination centers on leadership

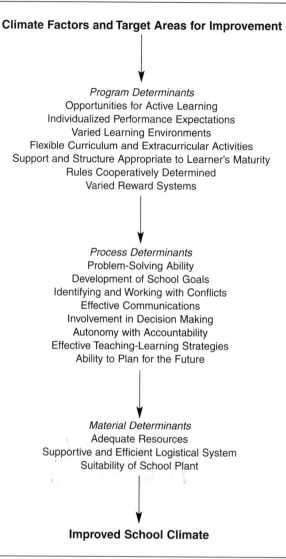

Climate Factors and Target Areas for Improvement

Program Determinants
Opportunities for Active Learning
Individualized Performance Expectations
Varied Learning Environments
Flexible Curriculum and Extracurricular Activities
Support and Structure Appropriate to Learner's Maturity
Rules Cooperatively Determined
Varied Reward Systems

Process Determinants
Problem-Solving Ability
Development of School Goals
Identifying and Working with Conflicts
Effective Communications
Involvement in Decision Making
Autonomy with Accountability
Effective Teaching-Learning Strategies
Ability to Plan for the Future

Material Determinants
Adequate Resources
Supportive and Efficient Logistical System
Suitability of School Plant

Improved School Climate

Figure 8.2   The School Climate Profile: Program, Process, and Material Determinants

SOURCE: Robert S. Fox et al. Phi Delta Kappa, *School Climate Improvement: A Challenge to the School Administrator* (1973). Reprinted by permission.

responsibilities in assessing improvement needs, working to determine cooperative goals, determining actions strategies, implementing strategies, and monitoring progress and improvement results.

3. Human resources administrators must assume leadership in the implementation of specific climate improvement projects. For each project, assessing improvement needs, setting objectives, implementing strategies, and controlling the improvement process are required leadership actions. (Phi Delta Kappa, 1973)

Thus, the route to school climate improvement depends largely on the extent to which program, process, and material determinants are being assessed, programmed, and monitored by school personnel. For example, the program determinant "individualized performance expectations" would be reflected in the attention given to the placement of students in appropriate learning environments scaled to their relative abilities, learning styles, and interests. Other considerations might include attention to teacher talents and interests in work assignments, the use of specially prepared teaching materials for individualizing instruction, and other program provisions that foster varied learning environments for students.

School Improvement Models and Strategies

Sweeney (1992) recommended several things that are needed for the improvement of climate in schools. He suggested that the first step in the process—awareness—is often the most difficult. "People need to understand what climate is, how it affects them and others, and what can be done to improve it" (p. 71). School personnel must identify the primary beliefs and values that should guide the school and what must be done to initiate a plan of action to implement these beliefs toward the goal of climate improvement.

Wilmore (1992) suggested three keys to the development of effective school climate: (1) curriculum and instruction, (2) student affairs, and (3) parental support. She contended that curriculum should be student centered and that one of the best ways to promote positive school climate and an effective school is through a viable student affairs program. She also recognized that schools are not successful without a strong system of support from parents. Wilmore (1992) maintained that parental support stems largely from a sincere belief that school personnel truly care about the personal development of their child. Other studies, including the 1997 study by the National Center for Educational Statistics, have supported Wilmore's contention that parental support is essential for positive school climates.

Human Resources Responsibilities in the Improvement of School Climate

This text emphasizes that all school administrative personnel are human resources administrators. As is true with every human resources process, the organizational climate process is a shared responsibility among school leaders at all levels. Regardless of the position of the school administrator, we believe that the following primary responsibilities must be assumed. This belief is supported by the literature concerning successful programs and practices in the area of organizational climate.

1. *The Development of a Set of Shared Goals.* "Goals are those statements that set forth the purposes of the school system. Goals serve to clarify the aims of the school system; they provide a focus for the organization and give it a meaningful direction.

Goals express what is important to the school system overall and are undergirded by the beliefs, values, traditions, and culture of the school system's community" (Norton et al., 1996, pp. 111–112). A primary process determinant of school climate is the development of a viable set of school goals. The significance of cooperative behavior as an important characteristic of school climate has been well established. In Barnard's classic work, *The Functions of the Executive* (1938), he set forth the belief that cooperation is essential for individuals in an organization. Cooperation necessitates commitment to a set of group goals and, as Barnard emphasized, the formulation of organizational purposes and objectives is one of the three primary functions of all organizational leaders. Thus, human resources administrators must assume leadership roles in developing a set of shared goals that express the school or school system's important and unique objectives. Once such goal statements are completed, a procedure for objectively examining these goals must be implemented.

2. *Self-Image and High Expectations.* We previously noted that effective schools, ones with healthy climates, hold high expectations for student and personnel performance. Levels of expectation should be such as to solicit the best performance that each teacher, student, or administrator has to offer. Viable goals provide a focus and give meaning to the people in the school. Such meaning is exemplified by the important work, personal motivations, and commitments of the school system's human element. The meanings that are important to the system make up the system's self-image. A positive self-image serves as a foundational component of an open, healthy school climate. Human resources leadership must work to develop a meaningful self-image for the organization, one that reflects the beliefs and values of importance to its stakeholders.

3. *Opportunities for Personal Growth and Development.* Healthy organizations understand that they will progress as people in the organization grow and develop. Schools with open, healthy climates tend to attract talented personnel who are motivated by opportunities to contribute and to be recognized for the important roles they play in the achievement of school purposes. Human resources administrators help to develop the school system's full potential by removing obstacles that inhibit growth opportunities, by assigning personnel in positions that allow human potential to be realized, and by establishing an environment that encourages creative activity. Such an environment enables personnel in the school to be innovative, to develop different, more efficient, and more effective methods of achieving school goals and objectives. New and creative ideas must have a chance for implementation, but without the freedom to fail under controlled conditions, such ideas will not likely be tested. Human resources leaders must work to provide opportunities for staff personnel to assume the major responsibility for their own personal growth. Such opportunities are more likely to exist in school systems that encourage the use of individual strengths, and in which staff personnel believe that their thoughts and creations are welcome and respected.

4. *Development of a Viable Set of Personnel Policies and Regulations.* Many people believe that a school district's personnel policies and regulations are a direct

reflection of how it values its human resources. Governance policies directly affect the work and life of school employees, and, therefore, human resources administrators must assume a leadership role in the development of such policies. School policies and regulations affect the school climate in numerous ways. Policies are an important means of implementing the established goals that direct programs and influence interpersonal relationships. Policies serve to release human potential by providing opportunities for discretionary action on the part of the professional staff. They serve an important communication role in helping all people understand the school system and its purposes, and, as we previously noted, a viable set of policies and regulations serves to release the strength and creativity of personnel and allows them to establish a basis for intelligent decision making within the system. In Chapter 9, we suggest that human resource administrators should be given the primary authority for developing viable personnel policy for the school district. Such a recommendation requires the HR director to be involved directly in all personnel policy decisions of the school district. This responsibility provides HR leaders an opportunity to directly affect the climate of the school they serve.

5. *Problem-Solving Capacity.* Schools with healthy climates, like schools with less healthy ones, regularly face problems. A primary difference is that schools with positive climates have an identifiable problem-solving capacity. Climate characteristics that facilitate the availability to meet and resolve problems include open channels of communication, effective suggestion systems, a research posture, and recruitment and selection policies that encourage the hiring of a diversified staff. Human resources personnel must clearly identify ways to increase the effectiveness of communication, educate others about these channels, and facilitate their use. Effective problem solution and effective communication are inextricably related. Problem solving requires that the best ideas be heard and that they be considered on the basis of their merit as opposed to their origin. Open systems work diligently to increase the flow of ideas both vertically and horizontally within the system.

Human resources leadership necessitates the development of a research posture within the school system. Problem solving often depends on the development of new knowledge. The effective human resources administrator is a consumer, facilitator, and disperser of good research, who realizes that creative solutions are often the outcome of research efforts that have objectively examined viable alternatives.

As we previously emphasized, a healthy school climate is not a product but a continuous process. Organizational climate is a people phenomenon, and people are the primary concern of human resources administration.

Summary

The human resources function by definition holds a primary responsibility for fostering an organizational climate that enhances goal achievement.

Organizational climate is of paramount importance to the operation of schools and their personnel because it affects every process of the HR function. Early work in the area of organizational climate by Halpin, Croft, and others opened the field for numerous investigations on the topic. Their OCDQ spurred hundreds of empirical studies designed to ascertain the type of climate in various schools and led to major studies to determine the characteristics of various climate types, the effects of climate on people behavior and student achievement, and the extent to which various types of climate influence innovation and change in organizations.

Various field studies have led to the development of frameworks that serve as models for improving climate in schools. Such models hold strong implications for leadership by the school principal. Virtually every study in the area of school climate links the type of climate to the leadership behavior of the school principal.

The improvement of school climate is the responsibility of all school personnel. Nevertheless, human resources units and administrators have specific responsibilities in the administration of organizational climate, including developing a set of shared goals, fostering a positive self-image for the school system, providing opportunities for personal growth and development, developing a viable set of personnel policies and procedures, and working to ensure a problem-solving capacity within the system.

Discussion Questions

1. Give thought to the climate of the school or school system that you know most about. What climate characteristics can you identify in each situation? After noting several climate characteristics for a particular school or system, attempt to label its climate type according to Halpin and Croft's or Hoy and Tarter's prototypes discussed in this chapter.

2. Discuss the approaches that today's schools are using to change the environments. Which factors tend to foster or inhibit positive climate in educational settings? Are these factors tied closely to monetary provisions or to factors more closely related to conditions of work, such as workload and administrative support?

3. This chapter suggests strongly that school principals have great influence on the school climate in their buildings. What changes might increase this influence in the next several years? Are there changes that might serve to reduce this influence?

4. Reexamine the several characteristics of the program, process, and material determinants associated with the CFK Ltd. School Climate Profile. Which of these characteristics do you view as most important in conditioning school climate? Support your response with specific examples.

Case Studies

CASE 8.1

MAKING THE WORST OF A GOOD SITUATION

Principal William McChesney was the newly selected principal for Antonio High School. He was follow-ing in the footsteps of Art Lown, who had served for six years. Under the leadership of Principal Lown, Antonio High School had gained a reputation as one of the best schools in the southwest region. The teaching staff at Antonio was viewed as highly creative; three on the faculty had been named teacher of the year in the state. Turnover in the high school was quite low, and Principal Lown was viewed as an administrator who was highly supportive and easily approachable. Faculty and parents regretted his departure to California to head a developing program for at-risk students.

During the first week at Antonio High School, Principal McChesney sent a questionnaire to faculty members asking for their input on what improvements might be made in the school's program and activities. The feedback from the faculty revealed their creativeness; many improvement ideas were presented. One member of the staff suggested that the principal's control over curriculum be lessened and delegated largely to faculty personnel in the respective school departments. Another recom-mended a representative faculty advisory committee for the purpose of developing school policies and procedures in order to improve faculty involvement in participative management.

Principal McChesney did not act directly on any of the several recommendations received. At the sec-ond monthly meeting of the faculty, he commented, "I'll take your ideas under advisement. I must say, however, that I was under the impression that I was entering a school with a happier family than is appar-ently the case." One faculty member raised her hand to speak, but McChesney indicated that he would be following up on this matter soon. Within the next two weeks, he talked with faculty members indi-vidually about their suggestions. For the most part, he probed the matter about their apparent "unhap-piness" with the present school operation. The consensus of faculty responses implied that there were really no major problems at Antonio, but that any school had some room for improvements.

Over the next several weeks, directives from McChesney's office centered on plans for focusing on performance evaluations, his desire to sit in on department meetings dealing with program and activi-ties within the school, and his intention to "flatten the organization" by eliminating the department heads by the end of the first semester. In addition, he sent a newly revised draft of recommended poli-cies and procedures for the faculty's information.

By the close of the first semester, two department heads had asked to be relieved from the role, and three faculty members sent letters requesting transfers to other schools. For the first time in the school's history, Antonio students held a "sit-in" in the school cafeteria; their protest focused on the lack of opportunity for input into the decision-making process. Both student and teacher absenteeism increased significantly as well.

As Principal McChesney sat in his office late one Friday afternoon, he contemplated the school situa-tion with some bewilderment. "How did this situation change in so short a time?" he thought to him-self. "What should I do now?"

Questions

1. In view of the somewhat limited information in Case 8.1, present your thoughts about what seems to be happening at Antonio High School.

2. At this point, what positive steps might Principal McChesney take to reverse current climate trends? Do you believe that such a reversal is possible in this setting? Why or why not?

3. Discuss the situation in which a new school administrator moves into a school. Are there rec-ommended procedures for entering such a new situation? Name two or more specific actions or behaviors that new administrators would be wise to consider on moving into a new leadership position.

CASE 8.2

WHAT'S REALLY IMPORTANT AROUND HERE?

Virginia Royce was in her second year of teaching at College View High School. Her performance ratings for year one were "very good" in all categories. She had gained the reputation as one of the school's most promising new teachers. At the close of school on a Friday in October, Mrs. Royce went to the principal's office and asked if Mr. Henson, the principal, was available. The secretary answered in the positive and indicated that she was certain that he could visit with her.

"Come in, Mrs. Royce," directed Principal Henson. "What's on your mind on this late Friday afternoon?" "Something has been troubling me for several weeks," answered Mrs. Royce. "So far this semester, six football players have been absent from my English class for the last period of the day on three occasions, and on two occasions they were absent for the full afternoon to play in out-of-town games, so they had to miss two other teachers' classes as well on those days. Pep rallies generally are held the last class period of the day before games; it all adds up to the question of, 'What's really important around here?'"

Questions

1. Assume the role of Principal Henson in Case 8.2. How might you answer Mrs. Royce?

2. In your opinion, is it sufficient to respond that both subject-matter classes and extracurricular activities are important at College View High School? What other factors must you consider in this case?

3. Use the concepts of open climates, use of criticism, and open channels of communication for conflict resolution set forth in this chapter and apply them to Case 8.2. Write out your action plan that you would use to resolve the conflict described in the case. (Note: Class members couldbe assigned roles in Case 8.2 and role-play the situation using the conflict concepts in the chapter.)

References

Akin, J. (1993). The effects of site culture on reform. *High School Magazine, 1*(1), 29.

Aon Consulting Worldwide, Inc. (1998). *America @ work.* Chicago: Author.

Barnard, C. I. (1938). *The functions of the executive.* Cambridge, MA: Harvard University Press.

Bennett, R. E. (1969). An analysis of the relationships of organizational climate to innovations in selected schools of Pennsylvania and New York. *Dissertation Abstracts, 30,* 942A.

Bentley, R. R., & Rempel, A. M. (1980). *The Purdue teacher opinionaire.* West Lafayette, IN: Purdue University Office of Technology Commercialization.

Bobbett, G. C., & French, R. L. (1992). *Evaluation of climate in "good" high schools in Tennessee, Kentucky, and North Carolina.* Paper presented at the annual meeting of the Southern Regional Council on Educational Administration, Atlanta, GA.

Buckingham, G. (2000, February). Same difference. *People Management, 6*(4), 45.

Bulach, C. R., & Malone, B. (1994). The relationship of school climate to the implementation of school reform. *ERS Spectrum, 12*(4), 3–8.

Butler, E. D., & Albery, M. J. (1991). *Tennessee school climate inventory: A resource manual.* Memphis, TN: Memphis State University, Center for Research in Educational Policy.

Christian, C. F. (1972). *Organizational climate of elementary schools and the introduction and utilization of innovative educational practices.* Unpublished doctoral dissertation, University of Nebraska, Lincoln.

Cunningham, W. G., & Cordeiro, P. A. (2000). *Educational administration.* Needham Heights, MA: Allyn & Bacon.

Deal, T. E., & Peterson, K. D. (1999). *Shaping school culture.* San Francisco: Jossey-Bass.

Decker, L. E., Decker, V. A., & Brown, P. M. (2007). *Diverse partnership for student success.* Lanham, MD: Rowman & Littlefield Education.

Deibert, J. P., & Hoy, W. K. (1977). "Custodial" high schools and self-actualization of students. *Educational Research Quarterly, 2,* 24–31.

Farrar, E., & Flakus-Mosqueda, P. (1986). State sponsored schoolwide improvement programs. What's going on in the school? *Phi Delta Kappan, 67,* 586–589.

Grossnickle, D. R. (1993). The school discipline climate survey: Toward a safe, orderly learning environment. *NASSP Bulletin, 77,* 60–66.

Halpin, A. W., & Croft, D. B. (1962). *The organizational climate of schools* (Contract SAE 543-8639). Washington, DC: U.S. Office of Education.

Harrison, R. (1985). *The 1975 handbook for group facilitation.* Newton, MA: Development Research Associates.

Herzberg, F., Mausner, B., & Snyderman, B. (1959). *The motivation to work.* New York: Wiley.

Hopkins, W., & Crain, K. (1985). *School climates: The key to an effective school.* Paper presented at the annual meeting of the National Association of Secondary School Principals, New Orleans, LA.

Hoy, W. K., & Appleberry, J. B. (1970). Teacher principal relationships in "humanistic" and "custodial" elementary schools. *Journal of Experimental Education, 39,* 27–31.

Hoy, W. K., & Clover, S. I. R. (1986). Elementary school climate: A revision of the OCDQ. *Educational Administration Quarterly, 22,* 93–110.

Hoy, W. K., & Miskel, C. G. (2001). *Educational administration: Theory, research & practice* (6th ed.). New York: McGraw-Hill.

Hoy, W. K., & Tarter, C. J. (1997). *Healthy schools: A handbook for change* (Elementary and Middle School Edition). Thousand Oaks, CA: Corwin.

Hoy, W. K., Tarter, C. J., & Kottkamp, R. B. (1991). *Open schools/healthy schools: Measuring organizational climate.* Newbury Park, CA: Corwin.

Kleiman, L. S. (2000). *Human resources management.* Cincinnati, OH: South-Western College Publishing.

Kottkamp, R. B., Mulhern, J. A., & Hoy, W. K. (1987). Secondary school climate: A revision of the OCDQ. *Educational Administration Quarterly, 23,* 32–48.

Kreitner. R. (2001). *Management* (8th ed.). Boston: Houghton Mifflin.

Laabs, J. J. (1996). Change. *Personnel Journal, 53*(7), 54–63.

Lunenburg, F. C. (1983). Pupil control ideology and self-concept as a learner. *Educational Research Quarterly, 8,* 33–39.

Marcum, R. L. (1966). *Organizational climate and adoption of educational innovations.* Unpublished doctoral dissertation, Utah State University, Logan.

National Association of Secondary School Principals (NASSP). (1987). *Comprehensive assessment of school environments.* Reston, VA: Author.

National Center for Educational Statistics. (1997). *Job satisfaction among America's teachers: Effects of workplace conditions, background characteristics, and teacher compensation.* NCES 97471. Washington, DC: Author.

Newman, F. M., & Associates. (1996). *Authentic instruction: Restructuring schools for intellectual quality.* San Francisco: Jossey-Bass.

Norton, M. S. (2001). Provide school and community orientation to retain your teachers and staff. *School Public Relations, 22*(2), 16–22.

Norton, M. S. (2005). *Executive leadership for effective administration.* Boston: Allyn & Bacon.

Norton, M. S., Webb, L. D., Dlugosh, L. L., & Sybouts, W. (1996). *The school superintendency: New responsibilities, new leadership.* Boston: Allyn & Bacon.

Pai, Y., & Adler, S. A. (2001). *Cultural foundations of education* (3rd ed.). Upper Saddle River, NJ: Prentice Hall.

Paredes, V., & Frazer, L. (1992). *School climate in AISD.* Austin, TX: Independent School District, Office of Research and Evaluation.

Patrick, J. E. (1995). *Correlation between administrative style and school climate.* (ERIC Document Reproduction Service No. ED387853)

Phi Delta Kappa. (1973). *School climate improvement: A challenge to the school administrator.* Bloomington, IN: Author.

Robbins, S. P. (2001). *Organizational behavior* (9th ed.). Upper Saddle River, NJ: Prentice Hall.

Rutherford, W. I. (1985). School principals as effective leaders. *Phi Delta Kappa, 67,* 31–34.

Short, P. M., & Greer, J. T. (1997). *Leadership and empowered schools: Themes from innovative efforts.* Columbus, OH: Merrill.

Stern, G. G. (1964). *High school characteristics index.* Syracuse, NY: Psychological Research Center, Syracuse University.

Stevens, M. P. (1990). School climate and staff development: Keys to school reform. *NASSP Bulletin, 74,* 66–70.

Sweeney, J. (1992). School climate: The key to excellence. *NASSP Bulletin, 76,* 69–73.

Taylor, D. L., & Tashakkori, A. (1994). *Predicting teachers' sense of efficacy and job satisfaction using school climate and participatory decision making.* Paper presented at the annual meeting of the Southwest Educational Research Association, San Antonio, TX.

Walberg, H. J., & Genova, W. J. (1982). Staff, school, and workshop influences on knowledge use in educational improvement efforts. *Journal of Educational Research, 76*(2), 69–80.

Wilmore, E. L. (1992). The "affective" middle level school: Keys to a nurturing school climate. *Schools in the Middle, 1*(4), 31–34.

Winter, J. S., & Sweeney, J. (1994). Improving school climate: Administrators are the key. *NASSP Bulletin, 73,* 65–69.

Wynn, S., & Carboni, L. W. (2006). *Principal leadership, school climate critical to retaining beginning teachers.* Paper presented at the American Educational Research Association annual meeting, San Francisco.

CHAPTER 9

The Legal World of Human Resources Administration

Policy and Regulation Development

Learning Objectives

After reading this chapter, you will be able to

- Define and identify policies, regulations, and bylaws in relation to school governance.
- Describe the benefits of a viable set of governance policies and regulations for the school district and the human resources function.
- Implement a codification system for classifying governance policies and regulations for the human resources function.
- Identify several strategies for developing policies and regulations in a school setting.
- Identify the characteristics of effective school policies.
- Explain the compliance aspects of school policy as related to federal and state laws and court rulings.
- Discuss several of the rulings of the courts that have greatly influenced the human resources function.
- Discuss court rulings related to due process, sexual harassment, teacher dismissal, drug-free workplace, and other important legal considerations for personnel practices in education.
- Describe much of the civil rights legislation and related laws concerning the liberty and property rights of employees.

Legal Considerations and the Human Resources Function

Organizations today are regulated and controlled by legislation, court rulings, and local policies and regulations, and school systems are no exception. The human resources function in school systems operates within a legal world. A statewide study of human resources directors revealed the following results (Norton, 2005):

1. The need for legal skill was ranked second only to human relations skill as a necessary job skill for the HR director.

2. Legal matters, including litigation, ranked third among those HR processes that consumed the greatest amount of the HR director's time.

3. Legal impacts on personnel ranked among the top 10 serious problems facing HR directors in the study.

4. Legal impacts on personnel tied for second among the frequent problems facing HR directors.

5. Lawsuits and litigation of personnel issues were listed among the top five issues, should they intensify, that would likely lead to directors leaving their position.

The following section discusses several rights of employees in school systems. First, it discusses rights related to the following six areas: (1) academic freedom, (2) sexual harassment, (3) employee dismissal, (4) drug-free workplace, (5) teacher transfers, and (6) due process. Second, it identifies and describes several laws specifically related to human resources legislation.

Employee Rights

An employee **right** is "the ability to engage in conduct that is protected by law or social sanction, free from interference by another party." Employees' **statutory rights** "are protected by specific laws enacted by government," and **contractual rights** "are based on the law of contracts" (Gómez-Mejía, Balkin, & Cardy, 2007, p. 467).

The following section discusses employee rights, responsibilities, and duties related to academic freedom of teachers and other educational personnel.

Rights, Responsibilities, and Duties: Academic Freedom

"Academic freedom includes the right of teachers to speak freely about their subjects, to experiment with new ideas, and to select appropriate teaching materials and methods. Courts have held that academic freedom is based on the First Amendment and is fundamental to our democratic society" (Fischer, Schimmel, & Stellman, 2003, p. 134). Academic freedom protection for teachers and the responsibility of teaching personnel to use good judgment in the classroom are included here. In one sense, academic freedom permits teachers to teach in a manner that they deem appropriate, yet the teacher must always be sensitive to the matter of indoctrination; teachers must be particularly careful about the students' freedom when teaching controversial issues and when conflicting values are present.

Administrators attempting to implement academic freedom policies need to proceed with judgment and caution. Figure 9.1 gives an example of a policy statement concerning academic freedom.

Policies Relating to Staff Protection: Sexual Harassment

Title VII of the Civil Rights Act of 1964 prohibits employment discrimination based on race, color, religion, sex, and national origin. In 1980, the Equal Employment Opportunity Commission (EEOC) provided guidelines that have served to define sexual harassment and clarify the responsibility of organizations concerning such activities. In brief, these guidelines defined **sexual harassment** as unwelcome sexual advances, requests, or demands for sexual favors and other verbal or physical conduct of a sexual nature that explicitly or implicitly are suggested as a term or condition of an individual's employment, are used as the basis for employment or academic decisions, have the purpose or result of unreasonably interfering with an individual's performance in the workplace or in a school setting, or result in a hostile or offensive work environment.

Sexual harassment in the workplace is considered a form of sexual harassment under Title VII of the Civil Rights Act of 1964. Sexual harassment of students is considered sexual harassment under Title IX of the Educational Amendments of 1972. "What this means . . . is that all employers—both large and small—must have a sexual harassment policy in place. They must train all employees on the policy. They must have clear procedures for reporting such behavior—including allowing

---

Garland School District

Code: GBE

Personnel Academic Freedom

This school district supports the teachers' freedom to think and to express ideas, to select appropriate instructional materials and methods of instruction, and to be free to take action within their professional domain. Such freedom carries with it the responsibility of using judgment and prudence to the end that it promotes the free exercise of intelligence and pupil learning. Through the use of good taste and professional judgment, teachers are free to conduct discussions of various issues that offer students experience in examining respective views of controversial questions.

Academic freedom must be exercised with the basic ethical responsibilities of the teaching profession and the level of student maturity in mind. These responsibilities are undergirded with a sincere concern for the welfare, growth, and development of students and the use of professional ethics and good judgment in selecting and employing materials and methods of instruction.

Figure 9.1   Sample Policy Concerning Personnel Academic Freedom employees access to management other than their supervisor. And they must communicate policy effectively and openly" (Cole, 2000).

Sexual harassment can fall into one of two general areas, quid pro quo and hostile environment. **Quid pro quo** harassment occurs when an employee or applicant is asked to provide sexual favors in order to obtain or retain employment. When individuals are harassed by intimidating conditions in the workplace, a **hostile environment** exists. In such cases, a female employee might be subject to unwelcome touching or placed in situations where she must listen to stories of the sexual exploitations of other employees.

The human resources unit of the school district should assume the leadership for establishing specific policies and regulations relating to sexual harassment involving both students and staff. Without a written policy prohibiting sexual harassment and outlining specific procedures for reporting and handling complaints, an employer is likely to be found just as guilty as if he or she had condoned the harassment. At least two other responsibilities accompany this leadership role: (1) the human resources unit should lead in the development of effective education programs that focus on the nature of sexual harassment, the district's policies on harassment, and individual employee's responsibilities for eliminating sexual harassment in the school district; and (2) the human resources unit should make certain that employee assistance programs and services are available for employees who have experienced sexual harassment and need psychological counseling.

Employee training activities that include programs for educating employees about the subject of harassment and serve to gather information about the status of harassment within the school setting are direct responsibilities of the human resources unit and administrators in the district. Such training programs serve as a preventative measure against sexual harassment and can result in focusing the attention of all employees on the problem and their responsibilities in such matters.

Wolkinson (2000) recommended six specific features of a comprehensive policy on sexual harassment: (1) it should identify what constitutes sexual harassment, (2) it should clearly communicate the message that sexual harassment will not be tolerated at the workplace, (3) it should designate a particular employee as EEO officer who can advise employees and to whom complaints may be made, (4) it should emphasize the need to investigate complaints immediately and thoroughly with all facts documented, (5) it should set forth vigorous disciplinary measures, and (6) it should include a plan for training all personnel, both administrators and employees (p. 818). Most authorities point out that remediation of sexual harassment in the workplace is largely a matter of good management. That is, systems that are practicing good management by placing emphasis on such matters as task accomplishment, individual and unit work responsibilities, and positive work conditions rather than matters such as personality issues will by themselves reduce sexual harassment and discrimination (Cole, 2000).

Cohan, Hergenrother, Johnson, Mandel, and Sawyer (1996) suggested the following strategies to combat sexual harassment in schools:

1. Establish a district-wide sexual harassment committee that includes members of the entire school community.

2. Create and disseminate a sexual harassment policy, including a grievance procedure for reporting incidences of alleged sexual harassment.

3. Include in the district mission the goal to eradicate sexual harassment and promote gender equity.

4. Become aware of attitudes and assumptions about sexual harassment and educate to change attitudes and behaviors.

5. Identify intolerable behaviors.

6. Distinguish between flirting and sexual harassment.

7. Educate the school community on an ongoing basis on recognizing and responding to sexual harassment; challenge gender stereotypes.

8. Educate all staff, students, and parents about the school district sexual harassment policy.

9. Communicate the school district commitment to ending sexual harassment.

10. Expect changes in attitudes and behaviors.

11. Incorporate messages against sexual harassment and in favor of gender equity into the entire school—classroom, hallway, and playground.

12. Demonstrate appropriate behavior. (pp. 74–75)

Figure 9.2 provides an example of a school district sexual harassment policy statement.

Employee Dismissal and Legal Considerations

Dismissal has been a much-discussed topic in human resources administration. "To secure the best results in our schools, we must have able-bodied, energetic, active, industrious teachers—teachers who can control themselves under the most trying circumstances" (Bloss, 1882, p. 82). As indicated by this statement made more than 100 years ago, teacher quality historically has been recognized as critical to effective teaching and learning. Dismissal has been a matter of historical importance as well. In 1882, Bloss reported to the governor of Indiana that, "the [county] superintendent may take every precaution, yet occasionally it happens that one is licensed who is unworthy to exercise the functions of a teacher" (p. 84). The 1882 School Law reference, Section 36 stated

> The county superintendent shall have the power to revoke licenses, granted by him or his predecessor, for incompetency, immorality, cruelty, or general neglect of the business of the school, and the revocation of the license of any teacher shall terminate the school which the said teacher may have been employed to teach. (Bloss, 1882, p. 84)

HUMAN RESOURCES

Anti-Discrimination and Harassment

Lincoln Public Schools is committed to providing a workplace and learning environment free of discrimination and harassment for students and employees. Accordingly, discrimination or harassment of any kind by supervisors or coworkers is prohibited. In addition, the District will endeavor to protect employees from reported discrimination or harassment in the workplace by students and other non-employees. Discrimination or harassment based on a person's race, color, religion, national origin, sex, disability, age, marital status, veteran status, or sexual orientation is specifically prohibited by Board of Education policy and/or federal and state law.

Date of Adoption (or Last Revision):   8-10-2004
Related Policies and Regulations:
Legal References: **Section 703 of Title VII of the
                                                 Civil Rights Act**

LINCOLN PUBLIC SCHOOLS   **POLICY AND REGULATION MANUAL**
LINCOLN, NEBRASKA

Figure 9.2   Sample Antidiscrimination and Harassment Policy

SOURCE: Reprinted with permission from the Lincoln, Nebraska Public School District.

More than 80 years ago, Tead and Metcalf (1920) underlined the momentous effects of dismissal on the discharged worker as follows:

> So heavy a penalty as the dismissal of a workman (involving to him a serious dislocation of his life, the perils and demoralization attendant on looking for work, probably uprooting of his home and the interruption of his children's schooling, possibly many weeks of penury or semi-starvation for his family and himself) ought to be regarded as a very serious matter. (p. 245)

Today, employee dismissal continues to be a difficult and often traumatic personnel action. Norton (2004) found that personnel directors in one state viewed dismissing incompetent staff as one of the 10 leading problems facing them as school administrators. Fischer and colleagues (2003) note that, "State laws, school board policies, and collective bargaining agreements set forth the specific reasons why teachers can be dismissed" (p. 36). The grounds of incompetence, willful neglect of duty, immorality, misconduct, and insubordination commonly are used for dismissal by most states.

A school board continuity policy remains only as a written statement until it is put into practice. Young (2008) points out clearly that, "Once the goals for maintaining continuity of personnel service have been set forth, implementation by school officials follows. . . . One of these actions is the preparation of a series of policy statements to guide members in designing and implementing specific programs" (p. 292).

The second step is to develop a set of related administrative procedures. The purpose of this discussion is to emphasize the need and significance of sound school board policy and regulations in this area that serve as significant legal documents in teacher dismissal cases. It is necessary to keep reviewing them and one's related responsibilities thoroughly before any dismissal hearings are held.

Often, a dismissal hearing charges a teacher with violating school system policy or school regulations. It is not enough to cite the rule or policy the teacher allegedly violated; it will be necessary to present a copy of the rule to the hearing officer or board. The administrative representative must be prepared to establish that the teacher in question was also furnished with a copy before the infraction took place or at least was well aware of the rule or policy. Authorities recommend that school officials keep records of policy distribution procedures and contract clauses whereby teachers agree to follow school system policy and regulations.

State statutes set forth both policies and regulations for teacher nonrenewal and dismissal. When a teacher's contract is not renewed at the end of the contract time, state statutes most often set forth the specific procedures to be followed. In such instances, state laws for tenure govern the procedures to be followed. **Tenure** is the protection given to teachers against arbitrary actions by school officials in the dismissal process. That is, tenured teachers can be dismissed only for those reasons set forth in the law. In any case, this does not mean that teachers have the right to lifetime employment. Rather, if being dismissed for cause, tenured teachers have the right of **due process**, a procedure that includes the notice of charges, a hearing on the charges, and the right to reply to the charges. However, in the case of nontenured teachers, most states simply require a notice to the teacher that the contract will not be renewed. Tenure cases are quite different. State statutes generally set forth procedures for dismissal of tenured teachers that include such features as notice, the right of a hearing, the right to be represented by counsel, and other provisions related to due process.

School board dismissal policies commonly include a brief board policy statement, followed by the specific statute as stated in law. Policy development guidelines usually recommend that statements from state statutes not be rewritten verbatim as board policy. Rather, a policy based on the statute should be written. However, because of the sensitive nature of dismissals and the high potential for litigation in the courts, the use of specific state statutes as district policy is common. It is clear that dismissal procedures and requirements will differ as laws of the various states differ. Figure 9.3 provides a dismissal policy based strictly on a state statute.

EPS File: GCQF Suspension and Dismissal of Certificated Staff Members (Including Reprimand)

Suspension and Dismissal

Employees are expected to comply with the policies adopted by the Governing Board or as set forth in approved administrative regulations. Dismissal shall be in accordance with the laws of the state.
The procedures for suspension and dismissal of teachers shall be those prescribed by the State's Revised Statutes.

Legal Refs: A.R.S. 15-508; 15-521; 15-536; 15-550

Adopted: Date of Manual Adoption OC 2578

                 Tempe Elementary Schools, Tempe, Arizona

Log No. 166

EPS File: GCPD-R1

Rules and Procedures for Disciplinary Action Involving a Teacher

1. *Purpose.* These rules are prescribed pursuant to Arizona Revised Statutes, Section 15-341(A)(26) and are intended to be utilized as a disciplinary mechanism to deal with violations of statutory duties, School District regulations, Governing Board policies, and the duties of a teacher that do not constitute cause for dismissal or certificate revocation. The Governing Board reserves the right to initiate termination proceedings or to non-renew contract for serious or multiple violations of these rules or for any incident of insubordination, unprofessional conduct, or other reasons that it determines sufficient to constitute cause for severance of the employer-employee relationship. Dismissal procedures for teachers are governed by the contract of employment, District policy, and the statutory provisions contained in A.R.S. Title 15, Article 5, Chapter 3.

2. *General Provisions.* These rules are intended to preserve the orderly and efficient administration of the school system and to serve as guidelines for the imposition of minor discipline not to exceed suspension without pay for a period of ten (10) days. Discipline may, but need not be imposed for violation of any of the following rules, that include statutory teaching duties, components of a teacher's job responsibility or any violation of Board policy, administrative rules or regulations, and any provision of the teacher or student handbooks.

Each teacher employed by the Governing Board in this District shall:
Statutory duties—A.R.S. 15-521.A.:

1. Enforce the course of study for his or her assigned class or classes.

2. Enforce the use of the adopted textbooks for his or her assigned class or classes.

3. Enforce the rules and regulations governing the schools prescribed by the Governing Board, the Arizona Department of Education, and any other lawfully empowered authority.

4. Hold pupils to strict account for disorderly conduct.

5. Exercise supervision over pupils on the playgrounds and during recess if assigned to such duty.

6. Make the decision to promote or retain a pupil in grade in a common school or to pass or fail a pupil in a course in high school.

7. Present his or her certificate to the County School Superintendent before assuming charge of a school, except as provided in Arizona Revised Statutes 15-502, Subsection B.

8. Make such reports as may be reasonably required by the Superintendent of Public Instruction, County School Superintendent, Governing Board, or School Administration.

(Continued)

(Continued)

3. *Procedures*

   A. *Disciplinary action alternatives.* Appropriate discipline is at the discretion of the Supervisor. The alternatives available include:

   1. Verbal warning;

   2. Verbal reprimand;

   3. Written reprimand;

   4. Suspension with pay;

   5. Suspension with pay and required remedial action, i.e., observation of other teacher, mandated in-service or educational program;

   6. Suspension without pay. A teacher may be given a suspension without pay for a period not to exceed ten (10) days;

   7. Termination. This remedy is reserved by law to the Governing Board, and procedures are described in applicable statutory provisions. The Governing Board may, if appropriate, determine that termination be imposed for serious or repeated violations of these rules. Notice of the Board's intent to dismiss and applicable procedures are not covered by these rules.

   B. *Notice of discipline*

   1. An administrator, after a reasonable investigation, is authorized to impose minor discipline in any category described in Paragraph A.3 through A.6 above subject to notice, hearing, and appeal rights described below. A reasonable investigation shall include some discussion with the employee to ascertain if grounds exist to justify imposition of discipline.

   2. When it is determined that grounds exist for disciplinary action, a written notice shall be sent to the teacher. The notice shall identify:
      a. The date the infraction occurred;
      b. The rule or duty violated;
      c. A summary of the factual information supporting the recommended discipline;
      d. The nature of the disciplinary action to be imposed.

   C. *Request for hearing.* A teacher who has received notice of discipline has the right to request a hearing in writing within five (5) school days after the date the teacher receives the notice. The request for a hearing shall be in writing and filed with the Personnel Office and shall contain the prior written notice of discipline.

   D. *Hearing tribunal.* The hearing will be held before the Superintendent or designee.

   E. *Hearing procedure*

   1. The hearing shall be scheduled within ten (10) school days after receipt of the teacher's request unless extended by mutual agreement of the parties.

   2. Notice of the hearing shall be served on the teacher and Supervisor by the Hearing Officer and shall contain:
      a. The time and place of the hearing.
      b. A copy or summary of the written disciplinary notice previously served on the teacher.
      c. Notice that disciplinary action will be imposed if the teacher fails to appear.
      d. A statement to advise the parties that they may present oral or written evidence relevant to the alleged violation of rules or policies.
      e. State that the hearing will be conducted informally without adhering to the rules of evidence.

     f. State that within seven (7) school days after the hearing a written decision shall be served on the parties.

     g. Advise the parties that they may, if they desire, be represented by another employee at the hearing.

  3. The hearing shall be held at the time and place stated in the notice. The designated person or persons shall conduct the hearing in an informal and orderly fashion recognizing the rights of all parties. A statement should be made by the Hearing Officer as to the purpose of the hearing. Parties shall be advised if a record shall be made by tape, stenographer, or the notes of the Hearing Officer. Any party may tape the hearing for his own use, but it will not be the official record.

  4. Subsequent to the hearing, the Hearing Officer shall prepare a written decision to be served on the parties within fifteen (15) calendar days.

F. *Decision.* The decision shall contain a brief summary of the hearing and a finding of whether the teacher committed a violation and if the discipline was appropriate. If it is found that the teacher committed the violation, the teacher's right to appeal the written decision to the Governing Board for review of the record shall be provided as part of the decision.

G. *Appeal to governing board*

  1. Any appeal to the Governing Board via the Superintendent must be in writing, filed within five (5) school days after service of the hearing decision, list the issue or issues upon which review is requested, and specify the relief sought from the Governing Board.

  2. All evidence the teacher wishes to have the Governing Board review shall be attached to the appeal. No new information, other than that already submitted at the hearing, will be allowed.

  3. The supervisor shall be served with a copy of the appeal and have five (5) days after service to file material and information submitted at the hearing and which are deemed appropriate in support of the discipline imposed.

  4. When the Superintendent receives the appeal, it shall be transmitted to the Governing Board.

  5. The Governing Board has no obligation to conduct another hearing or to receive new evidence not previously presented to the Hearing Officer in a minor discipline matter.

  6. The Board shall schedule an executive session to review the appeal. No additional testimony or input shall be allowed unless expressly requested by the Board.

  7. Written notice of the Board's decision shall be served on the parties. The Board shall have a reasonable time, not to exceed thirty (30) school days to review the matter and render its decision.

  8. Discipline shall be held in abeyance during the hearing and appeal procedures under these rules.

Cross refs: KK-R

               GBCB

               GBCC

Legal References: A.R.S. 15-34

Issued: _____ Tempe Elementary Schools
                                Tempe, Arizona

Figure 9.3   Suspension and Dismissal Policy Based on State Statute

SOURCE: Reprinted with permission from the Tempe Elementary School District, Classified Personnel Document, Tempe, Arizona.

Drug-Free Workplace Legislation

The cost of drug and alcohol abuse to industry was estimated to be almost $200 billion in 1996 (Harvey & Bowin, 1996), and the cost has likely increased since that date. Decreased productivity, increased absenteeism, increased threats to the safety of self and others, and increased loss or damage to property are among the major problems and costs associated with employee drug and alcohol abuse (Bolton, 1997). The schools have not been immune to the problems related to drug and alcohol abuse among employees. One study in education found that 90 of the 91 responding districts reported drinking and alcoholism to be the leading problem of troubled workers, and 63 of the 91 districts listed drugs or chemical dependency as a major problem area for troubled workers.

The 1988 Federal Drug-Free Workplace Act requires federal contractors and grantees who receive more than $25,000 in federal funds to certify that they will maintain a drug-free workplace and to adopt a drug-free work environment policy, disseminate it to all employees, and notify employees that a drug-free state is a condition of employment. School districts have attempted to meet this goal by adopting alcohol and substance abuse policies, instituting drug awareness programs, and increasing employee assistance program services directed at drug and alcohol use and abuse. The act specifically permits employers to adopt drug testing and drug-free workplace policies and to prohibit employees from using illegal drugs. Some districts have adopted mandatory drug testing for certain "safety-sensitive" positions (e.g., bus drivers). When these are adopted, the school district should notify employees that such testing is to be conducted and set forth in writing the testing procedures. In all cases, specific steps must be taken to safeguard the testing samples, follow up with additional tests in case of positive results, and maintain a status of confidentiality for the overall procedure.

School board policies and approved regulations related to drug and alcohol use have focused primarily on the elimination of alcohol or drug use on school district property, the establishment of disciplinary action in cases of the violation of alcohol and drug policies, the implementation of alcohol and drug awareness programs, procedures for alcohol and drug testing, employee assistance programs, and the establishment of employee rights, including appeal procedures. Figure 9.4 shows a sample policy with accompanying regulations in the area of a drug-free workplace.

The courts have been somewhat consistent in rulings relative to possession and use of alcohol and drugs by employees. For example, the courts might not support the dismissal of a teacher based solely on a conviction of possession of a small amount of marijuana without any evidence of unfitness of the teacher. However, they probably would uphold a dismissal based on evidence of a widely publicized conviction, combined with substantial evidence that the teacher's conduct had seriously undermined his or her fitness to teach (Fischer et al., 2003).

Legal Considerations Relative to Teacher Transfer

Human resources administration is faced with changes in personnel assignments, the placement of staff, the condition of having surpluses in some staff positions, voluntary and involuntary transfers, reduction in force (RIF), dismissals, and

Drug-Free Workplace

Codes: GBEC & ADB

The governing Board recognizes that drug dependency is a major health problem and its effect has serious safety and security repercussions for both students and staff. Therefore, it is this District's intent and obligation to provide a Drug-Free workplace.

No employee shall consume or use alcohol or a drug(s) (without medical authorization) while on District property, on the job or while responsible for the supervision of students. (Drug means any dangerous drug as defined in A.R.S. § 13-34-1).

Employees shall not report to work having consumed alcohol or drug(s) (without medical authorization) when such consumption can be detected or impair their ability to perform their assigned job.

Any employee who violates this policy is subject to disciplinary action in accordance with established policies and regulations.

The Superintendent shall establish a Drug-Free Awareness Program and inform all employees regarding that program and their rights, responsibilities and privileges under the law.

Adopted: 03/05/____

Legal Ref.   A.R.S. § 13-2911 13-3401 ET SEQ 15-341 (A) (1)
P.L. 100-690, Title V. Subtitle D.
P.L. 101-226 34 C.F.R. Part 86

I.   It is the District's intent and obligation to provide a drug-free workplace. Workplace includes:
  • Any school building or District premises;
  • Any property leased or used by the District for any educational or District business purposes during the time the employee is on duty;
  • Any school sponsored or approved activity, event or function where students or staff members are under the jurisdiction of the District; and
  • Any District-owned vehicles or District-approved vehicles used to transport staff members or students for school activities or District business.

II.   The unlawful manufacture, distribution, dispensation, possession, sale or consumption of intoxicating beverages, narcotics and any other illicit drug(s) is prohibited.

III.   All employees shall receive information about:
  • Dangers of alcohol and drug abuse in the workplace
  • Policies and regulations of the District for maintaining a drug-free workplace
  • Supervisory responsibilities in administering this policy and regulations
  • Alcohol and drug testing procedures
  • Penalties that may be imposed for alcohol and drug abuse violations occurring in the workplace
  • Alcohol and drug counseling and rehabilitation reentry programs available to staff

IV.   All employees must sign a statement indicating that they have received a copy of the current drug-free workplace policy and regulations. The signed statement will be placed in their personnel file.

  Employees must, as a condition of employment, abide by the terms of this policy and report any conviction under a criminal drug statute occurring in the workplace, as defined in I. above, not later than five (5) calendar days after such conviction. Failure to report a drug conviction under this paragraph may result in disciplinary action up to and including termination.

V.   Use of prescription and/or over-the-counter drugs
  A.   Employees shall report to their supervisor use of prescription drugs which may impair job performance and/or affect the safety of themselves and others.

  B.   Employees are expected to act responsibly with regard to use of over-the-counter drugs. It is the employee's responsibility to request reassignment or leave if use of over-the-counter drugs impairs job performance and/or affects the safety of themselves or others.

(Continued)

(Continued)

VI. Procedures when an employee appears impaired

   A. If the supervisor of an employee has probable cause that the employee's job performance has been impaired by the use of alcohol or drugs, and the Superintendent/designee concurs, the employee shall submit to alcohol/drug(s) testing.

   B. Probable cause exists where the facts and circumstances are sufficient to warrant the belief that the employee has consumed alcohol or used a drug(s) during a period of time when such consumption or use could affect job performance.

   C. If the supervisor is directed to have the employee evaluated, the supervisor or designee will contact the Office of Personnel Services to arrange for an immediate physical evaluation of the employee.

VII. Procedures for alcohol and drug testing

   A. The annually selected medical facilities shall be licensed and certified by the appropriate state or federal agency or by the College of American Pathologists. The collection facility shall comply with acceptable standards of the medical field relating to collection, storage and transportation of samples.

   B. Prior to testing, the director or supervisor shall confidentially inform the employee and provide a written affidavit of the reason(s) for testing referral. The employee shall be given an opportunity to provide an explanation of the facts and circumstances giving rise to the referral. The District may require the employee to immediately submit to testing.

   C. An employee who refuses to submit to alcohol and drug testing may be subject to termination of employment.

   D. When testing is required, the District shall assume the cost of the test provided the results are negative. The employee may elect to have a blood sample drawn and retained at the employee's expense.

   E. The employee may not be allowed to perform normal job responsibilities until test results are known.

   F. Immediately upon receipt of test results, the District shall notify the employee.

   G. If test results are negative, the sample(s) shall be destroyed.

   H. Employees with positive samples shall be informed of the right to a second testing of the reserved sample at a certified laboratory of their choice at their expense.

   I. The employee shall be informed of the right to a second testing of the reserved sample at a certified laboratory.

VIII. Appeal of test results

   The following procedures shall apply to any appeal of the test results:

   1. Any appeal of test findings shall postpone a recommendation pending outcome of the appeal.

   2. Any appeal shall be made in writing to the Superintendent/designee within two (2) working days following receipt of test results by the employee.

   3. The appeal shall specify the basis of the employee's challenge to the test findings.

   4. Any employee appealing the test findings shall arrange for a second testing of the sample at the employee's cost. In the event of a negative second test result, the District shall assume the cost of both tests.

   5. The Superintendent/designee shall meet with the employee and their representative and the person most able to respond to the employee's challenge, to determine if there is any validity to the employee's appeal.

6. If the Superintendent/designee determines that the employee's challenge is valid, any pay withheld during suspension, between the time test results are known and the time the Superintendent/designee makes a determination, shall be reinstated.

7. If the Superintendent/designee determines that the employee's challenge to the test findings is valid, disciplinary action shall not be taken unless there are documented independent grounds for such action.

IX. Disciplinary sanctions and appeals

Disciplinary sanctions may include the successful completion of an appropriate rehabilitation program, suspension and/or immediate termination of employment, and referral for prosecution.

A. Employees recommended for disciplinary action shall be advised of their due process rights, including the right to a hearing before the Superintendent/designee.

B. When an employee tests positive for alcohol/drug(s), and is disciplined but not dismissed, the employee will be referred to the employee's health care provider for assessment, counseling and rehabilitation or to an Employee Assistance Program.

C. Participation in rehabilitation or treatment may be required of an employee who has violated this policy. Failure to begin or complete a treatment or rehabilitation program may subject the employee to disciplinary action, including termination.

X. Employee Assistance Program Employees are encouraged to seek assistance if they have concerns about alcohol/drug(s) use. A staff member who requests assistance prior to the detection of a problem shall be directed to an appropriate Employee Assistance Program. An employee who is referred to an Employee Assistance program may be placed on some category of leave until the District receives medical and/or professional Certification of the employee's ability to resume job responsibilities.

XI. Confidentiality

A. An employee with an alcohol/drug(s) problem is entitled to confidentiality. Information relating to any testing incident shall be officially communicated within the District only on a need-to-know basis. Employees who violate this provision shall be subject to disciplinary action.

B. Employee records pertaining to this regulation shall be subject to normal District procedures relating to confidential personnel records and state law. Any report of a negative test shall be destroyed after final disposition of the matter.

XII. Convictions

All convictions, when known by the District, involving employees engaged in the performance of a Grant from the United States Government shall be processed by the District as follows: Within ten (10) days of receiving any notice of conviction, the District shall notify the U.S. Department of Education of such notice. Within thirty (30) days of receiving notice of conviction, the District shall take appropriate personnel action against the employee up to and including termination.

Adopted: 03/05/_____

Figure 9.4   Policy and Administrative Regulation Concerning a Drug-Free Workplace

SOURCE: Used with permission from the Creighton Elementary School District #14, Phoenix, AZ.

resignations. In each of these situations, legal rulings, guiding policy, and administrative regulations are of primary importance. Figure 9.5 is an example of a voluntary transfer administrative regulation. The specific procedures for the school district's posting of vacancies and application for the vacancies by internal district personnel are set forth in the regulation.

One basic legal ruling dictates how a teacher can be assigned to teach in a school or school system.

> Without consent, a school board cannot compel a teacher to teach subjects or grades other than called for in the contract of employment. If a contract states that a teacher is employed to teach second grade, the teacher cannot be made to teach first; if it states that a teacher is to teach mathematics, he or she cannot be made to teach biology. (Peterson, Rossmiller, & Volz, 1978, p. 428–429)

> As early as 1936, the courts ruled that teachers may be transferred to other schools within the school district; however, such transfers are justified only in cases of emergency and not because the transfer is expedient (*White vs. Board of Education of Lincoln County*, 184 S.E. 264, 103 A.L.R. 1376 [W.VA. 1936]).

6–4 Voluntary Transfer

a. An updated list of present vacancies and known vacancies for the following school year will be posted in all school buildings, at least every two weeks starting March 15. The posting of vacancies will continue up to 30 calendar days prior to the first contract day of the building with the vacancy. If all surplused teachers have not been assigned, posting shall continue past 30 days prior to the first contract day. The vacancy list shall include:

(1) Position title

(2) Building location

(3) Status, i.e., permanent, temporary, part-time or itinerant

(4) Qualifications: Courses to be taught and if elementary, grade and subject matter emphasis.

At all times, an updated list shall be available at the Human Resources Office.

b. Posting: If posted, no vacancy shall be permanently filled within five (5) working days of the date of posting.

c. Procedures: Every employee on continuing contract shall have the right to apply for any vacancy for which he/she is certificated and endorsed by contacting the Human Resources Office within the five (5) day posting period. All certificated employees applying for a voluntary transfer shall, after contacting the Human Resources Department, be allowed to submit a letter of application and resume to the principal or supervisor where the vacancy exists. All applicants shall receive written notification within five (5) days from the principal indicating receipt of their application for the position.
The Human Resources Department will notify all applicants, in writing, within ten (10) days of the closing date for the application when the screening process and subsequent interviewing will occur.
Applicants selected for an interview will be notified by the Human Resources Department. Other applicants will be notified, in writing, by the Human Resources Department within ten (10) days that they have not been selected for an interview. Interviewees not selected for the position will be notified by Human Resources within ten (10) days from the time the position has been filled.

d. Certificated employees exchange shall be defined as the exchange of assignments between two staff members in different buildings with the approval of both principals. Such exchange shall be for a one (1) year trial. At the end of one (1) year, a request for discontinuation of the exchange by any of the affected teachers or principals will be honored. An exchange extended beyond one (1) year shall become permanent.

Figure 9.5   Administrative Regulation for Voluntary Transfer

SOURCE: Professional Agreement, Voluntary Transfer Regulation. Reprinted with permission from the Lincoln, Nebraska Public Schools.

In a situation whereby a teaching vacancy occurs within a school district, direction is needed for determining just how the vacancy is to be filled and how the eligibility of current teachers within the system will be treated. Considerations must be given to how vacancies will be posted and made known to current teaching staff members, the nature of the vacancy, the length of the position posting, procedures for application for the opening, communication procedures regarding follow-up contacts, interview procedures, and a related addendum that focuses on teacher exchanges.

The reorganization of school districts, whereby some teachers of an original school district become employees of a reorganized school district, gives rise to the question of teachers' job security rights. A court in New Mexico ruled that a teacher who has acquired tenure in a district that has been consolidated into another school district does not lose tenure because of the result of a merger or consolidation of school districts. The teacher is entitled to all the benefits that were granted in the original district (*Henslely v. State Board of Education*, 376 P.2d, 968 [N.M. 1962]).

Legal Considerations Regarding the Use of Network and Internet

Rapid advancements in information technology are having major impacts on the human resources function. Although information technology has contributed positively to each of the major human resources processes, it brings about new responsibilities for the integration of data, information, methods of record storage and retrieval, and moral and ethical considerations related to uses of electronic technology. How is information to be collected? What information is to be collected and how is it to be stored and accessed? How are personnel records to be managed and by whom? How is the security of personnel records to be safeguarded? It is not the purpose here to set forth detailed responses to these kinds of questions.

To protect against abuses in the use of computers, school districts must develop viable policies and regulations for dealing with information technology in general and the human resources function specifically, including stipulations that allow computers to be used only for specified educational purposes. School board policies and regulations regarding records management minimally should include the following: (1) a statement of purpose, which provides guidelines for making information management decisions and improving the district's information effectiveness, increased efficiency, and improved information flow; (2) integration provisions that focus on a plan for coordinating the district's information system with all other subunits within the system; (3) personnel and unit assignments of responsibility, which are job responsibilities and the assignments of accountability for the information management system in the district; (4) input and retrieval processes that identify opportunities and set forth limitations of the system, including restrictions and ethical guidelines for users; (5) funding considerations that include the initiation of new programs and their maintenance; and (6) data, information, and files, with due attention to what information is to be collected and stored and how such information is to be retrieved and safeguarded. Figure 9.6 is an example of a district's statement for use of the computer network and Intranet. The statement is regulatory in nature and places emphasis on the user's responsibilities and personal ethics.

BB. Use of District Computer Network and Internet

District employees have access to the district computer network and the Internet for the enhancement and support of student instruction. It is important to remember that the equipment and the software are the property of the school district.

In using the computers and the Internet, employees are agreeing to the following:

1. Since copyright laws protect software, employees will not make unauthorized copies of software found on school computers by any means.

2. Employees will not give, lend, or sell copies of software to others unless the original software is clearly identified as shareware or in the public domain.

3. If an employee downloads public domain programs for personal use or non-commercially redistributes a public domain program, the employee assumes all risks regarding the determination of whether a program is in the public domain.

4. Employees are not permitted to knowingly access information that is profane, obscene or offensive toward a group or individual based upon race, gender, national origin or religion. Further, employees are prohibited from placing such information on the Internet.

5. Employees will protect the privacy of other computer users' areas by not accessing their passwords without written permission.

6. Employees will not copy, change, read, or use another person's files.

7. Employees will not attempt to gain unauthorized access to system programs or computer equipment.

8. Employees will not use computer systems to disturb or harass other computer users by sending unwanted mail or by other means.

9. Employees will not disclose their passwords and account names to anyone or attempt to ascertain or use anyone else's password and account name.

10. Employees will not attempt to login to the system as a system administrator.

11. Employees understand that the intended use of all computer equipment is to meet instructional objectives.

12. Employees will not waste or take supplies, such as paper, printer ribbons, toner, and diskettes that are provided by Lincoln Public Schools.

13. Employees will not use the network for financial gain or for any commercial or illegal activity.

14. Attempts to bypass security systems on computer workstations or servers, or vandalism will result in cancellation of privileges. Malicious attempts to harm or destroy data of another employee, or data that resides anywhere on the Lincoln Public Schools network or on the Internet, or the uploading or creation of computer viruses are forbidden.

15. Lincoln Public Schools will not be responsible for any liabilities, costs, expenses, or purchases incurred by the use of LPS telecommunications systems such as the Internet. This includes, but is not limited to, the purchase of on-line services or products. The employee is solely responsible for any such charges. The employee's signed application for an email account states that the employee is agreeing to indemnify the district for any expenses, including legal fees, arising out of their use of the system in violation of the agreement.

16. The Internet will be supplied for your use on an "as is, as available" basis. The Lincoln Public Schools does not imply or expressly warrant that any information you access will be valuable or fit for a particular purpose or that the system will operate error-free.

17. The Lincoln Public Schools is not responsible for the integrity of information accessed, or software downloaded from the Internet.

18. The system administrators reserve the right to refuse posting of files, and to remove files.

Any violation of any part of this agreement or any other activity which school authorities deem inappropriate will be subject to disciplinary action consistent with LPS due process procedures. Discipline could include but would not be limited to, the immediate suspension or termination of the employee's Internet account and computer privileges.

Figure 9.6   District Statement on Use of the District's Computer Network and Internet

SOURCE: Certificated Personnel Handbook. Use of District Computer Network and Internet. Reprinted with permission from the Lincoln, Nebraska Public Schools.

Can the school restrict the use of school computers? According to Fischer and colleagues (2003), "It depends on the message and the consequences" (p. 426). To protect against improper computer use, these authors recommend that policies be adopted that allow computers to be used only for educational purposes and that inappropriate uses be stipulated in the policy (e.g., harassment of students or staff, copyright violations, commercial purposes, access to pornographic material, etc.). In addition, those persons using computers in the school should agree to sign a statement that they understand the policy before being given authorization to do so.

Summary of Selected Legal Statutes, Including Various Civil Rights Acts, Relating to the Work of the Human Resources Function

Civil rights of employees are founded on both the rights set forth in the U.S. Constitution and other statutory rights determined by various courts and other official regulatory bodies. Such rights are stipulated in the First, Fifth, Ninth, and Fourteenth Amendments and in the provisions stated in various civil rights acts. Such provisions guarantee such rights as the freedom of speech, freedom of the press, the right to peaceful assembly, and protection against discrimination because of race, sex, religion, national origin, and other such reasons.

Civil Rights Act of 1870. This act stated that all persons should have the same rights as white citizens to make and enforce contracts, to be a party to litigation, and to the full and equal benefit of laws pertaining to security of persons and property.

Social Security Act (August 14, 1935). This act provides for the general welfare by establishing a system of federal old-age benefits, and by enabling the several states to make more adequate provisions for aged persons, dependent and crippled children, maternal and child welfare, public health, and the administration of their unemployment laws; to establish a Social Security Board; to raise revenue; and for other purposes.

Fair Labor Standards Act (June 25, 1938). This act establishes minimum wage, overtime pay, record keeping, and child labor standards affecting full-time and part-time workers in the private sector and in federal, state, and local governments.

Civil Rights Act of 1960. This act prohibited certain discriminatory actions and practices against black persons.

Equal Pay Act of 1963. This act declared that women and men must receive equal pay for equal work. It stated that "no employer having employees subject [to pay provisions] shall discriminate, within any establishment in which such employees are employed, between employees on the basis of sex by paying wages to employees in such establishment at a rate less than the rate at which he pays wages to employees of the opposite sex . . . for equal work on jobs the performance of which requires equal skill, effort, and responsibility, and which are performed under similar working conditions, except where such payment is made pursuant to: (i) a seniority system; (ii) a merit system, (iii) a system which measures earnings by quantity or quality of production; or (iv) a differential based on any other factor other than sex."

Civil Rights Act of 1964 and Title VII (P.L. 88-362). Title VII of the Civil Rights Act protects individuals against employment discrimination on the basis of race, color, religion, sex, or national origin and prohibits employers from limiting, segregating, or classifying employees in any way that would deprive or tend to deprive any individual of employment opportunities or otherwise adversely affect his or her status as an employee because of his or her race, color, religion, sex, or national origin.

The act prohibits discrimination against any individual in regard to recruiting, hiring and promotion, transfer, work assignments, performance measurements, the work environment, job training, discipline and discharge, wages and benefits, or any other term, condition, or privilege of employment. The act applies to employers with 15 or more employees, including state and national governments.

Age Discrimination in Employment Act (1967). This act protects individuals who are 40 years of age or older against discrimination because of age. However, the state or school boards may establish a retirement age for teachers. Furthermore, the retirement age for elementary and secondary teachers does not necessarily have to apply to other state employees (*Lewis v. Tucson School District No. 1*, 531 P.2d 199 [Ariz. 1975]).

The act set forth a broad ban against age discrimination and specifically prohibits (1) discrimination in hiring, promotions, wages, or firing or layoffs; (2) statements or specifications in job notices of age preference and limitations; (3) denial of benefits to older employees; and (4) mandatory retirement in most sectors. Age limits may be legally specified in circumstances where age has been shown to be a "bona fide" occupational qualification reasonably necessary to normal operation of the particular business (e.g., when public safety is at stake, such as airline pilots, bus drivers, etc.).

The Occupational Safety and Health Administration (OSHA) was created in 1970 when President Nixon signed the Occupational Safety and Health Administration Act. Its mission is to prevent work-related injuries, illnesses, and deaths by issuing and enforcing standards and rules for workplace safety and health. The agency is currently headed by Assistant Secretary of Labor Edwin G. Foulke, Jr. It has had far-reaching impacts on school district operations. The act covers a wide range of safety and health requirements, including overtime mandates, protection of individual privacy in records, equal access to justice, and health and safety standards relating to such occupations as agriculture and construction.

Rehabilitation Act of 1973. This national law protects qualified individuals from discrimination based on their disability. It was amended in 1992 to stipulate that the term "individuals with a disability" does not include individuals who are currently engaging in the illegal use of drugs.

Employee Retirement Income Security Act (1974). This federal legislation was established to prevent the retirement benefits of employees from being mismanaged.

Privacy Act of 1974. This act guaranteed the privacy of the files of employees of the U.S. federal government.

Workers' Compensation. Workers' compensation laws are designed to ensure that employees who are injured or disabled on the job are provided with fixed monetary awards, eliminating the need for litigation. All states require employers to provide workers' compensation in case of personal injury, disability, or death related to one's occupation. State workers' compensation statutes establish this framework for most employment. Related federal compensation acts include the Merchant Marine Act, the Black Lung Benefits Act, the Longshore and Harbor Workers' Compensation Act, and others.

Pregnancy Discrimination Act (1978). This act provides equal protection for female workers who are pregnant. Pregnancy is to be treated the same as any other disability in relation to all aspects of employment.

The Fourteenth Amendment to the Constitution provides that no state shall "deprive any person of life, liberty, or property without due process of law."

Consolidated Omnibus Budget Reconciliation Act (1986). This act states that the employee's health insurance coverage must be continued following termination and paid by the employee.

Immigration Reform and Control Act (1986). This law makes it illegal to knowingly hire an unauthorized alien, to continue to employ a person who becomes unauthorized, or to employ any person without taking steps to verify employability and identity of that person.

Family and Medical Leave Act (1993). Eligible employees are given the right to take 12 weeks of leave per year without pay in relation to the birth or first year of a child, adoption or foster placement of a child, or the illness of the employee or spouse, child, or parent. The Act applies to both sexes.

Health Insurance Portability and Accountability Act of 1996 (HIPAA). This act provides rights and protections for participants and beneficiaries in group health plans. The law identifies and clarifies transactions, enforcements, security, privacy, code sets, industry discussion and collaboration, and other resources.

The Development of Personnel Policies and Regulations

School boards are extensions of state legislatures and thus are legal bodies representing school districts within the many states. As such, school policies officially adopted by the local school board are considered as legal decisions as long as they do not conflict with the legal rulings set forth by state or national governance bodies. Therefore, it is imperative that human resources administrators have the necessary knowledge of and skills in policy drafting and implementation related to the important work of the HR function.

Many people express the belief that a school district's personnel policies and regulations are a direct reflection of how it values its human resources. Governing board policies directly affect the work and life of the school employees and the school district's clients. One premise of this text is that schools are people; the school's human resources determine in large part the extent to which the school system will achieve its purposes. The formal adoption of policy by the board of education gives the professional staff the necessary support and direction for the implementation of program initiatives. In a statewide study of HR directors by Norton (2004), personnel policy and regulation development tied with human resources record keeping as their third highest rated job responsibility; only the recruitment of personnel and human resources planning ranked higher.

This chapter emphasizes the development of policies and regulations that guide and facilitate the human resources function. It gives primary consideration to important differences between governing board policies and administrative regulations; the purposes served by a viable set of policies and regulations, the responsibilities of the school board, the human resources director, and other professional staff and laypersons in the development of policies and regulations; and ways in which personnel policies and regulations are developed. It discusses the characteristics of effective policies and regulations and gives examples of policies and regulations in selected personnel areas, along with court rulings that affect various personnel practices. The contents of this chapter are based on the assumption that the HR director's position in education will continue to move toward an executive role. As such, recommendations and development of viable personnel policy become increasingly important leadership roles for school administrators.

Goals, Policies, and Regulations

The terms goals, policies, and regulations are defined in various ways in the literature. It is important to differentiate among these terms and to clarify other terms often used in relation to them. Goals are statements that set forth the purposes of the school system. Goals serve to clarify the aims of the school system; they provide a focus for the organization and give it a meaningful direction. Goals express what is important to the school system overall and are supported by the beliefs, values, traditions, and culture of the school system's community. School goals are developed through cultural sanctions embedded in the school community, through lay judgments expressed through such bodies as the district's school board, and through the professional judgments of professional and support staffs of the school district.

Governing board policies are comprehensive statements of decisions, principles, or courses of action that serve toward the achievement of stated goals. They answer the question of *what* the school system is to do; essentially, they serve as guidelines for the administration of the school district. Thus, "It is important that the procedures should fulfill the policy, and the policy should clearly state the purpose and desire of the organization" (McConnell, 2005, p. 4). Policies are local adaptations of stated goals; they are developed through the actions of the school board with the leadership of the professional staff.

An administrative regulation or rule is a precise statement that answers the question of *how* a policy is to be applied or implemented. Regulations serve as methods for accomplishing policies. As McConnell (2005) stated, a policy "is a statement of the organization's position regarding a specific condition of employment—what the organization believes is the correct approach to fulfilling that condition of employment" (p. 16). Although administrative regulations are approved generally by the governing board, they are developed primarily through the professional judgments of the school district's staff with representative community input and ultimately by administrative decision. For our purposes, the terms regulation, rule, and procedure are used interchangeably.

Bylaws are procedures by which the school board governs itself. They are regulations that apply to the internal operations of the school board. Such matters as the election of board officers, voting procedures, agenda development, parliamentary procedure, and the order of business are examples of topics included in the bylaws of the governing board.

Compliance Aspects of Policy

Governing board policies, regulations, and bylaws are subject to state and national laws. A law is a rule recognized by the nation or state as binding on its members. Law emanates from actions by governing bodies such as the U.S. Congress or state legislatures or from rulings by courts of law.

It is not unusual for state laws or court actions to mandate school policy; that is, state statutes and court rulings often mandate what school systems must do regarding a specific educational matter. Seldom is the specific law written verbatim in the school district's policy manual. Rather, a policy statement based on the requirements of the law is written as a school policy and is accompanied by specific statute references or citations. There are exceptions to this provision. For example, in many states, policies and regulations concerning personnel dismissal are written verbatim from state statutes because dismissal cases frequently are litigated in court. Specific language is important as are the specific procedures that must be followed. As a result, school districts take all precautions to ensure that their policies and regulations are in compliance with federal and state laws. It should be clearly understood that local school district policy is inextricably related to the "laws of the land" as determined by the U.S. Constitution, U.S. Congress, state legislatures, the courts, and other agencies and legal bodies that implement legislative acts and court rulings. As we discussed earlier in this chapter, local school district policy must be in compliance with federal and state legislation exemplified by such acts as Title VII of the Civil Rights Act of 1964, which prohibits discrimination in hiring, compensation, and terms and conditions of employment on the basis of race, color, religion, national origin, or sex, and the EEOA of 1972, which extended race coverage stipulated in Title VII to include employees of state and local governments and educational institutions and created the EEOC with authority to prohibit discrimination and file suits against organizations believed to be discriminatory.

Statutes such as OSHA affect human resources policy by requiring schools and other organizations to comply with specific safety requirements within the working environment; governmental agencies such as the Department of Labor serve to enforce fair labor practices such as compensation for overtime work by employees. Both are specific examples of how law and agency regulations affect the development and adoption of local school district policy. The implications regarding compliance of school districts with federal and state laws are far-reaching. Policies of a school district that are not in compliance with federal and state statutes or with court rulings are likely to be challenged and declared unconstitutional. Noncompliance can result in litigation and possible monetary penalties.

The Benefits of Personnel Policies and Regulations

A viable set of personnel policies and regulations benefits the school system and the human resources function in numerous ways. Viable policies and regulations help to establish the division of labor between the school board and the professional staff. The school board, as the legislative body of the school system, has the responsibility of adopting policies that serve to guide the school program. In this way, the board of education "controls" the direction of the system through adopting policies that focus on what the school system is to do and what it wants to accomplish. The development and adoption of appropriate school policy are the primary responsibilities of the school board.

Viable school district policy fosters a more effective and accountable professional staff. School board policy serves to foster the compliance of the professional and support staff regarding the major aims of the school district; thus, staff accountability becomes more attainable. Without question, policy development is the school board's primary tool for ensuring district compliance and personal performance.

The school superintendent and the professional staff represent the executive body of school governance. A comprehensive set of well-developed policies and regulations is one of the human resources administrator's most valuable management tools. Viable school policies allow for discretionary actions by the professional staff. The implementation of board policy is administered through the development of specific regulations primarily through the leadership of the professional staff. Thus, good policies and regulations help the school board focus on its major legislative role and the professional staff to focus on its executive responsibilities. Policy provides the control that the school board must have to guide the school system and gives the professional staff the discretion it needs to operate the school program effectively.

School policies and regulations also serve to establish the basis for intelligent decision making and help to direct decision making at proper levels within the system. Without the direction that effective policies and regulations can provide, various units in the system invariably must seek a decision from a higher level unit before actions can be implemented. As a result, administrative effectiveness often is inhibited and organization efficiency and initiative are reduced.

A comprehensive set of school policies and regulations is the most important source of information about the goals and objectives of the school system. Policy statements and accompanying regulations serve to inform the public and the professional staff of the goals and objectives of the school system and serve as a foundation for effective system communication.

Viable policies and regulations help to avoid costly trial and error and serve to bring a sense of continuity to the organization. Board policies and regulations support the system's decision-making capability by providing a definite idea of what is to be accomplished and how to proceed administratively. Thus, viable policies release the strength and creativity of the school administrators and other employees. Employees understand the priorities set forth by the governing board and are able to implement their professional judgment with some degree of assurance and personal security.

District policies in such areas as personnel recruitment, selection, assignment, and staff development are vital to the quality of teaching and learning in the school district. These policies and administrative procedures have an impact on such matters as homework, student grading, instructional materials selection, student retention, student attendance, student discipline, early childhood programs, and other aspects of curriculum development in the school community as well.

In view of the fact that school boards are extensions of other legislative bodies, viable policies and regulations serve an important legal function for the board and the school district. In relation to governance practices and litigation stemming from personnel lawsuits, school policies and their dissemination serve as key evidence to document school board decisions and administrative practices. "In many, if not all, hearings and lawsuits regarding employees, the organization's policies and procedures become a key piece of evidence (sometimes for the employee and sometimes for the employer). Their absence also can affect a court's decision" (McConnell, 2005, p. 61).

Criteria That Identify Policies, Regulations, and Bylaws

A school policy was defined earlier as a comprehensive statement of decisions, principles, or courses of action that serve toward the achievement of stated goals. A **policy** is

1. An assertion of the intent and goals of the school system.

2. Related to a general area of major importance to the school system and citizenry.

3. Equivalent to legislation.

4. A broad statement that allows for freedom of interpretation and execution.

5. Applicable over long periods of time.

6. Mainly the concern of the school board, that is, only the school board can adopt policy.

7. An action undertaken to resolve or to give direction in ameliorating a problem of importance.

8. Related to the question, "What to do?"

An **administrative regulation** is

1. Related to a specific area or problem (it is a procedure to carry out or implement a policy).

2. Mainly the concern of the professional staff (it is executive in nature).

3. A precise statement calling for specific interpretation and execution.

4. Able to be altered without formal board action.

5. Related to the question, "How to do?"

A bylaw is a rule governing the school board's internal operations. It is a method by which the school board governs itself. A **bylaw** is

1. A combination of parliamentary procedures and state laws that apply to school boards.

2. Like any other rule in that it sets forth specific procedures, leaving little room for personal discretion.

3. A rule that applies to the internal operations of the school board only.

4. Related to the question, "How will the school board govern itself?"

Consider the following policy statement:

The school superintendent and persons delegated by the superintendent are given the responsibility to determine the personnel needs of the school district and to recruit qualified candidates to recommend for employment to the board. The school board will employ and retain the highest qualified personnel available. Concerted efforts shall be made to maintain a variation in staff relative to educational preparation, personal background, and previous experience. There shall be no discrimination against any candidate by reason of race, national origin, creed, marital status, age, or sex. It is the responsibility of the school superintendent to certify that persons nominated for employment shall meet all qualifications established by law and by the school board for the position for which the nomination is made.

The employment of any individual is not official until the contract is signed by the candidate and approved by the governing school board.

The above district policy specifies *what* ends the board desires concerning practices for employment and sets forth *what* is to be done relative to employee qualifications. The governance policy represents a broad statement that allows the professional staff discretion over specific recruiting and selection procedures. The policy is legislative in nature and is directly related to the question of *what* to do relative to the important end results of hiring school district personnel. Finally, although specific procedures regarding recruitment and selection might be changed and improved, the policy that guides the new procedures could remain as stated for a substantial period of time. The question of "what is to be accomplished?" could remain unchanged even though the question "how to do it?" might be altered to improve current practices.

Next, consider the administrative procedure illustrated in Figure 9.7 that sets forth steps for position application. This regulation relates specifically to the policy for personnel recruitment and selection; it is executive in nature, calling for specific procedures to be followed; it is possible to revise these procedures without having to change board policy; and it serves to answer the question of how selection of personnel is to be implemented.

Topical Headings for Personnel Policies and Regulations

Policy and regulation development in human resources administration is an ongoing process. Because of the ever-changing nature of the human resources function, new policies and regulations become necessary, current ones need revision, and some become obsolete and must be deleted. The most viable topical headings for policies and regulations evolve from the vision and needs of the local school district. Because policies are comprehensive statements of decisions, principles, or courses of action that serve toward the achievement of stated goals, ideally they evolve from local school and community initiatives.

The NEPN/NSBA Policy Codification System

The National Educational Policy Network of the National School Boards Association (NEPN/NSBA) and the Davies-Brickell System (DBS) are examples of

Code: 4111 Recruitment and Selection

To aid in obtaining the best available personnel for school positions, the following criteria and procedures will be utilized: Concerted efforts will be made to maintain a variation in staff relative to educational preparation, background, and previous experience through recruiting on a broad basis. All available sources of personnel supply, including college and university career placement offices, career-information-day programs, student-teacher information, advertisements in appropriate publications, and others that serve to identify a pool of qualified personnel for position openings will be used.

Written applications, official transcripts of college work, student teaching and teaching reports and recommendations, and personal interviews provide the primary data for personnel selection. The procedures for screening and selecting personnel for teaching positions are as follows:

1. Notices of position opening in teaching will be disseminated internally through the offices of school principals and externally through selected college and university teacher placement offices.

2. The central human resources office will collect and process applications; the official application form of the school district and other application materials, as required by the human resources office, must be completed and received before an applicant can be considered for a position.

3. The central human resources office will gather all evidence for purposes of screening applicants including the application form, evidence of certification or licensure for the position in question, teacher placement records of the applicant, official college transcripts, at least three professional references from former employers and/or supervisors, and other information of importance. In addition, the district's prescreening background-check form is to be completed and returned by the applicant.

4. Preliminary interviews of applicants who are best qualified will be conducted by the central human resources office, although other representatives may participate as interviewers as the case requires.

5. Finalists for the position, as determined by the human resources office, will be scheduled for interviews with appropriate building principals and /or supervisors. The human resources office, together with the appropriate building principal and/or supervisor, will decide if the position should be offered to a specific applicant.

6. When a position is offered tentatively and accepted pending school board approval, the human resources office will send its recommendation to the school superintendent. Upon the superintendent's approval, the nomination will be made to the school board for final approval.

7. All final applicants for a position will be notified of the decision reached by the school board.

Figure 9.7   Sample of an Administrative Regulation for Recruitment and Selection

educational policy systems that have been implemented in numerous school districts nationally. Both systems provide a comprehensive classification system to guide policy development in school districts. The **NEPN/NSBA**, which is the most widely used classification system nationally, is based on an "alpha" system; letters of the alphabet are used for coding policies and regulations (i.e., each major topical heading has a letter). The NEPN/NSBA system uses 11 major sections (or series) in its classification system. Section G is used for policies related to personnel. Thus, GCBC in the coding system refers to section G (personnel); the third subsection, C (professional staff); the second division, B (professional staff contracts and compensation); and the third subdivision, C (professional staff supplementary pay plans/overtime). Figure 9.8 reveals a partial listing of the subsections, divisions, and subdivisions of Section G.

Section G: Personnel

Section G of the NEPN/NSBA classification system contains policies, regulations, and exhibits on all school employees except for the superintendent (policies on the school chief are located in Section C, General Administration). The category is divided into three main divisions: GB has policies applying to all school employees or to general personnel matters; GC refers to instructional and administrative staff; and GD refers to support or classified staff.

GA	Personnel Goals/Priority Objectives
GAA	Evaluation of Personnel System
GB	General Personnel Policies
GBA	Open Hiring/Equal Employment Opportunity and Affirmative Action
GBAA	Sexual Discrimination and Harassment
GBAB	Pay Equity
GBB	Staff Involvement in Decision Making
GBC	Staff Compensation
GBCA	Merit/Performance Pay Programs
GBD	Communications with Staff (also BHC)
GBE	Staff Rights and Responsibilities
GBEA	Staff Ethics/Conflict of Interest
GBEB	Staff Conduct
GBEBA	Staff Dress Code
GBEBB	Staff Conduct with Students
GBEBC	Gifts to and Solicitations by Staff
GBEC	Drug-Free Workplace (also ADB)
GBED	Tobacco-Free Workplace (also ADC)/Staff No Smoking/Smoking
GBF	Staff Working on Federal/State Grants
GBG	Staff Welfare/Protection
GBGA	Staff Health
GBGB	Staff Personal Security and Safety
GBGC	Employee Assistance/Wellness Programs
GBGD	Workers' Compensation
GBH	Staff Participation in Community Activities
GBI	Staff Participation in Political Activities
GBJ	Personal Records and Files
GBJA	Confidential Information and Disclosure of Information
GBJB	Access to Personnel Files
GBK	Staff Concerns/Complaints/Grievances
GBL	Staff Awards and Recognition
GC	Professional Staff
GCA	Professional Staff Positions
GCAA	Instructional Staff Positions
GCAAA	Teacher Positions
GCAAB	Guidance and Health Staff Positions
GCAAC	Resource Staff Positions
GCAB	Administrative Staff Positions
GCB	Professional Staff Contracts and Compensation
GCBA	Instructional Staff Contracts/Compensation/Salary Schedules
GCBAA	Merit/Performance Pay for Instructional Staff
GCBB	Administrative Staff Contracts and Compensation/Salary Schedules
GCBBA	Merit/Performance Pay for Administrative Staff
GCBC	Professional Staff Supplementary Pay Plans/Overtime

Figure 9.8   Section G of the NEPN/NSBA Codification System

SOURCE: National School Boards Association, Alexandria, VA. Reprinted by permission.

The code GCAAB reveals that the entry is personnel (G), professional staff (C), professional staff positions (A), instructional staff positions (A), and guidance and health staff positions (B). New subsections, divisions, subdivisions, items, and subitems can be added to the policies by using appropriate letters.

The Davies-Brickell Codification System

The **Davies-Brickell System of Classification** uses a numerical code based on nine major series (e.g., 1000, Community Relations; 2000, Administration; 3000, Business and Noninstructional Operations; 4000, Personnel). The code 4151.1, for example, denotes the fourth major series, the first subseries, the fifth division, the first subdivision, and the first item. Similarly, the code 2346 denotes the second major series, the third subseries, the fourth division, and the sixth subdivision.

The use of Arabic numerals for coding systems provides the advantage of easy reading and referencing. One advantage of the alpha system is that it does not limit the number of entries in any one subsection, division, subdivision, item, or subitem to nine. In a numerical system, once nine entries under any one of the classifications have been reached, some structural revision becomes necessary. For this reason, some individuals prefer the alpha system that the NSBA uses. Because there are 26 letters in the alphabet, numerous divisions, subdivisions, items, and subitems can be utilized without the need to restructure. On the other hand, some persons find the use of letters for coding purposes to be less readable than numbers (e.g., 4146.2 vs. DADFB). In any case, a consistent codification system is of paramount importance. It enhances the development, readability, revision, and utilization of the school district's policy and regulation manual.

How Personnel Policies and Regulations Are Developed

Although quality varies considerably, most school districts have some form of a policy and regulation manual. Because policy development is a never-ending process, some school districts simplify completing this task by purchasing policies written by national organizations or policy consultants. Unless customized for the particular school district, such policy manuals tend to be no more than boilerplate products that do not reflect the real climate and educational needs of the system. Therefore, it is important that human resources administrators fully understand the process of policy development and be prepared to assume a major leadership role in that activity. In 2004, 75.6% of the personnel directors in one state reported that they had the primary responsibility for personnel policy and regulation development in their school districts (Norton, 2004).

Although most school districts have a nucleus of policy already established, the need to develop an entirely new set of policies is quite common. Even when school districts have a "complete" policy manual, it is not unusual to have one or more sections in need of complete revision. When major revisions are necessary, the question of who is to do the work arises. One approach is to have the school board appoint the school superintendent to do the policy work. The school superintendent is generally quite knowledgeable about the school district and its human resources purposes and needs. On the other hand, policy development is a monumental task, and such an arrangement tends to take much time away from other work of the superintendent's office. Another approach is to set up a series of task-force groups to do the policy work. Representative groups can benefit from personal involvement in policy development. Yet such an arrangement does not obviate the fact that policy development takes both time and skill. Professional staff members cannot always sacrifice the time necessary to do the work; nor are they always personally knowledgeable in the area of policy development.

Some school districts find it most expedient to use outside consultants to complete their policies. Policy consultants have special expertise for such work and are able to complete a quality product if it is founded on the district's culture and needs. Such an arrangement can be quite costly, however, because of the lengthy time commitments for such consulting. We caution against simply buying the policy statements from external organizations. Although such statements can result in a policy manual for the school district, unless such services are customized for the district, its goals, values, problems, needs, and situation, policies tend to be of a generic nature instead of exemplifying the real meaning and value of localized policies.

Another arrangement is to allow the central personnel unit to take the primary leadership in the development of policies and regulations in the area of human resources. The human resources director is highly knowledgeable about the personnel objectives and needs of the school district. These administrators necessarily must be fully acquainted with the legal aspects of personnel administration important to policy and regulation development.

We support the arrangement whereby the human resources director is given the primary authority to develop viable personnel policy for the school district. Such an arrangement does not set aside the fact that the school board remains as the final authority on all policy recommendations and the only body that can adopt policy officially for the school district. It also does not suggest that policy recommendations cannot evolve from any source or that participation in policy development should not include representatives from the school system's many publics. The following section explains one model for policy development that numerous school districts have used.

Model for Policy and Regulation Development

The human resources director might use the following model for completing a comprehensive study and revision of the school district's personnel policies and regulations:

Step 1. Examine various school and community documents and resources for information relative to what "policies" or decisions already have been determined. Sources of policies and regulations include school board minutes, school board manuals, teachers' manuals, board correspondence, board committee reports, staff committee reports, school publications, citizen committee reports, newspaper files, personal interviews with past and present members of the school board and staff, and legal documents related to the school district. Frequency of notations on certain personnel subjects may suggest the need for a definite district policy. Give special attention to specific goal statements set forth by the governing board.

Step 2. Check on established practices in the area of personnel administration. Operations of the school board and the district often reflect embedded practices that imply policy need areas. Unwritten policies often become formal statements of policy through such an analysis of practice.

Step 3. Investigate what other boards have done in the development of personnel policy. Such information serves as a guide to possible policy development rather than being directly applicable to the local district in question. Such information can be useful as a sounding board in revealing local policy needs. Additionally, complete a thorough examination of state statutes related to the administration of schools and other official documents for clues to topics that should be set forth as official school district policy.

Step 4. Consult the studies and writings of others in the area of school personnel administration. Guides and handbooks prepared by school board associations, state departments, and other organizations often are excellent sources of policy content. Once again, such information should be used as a place to start rather than serving as a blueprint for meeting local needs.

Step 5. Enlist the aid of all concerned. It is good practice to solicit input from citizen groups, professional and support personnel in the school district, and other stakeholders of the district. Such involvement is conducive to quality results and also to gaining the ultimate approval and effective implementation of the policies to be recommended.

Step 6. Organize study groups to examine policy needs and to recommend policy in various subsections and divisions of the personnel policy topical headings (e.g., the NEPN/NSBA section G topical headings). Include such representative personnel as teachers, support staff, patrons, administrators, and at least one school board member in the study groups. The final approval and adoption are facilitated with the sanction of at least one board member serving on the committee. Organize a steering committee of representatives most knowledgeable of policy development and the needs and purposes of human resources administration. These committee members serve as liaisons with study subgroups in checking for consistency in the policies developed.

Step 7. Have the school superintendent and the administrative cabinet review the policy work completed. The professional staff has an ongoing role as policies are being developed in the initial stages. Thus, administrator, teacher, and support staff groups can participate by completing their own review of needed policies, by providing suggestions to study groups, and by acting as sounding boards for initial study group recommendations.

Step 8. Have the school board review the policy work completed. As is the case with the administrator, teacher, and support staff groups, the school board needs to participate in the initial stages of personnel policy development in ways similar to those recommended in Step 7. In addition, the school board as a whole should review the semifinal policy draft and make recommendations for revision.

Step 9. Have the draft of the policies tested for legality. The school board attorney reviews the policy draft from a legal viewpoint. Legal clearance helps to build school board and district confidence and lends support to the final policy package.

Step 10. Use first and second readings of the personnel policy statements prior to official adoption by the school board. Policy is legally binding for all district personnel and in this sense is a legal contract between the school board and its personnel. Thus, due consideration necessitates attention to sunshine laws and other aspects of legal procedures.

The Language of School Policies and Regulations

Attention to the language of written policies can obviate many problems of interpretation and possible conflict. Because a variety of publics utilize policies and regulations, they must be readable and meaningful to all concerned. Poorly written, ambiguous policies tend to confuse rather than inform. Furthermore, because policies serve as legal extensions of the school board, precise language that is presented in a clear, straightforward manner is of paramount importance. In policy writing, the statement, "You get what you write," is a basic truth.

Consider the following personnel policy statement:

In order to provide quality education to all students within the school district, a yearly evaluation of all certificated staff will be conducted. Evaluations should commend staff and provide avenues for staff improvement. Staff evaluations will be used to consider contract renewal.

This policy statement might appear to be clear and concise on the surface, but certain language questions must be raised. For instance,

1. Is only one performance evaluation annually permissible under this policy?

2. Is this yearly evaluation to constitute the totality of evidence for contract renewal consideration?

3. Is this evaluation to serve both formative and summative purposes?

4. How is the statement "Evaluations should commend staff and provide avenues for staff improvement" to be interpreted?

5. Are statements other than commendations permissible?

6. Does the policy suggest that the school district itself will provide the avenues for staff improvement?

7. Who will be responsible for planning and administering the evaluation program?

Smith and Mazin (2004) underscored the importance of positive language in the writing of policies and regulations. Two examples of positive and negative wording are as follows:

Negative wording: Vacation requests not submitted at least 30 days in advance will be denied.

Positive wording: In order to properly schedule vacation times and assure that the organization meets its staffing requirements, employees should submit vacation requests 30 days in advance of the requested leave.

Negative wording: Due to the potential of infringing on the personal beliefs and basic ethics of individual students, teachers will avoid instruction, discussions, and use of instructional materials relative to controversial issues and topics related to sex, religion, and political beliefs.

Positive wording: The school district supports the teacher's freedom to think and express ideas, to select appropriate instructional materials and methods of instruction, and to be free to take action within their professional domain. Such freedom carries with it the responsibility of using judgment and prudence to the end that it promotes free exercise of intelligence and pupil learning.

Summary

Policy by its very nature is often surrounded by controversy. Because policy generally evolves from important issues, which are often in dispute, total consensus on specific policy is seldom the case. For this reason, some persons take the position of leaving well enough alone; after all, if one puts policy in writing, it has to be followed. Such a view overlooks the reality that all organizations are governed by policy, and educational systems are no exception. Without policies and regulations, the school district could scarcely be called a system. Policies and regulations serve to establish orderly operations within the school district and help to define the system's functions and organizational relationships.

Most people would agree that policy is designed to provide direction and purpose for the school system. Policy should be studied by human resources administrators because of its significant effects on the lives of the personnel in the system. The challenges surrounding the human resources processes of selection, assignment, evaluation, collective negotiations, compensation and welfare, protection, and others demand the direction and guidance that personnel policies and procedures can provide. As Davies and Brickell (1988) pointed out, "the whole process of policy formulation is rich with opportunities for stimulating good thinking about school goals and their relation to policies by the many persons and groups concerned with the schools" (p. iv).

It is quite clear that the human resources function in education is embedded in the legal world of legislation and court rulings. Policy and regulations of school districts increasingly reflect the actions taken by federal, state, and local agencies. The personnel processes of recruitment, selection, assignment, compensation, collective bargaining, evaluation, and others are all controlled in part by the results of legal actions taken by various official agencies.

This chapter has presented information that underscores the vital importance of policy and administrative regulation development for the human resources function. It has also discussed many of the legal rulings that influence the behavior of all human resources administrators.

Discussion Questions

1. You have been selected by your teacher colleagues to serve on a district-wide committee for the purpose of revising the school district's leave policy. All forms of absence from duty are concerns of the committee. Although the overriding concern is that of the development of a viable policy for all professional staff members, what are several specific provisions that you would want to have implemented as a teacher? For example, what stipulations would you see as important in the area of personal leave, sabbatical leave, and so forth?

2. Use the information provided in question 1 to set forth several specific provisions that you, as a member of the school board, would consider imperative to an effective policy on personnel leaves. Examine the differences, if any, between the stipulations arrived at for question 1 and question 2.

3. Information in the chapter indicated that the development of policies and regulations served to clarify the division of labor between the school board and the school superintendent. Discuss this contention in more detail. Why is such a division important in school operations? Isn't there some danger that such a division will result in conflicts between the board and the superintendent?

4. Obtain a copy of your school district's policy manual or that of another school district. Rate the following characteristics from low (1) to high (5) as they pertain to the policy manual examined: completeness, conciseness, clarity, distinctiveness, and consistency. (Review the discussion of these characteristics included in the chapter for further term clarification.)

5. Use the NEPN/NSBA system to determine each of the following topical headings. Write the topic of the series, subseries, division, subdivision, and so on, for each entry.
   a. GBEB
   b. GCAAA
   c. GCBBA
   d. GCB
   e. GCAB

6. An administrator comments that, "I do all I can to keep policies strictly informal. Put them in writing and you have to carry them out. I want to keep as much freedom to act as possible." How might you reply to such a statement?

Case Studies

PAY OR NO PLAY

Ce Ce Rose has taught instrumental music at East High School for six years. She holds a B.S. degree in music and will complete a master's degree at the end of the second term at State University.

Principal Hodson received a call from one of the school's patrons, Mrs. John Adams. Mrs. Adams, whose son is a sophomore at East, also is the mother of two daughters who both graduated from East and participated in the school's instrumental program.

"Miss Rose has informed my son, Mark, that he needs special help in order to retain his place in the school band," reported Mrs. Adams. "She implied to Mark that his trumpet playing was below the standard expected for the marching band," she remarked. "Miss Rose has made herself available for special lessons at $12.50 an hour. She'll work with Mark after school on Wednesdays and on two Saturday mornings a month."

Principal Hodson was silent for a moment. If this was true, this information was new to him.

"Aren't teachers supposed to give special help to students after school hours if needed?" asked Mrs. Adams. "I understand that she already is giving lessons to three other orchestra students."

"Well, many of our teachers do give help after regular classroom hours," said Principal Hodson, "and I do know that some of our teachers moonlight as tutors at night and on weekends."

"It seems to me that the charging for special lessons could lead to problems," commented Mrs. Adams.

"Mrs. Adams," said Principal Hodson, "let me search for more information on this matter. I'll get back to you at the earliest possible time. I appreciate your concern and thank you for contacting me on this matter."

Questions

1. Place yourself in Principal Hodson's role. What action plan would you implement in this situation?

2. Identify three or four issues of importance in this case.

3. Assuming that the school district has no written policy concerning the issues you identified in question 2, is a guiding policy needed to deal with such cases? Why or why not?

TEACHERS' ACADEMIC FREEDOM

On the opening day of school in September, Keefe, a tenured part-time English teacher, who is also head of a high school English department and coordinator for grades 7 through 12, gave each member of his senior English class a copy of the prestigious *Atlantic Monthly* magazine and asked the students to read the first article that night. Keefe discussed the article with his class—especially a particular word that was used in it. He explained the word's origin and context, and the reasons the author had included it (the word, admittedly highly offensive, was a vulgar term for an incestuous son). Keefe said that any student who felt the assignment personally distasteful could have an alternate one.

The next evening Keefe was called to a meeting of the school committee and asked to defend his use of the offensive word. (Parents had complained.) Following his explanation, a majority of the members of the committee asked him informally if he would agree not to use it again in the classroom. Keefe replied that he could not, in good conscience, agree. No formal action was taken at the meeting, but Keefe was suspended shortly thereafter, and school administrators proposed that he be discharged.

Claiming a violation of his civil rights, Keefe sought a temporary injunction before a federal district court forbidding any action on the part of the school board prior to a hearing on the alleged violation. The court refused to grant the injunction, and Keefe appealed to the United States Court of Appeals, First Circuit. His position was that, as a matter of law, his conduct did not warrant discipline and therefore there was no ground for any hearing. The position had two relevant parts:

1. His conduct was within his competence as a teacher, as a matter of academic freedom, whether the defendants (school board) approved or not.

2. He had no warning by any regulations then in force that his actions could bring about his discharge.

The school board denied Keefe's contentions, and the following statement appeared in court records:

They (the board) accept the existence of a principle of academic freedom to teach, but state that it is limited to proper classroom materials as reasonably determined by the school committee in the light of pertinent conditions, of which they cite in particular the age of the students. Asked by the court whether a teacher has a right to say to the school committee that it is wrong if, in fact, its decision was arbitrary, counsel candidly and commendably (and correctly) responded in the affirmative. This we consider to be the present issue. (Davies & Watt, 1970)

Questions

1. What do you believe about the freedom of teachers to select and use materials of instruction despite the objections of some parents?

2. Discuss your views of the position set forth by Keefe. Do the same with the statement by the school board that appeared in the court records.

SOURCE: From "Teachers' Academic Freedom" by D. R. Davies and H. Watt, August 1970, *School Board Policies*. Copyright © 1970 by Daniel R. Davies. Reprinted by permission. Davies and Watt based this discussion on the case of *Keefe v. Geanakos et al.* (1st Cir. 1969).

CASE 9.3

MISS NORTH'S DILEMMA

Miss North has served in the Jefferson school system for 19 years as an elementary teacher. Her employment record in the Jefferson schools shows that she taught at Longfellow Elementary School for five years, Mark Twain Elementary School for nine years, Whitman Elementary School for three years, and in her present position as grade 5 teacher at Emerson for two years. She has served under four different superintendents, including the present school head, Dr. Donnelly, who has been in Jefferson for two years.

During Miss North's two years at Emerson, one board member called Dr. Donnelly to inquire about Miss North. The board member stated that he had received many calls about Miss North in the last two days.

(Continued)

(Continued)

"I just wanted to let you know about the calls," said the board member. "You'll most likely be receiving some yourself soon. Better be on your guard."

Dr. Donnelly reviewed Miss North's permanent file. Evaluation reports on Miss North pointed out that it was felt that she was a strict teacher and did not have the most friendly classroom atmosphere, but most pupils performed better in her classroom than in one with more permissive surroundings.

One anecdotal notation in Miss North's file outlined a conversation between her and the assistant superintendent, Dr. Seward. Dr. Seward had telephoned Miss North to inform her that it would be necessary to transfer her from Mark Twain to Whitman. The reasons outlined for the action as recorded by Dr. Seward centered on an apparent feeling of growing parental dissatisfaction and the fact that several parents had requested that their children not be placed in her room the next year. Thus, the decision was reached to move Miss North to Whitman for a new start.

The record revealed that Miss North was greatly disturbed about the transfer decision. "I don't drive an automobile," Miss North had pointed out. "How do you expect me to get back and forth to school each day? Everyone knows what it means when you're placed at Whitman," Miss North had stated, according to Dr. Seward.

Mr. Smith, principal at Whitman Elementary School, was quoted by Dr. Seward as saying, "You never know how she will react from day to day. We've gotten along as well as can be expected. She doesn't have much patience for the slow learner, but her good kids can compete with most other grade-five pupils."

At a special board meeting later that week, a second member of the board of education mentioned the concern centering on Miss North. "Parents tell me that the pupils are afraid of her," one board member stated. "She apparently is 'cold' toward parents. In one instance, I was told that one of her pupils had written a note on the blackboard wishing her a happy birthday. Miss North insisted that the one who wrote it on the board erase it in front of the whole class. The parent of the child indicated that her embarrassed daughter didn't want to return to school."

Another board member stated, "This must be her 30th year of teaching in Jefferson. Doesn't she retire soon?"

The matter was referred by the board to Superintendent Donnelly for immediate study. After the meeting, Dr. Donnelly conferred with Mr. Malloy, principal at Emerson.

"She is a rather cold person, but I've received no official complaints from parents to date," said the principal. "However, my visit last week to her classroom revealed that some children are not responding. Her room was all business. The science lesson which I observed was well presented."

Dr. Seward apparently felt that it would be best to release Miss North. "She is starting one of her problems again. I think we've gone along with her long enough. Mr. Malloy would just as soon have her out of his building," Dr. Seward related to Dr. Donnelly. "She is a 'loner' in my opinion. She didn't even attend the faculty social last month."

Dr. Donnelly noted that the date was March 1 and school was to close on May 27. Obviously, the board was anticipating immediate action on the part of the administration.

Questions

1. Assume the role of Dr. Donnelly, school superintendent, and discuss/write your follow-up procedures and recommendations to the school board.

2. What policy and regulation matters are significant in this case? Why?

3. Explain how a viable set of policies and regulations might have proven of special value in this case.

References

Bloss, J. M. (1882). *Thirtieth report of the superintendent of public instruction of the state of Indiana to the governor.* Indianapolis: State of Indiana.

Bolton, J. E. (1997). *Human resources management for public and nonprofit organizations.* San Francisco: Jossey-Bass.

Cohan, A., Hergenrother, M. A., Johnson, Y. M., Mandel, L. S., & Sawyer, J. (1996). *Sexual harassment and abuse: A handbook for teachers and administrators.* Thousand Oaks, CA: Corwin.

Cole, J. (2000). Sexual harassment: New rules, new behavior. In Fred H. Maidment (Ed.), *Human Resources00/01* (10th ed., pp. 46–48). Reprinted from *Business Horizons,* March/April, 1999. Indiana University Kelly School of Business. Guilford, CT: Dushkin/McGraw-Hill.

Davies, D. R., & Brickell, H. M. (1988). *An instructional handbook on how to develop school board policies, by-laws, and administrative regulations.* Naco, AZ: Daniel R. Davies.

Davies, D. R., & Watt, H. (1970). *Teachers' academic freedom.* In D. R. Davies & H. Watt (Eds.), *School board policies.* Croft Consulting Services.

Equal Employment Opportunity Commission. (1980). Guidelines concerning sexual harassment: Title VII legislation, 703 of the Civil Rights Act. (P.L. 88-352).

Fischer, L., Schimmel, D., & Stellman, L. E. (2003). *Teachers and the law* (6th ed.). Boston, MA: Allyn & Bacon.

Gómez-Mejía, L. R., Balkin, D. B., & Cardy, R. L. (2007). *Managing human resources* (4th ed.). Columbus, OH: Prentice Hall, Pearson Education.

Harvey, D., & Bowin, R. B. (1996). *Human resource management: An experimental approach.* Upper Saddle River, NJ: Prentice Hall.

McConnell, J. H. (2005). *How to develop essential HR policies and procedures.* New York: American Management Association.

Norton, M. S. (2004). *The personnel administrator in Arizona: A research study.* Tempe: Arizona State University, Division of Educational Leadership & Policy Studies.

Norton, M. S. (2005). *Executive leadership for effective administration.* Boston, MA: Allyn & Bacon.

Peterson, L. J., Rossmiller, R. A., & Volz, M. M. (1978). *The law and public school operation* (2nd ed.). New York: Harper & Row.

Smith, S., & Mazin, R. (2004). *The HR administrator answer book.* New York: American Management Association.

Tead, O., & Metcalf, H. C. (1920). *Personnel administration.* New York: McGraw-Hill.

Wolkinson, B. (2000). EEO in the workplace: Employment law challenges. In E. E. Kasek & R. N. Block (Eds.), *Managing human resources in the 21st century.* Cincinnati, OH: South-Western College Publishing, Thompson Learning.

Young, I. P. (2008). *The human resource function in educational administration* (9th ed.). Columbus, OH: Pearson, Prentice Hall.

CHAPTER 10

Collective Bargaining and the Human Resources Function

Working With Employee Groups

Learning Objectives

After reading this chapter, you will be able to

- Describe the evolution of the empowerment of employee groups in education.
- Identify the responsibilities of human resources administrators in working with employee groups in the school district.
- Describe the collective bargaining process, including distributive and integrative or win-win approaches.
- Discuss the operational models for implementing the collective bargaining process.

Although collective bargaining is a way of life in education today, it was a repugnant idea in education less than 50 years ago. In 1960, for example, an attempt by the National Education Association (NEA) to pass a resolution at its national convention in Los Angeles stating that, "representative negotiations are compatible with the ethics and dignity of the teaching profession," was soundly rejected by the association's representatives (1961). The use of such terms as collective bargaining and teachers' union was slow to be accepted by a profession that viewed them as applicable only to organized labor. Today, the large majority of states and the District of Columbia have passed legislation approving bargaining in the public sector between boards of education and employee groups. Collective bargaining in education has become a way of life.

This chapter examines the work of the human resources function in relation to employee groups. The discussion centers on the development of influence within employee groups in education and its impact on human resources processes. It gives attention to collective bargaining and its implications for the work of human resources administrators. Human resources administrators are often directly involved in the collective bargaining process and commonly serve as the chief spokesperson for the school board bargaining team. The nature of the collective bargaining process, including both distributive and integrative approaches, is fully discussed. Special attention also is devoted to mediation strategies and to grievance procedures as these relate to collective bargaining in education.

One of the major problems with examining the status of collective bargaining in education was underscored by Hannaway and Rotherman (2006), who noted that despite the tremendous influence of teachers' unions, there has not been a significant study examining the role of collective bargaining in education for more than two decades. Much of the research related to collective bargaining in the public section was completed during the 1960s and early 1970s, a time when bargaining in education was in the initial stages.

Employee Unions Defined

Webb and Webb (1920) provided an early definition of the term "union" that remains viable today: "a continuous association of wage earners for the purpose of maintaining or improving the conditions of their working lives" (p. 10). The National Labor Relations Act (Wagner Act) of 1935 defined a union as any kind of a labor organization "in which employees participate and which exist for the purpose . . . of dealing with employees concerning grievances, labor disputes, wages, rates of pay, hours of employment, or conditions of work." Sixty-five years later, Lunenburg and Ornstein (2000) defined a union as "an organization of employees formed for the purpose of influencing an employer's decision concerning conditions of employment" (p. 548). "Teachers' unions have evolved to the point that few if any differences can be identified between them and employee unions in other settings" (Norton, 2005, p. 315). This chapter uses the terms "teachers' union" and "teachers' association" interchangeably.

Persons favoring unions in education argue that they serve several important purposes: (1) protection of teachers' rights, (2) extension of democracy in the workplace, and (3) promotion of teacher decision making and the development of better schools. Those who oppose unions in education argue that they are (1) self-serving and devoted only to higher salaries rather than to better education for students; (2) interested mainly in gaining more power in the governance of school programs and policy development; (3) inhibitors to needed educational reform, as they are only apologists for bad teachers; and (4) educational anachronisms and resistors to needed educational change (Nelson, Carlson, & Palonsky, 1996).

In 2006, membership in the National Education Association (NEA) numbered 3.2 million, far surpassing the estimated 1.3 million membership of the American Federation of Teachers (AFT). Are the NEA and the AFT unions as we know them in the private sector? As Norton, Webb, Dlugosh, and Sybouts (1996) pointed out,

(1) unions represent organizations of employees; (2) they strive to influence conditions of work for their membership; (3) they protect and enhance the economic welfare of members; (4) they demand the use of collective bargaining in determining salaries and conditions of work; (5) they lend strong support to members in matters relating to grievances and arbitration; and (6) they represent a continuous association of wage earners. (p. 275)

Both the NEA and the AFT reflect each of the foregoing criteria that describe a union. Today, the NEA is the largest employee union in the United States. More important, school superintendents and professors named the power of teacher and other school employee unions among the top 11 challenges facing public schools (Horace Mann League, 1996). In another study, 33.8% of the school superintendents reported that concerns about relations with teachers' unions were troublesome for them "very frequently," "frequently," or "somewhat frequently" (Norton, 2001). In the same study, school superintendents ranked the category "demands of the school staff" highest of six determinants of their workload.

Working Relationships: The Human Resources Function and Employee Groups

School boards generally expect that the school superintendent will represent them in the area of employee relations. In this sense, the superintendent serves as the director of the school district's employee relations, although various responsibilities are delegated to other units in the school system. (Norton et al., 1996, p. 279)

The four key responsibilities of the school superintendent in the area of employee relations are as follows:

1. The school superintendent must serve as the primary liaison between the school board and employee groups, and between the school board and school administration on matters of employee relations.

2. The school superintendent is responsible for the development of viable employee relations policy for the school district.

3. The school superintendent is responsible for providing instruction for school administrators and other personnel on the implementation of the master contract agreement and the administration of grievances related to the contract.

4. The superintendent serves as the school district's representative in matters of paramount importance concerning employee relations and school district practices in this area. (Norton et al., 1996, pp. 279–281)

For each of the listed employee relation responsibilities of the superintendent, the human resources unit of the school system and other human resources administrators provide vital support. For example, one study revealed that 41.5% of the state's human resources directors listed collective bargaining as a primary responsibility. Collective bargaining was ranked sixth among the processes that consumed the greatest amount of the HR director's time (Norton, 2004). Needed communication with teacher groups must be programmed so that school board members, district administrators, and employee groups are informed about the school district's goals, problems, and needs. In order to facilitate such communication, the human resources director should sit as a member of the superintendent's administrative cabinet. In this position, the human resources director is better prepared to inform school employees of the board of education's and school administration's personnel positions and also able to communicate the views of employees to the board.

One key responsibility of human resources administrators in the school district is to develop mutual support and trust between the school district's administrative staff and employees; in this sense, they become advocates of the district's employees. Efforts on the part of the human resources unit to gain optimal work conditions and proper salaries for employees promote cooperation, mutual trust, and a positive image of the school district. Furthermore, such leadership behavior lends to an atmosphere that serves to attract and retain quality personnel in the system.

Under the leadership of the school superintendent, human resources personnel serve a primary role in the fair and equitable implementation of the negotiated master agreement of the school district. The school principal plays a key role in the implementation of contract provisions and agreements because he or she works most directly with personnel at the local building level.

The human resources director frequently is delegated the responsibility of representing the school district in personnel matters such as contract grievances, affirmative action, the litigation of employment matters, due process procedures, and others. Because school personnel work for the school district and not for the employees' organization, the superintendent and the human resources administrators in the district must assume responsibility for the administration of all phases of the personnel function, including the development of a positive working relationship with school employees and employee groups.

Collective Bargaining: Definition and Basic Principles

An early definition of collective bargaining, and one that has remained relative to the process over the years, was stated by Lieberman and Moskow (1966): collective bargaining is "a process whereby employees as a group and the employers make offers and counter offers in good faith on conditions of their employment relations for the purpose of reaching mutually acceptable agreement" (p. 1). As early as 1967, the American Association of School Administrators (Redfern, 1967) defined collective bargaining as the process by which school teachers, through their designated representatives, negotiate with the board of education, or its designated representative(s), with reference to salary, working conditions and other matters of interest to negotiation practices. Collective bargaining and professional negotiations sometimes are used interchangeably. (p. 112)

Professional negotiations became the official policy of the NEA at the 1962 Denver Convention. A short time later, the NEA (1965) defined negotiations as

a set of procedures, written and officially adopted by the local association and the school board, which provides an orderly method for the school board and the local association to negotiate, through professional channels, on matters of mutual concern, to reach agreement on these matters and to establish educational channels for mediation and appeal in event of impasse. (p. 1)

Later definitions of negotiations are quite similar. Young (2008) stated that

collective negotiations is a process by which representatives of the school district meet with representatives of the school district employees in order to make proposals and counterproposals for the purpose of mutually agreeing on salaries, fringe benefits, and working conditions covering a specific period of time. (pp. 297–298)

An additional dimension, that of serving as a method for setting the procedures to be followed in settling disputes, is part of the negotiations definition set forth by Cunningham and Cordeiro (2000). For the purposes of this chapter, **collective bargaining** is the process whereby matters of employee relations are determined mutually by representatives of employee groups and their employer, within the limits of law or mutual agreement. Bargaining, under this definition, can occur under distributive or integrative approaches.

Regardless of the differences in phrasing of definitions, the process of collective bargaining most often is based on the following basic principles:

1. Employees have the right to form, join, and participate in the activities of organizations of their choosing for the purpose of representation on matters of employment relations.

2. An association has the right to request exclusive representation in negotiations when the majority of the employee membership so authorizes.

3. Representatives of the local association and the board of education meet to negotiate on matters relating to salaries, fringe benefits, and working conditions as set forth in cooperatively established ground rules or as set forth by law.

4. Recommendations (agreements) of the negotiation representatives, when ratified by the groups that they represent, result in the contractual agreements for the time period specified.

5. Failure to reach an agreement leads to impasse, in which case established appeal procedures are implemented to reach a settlement.

The Two Primary Bargaining Processes

The two primary approaches to collective bargaining described in the literature are distributive bargaining and integrative bargaining. Perry and Wilman's early description of these two bargaining strategies remains relevant today. Distributive bargaining is the collective bargaining processes exemplified by a labor-management model, which is primarily adversarial and designed to realize maximum-gain short-term bargaining through the use of authority, power, or withdrawal of services (Perry & Wilman, 1970). Distributive bargaining generally results in crisis bargaining and is the strategy most often associated with labor organizations. On the other hand, quasi-distributive bargaining is based on a desire to avoid a test of power.

The second major approach to bargaining, integrative bargaining, as described by Perry and Wilman (1970),

> is based on strong long-run mutual interests and important short-run problems. . . . A pure integrative bargaining strategy commonly leads to "problem solving" . . . problem solving has been concentrated in mature bargaining relationships in which external political and/or economic conditions force the parties to perceive a threat to their mutual survival in either continued conflict or continued reliance on short-run power as the basis for decision making. (pp. 62–65)

Quasi-integrative bargaining involves a quid pro quo, give-and-take process of compromise and thus has similarities to quasi-distributive strategies. However, quasi-integrative strategy places more emphasis on problem solving and is more closely associated with the win-win approach. A later section of this chapter discusses conditions that serve to determine when distributive or integrative strategies are more successful.

We note that both distributive bargaining and integrative bargaining have witnessed various adaptations as collective bargaining has evolved over the years. For example, terms such as power-based bargaining and fractional bargaining are associated with distributive bargaining methods. Power-based bargaining refers to bargaining based on an "all or nothing" concept. The threat or use of a strike is viewed as the primary pressure tactic for gaining employees' demands. The union might implement a lockout strategy or pose threats of firing employees as a weapon in their bargaining strategy. Fractional bargaining exists when clusters of employees within the same organization decide to bargain separately rather being part of the system as a whole. The cluster groups are of the opinion that they can do more for themselves than the union or organizational bargaining unit can do for them.

Integrative bargaining has assumed many different titles and varied procedures as well. Win-win bargaining, partnership bargaining, collaborative bargaining, problem-solving bargaining, mutual-gains bargaining, creative bargaining, consensus-based bargaining, and interest-based bargaining represent a few of the approaches based on integrative methods.

Win-win bargaining methods are discussed in detail later in this chapter. In brief, win-win bargaining centers on efforts to resolve mutual problems of interest to the school district as a whole. While working to arrive at creative solutions to issues that both parties encounter, the parties also emphasize attempts to improve relations between the school board and the employees.

Bargaining by Employee Groups: Historical Perspectives

The process of collective bargaining in education has evolved over several decades. Figure 10.1 outlines the early developments that had an impact on both the unity of employee groups and the legal pathways for negotiations in the public sector.

The competition for membership between the NEA and AFT in the early decades of the 20th century escalated efforts to serve the welfare of teachers and resulted in the acceleration of collective bargaining activities in education. Walter (1975) described the ultimate results of the AFT and NEA competition as follows:

> While the competition was at its strongest [for membership] and under the press of that competition, the NEA became a different organization. Its teachers clearly became the dominant power, and administration affiliates became much less influential. By the end of the sixties, fewer important differences remained between AFT and NEA. (p. 16)

Negotiations in education developed rapidly following the official stand by the NEA in 1962 insisting that teachers' associations have a right to negotiate with

---

1806	Philadelphia Cordwainers Case: Employee groups were found guilty of conspiracy to raise their wages. Such organized action was declared illegal by the courts.
1842	*Commonwealth v. Hunt:* In a decision relating to the use of group action by employees, the Supreme Court of Massachusetts ruled that labor organizations did not constitute unlawful bodies by the mere fact that they represented a combination of individuals or bodies. This decision enhanced group action by employees.
1845	First state association of teachers and school officials was established in Massachusetts.
1857	National Teachers Association (NTA) is founded.
1870	National Education Association (NEA) is founded.
1886	American Federation of Labor (AFL) is founded.
1886	Federal regulation of interstate commerce is established. Federal legislation passed to regulate interstate commerce proved to provide important support to union activity. This legislation served as the legal rationale for federal government intervention in disputes between management groups and employees on an interstate basis.
1890	Sherman Antitrust Act: The act expanded to find labor unions guilty of conspiracy to restrain trade by striking.

1914	Clayton Act: The act removed unions from application of antitrust laws. However, the United States Supreme Court did not apply antitrust laws until much later.
1926	Railroad Labor Act: The act represented a major step in the support of collective bargaining through legislation. Its constitutionality was reinforced four years later in a ruling by the Supreme Court.
1932	Norris-LaGuardia Act: The act supported the right of employees to form unions and placed restrictions on the courts concerning the issuance of injunctions to restrict labor activities. Refusal by employers to bargain with representatives of employee groups was determined to be an unfair labor practice and subject to punishment by law.
1935	National Labor Relations Act (Wagner Act): Congress established the right of employees to bargain with their employers on matters pertaining to wages, job-related benefits, and conditions of employment. The act concerned employees in the private sector only and excluded public employees. Most agree, however, that this act has affected employer-employee contract relations more significantly than any legislation passed to date. Even though the Wagner Act applied only to interstate commerce, it confirmed certain employee rights in the area of collective bargaining.
1938	Educational Policies Commission: The commission stated that the entire staff should take part in the formulation of the educational process.
1947	Labor Management Relations Act (Taft-Hartley Act): This act provided further expansion and clarification of employee rights in the bargaining process and added a set of unfair labor practices by unions. Although the act applied only to interstate commerce, its influence on legislation in the individual states and on bargaining in the public sector was far-reaching. Employee-employer bargaining under the Taft-Hartley Act is summarized as follows:

1. Collective bargaining is the performance of the mutual obligation of the employer and the representative of the employees to meet at reasonable times and confer in good faith with respect to wages, hours, and other terms and conditions of employment.

2. Collective bargaining also includes negotiation of an agreement or any question arising thereunder and the execution of a written contract incorporating any agreement reached if requested by either party.

3. Such an obligation (to bargain) does not compel either party to agree to a proposal or to require the making of a concession (Labor Management Relations Act, 1947).

1955	Merger of American Federation of Labor (AFL) and Congress of Industrial Organizations (CIO): Unionization was a powerful movement and an effective influence for bargaining in the private sector.
1959	Labor Management Reporting and Disclosure Act (Landrum-Griffin Act): The act established more effective controls over the operations and funds of unions. Governance practices such as voting rights, participation in union affairs, and the right to sue in case of rights violations were covered by the act. Financial reporting procedures, open or public expense accounting, election of union officers, and "democratic practices" were also included. Teacher organizations were excluded; however, the influence of the Landrum-Griffin Act on public employee groups has been significant.
1959	Wisconsin became the first state to enact legislation pertaining to negotiations in the public sector. A state labor relations board was established to oversee the administration of the act and assist in the resolution of disputes.
1962	American Federation of Teachers (AFT) victory: AFT Local No. 2 won the right to represent employees of the New York City public schools. This victory pushed the NEA to historical action at its Denver Convention in 1962.
1962	Denver Convention of the NEA: This convention marked the beginning of the NEA's official position on professional negotiations for teachers. Resolution 18 modified a 1961 resolution that called for the right of professional education associations "to participate in the determination of policies of common concern and other conditions for professional service" (NEA, 1961, pp. 216–217).

(Continued)

(Continued)

	Resolution 18, however, included the NEA's first official reference to the term "professional negotiations." The 1962 resolution set forth such strong wording as "the NEA insists on the right of professional associations through democratically selected representatives using professional channels to participate with boards of education in determination of policies of common concern including salary and other conditions for professional service" (NEA, 1962, p. 178).
1962	Presidential Executive Order 10988: The executive order by President John F. Kennedy opened the door for bargaining for federal employees. The order had significant effects on bargaining movements in the entire public sector. E.O. 10988 provided federal workers the right to join organizations of choice, provided for the recognition of organizations for purposes of negotiations, required federal agencies to meet and confer with recognized employee organizations about personnel policies and conditions of work, and established advisory arbitration of grievances in relation to agreements reached. As a result, government employee unions flourished. The order encouraged local and state government employees to take action to win negotiation rights as well.
1965–1968	Professional negotiations agreements: By 1965, an estimated 388 professional negotiations agreements in 35 states had been filed with the NEA. During 1967 and 1968, approximately 900,000 teachers were working under an estimated 2,200 agreements with at least some form of minimal formal acknowledgment of the existence of a teacher organization in the district (NEA, 1968). Professional negotiation legislation was passed in Oregon, Washington, Connecticut, California, and Massachusetts.
1969	Presidential Executive Order 11491: President Richard Nixon's order was designed to bring labor relations in closer relationship to practices in the private sector. The order modified and expanded the earlier order by President Kennedy. E.O. 11491 established exclusive recognition in the bargaining process, required the inclusion of a grievance procedure, established the Federal Labor Relations Council to interpret the provisions of the order, and established the Federal Service Impasse Panel. The order tended to lend additional support for legislation concerning collective negotiations in the public sector, including teacher groups.
1980–1990	By 1980, 32 states had enacted collective bargaining laws that encompassed some or all categories of educational employees in the public sector. This count included those states with "permissive legislation" whereby the employing agency could enter into contract discussions with employees, but such an action was not required. Peterson, Rossmiller, and Volz (1978) cited the case of *Norwalk Teachers Association v. Board of Education* in noting that "in the absence of a statute either authorizing or prohibiting collective bargaining by teachers the prevailing view today seems to be that teachers have that right" (p. 432). Although integrative approaches gained in popularity in education, distributive strategies remained most dominant.
1991–present	Some movement toward the increased use of integrative, or win-win, approaches to collective bargaining was witnessed during this time period. Although distributive, quid pro quo methods remained dominant, impasse problems and negative outcomes in the area of staff and community relationships motivated some school districts to implement less adversarial bargaining procedures. Best estimates indicate that approximately 7.5% of the nation's school districts have begun to use win-win methods.

Those districts using integrative bargaining typically report that the process tends to become a forum for everything that takes place in the school district; the scope of bargaining widened significantly. Thus, such topics as student discipline, curriculum, educational reform, decision-making processes, and teacher protection become agenda items. Also, negotiators who are effective in distributive bargaining situations often are found to be much less effective when integrative methods are utilized.

Overall, between 1991 and 1998, collective bargaining continued as a way of life for school personnel. By 2008, 38 states had passed collective bargaining legislation relative to the public sector. The scope of bargaining widened to include almost everything that happens within a school district. Although some movement toward integrative approaches was noted, distributive bargaining methods continued to dominate. |

Figure 10.1   Developments Influencing Bargaining: Historical Perspectives boards of education. Bargaining procedures in the private sector generally served as the blueprint for negotiations in education. Even though some have criticized the process of negotiations historically as inappropriate for education, by 1965 the die had been cast, and by 1968 negotiations had become an acceptable and expected practice in the field of education (NEA, 1968).

Collective negotiations in education were fostered and supported by several developments or conditions in the field that included the following:

1. A growing discontent with compensation levels on the part of teachers, who saw their salaries losing pace with professionals in other fields.

2. The increased sophistication of teacher groups and individual teachers in the actual processes of negotiations. Although teachers' expertise in collective negotiating increased, administrators and members of boards of education were reluctant to give credibility to the negotiations process and, in the 1950s and 1960s, all too often tended to ignore its impact on educational employee relations.

3. The increase of teacher strikes and threat of strikes. Before 1966, the NEA avoided references to strikes in its negotiation policy. Since that date, associations with NEA affiliation have been involved in numerous such actions. In 1979–1980, 242 teacher walkouts were reported (Diegmueller, 1991).

4. The mere growth in the number of negotiated agreements in education had a "spillover" effect on nonnegotiating districts and tended to cement the process as an expected right and practice. Once negotiations were initiated, withdrawal from the process was difficult.

5. Such developments as district reorganization, which resulted in larger school districts and more adequate financial resources; the changing composition of teacher groups, especially the increase in male teachers; the teacher supply and demand, with serious shortages of teachers in the 1960s; and the increased professional development of staffs, especially in the area of advanced preparation.

By 1984, the practice of collective bargaining was common in education and encompassed both professional and support staff personnel. Even in those states with no legislative provision for bargaining, the "meet and confer" concept was well established. The process of bargaining has not been restricted to teacher groups. Principals, supervisors, middle management personnel, and staff in other classifications have negotiated agreements in a growing number of school districts.

Collective Bargaining in Education and the Central Human Resources Unit

Human resources administration has been influenced by collective bargaining in two distinct ways: (1) the process of collective bargaining has affected virtually every process and activity within the human resources function, and (2) the human resources unit generally has assumed a major role in the administration of the bargaining process itself. Although collective bargaining approaches vary, the process is entrenched as a common practice in school systems today.

Human resources directors play a major role in three specific activities in the area of collective bargaining: proposal development, strategy development, and negotiations at the table. Many are involved in actual negotiations: almost 70.0% of the personnel administrators in one state reported that they served on the school district's collective bargaining team. In the same study, 58.6% of the directors served as chief spokesperson for the school board's negotiations team (Norton, 2004). The use of the human resources director as the chief negotiator or spokesperson for the board team varies among school districts. Smaller districts tend to use the school superintendent or a member of the school board more often than larger districts, which often use a professional negotiator (from outside or inside the school district) or the human resources director as the chief negotiator. It also has become common for the human resources director or the director of employment relations to coordinate the entire collective bargaining process for the school board. In the aforementioned study by Norton (2004), HR directors ranked collective bargaining as sixth among the responsibilities that were consuming the greatest amount of their time.

Because the involvement of human resources directors nationally in collective bargaining is well established, it is important to identify specific responsibilities or tasks related to negotiations in which a director must be competent. Figure 10.2 summarizes these competencies.

Figure 10.3 illustrates the influences and impacts of the negotiations process on the human resources function. An understanding of these relationships is essential for the effective functioning of the human resources program. For example, working conditions are a major negotiations consideration, and the "definition" of working conditions is expanding in scope.

In the following sections, we discuss integrative and distributive bargaining in detail.

Collective Bargaining in Education

As we noted previously in this chapter, in an effort to reduce conflicts and reach more mutually satisfying solutions to problems, various integrative approaches to collective bargaining have been introduced into education. Integrative bargaining, win-win bargaining, collaborative bargaining, partnership bargaining, creative bargaining, and joint problem solving are all names for bargaining approaches designed to eliminate adversarial relationships and to serve both parties in achieving their bargaining objectives, while at the same time feeling good about the results. Of course, although each of the above-named integrative bargaining approaches is founded on win-win methods, the strategies accompanying them tend to differ. For example, creative bargaining features the ingenuity of the bargaining parties in searching for various alternatives to reach agreement. Thus, the parties create new and different ways of approaching the manner in which negotiation is considered. Changes in contract provisions regarding the duration of

1.1. Ability to understand the methods and strategies of collective bargaining and the skills required in the process.

1.2. Ability to make all necessary preparations for negotiations by gathering information, establishing priorities, and interpreting parameters.

1.3. Ability to contribute to the resolution of a collective negotiations agreement.

1.4. Ability to prepare news releases for the media concerning bargaining progress reports.

1.5. Ability to interpret and communicate the negotiations agreement as it relates to the personnel function and employee contractual relations.

1.6. Ability to review and recommend revision of policies, regulations, and procedures as these relate to the "newly negotiated" agreement.

1.7. Ability to interpret, communicate, and evaluate the negotiated agreement as it relates to employer-employee relationships.

1.8. Ability to evaluate the negotiated agreements as these relate to future negotiations and school district policy development.

Figure 10.2   *Collective Bargaining Competencies of the Human Resources Director*
SOURCE: Norton & Farrar (2004), p. 109.

contracts, percentages applied to fringe benefit payments by management, or a new focus on work benefits as opposed to salary increases are examples of creative approaches. In contrast, partnership bargaining strives to develop a basic understanding between the parties.

Persons who have experienced win-win bargaining methods commonly note the following occurrences or results:

1. Integrative bargaining often results in a widening of the scope of the negotiations agenda. In some cases, the bargaining sessions become a "forum" for the discussion of a broad spectrum of concerns of the school district (e.g., student discipline, curriculum, educational reform, decision making, etc.).

2. Integrative bargaining tends to change the decision-making model within the district itself. That is, integrative bargaining fosters collaboration in the decision-making process. Site-based decision making, in turn, promotes collaborative bargaining.

3. Individuals who have previously served as negotiators in distributive or traditional bargaining may not be able to serve effectively in integrative processes. Integrative strategies depend greatly on the personalities of the persons involved; the openness of the process and the attitude of power-with versus power-over necessitate somewhat different personality characteristics than are useful in distributive approaches.

4. In school districts in which win-win bargaining approaches reportedly have been successful, morale, relationships, and trust have improved, while problems have decreased. However, positive happenings appear to be closely related to the personalities involved in the specific setting rather than to the

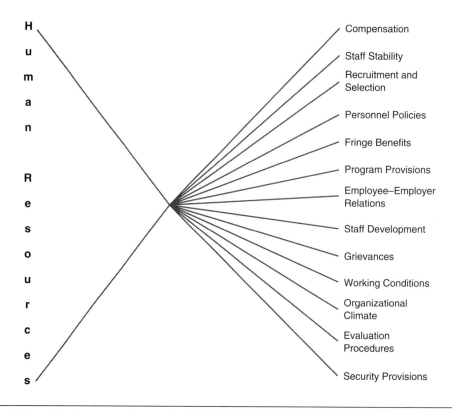

Figure 10.3   Collective Bargaining and Its Impact on the Human Resources Function

process itself. This consideration also supports the contention that negotiators experienced in distributive procedures may not be as successful in integrative approaches.

Distributive Bargaining

Quasi-distributive bargaining is based on a quid pro quo, give-and-take approach in which the utilization of power and bargaining strategy plays a major role. The general operations model for quasi-distributive bargaining, the model most frequently used in education, includes five major components:

1. Planning and preparation for collective bargaining.

2. Determination and recognition of the bargaining unit.

3. Determination of the composition of the bargaining team, including the chief spokesperson.

4. Determination of the initial bargaining procedures and appropriate table strategies.

5. Implementation of the contract agreement.

Planning Preparation

Initial Strategies
Impasse Procedures
Scope
Ground Rules
Goals and Objectives
Information/Data Gathering
Cost Analysis

Agreement Implementation

Evaluation
Considerations
Grievance
   Administration
Communication of
   Agreement
Ratification

Unit Recognition

Determination
   of Agent
Recognition of
   Unit
Composition
   of Unit

The Bargaining Process

Negotiation Strategies

Written Agreement
Reaching Agreement
Grievances Clauses
Proposals and
   Counterproposals
Table Tactics

Team Determination

Select Chief
   Spokesperson
Selection of
   Board Team
Selection of
   Employee Team

Figure 10.4   Collective Bargaining Components and Related Activities

Figure 10.4 illustrates the various activities related to each of these areas, which are discussed in the following sections.

Planning and Preparation for Collective Negotiations

Careful planning, including the development of clear goals, is of paramount importance for successful bargaining. Planning and preparation for collective negotiations include the following specific activities: (1) gathering the related information and data needed for decision making and cost analysis, (2) determining goals and objectives for negotiations, (3) establishing ground rules for conducting negotiations, (4) determining the scope of the negotiations, and (5) clarifying procedures in case of impasse.

Gathering Related Information for Decision Making and Cost Analysis

At the outset of the planning and preparation activities, communication with local implementers of the current contract agreement must be established. The school board bargaining team must gather and analyze all information that identifies problems related to the current agreement and the issues that most likely will, or should, be given serious attention in future bargaining sessions.

Several information sources should be used in preparing for bargaining, including (1) information from the school district administrative staff about their concerns and needs; (2) troublesome areas in the present contract agreement; (3) publications, reports, press releases, and public statements by the respective professional groups; (4) information concerning the agendas for bargaining and troublesome areas in bargaining in other school districts; (5) data relating to budgets and the financial plans of the school district; (6) input from the school district's various constituencies concerning attitudes and opinions on employer-employee matters; and (7) information on the results of arbitration or court actions under present contracts in other school districts. Once gathered, information must be analyzed in terms of related problems and their potential significance in the bargaining process. The possible impact on the school program, employer-employee relationships, budgets, and the school district's goals must be evaluated. Cost factors must include data on salaries, fringe benefits, program expenditures, human resources needs, administrative expenses, and other dimensions. Such information must be organized and properly recorded, and also must be easily retrievable for use during the planning and preparation phases of bargaining as well as during table negotiations. Thus, some form of a negotiations "bargaining book" should be organized in which information is organized by topic and labeled for convenient referencing and updating.

There is no question that preparation is the foundation on which successful collective bargaining is built. Empirical evidence suggests that it takes nine hours of preparation for each hour spent in actual table bargaining.

Determining Goals and Objectives for Collective Bargaining

An essential activity in planning and preparing for bargaining is the establishment of goals and objectives that serve as the foundation for all bargaining activities and provide the necessary guidelines for the entire process. The school board team must understand the bargaining objectives of the school board and the level of importance of each item to be considered.

Anticipating the requests of employee groups is another important consideration. Once these potential requests are identified, the board team must determine the probable level of importance to the employee group. Although this determination is difficult, clues to the importance of employee requests often exist in such information as employee grievances during the year, the substance of conferences and journals of state and national employee groups, and the negotiation requests by school districts that already are in the process of being settled or that have been settled for the ensuing year.

Consideration of the school board's objectives and a careful anticipation of the objectives of the employee group allow the board team to be proactive rather than merely reactive at the table. Such knowledge is essential in determining what the team wants to accomplish in the negotiations and what strategies best serve these purposes. Attempting to gather this information during table negotiations handicaps the team and severely inhibits its ability to react intelligently to requests or to question adequately the information provided by the other party.

A team's objectives should be ranked in some manner, perhaps as primary, secondary, or tertiary priorities. Such a ranking of objectives clarifies the expectations of the team and plays an important role in determining tactics and strategies during ongoing bargaining sessions.

Establishing Ground Rules for Conducting Collective Bargaining

Ground rules consist of the statements and agreements that govern the bargaining activities. Such rules encompass the establishment of the authority of the groups' representatives, time and place of meetings, length of table sessions, procedures for handling the agenda items, use of outside consultants, use of meeting minutes, use of open or closed meetings, quorum rules, use of a spokesperson, procedural rules, use of caucuses, use of press releases, ratification procedures, impasse provisions, a timeline for bargaining activities, and related guidelines.

Ground rules can be an unnecessary addendum to bargaining activities if they become dominant over primary issues of the negotiations and can inhibit later table bargaining process if they cause major disputes. Because of the negative effects of ground rules, their use has decreased. As team members become more sophisticated in the process of bargaining and if prior relationships have established mutual "trust," ground rules become less important to the process.

Nevertheless, when ground rules are used, the representative teams must agree on answers to such questions as the following:

Authority of Team Representatives

1. Can representatives sign agreements?

2. Are spokespersons serving as authoritative representatives of the respective groups?

3. When a tentative agreement is reached, will representatives work diligently within their own groups for its ratification?

Time and Place of Meetings

1. When and where will table sessions be held? During school hours? Weekends? Holidays? After school hours?

2. What will be the length of each session? Can this time be extended by mutual agreement?

3. If teams agree to meet during school hours, who pays for substitutes, if needed?

Agenda for Meetings

1. Is the agenda to be set in advance? Can new items be added?

2. How is the agenda to be handled?

3. What if teams cannot agree on the agenda for the next meeting? Who determines the agenda?

Team Members

1. How many team members can represent a group? Must representatives be members of the school district? Can a professional negotiator from the outside be utilized?

2. What are the expected roles of team members? Will there be a chief spokesperson for each team?

3. Can parties bring in outside consultants to report or to testify? Can members of the employer and employee units attend the table sessions?

4. Can a consultant take over the spokesperson's role?

Meetings and Meeting Records

1. How are the meeting events to be recorded? Can either party use a stenographer? Can sessions be audiotaped or videotaped? Who is to keep any records completed for the meetings?

2. Are meetings to be open or closed? If open, what kind of a group can teams bring to the meetings? Are the media to be invited? If the public is invited, what constitutes the public? Can an invited public person speak?

3. How are press releases to be handled?

4. What constitutes a quorum? Are Robert's Rules or a similar procedure to be utilized?

Procedural Considerations

1. During the table discussions, can either party break at any time for a caucus?

2. What constitutes agreement on a specific item? On the total contract package?

3. How will the tentative agreement be ratified by both parties?

4. How many days after the talks end must ratification be accomplished?

5. In case one or both parties fail to gain ratification, what are the time limits for renegotiations?

6. In case of impasse, who pays for mediation or fact-finding?

7. When will an impasse be declared? What constitutes an impasse date?

8. What happens if the teams reach impasse during renegotiations? Are mediation procedures reinstated? Is arbitration to be used? Is a strike to be held if not prohibited by law?

9. In what order will issues be addressed (e.g., language issues, economic issues, noneconomic issues, etc.)?

Even though ground rules are determined prior to the primary issues for discussion at the table, the answers to these questions do not necessarily come easily. It is not the intent here to discuss strategy positions appropriate for each question posed; however, it is important that both parties study the implications of various answers that might be determined.

Determining the Scope of Collective Bargaining

Although the scope of bargaining varies among the states and frequently is determined by statute or court decisions, many work conditions, in addition to salary and benefits, are negotiated in many states. These include, but are not limited to, such matters as class size, the school calendar, jury duty, probationary period, performance evaluations, overtime pay, use of school mail, use of bulletin boards, school library hours, grading frequency, teacher aides, substitutes, security, amounts of work, voluntary payroll deductions, leaves of absence for union activities, classroom management, use of school facilities for union meetings, number of holidays. Items considered as nonnegotiable in most states include the number of days or total hours of school, nondiscrimination, First Amendment issues, federal programs, teacher discipline if a constitutional issue, and special education placement procedures, although the courts have ruled that student progress is the primary measure of proper placement. It should be noted that the National Labor Relations Board (NLRB) over the years has ruled on mandatory and voluntary collective bargaining items. For example, from this national perspective, mandatory items, those that must be negotiated, include vacations and holidays, profit-sharing plans, polygraph testing of employees, in-plant food services and prices, and management rights. Voluntary items include pension and other benefits for those persons previously retired and union participation in the establishment of company product prices. Illegal bargaining items have been identified as discriminatory treatment, separation from employment based on race, and closed shop. A **closed shop** requires that the employee must be a member of the employees' representative union in order to be hired in the organization.

State laws concerning the scope of collective bargaining vary widely. In the absence of legal guidelines, precedent is most likely to determine what is negotiable. The obvious position of representatives of employee groups is that no limits should be placed on the items that are negotiable; every matter has some influence on conditions of employment. Board of education representatives, on the other hand, argue that the public interest must be protected and bargaining must not interfere with the board's right and responsibility to govern the school district. Consider such ground rule statements as the following: "Negotiations will encompass all educational matters of mutual concern"; "Negotiations shall encompass all matters pertaining to employment and the fulfillment of professional duties"; and "Negotiations will be determined by those matters presented to the board by the employee association." Clearly, these statements favor a broad scope for negotiations. Few matters in education, if any, would not be of some mutual concern or have some relation to employment, for example.

Preparation for collective bargaining, then, requires a careful examination of (1) existing statutes, court rulings, and legal opinions concerning the inclusions and limitations of bargaining items; (2) previously drafted preliminary statements of agreement; and (3) the role of various public groups in influencing the scope of collective bargaining and the procedures used for keeping such groups informed.

Clarifying Procedures in Case of Impasse

School boards and employee groups must determine well in advance of table discussions how an eventual impasse will be resolved. An impasse constitutes a difference or disagreement between the negotiating parties that has reached an unresolvable stage and brings a halt to table discussions.

Collective bargaining legislation, where enacted by the state, generally sets forth the specific means for resolving any impasse. With proper advanced planning and discussion, the parties involved are better able to design impasse procedures of a less disruptive, less traumatic nature than certain last-resort alternatives.

Procedures for resolving impasse in collective bargaining include mediation, fact-finding and advisory arbitration, voluntary binding arbitration, compulsory binding arbitration, last-best-offer arbitration, and strikes. Whereas some of these procedures are similar, there are certain important differences. Each procedure has associated advantages and disadvantages.

Mediation

Mediation is the most commonly used procedure for resolving impasses. An **impasse** occurs when the two parties become steadfast in their bargaining positions on one or more agenda items and a stalemate takes place. In mediation, a jointly appointed neutral third party serves as advisor for both parties. "The function of a mediator is to conciliate, counsel, persuade, dissuade, and assist the negotiating parties in any legitimate way so that they are able to reach an agreement. The function of the mediator is not to judge, decide, or arbitrate disagreements between the two sides" (Loughran, 1992, pp. 372–373). By conferring independently with both parties, the mediator seeks to determine the reasons for the disagreement, the issues that surround it, and, to the extent possible, what constitutes acceptability for each party. Through a process of interpretation and advisement, the mediator attempts to bring the parties back to the table to settle the issue at hand. The mediator most often provides specific recommendations and alternatives, but these are not binding on either group.

Some authorities believe that mediation is assuming a larger role in the resolution of disputes than the more traditional methods of arbitration. Through mediation, the parties involved continue to retain control of the negotiations process, as they ultimately have the opportunity to determine a solution of their own making. In fact, some states have mandated mediation before complainants go before the courts (Payne, Kohler, Cangemi, & Fuqua, 2000). Mediation almost always keeps both parties "talking," so it serves as a major strategy for successful bargaining. Mediation research has resulted in various findings of interest about what makes an effective mediator. For example, effective mediators (1) spend more time discussing possible solutions and terms of final agreements than unsuccessful mediators (Payne et al., 2000); (2) monitor the interaction, clarify party view, and solicit feedback on the part of both parties; (3) focus on key issues, provide ample opportunities for each party to speak, point out possible solutions, and refrain from closing an argument personally (Greatbatch & Dingwall, 1997); and (4) establish certain rules regarding the decorum of party members relative to personal attacks and other courtesies in participative behavior (Donohue, Allen, & Burrell, 1988). Perhaps a primary disadvantage of mediation is the extreme difficulty of the procedure itself. Because the impasse centers on complex issues and problems, mediation activities demand exemplary personal competence on the part of the mediator.

Fact-Finding and Advisory Arbitration

Fact-finding and advisory arbitration are usually considered synonymous, because almost identical procedures are generally involved in each. However, fact-finding is most often associated with impasses in table negotiations involving a future contract agreement, whereas advisory arbitration is generally associated with grievances and disputes under the present contract.

Fact-finding involves the selection of a neutral third party to serve as an investigator who studies all of the facts and circumstances that surround the impasse. As in mediation, fact-finding can proceed as an independent relationship between the fact-finder and the parties in dispute; however, arrangements often are made for a hearing in which both groups of negotiators present their cases.

In either the independent or formal hearing approach, the fact-finder prepares a report of the facts and recommendations for action based on the impartial findings. The representatives of each group study the findings and recommendations and respond with their acceptance or rejection. The fact-finder's recommendations are advisory only.

Voluntary Binding and Compulsory Arbitration

Voluntary binding and compulsory arbitration are procedures for resolving disagreements through the use of a neutral third party whose decision is mandated for both parties. In the absence of state law specifying compulsory binding arbitration, voluntary binding arbitration can be implemented by agreement of the disputing parties. Specific procedures, including the arrangement for paying the costs of arbitration, are usually set forth in the master agreement. Empirical evidence suggests that, on the average, an arbitrator spends one day in preparation and two days in "hearings." Charges for arbitrator services vary greatly; a range of $1,000–$3,000 per day is not unusual. Most commonly, costs are equally shared between the school district and the employee association. However, a procedure whereby the school district "pays" if it loses the grievance case and the grievant "pays" if the association loses the case also is used. The third party might be an individual, a group of individuals, or a panel board (e.g., board of industrial relations). Following an in-depth study of the issue and all relative information, the arbitrator or panel renders a decision that is final and binding.

The major advantage of compulsory arbitration is its potential to avoid more disruptive events, such as a strike. Many people consider it a disadvantage that compulsory arbitration places the settlement outside the jurisdiction of the bargaining parties, especially the governing board of education. Yet the removal of the two parties from the personally traumatic experiences of face-to-face table disputes and further professional alienation is an advantage in the minds of others.

Last-Best-Offer Arbitration

In last-best-offer arbitration, a neutral third party is called on to study the last best offers stated by each of the two parties in the table negotiations. Rather than reach a decision based on a "down-the-middle" compromise, the arbitrator reviews each last offer in view of the facts (e.g., salary trends, agreements settled in competitive school districts, ability to pay, supply and demand, etc.). In the final analysis, *one* of the two last best offers is recommended and considered binding on both parties.

An advantage of this procedure centers on the possible results of the competitive atmosphere it fosters. That is, because each party attempts to present a reasonable, well-intentioned best offer that an arbitrator might view most favorably, the result likely could be an agreement at the table itself, in which case the need for arbitration is obviated. Last-best-offer arbitration has been used extensively in baseball for resolving salary disputes. The primary areas of application are situations in which strikes cannot be tolerated by the public or those involving such problems as inordinate economic loss, danger to public health, or danger to personal safety.

Critics of the procedure point out that because only one group's offer can be recommended, the other group must live with an "unfair" decision.

Strikes

Strikes are actions that result in stoppage of work and services rendered by an employee group. The National School Boards Association (NSBA) supports legislation that makes strikes against public schools illegal and provides for mandatory penalties (NSBA, 1991). The NEA believes that the right to strike must be an integral part of any collective bargaining process (NEA, 1991). The American Association of School Administrators (AASA) historically has opposed strikes and has emphasized the responsibility of school leaders to keep the schools open with protective measures for both students and those personnel who report to work. The American Association of School Personnel Administrators (AASPA) set forth its views on school strikes as follows. First, the AASPA proposed that in case of a strike, retroactive contract settlements should be prohibited. Second, a secret ballot of all members of the bargaining unit should be taken prior to any strike to accept or reject the school board team's last offer. If approved, the contract would be considered binding; if rejected, alternatives of a strike or further negotiations are in order. Third, the AASPA recommended the implementation of a procedure for governing strikes, including a cooling-off period. Before any strike, a fact-finder would be selected to study all issues and attempt to alleviate the dispute (AASPA, 1978).

From the school board's point of view, planning for a possible strike must be part of the preparation for collective bargaining. The following are essential activities included in such preparation:

1. Well in advance of table negotiations or any indication of a possible strike, a comprehensive plan must be developed to retain the services necessary to operate the schools and to resolve the strike issues as expeditiously as possible.

2. An effective means must be established for communicating important information to both internal and external groups. Alternative communication methods and means of contact must also be identified in anticipation of an interruption of the usual communication channels.

3. A central office or unit should be organized to serve as the coordination and control center for information-gathering, decision-making, and implementation procedures. Key personnel who will serve in the central office must be identified in advance and their roles clearly delineated.

4. Resource pools of personnel who can keep the schools open and operating should be identified. This consideration includes the identification of employees who likely would cross picket lines and others who would be employable on a temporary basis.

5. Information concerning the legality of strike activities must be gathered, studied, and distributed appropriately. Legal information concerning strike activities in the state, restrictions of law, penalties, legal implications, restraining orders, the job status of strikers, and so forth, must be clarified. Legal alternatives available for board action must be investigated.

6. Building administrators and supervisors should develop local plans for dealing with the strike situation. They must clarify responsibilities and identify program alternatives that meet instructional goals. Guidelines for establishing the safety and welfare of students and other personnel must be stated and understood.

7. Local security personnel must be kept well informed of the ongoing conditions and potential problems that might occur. A straightforward approach with the media concerning developments and issues has proved to be the best policy.

8. Procedures must be determined for establishing meaningful communication with the employee group representatives. Serious efforts to keep talking in relation to the issues in dispute must be made. A well-organized, creative means for fostering ongoing internal discussions of the issues must be established in advance. Such communication must be positive and focus on a sincere attitude of resolution and possible agreement.

Court rulings most frequently have supported the opinion that strikes by employees in the public sector are illegal. However, strikes by public employees continue, as do other strategies to bring about changes in compensation and working conditions. "Firefighters have been known to catch the 'red rash,' police come down with the 'blue flu,' teachers have suffered from 'chalk-dust fever,' and state workers such as in Pennsylvania have called in with 'budgetitis'" (Milakovich & Gordon, 2001, p. 315).

Teachers' groups nationally have used various means to protest salary, working conditions, and other issues. For example, besides lengthy strikes, teachers nationally have staged three-day walkouts, have had one-day "blueouts" in which all teachers call in sick, have stacked contracts without signatures, have sponsored television commercials that portray their views of the state of education, have had work slowdowns, and have used other strategies to gain public support in order to prompt positive action from state legislators and to pressure school boards. As is basically the case with teacher strikes, the foregoing actions are designed to achieve various purposes. Their primary purpose, however, is to gain an advantage in the bargaining process by having the other party change its present position on a bargaining issue or issues.

Although teacher strikes historically have proved to be both problematic and disruptive for the school district and community in which they occur, many groups and individuals believe that teachers should have the same right to strike as employees in the private sector. Figure 10.5 lays out the pros and cons concerning the rights of teachers to strike.

Determination and Recognition of the Bargaining Unit

Before collective bargaining at the table can be initiated, the employee groups to be included in the bargaining unit and their official memberships must be determined. A school district consists of several different employee groups and clusters of employees within those groups. For example, teachers, librarians, nurses, counselors, and psychologists are among the professional staff personnel. Support staff personnel such as clerks, secretaries, maintenance workers, transportation staff, custodians, and foodservice workers represent employee groups and clusters. The bargaining unit to which each of these employee groups belongs is of paramount importance for purpose of negotiations. A **bargaining unit** is a group of employees certified as the appropriate unit for collective negotiations. This unit is the one to which the negotiated contractual agreements will apply. It is not unusual for a

Pros	Cons
1. The Fourteenth Amendment of the U.S. Constitution provides protection under the law. Teachers' groups and others in the public sector should have the same rights as those in the private sector.	1. The Constitution of the United States or state laws do not give any equal protection under the law. Strikes by government employees have been declared unlawful in court cases.
2. In a democratic society, citizens are given rights related to academic freedom, personal participation in policy matters, and guarantees of personal respect. Restrictions on rights to negotiate or to protest unfair treatment are contrary to these rights.	2. Collective bargaining in the private sector is completely different from collective bargaining in the public sector. Collective bargaining is a labor-management activity appropriate for the political environment of the private sector only. Strikes and collective bargaining are not amenable to the concepts of public service and professionalism of teachers.
3. Both state and federal legislation have increasingly underscored the rights of teachers and other employees in the public sector, thus confirming the rights of all employees and employee groups.	3. As stated previously, no rights to strike are stated in the U.S. Constitution or in constitutions of the various states. Illegal acts such as strikes against government agencies cannot be tolerated.
4. The efforts of teachers and other groups to improve the education for children should be applauded, not curtailed.	4. Actions of teachers, such as the use of strikes for personal gain, take away from quality time of instruction of children in the classroom. Teachers, as professionals, should find other, less abrasive methods that do not detract from the time that should be spent with children in the classroom.
5. Those persons who hold the belief that teachers' groups or other public employees should not participate in decisions regarding how government should best serve its people do not support the ideals of a democratic society.	5. Efficient and effective government depends on the ability to exercise its authority for the good of all the people. The sovereignty of those institutions, such as education, must be protected so as to retain order and prevent chaos.
6. Without the right to strike, teachers' unions cannot fulfill their primary goal of caring for the welfare of its members and the improvement of education. Thus, education will lose out in the increasing competition for the tax dollar. Many other groups simply do not want education to get its rightful share of the tax dollar.	6. There are numerous more effective ways for teachers to achieve their ends regarding compensation and work conditions. Cooperative efforts are far more productive in the long run than adversarial relationships exemplified by collective bargaining and employee strikes.
7. Collective bargaining and strikes have led to educational improvements such as reduction in class sizes, more time for planning, better compensation for teachers, more state aid, and other educational benefits. Without the strength of collective bargaining and the right to strike, compensation for teachers will continue to lag behind other comparable professions.	7. Research shows clearly that collective bargaining and negative strategies such as sanctions and strikes do not result in improved teacher compensation. In fact, some studies have revealed that school districts that do not use collective bargaining fare as well in salary gains as districts that do bargain.
8. In view of past history, teachers have no other alternative but to strike as a last resort. In cases of impasse, various methods of arbitration often end in compromises that are untenable for teachers' groups. In many cases, boards of education and other groups have blocked such strategies as binding arbitration to resolve impasse.	8. The argument that teachers have no other alternative but to strike is faulty. Other public employee groups, such as firefighters, have found binding arbitration to be most successful, making disruptive strikes unnecessary.

Figure 10.5   Teachers' Right to Strike

school district to have several bargaining units, although a common practice is that one unit represents the combination of teaching and nonadministrative professional personnel. Bargaining indeed is "collective" in that various groups and clusters are being represented as one group in the process.

Procedures to determine the bargaining unit often are established by statute. In the absence of statute, the school board and employee groups most often mutually determine the procedures for deciding which employees to include in the bargaining unit.

Loughran (1992) points out that thousands of cases regarding the "appropriate bargaining unit" have been the subject of NLRB and court decisions. He concludes that it is generally sufficient if the appropriate unit for bargaining purposes meets at least one of the following criteria:

1. The unit is the one certified by the NLRB.

2. The unit is the one the employer and union have historically recognized.

3. The unit is the one the employer and union agree to recognize as the appropriate bargaining unit. (p. 14)

Two criteria serve important roles in determining which employees will belong to a particular unit: community of interest (Lieberman & Moskow, 1966) and fragmentation (Walter, 1975). Employees who share common employment interests and concerns, who desire to be in the same bargaining unit, and who receive similar compensation and have similar working conditions represent examples of a **community of interest**.

The larger the unit, the more difficult it is to establish a community of interest. Yet small bargaining units present problems for both employees and employers. From the employees' viewpoint, very small units are far less likely to carry the bargaining strength of units with larger representation. Consider, for example, a school district with several elementary, middle, and high schools. If schools in the school district were composed of members with dissimilar interests, negotiations would be further complicated. The task for employer groups, then, is to establish bargaining units based on the community interest principle and, at the same time, to attempt to avoid "fragmentation of their workforce into many separate bargaining units . . . since it requires the employer to bargain many times, generally over the same questions, but with different groups of employees" (Walter, 1975, p. 25).

In actual practice, unit determination is decided generally by (1) state statutes and law, (2) agreements reached by the school board and the various employee groups, (3) an external agency such as a labor relations board or other outside authority, or (4) the unilateral decision of the school board.

The Bargaining Agent

The **bargaining agent** is the employee organization designated as the official representative of all employees in the bargaining unit. Two types of recognition are generally found in education: exclusive and multiple representation.

Exclusive representation is the certification of one particular employee organization to represent all employees in the unit. The general procedures for determining exclusive recognition include (1) the request by an employee organization to be the bargaining agent for all employees in the bargaining unit, (2) an election or other means of determining majority preference, (3) results of an election in which at least 51% vote yes, and (4) certification by the school board that the organization has exclusive bargaining rights.

One nonvoting method of determining the bargaining agent is to recognize the organization that for the last two or three years has enrolled a majority of the school employees as members.

Strahan's (1969) early description of multiple representation is quite appropriate today. It assumes one of the following forms:

1. Joint negotiating committee with proportional representation based on the size of membership in the organization.

2. Completely separate negotiations with each organization represented.

3. Joint negotiating committee with equal representation of the recognized organizations in the school.

Exclusive recognition is most widely used in education for the following reasons: (1) it is supported by both the NEA and the AFT, (2) it is mandated for the public sector in many states and is the form of recognition most generally accepted when statutes do not specify what form of recognition is to be given, and (3) private business and industry serve as examples that exclusive recognition is most effective (Rebore, 2001, p. 298).

Determination of the Composition of the Negotiations Team

The selection of the bargaining team is a critical decision for successful negotiations. Each party must have individuals at the table who can answer the questions that will arise and who can complete the process effectively. The size of the team will vary; it depends considerably on the size of the school system and the representations needed. Experience in the collective bargaining process appears to be an important criterion for team member selection. For example, experienced team members tend to spend much less time on such matters as ground rules. Edson (2000) contends that the biggest mistake inexperienced negotiators make is not listening; they often are good at talking, but lack listening skills. Each of the foregoing contentions holds implications for the bargaining situation at hand and the proposed bargaining strategies desired.

Mnookin (2000) points out two significant myths that surround the collective bargaining process as follows. *Myth #1: There is no relevant theory for negotiations.* In fact, the core idea relative to collective bargaining involves the opportunity "to expand the pie"; that is, the process has the potential to make both parties better off. *Myth #2: Negotiations can't be taught.* In fact, negotiation skills definitely can be taught. Although people do develop habits during negotiations that sometimes serve them well, when they don't they have no idea why not. Thus, people who serve on collective bargaining teams should be well prepared to do so as evidenced by appropriate participation in related negotiations courses and workshops along with extensive reading and observation activities concerning the negotiations process.

The following criteria help to determine the selection of individuals for the bargaining team:

1. *Time.* Do the individual's schedule and responsibilities allow the time required to serve on the team?

2. *Temperament.* Does the individual have the emotional stability and personal poise necessary for serving on the team?

3. *Tenacity.* Will the individual "stay with it" and work through the complex and tenuous process?

4. *Technical Know-How.* Does the individual have the necessary understanding of the process of bargaining and knowledge of the content information required in the collective negotiations?

5. *Talent.* Does the individual have the talent for participating in the art of collective bargaining?

The inclusion of school board members, the school superintendent, the human resources director, the board attorney, or an outside professional negotiator on the board of education's team will depend largely on the unique characteristics within each school district. Figure 10.6 summarizes the advantages and disadvantages in using each of these persons.

The size recommendations that do exist most often specify from three to five members. Some individuals view a five-member team as ideal because it is large enough to provide for representative resource personnel and meet the need for different types of individuals with various competencies, yet it is not so large as to be unwieldy. Those who suggest that team size be limited to three members stress that this number facilitates the process and enables the teams to progress under less formal conditions. In addition, members can concentrate on assigned roles as spokesperson, recorder, and observer.

The **spokesperson** is the chief negotiator for the team and serves as team captain. The chief spokesperson plays an essential role in the success of the bargaining process. A state study reported that the school superintendent served as the chief negotiator for the board's bargaining team in 56.8% of the participating school districts in the state. A professional negotiator or other school administrator served as chief spokesperson in 9.5% and 12.2%, respectively, of the reporting districts (Norton, 2001). The focus of unity for the team, the spokesperson generally serves as the single "voice" of the team's position.

The **team observer** listens and watches for clues and behaviors communicated by members of the other party. Verbal statements and body language are monitored for clues about priority of issues, major concerns, closing arguments, and possible

Role or Position	Advantages	Disadvantages
School Board Member	• Participation may help the board understand the nature of the bargaining process and its complexity. • Participation can gain the confidence of the total board that their real interests are being protected. • May have more time than other school district personnel who might represent the board's team.	• Board members on the team are viewed as members of the board, rather than as members of the bargaining team; may tend to speak for the board instead of participating in the bargaining process. • May not be skilled in the art of collective bargaining. • Conditions surrounding the bargaining process may cause board members to lose objectivity; board members ultimately must decide on ratification of the agreement.
School Superintendent	• Most knowledgeable of the entire school system; expertise is invaluable at the bargaining table. • School board generally views the superintendent as having the competence required for successful bargaining. • Because of position responsibilities, he or she is in best position to view the school system as a whole and to conceptualize the system's goals, objectives, and human resources needs.	• Time commitment required may interfere with other primary responsibilities. • Involvement in bargaining for the school board might foster poor attitudes and adversary relations with employees. • Representatives of the employee unit tend to want responses from the administrative authority rather than bargaining strategy responses. • Membership tends to place the superintendent in an untenable position—an equal at the table one day and chief school administrator the next.
Human Resources Director	• Likely to have the best understanding of employee relations in the school district. • Normally well prepared and highly skilled in collective bargaining and school law. • Has key information relative to the primary agenda items to be encountered in the bargaining process. • Possesses the experience and knowledge relative to human needs and their importance in fulfilling the goals and objectives of the school district.	• Role as an adversary at the bargaining table conflicts with responsibilities of personal counselor and promoter of positive human relations in the school system. • Time commitments detract from other major HR responsibilities. • Although they are knowledgeable of employee relations and bargaining, an assignment of resource consultant might be more advantageous to the school board's bargaining team. • May not be knowledgeable of the school system and its educational programs and needs.

(Continued)

(Continued)

Role or Position	Advantages	Disadvantages
School Board Attorney	• Can provide important advice and counsel relative to the legal aspects of collective bargaining. • Can help insert language in the contract agreement that eliminates unclear statements and possible misinterpretation due to poor contract language. • Can provide legal advice in ongoing negotiations at time of deliberations rather than after the fact.	• Legal expertise does not automatically translate into expertise in collective bargaining. • May prove costly in both time and money.
Professional Negotiator	• Often can save time because of knowledge of collective bargaining and the importance or unimportance of bargaining activities. • Allows internal personnel to concentrate on other important educational matters. • Has strong incentive to be highly effective in order to be asked to serve again and build a reputation needed for expanded employment contracts.	• Professional fees are costly. • Is usually unfamiliar with the school system. • Does not remain to help implement the contract agreement or to face possible grievances. • Problems can arise concerning payment arrangements; hourly contract arrangement with professional negotiator carries certain disadvantages, whereas a set fee can pose problems of performance. • In lengthy negotiations that encounter impasse or work stoppage, the school district encounters the problem of paying the professional or being without counsel and advice.

Figure 10.6   Pros and Cons of Using Various Team Members on the Bargaining Team

closure. The **recorder** maintains written information concerning strategy and positions as well as facts, decisions, and events surrounding each negotiations session.

Initial Bargaining Procedures and Appropriate Table Strategies

The decision about whether to use a distributive approach or an integrative approach to bargaining depends on the situation at hand. Schoonmaker (1989) suggested that certain conditions warrant a distributive bargaining approach, whereas a joint problem-solving approach should be emphasized when other conditions are present. For example,

Emphasize distributive bargaining when
- Your interests clearly conflict.
- You are much more powerful.
- You do not need or want a long-term harmonious relationship.
- You do not trust the other party.
- The agreement is easy to implement.
- The other party is pure bargaining.

Emphasize joint problem solving when
- You have common interests.
- You are weaker or power is approximately equal.
- You need or want a continuing, harmonious relationship.
- You trust the other party.
- Implementing the agreement may be difficult.
- The other party is problem solving. (pp. 12–13)

Once quasi-distributive bargaining has been initiated and negotiation items have been submitted by the employee group, **good faith bargaining** requires that the board of education team respond. A first response on any one item might be we agree, we will consider it, we cannot agree, or that item is not negotiable, accompanied by appropriate reasons. Good faith has been interpreted from various perspectives by writers, the courts, and the NLRB. Agreement as to what behaviors tend to demonstrate good faith emphasizes the intentions of both parties to meet with the specific purpose of attempting to reach an agreement. Therefore, such actions as surface bargaining, Bulwarism, or refusing to advance any proposals are looked on as negative factors in demonstrating good faith. **Surface bargaining** takes place when one party simply goes through the motions of bargaining without any real intentions of reaching an agreement. The term **Bulwarism** describes the placement of a proposal on the table accompanied with a statement to the effect that "it is this way or nothing," which constitutes as absolute refusal to negotiate on the matter.

As Dessler (2001) noted, "Although no one is required to make a concession, the courts' and NLRB's definitions of good faith suggest that a willingness to compromise is an essential ingredient in good faith bargaining" (p. 231). Experienced negotiators concentrate on listening to the other team's responses to try to uncover their key issues, major concerns, and position statements. As a matter of bargaining strategy, listening as opposed to always talking looms important. "If one party has five reasons for doing something, is this more persuasive than having only one? Apparently not, skilled negotiators used an average of 1.8 reasons; average negotiators used 3.0" (Cascio, 2003, p. 517). Sometimes, not responding is an effective negotiations strategy. That is, listening may be more effective than talking in some instances.

The goal of collective bargaining is not to win a debate, but rather to reach an agreement on the proposals. The tactics that serve best are the ones that include a possible response to a proposal, or a solution to differences between the two parties. A reasonable proposal or counterproposal has the potential of resolving the issue or settling the existing differences.

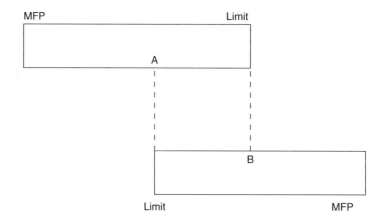

Figure 10.7   Reaching an Agreement: Range of Settlement

SOURCE: Kennedy, Benson, & McMillan (1982).

Kennedy, Benson, and McMillan (1982) discussed compromise toward the goal of reaching agreement in relation to team movement and "distance between the two parties." They illustrated the distance in terms of movement and suggested that each team has a limit and "break point." The range of settlement lies between a team's most favorable position (MFP) and that break point or limit (see Figure 10.7). If the teams' limits do not overlap, reaching agreement is highly unlikely. If the first team's range overlaps the second team's MFP, the first team holds a decided advantage in the negotiations process.

Movement in negotiations implies flexibility; flexibility requires compromise. The Latin term quid pro quo means something for something or, in negotiation terminology, to get something for giving something. In negotiations, each team moves closer to an agreement by giving something of value in return for receiving a desired goal. Thus, both teams use the tactics involving submission of proposals and counterproposals in a give-and-take process to try to reach a tentative agreement.

Although there is no one best way to negotiate, and bargaining is more art than science, empirical evidence suggests a number of guidelines for distributive bargaining that deserve consideration.

1. Always bargain from the viewpoint of the total contract amount. Never agree on economic items separately.

2. Do not submit a proposal or counterproposal and then attempt to retract it. Do not "show your hand" before you need to do so.

3. Be cautious about stating that your team is anxious to settle early. When this becomes known, then the "ransom" often goes higher.

4. Remember that collective bargaining is a process of compromise. Generally, it is not good in the long run to "win it all." Seasoned negotiators try to build long-term relationships that include mutual trust and respect. Any agreement must have mutuality of benefit. Do not bluff. A team must be prepared

to carry out threats. Try to develop a high degree of credibility through a positive relationship.

5. In bargaining, say what you mean and mean what you say. Be certain that you write what you mean in any tentative or final agreement.

6. Do not present items for bargaining that are already within a group's jurisdiction (e.g., school board's legislative rights, administration's evaluation responsibilities, employees' academic freedom).

7. Team representatives negotiate with team representatives. The board of education, for example, should not take its case directly to the employee association.

8. Listen. A good negotiator spends the majority of his or her time listening to the other team's responses, rationale, key issues, and major concerns. Responses such as "Tell me more," "I didn't know that," and "Why?" help the negotiator learn more of the other team's position statements and closing arguments.

9. Use closed-ended questions to bring issues into focus. Keep dialogue going. When teams stop talking, bargaining breaks down. The sophisticated negotiator wants to reach an agreement.

10. Develop signaling techniques, such as cuecards, that serve your team (e.g., OBS, return to original bargaining statement; CQ, state the closing question; etc.). Verbal signaling, sending an intended message to the other team, is a necessary tactic as well. But be careful about body language. Hesitation in responding, for example, sends a message that you might accept the proposal.

11. Use reason rather than rhetoric to explain your stand. State your case and stay with the facts.

12. Realize that timing is a major aspect of bargaining. At the outset, very little is agreed to. In the course of bargaining, teams tell each other their priorities and what they want.

13. Use the term "we" for the team's position and never the personal "I" at the table. Team representatives do not have a position; they represent the larger group.

14. Personal poise and behavior are of major importance. Self-control is essential. As we presented previously, team members must be selected on the basis of their availability, temperament, tenacity, technical know-how, and talent.

The Contract Agreement

The bargaining contract or master agreement is the ratified document that specifies the terms of the negotiated contract. The contract agreement is used to guide employee relations. Contract language represents the final product of the negotiations. It is what both parties must live with for the contract period. Carelessness in the use of words can lead to serious problems, including arbitration. The phrase "you get what you write" applies directly to the written agreement.

Information included in the written agreement varies considerably in practice. However, most agreements include (1) a statement of recognition; (2) the nature of the agreement, its scope, time considerations, and communication channels; (3) the specific stipulations or articles of agreement; (4) mutual understandings concerning the agreement, including the responsibilities of both parties; and (5) impasse procedures.

The statement of recognition stipulates the one specific organization or arrangement for the bargaining representation of the defined employee unit. The section that centers on the nature of the agreement includes the curtailment of any further negotiations until the approved agreement has elapsed, and provisions for ongoing communication between the two parties. The specific agreement stipulations or articles include the agreements reached concerning compensation, employee benefits, and other conditions of employment. Included in the section concerned with mutual understandings and responsibilities are the obligations of both parties for implementation of the agreement, the responsibilities to administer professional working relationships and thus to provide high-quality education, and in some cases a statement concerning strikes. Grievance and impasse procedures are significant considerations of any written agreement as well.

Grievances

A **grievance** is a problem or complaint related to the contract agreement. It represents a violation, or purported violation, of the agreement. A significant difference exists between a general complaint by an employee on a matter of school policy and a grievance based on an alleged violation of the negotiation agreement. Whereas both kinds of employee problems are important for effective human resources practices, the grievances discussed here focus on disagreements related specifically to the negotiated agreement. The grievance procedure is essentially a part of the ongoing collective bargaining process. Even though the written bargaining agreement should stipulate no further bargaining until the current contract expires (referred to as the zipper clause), the use of the grievance is one way in which the negotiations process continues. Thus, designing grievance procedures that define time limitations, preliminary steps, and procedures is of crucial importance.

In many cases, procedures for grievances are stipulated in law. The following grievance procedures are generally applicable. (1) A written grievance is filed that includes a description of the basis for the grievance; a statement of any prior informal steps taken to attempt to resolve the issue; a statement of reasons as to why the alleged actions were unfair, arbitrary, or contrary to contract provisions; and actions that the aggrieved employee believes necessary to resolve the issue. (2) The immediate supervisor prepares a written statement concerning the grounds of the grievance and recommended solutions as appropriate to the case. (3) If not resolved, the next higher level of authority (e.g., human resources director, superintendent, or other appropriate staff member) conducts a further investigation and renders a decision with a recommended solution. (4) If the issue is not resolved in the foregoing investigation, a review board or the board of education considers the case. The recommendation by the review board is considered final. If it is not accepted by the grievant, arbitration by a third party or litigation is a possible alternative (see Figure 10.8).

A grievance procedure should provide for due process and ensure that legitimate grievances and problems are heard, reviewed, and resolved. A properly designed procedure helps to place problems and complaints in the proper channels of supervisory relationships for possible solution at the most appropriate level of administration. Such procedures provide employees with a fair consideration of grievances without reprisal and also safeguard the rights of supervisory personnel.

Impact of Collective Bargaining on Education

The effects of collective bargaining on education have been the subject of much discussion and research. Although the bargaining process is present in virtually every human resources process, the key question is its impact on employee compensation levels and conditions of work. Somewhat surprising are the findings of several research studies that collective bargaining has had little or no effect on compensation levels in education, and in fact, some studies indicate that school districts that do not negotiate have as good or better records of salary increases. Other studies, however, have disagreed with these findings. The research that attempts to isolate the effects of collective bargaining on competition levels is confounded by the difficulty of controlling for the many variables that influence the determination of salary levels. For example, the influence of bargaining districts on nonbargaining districts, sometimes termed **spillover**, is virtually impossible to measure. It should be noted that the large majority of the research related to the impact of collective bargaining in education was conducted in the 1970s and early 1980s. A brief summary of the more noted impact studies follows:

> **1970:** Perry and Wilman's investigation of 24 school districts from New York to California found that negotiations had resulted in (1) an increase in the absolute and relative size of the total amount of resources allocated to teacher compensation within the district budget, and (2) an increase in the absolute and relative size of yearly service increments and differentials for academic training beyond the B.A. degree.

> **1970:** Kasper's study concluded that there is no statistically significant positive effect of teacher negotiations on salaries, once other variables such as income and urbanization are taken into account.

> **1973:** Hall and Carroll studied more than 100 elementary school districts in Cook County, Illinois, involved in negotiations. Salary increases in the schools investigated averaged $165 per year, and the study noted that teacher bargaining is associated with larger student-teacher ratios.

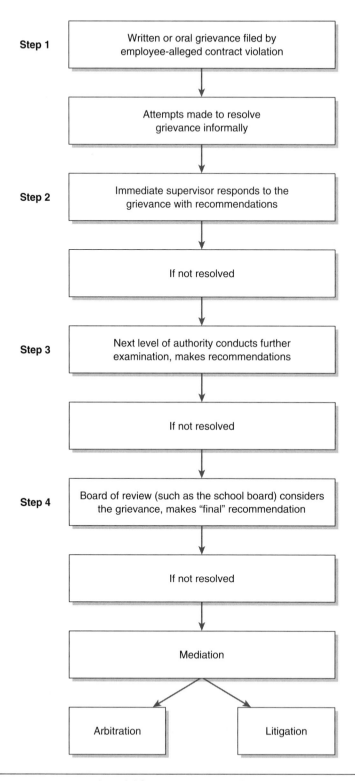

Figure 10.8   Operational Model for Grievance Procedure

1974: Balfour studied New York school districts and concluded that the presence of substantive bargaining procedures, any type of union recognition or teacher union membership had no significant positive effect on teachers' salaries or rate of change.

1975: Moore studied 181 K–12 school districts in Nebraska. His study revealed that negotiating districts paid salaries that averaged $609 higher than nonnegotiating districts.

1977: Zuelke and Frohreich collected data from 50 randomly selected small and medium-sized school districts in Wisconsin. Their research indicated that collective negotiations had, in most cases, a significant negative effect on teachers' salaries.

1978: According to the Public Service Research Council in Vienna, Virginia, for a 10-year period between 1969–1970 and 1979–1980, there were 30 states with teacher bargaining legislation. Over this period, the increase in U.S. average classroom teacher salary was 89%. Of the 30 states with bargaining legislation, 15 (50%) experienced a rate of change greater than the national average. Of the 20 states without teacher bargaining legislation, 13 (65%) experienced a rate of change greater than the national average, and seven states (35%) were below it. The average increase in teacher salaries in the states without teacher bargaining legislation was 92.3%. For states with legislation, the average change was 87.2%. (p. 3)

1978: Gallagher's study of negotiations in Illinois indicated a significant positive relationship between collective negotiations and teacher salary levels with differentials of 1.3%–4.5% between bargaining and nonbargaining districts.

1979: Kahn's study concluded that unions have a significant wage effect in both the short run and the long run.

1979: In Marshall's study of collective bargaining on faculty salaries in higher education, the author concluded that little, if any, difference existed between salary increases at union and nonunion institutions.

1980: The Bureau of Labor Statistics reported that in the most recent three years for which data were available, the major issue in 70% of all public sector strikes was "general wage changes."

1981: Wynn examined the rate of change in K–12 public school teachers' salaries between 1960–1961 and 1979–1980. The study findings revealed that 52% of the states with intensive collective bargaining gained more than the national average, whereas 77% of the nonintensive bargaining states did better than the national average.

1981: Freeman found that unionism raises the share of compensation allotted to fringe benefits, particularly vacation pay and life and accident insurance.

1984: Eberts studied 6,000 teachers and principals randomly selected from elementary schools nationally, and concluded that collective negotiations had resulted in a reduction of instructional time, an increase in preparation time, an increase in experience and educational levels of teachers, and an increase in the number of teachers and administrators per student.

1985 to the present time: The difficulty of isolating the many variables surrounding the collective bargaining process has tended to limit quantitative research studies in this area. Among the reasons for curtailed research in this area are contemporary practices between those states that have passed legislation related to bargaining in the public sector and those that have not done so, the effect of spillover between those school districts that bargain and those that do not, and the wide variety of distributive and integrative bargaining methods. Empirical evidence does reveal that most school districts have incorporated some form of school board and employee association negotiation on salary and conditions of work; collective bargaining has become a way of life in the work of school leaders, and it continues as one of the primary responsibilities of the central human resources unit of the school district.

Summary

Collective negotiation is a process whereby matters of employment relations are determined mutually by representatives of employee groups and their employer within the limits of law or mutual agreement. Collective bargaining in the private and public sectors has historically influenced the development of the practice in education.

The human resources unit in education is involved in collective bargaining in two specific ways. First, the human resources director assumes many of the responsibilities in the negotiations process itself. Second, the process of bargaining affects virtually every other facet of the human resources function. In order to be effective in the role, the human resources director must have a complete understanding of the tasks related to the bargaining process and must possess specific personal competencies appropriate for these tasks.

The collective bargaining process includes (1) planning and preparation for collective negotiations; (2) determination and recognition of the bargaining unit; (3) determination of the negotiations team, including the chief spokesperson; (4) determination of the initial bargaining procedures and appropriate table strategies; and (5) implementation of the contract agreement.

Planning and preparation for collective bargaining include establishing goals and objectives for bargaining, establishing ground rules, determining the scope of bargaining, gathering information, analyzing costs, determining initial strategies, and clarifying impasse procedures.

The membership of the bargaining unit must be verified and the bargaining agent certified. Team representation constitutes an important matter. Available time, personal temperament, individual tenacity, technical know-how, and talent are criteria that should guide the selection of individual team members.

The members of each group must ratify the tentative agreement reached by the negotiating parties. Once it is ratified, steps must be taken to communicate the provisions of the agreement. Grievance procedures that have been identified in the master agreement are implemented in case of a violation or grievance related to the contract.

Table tactics depend in large part on the bargaining strategies in place. In general, education most often has adopted the quasi-distributive strategy, in which both parties attempt to avoid a test of power and, through a procedure of proposals and counterproposals, withhold concessions on all major issues until the last possible moment. Integrative bargaining, for many reasons, has been initiated in school district bargaining and has gained increasing popularity. This approach focuses on a win-win result through problem solving.

Discussion Questions

1. Collective bargaining has been described as an indispensable process in democratic societies. What evidence supports this contention?

2. Consider the distributive bargaining strategy as compared to the integrative strategy. What evidence, if any, is available presently to suggest that the integrative approach is gaining ground in education? What factors have influenced increases or decreases in the use of the integrative strategy?

3. This chapter recommended that school board representatives negotiate directly with the teachers' group representatives. That is, the school board as a whole should not take its case directly to the teachers' organization; nor should the teachers' team take its case to the school board as a whole. Why does this recommendation make sense? What kinds of problems evolve from such actions?

4. Divide the class into appropriate triads that represent bargaining teams for the school board and for the teachers. Each of the teams has 30 minutes to consider the following situation.

   The teachers' organization bargaining team plans to request three personal-leave days as a negotiation item. Presently, teachers have 10 days of sick leave available per year, accumulative to 180 days. Professional leave is available with administrative approval for three days per year, and the teacher may take three days for deaths in the family.

   a. During the 30-minute time period, each of the teacher teams drafts its version of the personal-leave proposal as it will be presented at the table.
   b. Board teams are aware of the general nature of the teachers' request as presented here, but have not seen the specific proposal that ultimately will be presented. Thus, during the 30-minute time period, each school board team discusses the general proposal and considers its position on its provisions for compensation, approval authority, days such leave could be taken, limitation on the number of approvals, trade-offs, and so on.
   c. After the 30-minute individual team sessions, the triads meet as board and teacher teams. Each teacher team presents its proposal and the

board team reacts to it. Triads take another 30 minutes to "negotiate" a tentative agreement on this matter.

d. Each bargaining triad reports its results to the class as a whole.

e. Consider the rationale and strategies associated with distributive and integrative bargaining methods. Discuss why an effective negotiator in one method may not be effective in the other method.

Case Studies

CASE 10.1

A WIN-WIN END RUN

Union School District had bargained with teachers on a meet-and-confer basis for four years. Because there were no state statutes to require collective bargaining between school boards and employee groups, practices varied widely throughout the state.

In the Union District, the human resources director had served as the school board's chief spokesperson for the last four years. Bargaining had gone well until last year when an impasse was declared and a mediator was called in to help resolve the matter of extra-duty assignments.

Budget restraints in the district were such that an override election was necessary last year to meet this year's operating expenses. The school board considered the possibility of receiving a favorable vote on a second override to be highly questionable.

"I think we should move to a win-win, problem-solving approach in our negotiations with teachers this year," offered Merlin George, human resources director. "In view of the current economics, I can't see our past approaches to negotiations effective this year. I would be glad to serve as a resource person this year, but I recommend that someone else serve as chief spokesperson this year."

In the final analysis, the school board and superintendent agreed to George's recommendations. Thelma Morton, the school business manager, was named as negotiations team leader for the school board. Overall, teachers were receptive to the proposal for win-win bargaining.

As bargaining for the year proceeded, Thelma spent considerable time giving facts and figures relating to a tight budget and lack of needed legislative financial support. She underlined the fact that 90% of the operations budget already was directed to staff salaries and benefits. She informed the teachers' team that the voters would not stand for another override election. "Such an attempt would bring down the wrath of the community on the schools," Thelma contended.

After several weeks of conversation between the school board and teachers' bargaining teams, Thelma met with the school superintendent and Merlin George to brief them on progress to date.

"I've spelled out the budget situation for the teachers," stated Thelma. "I think it's time to present the recommendation to the teachers that it would be the best win-win strategy for all of us to forgo any salary increases for next year; only salary increments based on experience or degree credits using the present salary schedule would be provided. I think that I've got the teachers' team convinced that we're in a dire situation. Timing is good; just last week the factory workers at Specialty Supply accepted a cut in hourly pay," she noted. "Are you both agreeable to my plan?"

Questions

1. Assume the position of Merlin George in this case. How would you respond to Thelma Morton?

2. What evidence in the case justifies this situation as win-win bargaining?

3. Knowing the economic conditions prior to bargaining in this case, what approaches and recommendations for bargaining might you have suggested?

References

American Association of School Personnel Administrators. (1978). *Trends in collective bargaining in public education.* Seven Hills, OH: Author.

Balfour, G.A. (1974). More evidence that unions do not achieve higher salaries for teachers. *Journal of Collective Negotiations in the Public Sector, 3,* 289–303.

Bureau of Labor Statistics. (1980). *Work stoppings in government* (Bulletin 2110). Washington, DC: Author.

Cascio, W. F. (2003). *Managing human resources* (6th ed.). New York: McGraw Hill/Irwin.

Cunningham, W. G., & Cordeiro, P. A. (2000). *Educational administration.* Boston: Allyn & Bacon.

Dessler, G. (2001). *A framework for human resource management* (2nd ed.). Upper Saddle River, NJ: Prentice Hall.

Diegmueller, K. (1991, April 17). Tight budgets escalate school labor tensions. *Education Week,* p. 14.

Donohue, W. A., Allen, M., & Burrell, N. (1988, March). Mediator communicative competence. *Communication Monographs, 55,* 1204–1219.

Eberts, R. W. (1984). Union effects on teacher productivity. *Industrial and Labor Relations Journal, 37,* 346–358.

Edson, L. (2000, April). The negotiation industry. *Across the Board, 37*(4), 14–23.

Freeman, R. B. (1981). The effect of unionism on fringe benefits. *Industrial and Labor Review, 34,* 489–509.

Gallagher, D. G. (1978). De facto bargaining and teacher salary levels. *Journal of Collective Negotiations in the Public Sector, 7,* 245–254.

Greatbatch, A., & Dingwall, R. (1997, February). Argumentative talk in divorce mediation sessions. *Sociological Review, 62*(1), 151–171.

Hall, P. (2000). Feel the width. *People Management, Viewpoint, 6*(1), 23.

Hannaway, J., & Rotherman, A. J. (2006). *Collective bargaining in education.* Cambridge, MA: Harvard Education Press, Graduate School of Education.

Horace Mann League. (1996, March 15). Survey of 600 superintendents and professors. *Education Daily,* p. 4.

International Labour Office. (1997, November). *World employment report.* Geneva: Bureau of Public Information.

Kahn, L. (1979). Unionism and relative wages: Direct and indirect effects. *Industrial and Labor Relations Review, 32,* 520–532.

Kasper, H. (1970). The effects of collective bargaining on public school teachers' salaries. *Industrial and Labor Relations Review, 24,* 57–72.

Kennedy, G., Benson, J., & McMillan, J. (1982). *Managing negotiations.* Englewood Cliffs, NJ: Prentice Hall.

Lieberman, M., & Moskow, M. H. (1966). *Collective negotiations for teachers.* Washington, DC: Office of Professional Development and Welfare.

Loughran, C. S. (1992). *Negotiating a labor contract: A management handbook* (2nd ed.). Washington, DC: The Bureau of National Affairs, Inc.

Lunenburg, F. C., & Ornstein, A. C. (2000). *Educational administration: Concepts and practices* (3rd ed.). Belmont, CA: Wadsworth.

Marshall, A. (1979). The effects of collective bargaining on faculty salaries in higher education. *Journal of Higher Education, 50,* 310.

Milakovich, M. E., & Gordon, G. J. (2001). *Public administration in America.* Belmont, CA: Thomson Learning.

Mnookin, R. H. (2000, April). Negotiation: The advanced course. *Across the Board, 37*(4), 21–22.

Moore, G. A. (1975). *Some salary effects of professional negotiations in public schools—The Nebraska experience.* Lincoln: University of Nebraska.

National Education Association. (1961). *Addresses and proceedings.* Washington, DC: Author.

National Education Association. (1962). *Addresses and proceedings.* Washington, DC: Author.

National Education Association. (1965). *Guidelines for professional negotiation.* Washington, DC: Office of Professional Development and Welfare.

National Education Association. (1968). Listing of 1967–68 agreements. *Negotiations Research Digest, 1*(10), E1–E29.

National Education Association. (1991, September). The 1991–1992 resolutions of the National Education Association. *NEA Today,* pp. 15–25.

National School Boards Association. (1991, March 6). Resolutions, proposed changes for 1991–92. *School Board News,* pp. 2–7.

Nelson, J. L., Carlson, K., & Palonsky, S. B. (1996). *Critical issues in education* (3rd ed.). New York: McGraw-Hill.

News from home, California. (2005, March 3). *Arizona Republic,* p. D1.

Norton, M. S. (2001). *The school superintendency in Arizona.* Tempe: Arizona State University, Division of Educational Leadership & Policy Studies.

Norton M. S. (2004). *The personnel administrator in Arizona: A research study.* Tempe: Arizona State University, Division of Educational Leadership & Policy Studies.

Norton, M. S. (2005). *Executive leadership for effective administration.* Boston: Allyn & Bacon.

Norton, M. S., & Farrar, R. D. (2004). *Competency-based preparations of educational administrators—Tasks, competencies and indicators of competency.* Tempe: Arizona State University, Division of Educational Leadership & Policy Studies.

Norton, M. S., Webb, L. D., Dlugosh, L. L., & Sybouts, W. (1996). *The school superintendency.* Boston: Allyn & Bacon.

Payne, K., Kohler, P., Cangemi, J. P., & Fuqua, H., Jr. (2000). Communication and strategies in the mediation of disputes. *Collective Negotiations in the Public Sector, 29*(1), 29–47.

Perry, C. R., & Wilman, A. W. (1970). *The impact of negotiations in public education.* Worthington, OH: Charles A. Jones.

Public Service Research Council. (1978). *Report on states with and without bargaining legislation.* Vienna, VA: Author.

Rebore, R. W. (2001). *Personnel administration in education: A management approach* (6th ed.). Englewood Cliffs, NJ: Prentice Hall.

Redfern, G. G. (1967). *Ways and means of PN: Professional negotiations and the school administrator.* Arlington, VA: American Association of School Administrators.

Schoonmaker, A. N. (1989). *Negotiate to win.* Upper Saddle River, NJ: Prentice Hall.

Strahan, R. D. (1969). *Legal guidelines for the management of collective agreements in education.* Houston, TX: Gulf School Research Development Association.

Walter, R. L. (1975). *The teacher and collective bargaining.* Lincoln, NE: Educators Publications.

Webb, S., & Webb, B. (1920). *History of trade unionism* (part 1). New York: Longman, Green.

Wesley, E. B. (1957). *NEA: The first hundred years.* New York: Harper.

Wynn, R. (1981). The relationship of collective bargaining and teacher salaries, 1960–1980. *Phi Delta Kappan, 63,* 237–242.

Young, I. P. (2008). *The human resource function in educational administration* (9th ed.). Upper Saddle River, NJ: Pearson Merrill Prentice Hall.

Zuelke, D. C., & Frohreich, L. E. (1977). The impact of comprehensive collective negotiations on teachers' salaries: Some evidence from Wisconsin. *Journal of Collective Negotiations in the Public Sector, 6*(1), 81–88.

CHAPTER 11

The Compensation Process

An Operations Model

Learning Objectives

After reading this chapter, you will be able to

- Identify the problems related to school finance in education historically.
- Identify the various approaches to personnel compensation in education.
- Determine the differences between salary, wages, and psychic income.
- Identify the various methods of compensation for extracurricular assignments.
- Calculate compensation on various salary scales.
- Apply an operational model for the school finance process in education.

School Finance: The Number One Problem Facing Education

Chapter 1 underscored school finance as a leading problem facing education today. Finance has been the leading problem for education historically. In his 1882 annual report to the Governor of the state of Indiana, the Superintendent of Public Instruction, John M. Bloss, stated "The compensation offered is too small to induce teachers to remain in the profession" (p. 156). More than 100 years later, in its latest *Study of the American School Superintendency* (2000), the American Association of School Administrators reported that 96.7% of the nation's school superintendents named financial issues as the most difficult problem facing them. School boards nationally have named financial issues as the top-ranking problem every year since 1992 regardless of the size of the school district. State studies reveal the same findings.

In a statewide study of school superintendents (Norton, 2004), 82.4% of the participating school superintendents named financial issues as a "highly difficult" or "difficult" problem. In the same superintendents' study, inadequate finance led to the listing of issues that inhibited their effectiveness in the role. Concern about financial matters and levy issues also led the school superintendents' listing as being the most frequent troublesome problem facing them. The compensation of personnel is highly significant for the accomplishment of a school district's stated goals. It is generally known that approximately 85% of a school's operations budget is expended on staff compensation.

An effective compensation process is designed to assist in motivating personnel to (1) join the school system; (2) continue to develop their potential knowledge, attitudes, and skills; and (3) remain in the school system and serve purposefully in the accomplishment of its goals and objectives.

Education Is Big Business

In the 2006–2007 school year, the nation's public elementary and secondary schools enrolled 48,948,000 students. As Table 11.1 shows, public school educational expenditures were estimated at $451.7 billion or $9,008 per pupil. The U.S. Department of Education, National Center for Educational Statistics, estimated that low-alternative per pupil costs will escalate to $10,654 by the 2015–2016 school year (National Center for Educational Statistics, 2007). Yet, comparative expenditure statistics for tobacco, alcohol, gambling, and other less necessary items in the U.S. indicate that the nation can afford any educational program that it chooses to support. Compared to the actual national expenditures of $451.7 billion for public education in 2006–2007, tobacco sales alone by the four largest tobacco companies in America totaled an estimated $111 billion during the same time period.

Table 11.1   Projections of Educational Expenditures to 2015

School Year	Enrollment (in thousands)	Current Dollars	
		In Billions	Per Pupil
1990–1991	41,217	202.0	4,902
1993–1994	43,465	231.5	5,327
1996–1997	45,611	270.2	5,923
1999–2000	46,857	323.9	6,912
2002–2003	48,183	387.6	8,044
2005–2006*	48,710	447.4	9,185
2008–2009*	49,167	511.6	10,406
2012–2013*	49,938		
2015–2016*	51,220		

SOURCE: U.S. Department of Education, National Center for Educational Statistics. National Public Education Survey, 1990–91 through 2003–04. Table prepared November, 2005.

*Projected.

Competition for the Tax Dollar

Throughout history, groups and individuals have been interested in the politics and power influences that result in decisions about how values and resources are allocated over a period of time. How decisions about educational issues are determined and who makes these decisions are central to what is generally referred to as the politics of education. Just about every group in the United States has something to say about improving the quality of education. Politically, governmental agencies, study groups, educational associations, and a variety of other groups have set forth actions designed to make the schools better and more relevant to society's needs. Educators have encouraged more involvement in the school's activities by the school system's stakeholders with the hope that such participation would lead to a better understanding of the educational needs. The more the citizenry has become involved in the activities of the school, the more questions are asked about the school and its operations. In recent years, the schools' stakeholders and others have become more critical of what they view as unresponsiveness of the school's administration and the need for higher levels of student achievement. The new participation has taken such serious forms of shared control as (1) different clientele running for school board positions, (2) advisory committees at the local school level, and (3) taskforce groups of citizens working directly with the administration on such matters as school budgets.

The calls for more involvement in and control of schools have not been restricted to parents. The taxpayers generally have placed political pressure on the states to assume more responsibility for financing education, to change the ways of distributing school funds, to set tax ceilings for funding school costs, and to support compensation practices based on pay-for-performance methods.

Resistance on the part of taxpayers to pay higher rates of local property tax has resulted in a larger proportion of financial support being assumed at the state level. Individual states presently pay more than 50% of the public elementary and secondary education costs. The result has been an ongoing concern for the loss of local school control and the increasing number of state requirements and mandates.

The involvement of various publics in the financial administration of America's schools has brought several truths to the forefront, including the following: (1) the greater the diversity of publics involved in the politics of any governmental area, the less likely will be the continuance of low-pressure politics, and (2) the greater the differences of opinion of the various diverse publics on educational goals and financing, the less likely is it that consensus will be realized. In the past, political consensus was more easily reached through extralegal social networks, including the resolution of problems by neighbors over the backyard fence. Today, problems of school finance are usually resolved by formal bodies such as legislatures and the courts.

The foregoing discussion underscores the fact that educational finance has been forcibly moved further away from local policy decisions and more into the political arena with other agencies that compete for the same public tax dollar. As a result, the political problems related to competition for the funding of education are no different than the political problems faced by other institutions, programs, and national needs of the United States (e.g., public welfare, transportation, highways, government agencies, safety, the justice system, etc.).

Operational Model for the Compensation Process

The following section presents an operational model for guiding the compensation process. It discusses in detail each of the following four steps: (1) developing compensation policies, (2) establishing the position structure, (3) determining the economic values of personnel positions, and (4) establishing administrative procedures for implementing the compensation process.

It is important to keep in mind that personnel compensation includes much more than salaries. Employee compensation includes legal requirements for workers' compensation insurance, unemployment insurance, social security, retirement benefits, disability pay, survivor's benefits, health insurance payments, and other types of fringe benefit payments assumed by the school district.

Developing Compensation Policies

An adopted school board compensation policy serves several important purposes. A **compensation policy** is a statement adopted by the school board that sets forth the goals and objectives that direct the compensation process for the school district. First and foremost, a compensation policy provides the guidelines for what the compensation process is to accomplish. For example, if the school district's policy states, "employee compensation is to be competitive so that the school district is able to employ quality personnel in the various teaching, administrative, and support positions," the policy provides support for the implementation of a compensation process that indeed serves to attract and retain quality personnel.

Examples of contents often included in a school board compensation policy are as follows:

1. Attract and retain personnel who are capable of performing effectively in the positions needed in the school district.

2. Contribute to the attainment of the school district's goals and objectives.

3. Be competitive so that the school district is able to employ quality personnel in the various teaching, administration, and support service areas.

4. Compensate all personnel equitably in proportion to the knowledge and skills, education level, and supervisory responsibilities required in the position.

5. Include the compensation factors of salary, benefits, and psychic income.

6. Contribute to the economic, social, and psychological satisfaction of the district's employees.

7. Compensate appropriately for extracurricular assignments not included in the salary and wage package of the employee.

Figure 11.1 is an example of a school board policy concerning professional staff contracts and compensation, along with an accompanying administrative regulation. The contents of the administrative regulation center on the procedural aspects of employment contracts and compensation as related to days of absence and how absences will be calculated for salary purposes.

Professional Staff Salary Schedules

Administrators

The Board will enter into an individual contract with each member of the administrative staff commensurate with the requirements of the position. This contract shall describe the general services to be rendered by the employee in return for financial and other considerations. Additionally, the employee's job description, detailing the more specific performance responsibilities of the contracted position and the mode of evaluating performance, shall be incorporated into the contract by reference. All terms and conditions of contracts with administrative staff members are to conform with the requirements of the Arizona Revised Statutes.

Other Certificated Personnel

The salary schedule pertains to personnel holding provisional, basic, or standard certificates at the elementary or secondary levels.

Initial Placement on Salary Schedule. New teachers entering the system with prior teaching service, who have met academic and professional qualifications for Arizona State Department of Education certification, will be given a maximum credit of _____ years for substantiated experience, i.e., placed on the _____ step of the salary schedule. Previous verified experience recognized for the purpose of placement on the salary schedule is defined as any previous full-time certificated teaching in any public school. For a teacher to receive credit for previous teaching experience, the teacher must furnish the office of the Superintendent full information concerning the previous teaching records. When the experience has been verified, credit will be given by the District.

Substitutes

Pay for substitute teaching will be established by the Board.

Advancement on Salary Schedule

Vertical and horizontal advancement on the salary schedule will be in accordance with the salary schedule currently in effect. Vertical advancement is limited to one (1) step per year.
Reasons for denial of vertical advancement on the salary schedule include but are not limited to:

- Lack of adequate disciplinary control.
- Insufficient effort and time given to assigned duties or failure to engage in a reasonable amount of extracurricular activity.
- Lack of cooperation with the administration in carrying out adopted policies of the school.
- Unprofessional conduct.

Other Contract Provisions

Any person who does not work the full term as set up by salary schedule shall be paid on a prorated basis for the number of days to be worked for the remainder of the school year; this shall include school days taught plus the number of days required for orientation.
For newly hired, critical, and difficult to fill certificated personnel placed on the teachers' salary schedule, differentials above the stated schedule may be paid.

Adopted: date of manual adoption

Legal Ref.:   A.R.S. 15-502, 15-941

Cross Ref.:   GCO-RB—Evaluation of Professional Staff Members

Professional Staff Contracts and Compensation

Salaries in the District will be differentiated in relationship to duties and responsibilities.
The Superintendent will provide recommendations on salaries and fringe benefits to the Board each year.
After receipt of the Superintendent's recommendations, the Board will annually establish the salaries and benefits for all employees within the budgetary constraints of the District.

Adopted: date of manual adoption

Legal Ref.:   A.R.S. 15-502, 15-503, 15-952

Figure 11.1   Example of Professional Staff Contracts and Compensation Policy

SOURCE: Arizona School Boards Association (2007).

A variety of factors influences the contents of a compensation policy. School finance legislation, mandates of the State Board of Education, federal legislative directives, positions of pressure groups, and collective bargaining agreements are among the factors that influence a policy statement. For example, school finance legislation sets conditions and limits concerning school district expenditures, state school boards specify directives for expenditure controls, federal legislation often determines the categorical areas for approved educational expenditures, various pressure groups tend to influence the priorities of educational spending, and collective bargaining tends to dictate specific salary and benefits provisions for employees.

The influence of the collective bargaining process on compensation levels for employees in education has been the topic of much discussion, and the matter remains in question. Some authorities credit the process of collective bargaining as having had a greater influence on the human resources function processes than any other development in the field. Somewhat surprising, however, were the findings of several early research studies that collective bargaining has had little or no effect on compensation levels in education. In fact, some studies found that school districts that do not negotiate salaries and benefits had as good or better records of salary increases than those districts that did bargain (Balfour, 1974; Kahn, 1979; Kasper, 1970; Public Service Research Council, 1978; Wynn, 1981; Zuelke & Frohreich, 1977). Other early studies found that collective bargaining had some positive effect on salary increases (Freeman, 1981; Gallagher, 1978; Moore, 1975). Research that attempts to isolate the effects of collective bargaining on compensation levels is confounded by the difficulty of controlling for the many variables that influence the determination of salary levels, including what is termed **spillover**. Spillover is the influence that bargaining districts might have on the salary of nonbargaining districts. Nonbargaining districts, for example, might increase their salary levels in order to remain competitive with other districts that have engaged in collective bargaining. In this initial step of the compensation process, specific goals and objectives are determined, timelines are established, compensation process responsibilities are assigned, and personnel inventories are examined.

Establishing the Position Structure

Chapter 4 presented the topics of job analysis, job grading, and job ascription. As stated by the compensation policy in Figure 11.1, employee salaries generally are differentiated according to duties and responsibilities. Classified personnel positions, for example, often are categorized into several different levels. In the case of clerical personnel, such classifications as Clerk 1, Clerk 2, Secretary 1, Secretary 2, Administrative Assistant, and so forth are typical. As position responsibilities require more preparation and experience, additional supervisory responsibilities, and increased levels of competency, compensation levels are differentiated accordingly. This process is termed **job grading**. **Job assessment** is the ascription of a monetary value of a position on the basis of job grading.

Job Assessment: Determining the Value of Employee Positions

Compensation structure commonly includes five kinds of compensation: (1) salary, which is generally contractual with a greater assurance of steady compensation; (2) wages, which are generally compensation for services provided by support personnel who have no guarantee of permanent employment; (3) collateral benefits or fringe benefits, which are direct forms of compensation that generally do not require additional services beyond those of the basic contract; (4) nonsalary pay or extracurricular compensation, which are extra compensation that includes additional income and also includes incentive pay or merit; and (5) psychic income, which is nonmonetary pay, such as rewards, recognitions, authority, and privileges.

Collateral or fringe benefits for personnel in education have increased substantially over the years. Four specific categories of benefits are (1) financial security, (2) professional development, (3) health and recreation, and (4) service-connected personnel needs. Figure 11.2 identifies several selected benefit provisions within each of the four categories.

The **cost of benefits (COB)** has become a serious financial problem for most school districts. Such provisions as increasing health costs, insurance protection, educational travel, and others have resulted in decreases in the proportion of financial support paid by school boards. The employee is being asked to assume a greater proportion of benefits costs.

I. Security Benefits

Sick Leave, Personal Leave, Retirement Benefits, Bereavement Leave, Leave for Jury Duty, Military Leave, Extended Leave, Tax-sheltered Annuities, Severance Pay, Life Insurance, Credit Union Services, Workers' Compensation, Unemployment Compensation, Savings Plans, Other Insurance Protections and Leave Benefits.

II. Health Benefits

Health Insurance, Dental Insurance, Vision Insurance, Health Services, Medical Leave, Employee Assistance Programs, Prescription Drug Insurance, Security Provisions.

III. Service-Connected Liabilities

Legal Services (commonly provided by professional association), Professional Liability Insurance, Travel Insurance, Workers' Compensation, Personal Property Insurance.

IV. Service-Connected Personal Benefits

Travel Expenses, Moving Costs, Parking Facilities, Cafeteria Privileges, Child-care Facilities, Free or Reduced Cost Services, Professional Membership Dues Payments.

V. Professional Development Benefits

Professional Growth Programs, Tuition Defrayment Payments, Conference Expenses, Sabbatical Leave Provisions, Professional Business Leave, Mentoring Services, Educational Trips, Professional Development Resources, Professional Leave Opportunities, Career Ladder and Master Teacher Incentives, Business Partnerships, Administrator Academies for Prospective School Administrators, Association Business Leave, and other types of leaves for personal and professional growth purposes.

Figure 11.2   Types of Fringe Benefits in Educational Systems

Several factors have been identified that, over time, determine the general level of employee salaries. These factors include

1. Compensation legislation.

2. Mandates from state boards and the courts.

3. Prevailing salaries of related occupations.

4. Collective bargaining.

5. Employee supply and demand.

6. Ability to pay.

7. Standard cost of living.

8. National productivity.

9. Collateral considerations, including recruitment difficulty, ability to retain employees, and so on.

The following section briefly discusses each of these factors.

Compensation Legislation

The Fair Labor Standards Act (FLSA) of 1938 is a primary example of compensation legislation that strictly governs compensation practices. The Equal Pay Act (EPA) of 1963, which is part of the FLSA, prohibits sex-based wage discrimination between men and women in the same establishment who are performing under similar working conditions. Specifically, the EPA states that

No employer having employees subject to any provision of this section shall discriminate, within any establishment in which such employees are employed, between employees on the basis of sex by paying wages to employees in such establishment at a rate less than the rate at which he pays wages to employees of the opposite sex in such establishment for equal pay on jobs the performance of which requires equal skill, effort, and responsibility, and which are performed under similar working conditions, except where such payment is made pursuant to (i) a seniority system; (ii) a merit system; (iii) a system which measures earnings by quantity or quality production, or (iv) a differential based on any other factor other than sex: *Provided,* That an employer who pays a wage rate differential in violation of this subsection shall not, in order to comply with the provisions of this subsection, reduce the wage of any employee.

The Individuals with Disabilities Education Act (IDEA) is another example of federal legislation that provides states with funding for certain program provisions and procedural guarantees (Bartlett, Etscheidt, & Weisenstein, 2007). The IDEA is essentially a contract between the federal government and each state, whereby the state agrees to follow certain regulations in exchange for funds. Local applications must include descriptions of facilities, personnel, and services available; guarantees that federal guidelines are being followed; plans for parental participation; accounting systems; and agreement to furnish data required by the state for its reports.

Mandates From State School Boards and the Courts

Most states establish minimum salary levels for administrators, teachers, and other staff personnel. Restrictions on the local tax levies that can be applied by school boards for operational and capital outlay funds are common. Such restrictions have two primary purposes: (1) attempting to equalize educational support among school districts that differ greatly in their ability to pay, and (2) to control the school board's ability to increase taxes on local properties at will.

The federal government has passed many other laws that have influenced compensation practices in education. The No Child Left Behind Act (NCLB) is a prime example. The NCLB is a comprehensive, detailed, and specific statement that stipulates, for example, the procedures and requirements for receiving funding for special program purposes:

Sec. 1231. Statement of Purpose.

It is the purpose of this subpart to help break the cycle of poverty and illiteracy by

(1) Improving the educational opportunity of the Nation's low-income families by integrating early childhood, adult literacy or adult education, and parenting education into a unified family literacy program to be referred to as Even Start. (U.S. Department of Education, 2004)

Specific requirements for meeting the qualifications for funding, application stipulations, funding controls, and program assessment are among the other controls set forth in the NCLB.

Prevailing Salaries of Related Occupations

Comparing salaries among various occupations poses several problems related to job similarities, preparation requirements, licensing, contract arrangements, importance of the work, and other topics. For example, is it appropriate to compare the salary of teachers to nurses, firefighters, postal workers, accountants, or social workers? Perhaps an examination of teachers' salaries and several other public service occupations might provide some insight into how the citizenry view their relative importance. Table 11.2 shows the mean annual salaries of several public service positions and the mean annual salaries of teachers as reported by the U.S. Department of Labor in 2005.

As Table 11.2 shows, the mean salary of kindergarten teachers in 2005 was $45,250; elementary school teachers earned $46,990; middle school teachers earned $47,890; and secondary school teachers earned $49,240. Comparatively, social workers earned a mean annual salary of $42,720, health educators earned $43,440, and persons in the clergy earned $41,700. Each of these occupations earned lower

Table 11.2   Comparative Occupational Salaries, 2005

Occupation	Average Annual Salary
Kindergarten Teachers	$ 45,250
Elementary School Teachers	$ 46,990
Middle School Teachers	$ 47,890
Secondary School Teachers	$ 49,240
Special Education Teachers	
Elementary	$ 47,820
Middle School	$ 50,340
Secondary School	$ 50,880
Education, Vocational, & School Counselors	$ 48,530
Registered Nurses	$ 56,880
Dental Hygienist	$ 60,620
Fire Fighters	$ 40,420
Police & Patrol Officers	$ 47,270
Chefs and Head Cooks	$ 35,840
Flight Attendants	$ 53,740
Fish and Game Wardens	$ 43,360
Foresters	$ 51,030
Chemists	$ 63,470
Social Workers	$ 42,720
Health Educators	$ 43,440
Court Reporters	$ 45,420
Clergy	$ 41,700
Janitor	$ 21,120
Radio & TV Announcers	$ 39,350
Optometrists	$ 84,030
Educational Administrators Elementary & Secondary	$ 78,590
Instructional Coordinator	$ 53,360
Human Resources Director (Education)	$ 68,100
Human Resource Director (Other)	$ 89,950
Managers of Business/Industry	$ 77,780
Administration Service Managers	$ 69,540

SOURCE: Bureau of Labor Statistics (2005).

salaries than teachers at any level. However, flight attendants earned salaries of $53,740, dental hygienists earned $60,620, registered nurses earned $56,880, chemists earned $63,470, mathematicians earned $81,150, and optometrists earned $84,030. Each of these occupations exceeded the highest mean salary earned by teachers at any school level.

In 2005, human resources managers in business or industry earned a mean salary of $89,950 annually, whereas human resources directors in education earned $68,100. Elementary and secondary school administrators earned annual mean salaries of $78,590, whereas managers in other occupations earned $77,780.

One way to examine teachers' salaries in relation to gains over the years is to compare mean salaries longitudinally. By using constant dollars for 1994, the National Center for Educational Statistics presented salary statistics for the years between 1960 and 1994.[1] The data showed that the mean salary for elementary teachers in 1972 was approximately $36,000 using 1994 constant dollars. Twenty-two years later in 1994, the mean salary for secondary teachers was approximately $37,000 using 1994 constant dollars, only $1,000 more. Although the mean salary of teachers was higher in 1994 than in 1960, most of the gain since 1981 only recouped losses incurred during the 1970s (National Center for Educational Statistics, 1994).

Prevailing salary schedules of school districts are another factor that influences compensation. There is a spillover effect when one school district gives a sizable salary increase to teachers. The tendency is for neighboring school districts to match the compensation in order to remain competitive for attracting and retaining personnel. It is common practice for human resources personnel from various regional school districts to meet periodically, and salary increases for the ensuing year are often a topic of discussion.

Collective Bargaining

We noted in Chapter 10 that results from studies of the impact of collective bargaining on teacher compensation are mixed. Early collective bargaining study results in education ranged from some impact, to no impact, to a negative impact. Early studies of the impact of unionism on salary increases are inconclusive as well. Empirical evidence suggests that organizations that used collective bargaining saw less than a 2% advantage over nonbargaining organizations.

Some research studies suggest that collective bargaining has resulted in increased fringe benefits for personnel. However, such gains tend to be offset by increases in class size.

Supply and Demand for Personnel

The concept of supply and demand as it applies to education is complex. From a theoretical perspective, if the personnel supply is low and demand for personnel is high, competition for the available supply substantially raises personnel compensation. On the other hand, if the available supply is high and the demand is low, the lack of competition results in lower compensation levels. The need for a reduction in force (RIF) was prominent in many school districts nationally in the mid-1970s and early 1980s. During this time period, the mean teacher salary for secondary school teachers was approximately $32,000 using 1994 constant dollars. By 1994, teacher shortages confronted many school districts, and the mean salary for secondary teachers reached $37,000 annually (National Center for Educational Statistics, 1994). However, the consideration of supply and demand in education varies widely throughout the states and is influenced by many factors such as the following:

1. As the nation entered the 21st century, more individuals were entering preparation programs than there were teaching jobs. There were more institutions preparing teachers than ever before in history. Yet, of the number of prospective teachers completing preparation programs, only approximately 60% assumed teaching positions (Feistritzer, 1984). In addition, 30%–50% of new teachers were leaving the teaching profession within the first five years (American Council on Education, 1999).

2. The supply and demand phenomenon in education is influenced by increases or declines of student enrollment in school districts. Immigration and migration statistics bring about special demand considerations. Decisions about such factors as pupil teacher ratios and teacher retirement percentages alter teacher needs as well.

3. The demand for teachers is influenced by both geographical and community factors. For example, urban and poor communities have the greatest need for teachers (Yasin, 1998). There are now more than three million teachers in the United States. Of this number, approximately 40% teach in California, Florida, Illinois, New York, Ohio, and Texas. Bradley (1999) reported that five states, "Connecticut, Minnesota, New York, Pennsylvania, and Wisconsin historically have produced more teachers than they need. . . . Others such as California, Florida, Nevada, and Texas require more teachers than they produce."

4. There is growing evidence that teacher shortages are due in part to the lack of quality human resources programs. For example, Gold (1996) pointed out that the establishment of induction programs that provide new teachers with direct support from a mentor or master teacher can reduce attrition rates substantially. Pilot induction programs in California reportedly reduced teacher turnover rates by two-thirds. Over a five-year period, turnover rates of new teachers were reduced to 9% compared to a 37% rate for teachers who did not participate in the induction program. Such evidence underscores the fact that teacher supply and demand problems are not always directly tied to compensation; many other nonsalary factors influence the need for teachers.

Ability to Pay

Early finance studies in education underscored the fact that the ability to pay for education varied among the states in a ratio of 6 to 1. That is, some states require six times the effort of some other states to raise the same amount of dollars for education. The ability to pay for educational services differs widely among the "rich" and "poor" school districts as well. State foundational finance programs are examples of funding programs that have been established in an attempt to equalize the amount of money spent per pupil for education regardless of the school district in which a child resides.

Variations in property values, tax regulations, and the public's valuing of education are among the factors that help determine compensation levels for education. We noted previously that federal, state, and local legislation places many restrictions or limitations on local expenditures for education. How a community values education is another matter. Willingness to pay local and state taxes looms large in ability to pay. For example, there are communities today that do not organize their own public school programs. In most of these cases, although these school districts do have the ability to pay for public education, it is less costly for them to pay tuition charges and send their children to schools in surrounding school districts.

Standard Cost of Living

Consider the situation of an experienced teacher living in Phoenix, Arizona, who is earning $50,000 annually. The teacher is considering taking a similar teaching position in Los Angeles, California. The cost of living in California is 13.1% higher than in Phoenix. Therefore, if the teacher took the same type of teaching position in Los Angeles, he or she is likely to earn $56,550. The cost of living in Lincoln, Nebraska, is 2% lower than Phoenix, Arizona. If the same teacher were to take a teaching position in Lincoln, Nebraska, he or she would have to earn a salary of $49,000 in order to maintain the current standard of living.

The **cost of living adjustment** (COLA) is an important consideration in decisions about salaries of personnel in educational employment. In instances when existing economic factors prohibit any increases in the base salary schedule, the teacher generally receives only the experience increment increase set forth on the next step of the salary schedule. Depending on the change that takes place in the community's cost of living, the increment earned by the teacher might not even cover the increased cost of living. In this sense, the teacher's salary has been reduced.

The **ability to pay principle** also relates to other aspects of compensation, including the payment of taxes. "Under this notion, persons with higher status are presumed more able to pay and should be made to contribute more than persons of lesser status" (Thompson, Wood, & Honeyman, 1994, p. 178). The underlying rationale is that those who are least able to pay are likely the ones who need education the most. Income tax assessments are based on this progressive tax concept.

School board members commonly are well versed in the importance of the cost of living and employee compensation. Nevertheless, teachers' associations generally include a cost of living adjustment clause on the agenda during the collective bargaining process.

National Productivity

The individual contributions of education have been demonstrated extensively. Strong arguments have been set forth concerning the contributions of education as a vital investment in the support of a democracy, as a foundational factor for a business system of free enterprise, and as a significant contribution to the personal welfare of each citizen.

Education's importance in national productivity has been argued historically. Is education an investment or an expense? One position argues that "education produces human capital, contributes to national economic health, and in large part determines the economic and social welfare of the nation" (Thompson et al., 1994, pp. 23–24). The more educated the citizenry, the higher standards of living it demands. Educated citizens want more and better products. Thus, national productivity benefits through a national investment in education. "Because no way has been found by which to precisely measure the productivity output of educational investment relative to the input variable of fiscal resources, economists often rely on estimation of 'residual' effects in the economy" (Thompson et al., 1994, p. 30). Economists have used various approaches in attempts to show the relationship of economic growth and investments in education. An early study by Denison (1983) concluded that the contribution of education is higher in the United States than in any country. "Although precise quantifications of investment-expense is elusive, education and economic growth seem closely and consistently tied together" (Thompson et al., 1994, p. 32). In the final analysis, the value of education in the eyes of society is expressed in the level of resources committed to it.

Collateral Considerations That Affect Compensation

Many other collateral factors influence the level of compensation for school districts. Location, status, reputation, recruitment, retention, and demographics are among the factors that tend to increase or decrease salary levels. School districts located in poor economic areas are most likely to have lower property valuations for tax purposes. As a result, compensation levels in these school districts are problematic. Recruitment of employees and retention are also more difficult if competitive salaries cannot be paid or adequate instructional resources cannot be provided.

In some states, schools that do not meet student achievement standards are viewed as underperforming. This reputation inhibits the school's ability to recruit and retain quality personnel.

Although the practice is less common than in previous years, some school districts require that employees reside within the school district in which they teach. In some instances, the cost of housing in the school district is beyond what a beginning teacher is able to afford. School district demographics also affect compensation levels. Schools with high numbers of minority students more frequently offer incentives to attract new teaching personnel to the school district.

In view of the contemporary concept of **choice** as it relates to school attendance, competition for students is more in evidence. In a state that supports education at an $8,000 per pupil level, a school district that loses 100 students to a neighboring school district loses $800,000 in financial support, money it could have used to advantage for the support of employee compensation.

Cost of benefits (COB) weighs heavily on the school district's budget and on employee compensation. Costs related to **collateral or fringe benefits** for employees have become problematic for most school districts nationally. Collateral benefits commonly include five categories of employee collateral payments: (1) financial security—protection from loss of income when absent from work, retirement, and security of dependents in case of employee disability or death; (2) professional development—benefits that provide growth opportunities for employees; (3) health and welfare—benefits that provide for medical care and services and other health related programs; (4) employment-related liabilities—protection against expenses or losses incurred through job performance; and (5) service-related employee needs such as travel expenses and parking facilities.

Not all collateral benefits, of course, are provided by each school district. Nevertheless, examples of financial security benefits provided in many school districts include sick leave, bereavement leave, personal leave, professional leave, retirement plans, life insurance, workers' compensation, tax-sheltered annuities, employee credit unions, and severance pay. Professional development benefits include in-service training and professional development programs, sabbatical leave, education cost plans, conference and workshop attendance, educational travel programs, participation in professional activities and associations, teacher exchange programs, and others.

Because of the increasing costs of employee benefits in all benefit categories, some school districts are discontinuing certain fringe benefits or increasing the proportional fee the employee is required to pay. Some districts are implementing cafeteria benefit plans, whereby the employee receives a specific dollar amount for benefits and must decide which benefits to purchase. A variation is to include a benefit increment in the employee's salary; the employee must decide whether to retain that benefit increment as salary or to spend it for specific benefits.

Establishing Administrative Procedures for Implementation of the Compensation Process

Compensation administrative procedures tie directly to the compensation policies adopted by the school board. The compensation policy, set forth in Figure 11.1, stated two specific aims to be accomplished: (1) salaries in the district will be differentiated according to duties and responsibilities, and (2) the superintendent will provide recommendations on salaries and fringe benefits to the board each year. Thus, the administrative procedures related to job analyses, job descriptions, job grading, and job assessment encompass the general administrative responsibilities in this step of the compensation model. Chapter 4 discussed these activities, and Chapter 12 will discuss them once again in relation to classified personnel.

Chapter 1 discussed competency-based administration. The human resources director assumes several major administrative tasks in relation to wage and salary administration. Three examples of such tasks, along with selected competencies and indicators of competency, are as follows:

Task 1—To assist in the development of the district policy on wages and salaries.
Related competencies for Task 1:

1.0. Ability to secure information that will be helpful in the development of a district philosophy on wages and salaries.

Indicators of competency for Competency 1.0:

1.1. Provides leadership in the development and revision of salaries and wage policies.

1.2. Writes guidelines for salary and wage determination.

Task 2—To develop and administer a broad basic program of personnel wages and salaries.
Related competencies for Task 2:

2.0. Ability to obtain appropriate data for completing job analyses, job grading, and job assessment.

Indicators of competency for Competency 2.0:

2.1. Collects information for completing job analyses.

2.2. Assists in the synthesis of job analyses results.

2.3. Assists in the computation of projected wage and salary schedules.

Task 3—To participate in the collective bargaining process.
Related competencies for Task 3:

3.0. Ability to understand the nature of collective bargaining and possess the skills required for effective bargaining.

Indicators of competency for Competency 3.0:

3.1. Understands the bargaining strategies used in the distributive and integrative bargaining processes.

3.2. Participates in training conferences and workshops on contemporary collective bargaining methods in education.

3.3. Participates directly in the collective bargaining planning process.

3.4. Assumes leadership responsibilities in the controlling and evaluating activities related to the bargaining process of the school district.

The administration of the competency process is a shared responsibility among the offices of the school superintendent, business, human resources, support personnel, and others. It is clear that the human resources director must be knowledgeable of the contemporary compensation programs and be instrumental in serving to determine the compensation plan most appropriate and acceptable for the school district. Later sections of this chapter discuss the single salary schedule, along with several contemporary compensation methods used in school districts.

As is the case with any of the HR processes, the compensation process requires strategic planning. Both the internal and external factors that influence compensation must be examined. Data for each of the factors that influence salary levels must be gathered and analyzed. For example, economic factors such as the COLA must be determined for the school district. Such strategic planning is not something that is done at some scheduled time during the year; rather, it is an ongoing activity that culminates with specific decisions concerning the economic growth level for an employee or job family, the logic and equity of compensation among and between the various range levels of a job family or administrative structure (e.g., elementary, middle school, high school positions, etc.), and earning potentials of specific positions and job families relative to other internal positions and potential compensation for comparable positions outside the school district. Each of these administrative considerations necessitates data gathering and analysis, projections about the financial circumstances facing the district, decisions about educational priorities, and administrative judgments about priorities and work production.

The following five guidelines serve as a summary of the administration of compensation procedures:

1. *Equity in Position Grading and Assessment.* Positions within each job family must be analyzed accurately relative to the importance of position responsibilities and required competency. Position grading and assessment requires input from appropriate personnel within the school district, including the employees themselves. Such administrative activities should tie closely to the activities of job analysis and job descriptions related to the HR planning process.

2. *Competitive Assessment.* Salary ascriptions for a position or position family must be such that compensation enables the district to attract and retain quality personnel. School and school district stability depend on a compensation process that is competitive with other school districts and business and industry positions that compete for quality employees in the same job families.

3. *Career Opportunities and Incentive Rewards.* Compensation programs should provide opportunities for employee advancement, both vertically in the organization and on the job itself. That is, effective compensation programs are essential for fostering continuous personal and professional growth on the job.

4. *Control and Evaluation of the Compensation Process.* Accountability of the compensation process can be assessed through activities that measure the outcomes of the goals and objectives of the process. Data on the results of recruitment and selection, employee retention, job satisfaction, and so forth serve as indicators of

the competitiveness of the compensation process. For example, to what extent are teachers leaving the school district for similar positions or joining the school district for reasons of salary? To what extent is the compensation program for support personnel competing for qualified personnel with other school districts or businesses and industries?

Controlling the Compensation Process

Controlling and evaluating the compensation process is the final step of the compensation process model, although it is an ongoing process instead of an end-of-the-line activity.

Were the goals and objectives set forth in the compensation planning activity achieved? What hard data are needed to demonstrate these accomplishments? Accountability measures presented in the preceding section serve as examples of evaluations that should be administered. Is it possible, for example, to relate specific outcomes of student achievement to compensation objectives of hiring quality personnel or to the incentive programs administered by the school district during the year? To what extent did the performance-based pay program result in an increase or decrease in teacher job satisfaction?

Compensation program audits are essential. An audit of the compensation plan includes a review and analysis of all the factors surrounding the planning, implementation, administration, and budgeting of the compensation process. State statutes usually control the process of an accounting audit of the income and expenditures of a school district. Income and expenditure controls, budgetary impacts, costing procedures, and problem areas must be determined and reported to the school board and other appropriate state and federal agencies. Accredited auditing firms are selected to perform the financial audits of the school district; such an audit includes all aspects of the school district's financial affairs, including the operation budget, building and equipment budget, and special audits of federal programs as set forth by federal regulations.

Trends in Salary Scheduling: Alternative Compensation Programs

Merit pay, bonus pay, career ladders, competency-based performance, skill-based pay, incentive pay, differentiated staffing, career ladders, and collective performance incentives are among the terms used today to describe various approaches for the compensation of personnel in school systems. **Merit pay** is a one-time compensation for meritorious performance based on predetermined work standards; it is paying the employee according to certain standards related to the quantity and quality of the work.

Each of the foregoing approaches centers on compensation supplements for exemplary employee performance or special achievements. Merit pay practices became popular in business and industry during the scientific management era of the early 1900s, continued through the 1920s, and reached a peak in the 1950s. Proponents of the merit pay concept believed that it would serve to motivate employee productivity and also would be instrumental in retaining employees in the organization. Over the years, merit pay has followed cycles that alternate between highs and lows according to societal pressures for paying employees on the basis of personal productivity. School districts have not yet been able to implement merit-pay systems with positive results in all instances. Problems related to the lack of success of merit plans have included questions concerning the objectivity of their implementation, staff disgruntlement concerning fairness in the administration of the merit plan, concerns about the validity and reliability of teacher performance evaluation instruments and evaluators' judgments, personnel differences over the importance of stated district performance objectives, and differences in personal views about the question of "what is teaching." Because merit-pay plans are costly, they require state funding for their implementation in most instances.

Several trends can be identified concerning salary scheduling, although a variety of arrangements for annual increments and degree or college preparation increments are being practiced. The following are among the trends in the implementation of salary schedules and alternative compensation programs:

1. The **single salary schedule** has been retained as a minimum base schedule with annual changes as determined by collective bargaining procedures and employee and school board master agreements. However, changes in the experience increments and preparation increments have varied considerably over the years. For example, preparation increments in salary schedules commonly include six or more levels (e.g., B.S. degree, B.S. + 15, B.S. + 30, M.A. degree, M.A. + 15, M.A. + 30, Ed.D. degree, etc.). Index salary schedules also are evident in compensation programs nationally.

2. Salary schedules have been designed to encourage employees to obtain continuous college or professional growth credits. Some salary schedules have included as many as seven or eight preparation increments. Although college credit hours and advanced degrees are the primary criteria for determining preparation increments, professional growth credits earned by employees are used for preparation increments as well in some school districts.

3. Annual increments or steps for teaching experience commonly have been reduced for the B.S. degree and for the Master's degree. Some schedules limit increases on the B.S. degree salary scale to five years. The rationale is to encourage those with B.S. degrees to continue work toward obtaining a Master's degree. In some school districts, credit for preparation on the salary schedule is granted only if the employee obtains the degree in the area of teaching responsibility. It is more common for school districts that need to attract new teachers to place an emphasis on the base salary and greater increments for the first few years of teaching, although this practice does receive criticism. Why pay more to the new teacher who might not remain with the district after the first year? Many school districts are designing salary schedules that allow teachers to double their beginning salary in

approximately 12 years. Districts that need to retain experienced teachers place more emphasis on greater increments for experienced personnel who have remained loyal to the school district. Such decisions are usually determined by the power of consensus or collective bargaining results.

4. School districts nationally have implemented various forms of **performance-based pay** plans. Such programs as master teacher or career ladder programs, which center on professional development, are typical of this practice. Career ladder compensation programs are common in many school districts nationally. Such programs have three primary purposes: (1) to encourage teachers toward professional development from the entry teaching level to advanced levels of professional practice (e.g., entry, professional, senior, master), (2) to reward teachers for increasing personal and professional knowledge and skills, and (3) to provide opportunities to realize increased professional pride and encourage teacher retention in the profession. In most instances, career ladder programs are subsidized by state funding. Each step on the career ladder carries specific stipulations concerning requirements, qualifications, certifications, and contract salary specifications. For example, each step on the career ladder sets forth the required contract days, base salary, and supplemental compensation to be received on completion of the requirements.

5. **Incentive pay** links closely to merit pay in that it is compensation allocated in addition to base salary for special work accomplishments or for meeting performance objectives. The purpose of performance pay plans is to encourage improvements in student test results and to achieve other standards and requirement of the NCLB. Performance-based plans have become more common in the compensation of school employees. A common reason for allocating incentive pay is meeting or exceeding student performance goals. Although the practice remains controversial in many respects, teachers who improve student achievement scores (e.g., achievement standards for a specific grade level) may receive incentive pay. In some cases, achievement incentive awards are centered on the performance of the entire school staff as opposed to the individual teacher. Such compensation systems that pay selected teachers or are based on the collective performance of the school in relation to overall student achievement are commonly termed bonus pay or **gain sharing**. Compensation for the school principal and the immediate supervisor in some school districts is based on performance-based systems. For example, the principal and the immediate supervisor reach an agreement on the goals and objectives to be accomplished by the principal during the school year. The school principal establishes specific evidence of accomplishments for each stated objective by using a portfolio of results or other accountability measures. The principal's supervisors and other appropriate personnel assess the accomplishments and ascribe monetary recommendations for the principal for the ensuing year. Although compensation plans that base teacher pay on classroom performance that centers on student achievement are controversial, some school leaders report that the extra pay included in such plans serves to improve the recruitment of new teachers and that test scores have indeed improved. Some school leaders have reported that performance pay plans have been a positive step in the eyes of the community's stakeholders (Koeppel, 2005).

6. **Knowledge- and skill-based pay systems**, in which employees' pay is based more on what they know and how they implement the knowledge and skills at work, also are emerging is school districts nationally. Pay systems using the knowledge- and skill-based system commonly do not guarantee more money for more experience. Rather, these compensation plans compensate employees according to the knowledge and skill levels demonstrated on the job. The employees with the most advanced skills, as related to their position requirements, receive the most pay. This compensation method is exemplified by the practices used commonly in classified and support personnel programs. For example, the knowledge and skill requirements for the position of Clerk 1 would differ from a Secretary 1 position.

7. Supplements for collateral or extracurricular assignments are commonly provided.

8. More attention is being given to **index salary schedules** that are often more favorable than the single salary schedule and for the more experienced career teacher in the school district. Index salary schedules are discussed later in this chapter.

History of the Single Salary Schedule

Near the turn of the 20th century, national population growth, increasing urbanization, the low level of teacher preparation, and rising taxes throughout the nation were among the many concerns of the citizenry. Many elementary school teachers of the time held only high school diplomas. The typical ideal for teacher preparation was two years of normal school training. Contrary to popular belief, teacher evaluation was a major topic in the 1910s and 1920s. There was a great push to establish merit pay system in all organizations.

There were no organized procedures for administering the salaries of teachers. The answer was the introduction of the single salary schedule. The NEA is credited with the sponsorship of the first single salary schedule in 1923, more than 80 years ago. The single salary schedule served several important concerns. (1) It provided different compensation in terms of degrees earned and encouraged those persons without degrees to earn the "high pay" provided by having a B.S. degree. (2) It gave credit for longevity in teaching by providing annual pay increments for each year of experience. (3) It solved the problem of administering the compensation for the increasing numbers of personnel in the school system; the salary schedule determined individual payments. The salary schedule was viewed as giving fair treatment to all personnel. Furthermore, it removed the determination of individual salary payments from the jurisdiction of school administrators whom many felt could not be trusted to make salary recommendations. (4) Initiation of the salary schedule halted the strong push for merit-pay programs in education, a practice that the NEA strongly opposed at the time.

Three Basic Models of Salary Schedules

Although competency-based pay is receiving more attention in organizations today, the single salary schedule continues to dominate methods for compensation allocations in school districts nationally.

The single salary schedule concept established the administrative procedure for the compensation of employees in education. The most common number of increment steps in the early salary schedules was 16. The highest degree level was that of the B.S. degree. The 16 small salary increments served two primary purposes. First, the annual increases were thought to help retain teachers in the school system and also provide some level of satisfaction as teachers gained additional experience. Second, the longitudinal increases for degree attainment encouraged the continuous preparation and growth of teaching personnel. Nondegreed teachers, who could earn nine college credit hours during the summer months, could earn 135 credits over a 15-year time period or enough credits for a B.S. degree.

Today, the single salary schedule still dominates the structure for employment compensation. However, many variations have been developed and implemented over the years. Commonly, the number of salary increments for the B.S. degree has been reduced and the number of longitudinal degree or college credit hour increments has increased substantially. One benefit of the single salary schedule is in the ability to automate various modifications in the existing salary that take place when the base salary is changed. Through the use of a computer spreadsheet with each cell in the schedule referenced to another cell, changing the present base salary can reveal the changed values for all other cells containing calculated values (Thompson et al., 1994).

The reduction of increment steps at lower degree levels encourages employees to continue their formal degree work. The increase in the longitudinal increments, such as additional salary increases for a B.S. + 15 credit hours or an M.A. + 30 hours, provides motivation for continuous staff development.

Table 11.3 is a basic model of a compound index salary schedule. The compound salary schedule is based on the assumption that experience increments are the same for each year of teaching. Sample salary calculations for each of the three salary schedules—single, simple index, and compound index—are illustrated in the following section.

Problem #1: Single Salary Schedule. Assume the following information. The base salary (B) for the salary schedule is $36,000, the experience increment (E) is $500, the preparation increment (P) is $600, the teacher has five years' experience, and he or she has an M.A. degree + 30 hours.

$$\text{Salary calculation: salary} = B + 5E + 2P$$
$$S = \$36,000 + 5\ (\$500) + 2\ (\$600)$$
$$S = \$36,000 + \$2,500 + \$1,200$$
$$S = \$39,700$$

Table 11.3   Compound Index Salary Schedule Model

Years of Experience	Preparation Level		
	B.A.	M.A.	M.A. + 30
0	(B) Base Salary	$B \times P''$	$B \times P''^2$
1	$B \times E''^1$	$B \times E''^1 \times P''$	$B \times E''^1 \times P''^2$
2	$B \times E''^2$	$B \times E''^2 \times P''$	$B \times E''^2 \times P''^2$
3	$B \times E''^3$	$B \times E''^3 \times P''$	$B \times E''^3 \times P''^2$
4	$B \times E''^4$	$B \times E''^4 \times P''$	$B \times E''^4 \times P''^2$
5	$B \times E''^5$	$B \times E''^5 \times P''$	$B \times E''^5 \times P''^2$
6	$B \times E''^6$	$B \times E''^6 \times P''$	$B \times E''^6 \times P''^2$
7	$B \times E''^7$	$B \times E''^7 \times P''$	$B \times E''^7 \times P''^2$
8	$B \times E''^8$	$B \times E''^8 \times P''$	$B \times E''^8 \times P''^2$
9	$B \times E''^9$	$B \times E''^9 \times P''$	$B \times E''^9 \times P''^2$
10	$B \times E''^{10}$	$B \times E''^{10} \times P''$	$B \times E''^{10} \times P''^2$
11	$B \times E''^{11}$	$B \times E''^{11} \times P''$	$B \times E''^{11} \times P''^2$
12	$B \times E''^{12}$	$B \times E''^{12} \times P''$	$B \times E''^{12} \times P''^2$

Problem #2: Simple Index Salary Schedule. Assume the following information. The base salary (B′) for the salary schedule is $36,000, the experience increment (E′) is 5%, the preparation increment (P′) is 6%, the teacher has five years' experience, and he or she has an M.A. degree + 30 hours.

Note that the prime notation (e.g., B′, 5E′, etc.) is for the purposes of distinguishing the formulas only; it is not a mathematical calculation. The calculation is additive.

$$\text{Salary calculation: salary} = B' + 5E' + 2P'$$
$$S = \$36{,}000 + 5\,(0.05)(\$36{,}000) + 2\,(0.06)(\$36{,}000)$$
$$S = \$36{,}000 + \$9{,}000 + \$4{,}320 = \$49{,}320$$

Problem #3: Compound Index Salary Schedule. Assume the following information. The base salary (B″) for the salary schedule is $36,000, the experience increment (E″) is 5%, the preparation increment (P″) is 6%, the teacher has five years' experience, and he or she has an M.A. + 30 hours. Note that the salary calculation is multiplicative and the base salary is only included once in the calculation. Also note that the calculation requires that 5% and 6% be written as 1.05 and 1.06 in order to avoid reducing the salary result.

$$\text{Salary calculation: salary} = B'' \times E''^5 \times P''^2$$
$$S = \$36{,}000 \times (1.05)^5 \times (1.06)^2$$
$$S = \$36{,}000 \times 1.28 \times 1.12$$
$$S = \$51{,}609$$

As we previously noted, index salary schedules are increasing in some school districts. Slight increases in the percents used for the experience increment and the preparation increment can increase the salary payments substantially. Thus, even in instances when the base salary remains constant, if the experience increment and the preparation increment are increased, substantial salary increases result.

Summary

School finance and teacher compensation have been leading topics in education historically. School superintendents, teachers, and school boards consistently name school finance as the number one problem facing them. Although expenditures for education in the United States have increased significantly over the years, available funds never seem to meet the needs expressed by school personnel and others in the work of educating the nation's children and youth.

Education is indeed a big business. In 2006–2007, the public schools in the U.S. enrolled 48,940,000 students; the expenditures for education in the same year totaled $451.7 billion. Early public education was supported primarily by local initiatives, but now, state financial support leads the way. In view of the increased involvement of the state and federal government in education, competition for the public's tax dollar has become fierce. Education must compete with other institutions and programs that depend on state and federal tax dollars for their operations.

The chapter presented a comprehensive compensation operations model that included activities related to the adoption of school policies for the compensation process, the establishment of position structures within the school system, the determination of economic values for the various position clusters in the system, the establishment of administrative procedures for implementing the compensation process, and controlling the compensation process.

The history of the salary schedule and its status as the primary method of allocating employee salaries were discussed in detail. Salary levels for teachers and other school employees are now determined primarily on the basis of time in the position (work experience) and the preparation level (degrees and credit hours) attained. Although some forms of merit pay, competency-based performance pay, and other incentive compensation methods have been introduced in recent years, merit pay as such has not become a primary compensation method in America's schools. This is not to say that merit pay is a new entity in education. On the contrary, merit pay was introduced in education in the early decades of the 20th century.

This chapter gave consideration to other aspects of the compensation process including collateral benefits, both mandated and voluntary, for personnel. The factors that tend to determine the compensation levels for educational personnel were identified and discussed in detail.

Note

1.   No specific data were available for the years after 1994. The 1960–1994 statistics were used because of their availability and because they served to demonstrate the constancy of teachers' salaries for a period of 34 years.

Discussion Questions

1. Class Exercise and Discussion—Resolved: "If education is to realize improved salary levels, performance-based compensation programs must be implemented." Class members should be divided for a debate activity. One group assumes a "pro" position and the other a "con" position on the foregoing resolution.

2. Consider the aspects of the single salary schedule as practiced in education today. What are the positive aspects of the single salary schedule? What are the negative aspects?

3. Review the salary statistics for the various occupations as discussed in the chapter. Can a fair and objective comparison be made between the salaries of teachers and those of other occupations? Why or why not?

4. Discuss the question, "Who should pay for public education?" Provide a rationale for your answers.

Case Studies

CASE 11.1

WHOSE SIDE ARE YOU ON?

MEMO

TO: Ted Henson, Principal, Wymore Middle School

FROM: Rita Romero and Jim Miller, Faculty Members

RE: Teachers' concern regarding the merit pay decision

Date: March 4

Several of us on the faculty have been discussing what we view as a detrimental move for the Wymore School District teaching personnel. That is, the talks that apparently have been taking place on merit pay for teachers.

Although our information is sketchy, we understand that the Wymore Administrative Council is considering the recommendation of merit pay for teachers. If this is true, we are wondering why the teachers have not been involved in the discussions on this matter.

Specifically, members of our school's faculty are interested in learning your personal views on the matter of merit pay. Would you support such a movement for our school district? If so, why?

It seems that some immediate attention should be given to this matter since the concern of faculty members is increasing daily. As you most likely know, merit pay in education has not been well received and likely would not be acceptable to the teaching personnel in the Wymore district.

Rita and I both serve on the Teachers' Association Welfare Committee. Since your opinion would weigh heavily on any decision about merit pay for Wymore, we would like to know how you stand on this issue. Please let us hear from you.

Sincerely,

Rita Romero, Grade 8 Teacher

Jim Miller, Fine Arts

Questions

1. Assume the role of Principal Henson. Discuss the actions that you would take in responding to the teachers who sent the memorandum to you. If you would respond by memo, draft the actual memo that you would send. If you would plan to meet personally with the two teachers or would plan to address the school faculty as a whole, set forth the specific comments or position that you would take on this matter.

2. Should the principal be neutral on such matters? Why or why not?

CASE 11.2

WHAT ARE YOUR PRIORITIES?

Wymore Middle School

Wymore, Lafayette

Memorandum

To: All Principals

From: Pat Herr, Superintendent

RE: Allocation of Funds

As you know, the school board has asked us to take steps to revise our teacher evaluation instrument and process to correspond with the new incentive pay program. As stated in the school board's recently adopted policy, "School principals will recommend teachers for incentive pay above regular contract for meritorious performance based on criteria to be determined by the school superintendent and others on the administrative staff."

I plan to present a plan to the school board at its next monthly meeting and would like to include effective classroom instruction as one of the priorities for determining incentive pay. I want to consolidate the information and ideas I receive from all school principals into the final plan.

Therefore, I would like your ideas on this matter as soon as possible. In short, what do you believe should be the priority criteria for determining incentive payments for the teaching staff? The performance evaluation instrument that we develop will have to include the performance criteria that are ultimately determined.

Thank you.

(Continued)

(Continued)

Question

1. Assume the role of one of the principals in the Wymore School District. Draft your response to Superintendent Herr. Be specific in your response by identifying several performance criteria that you recommend, prioritize the recommendations, and provide a brief rationale for your selections.

CASE 11.3

ON THE SPOT

As director of the district's human resources unit, you were asked to attend a study session of the Wymore School Board centering on teacher salaries for the ensuing year. At one point in the meeting, Amare Adams, a school board member, commented: "At the recent meeting of the State School Boards Association, one presenter mentioned something about single salary schedules and index salary schedules. What is the difference between these kinds of salary schedules?" All eyes turn to you for an expected response.

Assume the role of the human resources director in this case. How would you respond to the question posed by the school board member? (Note: If you know the answer to the question, take a few minutes to describe your answer in writing. If you do not have the answer at hand, review the section on salary schedules and then draft your brief response.)

References

American Association of School Administrators. (2000). *The study of the American school superintendency.* Arlington, VA: Author.

American Council on Education. (1999). Facts in brief: Birth rates impact current and future enrollment trends. *Higher Education and National Affairs, 48*(17), 1–18.

Balfour, G.A. (1974). More evidence that unions do not achieve higher salaries for teachers. *Journal of Collective Negotiations in the Public Sector, 3,* 289–303.

Bartlett, L. D., Etscheidt, S., & Weisenstein, G. R. (2007). *Special education law and practice in public schools* (2nd ed.). Upper Saddle River, NJ: Merrill Prentice Hall.

Bloss, J. M. (1882). *Thirtieth report of the superintendent of public instruction of the state of Indiana to the Governor.* Indianapolis: State of Indiana.

Bradley, A. (1999, March 10). States' uneven teacher supply complicates staffing of schools. *Education Week,* p. 1.

Bureau of Labor Statistics. (2005). *Occupational employee statistics: National occupational employment wage statistics.* Washington, DC: U.S. Department of Labor.

Denison, E. (1983). The interruption of productivity growth in the United States. *The Economic Journal, 93,* 56–77.

Feistritzer, C. E. (1984). *The making of a teacher: A report on teacher education and certification.* Washington, DC: National Center for Educational Statistics.

Freeman, R. B. (1981). The effect of unionism on fringe benefits. *Industrial and Labor Review, 34,* 489–509.

Gallagher, D. G. (1978). De facto bargaining and teacher salary levels. *Journal of Collective Negotiations in the Public Sector, 7,* 245–254.

Gold, Y. (1996). Beginning teacher support: Attrition, mentoring, and induction. In J. Sikula (Ed.), *Handbook of research on teacher education* (2nd ed., pp. 548–594). New York: Macmillan.

Kahn, L. (1979). Unionism and relative wages: Direct and indirect effects. *Industrial and Labor Relations Review, 32,* 520–532.

Kasper, H. (1970). The effects of collective bargaining on public school teachers' salaries. *Industrial and Labor Relations Review, 24,* 57–72.

Koeppel, G. (2005, September 21). Kyrene honing performance pay. *Arizona Republic,* p. 1.

Moore, G. A. (1975). *Some salary effects of professional negotiations in public schools—The Nebraska experience.* Lincoln: University of Nebraska.

National Center for Educational Statistics. (1994). *Digest of education statistics.* Washington, DC: Author.

National Center for Educational Statistics. (2007). *Projections of education statistics to 2015.* Washington, DC: Author.

Norton, M. S. (2004). *The human resources director in Arizona: A research study.* Tempe: Arizona State University, Division of Educational Leadership & Policy Studies.

Public Service Research Council. (1978). *Report on states with and without bargaining legislation.* Vienna, VA: Author.

Thompson, D. C., Wood, R. C., & Honeyman, D. S. (1994). *Fiscal leadership for schools: Concepts and practices.* White Plains, NY: Longman.

U.S. Department of Education. (2004). *Elementary and secondary education: Subpart III—William F. Goodling Even Start Family Literacy Programs.* Retrieved December 19, 2007, from http://www.ed.gov/policy/elsec/leg/esea02/pg6.html#sec1231

Wynn, R. (1981). The relationship of collective bargaining and teacher salaries, 1960–1980. *Phi Delta Kappan, 63,* 237–242.

Yasin, S. (1998). Teacher shortages across the nation: Implications for SCDEs. *Briefs, 19*(12), 1.

Zuelke, D. C., & Frohreich, L. E. (1977). The impact of comprehensive collective negotiations on teachers' salaries: Some evidence from Wisconsin. *Journal of Collective Negotiations in the Public Sector, 6*(1), 81–88.

CHAPTER 12

The Classified Staff

An Important Human Resources
Administration Responsibility

Learning Objectives

After reading this chapter, you will be able to

- Identify the common support personnel groups within school districts.
- Understand the procedures for classifying support personnel job families in school districts.
- Understand the recruitment and selection processes for employing support personnel.
- Identify the common preemployment requirements for classified personnel.
- Set forth the procedures for assessing the training needs of classified personnel.
- Set forth the procedures for providing development programs, on-the-job training, and certification programs for classified personnel.
- Describe various accountability measures implemented for assessing and controlling classified personnel development activities.
- Design various personnel forms for use in the writing of job descriptions, performance evaluations, and professional development plans of classified personnel.

Classified personnel or support staff are those employees who commonly do not perform instructional responsibilities directly related to the instructional programs of the school system, but do perform support services of paramount importance to the accomplishment of educational goals. Classified employees commonly are those employees whose jobs are assigned to titles, job families or categories, and pay grades. Classified personnel generally do not require professional educator's licenses issued by state boards of education, but there are exceptions, depending on state regulations and school board policies. For example, some school districts require that teacher aides, who work in Title I programs, have a two-year degree, 60 hours of college credit, or pass a special proficiency examination.

Support personnel typically constitute 30%–50% of the total school district staff. In a large school system of 24,000 students and a pupil-teacher ratio of 20 to 1, for example, a teaching staff of 1,200 would be required. In addition, 360–600 classified staff personnel commonly would be employed in the school system. Although the classified personnel job titles among school systems do differ because of school size, board policy, and school system needs, job titles typically extend far beyond those of secretary, custodian, food service worker, and bus driver.

Typical job families include (1) para-educators, (2) office professionals, (3) professional and technical, (4) transportation, (5) maintenance, (6) custodial staff, (7) food service, (8) grounds and warehouse services, and (9) classified supervisors, managers, and administrators.

Classified personnel positions under the job family of food services in the West Contra Costa Unified School District in California, for example, include food production lead worker, food service aide, food service clerk, food service operation assistant, food transport driver, school lunch cashier, school lunch worker 1, and school lunch worker 2. In all, the school district lists more than 200 different classified job titles. The Mesa Public School District in Mesa, Arizona, one of the state's largest school districts, lists 268 classified job titles. Table 12.1 reveals a sample of the classified job tiles of the West Contra Costa Unified School District. Because of the several different positions within position families, as illustrated in Table 12.1 and by the foregoing food services example, job analysis, job grading, and job assessment serve important purposes in classifying and compensating classified personnel.

Classified personnel carry a wide variety of job titles, and their employment status varies as well. For example, a **full-time regular classified employee (FTR)** typically is hired for nine to 12 months and the employee is expected to work a minimum number of hours during the time period. The full-time equivalent (FTE) of such a position is considered to be at least 0.53 FTE. These employees are eligible for the school district benefits available to all regular classified employees, subject to the qualifying conditions set forth for each benefit, prorated to a 1.00 FTE.

Part-time regular employees (PTR) are employed in positions created to last less than the minimum hours required of a FTR employee over a 12-month period. Such an employee is not generally eligible for benefits. A **temporary classified employee** is employed in a job created to last for a short time period, generally less than nine months regardless of the hours worked per week. This employee is not generally eligible for benefits. Other types of employees include the **casual employee** and, in some situations, the student employee.

A casual employee position is created to meet a specific operational need in the school district for a limited number of hours during a nine to 12-month period. In some instances, and under specific legal regulations set forth by law and school board policies, students are hired to work in the school cafeteria, provide clerical service or do other low-skill tasks in support of a particular school or school district service.

Table 12.1 Selected List of Classified Job Titles and Salary Range Codes

Job Family	Job Title	Salary Code Range
Business/Accounting	Account Clerk 1	45
	Account Clerk 2	49
	Accountant II	63
	Accounting Technician	63
	Budget Control Clerk	53
	Buyer	57
	Senior Buyer	61
	Payroll Clerk	53
	Payroll Technician	59
	Payroll Technician Assistant	51
	Senior Account Clerk	53
Maintenance and Facilities Upkeep/Repair	Carpenter	66
	Head Custodian	55
	Custodian	48
	Electrician	66
	Electrician Assistant	61
	Electronics Repair Worker	66
	Field Maintenance Grounds Keeper	57
	Furniture Repair Worker	66
	Gardener	56
	Gardener Tree Topper	61
	Locksmith	66
	Locksmith Assistant	61
	Office Machines Repair	63
	Painter	66
	Painter Assistant	61
	Heating and Ventilation Mechanic	66
	Journeyman Plumber	66
	Roofer	66
	Sheet Metal Worker	66
Clerk/Secretarial	Typist Clerk 1	43
	Typist Clerk 2	47
	Textbook Clerk	47
	Attendance Clerk	47
	Bindery Service Clerk	43

Job Family	Job Title	Salary Code Range
	Library Resource Secretary	55
	Operations Secretary	61
	Staff Secretary	57
	Staff Secretary Bilingual	58
	Secretary Administrative Services	61
	Pre-School Secretary	55
Instructional/Service Aide and Assistant	Child Care Aide	44
	Counselor Aide	44
	Instructional Aide	39
	Instructional Aide, Adult Education	43
	Instructional Assistant, Special Education	43
	Instructional Materials Specialist	55
	Interpreter for the Deaf	55
	Library Assistant	56
	Parent Aide	39
	Parent Liaison Worker	53
	Pre-school Community Worker	52
	After School Group Leader	46
	Chief Attendance Technician	59
	Bilingual Paraprofessional	48

SOURCE: Adapted from the West Contra Costa School District Classified Personnel Salary Schedule, Richmond, CA (2006).

The Director of Classified Personnel

It is a common practice that classified personnel be supervised by a different director than certificated personnel. In other instances, the supervision of classified personnel is a responsibility assumed by an administrator who supervises both certificated and classified employees. How the classified personnel unit is organized depends on the nature of the school district, its size, resources, and practices relative to outsourcing certain services (e.g., food services, facility maintenance, transportation, business operations, etc.). Figure 12.1 is an example of a job description for a Director of Classified Personnel. Note specifically the essential duties prescribed for the position, which include recruitment and selection,

Primary Responsibilities

Provides administrative and technical support and direction for all operations related to support personnel including Maintenance, Operations, Grounds, Transportation, Food Services, Printing Services, Secretarial Services, and Facilities. Supervises, directs and evaluates classified personnel. Oversees and participates in human resources activities including employment, compensation, record keeping, policy development and interpretation, and performance management, Establishes departmental goals and expectations relative to goals achievement and employee performance.

Reports to: Superintendent of Schools

Supervises: Classified personnel and classified personnel department supervisors

Qualifications: **Skills and Commitment**

1. Education and/or experience equivalent to a Bachelor's degree; a minimum of two (2) years of work experience in the area of classified personnel which includes supervisory experience.

2. Knowledge of the principles, practices and techniques of human resources administration.

3. Knowledge and leadership skill as related to supervisory principles and practices including human motivation, human relations and organizational development.

4. Knowledge and skill in the processes of recruitment selection, assignment, evaluation and development of personnel.

5. Knowledge of federal, state and local laws, policies and regulations relative to classified personnel administration.

6. Ability to establish a positive climate and positive effective working relations within the classified personnel unit.

7. Ability to gather and analyze data and information relative to the operation and effectiveness of the classified personnel unit.

8. Ability to establish an effective system of communication within the classified personnel unit.

9. Understands and implements the concept of total quality management, including business practices and program budgeting, and has commitment to: The school district's vision and mission, fostering the professional growth of all personnel, establishing effective working relationships with other units and personnel in the school district, and valuing the worth and dignity of all personnel.

Responsibilities:

1. Recommends, implements and administers district policies and regulations related to the assigned areas of classified personnel, Recruits, selects, trains, supervises, directs and evaluates classified staff.

2. Recommends salary placement and approves all transfers. Coordinates the Workman's Compensation program and manages assigned efficient and economical use of funds, manpower, materials, facilities and time.

3. Oversees and recommends the issuance of contracts and requests for salary advancement according to district policy. Supervises the appropriate certification and certification renewal notification as required. Administers salary programs and work schedules for certificated employees. Directs the evaluation process for all classified personnel.

4. Administers job analyses and develops job descriptions for all job titles within the classified personnel unit.

5. Reviews recommendations from job family supervisors relative to renewal and/or non-renewal of job continuation.

6. Develops short and long-range goals and objectives for each classified personnel department. Establishes an evaluation program for assessing the performance of each department relative to the accomplishment of stated goals and objectives.

7. Reports to the school superintendent and to the Board of Education regarding the condition of facilities and grounds and the status of building maintenance.

8. Provides assistance in contract negotiations for the building of new school facilities and other capital projects that are outsourced by the school district.

9. Reviews and analyzes reports, legislation, court cases and related personnel actions and makes recommendations to the school superintendent regarding appropriate actions that might be required.

Contract/Compensation:

Contract: 12 months Administrative

Compensation: Determined annually by the Board of Education

Figure 12.1   Director of Human Resources Support Services

---

personnel assignment, wage and salary scheduling, classified policies and regulations development, employee induction, collective bargaining with classified personnel, counseling, salary and incentive administration, and several other human resources processes and activities discussed throughout this text.

The Classified Job Analysis

The importance of the job analysis and its content was discussed previously in Chapter 4. The following discussion considers the application of the job analysis as it applies to position grading and ultimate assessment of compensation levels. Figure 12.2 is an example of an ability-level **classification value system**. For each entry on the form, several knowledge, skill, or responsibility levels are identified. A point value is assigned to each level. Total point values are determined in some appropriate manner so that the position being analyzed can be classified objectively. That is, the director of classified personnel and others in the human resources unit determine the appropriate point level by consensus or the director and other experienced workers in the specific classification collaborate relative to an appropriate point value for each entry.

Job Grading and Salary Ranges

The analysis of each position within a certain job family is graded and classified (e.g., clerk 1, clerk 2, secretary, administrative secretary, etc.). The analysis is completed for each job family (e.g., food services, maintenance, facilities, business, etc.). Then, compensation levels are ascribed for each of the classification levels. As discussed in Chapter 11, prevailing wages, collective bargaining, supply and demand, and other factors determine the general compensation levels assigned to each job.

	Point Level
Skill and Knowledge *The employee:*	
a. requires no specialized skill/knowledge.	1
b. requires specialized skill/knowledge common to all in the broad category under consideration (e.g., clerical, secretarial, administrative secretary).	2
c. requires a specialized skill/knowledge not common to all in the category being considered.	3
d. requires a high level of skill/knowledge not common to all in the category being considered.	4
Environmental Factors *The environment:*	
a. is usually calm with little or no stress; has few or no interruptions; has little or no emotional pressure.	1
b. exhibits normal stress; has normal interruptions; has normal emotional pressure.	2
c. has abnormal stress, interruptions, and/or emotional pressures.	3
d. exhibits considerable stress; has considerable interruptions; exhibits a considerable amount of emotional pressures.	4
Level of Responsibility *The employee:*	
a. is responsible only for the satisfactory performance of his or her own work which is assigned to him or her by another and which is routine.	1
b. is responsible only for the performance of his or her own work; however, he or she must do some work independently and complete tasks upon his or her own initiative.	2
c. is responsible for the direction of an office and/or unit of employees and makes decisions which are in line with adopted system policy.	3
d. is responsible for the function of a subdivision or division of the system and helps develop policy which aids in making decisions that aid the division and system in goal achievement.	4
Level of Supervision *The employee:*	
a. supervises no one.	1
b. supervises from one to three employees all of whom do the same type of work.	2
c. supervises three or more employees, all doing the same type of work, or fewer than five employees doing diversified work.	3
d. supervises persons doing diversified work in a unit or division or supervises a major division of the school district.	4

	Point Level
Human Relations *The position:*	
a. requires contact with a limited number of employees and has little or no contact with students or the public.	1
b. requires contact with many types of school or school system employees.	2
c. requires contact with many types of school or school system employees, including students.	3
d. requires considerable contact with all types of school and school system employees, including students, parents, and the general public.	4
Level of Education *The position:*	
a. requires an elementary and/or secondary school education.	1
b. requires post-high school education and training, including an Associate Degree or equivalent.	2
c. requires a B.S. degree with specialization in some fields related to the job category.	3
d. requires graduate work beyond a B.S. degree in a specialized field.	4
Level of Experience *The position:*	
a. requires little or no experience; will be mastered within a short period of time on the job.	1
b. requires some experience in a like position requiring similar knowledge and skills.	2
c. requires one or two years of related experience in a similar position in or outside the school system.	3
d. requires related and/or similar experience of sufficient depth to establish levels of work and assign responsibilities for positions subordinate to his/her own.	4
Availability *For this position the supply is:*	
a. plentiful	1
b. adequate	2
c. limited	3
d. limited or almost non-existent	4
Total Points	
Average Points	

Figure 12.2   Ability-Level Classification Value System

Table 12.2 Classified Salary Schedule Relative to Range Category (Hourly wages)

Range	1	2	3	4	5	8	10	13
Range 8	7.53	7.73	7.91	8.09	8.31	8.93	9.37	10.17
Range 10	7.91	8.09	8.31	8.53	8.72	9.37	9.85	10.68
Range 12	8.31	8.53	8.72	9.14	9.37	10.09	10.87	11.51
Range 14	8.72	8.93	9.14	9.37	9.62	10.33	10.87	11.81
Range 16	9.14	9.37	9.62	9.85	10.09	11.41	11.96	12.67
Range 18	9.62	9.85	10.09	10.33	10.59	11.69	12.59	13.32
Range 20	10.09	10.33	10.59	10.87	11.14	12.24	13.23	14.32
Range 22	10.59	10.87	11.14	11.41	11.95	12.87	13.52	14.68
Range 24	11.14	11.41	11.69	11.96	12.24	13.23	13.87	15.05
Range 26	11.69	11.98	12.24	12.59	12.89	13.87	14.57	15.82
Range 28	12.24	12.59	12.89	13.23	13.53	14.57	15.28	16.62
Range 30	12.89	13.23	13.53	13.87	14.20	15.28	16.04	17.42
Range 32	13.53	13.87	14.20	14.57	14.92	16.04	16.84	18.27
Range 34	14.20	14.57	14.92	15.28	15.66	16.84	17.68	19.19
Range 36	14.92	15.28	15.66	16.04	16.42	17.68	18.56	20.18
Range 38	15.66	16.04	16.42	16.84	17.24	18.56	19.51	21.20
Range 40	16.42	16.84	17.24	17.68	18.11	19.51	20.46	22.22
Range 42	17.24	17.68	18.11	18.56	19.02	20.46	21.47	23.34
Range 45	18.56	19.07	19.53	20.01	20.50	22.08	23.19	25.21

SOURCE: Adapted from the Classified Employee Salary Schedule, 2006–2007. Mesa Public School District, Mesa, Arizona.

As shown in the classified salary schedule in Table 12.2, hourly pay ranges are ascribed for each job title for Ranges 8 through 45. Range 8 jobs require lower knowledge, skill, and responsibility levels than jobs at higher range levels. A part-time custodian, for example, is placed in Range 8, whereas an audio-visual clerk is placed in Range 17, and a senior accountant is placed in Range 40.

As shown in Table 12.2, a new employee with no experience would begin in a Range 8 job on Step 1 and receive a wage of $7.53 per hour. In the fifth year of employment, the employee would receive $8.31 an hour. Similarly, a senior accountant, a Range 40 job, after 13 years of experience would receive $22.22 an hour.

One of the primary problems in the classified personnel area is that of employee turnover. Statistical reports of classified employee turnover vary widely among school districts. However, empirical evidence suggests that classified employee turnover is approximately 25% each year. As would be expected, the turnover rate of part-time classified employees is typically twice that of full-time classified workers. The leading reason for turnover, according to administrators of classified personnel units, is low salary. Consider the salary of a Journey Plumber in the school district that pays Range 38 employees $21.20 per hour after 13 years of experience. Then assume, the plumber works 8 hours each day and is paid for 52 weeks each year by the school district (see Table 12.2). The annual salary of this classified employee would be $27,560. Using the lowest average salary for Journey Plumbers in private business of $42,000–$48,000 annually (Bureau of Labor Statistics, 2005), private plumbers earn $14,440 more than would be earned in the school district. It is clear that salary influences both the ability to recruit and to retain quality classified personnel in school districts.

Recruitment of Classified Personnel

Sources for recruiting classified personnel include newspaper advertisements; Web sites; job hotlines; job boards; job fairs; employment services, such as departments of economic security and workforce development; movie theater advertisements; family, friend, or employee referrals; and walk-ins. Commonly, classified personnel are contract employees or **noncontract** employees. Contract employees generally are for one year only and have no reasonable expectation of continued employment beyond the term of the written contract. Noncontract employees are employed on the basis of school system's need and may be terminated at any time by a decision of the school district or the employee for any reason not contrary to law.

For many reasons, contemporary applications for classified employment are comprehensive and detailed. For example, most application forms include personal information regarding previous dismissals from employment, gaps in employment, and previous job disciplinary actions, as well as information regarding criminal activity.

Figure 12.3 is an example of a classified employment application that includes the following information categories: (1) personal information regarding name, address, citizenship, languages spoken, work authorization, and availability; (2) personal data regarding driving status and licensing; (3) work experience including position and salary; (4) education; (5) professional experience and training, circumstances of work, and reasons for leaving other positions; (6) personal references; (7) Selective Service registration; (8) criminal activity report; and (9) conviction information. Note that if the individual is considered for an offer of employment, the employee is informed that a background investigation will be conducted to determine his or her eligibility, qualifications, and suitability for employment. In addition, the application points out that all applicants who are offered employment will be fingerprinted at the time of hire.

Minimum qualifications for each position must be listed in the vacancy announcement, and it should be made clear that individuals should not apply for a position if minimum requirements are not met. The information provided to potential applicants should clearly indicate procedures for the selection process, including the requirements for interviewing, testing, and verifying qualifications.

Wymore Public Schools

Human Resources Department

Madison, Lafayette

Application for Classified Employment

Classified contract positions are for one year only. The employment of any non-contract employee is on an "at will" basis meaning that the employment relationship may be terminated at any time by either the employee or the district for any reason not prohibited by law.

Last Name	First	Middle

Address_____

             Street   City   State   Zip

Home Phone _____   Cell Phone _____

Social Security # _____

Date of Application: _____

Are you legally eligible to work in the United States?   Yes ___   No ___

Do you presently have work authorization that would allow
you to begin work at Wymore Public Schools immediately?   Yes ___   No ___

Position(s) desired (indicate one or more):   a. _____

                                           b. _____

                                           c. _____

Full-time _____   Part-time _____   Temporary _____

Note:

The Wymore School District is an equal opportunity organization and does not discriminate on the basis of age, race, color, religion, sex, marital status, handicap/disability, or national origin. The Wymore School District maintains a drug-free workplace and reserves the right to test employees for use of alcohol or drugs whenever reasonable suspicion exists that the employee has violated the drug-free workplace policy.

As required by state law, applicants are advised that smoking is prohibited in Wymore Public Schools facilities and vehicles.

Any applicant with a disability who needs reasonable accommodation in any step of the application process should notify a representative in the Human Resources Classified Unit.

Personal Data

1. Name _____ Date_____

2. Do you have a driver's license?   Yes ___   No ___

3. Do you have a commercial driver's license?   Yes ___   No ___

              If yes, what class?_____

Work Experience

4. List current and/or previous employers. Put most recent experience first. The district will contact your current employer for a reference.

Applicants for positions in Transportation must list all employers for the two years prior to the date of this application. Transportation applicants must also sign a "Consent for Information from Previous Employers on Alcohol and Controlled Substance Testing" form.

Dates	Employer's Name	Phone	Position	Reason for Leaving

5. Are you a former Wymore employee? Yes ___ No ___

Education

6. List schools attended and special training received.
   Circle highest year completed: High School 7 8 9 10 11 12
   College 13 14 15 16

	Name	Location	Dates Attended	Year Graduated	Diploma	GED	None
High school							
College or technical school							

Indicate college hours completed or degree awarded _____

Professional Experience or Training

7. Describe additional training not listed above (i.e., trade school, business school, technical institute, etc.)

8. Have you ever been dismissed or non-renewed from a position? If yes, explain:

(Continued)

(Continued)

9. Have you ever resigned from a position rather than being dismissed? If yes, explain:

10. Have you ever been disciplined for any reason which resulted in suspension from work (with or without pay)? If yes, explain:

Personal References

Give the names and complete addresses of at least three references who are familiar with your personality, character, and work habits (please do not list relatives as references).

Name	Years Known	Official Position	Phone

Criminal Activity Report

Because of the responsibility the Wymore School District has to its school children and community, the following information is needed from all applicants. Failure to disclose all information may mean disqualification from consideration for employment.

1. Name _____

2. Other names used _____

3. Have you ever been convicted of any misdemeanor or offense other than traffic violations?   Yes ___ No ___

4. Have you ever been convicted of a DUI offense?   Yes ___ No ___

5. Have you ever been convicted of a felony?   Yes ___ No ___

6. Have you even been convicted of a sex or drug offense?   Yes ___ No ___

7. Have you ever been convicted of a dangerous crime against children?   Yes ___ No ___

8. Have you ever been arrested for any offense which has not been resolved? Yes ___ No ___

Under penalty of criminal prosecution and dismissal, I hereby certify that the information presented in this application is true, accurate and complete. I understand and agree that misrepresentation or omission of relevant facts would be good cause for rejection of my application or, if I have been employed, for immediate termination of my employment.

_____   _____
Signature   Date

Figure 12.3   Application for Classified Employment

Appraising Candidates in Relation to the Selection Criteria

Figure 12.4 shows a qualifications form used as part of the recruitment process for prescreening purposes. A consent to conduct a background investigation and release waiver form is shown in Figure 12.5. Some school districts also require a consumer report of the applicant for the purposes of evaluating the employment, promotion, reassignment, or retention of the individual. In some cases, a Notice to Consumer Report is also required. Such reports frequently are limited to consumer information relative to criminal history.

Classified Employee Selection Process

The selection process for classified employees is quite similar to the selection process set forth in Chapter 5 for certified personnel. The steps in the selection process include (1) designing and organizing the selection process, (2) defining behavioral characteristics to be appraised, (3) compiling appropriate selection data, (4) appraising candidates in relation to the selection criteria, (5) preparing eligibility lists, (6) nominating the selected candidates for hiring, (7) contracting approval by the school board, and (8) assessing the selection results.

Designing and Organizing the Selection Process

As we stated in Chapter 5, an effective selection process is guided by a viable selection policy, specific goals and objectives, and strategic plans for the implementation of the process under the direction of qualified administrative leaders. The director of classified personnel most often directs the recruitment and screening program for classified personnel, working closely with school principals and other administrators in their selection and assignment. Although the central human resources department assumes the primary responsibility for recruiting and developing applicant pools for position needs, school principals and other supervisory personnel play a major role in the ultimate selection process.

Designing the selection process includes inventorying position needs, budgeting, designing application forms, assigning selection responsibilities, designing interview and testing instruments, and establishing target dates for each step of the selection process. Plans are made for identifying eligible candidates from the recruitment pool and conducting selection interviews.

Defining Behavior Characteristics to Be Appraised

Job descriptions are important statements relative to personnel selection. "The creation of position descriptions that set forth the responsibilities and qualifications needed by personnel in their respective roles is also an important planning task. A position description provides a clear statement of facts pertaining to the

---

Wymore School District

Qualifications

Date:_____

Name: _____ SS# _____

Current address or school location

_____ Phone: (   ) _____

_____ E-mail: _____

Position applying for: _____

Current WSD employee: No ____   Yes, Position _____

Former WSD employee: No ____   Yes, Dates _____

Current application on file: No ____   Yes, Date Submitted _____

In reference to the position that you are applying for, please provide the following information: Describe how your previous work experience has prepared you for this position:

Explain how previous jobs or work experience required you to perform similar job duties:

Describe the qualities or abilities you possess that will contribute positively to the Wymore Public Schools:

Tell about a work experience in which you used your personal initiative to achieve an important objective or to resolve an existing problem:

Figure 12.4   Screening Application Form for Classified Position

---

Wymore Public District

Consent to Conduct Background Investigation and Release Waiver

I. I, _____, have applied for employment with
        Print Name   Wymore Public Schools

II. I understand that in order for the District to determine my eligibility for employment, they will conduct a background investigation if I am considered for an offer of employment. The investigation may include asking my current and former employer about my education, training, experience, job performance, professional conduct and evaluations, as well as confirming my dates of employment, position(s) held, reason(s) for leaving, whether I would be eligible for rehire, reasons for not rehiring (if applicable) and similar information.
I hereby give my consent for any employer to release any information requested in connection with this background investigation. By my signature below, I hereby waive my right to review this reference, and I understand that the contents of this reference will not be available to me now, or at any future time.
A photocopy or facsimile ("fax") copy of this form that shows my signature shall be considered as valid as an original.

Dated this _____ day of _____, 20_____

Applicant's signature: _____

Figure 12.5   Consent to Conduct Background Investigation and Release Waiver Form

SOURCE: Reprinted with permission from the Mesa Public Schools, Mesa, AZ.

duty specifications of the position, the context in which the position takes place, and the personal qualifications required by the employee" (Norton & Kelly, 1997, p. 99).

Figure 12.6 shows an example of a job description for a school bus driver. As previously noted, the job description evolves from the job analysis, which sets forth the specific content of the job, necessary qualifications as related to knowledge and skill requirements, and other factors related to the environment in which the job takes place. Note the job responsibilities set forth in the job description in Figure 12.6. The bus driver is responsible for transporting students to and from school, and must also inspect the bus for safety purposes, keep the bus clean inside and out, maintain proper fluid levels, keep written log records, maintain order of students, and prepare bus repair orders. Student safety is emphasized. Yet, the National Association of School Resource Officers (2004) reported that approximately 67% of school-based police officers stated that school bus drivers and transportation personnel, in the last three years, have not had training on security measures and related topics. Each responsibility set forth in the job description for bus drivers identifies important criteria that must be considered in the selection of transportation personnel.

An effective selection process requires an impartial method of ranking candidates who have been identified through the development of an eligibility list of qualified candidates. **Application screening** is a procedure used to qualify applicants for admission to the formal candidacy process. Applications are screened to determine if applicants do indeed meet the minimal qualifications required (e.g., experience, education, training, references, etc.) for the position in question.

Wymore School District

Job Title: Bus Driver   Job Code 2407   Pay Range 38

Job Description

Definition: Operates a school bus over designated routes within an established time schedule; transports students to and from school and on special event trips in a safe manner.

Essential Functions: (Essential functions, as defined under the Americans with Disabilities Act, may include any of the following tasks, knowledge, skills, and other characteristics. This list is illustrative only, and is not a comprehensive listing of all functions and tasks performed by incumbents of this class.)

Tasks: Transports students to and from school and on special events trips in a safe manner. Performs daily inspection of bus and prepares reports concerning maintenance needs; ensures bus is in good running condition by checking brakes, lights and inside vehicle. Checks and monitors the condition of the bus before and after the shift, ensures it is safe to operate; keeps bus clean inside and out; sweeps and mops floors, cleans windows to ensure good visibility. Inspects and maintains fluid levels; prepares repair orders, keeps written records and log sheets. Interacts with students, maintaining good student/driver relationships; maintains order and ensures safety and comfort of students; completes misconduct forms if necessary; performs other related duties as assigned.

Knowledge, Skills and Other Characteristics:

Knowledge of safe driving practices and techniques, and motor laws.

Knowledge of basic first aid procedures and methods.

Knowledge of safety and maintenance requirements of bus and other student transportation equipment.

Skill in developing and maintaining effective working relationships.

Skill in both verbal and written communication.

Ability to operate a passenger bus.

Ability to obtain a Class B Commercial Driver's License (CDL), Passenger endorsement, and DPS Bus Driver Certification.

Ability to pass physical and obtain CPR certification.

Working Conditions:

Dangerous machinery and/or hazardous chemicals.

Exposure to extreme weather conditions.

Physical Effort:

Lifts, moves, or carries up to 80 pounds.

Drives District vehicle.

Bends, stoops, climbs, enters and exits bus by use of steps.

Minimum Qualifications:

Education and/or experience equivalent to a high school diploma or GED are required. Approximate valid class driver's license and education and/or experience equivalent to four years of driving experience. Must be minimally 21 years of age with a good driving record.

Reporting Relationships:

A. Reports to: Director of Transportation

B. Supervises: N/A

Figure 12.6   Job Description for Bus Driver

SOURCE: Adapted from Tempe Elementary School District, School District #3, Transporter of Learners Drivers, Tempe, Arizona.

Depending on the number of applicants who meet the minimal job requirements, applicants are reviewed again to determine those with the highest qualifications. Those with the highest qualification scores are then approved for additional testing, selection interviews, or other evaluations that lead to final selections.

Written examinations, interviews, performance tests, simulation exercises, and other evaluation activities are used in the selection process. A written examination tests specific technical knowledge related to the specific job. Selection interviews evaluate the candidate's knowledge and skills and other qualifying factors for the position. Performance tests provide opportunities for the candidate to demonstrate a skill or knowledge essential to the job. Simulation exercises often place the candidate in the specific job role and ask him or her to role-play a response to a given case situation that has occurred on the job.

After all data have been collected and evaluated, a system of reaching consensus is implemented and employee eligibility lists are prepared.

Employee Eligibility Lists and Nominating Candidates for Hiring

Employee eligibility lists consist of the consensus ratings of the selection team. Recommendations for employees to be hired are listed, generally in rank order, depending on the number of openings. In most cases, recommendations of the classified nominees for hire are presented formally to the school board for approval. However, some school districts present to the school board only those classified personnel who are considered regular staff employees and are on contract. Part-time personnel in some school districts need only the approval of the assistant superintendent or director of human resources.

Letters of acceptance are sent to those candidates who have been selected and, as fits the case, are notified that they must show authorization to work in the United States, obtain the required immunizations, complete a formal background check, and be fingerprinted. For some positions, the person hired might be required to pass a medical examination and drug screening.

Letters of nonacceptance should be sent to those candidates who had acceptable qualifications but were not selected for a particular position. In such cases, they are notified that their application will be kept on file for a specified period of time. Most all authorities agree that unqualified applicants and those applicants whom the school system does not intend to hire should be notified as well.

A probationary time period is commonly required of all classified personnel. Once the probationary period has been completed satisfactorily, the employee is considered a permanent employee typically on a one-year basis.

Assessing the Classified Employee Selection Process

The accountability of the selection process can be assessed in several ways. A first measure is the number of applicants selected from the recruitment pool that eventually became active candidates in the selection process. A second measure is the number of candidates who became finalists and were ultimately selected. Over time, how many of the selected candidates were effective employees and remained in the school system after the first year? How many selected candidates remained in the school system after three years of service? Such measurements serve to determine the extent to which selection goals were achieved.

Classified employee effectiveness is inextricably tied to the school district's training program and performance evaluation activities. The following section discusses these dimensions of the classified employee program.

The Classified Employee Training Program

Employee development and training are of paramount importance in classified employee programs. The purposes of these programs are to (1) encourage and support needs-based and career development opportunities for all classified personnel, (2) improve the level of job production and skill performance of the individual employee, (3) provide an opportunity for the supervisor and classified employee to develop mutual performance goals, and (4) develop a plan of assistance for correcting the deficiencies within the school system generally and the deficiencies of individual employees. Development and training experiences for classified personnel are job embedded; they center on knowledge and skills that the employee can implement to improve job performance. As Cunningham and Cordeiro (2000) noted, "Successful organizations promote and demand continuous professional development throughout one's career" (p. 300).

> A needs analysis should precede the planning and execution of a training program. . . . A needs analysis typically has a threefold focus: organizational analysis (analyzing the needs of the entire school district now and in the future), operational analysis (analyzing the needs of a specific group of jobs or positions), and individual analysis (analyzing the needs of the specific individual. (Lunenburg & Ornstein, 2004, p. 593)

Requirements for personnel development and training credits vary among school systems, but a common practice is to require a specified number of training credits for moving up the salary scale and becoming eligible for reclassification in a particular job family. Some examples of the variety of training classes commonly offered are basic development classes, those required of all classified employees in the job family; elective development classes, those classes that can be taken to fulfill job requirements; and advanced development classes, those classes geared for credit toward reclassification. Figure 12.7 shows an example of food and nutrition services training program classes. Note that basic classes center on information and skills that every classified employee in the job family should possess: (1) communication skills, (2) conflict management skills, (3) food safety and sanitation, (4) safety in the workplace, (5) building healthy school meals, and others.

Staff Development

Food and Nutrition Services Training Program Classes

Number Title

Basic Classes

Communication Skills
Conflict Management #1
Food Safety and Nutrition #1
Food Services Cashiering
Child Nutrition and Dietary Needs
Safety in the Workplace
Computrition Food Management System
Building Healthy School Meals #1

Advanced Classes

Teambuilding #1
Listening Skills
Food Services Operational Management
Marketing: Menu Planning
Supervisory and Training Skills
Central Kitchen Equipment
Communication Styles: Men and Women in the Workplace #1

Elective Classes

PC Windows Introduction #1
PC Windows Introduction #2
Managing PC Files and Folders #1
Excel Introduction for Classified Staff #1
Word Introduction for Classified Staff #1
Cultural Competence and School Issues
Workplace Courtesy and Communication
Stress Busters: How to Remove Your Stress-Builders
English and Grammar
Writing for Results
Multicultural Awareness and Sensitivity
Facilitation Skills and Change Strategies
Leadership Skills
Time Management, Goal Setting, and Organization
Valuing Diversity
Personal Safety
Working and Living in a Multicultural World
Nutrition and Exercise for a Healthy Life

Figure 12.7 Food and Nutrition Services Training Program Classes

SOURCE: Staff Development, Food and Nutrition Services Training Program Classes, Kent School District, Kent, Washington. Copyright by Kent School District, 1995–2001 (http://www.kent.k12 .wa.us/sd/sd_emp.training?vPROG=FNS).

Elective classes focus on topics of personal interest and needs such as the development of computer skills, cultural competence, valuing diversity, English and grammar, time management, and others. Advanced classes emphasize leadership and management topics such as teambuilding, listening skills, supervisory and training skills, marketing and menu planning, and food service operation management.

Figure 12.8 is an example of a professional growth and development plan for classified personnel. The growth plan begins at the outset of the school year with an identified performance area related to the specific job. Goals are determined, and desired outcomes are specified. Initial planning includes the identification of activities that will be pursued toward the accomplishment of stated goals. The employee's evaluator completes a midterm progress check and determines performance adjustments with the employee as needed. The final evaluation report includes evidence of the completion of the growth plan and the extent to which the goal targets were met.

The National Staff Development and Training Association (NSDTA), established in 1983, is an affiliate of the American Public Human Services Association, headquartered in Washington, D.C. The NSDTA is a leader in providing staff development activities for both certificated and classified personnel. The mission of the NSDTA is to build professional and organizational capacity in the human services through national networking of membership and sharing ideas and resources on organizational development and training. The association sponsors an annual

---

Wymore School District
Professional Growth/Development Plan

Name: _____   Job Title: _____

Worksite: _____   Date: _____

Performance Area:

(See Evaluation Job Requirements)
☐ Standard 1   ☐ Growth Plan
☐ Standard 2   ☐ Corrective Action Plan
☐ Standard 3   Standard Number: _____
☐ Standard 4

Performance Criteria

Present Stage of Development

☐ Awareness   ☐ Preparation   ☐ Implementation   ☐ Refinement

I.   Professional Goal Addressed:

II. Personal Goal:

III. Objective, Desired Outcome:

☐ To acquire & apply knowledge, understanding, skills, & abilities to achieve stated goal.
☐ Other, explain:

IV. Activities for Implementation:

V. Documentation of Progress

Explain:

☐ Reflections   _____

_____

☐ Product   _____

_____

☐ Demonstration   _____

_____

VI. Mid-term Check
Evaluator's Comments:
VII. Evidence of Project Completion:

VIII. The Target Was:

Achieved   ____

Continued   ____

Revised   ____

IX. Evaluator's Comments:

X. Employee's Comments:

Signature of Employee: _____   Date: _____

Signature of Evaluator: _____   Date: _____

Figure 12.8   Professional Growth Plan

SOURCE: Adapted from Anderson County Professional Growth/Development Plan. Anderson County Public School District, Lawrenceburg, Kentucky.

institute that features a variety of workshops, seminars, and other network opportunities. Activities of the association include consultation and technical assistance, professional networking, guidelines for training evaluation, and other development and training programs.

Most states have organized personnel associations that provide ongoing staff development programs for classified personnel. As is the case with certificated personnel, classified personnel commonly have organized associations with the local district and the state that provide special services for members. One objective of these associations is to improve the salary and working conditions for classified personnel. Another important service is to provide staff development and training programs for members.

Employee Evaluation

As Young (2008) noted, "Appraisal of performance relative to assigned duties, in general, has never been more popular and has never received more attention in the popular press than it has in recent times. . . . Stakeholders involved with the educational process no longer expect some means of performance appraisal be performed for employees but demand that the assessment of all educational employees be conducted on a continuing basis" (pp. 207–208).

Performance evaluations typically are completed annually, but may be completed more frequently if the first evaluation indicates the need for a follow-up evaluation. Classified evaluation procedures are as follows:

1. The evaluator meets individually or with groups of classified employees to explain the evaluation process and to answer questions about the evaluation purposes, procedures, and responsibilities of the employee and evaluator in the process. In most cases, copies of the evaluation instruments are distributed in advance of the scheduled evaluation. (Note: Figure 12.9 is an example of a classified human resources evaluation summary form. The evaluation form lists 23 factors relative to the performance of all classified personnel. It also lists additional factors for secretarial or clerical and supervisory personnel. The report includes a summary of job strengths and performance deficiencies, a record of goals or improvement programs, an overall evaluation score, and recommendations for reemployment.)

2. A formative evaluation observation is scheduled and implemented. Formative procedures serve to identify both the employee's strengths and improvement areas. In most cases, the employee's immediate supervisor serves as the evaluator. "Although employee performance appraisal is commonly delegated to the central human resources office and to local school principals, the school district's executive leader is held accountable ultimately for the appraisal of all employees, including teachers, administrators, and classified personnel" (Norton, 2005, p. 206). Following the employee evaluation, a follow-up conference is scheduled with the employee to review the evaluation results. If the employee's overall work performance has proven to be "unsatisfactory," the evaluator either informs the employee that he or she will not be recommended for reemployment or schedules a follow-up

(Text continues on page 398)

Classified Personnel Evaluation

Employee's Name: _____

Worksite/School _____ Date: _____

Supervisor: _____

Position: ☐ Bus Driver   ☐ Custodian   ☐ Para Educator
  ☐ Clerical Personnel   ☐ Food Service Employee
  ☐ Maintenance Personnel   ☐ Transportation
  ☐ Facilities/Grounds   ☐ Other: _____

I. Job Knowledge

Evaluate skill/knowledge of the information, procedures, materials, equipment, techniques, etc. required for the position.

1. Has necessary skills to complete tasks required in current job.

	Self	*Evaluator*
Met		
Needs Growth		
Does Not Meet		

2. Understands and completes all records, reports and documents required.

	Self	*Evaluator*
Met		
Needs Growth		
Does Not Meet		

3. Has working knowledge of equipment, material that is necessary for completion of assigned work.

	Self	*Evaluator*
Met		
Needs Growth		
Does Not Meet		

(Continued)

(Continued)

4. Attends appropriate in-service programs.

	Self	Evaluator
Met		
Needs Growth		
Does Not Meet		

5. Adheres to Board policies.

	Self	Evaluator
Met		
Needs Growth		
Does Not Meet		

Overall Rating: ☐ Self   ☐ Evaluator

II. Productivity and Quality of Work

1. Completes the required tasks.

	Self	Evaluator
Met		
Needs Growth		
Does Not Meet		

2. Completes tasks accurately.

	Self	Evaluator
Met		
Needs Growth		
Does Not Meet		

3. Completes tasks in a timely manner.

	Self	Evaluator
Met		
Needs Growth		
Does Not Meet		

4. Uses proper safety measures when working.

	Self	Evaluator
Met		
Needs Growth		
Does Not Meet		

5. Takes initiative in seeking and completing tasks without supervision.

	Self	Evaluator
Met		
Needs Growth		
Does Not Meet		

Overall Rating: ☐ Self   ☐ Evaluator

III. Responsibility, Dependability, and Attendance

1. Uses discretion with confidential or privileged information.

	Self	Evaluator
Met		
Needs Growth		
Does Not Meet		

2. Follows directions.

	Self	Evaluator
Met		
Needs Growth		
Does Not Meet		

3. Uses good judgment in performing responsibilities.

	Self	Evaluator
Met		
Needs Growth		
Does Not Meet		

(Continued)

(Continued)

4. Organizes work responsibilities and sets priorities.

	Self	*Evaluator*
Met		
Needs Growth		
Does Not Meet		

5. Has a good attendance record.

	Self	*Evaluator*
Met		
Needs Growth		
Does Not Meet		

6. Reports to work punctually.

	Self	*Evaluator*
Met		
Needs Growth		
Does Not Meet		

Overall Rating: ☐ Self ☐ Evaluator

IV. Interpersonal Relations

1. Deals with students and parents in a positive, constructive manner.

	Self	*Evaluator*
Met		
Needs Growth		
Does Not Meet		

2. Deals with colleagues and supervisors in a positive, constructive manner.

	Self	*Evaluator*
Met		
Needs Growth		
Does Not Meet		

3. Cooperates in accomplishing school and District goals and objectives.

	Self	*Evaluator*
Met		
Needs Growth		
Does Not Meet		

4. Handles problems in a constructive and fair manner.

	Self	*Evaluator*
Met		
Needs Growth		
Does Not Meet		

5. Works through line/staff relationships when addressing problems.

	Self	*Evaluator*
Met		
Needs Growth		
Does Not Meet		

6. Offers differing opinions in a constructive and helpful manner.

	Self	*Evaluator*
Met		
Needs Growth		
Does Not Meet		

7. Demonstrates effective written and verbal communication.

	Self	*Evaluator*
Met		
Needs Growth		
Does Not Meet		

Overall Rating: ☐ Self   ☐ Evaluator

Comments of the Evaluator:

Figure 12.9   Classified Personnel Evaluation Form

SOURCE: Adapted from Anderson County Public School District, Classified Personnel Evaluation, Lawrenceburg, Kentucky.

summative evaluation. For others, both the strengths of the employee's work performance and the deficiencies are discussed. The employee receives a written notice of the categories marked "not satisfactory" or "requires improvement." The evaluator and employee discuss growth plans for the purposes of setting improvement goals and identifying the responsibilities of the employee and school district supervisory personnel in the improvement process. Both the employee and the evaluator sign the evaluation form.

3. Following the performance evaluation, an employee implements a professional growth and development plan. The plan centers on extending and implementing the employee's strengths and providing opportunities for continuous improvement of work performance (see Figure 12.9).

Controlling Classified Employee Development Results

Accountability of the development process calls for both soft and hard data reports. Soft accountability measures include statistics on the number of employees engaged in continuing development programs and feedback from employees concerning their assessments of the value of development activities.

How many classified employees were reclassified into higher level jobs in a job family as a result of their completion of specified development program requirements and passing required tests? Did accidents or injuries related to bus transportation decrease after bus drivers completed the driving and safety programs provided by the school district? Did the required inspections of the food service units in schools throughout the school system reveal a significant decrease in sanitation and safety violations after food service workers completed the basic classes provided in food safety and sanitation? Have the development programs in the job family of supervision and leadership resulted in the development of a qualified pool of candidates for classified personnel administrative positions? Specific answers to the foregoing questions provide hard data accountability measures.

Consider the following scenario:

A school district is having difficulty hiring qualified supervisory personnel for various classified job families. The director of classified personnel and appropriate others in the school system agree to establish a "grow your own" development program for supervisory leadership. Procedures for initiating the development program begin by reviewing the performance evaluations of present classified personnel. Twenty-five of the employees with the highest performance ratings are invited to participate in the supervisory leadership development program.

Courses related to leadership, team building, conflict management, discipline strategies, communication skills, multicultural awareness, decision making, human motivation, business practices, human relations, and others are programmed for

22 of the employees who accepted the invitation to participate in the program. Twenty of the 22 employees successfully complete the required leadership program and become candidates in the recruitment pool for supervisory positions, a 90.9% completion record. Within three years, 10 of the 20 employees in the recruitment pool are selected for supervisory positions in the various classified personnel areas, a 50% placement record.

Such hard data would provide quality support for the accountability of the supervisory development program activities. The school superintendent and school board would be quite likely to support the continuation of the leadership development activities.

Summary

Classified personnel constitute between one-third and one-half of the total staff of most school districts, and therefore it is of paramount importance that effective human resources policies and practices are operative. Human resources practices for classified personnel parallel those of certificated personnel in many ways. The primary human resources processes of planning, recruitment, selection, induction, assignment, development, collective bargaining, compensation, stability, evaluation, organizational climate, and protection are all part of the responsibilities of human resources administrators who work with classified personnel.

Based on the school board policies and administrative regulations, the classified personnel unit implements job analysis procedures that lead to the development of job families and ultimately to position classifications. Each position classification is graded and assigned a salary range according to the level of responsibility, education, and skill required. On the basis of such indicators as job classification, supply and demand, ability to pay, economic factors, prevailing wages, and other job factors, each job is valued and salary schedules are assigned.

Professional and personal growth and development are important for continuous program improvement regarding effective human performance in an environment of continuous change. The adage that "classified support systems will succeed as classified personnel progress" directly reflects the concept of development programs for classified personnel. Opportunities for personal development are provided through formal classes, on-the-job experiences, technical institutes, job-related conferences and workshops, and other employee involvement activities.

Performance appraisals, both formative and summative, are important activities in all classified personnel programs. Evaluation programs serve several purposes including (1) the determination of the extent to which the classified employee is meeting the standards set forth for the job in question, (2) the identification of "growth needs" of the employee for the purpose of developing and implementing the personal growth plan, (3) providing an opportunity for the employee and the supervisor to review the job requirements and the possible changes that should be made to improve the employee's ability to succeed, and (4) to provide objective data and information for making decisions relative to the retention or nonretention of employees.

Discussion Questions

1. The chapter emphasized the importance of job analyses procedures in the administration of the classified personnel. Review the purposes of a job analysis and then describe how a job analysis relates to the human resources processes of recruitment, selection, assignment, compensation, and staff development.

2. Consider the human resources processes of recruitment, selection, staff development, and performance evaluation as they relate to the administration of classified personnel. Describe at least two specific measures that would provide hard data for demonstrating the accountability of two or more of the processes listed.

3. Statistics reveal that 20%–30% of the classified personnel are leaving the school district after the first year of service. What steps might you take to reduce the percent of turnover of classified personnel in the school district?

4. Review the job description of the classified personnel director set forth in Figure 12.2 and also the primary responsibilities required in the role as discussed in the chapter. Develop a 30-credit-hour preparation program that you believe would be appropriate for a person who assumes this position. What courses and experiences would be appropriate in such a preparation program?

5. (Class Discussion) The topic of classified personnel often is "slighted" in textbooks and discussions of human resources in education. Discuss Chapter 12 in terms of new knowledge. What considerations relative to the work of classified personnel were new to you? What aspects of the work of classified personnel were of most interest to you as a present or potential school administrator?

6. Low salary for classified personnel was a topic of discussion in the chapter. Are the reasons for low salary levels for classified personnel the same or different than those for certificated personnel? Give reasons for your contentions on this matter.

7. Consider the topic of the performance evaluation process for classified personnel. Discuss the accountability measures that could be implemented to assess the outcomes of the process.

8. Employee development and training are activities of paramount importance to the classified personnel program. First, consider the role of the director of classified personnel in development and training activities for employees. Then, consider the roles of classified employee supervisors and school principals in this regard. What steps are needed to ensure an effectively organized and implemented development and training program in a school district?

Case Studies

CASE 12.1

A CHANCE TO PARTICIPATE
WYMORE SCHOOL DISTRICT
OFFICE OF THE SUPERINTENDENT

To: Pat Ramirez, Director of Classified Personnel

From: O. K. Erickson, Supt.

Re: Annual Performance Evaluation

Date: April 20

In follow-up of the School Board's action last month, I am requesting the input of each central office administrator concerning the content, makeup, and procedures for their annual performance evaluation. Thus, I need your ideas relative to the following matters:

1. What specific performance areas should be involved in your annual evaluation? Who else might be included in helping determine these areas and related evaluation criteria?

2. Who, specifically, should be involved in evaluating your performance in the areas that you recommend?

3. What other ideas, beliefs, or suggestions might you have regarding the evaluation of your specific job?

4. What is important and why?

Please give this request priority attention since it is getting late and we must act soon on this matter. Thanks.

Questions

1. Assume the role of Pat Ramirez and write your response to the school superintendent's request.

2. In answering Question 3, give special attention to specific ideas relative to the methods of evaluation that you believe should be implemented.

CASE 12.2

A CASE OF MERITORIOUS PERFORMANCE
WYMORE CLASSIFIED PERSONNEL ASSOCIATION

MEMO

To: Pat Ramirez, Director of Classified Personnel

From: Nancy Evans and Raul Romero, Co-Chairs, Wymore Classified Personnel Association

(Continued)

(Continued)

Re: Employees' Concern Regarding Merit Pay Movement

Date: April 14

We are representing the Wymore Classified Personnel Association in presenting our concern about what we believe is a detrimental move for Wymore classified personnel. That is, talks that apparently have been taking place on performance-based pay for classified personnel. Although nothing has been voted on to date, we have yet to be brought into the picture for our views on this matter.

It seems that some immediate attention should be given to this matter since the classified personnel concern is increasing daily. As you know, merit pay in school systems has not been well received and likely would not work here for classified personnel either.

Since your opinion would weigh heavily on any decision about performance-based pay for Wymore, we would like to know how you stand on this issue. What are your personal views on the matter of performance pay? Are you supporting such a movement for our school system, and why?

Since our Association meets in early May, we hope to be able to report your response to the Association members at the next meeting.

Nancy Evans, Cafeteria Manager, Wymore High School

Raul Romero, Journey Plumber, Wymore School District

Questions

1. Assume the role of Pat Ramirez and write your response to the memo received from Nancy Evans and Raul Romero. If you choose another method of responding to the request such as a face-to-face meeting with the association representatives, set forth in writing the nature of your remarks, questions, recommendations, and so forth that you will discuss at the meeting.

2. What are the implications of the contents of the memo received from the Association representatives relative to supervisor and administration and employee communication, employee participation, collective bargaining, and other aspects of employee relationships?

References

Bureau of Labor Statistics (2005). *Occupational employee statistics: National occupational employment wage statistics.* Washington, DC: U.S. Department of Labor.

Cunningham, W. G., & Cordeiro, P. A. (2000). *Educational administration: A problem-based approach.* Needham Heights, MA: Allyn & Bacon.

Lunenburg, F. C., & Ornstein, A. C. (2004). *Educational administration: Concepts and practices* (4th ed.). Belmont, CA: Wadsworth Thompson Learning.

National Association of School Resource Officers. (2004). *School safety left behind? 2004 national SRO survey results: Law enforcement survey.* St. Paul, MN: Author.

Norton, M. S. (2005). *Executive leadership for effective administration.* Boston: Allyn & Bacon.

Norton, M. S., & Kelly, L. K. (1997). *Resource allocation: Managing money and people.* Larchmont, NY: Eye on Education.

Vaughn, R. H. (1999). *The professional trainer: A human resources development guide.* Euclid, OH: Williams Publishing.

Young, I. P. (2008). *The human resource function in educational administration* (9th ed.). Upper Saddle River, NJ: Pearson Merrill Prentice Hall.

Glossary

Ability to pay principle   A tax principle based on the notion that persons with higher status are presumed more able to pay and should be made to contribute more than persons of lesser status.

Absenteeism   Failure on the part of the employee to be at work as scheduled regardless of the reason for such absence.

Accountability   The act of showing proof of results in relation to a specific intervention or program activity.

Administrative regulation   A precise statement that answers the question of how a policy is to be implemented.

Advanced development classes   Training classes geared for credit toward the reclassification of personnel.

Advanced preparation   A form of preparation whose goals and objectives are related to anticipated future needs of the school system or needs brought about by changes in workplace assignments.

Andragogy   The art and science of helping adults learn.

Application screening   The procedure used to qualify applicants for admission to the formal candidacy process.

Authoritarian leadership   An autocratic, controlling type of leadership.

Bargaining agent   The employee organization designated as the official representative of all employees in the bargaining unit.

Bargaining contract or master agreement   Ratified document that specifies the terms of the negotiated agreement.

Bargaining unit   The group of employees certified as the appropriate unit for collective negotiations. The unit is the one to which the negotiated contract agreement applies.

Basic development classes   Training classes commonly required of all classified employees of a specific job family.

Behavior costing   A term used for attaching economic estimates to the consequences of employee behaviors.

Behavior interview   An interview method whereby the candidate is assessed on specific criteria related to his or her subject-matter area or grade level of instruction.

Behavior modification   A concept that suggests that providing positive feedback of job results will reinforce that behavior. Undesirable behavior is dealt with by merely ignoring it, whereby the behavior is made extinct.

Boomerang hiring   The rehiring of former teachers in an effort to help resolve a teacher shortage.

Bulwarism   A term used to describe the placement of a proposal on the bargaining table accompanied by a statement to the effect that it is this or nothing.

Bylaws   Procedures by which the school board governs itself. They apply to the internal operations of the school board.

Capacity of equilibrium A term credited to Chester Barnard for satisfying both the system productivity and the need dispositions of personnel in the system.

Career ladder   An alternate compensation method that centers on the promotion of professional development of employees.

Casual employee   An employee hired to meet a specific operation need in the school district for a limited number of hours during a 9- to 12-month period.

Challenge   A task or summons that is surrounded with difficulties, but one that is often provocative and stimulating.

Choice   As used in relation to student attendance in school, choice contends that students have the right to attend any school in the school district of their choice and should not be restricted to attending a school only within a designed boundary. The choice argument extends to attending private schools with state support as well.

Classification value system   A rating system used for classified personnel that places a value on various jobs according to such factors as knowledge and skills required, responsibility levels, and related requirements of the job.

Classified personnel or support staff   Employees who commonly do not perform responsibilities directly related to the instructional program, but do perform support services of paramount importance to the accomplishment of educational goals. The term "noncertificated staff" is also used to identify classified personnel.

Clinical supervision cycle   The several steps involved in clinical supervision involving the teacher or employee and an immediate supervisor. Step one is the development of a cooperative relationship between the teacher and the supervisor.

Closed climate   A school climate characterized by low staff morale, limited and inadequate communication, and limited socialization.

Closed shop   A requirement that an employee must be a member of the employees' representative union in order to be hired in the organization.

Closed system   A system that does not have appropriate relations with its environment. The system is focused exclusively on its internal environment.

Coaching   The art of counseling professionals or clients within a full range of backgrounds.

Coactive power   In Mary Parker Follett's conception, coactive power is power with instead of power over; it includes such activities as coordination, cooperation, and integrative decision-making methods.

Coercive control   In Mary Parker Follett's conception, coercive control is autocratic management methods, which she called the curse of the universe.

Cohort survival method   A method for forecasting future population or student enrollment figures based on certain assumptions about longitudinal statistics relative to birth rates, death rates, student migration, grade retention, and other population data.

Collaborating   Using all possible resources in order to achieve the best results relative to a plan, activity, or decision.

Collateral or fringe benefits   Benefits provided to employees that do not require additional time or effort; nonmonetary compensation.

Collective bargaining   The process whereby matters of employee relations are determined mutually by representatives of employee groups and their employer, within the limits of law or mutual agreement.

Competencies   Abilities needed to accomplish a task at a satisfactory level of performance.

Conflict   An antagonistic state or action as exemplified by divergent ideas and interests of individuals or groups.

Contract and noncontract employees   Classified contract employees generally are for one year only and have no reasonable expectation of continued employment beyond the term of the written contract. That is, the employee's contract must be approved on an annual basis. Noncontract employees are employed on the basis of a school system's need and may be terminated at any time by the decision of the school district for any reason not contrary to law.

Community of interest   Employees who share common employment interests and concerns, who desire to be in the same bargaining unit, and who have similar working conditions.

Compensation policy   A statement adopted by the board of education that sets forth the goals and objectives that direct the compensation process for the school district. It provides the guidelines for what the compensation process is to accomplish.

Competency-based compensation plan   A compensation plan based on the accomplishment of goals that are agreed on mutually by the administrator and the immediate supervisor.

Contract agreement   A ratified document that specifies the terms of the negotiated agreement between the school board and the employees' association.

Contractual rights   Employee rights that are based on the law of contracts.

Cooperating   The positive and mutual involvement of individuals relative to a plan, activity, or decision.

Cost of benefits (COB)   School district expenses related to the provisions for employee collateral or fringe benefits

Cost of living adjustment (COLA)   An increment in salary related to changes in the existing economic conditions of the community.

Critical theory   An era of thought that challenges traditional assumptions about the administration of organizations and leadership behaviors. It questions the values on which many of the prevailing assumptions about gender, power relations, and other relationships that influence follower behavior are based.

Culture   The set of important assumptions, beliefs, values, and attitudes that members of the school or school system share.

Democratic leadership   A cooperative, empowering type of leadership viewed as the humanistic approach to people management.

Designing   The creation of plans of action directed toward specific goals.

Disengaged climate   A climate in which relationship behaviors among personnel are negative. Teachers are not engaged in the tasks, and teacher behaviors are exemplified by divisiveness, intolerance, and noncommitment.

Disengagement   A teacher's tendency not to be "with it." Disengaged teachers are going through the motions but are not in gear with respect to the tasks at hand.

Distributive bargaining   Modeled after the bargaining process used mainly in the private sector. It is designed to realize maximum gain through use of authority, power, sanctions, or withdrawal of services.

Diversity   Characteristics that make people different from one another. Includes such characteristics as race, gender, age, ethnicity, education, and physical attributes.

Due process   A procedure that includes the notification of charges, a hearing on such charges, and the right to respond to the charges.

Effectiveness   Characteristics relative to the structural dimension of an organization. It is the extent to which the observed behavior of the worker is congruent with the expectations of the organization.

Efficiency   The extent to which the worker's behavior is congruent with the employee's need dispositions.

Efficiency dimension   A term coined by Chester Barnard to describe the behaviors of a social system that foster group maintenance, mutual trust, respect, positive relationships, and personal friendships.

Elective development classes   Training classes taken to fulfill specific job requirements.

Employee right   The ability to engage in conduct that is protected by law or social sanction, free from interference by another party.

Engaged climate   A climate in which attention to tasks is high and the faculty is professionally responsive despite the principal's restrictive behaviors.

Environmental scan   An examination of the school's internal and external environments that identifies the system's strengths and weaknesses and its opportunities and threats. Scanning information supports the development of a rationale for operating assumptions.

Exclusive representation   The certification of one particular employee organization to represent all employees in the bargaining unit.

Exit interview   An interview administered to an employee who has decided to leave the school system voluntarily.

Fact-finding   The process of selecting a neutral third party who serves as an investigator in studying all the facts and circumstances that surround an impasse and submits a recommendation that both parties take in advisement.

Feedback   Measures relative to performance and attitudinal changes.

Forecasting   An activity that centers on looking to the future and assessing probabilities.

Formal classroom observation   A classroom observation conducted by a qualified observer for the purpose of assessing a teacher's performance level on the basis of the criteria approved by the school and school district. It can be either a formative or a summative evaluation.

Formal organization   The units, departments, and staff members that make up the official organizational structure of the system.

Formative evaluation   An evaluation that has goals that center on professional development as opposed to employment continuation or dismissal.

Fractional bargaining   Exists when clusters of employees within the same organization decide to bargain separately rather than being a part of the system as a whole.

Full-time regular classified staff (FTR)   Employees who are typically hired for 9 to 12 months and are expected to work a minimum number of hours during the time period.

Gain sharing   Bonus payments given to a teaching staff based on the collective performance on such measures as gains in student achievement or other standards.

Goals   Statements that set forth the purposes of the school system.

Good-faith bargaining   Requirement that both parties enter the bargaining process with the intent to reach an agreement. Good-faith bargaining requires the school board team to respond to each of the employee team's proposals by indicating that it agrees, it will consider the proposal, it cannot agree, or the item is not negotiable.

Governing board policies   The comprehensive statements of decisions, principles, or courses of action that serve toward the achievement of stated goals. Policies answer the question of "what the school system is to do."

Grievance   A problem or complaint related to the master agreement. It represents a violation, or purported violation, of the bargaining contract.

Ground rules   The statements and agreements that govern the bargaining activities.

Group interview   An interview method that involves the entire search committee and others. It uses question and answer activities, demonstrations of teaching, simulation exercises, and other strategies to assess the candidate's qualifications.

Hard data measurements   Quantitative measurements used to assess the outcome of an activity or program. Results are based on statistical differences rather than personal emotions and opinions.

Hostile environment   A work situation in which individuals are harassed by intimidating conditions in the workplace. An employee might be subject to unwelcome touching or placed in situations where he or she must listen to stories of sexual exploitations of other employees.

Human capital   The human resources in the system viewed from the perspective of assets and investments.

Human resources   The people in the system and their knowledge, skills, and individual assets.

Human resources administration   The processes that are planned and implemented in the school system to establish an effective system of human resources and to foster an organizational climate that enhances the accomplishment of the system's educational mission, fosters the personal and professional objectives of the employees, and engages the support of the school community in which the school system is embedded.

Hygienes   Factors such as bad company policy and administration, poor methods of employee supervision, and poor employee-supervisor relations that Herzberg associated with job dissatisfaction.

Idiographic dimension   The human or people dimension of a social system, comprising individuals, their personalities, and their individual need dispositions.

Impasse   Situation in which two bargaining parties become steadfast in their positions on one or more agenda items and a stalemate takes place.

Incentive pay   A pay system that links closely to merit pay in that it is compensation allocated in addition to base salary for special work accomplishments or for meeting performance objectives.

Index salary schedule   A salary schedule that uses percent increments for experience and preparation. Simple index and compound index schedules exemplify such salary schedules.

Indicators of competency   Overt behaviors or products that illustrate one's capacity to perform competently.

Informal classroom observation   A classroom observation that often takes the form of a "walk-through" assessment. Although the informal observation generally is not related to job continuation or compensation decisions, feedback on the teacher's strengths and needs is provided.

Informal organization Groups or individual staff members in the system who influence policy, procedures, and decisions in the system but who are not in official line positions.

Inputs Environmental resources in the form of human, physical, financial, and knowledge bases; these are transformed by means of available tools and technology to produce outputs that represent products, services, and behaviors.

In-service training A planned program provided for improving the skills and knowledge of employees on the job.

Integrative bargaining A win-win approach to collective bargaining. Interest-based, problem-solving, consensus-based, and collaborative bargaining are integrative bargaining approaches.

Intimacy The teachers' enjoyment of friendly relationships with one another.

Issue A matter that is in dispute between two or more parties.

Job embedded training and development Training and development programs and experiences that center on the knowledge and skills that can be implemented by the employee to improve job performance.

Job-person-job fit A state of congruence between job demands and resources on the one hand and individual abilities and proclivities on the other.

Judgmental techniques Executive judgments, succession techniques, and vacancy analysis procedures used in the forecasting of employee demand.

Knowledge- and skill-based pay systems Compensation plans that compensate employees according to the knowledge and skill levels demonstrated on the job.

Knowledge management The processing of information readily from one unit to another.

Laissez-faire leadership A leadership style in which the leader assumes more of a functionary role and carries out the will of the governing board or the populace.

Last-best-offer arbitration A form of arbitration in which a neutral third party is called on to study the last best offers made by each of the two parties in the table negotiations. The arbitrator studies the facts related to both offers and selects one of the two best offers, which is binding on both parties.

Law A rule recognized by the nation or state as binding on its members.

Line administrators School personnel in the hierarchical line of authority in the system.

Long interview technique An interview method that uses a variety of strategies to determine the candidate's strengths and weaknesses. Candidates interact with committee members and appropriate others during the interview time period.

Markovian analysis A quantitative technique for forecasting employee transition within the system.

Mediation   A system in which a jointly appointed neutral third party serves as advisor for both parties in an attempt to conciliate, counsel, persuade, dissuade, and assist the negotiation parties so that they are able to reach an agreement.

Mentor   An experienced professional who guides the personal development of a less experienced individual through coaching and advising.

Merit pay   A one-time compensation for meritorious performance based on predetermined work standards.

Micromanagement   The practice of school boards spending too much time on matters of administrative procedure rather than on school policy.

Motivators   Factors such as job recognition, achievement, and doing meaningful work that Herzberg associated with job satisfaction.

Nomothetic dimension   The structural or normative dimension of a social system, comprising its institutions, related roles, and role expectations.

Open climate   A school climate in which staff members enjoy high morale, work well together, and have friendly relationships, but do not engage in high levels of socialization.

Open system   Any organization that is open to the environments in which it is a part. It views the system in terms of its interrelated parts and their relationship to one another and to the system as a whole.

Organizational analysis   The process of determining the congruence between the overall personality, goals, values, and interpersonal skills of the candidate and the climate or culture of the organization.

Organizational climate   The collective personality of a school or school system; the atmosphere that prevails in the system as characterized by the social and professional interactions of the people.

Outputs   Products, services, and human behaviors produced as a result of system inputs that are transformed through the use of available tools and system technology.

Participating   Cooperating with those affected by a plan for the best implementation of the results.

Partnership bargaining   A type of bargaining based on cooperative win-win bargaining approaches. One of the integrative bargaining strategies.

Part-time regular classified staff (PTR)   Employees in positions created to last fewer than the minimum hours required of FTR employees over a 12-month period. Such an employee usually is not eligible for benefits.

Pedagogy   The art and science of teaching children.

Performance-based pay   An alternative compensation program in which the employee receives bonus payments for meeting certain production or achievement goals agreed on by the employee and the administrative supervisor.

Performance interview   An interview method that uses participative or simulation activities to assess the candidate's qualifications. The candidate might be asked to demonstrate a teaching method for a particular grade or subject-matter area.

Performance management   A process that includes the implementation of performance objectives, determining methods for assessing performance results, developing employee growth plans, reviewing progress, coaching, and rewarding employees for positive contributions.

Person-job fit   A measure of how well an applicant is qualified for a position opening, used to narrow the applicant pool to those who are best qualified.

Person-organization fit   A measure of how well an applicant meets the requirements of the job and how well he or she fits the organization, used to further narrow the applicant pool.

Personnel   The human component of the system; persons who hold the various certificated and classified positions in the system.

Personnel recruitment   The human resources process that informs personnel of positions available and assesses their interest and qualifications.

Plan   A product of the planning process; it is a fixed entity that is time and place specific.

Planning   The comprehensive, continuous process characterized by flexibility and responsiveness to change.

Policy   A comprehensive statement of decisions, principles, or courses of action that serve toward the accomplishment of stated goals.

Position analysis   The process of examining the contents of a position and breaking it down into its primary tasks. It is a scientific, in-depth analysis of a position, its constituent parts, and surrounding conditions.

Position assessment   An activity that ascribes monetary values to each position.

Position description   It evolves from a position analysis and commonly includes the position title, major duties, evaluation responsibilities, coordination activities, position qualifications, and the supervision given and received.

Position/job grading   An activity that centers on the analysis of a position or family of positions and determining the range level for each specific position.

Potential analysis   An attempt to determine the extent to which an individual's present or future competencies will develop or could develop.

Power-based bargaining   A collective bargaining method that is based on an "all or nothing" concept.

Power rewards   Employee rewards that avoid excessive dependence on monetary factors.

Principle of definition   One of the principles of effective production set forth by Fayol and other contributors to the scientific management era. Every worker performs a single function.

Principle of organization   Another principle that evolved from the scientific management era. All duties and responsibilities should be clearly and completely defined in writing; this is the initial concept of personnel job descriptions.

Problem   A condition or situation needing a solution. A question raised for inquiry or consideration.

Program, process, and material determinants   Factors that serve to determine the route to school climate improvement such as individualized performance expectations, procedures and methods utilized relative to learner needs, and instructional resources available.

Quantitative techniques   Statistical procedures used for forecasting personnel supply and demand.

Quasi-distributive bargaining   A bargaining process based on a quid pro quo, give-and-take approach in which the utilization of power and bargaining strategy plays a major role.

Quasi-integrative bargaining   A bargaining process that involves a quid pro quo, give-and-take process of compromise and is similar to quasi-distributive approaches. It places emphasis on problem-solving solutions.

Quid pro quo harassment   Harassment that occurs when an employee or applicant is asked to provide sexual favors in order to obtain or to retain employment.

Rationality   A term related to Weber's concept of a bureaucracy and the belief that human judgment is unreliable because of biases and emotionalism. Thus, depersonalization within an organization is of primary importance for rationality.

Recorder   The bargaining member who maintains written information concerning strategy and positions of each bargaining team including facts, decisions, and events surrounding each bargaining session.

Recruitment   The human resources process that informs personnel of positions available and assesses their interest and qualifications.

Re-recruitment   Efforts extended by school leaders to retain key personnel in the school or school system.

Return on investment (ROI)   The gain or positive change realized from an investment of human and monetary expenditures.

Scientific management era   A historical time period in America that featured a structured management process. The manager was responsible for planning and supervising the work, and the employee was to carry out the plan under controlled procedures.

Selection   The human resources process of making decisions about the hiring of personnel.

Selectmen   The title given to the influential persons asked to supervise the operations of America's early schools. Selectmen were the forerunners of school board members in the United States.

Sexual harassment   Unwelcome sexual advances, requests or demands, and other verbal conduct of a sexual nature that explicitly or implicitly are suggested as a term or condition of an individual's employment.

Short interview technique   A method that is often conducted as a telephone interview. The applicant's professional qualifications serve as an opener for the interview.

Single salary schedule   The salary schedule that is based on a base salary, years of experience, and the level of preparation of the employee.

Skill   The ability needed to accomplish a task at a satisfactory level of performance.

Social system   Composed of a multitude of subsystems and characterized by a number of sociopsychological factors often referred to as the system's culture.

Soft measures   Personal or group attitudes and opinions regarding the usefulness of certain program change or employee development experience. Assessments are based on attitudes and perceptions of outcomes rather than statistical results.

Spillover   The influence of bargaining district results on nonbargaining school districts.

Spokesperson   The chief negotiator for the bargaining team, who serves as the team captain.

Staff administrator   An administrator who is not in the direct hierarchical line of authority; a support or advisory position.

Strategic human resources planning   A planning activity that focuses on the effective utilization of human resources and their contributions toward the accomplishment of educational goals.

Strategic plan   A long-term plan outlining actions needed to achieve planned results.

Strategic staffing   Another term for the re-recruitment of personnel that centers on the retention of quality employees.

Strategizing   The defining of activities to meet stated system goals.

Strategy   The process that serves to determine what decisions, programs, activities, and resources are necessary to achieve the desired results.

Staff administrator   An administrator who is not in the direct line of authority in the system and whose responsibilities are created primarily to serve and support the major line administrators.

Staff development   The HR process of providing opportunities for employees to improve their knowledge, skills, and performance in line with the goals and values of the organization and in relation to the interests and needs of the employee.

Statutory rights   Employee rights protected by specific laws enacted by government bodies.

Strike   An action that results in stoppage of work and services rendered by the employee group.

Structured interview   An interview that uses pre-prepared questions and specific "look-fors" to assess the candidate's personal qualities relative to such factors as empathy, focus, innovation, mission, and others.

Subject specialty interview   An interview that centers on the candidate's knowledge of the subject matter and experience for the teaching of a specific subject.

Summative evaluation   Performance evaluation goals are associated with making decisions about job continuation, tenure, placement on specific tracks of the school system's evaluation plan, and defining teacher compensation levels.

Superordinate goals   Goals that supersede the personal self-interests of the individual and of the company. A goal that expresses the best interests of all concerned.

Surface bargaining   A bargaining technique in which one party simply goes through the motions of bargaining without any real intention of reaching an agreement.

SWOT   The strengths and weaknesses of the internal environment and the opportunities and threats of the external environment as perceived through the administration of environmental scans.

Syntality   The collective behavior of a school; the school's personality.

Talent management   An effort to measure an employee's individual work performance against the specific objectives determined by the organization and the individual. Talent management also includes efforts to retain quality personnel and develop succession planning.

Task   The specific responsibilities, obligations, or requirements of a given role or administrative position.

Task management   A process that centers on the concept of efficiency by finding the best way to do a task at the lowest possible cost.

Teacher center   An enriched environment of resources, personal involvement, and peer communication. Conceptually constitutes a teaching resource bank.

Team observer   The bargaining member who listens and watches for clues and behaviors communicated by members of the other bargaining party.

Temporary classified employee   An employee in a job created to last for a short time, generally less than nine months regardless of the hours worked per week.

Tenure   The protection given to teachers from arbitrary action by school officials in the dismissal process.

Theory Y   A theory of human motivation and behavior set forth by Douglas McGregor that views humans as being intelligent, self-directed, committed, responsible, and creative.

Township institutes   Teacher training programs that taught lessons on the basics, globes, and "school keeping" prior to the establishment of the normal school in America.

Toxic climate   A climate in which workers have excessive workloads, tight deadlines, unreasonable supervisors, unrealistic targets for productivity, and unattainable goals.

Transformational process   The available tools and technology used to transform and produce system outputs in the form of products, services, and changed human behaviors.

Trend   A general movement of detectable change in thinking or practice. An emerging practice in the field that later may become a prevailing tendency.

Vacancy analysis   The technique of making judgments about the likely movements of employees in the short- and long-range future.

Virtual teams   Employee teams that use various technologies to work cooperatively when separated from one another.

Voluntary binding and compulsory binding arbitration   Procedures for resolving disagreements through the use of a neutral third party, whose decision is mandated for both parties.

Workplace flexibility   The implementation of flexible work arrangements, variations in hours, use of virtual means of communications, outsourcing, and other strategies for the purpose of establishing a better balance between work and the employee's personal life.

Index

AARP. *See* American Association of Retired Persons (AARP)

AASA. *See* American Association of School Administrators (AASA)

AASPA. *See* American Association of School Personnel Administration (AASPA)

Absenteeism, 23–24, 184–186. *See also* Stability process

Academic freedom, 263–264

Accountability, demands for:
  absenteeism, 23–24
  behavior costing, 22
  defined, 21
  operational model for assessing accountability effectiveness, 25–27
  return on investment (ROI), 22

Achievement, impact of school climate on student, 245–256

Achievement-motivated people, 158

Adler, S. A., 235

Administration and Education, 81

Administrative Behavior, 54

Administrative personnel, retention of, 182–184. *See also* Personnel

Administrative regulation, 283, 286. *See also* Policies and regulations, personnel

Administrators:
  changing leadership role of, 28–29
  employee relations and, 303
  shortages of, 17
  supply and demand, 16–17
  talent management and, 34–36
  See also Human resources director; Position analysis; Position description; Superintendent

Adults, as learners, 215–217

Advanced preparation, 195

Advisory arbitration, 319

Affiliation-motivated people, 158

AFL. *See* American Federation of Labor (AFL)

AFT. *See* American Federation of Teachers (AFT)

Age Discrimination in Employment Act (1967), 280

Aitkin, R., 92

Akin, J., 249

Albery, M. J., 241

Alderfer, C. P., 156

Allegra, A., 203–204

Allen, M., 319

Alley, J., 184–185

American Association of Retired Persons (AARP), 15

American Association of School Administrators (AASA), 303, 320

American Association of School Personnel Administration (AASPA), 70–71, 321

American Federation of Labor (AFL), 306–307

American Federation of Teachers (AFT), 302, 306–307

American Public Human Services Association, 390–391

Andragogy, 216

Aon Consulting Worldwide's Loyalty Institute, 187, 248

Appleberry, J. B., 245

Applicant pool, 110, 120–122

Application, for recruitment, 122–124

Application screening, 385. *See also* Screening application form, for classified position

Argyris, C., 58

Armour, S., 15, 19

Assessment center, 141, 211–213, 223

Assessment instruments, climate, 238–241

Assignment process, 61–62

Attendance. *See* Absenteeism
Attitudinal feedback, 158–159
Attrition, 97
Attrition analysis, 112
Authoritarian leadership, 50
Automation and technology,
    developments in, 9–10
Avery, P., 184–185

Background check, 143–145, 385 (fig.),
    387. *See also* Protection process
Baird, L., 84
Baker, D. P., 17
Balfour, G. A., 335, 347
Balkin, D. B., 14, 263
Barak, L., 184–185
Bargaining agent, 324–325
Bargaining contract, 331–333
Bargaining unit, 322, 324–328
Barnard, C. I., 12, 53–54, 72, 154, 254
Barnard, H., 44
Bartlett, L. D., 349
Bathurst, P., 194
Bayesian estimation process (BEP), 100
Behavior, impact of school climate on
    personnel, 246–247
Behavior costing, 21
Behavior modification, 155, 158
Behavior of Organisms, The, 157
Behavioral science movement:
    Barnard, C., 53–54
    Fiedler, F., 56–57
    Griffiths, D. E., 55–56
    Halpin, A. W., 54–55
    Hodgkinson, C., 57
    Likert, R., 57–58
    Postmodernism, 58–60
    Simon, H. A., 54
Belles on Their Toes, 46
Bennett, R. E., 249
Benson, J., 330
Bently, R. R., 239
BEP. *See* Bayesian estimation
    process (BEP)
Berglas, W. W., 17, 125, 165–166
Bertalanffy, V. L., 59
Binding arbitration. *See* Voluntary binding
Biographical data measures, 23, 141
Bjork, L., 7, 9, 183
Black Lung Benefits Act, 281
Block, R. N., 109
Bloss, J. M., 44, 195, 266, 342
Bobbett, G. C., 241, 245
Boomerang hiring, 20

Bowin, R. B., 272
Bradley, A., 353
Brayfield, A. H., 156
Breaugh, J. A., 122
Breuer, N. L., 165, 172
Bria, R., 169–171
Brickell, H. M., 290, 294, 297
Bridges, E., 58
Brockett, R. G., 216
Brown, M., 212
Brown, P. M., 235
Brummet, R. L., 21
Brunner, C. C., 7, 183
Buckingham, G., 246
Bulach, C. R., 241, 245, 249
Bulwarism, 329
Bureau of Census, 15
Bureau of Labor Statistics, 15–16
Burns, S., 89
Burrell, N., 319
Bush, C., 204
Bush, G. W., 32
Butler, E. D., 241
Bylaws, 283, 286–287. *See also* Policies
    and regulations, personnel

Callahan, R. E., 45
Campbell, R., 58
Cangemi, J. P., 319
Capacity of equilibrium, 12
Cardy, R. L., 14, 263
Career development planning, 214
Career Service, 204
Carlson, K., 301
Cascio, W. F., 21–22, 329
Casual employee, 371
Central human resources unit:
    collective bargaining and, 309–312
    organization of, 65
    position description, 67–69
    titles, 66–67
Centralization, of human resources
    function, 65–68
CFK Ltd. School Climate Profile, 240
Challenges, facing education and
    human resources function, 10
    accountability, new demands
        for, 21–27
    defined, 11
    diversity in workplace, increasing, 14–16
    employee demands for balanced work
        life, 18–21
    internal and external environments of
        school system, influence of, 11–14

relationship between and among, issues and trends, 4
supply and demand, teacher and administrator, 16–17
Chandler Unified School District, 90–91
Charles F. Kettering School Climate Profile, 240, 251–253
Cheaper by the Dozen, 46
Checklists, 223
Chemers, M. M., 56
Choice, related to school attendance, 355
Christian, C. F., 249
CIO. *See* Congress of Industrial Organizations (CIO)
Citrin, R. S., 175
Civil Rights Act (1870), 279
Civil Rights Act (1960), 280
Civil Rights Act (1964), 264, 284
Civil Rights Act (1964) and Title VII, 280
Clark, R., 144
Class size, 9
Classification value system, 375–378
Classified job analysis, 375–378
Classified personnel evaluation, 393–397 (fig.)
Classified personnel (support staff), 370–399
    appraising candidates in relation to selection criteria, 383–385
    classified job analysis, 375–378
    classified salary schedule relative to range category (hourly wages), 378 (table)
    controlling development results, 398–399
    defined, 370–371
    director of classified personnel, 373–375
    employee evaluation, 392–398
    employment application form for, 379–392
    job families, 371–375, 378–379
    job grading and salary ranges, 375, 378–379
    job titles, 371–375
    recruitment of, 379–382
    selection process, 383–387
    training programs, 388–392
Classified salary schedule relative to range category (hourly wages), 378 (table)
Classroom observation:
    assessment instruments, 225–226
    evaluators, 223–225
    follow-up conferencing and feedback, 227
    timely observations, 225, 227
Classroom walk-through evaluation form, 222 (fig.)
Clayton Act (1914), 307
Cleve, J. V., 19
Clifton, D. O., 139, 195
Climate:
    characteristics of schools with positive, 244
    dealing with conflict, 247–248
    defined, 237
    human resources responsibilities in improvement of school, 253–255
    importance of healthy school, 236–238
    improvement of, 251–255
    links between culture and, 236–237
    measurement of, 238–243
    organizational change and innovation and, 249–251
    personnel behavior and, 246–247
    program, process, and material determinants of school, 251–253, 252 (fig.)
    research studies on school, 243–251
    school improvement models and strategies, 253
    school life and staff commitment, 248–249
    student achievement and, 245–256
Climate assessment instrument, 238–241
Clinical supervision, 213–214
Clinical supervision cycle, 214
Closed climate, 239
Closed shop, 317
Closed system, 59
Clover, S. I. R., 246
Coaching:
    defined, 203
    mentoring and, 203–206
Coactive power, 48
COB. *See* Cost of benefits (COB)
Coca-Cola Retailing Council, 165
Coercive control, 48
Cohan, A., 265
Cohort survival method, 99–100
COLA. *See* Cost of living adjustment (COLA)
Cole, J., 265
Cole, L. L., 187
Collaborating, 81
Collaborative bargaining, 305
Collateral benefits, 348, 356. *See also* Fringe benefits
Collective bargaining:
    bargaining agent, 324–325

bargaining contract, 331–333
by employee groups, 306–309
central human resources unit
    and, 309–312
clarifying procedures in case of
    impasse, 318–322
contract agreement, 331–333
defined, 62–63, 304
definition and basic principles, 303–305
distributive bargaining, 63, 305, 312–313
gathering information for decision
    making and cost analysis, 313–314
goals and objective for, 314–315
grievances, 332–334
ground rules for conducting, 315–317
historical perspectives, 306–309
impact of, on education, 333–336
impact studies, 333–336
in education, 310–322
influence of, on compensation
    levels, 347
initial bargaining procedures and
    appropriate table strategies,
    328–331
master agreement, 331–333
myths surrounding process of, 325–326
negotiations team composition, 325
planning and preparation for
    negotiations, 313
primary processes, 305–306
scope of, 317–318
teacher compensation and, 352
unions defined, 301–302
unions, 300
working relationships, 302–303
See also entries for specific approaches
Collier, J. G., 19
Commonwealth v. Hunt, 306
Community of interest, 324
Comparative occupational
    salaries, 351 (fig.)
Compensation policy, 345–347
Compensation process:
    administrative procedures for, 356–359
    basic models of salary schedules,
        363–365
    collateral considerations affecting
        compensation, 355–356
    competition for tax dollar, 344
    controlling, 359
    defined, 64
    education as big business, 343
    educational expenditures, 343

fringe benefits in educational
    system, 348–349
mandates from state school
    boards and courts, 350
operational model for,
single-salary schedule, 360, 362–364
trends in salary scheduling, 359–362
See also Salary
Compensation process, operational
    model for:
    ability to pay, 353–354
    collective bargaining, 347, 352
    developing policies, 345–347
    job assessment, 348–349
    legislation, 349–350
    national productivity, 355
    operational model for, 345–356
    position structure, 347
    salaries of related occupations, 350–352
    school finance, 342–343
    standard cost of living, 354
    supply and demand for
        personnel, 352–353
Competency-based pay, 363. *See also*
    Compensation process; Salary
Competency-based performance, 31–33
Compound index salary schedule, 363–365
*Comprehensive Assessment of School
    Environments,* 241
Compulsory arbitration, 319–320
Computer programs, 9–10
Conference of Teacher Examiners, 70
Conflict:
    climate and, 247–248
    dealing with, 177–179
    See also Protection process; Turnover
Congress of Industrial Organizations
    (CIO), 307
Conscientiousness test, 23, 141
Consensus-based bargaining, 305
Consideration domain, 14
Consolidated Omnibus Budget
    Reconciliation Act (1986), 281
Consultants, 202–203. *See also* Coaching
Contingency leaderships, 56–57
Contract agreement, 331–333
Contract approval, 143–144
Contract employee, 379
Contracts and compensation policy,
    example of, 346 (fig.)
Contractual rights, 263
Coons, A. E., 54
Cooperating, 81

Coordination, views of, 48–49
Cordeiro, P. A., 235, 304, 388
Cost of benefits (COB), 64, 348, 356
Cost of living, standard, 354
Cost of living adjustment (COLA), 354
Costing, behavior, 21
Costs:
    for employee turnover, 165
    for recruiting, 125
    See also Funding
Council of Professors of Instructional
        Supervision, 201
Crain, K., 245
Creative bargaining, 305
Creative Experience, 48
Criterion-reference evaluation, 223, 225
Critical theory, 58
Crockett, W. H., 156
Croft, D. B., 54, 238–239, 240, 249, 256
Crook, J., 175
Culture:
    benefits of, 235–236
    defined, 235, 237
    links between, and climate, 236
Cunningham, W. G., 388, 235, 304
Customer loyalty, 179–180

Davies, D. R., 290, 294, 297
Davies-Brickell System (DBS), 287, 290
DBS. *See* Davies-Brickell
        System (DBS)
Deal, T. E., 235
Decentralization, of human resources
        function, 65, 69–70
Decker, L. E., 235
Decker, V. A., 235
DeGive, G., 84
Deibert, J. P., 245
Democratic leadership, 50
Demographic changes, 15–16, 18.
        See also Diversity
Denison, E., 355
Dennis Corporation, 36
Department of Labor, 215–216, 284
Designing, 81
Dessler, G., 329
Develop Strategic Objectives, 88, 91–92
Develop Strategies, 88, 92–93
Development process, 61
Dickson, W., 47, 49
Diegmueller, K., 309
Dillion-Peterson, B., 201
Dingwall, R., 319

Director of classified personnel, 373–375
Diseases, 187–188
Disengagement, 238
Distance education, 10, 19–21
Distributive bargaining, 63, 305, 312–313
District philosophy, of performance
        evaluation, 218
Diversity, 14–16
Dlugosh, L. L., 250, 254, 302
Donohue, W. A., 319
Doolittle, T. M., 174
Douglass, H., 169–172
Doyle, A., 143–144
Drive-reinforcement theory, 155
Drug-free workplace legislation, 272–275
Due process, 268
Durden, P. C., 212
Dyer, L., 95
Dynamic equilibrium, 239

EAPs. *See* Employee assistance
        programs (EAPs)
Ebmeier, H., 208
Edson, L., 325
Educational Amendments (1972), 264
Educational Policies Commission, 307
EEOC. *See* Equal Employment
        Opportunity Commission (EEOC)
Effective and efficient system, 61
Effective human resources, 61
Effectiveness, 12
Efficiency dimension, 12–13
Elementary and Secondary Education Act
        (ESEA), 32, 34–36
Elementary school teacher load, 170–172
Eligibility tests, 143–144
Employee assistance programs (EAPs),
        165, 174–176
Employee demands, for balanced
        work life, 18–21
Employee dismissal, legal considerations
        and, 266–271
Employee eligibility list, 387
Employee evaluation, for classified
        personnel, 392–398
Employee groups, 302–303
Employee Retirement Income
        Security Act (1974), 281
Employee rights, 263
Employee unions. *See* Unions
Engelhardt, N. L., 99
Environmental inputs, 59
Environmental scan, 85

Environmental Scanning, 85–88
Environments of school system, internal
    and external, 11–14
Equal Employment Opportunity
    Commission (EEOC), 142, 264, 284
Equal Pay Act (1963), 280, 349
Equifinality, 239
ERG theory (existence, relatedness,
    and growth), 156
ESEA. *See* Elementary and Secondary
    Education Act (ESEA)
Ethical administration, standards of, 70–71
Etscheidt, S., 349
Ettore, B., 125
Etzioni, A., 58
Evaluation process, 61, 218 (fig.). *See also*
    Performance evaluation process
Evaluators, qualified, 223–225
Exclusive representation, 324–325
Exit interview, 144–147
Expectancy theory of motivation, 156
Expenditures, educational, 343
Expenses, educational, for teachers, 18
Exploitive-Authoritative organization, 57
External Scanning, 85–87
Extracurricular compensation, 348

Fact-finding, 319
Fair Credit Reporting Act (FCRA), 144
Fair Labor Standards Act (FLSA), 280, 349
Family and Medical Leave Act (1993), 282
Far West Laboratory (San Francisco), 215
Farrar, E., 244
Farrar, R. D., 311
Fayol, H., 45–46, 72
FCRA. *See* Fair Credit Reporting
    Act (FCRA)
Federal Drug-Free Workplace Act (1988),
    272–275
Federal government, and influence of
    educational programs, 4
Feedback, 59–60
Feistrizer, C. E., 353
Feuer, M. J., 97
Fiedler, F., 56–57
Finance, school, 342–343
Fingerprint card, 144, 387
Fingerprint policy, 144
Fischer, L., 143, 263, 267, 272, 279
Flakus-Mosqueda, P., 244
Flamholtz, E. G., 21
Flexible scheduling, 18–19. *See also*
    Workplace flexibility

FLSA. *See* Fair Labor Standards Act (FLSA)
Follet, M. P., 47–49, 72, 243
Food and nutrition services training
    program, example, 388–389
Forecasting, 81
    defined, 96
    personnel needs, 96–98, 100
    student enrollments, 98–100
Formal classroom observation, 223
Formal organization, 12
Formative evaluation observation, 392
Formative evaluation
    system, 62, 217–218
Foulke, E. G., 281
Fox, Robert S., 252
Fraction bargaining, 305
Frazer, L., 245
Freeman, R. B., 347
French, R. L., 241, 245
Fringe benefits, 348, 356
Frohreich, L. E., 335, 347
FTA. *See* Future Teacher
    of America (FTA)
Full-time equivalent (FTE), 371
Full-time regular classified
    employee (FTR), 371
Functions of the Executive, The, 53, 254
Funding:
    No Child Left Behind Act (NCLB)
        and, 32–34
    for recruitment, 112
Fuqua, H., 319
Future Teachers of America (FTA), 119

Gain sharing, 361
Gallagher, D. G., 335, 347
Gallup Organization, 139
Galpin, T., 126, 182
Gantt, H., 45–47, 72
Gantt on Management, 46
Gap Analysis, 88, 92
Garland School District, 264
Gayle, J. S., 20
General and Industrial Management, 45
General intelligence test.
        See Intelligence test
Genova, W. J., 244
Getzels, J. W., 12, 53, 153–154, 197
Gilbreth, F., 45–46, 72
Gilbreth, L., 45–46, 72
Glass, T. E., 7, 9, 183
Goals:
    defined, 282

determining, for collective
  bargaining, 314–315
  See also Policies and regulations,
    personnel
Gold, Y., 353
Gomez-Mejia, L. R., 14, 263
Good faith bargaining, 329
Goodstein, L. D., 80
Gordon, G. J., 322
Governance and leadership, school, 4–5
Governing board policies, 283
Graphic ranking, 223
Greatbatch, A., 319
Green, K., 18
Greer, J. T., 57, 244
Grievances, 332–334
Griffths, D. E., 55–56
Grossnickle, D. R., 241
Ground rules, 315–317
Group interview, 139
Group Openness and Trust Scale, 241
Growth and development plan, for
  classified personnel, 390–391
Guaglianone, C. L., 8
Guba, E. G., 12, 53, 153–154, 197

Hall, P., 333
Hall, W., 139
Halpin, A. W., 54–55, 238–240, 249, 256
Hanlon, J. M., 81
Hanson, E. M., 142
Harris, B. M., 195
Harrison, R., 240
Harrison Instrument for Diagnosing
  Organizational Ideology, 240
Harvey, D., 272
Hawthorne effect, 47
Health Insurance Portability and
  Accountability Act (HIPPA), 282
Healthy Schools, 241
Hemphill, J. K., 54
Henslely v. State Board of Education, 277
Hepatitus, B., 187
Hergenrother, M. A., 265
Hertling, E., 8
Herzberg, F., 47, 50–52, 72,
  154, 159, 246
Hierarchy of Needs, Maslow's, 155–156
High school, advent of public, 44
High School Characteristics
  Index (HSCI), 239
HIPPA. *See* Health Insurance Portability
  and Accountability Act (HIPPA)

HIV. *See* Human Immunodeficiency
  Virus (HIV)
Hodgkinson, C., 57
Honeyman, D. S., 354–355
Hopkins, W., 245
Hostile environment, 265
Hoy, W. K., 240–241, 245–247, 250
HR director, and employee relations, 303
HR Focus, 36, 179
HSCI. *See* High School Characteristics
  Index (HSCI)
Human dimension, 14
Human Immunodeficiency
  Virus (HIV), 187–188
Human motivation theories, 154–159
Human Organization, The, 57
Human relations movement:
  contributors to, 48–53
  impact on human resources function
    and, 47–53
Human resources administration, 234
Human resources utilization, 60–61
Human resources:
  defined, 3
  defined as function in education, 2–4
Human resources administration, 3
Human resources administrator.
  See Administrators
Human resources development, 60–61
Human resources director, and
  employee relations, 303
Human resources environment, 60–61
Human resources function, growth of, 8
Human resources operational
  plans, 94–95
Human resources planning, 61
Human Side of Enterprise, The, 52, 156
Hunter, J. F., 141
Hygienes, 51, 246

IDEA. *See* Individuals with Disabilities
  Education Act (IDEA)
Idiographic dimension, 153–154
Imants, J., 185
Immigration Reform and
  Control Act (1986), 281
Impasse:
  defined, 318
  fact-finding and advisory
    arbitration, 319
  last-best-offer arbitration, 320
  mediation, 318–319
  strikes, 320–322, 323 (fig.)

voluntary binding an compulsory
arbitration, 319–320
See also Collective bargaining
Implementation, 85–86, 95
Incentive pay, 361
Index salary schedule, 362–365
Indicators of competency, 32
Individual personality, 153–154
Individuals with Disabilities
Education Act (IDEA), 349
Induction process, 61–62, 126
bases purposes of, 159–160
defined, 159, 164
mentoring program, 162
operational procedures for, 160
orientation for beginning teacher and
others new to school
system, 164–165
personnel information
handbook, 163–164
policy and administrative
manual, 162–163
postemployment induction,
161–162
preemployment activities, 160–161
what research says, 165–166
Informal organization, 12
Innovation, impact of school
climate on, 249–251
Inputs, 59–60
In-service education, 195
In-service training, 195
Institutional role (R), 153–154
Integrative bargaining, 35, 63, 311
Integrity test, 23, 141
Intelligence test, 23, 141
Interest-based bargaining, 305
Internal Scanning, 85–88
Internet, legal considerations
regarding, 277–279
Interpersonal dimension, 14
Interstate School Leaders Licensure
Consortium (ISLLC), 29–31, 140
Interview:
exit, 144–147
recruitment, 120–121
selection, 387
techniques, 138–140
Interview guide, 137–138
Interviewer, training of, 138
Interviewing, legal considerations
and, 142
Intimacy, 238

Issues, facing education and human
resources function:
automation and technology, 9–10
defined, 3
demands on professional personnel, 8–9
external mandates and legal impacts, 9
performance, effective human, 7–8
relationship between and among,
challenges and trends, 3–4
relationships and cooperation, among
school administrators
and teachers, 6
school financing, adequate, 8
school governance and leadership, 4–5
*See also entries for specific issues and
specific problems*

Jacobson, S., 185
Jantzi, D., 92
Job analysis, classified, 373–378
Job assessment, 347–349
Job description, of school bus
driver, 383–386
Job families, of classified employees,
371–373, 375, 378–379. *See also*
Classified personnel (support staff)
Job grading, 347, 375, 378–379
Job insecurity, 8
Job portfolio, 225
Job rotation, 214–215
Job satisfaction:
administrators, 6
teachers, 6, 17
Two-Factor Theory of Job
Satisfaction, 50
Job titles. *See* Job families, of classified
employees
Johnson, I. M., 265
Judgmental techniques, for forecasting, 97

Kahn, L., 335, 347
Kaman, J., 15
Kasper, H., 333, 347
Kazanas, H. C., 97
Kelly, L. K., 89, 122, 385
Kennedy, C., 183
Kennedy, G., 330
Kennedy, J. F., 309
Kimball, K., 8
Kinicki, A., 80
Kleiman, L. S., 235
Kleinmann, M., 23, 140
Knowledge management, 29

Knowlege-based pay system, 362
Knowles, M., 216–217
Koeppel, G., 361
Kohler, D., 319
Kossek, E. E., 109
Kottkamp, R. B., 240
Kowalski, T. J., 135–136
Krazewski, L. J., 96
Kreitner, R., 80, 238

Laabs, J. J., 248
Labor Management Relations Act
    (Taft-Hartley Act), 307
Labor Management Reporting and
    Disclosure Act (Landrum-Griffin
    Act), 307
Laissez-faire leadership, 50
Landrum-Griffin Act, 307
Laramie County School District #1
    (Wyoming), 225–226
Last-best-offer arbitration, 320
Law, defined, 283. *See also* Legal
    considerations; Policies and
    regulations, personnel
LBDQ. *See* Leadership Behavior
    Description Questionnaire (LBDQ)
Leadership Behavior Description
    Questionnaire (LBDQ), 54–55
Leadership styles, 54–57
Learning programs:
    knowledge management and, 29
    outsourcing of, 20–21
Legal considerations:
    drug-free workplace legislation, 272–275
    employee dismissal and, 266–271
    employee rights, 263
    interviewing and, 142
    language of school policies and
        regulations, 293–294
    legal statutes, summary of, 279–282
    model for development of, 291–293
    network and Internet, 277–279
    personnel policies and
        regulations, 282–290
    policies relating to staff protection:
        sexual harassment, 264–266
    process of personnel policies and
        regulations, 290–291
    rights, responsibilities, and duties:
        academic freedom, 263–264
    teacher transfer and, 272, 275–277
    See also Compensation process
Legal impacts, and external mandates, 9

Legal statutes, summary of, 279–282
Leggett, S., 99
Legislation. *See* Legal considerations; U.S.
    Constitution; specific laws
Leithwood, F., 92
Lemke, J. C., 17, 125
Letters of acceptance, 387
Letters of nonacceptance, 387
Letters of reference, 135–137
Lewin, K., 47, 50, 72
Lewis v. Tucson School District No. 1, 280
Lieberman, M., 303, 324
Likert, R., 21, 57–58
Line administrator, 65–66
Linking Pin organization, 58
Linn, H. E., 98
Lippitt, R., 47, 50
Load. *See* Teacher workload
Local school ward boards, 4
Lohaus, D., 23, 140
Long interview technique, 138–139
Longshore and Harbor Workers'
    Compensation Act, 281
Losey, M., 27
Loughran, C. S., 318, 324
Lunenburg, F. C., 245, 301, 388

Mahoney, D., 126
*Making Schools Smarter: A System for
    Monitoring School District Progress,* 92
Malone, B., 241, 245, 249
Management by objectives (MBO), 156
Managing by Objectives, 156
Mandel, L. S., 265
March, J., 58
Marcum, R. L., 249
Marginal staff, working with, 172–173,
    176–177
Markovian analysis, for forecasting, 97–98
Maslow, A. H., 155–156
Master agreement, 331–333
Mausner, B., 50–51, 154, 246
Mayo, E., 47–50, 72
Mazin, R., 294
MBO. *See* Management by
    objectives (MBO)
McClellan, R. I., 184
McClelland, D. C., 158–159
McConnell, J. H., 283, 285
McDaniel, P., 135–136
McGregor, D., 47, 50, 52–53, 72, 154, 156
McMillan, J., 330
Mediation, 318–319

Mentor and mentoring:
  assessment centers, 211–213
  career development planning, 214
  clinical supervision, 213–214
  coaching and, 203–206
  defined, 162
  functions of, 204
  induction process, 162
  job rotation, 214–215
  peer-assisted leadership (PAL), 215
  personnel appraisal methods, 214
  primary phase of, 205
  purposes of, 205
  qualifications for, 206
  quality circles, 209–210
  Talent development plan (TDP)
    process, 205–215
  taskforces and shadow groups, 214
  teacher centers, 210–211
Mentor-protégé relationship, 204–205,
  207. *See also* Talent development
  plan (TDP)
Merchant Marine Act, 281
Merit pay, 359–360
Merriam, S. B., 216
Merrill, R. J., 183
Mesa Public School District (Arizona), 371
Mesa Public School
  District (Arizona), 219–223
Meshoulam, I., 84
Metcalf, H. C., 267
Midvale School Works, 46
Milakovich, M. E., 322
Minsberg, H., 58
Miskel, C. G., 247, 250
Mission statement, of strategic plan, 88–91
Mnookin, R. H., 325
Moore, G. A., 335
Moore, L. E., 347
Moos, B., 18
Morgan, G., 58–59
Moskow, M. H., 303, 324
Motivation, 155–159
Motivation to Work, The, 50
Motivation-hygiene theory, 159
Motivators, 51–52
Muchinsky, P. M., 62, 109
Mulhern, J. A., 240
Multiple regression statistics, 141
Multiple representation, 324–325
Multiyear planning format, 87
Murray, M., 15
Mutual-gains bargaining, 305

Narrative system, 223, 225
NASSP. *See* National Association of
  Secondary School Principals (NASSP)
National Association of School Resource
  Officers, 385
National Association of Secondary
  School Principals (NASSP), 211
National Center for Educational
  Statistics, 343
National Development Center, 200
National Education Association (NEA),
  300, 302, 304, 306–307, 320, 362
National Education Policy Network of the
  National School Boards Association
  (NEPN/NSBA), 287–290
National Labor Relations Act (Wagner
  Act), 301, 307
National Labor Relations
  Board (NLRB), 317, 329
National productivity, 355
National School Boards Association
  (NSBA), 320
National Staff Development and Training
  Association (NSDTA), 70–71, 390
National Teachers Association (NTA), 306
NCLB. *See* No Child Left Behind
  Act (NCLB)
NEA. *See* National Education
  Association (NEA)
Need disposition, 153–154
Needs theory, 156
Negotiations, 304
  composition of teams, 325
  planning and preparation
    for collective, 313
  See also Collective bargaining
Nelson, J. L., 301
Nelson, P., 195
NEPN/NSBA. *See* National Education
  Policy Network of the National
  School Boards Association
  (NEPN/NSBA)
Network and Internet, legal
  consideration and, 277–279
New Patterns of Management, 57
Newman, F. M., 245
Niehaus, R. J., 97
Nixon, R. M., 308
NLRB. *See* National Labor
  Relations Board (NLRB)
No Child Left Behind Act (NCLB),
  19, 32, 350
Nolan, T. M., 80

Nomothetic dimension, 12–14

Noncontract employee, 379

Nonsalary pay, 348

Norm-reference evaluation, 223

Norris-LaGuardia Act (1932), 307

Norton, M. S., 6–9, 16, 19, 23, 29, 32, 60, 66, 69, 80–81, 89, 94–95, 111–112, 122, 126, 133, 165, 169–179, 183–185, 236, 246, 250, 254, 267, 282, 290, 301–303, 310–311, 326, 342, 385, 392

Norton/Bria Formula, 169–179

Norwalk Teachers Association v. Board of Education, 308

NSBA. *See* National School Boards Association (NSBA)

NSDTA. *See* National Staff Development and Training Association (NSDTA)

NTA. *See* National Teachers Association (NTA)

Occupational Safety and Health Administration (OSHA), 187, 281, 284

Occupational salaries, comparative, 351

OCDQ. *See* Organizational Climate Description Questionnaire (OCDQ)

OHI-S. *See* Organizational Health Inventory (OHI-S)

Open climate, 177–178, 238–239, 246

Open system, 12, 59, 238–239. *See also* Open climate

Operant conditioning, 155

Operational model, for assessing accountability effectiveness, 25–27

Operational model, for selection process: assessing selection results, 144, 146
compiling appropriate selection data, 135–142
defining behavioral characteristics for appraisal, 135–136
designing and organizing, 133–135
preparing eligibility lists and nominations for submission to board of education, 143–144

Operational plan, 85–86
defined, 93
example of, 219–223 (fig.)
school operational plan, 94
system operational plan, 94–95
teacher retention, 181–182

Operational procedures, for staff induction, 160

Organizational change and innovation, impact of school climate on, 249–251

Organizational climate, 61, 63–64, 126, 236. *See also* Climate

Organizational Climate Description Questionnaire (OCDQ), 54, 238–242, 246, 249

Organizational Health Inventory (OHI-S), 240

Organizational type, 57

Organizing, 81

Orientation, for beginning teacher and others new to school system, 164–165

Ornstein, A. C., 301, 388

OSHA. *See* Occupational Safety and Health Administration (OSHA)

Ouchi, W., 157

Outputs, 59–60

Outsourcing, of learning programs, 20–21

Pai, Y., 235

PAL. *See* Peer-assisted leadership (PAL)

Palonsky, S. B., 301

Paredes, V., 245

Participating, 81

Participative organization, 57

Partnership bargaining, 305

Part-time regular employee (PTR), 371

Path-goal theory, 156. *See also* Management by objectives (MBO)

Patrick, J. E., 246

Pay systems. *See* Compensation process

Payne, K., 319

Pedagogy, 216

Peer-assisted leadership (PAL), 215

Peoria School Improvement Climate Study, 241–242

Performance, effective human, 7–8

Performance evaluation process, 62
classroom observation, 223–227
district philosophy, 218
example of classroom walk-through evaluation form, 222 (fig.)
example of operational plan, 219–223 (fig.)
example of philosophy of evaluation, 218 (fig.)
purposes of, 217–218
See also Employee evaluation

Performance interview, 138

Performance tests, for teachers, 7–8

Performance-based pay, 361

Perie, M., 17

Perry, C. R., 305, 333
Personal competency, 61
Personal reference. *See* References
Person-job fit, 109, 135
Personnel:
    appraisal methods for, 214
    defined, 3
    demands on, 8–9
    forecasting for, 100
    forecasting needs of, 96–98
    impact of school climate on, 246–247
    scientific management era and impact
        on practices, 45–47
    supply and demand for, 352–353
Personnel administration, 5, 43–44
Personnel attrition, 97–98
Personnel information handbook, 163–164
Personnel policies and regulations. *See*
    Policies and regulations, personnel
Personnel recruitment. *See* Recruitment
Person-organization fit, 109, 135
Persons-oriented domain, 14
Peterson, K. D., 235, 308
Peterson, L. J., 137, 276, 308
Pfiffer, J. W., 80
Philadelphia Cordwainers case, 306
Pitkoff, E., 185
Plan and forecast, to organize, to
    command, to coordinate, and to
    control (POCCC), 45
Planning, definition and background of,
    79–82. *See also* Strategic human
    resources planning
Planning, organization, staffing, directing,
    coordinating, reporting, and
    budgeting (POSDCoRB), 45–46
Plans and planning:
    characteristics of strategic, 83
    defined, 79
    integrating, into strategic plan, 84–95
    recruitment, 110–111
POCCC. *See* Plan and forecast, to
    organize, to command, to coordinate,
    and to control (POCCC)
Podgursky, M., 184
Policies and regulations, personnel:
    benefits of, 284–285
    compliance aspects of policy, 283–284
    criteria that identify, 286–287
    development of, 282–290
    goals, policies, and regulations, 283
    importance of, 282
    language of, 293–294

NEPN/NSBA policy codification
    system, 287–290
    process of, 61, 64
    topical headings for, 287
    See also Legal considerations
Policy, defined, 286
Policy and administrative manual, 162–163
Pool, applicant, 110, 120–122
Porwoll, P. J., 185
POSDCoRB. *See* Planning, organization,
    staffing, directing, coordinating,
    reporting, and budgeting
    (POSDCoRB)
Position analysis, 67–68, 112–115
Position assessment, 115
Position assignment, 166–168
Position description, 68–69, 119
    defined, 115, 133
    example of, 116–118 (illus.)
Position grading, 113, 115
Postemployment process, and induction
    process, 161–162
Postmodern behavioral science era, 58–60
Potential analysis, 140–141
Pounder, D. G., 183
Power-based bargaining, 305
Preemployment activities, and induction
    process, 160–161
Pregnancy Discrimination Act (1978), 281
Presidential Executive Order
    10988 (1962), 308
Presidential Executive Order
    11491 (1969), 308
Principal, 69–70. *See also* Position analysis;
    Position description
Principals, retention of, 183
Principle of definition, 45
Principle of organization, 45
*Principles of Scientific
    Management, The,* 45
Privacy Act, 143–144, 281
Probationary period, 387
Problem, defined, 3. *See also* specific
    issues; specific problems
Problem-solving bargaining, 305
Productivity, national, 355
Professional staff development. *See* Staff
    development
Program, process, and material
    determinants, 251, 252 (fig.), 253
Protection process, 61, 63, 186–188. *See
    also* Sexual harassment
Psychic income, 348

PTO. *See* Purdue Teacher Opinionaire (PTO)
PTR. *See* Part-time regular employee (PTR)
Public high school, advent of, 44
Purdue Evaluation Scale (PES), 239–240
Purdue Research Foundation, 239
Purdue Teacher Opinionaire (PTO), 239
Pyle, W. C., 21

Qualitative techniques, for forecasting, 97
Quality circles, 209–210
Quasi-distributive bargaining, 63, 305, 312
Quasi-integrative bargaining, 305
Quid pro quo strategy:
    harassment and, 265
    in negotiations, 63, 330

Raia, A. P., 156
Railroad Labor Act (1926), 307
Ranking system, 225
Rating system, 225–226
Rationality, 46
Reactive program, staff development as, 195–196
Rebore, R. W., 325
Recruitment, 22
    classified personnel (support staff), 379–382
    operations model for process of, 109–128
    process for, 61
    sample policy for, 110–111
    screening for, 108–109
Redfern, G. G., 303
References, letters of, 135–136
Regression statistics, standard multiple, 141
Regulations, 100–101
Rehabilitation Act (1973), 281
Reitzug, U. C., 135–136
Rempel, A. M., 239
Re-recruitment, 7–8, 125–128
Research:
    induction process, 165–166
    organizational harmony and, 243
    on school climate, 243–251
Rest pause, 49
Retention:
    administrative personnel, 182–184
    principals, 183
    teachers, 179–182
    why principals leave position, 183

Return on investment (ROI), 21, 200
Revised Versions of the OCDQ, 240
Reward practices, 126
Rights, 263–264. *See also* Legal considerations; specific laws
Ritzman, L. P., 96
Robbins, S. P., 235
Robertson, J., 18
Robinson, D. C., 28, 126, 182
Robinson, J., 28
Roethlisberger, F., 47, 49
ROI. *See* Return on investment (ROI)
Roithmayr, T., 35–36
Rossmiller, R. A., 127, 276, 308
Rothwell, W. J., 97
RPTIM model, 200–202
Rumsey, M. T., 175
Russell, F., 200–201
Rutherford, W. I., 244

Safety. *See* Protection process
Salary, 348
    comparative, of related occupations, 350–352
    job grading and, 375, 378–379
    teacher, 7–8
    teachers and administrators, 17
    See also Compensation process
Salary scheduling:
    basic models of, 363–365
    trends in, 359–360
Sawyer, J., 265
Scanning. *See* Environmental Scanning
Schimmel, D., 143, 263
Schmidt, F. L., 141
Schmidt, G., 51–52
School climate. *See* Climate
School Climate and Context Inventory, 241
School Climate Improvements: A Challenge to the School Administrator, 251
School Climate Profile, 240
School Climate Profile: Program, Process, and Material Determinants, 252 (fig.)
School Discipline Climate Survey: Toward a Safe Orderly Learning Environment, 241
School finance, 342–343
School governance and leadership, 4–5
School improvement:
    human resources responsibilities for, 253–255
    models and strategies for, 253
School life. *See* Climate

School operational plan, 94
School organization, evolutionary
    stage of, 83–84
Schoonmaker, A. N., 328
Schramm, J., 28
Schultz, R. R., 99
Scientific management era, 45–47
Scott, K. D., 184
Screening application form, for classified
    position, 384 (fig.)
Screening strategies, for recruitment,
    120–121
Security. *See* Protection process
Selection data:
    interview guide, 137–138
    letters of reference, 136–137
    selection interview techniques, 138–140
Selection interview, 387
Selection policy, 133–135
Selection process, 61–62
    assessing selection results,
        144, 146, 387–388
    background check, 143–145
    classified employees, 383, 385–387
    compiling appropriate selection
        data, 135–142
    defining behavioral characteristics to be
        appraised, 135–136, 383, 385–387
    designing and organizing, 133–135, 383
    interviewing, 387
    legal considerations and interviewing
        activity, 142
    plans for implementation of, 135
    preparing eligibility lists and
        nominations for submission to
        board of education: contract
        approval, 143–144
    re-recruitment and, 8
    scanning techniques for reviewing
        resumes, 10
    testing in, 140–141
Selectmen, 4, 43
Self-development, staff development
    and, 196
Self-referenced evaluation, 223, 225
Sergiovanni, T., 51–52
Sexual harassment, 264–266
Seyfarth, J. T., 99–100
Shadow group, 214
Sheridan, J. A., 97
Sherman Antitrust Act (1890), 306
Short, P. M., 57, 244
Short interview technique, 138

Shortages, of teachers and
    administrators, 7, 16–18
Sibson, R. E., 80
Sick leave. *See* Absenteeism
Simon, H. A., 54
Simple index salary schedule, 364
Single-salary schedule, 360, 362–364
Sirotnek, K. A., 8, 212
Situational leadership, 57
Skill-based pay system, 362
Skinner, B. F., 157–158
Smith, R., 294
Smith, R. E., 90, 176, 178, 204, 227
Snyder, C., 204
Snyderman, B., 50–51, 154, 246
Soar With Your Strengths, 195
Social Security Act (1935), 279
Social system, 12, 153–154
Socialization, 126
Spillover, 333, 347
Spitzer, D. R., 126
Spokesperson, 326
Stability process, 61, 63
    dealing with conflict and
        controversy, 177–179
    defined, 172
    employee assistance programs
        (EAPs), 174–176
    strategies for reducing teacher
        turnover, 180
    teacher retention and, 179
    working with troubled and marginal
        staff members, 172, 176–177
Staff, 195
    mix of, 84
    operational model for selection
        process, 133–146
    school life and commitment of, 248–249
    working with troubled and marginal
        members of, 172–173
    See also Recruitment
Staff administrator, 65–66
Staff assignment process:
    defined, 166
    position assignment, 166–168
    sample policy, 168 (illus.)
    teacher workload, 168–172
Staff development:
    adults as learners, 215–217
    defined, 195
    example of process, 197 (illus.)
    importance of, 194
    mentor qualifications, 206

mentoring relationship phases, 205
methods and strategies for, 202–205
operational procedures for, 199–217
primary phases of mentoring
    relationship, 205
process of, 64
purposes of, 197–198
reactive program, 195–196
RPTIM model for, 200–202
self-development and, 196
Talent development plan (TDP) in
    mentoring process, 205–215
TDP in mentoring process, 205–215
training *versus*, 195
trends in, 198
Staff induction. *See* Induction process
Standard multiple regression statistics, 141
Starke, A. M., 159
State educational jurisdiction, 4
Statutory rights, 263
Steen, M., 19
Stellman, L. E., 263
Stephen, A., 35–36
Stern, G. G., 239
Stevens, M. P., 249
Strahan, R. D., 325
Strategic and Operational Planning, 85–86
    operational plans, 93–95
    strategic plan, 88–93
Strategic human resources planning, 80–83
Strategic plan:
    defined, 81
    integrating planning into, 84–95
    mission statement, 88–91
Strategizing, 81
Strategy, defined, 79
Strellman, L. R., 143
Strengths, Weaknesses, Opportunities,
    Threats (SWOT), 85, 87
Strevell, W. H., 98
Strikes, 6, 320–322, 323 (fig.)
Strong, W. B., 99
Structured employment interviews, 23, 141
Structured interview, 139
Student achievement, impact of school
    climate on, 245–246
Student enrollments,
    forecasting, 98–100
Stum, D. L., 179–180
Subject-specialty interview, 139
Successful accomplishment of
    system goals, 61
Summative evaluation system, 62, 217–218

Superintendent, and employee
    relations, 302–303
Superordinate goals, 54
Supply and demand, of personnel,
    16–17, 352–353
Support staff. *See* Classified personnel
    (support staff)
Surface bargaining, 329
Sweeney, J., 244–245, 253
SWOT. *See* Strengths, Weaknesses,
    Opportunities, Threats (SWOT)
Sybouts, W., 250, 254, 302
Syntality, 236
Syracuse University Psychological
    Research Center, 239
System operational plan, 94–95
System plan, correlation with, 95–96
Systems theory, 58–60

Taft-Hartley Act, 307
Talent Attraction and Selection System
    (TASS), 138–139
Talent development plan (TDP):
    assessment centers, 211–213
    career development planning, 214
    clinical supervision, 213–214
    defined, 205
    establishing goals and objectives and
        determining action plan, 208–209
    job rotation, 214–215
    mentoring process, 205–216
    peer-assisted leadership (PAL), 215
    personnel appraisal methods, 214
    quality circles, 209–210
    steps in, 206–208
    taskforces and shadow groups, 214
    teacher centers, 210–211
Talent management, and human resources
    administrator, 34–36, 195
Tarter, C. J., 240–241
Tashakkori, A., 244
Task, 32
Task management, 45
Taskforce group, 214
TASS. *See* Talent Attraction and Selection
    System (TASS)
Tax dollars, competition for, 344
Taylor, D. L., 243–244
Taylor, F., 45–47, 72
TDP. *See* Talent development plan (TDP)
Teacher and Administrator
    SRI Perceivers, 139
Teacher centers, 210–211

Teacher workload:
  defined, 168
  Douglass Teacher Load
      Formula, 169–171
  Norton/Bria Formula, 169–172
Teacher-in-service program, 24
Teacher(s):
  absenteeism among, 184–186
  re-recruitment and, 7–8
  retention of, 179–182
  salaries for, 8–9
  shortages of, 7–9, 16–18
  supply and demand, 16–17
  transfer of, 272, 275–277
  turnover, 24, 180, 182
Teachers' union. *See* Unions
Teacher-to-teacher relationships, 6
Tead, O., 267
Team observer, 326
Technology and automation,
      developments in, 9–10, 20
Tempe Elementary School District, 188
Temporary classified employee, 371
Tennessee School Climate Inventory, 241
Tenure, 268
Theory Y, 47, 52–53, 156
Theory Z, 157
Thompson, D. C., 354–355
Thompson, S. R., 200–201
Threats. *See* Protection process
Timely observations, 225, 227
*Towards a Philosophy of
      Administration,* 57
Township institutes, 44
Toxic climate, 239
Training:
  program for classified employees,
      388–392
  staff development *versus,* 195
Transfer, teacher, 272, 275–277
Transformation process, 59–60
Transformational process, 60
Travers, C. J., 173
Trends, in human resources
      administration, 34–36
  administrative standards, 29–31
  competency-based performance, 31–33
  defined, 27
  leadership role of administrator,
      changing, 28–29
  No Child Left Behind Act
      (NCLB), 19, 32
  relationships between and among issues,
      challenges, and, 3–4

staff development, 198
talent management as, 195
Troubled staff, working with, 172–173
Turnover, 24, 182
  costs of employee, 165
  strategies for reducing, 180
Two-Factor Theory of Job
      Satisfaction, 50–51

Uerling, D. F., 212
Unicomb, R., 184
Unions, 300–302. *See also* Collective
      bargaining
Urwick, L., 45
U.S. Constitution:
  Fifth Amendment, 279
  First Amendment, 279
  Fourteenth Amendment,
      63, 279, 281
  Ninth Amendment, 279
  Tenth Amendment, 4
  See also Legal considerations

Vacancy analysis, 97–98
Van Zoelen, A., 185
Villanova, P., 62, 109
Violence. *See* Protection process
Virtual teams, 20
Voluntary binding, 319–320
Voluntary transfer, 275–276
Volz, M. M., 137, 276
Vroom, V. H., 156
Vukovich, E., 137

Wages, 348. *See also* Compensation
      process; Salary
Wagner Act. *See* National Labor Relations
      Act (Wagner Act)
Walberg, H. J., 244
Walter, R. L., 306, 324
Ward boards, 4
Weaknesses, 85, 87
Webb, B., 301
Webb, L. D., 60, 126, 250, 254, 302
Webb, S., 301
Weber, M., 45–46, 54, 72
Weisenstein, G. R., 349
Welfare process, 61
Wendel, F. C., 212
West Contra Costa Unified School
      District (California), 371
Western Electric Company, 49
Whitaker, K., 8, 183
White, R., 47, 50

*White vs. Board of Education of
    Lincoln County,* 276
Wilman, A. W., 305, 333
Wilmore, E. L., 253
Winn, S., 175
Winter, J. S., 244–245
Win-win bargaining, 6, 305–306
Wolkinson, B., 265
Women, and workplace
    flexibility, 19–20
Wood, R. C., 354–355
Woods, F. H., 200–201
Work and Motivation, 156
Work journal, 223
Work portfolio, 223, 225

Work sample test, 23, 141
Workers' Compensation, 281
Workload, teacher, 168–172
Workplace conditions, 52
Workplace flexibility, 18–21
Wymore School District, 68–69,
    380–382, 384–386, 390
Wynn, R., 347

Yasin, S., 353
Yerkes, D. M., 8
Young, I. P., 3, 81, 100, 111, 172,
    225, 268, 392

Zuelke, D. C., 335, 347

About the Author

M. Scott Norton, a former public school teacher, coordinator of curriculum, assistant superintendent, and superintendent of schools, served as Professor in and Vice-Chair of the Department of Educational Administration and Supervision at the University of Nebraska, Lincoln, later becoming Professor and Chair of the Department of Educational Administration and Supervision at Arizona State University, where he is currently Professor Emeritus. He teaches graduate classes in human resources administration, school superintendency, school principalship, educational leadership, and competency-based administration.

Dr. Norton is coauthor of college textbooks in the areas of human resources administration, the school superintendency, and administrative management and author of a textbook in the area of effective leadership for effective administration. He has published widely in national journals in such areas as teacher retention, organizational climate, teacher workload, the role of the department chair in educational administration, employee assistance programs, selection and recruitment practices, the school principalship, distance education, and others.

He has received several state and national awards honoring his service and contributions to the field of educational administration from such organizations as the American Association of School Administrators, the University Council for Educational Administration, the Arizona School Administrators Association, the Arizona Educational Research Organization, Arizona State University College of Education Dean's Award for excellence in service to the field, and the distinguished service award from the Arizona Educational Information Service.

Dr. Norton's state and national leadership positions have included service as Executive Director of the Nebraska Association of School Administrators, a member of the Board of Directors for the Nebraska Congress of Parents and Teachers, President of the Arizona School Administrators Higher Education Division, Arizona School Administrators Board of Directors, Staff Associate for the University Council of School Administrators, Treasurer for the University Council for Educational Administration, and Nebraska State Representative for the National Association of Secondary School Principals. Presently he serves on the editorial board for the *Journal of School Public Relations*.